INNOVATIONS IN FEMINIST
PSYCHOLOGICAL RESEARCH

Innovations in Feminist Psychological Research

Ellen B. Kimmel and Mary Crawford

Editors

CAMBRIDGE
UNIVERSITY PRESS

Published by the Press Syndicate of the University of Cambridge
The Pitt Building, Trumpington Street, Cambridge CB2 1RP, England
40 West 20th Street, New York, NY 10011, USA
10 Stamford Road, Oakleigh, Melbourne, Victoria 3166, Australia

First published 1999

Printed in the United States of America

Library of Congress Cataloging-in-Publication Data

Innovations in Feminist Psychological Research / edited by
Ellen B. Kimmel and Mary Crawford. p. cm.
Includes bibliographical references and index.
ISBN 0-521-78640-1
1. Psychology—Research—Methodology. 2. Psychology, Experimental.
3. Feminist psychology. I. Kimmel, Ellen B., 1939– II. Crawford, Mary
(Mary E.)

BF76.5.I565 1999
155.3'33'072—dc21   99-088421

ISBN 0-521-78640-1

The essays in this book have also been published,
without frontmatter and index, in the quarterly journal
Psychology of Women Quarterly, Volume 23, No. 1, and No. 2,
which is available by subscription

CONTENTS

Contents   v

PREFACE

Feminist principles of seeking equality, promoting inclusiveness, honoring the personal, attending to context, characterizing power, and advocating change may be practiced in a multiplicity of settings. The practice of research is especially relevant to feminist goals because it can reveal hidden assumptions that privilege some at the expense of others and it can dispel myths that misrepresent women's lives. In other words, research can illuminate issues of privilege and can empower the voice of those who have been marginalized. Research intended to recover that which is distorted and suppressed is therefore inherently feminist.

However, there is tremendous resistance to this kind of oppositional knowledge, and information brought forth in this manner must be continually rediscovered because it is regularly dismissed from the pages of social consciousness. Conducting research inspired by feminist principles is further complicated, because research typically both derives from and re-affirms the society in which the research is conducted, i.e. it is socially constructed. How can one engage in social change when the very activity of research is itself a reflection of the status quo? One solution to this problem is to set out intentionally from the beginning to challenge systems of exclusion and inequity by making hidden meanings and vested interests figural. That is to say, making feminist research frankly political. Another solution to this problem is to structure for diversity.

Contributions to oppositional knowledge emerge from a wide range of methodologies and applications. In accord with the feminist principle of inclusiveness, this volume is structured to encompass diverse participants, topics, and formats. The entries include projects that rely on a variety of methodologies not typically seen in mainstream psychology, including narrative, life histories, focus groups, Q-methodology, concept mapping, case study, discourse analysis, and collective drama. Some projects attend solely to the qualitative features of meaning and how it is negotiated while others incorporate quantitative analyses.

Ellen Kimmel and Mary Crawford took on the task of coordinating an American Psychological Association Division 35 Psychology of Women task force on innovative research while I was president, 1995-1996. Their work with contributors to this volume is itself an innovative approach to method and process. There is a reflexivity about the process of doing the research and the interplay and negotiations of all the participants, researcher and respondent alike. For example, the commentaries that follow each entry offer a further consideration of the research process, what it means, and how it is situated. The topics of study reflect feminist efforts to honor the personal and to recover that which has been silenced. The studies additionally demonstrate a relaxing of boundaries between the knower and the known and an appreciation that knowledge is situated in context.

Cheryl Brown Travis
September 1999

INTRODUCTION

FEMINIST RESEARCH: QUESTIONS AND METHODS

Nancy Felipe Russo
Arizona State University

> Feminism:
> 1. A doctrine advocating political, economic, and social equality of the sexes.
> 2. Organized activity on behalf of women's rights and interests.
> *Webster's New Encyclopedic Dictionary* (1993, p. 369).

Although the dictionary definition of "feminism" appears straightforward, the devil is in the details. Feminism encompasses diverse frameworks, ideologies, attitudes, and analyses of the political, economic, and social inequalities between women and men (Donovan, 1992; Henley, Meng, O'Brien, McCarthy, & Sockloskie, 1998; Russo, 1998; Russo & Dabul, 1994; Tong, 1998; Walby, 1990). In this pluralistic context, the need for diversity in research methods would seem as obvious as the conclusion that any method that can be used on behalf of women's rights and interests is by definition a potential feminist tool. The issues to focus on then become: "What are the urgent feminist questions?" and "What methods do we need to answer them?" As knowledge cannot be separated from the method used to generate it, these issues are inextricably intertwined.

To me, the excitement that feminism brings to psychology comes out of the questions that feminism brings to our enterprise. The works of feminist psychologists who were trained in the traditional methods of scientific psychology provide many examples of just how useful a scientific lens can be when turned on a feminist question (Madden & Russo, 1997; Russo & Dabul, 1994; Worell & Etaugh, 1994). There are numerous demonstrations of the usefulness of an experimental approach. For example, recent articles published in the *Psychology of Women Quarterly* (*PWQ*) have documented how empowering and legitimizing token women leaders can enhance their leadership effectiveness (Yoder, Schleicher, & McDonald, 1998) and how so-called "harmless" flirting, even when welcomed by the recipient, can

Address correspondence to: Nancy Felipe Russo, Psychology Department, Box 871104, ASU, Tempe, AZ 85287–1104. E-mail: nancy.russo@asu.edu have negative consequences for college women's self confidence (Satterfield & Muehlenhard, 1997).

But feminists have expressed dissatisfaction with traditional psychological methods for good reason, and this dissatisfaction goes beyond simply eliminating the biases that pervade the traditional research process (Denmark, Russo, Frieze, & Sechzer, 1988; McHugh, Koeske, & Frieze, 1986; Russo & Dabul, 1994). However useful traditional methods may be for answering certain kinds of important feminist questions, other questions need to be addressed—questions about women's lived experiences, how we think about our lives and our selves, about the meanings of events and relationships in our lives, and how we differ in our constructions and interactions in the world—and such questions simply cannot be answered with old-fashioned methods. So the search is on to identify and develop the methods we need to answer them. To facilitate this process, Mary Crawford and Ellen Kimmel developed a two-part series of special issues of PWQ devoted to research and commentary on innovative methods that formed the basis for this book. Their series was unique in the history of the journal: in addition to presenting descriptions of their research methods and findings, the authors reflect on their thoughts and feelings about the research process and each other. They present the "human side" to research that underlies every step and action of the process. There is also a commentary on each article that expands and reflects on the researchers' ideas and actions and presents an additional point of view on the process. Taken as a whole, this work is an invaluable pedagogical resource for a variety of research training venues, from traditional classrooms to research training workshops.

Feminists will continue to debate the merits of various methodological approaches for answering different questions, and this book will help inform those discussions. As George Homans observed long ago, "People who write about methodology often forget that it is a matter of strategy, not of morals" (1949, p. 330). It is my hope that in such debates we keep our focus on the feminist goals of our research with the objective of strategically crafting our methods to attain them. We must also remember that any method that generates feminist knowledge can also be an anti-feminist tool. Witness the effectiveness to which anti-abortion activists have used qualitative methods to construct a "post-abortion syndrome" and argue against women's right to legal abortion (see Russo, 1995, for a discussion of these activities).

A Personal Note

As Crawford and Kimmel point out, an emphasis on the researcher's personal reflexivity (Wilkinson, 1988) has been a hallmark of innovative feminist research methods. Given that publication is a key goal of the research process, it seems appropriate to include reflections on the role of a feminist journal editor. The editor role is, by definition, one with power (to edit is to have the power to change another's words, after all). It also has tremendous and sometimes conflicting responsibilities: to the authors, who need that line on their vita to tip the scales in favor of promotion; to the journal's sponsor (in our case Division 35), which entrusts the editor with the charge of managing and maintaining the reputation of this important publication; to the field itself, which prospers depending on the quality of its knowledge base and the respect that is held for its research; and to women in general, who may benefit or be harmed by the application of the research findings, to name only a few of them.

Given such power and awesome responsibility for a feminist editor, it is humbling (even scary) to be the person charged with ensuring the process proceeds in a fair and appropriate way. In the case of *PWQ*, I have had the advice and support of a terrific editorial board, and all manuscripts undergo the scrutiny of a thorough peer-review process. Nevertheless, in the final analysis it is the editor's responsibility to decide if a manuscript is to be published. Indeed, feminist psychologists have been quite clear that they expect editors to be responsible and accountable for material published in journals.

Several issues arose in editing the journal series which provide examples of the challenges that can arise to a feminist editor who must make decisions in the context of limited resources. These special issues were longer than the typical *PWQ* issue. To accommodate the wealth of material generated by this project it was necessary to get creative. Thanks to the generosity of Division 35's Executive Committee, additional funds were voted to support publication of the special issues and to minimize the publication lag that having two back-to-back issues generates. Even so, we continued to have a substantial publication queue that required the cooperation and ingenuity of everyone involved. Thus, I had to overrule Crawford and Kimmel's wish to publish biographies and first names of authors of references—but their goals were met by my publishing the material on a special web site that I manage at http://www.public.asu.edu/~atnfr.[1] This also meant that authors cut and re-cut their articles. People were splendid in their cooperation. On behalf of the editorial board I want to thank each and every one of them for making all of this work.

This book provides a rare look behind the scenes in the research process. I am proud to be a part of this important project. On behalf of the book editors and the *PWQ* editorial board, I want to thank the individuals who provided peer review of the manuscripts, including Jane Aiken, Linda Beckman, Janis Bohan, Rebecca Campbell, Lou Carey, Roger Chaffin, Pauline Clance, Carole Corcoran, Judith Daniluk, Sara Davis, Mary Ann Dutton, Michelle Fine, Constance Fischer, Diane Follingstad, Margery Franklin, Michael Garko, Mary Gergen, Chris Griffin, Rachel Hare-Mustin, Carol Hollenshead, Wendy Hollway, Janet Hyde, Arnold Kahn, Celia Kitzinger, Elizabeth Klonoff, Hope Landrine, Hilary Lips, Bernice Lott, M. Brinton Lykes, Deborah Mahlstedt, Jeanne Marecek, Margaret Matlin, Jill Morowski, Charlotte Patterson, Natalie Porter, Catherine Renner, Lillian Range, Stephanie Riger, Paige Smith, Deborah Tolman, Rhoda Unger, Jane Ussher, Sue Wilkinson, Judith Worell, Gail Wyatt, and Karen Wyche.

Although an editor's role can be time-consuming and filled with conflict, frustrations, and headaches, all seem like minor annoyances when set beside the satisfaction that comes from being part of the exciting process of generating and preserving our feminist knowledge and supporting the careers of our excellent feminist psychologists.

NOTE

1. I want to thank Angela DuMont and Mark Blair for developing the web site on "Innovative Methods."

REFERENCES

Denmark, F. L., Russo, N. F., Frieze, I., & Sechzer, J. (1988). Guidelines for avoiding sexism in psychological research: A report of the Committee on Nonsexist Research. *American Psychologist, 43,* 582–585.

Donovan, J. (1992). *Feminist theory: The intellectual traditions of American feminism* (2nd ed.). New York: Continuum.

Henley, N. M., Meng, K., O'Brien, D., McCarthy, W. J., & Sockloskie, R. J. (1998) Developing a scale to measure the diversity of feminist attitudes. *Psychology of Women Quarterly, 22,* 317–348.

Homans, G. (1949). The strategy of industrial sociology. *American Journal of Sociology, 54,* 330–337.

Madden, M., & Russo, N. F. (1997). *Women in the curriculum: Psychology.* Towsen, MD: National Center for Curriculum Transformation Resources on Women.

McHugh, M., Koeske, R. D., & Frieze, I. H. (1986). Issues to consider in conducting a nonsexist psychology: A review with recommendations. *American Psychologist, 41,* 879–890.

Russo, N. F. (1995). Understanding emotional responses after abortion. In J. C. Chrisler, C. Golden, & P. Rozee (Eds.), *Lectures on the psychology of women* (pp. 260–273). New York: McGraw-Hill.

Russo, N. F. (1998). Measuring feminist attitudes: Just what does it mean to be a feminist? *Psychology of Women Quarterly, 22,* 313–315.

Russo, N. F., & Dabul, A. J. (1994). Feminism and psychology: A dynamic interaction. In E. J. Trickett, R. Watts, & D. Birman, *Human diversity: Perspectives on people in context* (pp. 81–100). San Francisco: Jossey-Bass.

Satterfield, A., & Muehlenhard, C. L. (1997). Shaken confidence: The effects on authority figure's flirtatiousness on women's and men's self-rated creativity. *Psychology of Women Quarterly, 21,* 395–416.

Tong, R. (1998). *Feminist thought: A more comprehensive introduction.* Boulder, CO: Oxford Westview Press.

Walby, S. (1990). *Theorizing patriarchy.* Oxford: Basil Blackwell.

Webster's new encyclopedic dictionary (1993). New York: Black Dog and Levanthal Publishers.

Wilkinson, S. (1988). The role of reflexivity in feminist psychology. *Women's Studies International Forum, 11,* 493–502.

Worell, J., & Etaugh, C. (1994). Transformations: Reconceptualizing theory and research with women [Special issue]. *Psychology of Women Quarterly, 18*(4).

Yoder, J., Schleicher, T. L., & McDonald, T. (1998). Empowering token women leaders: The importance of organizationally legitimated credibility. *Psychology of Women Quarterly, 22,* 209–222.

PROMOTING METHODOLOGICAL DIVERSITY IN FEMINIST RESEARCH

Mary Crawford
University of Connecticut

Ellen B. Kimmel
University of South Florida

Most feminist psychologists are more or less familiar with the feminist critiques of positivist science over the past 25 years or so. Just as we feminist psychologists have been reluctant to change our pedagogy, however (see Forrest & Rosenberg, 1997), so have we been loath to deviate from our traditional research methods. Radical feminists have condemned science as incorrigible. If science is indeed socially constructed, however, then it must be open to reconstruction. *Either/or* can become *and;* both the traditional methods of psychology and methods yet unimagined can serve feminist ends.

Innovation in feminist research methods is a project whose time has come. Just as feminist teachers are being driven to change their pedagogy by their values and the emerging scholarship on girls, women, and learning (e.g., Kimmel & Worell, 1997), so are feminist researchers seeking to expand the ways they raise and answer questions, to think differently about the process of doing research, and to seek ways to make it more useful. The time to promote innovation is now; as evidence, we note the special issues on this theme by both the *Journal of Social Issues* and the *American Journal of Community Psychology,* and the overwhelming response to the First Annual CUNY (City University of New York) Conference in Qualitative Methods in Psychology in 1997. In 1994, Cheryl Travis, then president of Division 35, had the prescience to see the need and act on it by appointing a Task Force on Research Methods. Nancy Felipe Russo, editor of the *Psychology of Women Quarterly,* provided a means for the work of the Task Force to reach a wide audience by publishing a double special issue of *PWQ* (March and June 1999).

Address correspondence and reprint requests to: Mary Crawford, Women's Studies, Box U-181, University of Connecticut, Storrs, CT 06269. E-mail: mcrawford@psych.psy.uconn.edu

1

Both were well aware of the need to support methodological innovation, as their Preface and Introduction to this volume indicate.

A FEW INNOVATIONS OF OUR OWN

In working on this project we (EK and MC) have collaborated as equals, a way of working that may itself be a characteristically feminist method. Our first decision was to avoid perpetuating the tired quantitative/qualitative dichotomy by naming our working group the Task Force on *Innovative* Methods. Is there anything new under the methodological sun? We do not pretend that there is, despite our emphasis on innovation. As Mary Gergen, Joan Chrisler, and Alice LoCicero point out in the final article, innovation is a relative term, dependent for its meaning on the immediate and historical contexts. What the authors in this volume have done is resurrect old strategies, elaborate and/or refine others, combine them in unique ways, or adapt to feminist ends diverse methods either forgotten, never known, or cast out by psychology.

Some psychologists in the United Kingdom, New Zealand, and Canada have been quicker than those in the United States in responding to the need to adopt a broader range of research strategies. For that reason, we made a special effort to solicit manuscripts from authors beyond our national boundaries and are pleased that they responded or volunteered. We felt it important to increase international communication and to benefit from the cross-fertilization of ideas such contact affords. We did not go outside the discipline of psychology, however, because we wished to showcase work within the field and document that such work can be accomplished despite considerable constraints.

An important goal was that this volume should serve as a teaching tool. At this moment in history, psychologists are perpetuating the status quo in research-methods courses and textbooks, ensuring that the next generation will be no more enlightened than the last (Campbell & Schramm, 1995; Ewick, 1994). We hope to disrupt these practices by providing a text that can be a resource for critical pedagogy on innovative methods in graduate and undergraduate courses.

How does one teach a methods course (and feminists should insist on doing so) that opens rather than closes off possibilities? How can feminists eschew the indoctrination against an expanded repertoire of methodological approaches often present in traditional courses? Ewick (1994) strongly urges avoiding a linear approach to designing methods syllabi, wherein a week or two is devoted to each of a series of discrete tasks or methods. Instead, one might present methodological "case studies" using diverse methods on a substantive topic. This permits a comparative exploration of alternative designs, assumptions, formulations, and interpretations. Students would learn what we more experienced researchers consciously or unconsciously understand, that we cannot unlink *what* we know from *how* we know it.

Another innovation here is that we have given equal weight to works presenting specific methods and those exploring the research process. As we discuss in the text that follows, reflexivity of process is a hallmark of feminist research. We hope that this volume will serve as a resource for teachers who wish to induct their students into the "webbed" world of research. To that end we have incorporated commentaries on each article and an extensive resource guide for research, publication, and teaching prepared by Mary Gergen, Joan C. Chrisler, and Alice LoCicero.

As can be seen from the articles, commentaries, and resource guide, research is not linear, desiccated, ahistorical, or free of human emotion and values. Rather, it is dynamic, with each aspect connected to the others. Decisions are made and remade as investigators use ingenuity to develop strategies for building knowledge. The commentaries, in particular, help the reader penetrate some of the complexities of conducting research and understanding the process. Intended to be used as "teaching notes," they highlight the dilemmas, struggles, and humanness of participating in feminist research.

There are other innovations in this volume. We were more flexible in the length requirement. The "lab report" format of APA's *Publication Manual* (American Psychological Association, 1994) was developed for standard methods; innovation may take more explanation, and qualitative methods in particular resist condensation. Moreover, we chose to include the voices of some of the next generation of feminist psychologists, in the form of a group of Janet Hyde's students (see the article by Jaffee et al.), who comment on some of the method and process articles. Their commentary is a sobering and realistic assessment of obstacles to change, both within individuals and within the institutions of psychology.

COMMONALITIES IN FEMINIST METHODS

Feminism is a perspective, not a method (Harding, 1987; Peplau & Conrad, 1989; Reinharz, 1992) or a topic (Grossman et al., 1997). Despite their diversity, the works in this collection have some common themes stemming from their feminist orientation. We identify three such themes; readers may find others.

Reflexivity

Innovative feminist research methods are characterized by an awareness of the personhood and involvement of the researcher (Reinharz, 1992)—what Sue Wilkinson (1988) has called *personal reflexivity*. It is a kind of "disciplined self-reflection" on who we are, how our identities—as individuals in Western society, members of particular ethnic or religious groups, gendered beings, and feminists—influence our work and, in turn, how our work influences these aspects of self. As a small contribution to personal reflexivity, we asked contributors to submit brief biographies, a first for the *Psychology of Women Quarterly*. Though standard psychological rhetoric has long denied it, research—the topics chosen, the theories and methods favored, the meanings made of our "data"—is deeply and reciprocally connected to our own values and self-interest. Personal reflexivity involves an ongoing exploration of these connections along with the recognition that psychological theories apply just as much to ourselves as to our "subjects."

These biographies are published on a special Web page that was constructed in conjunction with this volume to present information, comments, insights, and elaborations that could not be included because of space and financial limitations.

That Web site, which is managed by Nancy Felipe Russo at Arizona State University, links to a discussion group established in conjunction with this effort that is open to all individuals who wish to discuss and debate the issues involved in developing innovative methods in research and share ideas and strategies for testing them.

A broader kind of reflexivity is also evident in this collection. Perhaps because her perspective has sometimes defined her as the "other" in the psychological community, the feminist researcher has developed *functional reflexivity* (Wilkinson, 1988), that is, a sociological perspective on her discipline and how its dominant paradigms are sustained by powerful institutions (Reinharz, 1992; Unger, 1983). For example, the dominant paradigm exercises control by naming. Why was feminist research, with its values openly presented and defended, initially characterized as subjective, politically motivated, and untrustworthy (Crawford, 1997)? A small but significant aspect of naming is dictated by APA reference style. We allowed authors the option of including first names in their reference list. Critics have pointed out that the standard format (last names, first initials) contributes to the invisibility of women; changing this practice seems to be one aspect of functional reflexivity. The editor overruled us on this one, however, out of concern for space and cost restraints. Instead, she has included on the Web site an integrated reference list of the citations using first names that were provided by the authors (see http://www.public.asu.edu/~atnfr).

Methods That Serve—Not Drive—the Inquiry

In feminist research across the disciplines, there is little methodological elitism and a great deal of individual creativity and variety (Reinharz, 1992). Within and across projects, such research is characterized by the use of multiple methods and transgression of disciplinary boundaries. In 1989, Jeanne Marecek and I (MC) predicted that this methodological ferment would increase as psychology moves toward conceptualizing gender as a process and becomes more open to epistemological reflection (Crawford & Marecek, 1989). Earlier, Carolyn Sherif (1982, cited in Reinharz, 1992) predicted that a feminist methodology would be at hand when we recognized the need for cross-disciplinary inquiry and the integration of historical, political, and economic analyses with psychological ones.

Social Change Orientation

Advocacy and scholarship are *not* incompatible activities, despite what we have been socialized to believe (Reinharz, 1992; Unger, 1982). Feminist researchers do not just "collect data," they create knowledge, make social judgments about the applicability of that knowledge, and advocate for social change to benefit girls and women. Eroding polarized distinctions, they produce work that is both basic and applied, theoretical and practical, abstract and compellingly concrete. Again, the either/or becomes the and, synthesizing a *passionate scholarship* (DuBois, 1983). Always, the ultimate aim is to contribute to a transformation of gender relations and the gender system. To that end, the articles in this volume pay close attention to the voices and lives of girls and women and recognize the diversity of their experience.

THE POTENTIAL FOR CHANGE

We hope that this compendium will be useful to the women and men who create psychological knowledge. Feminist psychology has cared about methods from its start (Marecek, 1989). And feminist psychologists are perhaps more open to changing methods because they have had less to gain from the dominant paradigm (Unger, 1982; Wilkinson, 1988). As Rhoda Unger (1983) noted, they "are in a position of being the younger generation whatever their ages. They may have less commitment to prevailing ideology both because they are in a good position to recognize its flaws and because they have not received many rewards for having been committed to it" (p. 25).

We do not, however, wish to impose a new and ever-more-impossible set of methodological standards. Feminist psychologists are already working a double shift. As psychologists in academic and applied settings, we want to design and carry out research that meets all the conventional standards: Research that is free of major design problems, avoids sampling biases, has appropriate control groups, provides a definitive test of theory-derived hypotheses, provides results that lead to the development of rigorous causal models, and gets published in the "right" journals, leading to major funding. The APA *Publication Manual* (1994) admonishes us early on that

> No amount of skill in writing can disguise research that is poorly designed or managed. Indeed such defects are a major cause for the rejection of manuscripts. Before committing a report to manuscript form, you as a would-be author should critically review the quality of research and ask if the research is sufficiently important and free from flaws to justify publication.... No matter how well written, a paper that reflects poor methods is unacceptable (p. 2).

At the same time, as feminists, we articulate an additional set of goals. We want to recognize and acknowledge the role of values in research and to ground our work in feminist, not androcentric, theories and models. We want to expand the definition of good design and include our own values when making judgments about what is important. We want to focus on girls' and women's lived experience and the conditions of their lives and to behave in keeping with feminist values. We want to create a rapport, even a dialogue, with those who give their time to participate in our research. We want to give away our results to our participants so that they can benefit. We care about diversity more than homogeneity. We want our research to be powerful not only in the statistical sense but in its potential for bettering the lot of girls and women. Indeed, we want to do research that will change the world.

The collection is not an admonition to become a "research superwoman" (or superman) who becomes worn out trying to meet incompatible goals, however. Feminism and psychology have forged an uneasy alliance (Burman, 1997; Crawford, 1997). Each of the projects in this collection illustrates in its own particular way the creative tension of that ongoing alliance. The tension is palpable in the lives of feminist psychologists who strive to do research that is "connected to their personal beliefs and understandings, viable for their professional lives, safe for their students, and valuable to the participants and their communities" (Grossman et al., 1997). Our hope is that the examples, analysis, and resources presented here make such strivings a little easier and more rewarding.

REFERENCES

Burman, E. (Ed.). (1997). *Deconstructing feminist psychology*. London: Sage.

Campbell, R., & Schramm, P. J. (1995). Feminist research methods: A content analysis of psychology and social science textbooks. *Psychology of Women Quarterly, 19,* 85–106.

Crawford, M. (1997, April). *Feminism and psychology: An uneasy alliance*. Invited address presented at the meeting of the British Psychological Society, Edinburgh, Scotland.

Crawford, M., & Marecek, J. (1989). Psychology reconstructs the female. *Psychology of Women Quarterly, 13,* 147–166.

DuBois, B. (1983). Passionate scholarship: Notes on values, knowing, and method in feminist social science. In R. D. Klein & G. Bowles (Eds.), *Theories of women's studies* (pp. 105–116). Boston: Routledge & Kegan Paul.

Ewick, P. (1994). Integrating feminist epistemologies in undergraduate research methods. *Gender and Society, 8,* 92–108.

Forrest, L., & Rosenberg, F. (1997). A review of the feminist pedagogy literature: The neglected child of feminist psychology. *Applied and Preventive Psychology, 6,* 179–192.

Grossman, F. K., Gilbert, L. A., Genero, N. P., Hawes, S. E., Hyde, J. S., & Marecek, J. (1997). Feminist research: Practice and problems. In J. Worell & N. G. Johnson (Eds.), *Shaping the future of feminist psychology: Education, research, and practice* (pp. 73–92). Washington, DC: American Psychological Association.

Harding, S. (Ed.). (1987). *Feminism and methodology*. Bloomington, IN: Indiana University Press.

Kimmel, E., & Worell, J. (1997). Practicing what we preach: Principles and strategies of feminist pedagogy. In J. Worell & N. G. Johnson (Eds.), *Shaping the future of feminist psychology: Education, research, and practice* (pp. 121–154). Washington, DC: American Psychological Association.

Marecek, J. (1989). Introduction to special issue: Theory and method in feminist psychology. *Psychology of Women Quarterly, 13,* 367–378.

Peplau, L. A., & Conrad, E. (1989). Beyond nonsexist research: The perils of feminist methods in psychology. *Psychology of Women Quarterly, 13,* 379–400.

Publication manual of the American Psychological Association (4th ed). (1994). Washington, DC: American Psychological Association.

Reinharz, S. (1992). *Feminist methods in social research*. New York: Oxford University Press.

Unger, R. (1982). Advocacy versus scholarship revisited: Issues in the psychology of women. *Psychology of Women Quarterly, 7,* 5–17.

Unger, R. (1983). Through the looking glass: No wonderland yet! (The reciprocal relationship between methodology and models of reality). *Psychology of Women Quarterly, 8,* 9–32.

Wilkinson, S. (1988). The role of reflexivity in feminist psychology. *Women's Studies International Forum, 11,* 493–502.

DIMENSIONS OF DESIRE

*Bridging Qualitative and Quantitative
Methods in a Study of Female
Adolescent Sexuality*

Deborah L. Tolman and Laura A. Szalacha
Wellesley College Center for Research on Women

This study provides an example of how feminist psychology can bridge qualitative and quantitative methods while keeping lived experience at the center of an inquiry. The goal of the study was to begin to understand adolescent girls' experiences of sexual desire. We describe three separate and synergistically related analyses of interviews with 30 adolescent girls. We begin with a qualitative analysis of their voiced experiences of sexual desire; follow with a quantitative analysis of the differences in how urban and suburban girls describe these experiences, assessing the role of reported sexual violation; and conclude with a second qualitative analysis exploring the interaction between social location and reported sexual violation. These three analyses enabled us to understand qualitatively and to quantify interrelated dimensions of desire as described by adolescent girls.

The meaning and importance of women's sexuality and its systematic suppression (Rich, 1980) has been central in second-wave feminist research, theory, and politics (e.g., Snitow, Stansell, & Thompson, 1983; Vance, 1984). This study is a response to an acute absence of acknowledgment in psychological research of sexual desire as a normative aspect of female adolescent development (Tolman, 1994a). The work of several feminist scholars has suggested that girls' experiences of sexuality

This research was supported in part by a grant from the Spencer Foundation Small Grants Program. The authors wish to thank Michelle Porche, John B. Willett, Vita Rabinowitz, Elizabeth Debold, Joy Moreton, Margaret Keiley, and Judith D. Singer for their consultation and assistance, as well as the editors of this volume and two anonymous reviewers for their helpful comments.

Address correspondence and reprint requests to: D. Tolman, Center for Research on Women, Wellesley College, Wellesley, MA 02481-8203. E-mail: dtolman@wellesley.edu and sexual desire in particular are a significant, albeit neglected, force in girls' development (e.g., Cowie & Lees, 1987; Nava, 1987; Thompson, 1984, 1995) and as such are potentially crucial in girls' developing a sense of entitlement and empowerment (Fine, 1988; Tolman, 1994b). Feminist social psychologist Michelle Fine identified a "missing discourse of desire" in adults' discussions of girls' sexuality (Fine, 1988). Her research suggested that girls do know and speak of desire, despite anxious or even well-meaning denial of female adolescent sexual desire on the part of the adults in their lives. Fine's research raised the question of how girls speak about and experience their own sexual feelings. The goal of this study was to begin to understand the dimensions of the experience of sexual desire for adolescent girls.

There are several intertwining reasons that psychology, even feminist psychology, has not made significant inroads into the question of adolescent girls' sexual feelings. Feminist scholars have theorized how patriarchal suppression of female sexuality is a key aspect of women's oppression (i.e., Rich, 1980; Vance, 1984). Despite extensive inquiry into female adolescent sexual *behavior* (e.g., Delameter & Mac-Corquodale, 1979; Lees, 1986; Levinson, 1986; Scott-Jones & Turner, 1988) and a history of theorizing sexuality development (e.g., Benjamin, 1988; Freud, 1905; Jordan, 1987), there have been no studies that include the question of girls' sexual desire (Thompson, 1984; Tolman, 1994a). Buried within an ostensibly objective stance is the historical denial and denigration of female adolescent sexuality (Tolman, 1996). These studies also belie the politics of adolescent pregnancy as they trickle down into the research world. Conducted primarily by sociologists and demographers, such studies offer a limited conception of girls' sexuality. They focus on whether or not and when girls have had sexual intercourse and whether or not they have used effective measures of contraception and seek to identify trends in the outcomes of girls' choices about heterosexual intercourse. The agenda of such studies has not been to understand or support the development of healthy sexuality among girls (Tolman, in press). To achieve the goals of marking behavioral trends and distinguishing between "good" and "bad" groups of girls, these studies almost exclusively rely on survey method. This methodology has framed and limited for girls what the pertinent questions and possible answers are about what is important in the development of their sexuality.

The current study represents a different research agenda by locating a question about girls' sexuality development within a query about girls' healthy psychological development. Moving away from a focus on sexual intercourse, sexual behavior, sexual attitudes, or even sexual outcomes, our research question is phenomenological: How do girls describe their sexual experiences and sexual feelings and in what ways do they speak about their own bodies in telling their stories of desire? This theoretical shift ushers in a movement away from survey methods toward methods that provide research participants with opportunities to convey the meanings they make of their experiences. It also requires the explicit use of a feminist methodological approach.

Qualitative, phenomenological methods that enable understanding of people's experiences (Denzin & Lincoln, 1994; Packer & Addison, 1989) and the feminist perspective necessary to inform inquiry into an aspect of female experience that is systematically denigrated and denied in a patriarchal society (Irigaray, 1981; Omolade, 1983; Rich, 1980) do not yet enjoy wide respect within psychology

(Morowski, 1994). Even within feminist psychology, the question of what constitutes feminist methods continues to be intensely debated and unresolved (Crawford & Marecek, 1989; Fine, 1992; Marecek, 1989; Riger, 1992). This debate has often revolved around two approaches to understanding feminist methodology and the role of methods in feminist transformation of psychology. One approach to feminist methods is to work within psychology's methodological traditions, using conventional quantitative methods to answer research questions driven by feminist theory. Such research is more easily accepted by the discipline and thus has been thought by some to have more potential to transform it (Lykes & Stewart, 1986). The second approach holds that feminist methods are subject centered and therefore necessarily qualitative, disruptive of the tradition of objective experimental and survey methods in the field (Fine & Gordon, 1989). Such methods are aimed at generating knowledge about women's lives previously not produced by psychologists, thus transforming the information as well as the practices that constitute psychological knowledge and its production.

These two approaches have consistently been positioned in opposition to one another and framed as a choice in practice for feminist researchers. These very different perspectives on feminist methodology have contributed to the debate about the very concept of feminist methods itself. By demonstrating how both qualitative and quantitative methods can be used synergistically in a way that balances and integrates the concerns and demands of both feminist perspectives on methods, we hope that the methodological approach to learning about adolescent girls' experiences of sexual desire described in this article may serve as a contribution to defusing and reconfiguring this often divisive debate within feminist psychology.

The disagreements about methodology within feminist psychology reflect larger concerns within psychology and within the social sciences as a whole about what constitutes good research in the wake of poststructuralism and the ensuing postmodern debates about research paradigms (e.g., Cook & Reichardt, 1979; Sechrest & Sidani, 1995; Shadish, 1995; Weedon, 1987). In offering an approach that integrates qualitative and quantitative methods in a feminist research project, we begin by contextualizing the feminist debates within these larger issues. The debate on the relative value, appropriateness, and possible integration of quantitative and qualitative research paradigms has been a part of research in psychology's landscape for almost two decades (Cook & Reichardt, 1979; Healy & Sewart, 1991; Jayaratne & Stewart, 1991). Quantitative and qualitative approaches are often understood as separate paradigms of research, with radically differing assumptions, requirements, and procedures that are rooted in completely different epistemologies. One position of the philosophical debate contends that the integration of quantitative and qualitative paradigms is impossible, as they represent irreconcilable worldviews (e.g., Guba & Lincoln, 1989; Mishler, 1986). The opposite position, maintained on both philosophic and pragmatic grounds, is that not only *can* the two paradigms be combined at the hands-on level of research practice, at the sociological level of methodological assumptions, and at the metaphysical level of metatheoretical assumptions, they *should* be so combined, because these concerns are superseded in importance by political goals about how research findings should be used (Firestone, 1993; Tashakkori & Teddlie, 1998).

Finally, there are those who maintain that the point is not to accommodate or reconcile distinct paradigms but to recognize each as unique, historically situated forms of insight.[2] Lee Schulman (1986) argued that each research paradigm is bound by the programs and departments that teach them. Each research paradigm has grown "out of a particular perspective, a bias of either convention or discipline, necessarily illuminating some part of the field of teaching while ignoring the rest" and that "the danger for any field of social science or educational research lies in its potential corruption (or worse, trivialization) by a single paradigmatic view" (pp. 2–3). Rather than force a dichotomous choice, Kidder and Fine (1987) have suggested that researchers both avoid "homogenizing research methods and cultures," and strive to be "bicultural" (p. 57). Sktric (1990) suggested that the goal of researchers should be to understand both quantitative and qualitative paradigms, to learn to speak to them and through them, and to recognize that each are ways of seeing that simultaneously reveal and conceal.[3]

Unfortunately, the ongoing philosophical debate and discussion, although alive at conferences, on faculties, and in some journals, are rarely incorporated explicitly into actual research. At the same time, the substantive combination of qualitative and quantitative methods has gone forward, despite or in lieu of this epistemological unrest (Shadish, 1995). Guided mostly by pragmatic perspectives such as those of Patton (1990a) and Greene (1994), the qualitative/quantitative "joint venture" has become a feature in many disciplines, most notably in public health (e.g., Carlson, 1996; Keenan, 1996), program evaluation (e.g., House, 1994; Patton, 1990a, 1990b; Reichardt & Rallis, 1994), education (e.g., Goldfarb, 1995) and, to some extent, in psychology (e.g., Debats, 1995; Gladue, 1991; Hines, 1993; Way, Stauber, & Nakkula, 1994). Indeed, some have claimed that "methodological pluralism is an absolutely necessary strategy in the face of overwhelming cognitive limitations and biases inherent in human mental processing and responding" (Sechrest & Sidani, 1995, p. 80). The challenge of grappling with increasingly complex social problems, particularly those that confront activist and applied psychologies like feminist psychology, demands that we investigate further the hidden potential in combining quantitative and qualitative research methods.

The combination of methods has appeared in several recognizable forms. A "pseudo-combination" is a study conducted wholly under one rubric, with the other type of method serving simply as a support or illustration. The "logic-in-use" (Kaplan, 1964) of the study largely ignores one of the two approaches. Quantitative studies of this sort often have some illuminating portraits to "liven up the numbers" or to add richness. Qualitative studies may provide some "quasi-statistics" (Becker, 1986), which serve to add the legitimacy that numbers have traditionally commanded.

There are, however, studies in which both approaches are genuinely and equitably used. One possibility is a concurrent approach (Whitbourne & Powers, 1994). In this type of study, there is a peaceful coexistence or parallel process wherein two studies are conducted simultaneously, though each is whole and separate from the other. The chief difficulty lies in the integration of the findings of two very different, almost separate studies. Kidder and Fine (1987) cautioned that different methods within different paradigms are not simply addressing the same questions differently. Instead, they are addressing different questions, revealing different levels of activity, and leading to different knowledge, interpretations, and explanations. Such differences raise thorny questions of how to square or interpret contradictory findings. A second possibility for an integrated design is a sequential approach, in which a study is conducted in phases, using one method for one part of the study and then another method for another part. Most often this has taken the form of an exploratory qualitative study, which gives rise to the formulation of an instrument and then a confirmatory quantitative study. It can also be, however, that one would conduct a quantitative survey in order to provide profiles to frame questions and sampling for a qualitative phase. It is important to note that in this approach, neither the qualitative nor the quantitative method is superior and neither sequence is preferred (Maxwell, 1996). A third possibility is what Patton (1990b) suggested as "methodological mixes," in which one combines various methods simultaneously. This "technical eclecticism" requires a pragmatic point of view; methods, regardless of whether they originate in a qualitative or quantitative paradigm, are irrelevant to the question of what makes research viable. Finally, there is also the possibility of a wholly "integrated approach," wherein one combines both quantitative and qualitative approaches throughout the entire process from the formation of research questions, to decisions about sampling, to data collection and analyses. A real advantage in this option is the possibility of a methodological dialogue—an ongoing, dialectically informative interaction at each point of the research.

The study we report here does not fit neatly into any of these specific strategies for combining qualitative and quantitative methods; rather, the blend of qualitative and quantitative methods at which we have arrived is a kind of sequential integration. What distinguishes this approach is that it is explicitly feminist in nature; what drove our decisions was a feminist organizing principle of listening to and taking women's voices seriously (Andersen, Armitage, Jack, & Wittner, 1990; Belenky, Clinchy, Goldberger, & Tarule, 1986; Gilligan, 1982; Oakley, 1981), particularly in data collection and data reduction, as well as in data analysis and interpretation. Working with a single database, a set of intensive, semi-structured interviews with 30 adolescent girls attending public schools in urban and suburban settings, we posed and answered a series of questions grounded in feminist theory and research on female adolescent sexuality. Our method of data collection is anchored in a qualitative epistemology and methodology, and we use multiple methods of data analysis, including careful interpretations of narrative data and also more reductive, statistical methods of analysis, to answer an array of related feminist questions about female adolescent experiences of sexual desire. By choosing the method of data analysis that enabled us to answer each emerging question, the result has been an eclectic merging of both approaches to feminist methodology, producing a kind of feminist eclecticism that has at its heart the perspectives and experiences of these young women.

METHOD

Participants

The design of this study was grounded in the possibility that both qualitative and quantitative analyses would be performed. Tolman chose a random sample size of 30,[4] balancing concerns that the sample be large enough to conduct statistical analyses, while at the same time producing a manageable amount of rich narrative data.[5] Tolman collected data from eleventh grade girls, who ranged in age from

15–19, at an urban public high school ($n = 15$) and a suburban public high school ($n = 15$).[6] The sample thus represents an age group in which sexual activity is part of the social landscape and includes girls who are subject to various sexual stereotypes: Urban girls (often girls of color) are considered to be overly sexual, whereas suburban girls are thought of as asexual (Tolman, 1996). The design was meant to enable a challenge of such stereotypes of girls and to open the question of what normal sexuality is for all adolescent girls. In the urban school sample there were seven Black, three Latina, and five White girls.[7] In the suburban school, we spoke with 14 White girls and 1 Latina girl. The suburban girls are from Protestant, Catholic, and Jewish families, whereas the urban girls are from Protestant and Catholic backgrounds. One of the girls is a self-described lesbian, and two describe desire for both boys and girls.

In this analysis, we focus on the differences between and similarities among girls who live in an urban and a suburban social location. Tolman did not collect specific data on socioeconomic status (SES) for several reasons. As we will discuss in the text that follows, because Tolman was asking girls to speak about something that is essentially unspeakable, she made careful choices about what she did and did not ask so as to enhance the development of trust. Rather than collect conventional socioeconomic data on participants' parental, educational, and occupational background, which in the context of these interviews could have been experienced by the girls as alienating, she asked them to tell her in their own words about their families and social contexts. Based on their descriptions of their parents' work lives and their daily experiences with crime, housing, and need for social services in their neighborhoods and communities, Tolman concluded that although there was some variation within each group, the urban girls were all from poor and working-class families, and the suburban girls were all living in middle- and upper-middle-class families. In addition to girls' descriptions, differences such as levels in obvious poverty, explicit violence, community and educational resources, neighborhood stability and general well-being were discernable from observation, substantiating the girls' reports of their environments. We conclude that the urban/suburban difference in this case is a reasonable reflection of gross class differences in terms of the experiences and meanings associated with these girls' daily lives. Because these class designations are not precise, we understand and interpret our data in terms of differences in social locations rather than class per se, with these two distinct social locations offering a meaningful interpretive context for understanding how girls speak about, make meaning of, and experience their sexuality. In other analyses from this study, Tolman has integrated cultural characteristics in interpreting these data (e.g., Tolman, 1994a, 1996).

Procedure

A key component of this feminist inquiry is the method of data collection. Grounded in an explicitly feminist method of data collection (Brown & Gilligan, 1992, Taylor, Gilligan, & Sullivan, 1996; Way, 1995), Tolman invited in-depth narrative and descriptive data from girls on their thoughts about and subjective experiences of sexuality, including sexual desire, sexual pleasure, feeling sexy, and sexual fantasies, during private, one-on-one, semi-structured clinical interviews that lasted from 45 minutes to 2 hours. One of the primary tools of oppression of women is the maintenance of silence about their experiences and perspectives (Lorde, 1984; Rich, 1980). Acknowledging the possibility of female adolescent sexual agency, desire, pleasure, and fantasies through the act of asking about these realms of experience renders this approach a feminist research method. This method departs from a survey design by creating an opportunity for girls to put into words and to name their experience in and questions about a realm of their lives that remains unspoken in the larger culture. Thus, as a form of data collection, it enables us to learn from girls what might otherwise remain an unknown perspective on this part of their lives.

Each interview included a standard set of questions; follow-up questions guided by a feminist relational approach to psychological inquiry were asked in direct response to the specific contours of each interviewee's particular experiences (Brown & Gilligan, 1992; Way, 1995). The consent of participants and their parents (for girls who were under 18) was obtained prior to the interview. All interviews were tape-recorded and transcribed. Confidentiality and anonymity in reporting were ensured. No girl disclosed an experience of current sexual abuse or violence. The girls who disclosed past sexual abuse and dating violence were referred, with their permission, into appropriate therapeutic situations when they so wished.

This study as a whole has three iterations that are organized by three separate and synergistically related research questions, which emerged sequentially in response to the findings generated by pursuing the previous research question. These three questions demanded three different methods of analysis of our interview data. Together, the results emerging from these three analyses shed a multilayered light on adolescent girls' experiences of sexual desire.

DATA ANALYSIS AND RESULTS: QUESTION 1

Question 1: How Do Girls Describe Their Experiences of Sexual Desire?

The aim of this component of the study was to understand how the girls in this sample experience and describe their own sexual desire and to learn about the place of their bodies in this experience. The focus on the embodied nature of sexual desire was grounded in a view that psychological health and vitality, self-knowledge, and lived relationships are anchored in the body (Gilligan, Brown, & Rogers, 1989; Young, 1992) and that the meanings we make of our bodily experiences are socially constructed (Rubin, 1985). The findings from this component have been previously reported (Debold, Tolman, & Brown, 1996; Tolman, 1994a, 1994b, 1996; Tolman & Higgins, 1996), but in order to present the interlocking quality of the evolving methodological choices we made in this study, we will describe the methods and results of this analysis.

Data Analysis

The data were analyzed by combining two methods of qualitative analysis. This approach to data analysis was also used in part in answering Question 3 of this study, so we provide a complete description of our approach at this juncture. Tolman identified one narrative in which the girls told a story about an experience of sexual desire to analyze in depth using a method of narrative analysis called The Listening Guide, a feminist interpretive method (Brown, Debold, Gilligan, & Tappan, 1991; Brown, Tappan, Gilligan, Miller, & Argyris, 1989; Gilligan et al., 1989; Rogers & Gilligan, 1988). Acknowledging the multilayered nature of narratives and of the psyche, the "polyphonic and complex" nature of voice and experience (Brown & Gilligan, 1992, p. 15) highlights how there is no single way to understand any given narrative. Therefore, each narrative is read or "listened to" several distinct times; for each listening, the researcher focuses on or "listens for" a given aspect of the experience under study, underlining with a colored pencil the parts of the narrative in which the identified "voice" is expressed. A voice is a way of speaking that has an identifiable set of coherent features. Throughout this process, the researcher continuously checks and records her own thoughts, emotional and embodied feelings, and reactions as part of the data analysis. This method is grounded in a feminist standpoint (Nielsen, 1990), acknowledging that patriarchal culture silences and obscures women's experiences by providing the listener with an organized way to respond to the coded or indirect language of girls and women, especially for topics such as sexuality about which girls and women are not supposed to speak. This psychological approach to data analysis is accomplished in part because this method is explicitly relational, in that the researcher brings her self-knowledge into the process of listening by using clinical methods of empathy to contribute to her understanding of what a girl is saying. This relational practice increases the listener's ability to avoid bias or "voicing over" a girl's story with her own reactions, much like a skilled therapist can use countertransference to inform rather than overwhelm psychotherapy (Tolman, 1992).

In this analysis, Tolman listened for four voices associated with girls' experience of sexual desire: A voice of the self, an erotic voice, a voice of the body, and a voice of response to one's own desire. In listening for self, a standard voice of The Listening Guide, the reader attends to the interviewee as the narrator of the story by following the verbal markers for self, such as "I" or "me." Listening for the self is an efficient way of laying bare in what relationship the narrator places herself to her experience. The listening for self reveals agency and absence of agency, as well as the narrator's experience of herself as a subject and as an object, in the narrative context. Tolman then identified two desire voices, an erotic voice and a voice of responses to one's own desire, which are specific to analyzing what girls say about sexuality, using a grounded-theory approach (Strauss, 1987). Listening for an erotic voice tracks the ways in which girls speak about how sexual desire felt and what it was like for them, such as the intensity or specific quality of their sexual feelings. Listening for a voice of response to their sexual desire tracks how girls describe their thoughts and behavior in reaction to feeling their own sexual desire. Finally, listening for the voice of the body tracks how girls describe the explicitly embodied character of their desire and sexuality experiences.

The result of these sequential listenings and underlinings is a visual map of the different layers of a given experience in a narrative. The way that each voice maps in relation to the other voices is observed and recorded. Then the underlined parts of the narrative are transferred onto worksheets, so that interpretations can be made for what the narrator is saying in close proximity to her actual words. This tracking system enables the researcher to create a trail of evidence (Brown et al., 1989) for the interpretation that is developed. The result is a voice-centered interpretation of girls' narratives of sexual desire, which presents one way to understand these stories, a way that privileges feminist questions of agency, body, and relationship. By providing ample text in reporting results of such analyses (e.g., Brown & Gilligan, 1992; Tolman, 1994a, 1994b), the researcher enables others to develop alternative interpretations informed by different theoretical perspectives.

The second form of data analysis used was the construction of a conceptually clustered matrix for identifying patterns within and between groups (Miles & Huberman, 1984). Using the voice of self, the voice of the body, the erotic voice, and the voice of response as the frame for organizing the interpretations of these narrative data, Tolman incorporated the difference of urban and suburban social locations into the construction of this matrix. This way of organizing the qualitative data revealed how these two groups of girls voiced similar experiences of sexual desire and how their experiences had different qualities. This method also highlights individual variation within each group of girls, so that exceptions to patterns can be examined and understood as part of the diversity of experience for each group of girls.

Results

As Tolman has reported, about two thirds of the entire sample said they felt desire; the remainder said they were confused about whether or not they felt desire, or that they did not feel desire. There were several patterns in the data that were the same for both urban and suburban girls. In the stories of all of the girls who said they felt desire, an erotic voice was audible and characterized by the power, intensity, and urgency of their feeling. All of these girls described their experience of sexual desire in physical terms, defying the common conception of girls' desire as relational rather than embodied by expressing an audible "voice of the body." At the same time, there was an overall pattern for both the urban and suburban girls who voiced desire in these ways to question their entitlement to their own sexual feelings and to express doubt about the possibility of acting directly on their own desire and then being considered good or normal.

Although an erotic voice and a voice of the body sounded similar for urban and suburban girls, differences emerged in how they described their responses to their sexual desire—a kind of "main effect" of social location. One way to characterize this difference is that urban girls describe an agency in the service of protection, whereas suburban girls tell of an agency in the service of pleasure. In this analysis, Tolman heard the urban girls voice self-control and caution and conflict between the voices of their bodies and what they know and say about the reality of their vulnerabilities to AIDS, pregnancy, and getting a bad reputation. Most of these girls make a conscious choice to sacrifice pleasure to protect themselves from danger, at the cost of a severed connection with themselves and little real safety. For instance, Inez describes how, when her body says "yes" and her mind says "no," which she understands as her "mind lookin' towards my body," protecting her from the relational and physical dangers that can result from her own strong feelings.

In contrast, the suburban girls who said they felt desire all speak of a sexual curiosity that is hardly audible among the comparable group of urban girls. This curiosity is tempered by their wish to control themselves when they feel desire. Rather than speaking directly about the problems of physical or social vulnerability like the urban girls did, these suburban girls voice a more internal conflict in relation to their sexual desire, a discrepancy between what they describe feeling in their bodies and the cultural messages about female sexuality and appropriate female sexual behavior that they had internalized. For instance, while Emily offers a detailed description of what desire feels like to her, she also explains that "I don't like to think of myself as feeling really sexual . . . I don't like to think of myself as being like someone who needs to have their desires fulfilled . . . I mean I understand that it's wrong and that everybody has needs, but I just feel like self-conscious when I think about it, and I don't feel self-conscious when I say that we do these things, but I feel self-conscious about saying I need this kind of a thing."

This qualitative difference between the urban and suburban girls was a striking one. Drawing on the realities of their distinct social locations, we interpreted these differences as reflecting and relating to differentials in girls' sense of safety and violence, and the meanings and implications of girls knowing and exploring their sexuality in urban and suburban contexts. The urban girls live in overtly dangerous neighborhoods, where the consequences of their responses to their own sexuality can have enormous negative social, educational, and economic consequences, whereas the suburban girls live in a relatively safe environment, where the consequences of their sexuality are more psychological and internal and less threatening to their material futures. This analysis suggests the crucial importance of young women's social locations in how they experience their own bodies. Two constructions of how these girls understand their own sexual desire emerged: as perceived vulnerability and as possible pleasure.

Although the qualitative significance of this difference was apparent in the distinct voices of these two groups of girls, we wanted to know more about this difference: What is the magnitude of the difference between how urban and suburban girls experience sexual desire? Can this difference be understood quantitatively as well as qualitatively? The content of the difference, focusing on the interplay between pleasure and vulnerability associated with sexuality for girls, contributes new questions as well: Might personal experience with sexual violence play a role in girls' associations of their own desire with pleasure or vulnerability—or a balance between the two? Is such an association different depending on girls' social location? These questions called for a quantitative analysis.

DATA ANALYSIS AND RESULTS: QUESTIONS 2A & 2B

Question 2a: What Is the Size and Significance of the Difference Between Urban and Suburban Girls' Experiences of Their Own Sexual Desire?
Question 2b: Is There an Interaction Between Social Location and Reported Experience of Sexual Abuse or Violence in Whether Urban and Suburban Girls Associate Their Own Desire with Pleasure, Vulnerability, or Both?

The goal of this component of the study was to explore the difference we had identified between the urban and suburban girls' descriptions of desire. We wanted to understand how pleasure and vulnerability were associated differently for these two groups of girls. Evaluating whether there was an interactive effect of sexual abuse or violence through a quantitative analysis would provide useful insights into these dimensions of desire.

Data Analysis

Our challenge was to choose or develop a feminist approach to data reduction so that our interview data could be analyzed statistically. In the qualitative analysis, we had listened intensively to the nuances in a single narrative told by each of these girls, learning about the complexity of their experiences. In order to develop a broader understanding of the patterns in their experiences that could tell us more about what sexual desire is like for girls, we wanted to include more data in this next level of analysis. We shifted from intensive listening to reductive thematic coding as a strategy for including many more narratives in the analysis.

Because we had engaged in a feminist process of listening to girls voice their selves, desire, and bodies, we were able to code their narratives based on the emic themes and categories that we had learned *from them* were significant aspects of their experiences of sexual desire. One of the challenges for us was to continue to represent the complexity we noted in girls' voiced experience. The qualitative analysis had suggested two broad dimensions of girls' experience of desire: pleasure and vulnerability. Individual girls were not easily categorized simply as those who associated desire with pleasure and those who associated desire with vulnerability. In fact, no girl told desire narratives only about pleasure or desire narratives only about vulnerability. Therefore, we shifted our unit of analysis from girl ($N = 30$) to narrative ($N = 128$). We thus avoided collapsing data from multiple narratives told by each girl into a single "pleasure" or "vulnerability" score for her by identifying predominant themes of pleasure, vulnerability, or an equal presence of pleasure and vulnerability for all narratives about desire told by each girl. Increasing the database for each girl by including all of her desire narratives for this analysis met the feminist challenge to preserve the contradictory, complex quality of these girls' lived experiences while reducing our data.

This shift in level of analysis poses two possible problems. The first is whether differences in numbers of narratives told by urban and suburban girls could account for any differences we might find in the expression of pleasure and vulnerability in the narratives told by these two groups. As Table 1 illustrates, there were no significant differences in numbers of desire narratives told by urban versus suburban girls. The second problem is whether using multiple narratives from each girl as the basis of our analysis violates the assumption of independence of observations for linear modeling.[8] We have accounted for the clustering of multiple measurements for each girl in later analyses by estimating a series of fixed-effects logistic regression models. This analytic approach allows us to control for the number of narratives told by each girl and thereby reject the possibility that the differences among groups of girls that we have identified can be attributable to differences in how many narratives each girl or each group of girls told.

We coded the 128 narratives for themes of vulnerability and pleasure that girls associated with their experiences of sexual desire. To recognize the complex nature of both vulnerability and pleasure and to preserve the complexity of the girls' experi-

Table 1

General Characteristics of the Participants (N = 28) and Their Narratives (N = 128)

Characteristics	Total Number of Girls[a]	Total Number of Narratives	Mean Number of Narratives per Girl	SD	t
Urban	14	53	3.78	2.00	
Suburban	14	75	5.35	2.87	1.67[b]
Reported sexual violence	13	56	4.53	2.53	
Did not report sexual violence	15	72	4.60	2.66	.062[c]

[a]Although the total number of participants was 30 girls, 2 of the girls did not tell any desire narratives at all.
[b]p = .105
[c]p = .95

ences, we included six different types or domains of pleasure and vulnerability within each theme, derived from examining their narratives: Personal identity, interpersonal relationships, social relationships, physical, psychological, and other. For example, the theme of vulnerability can represent the physical danger of sexually transmitted disease, the interpersonal risk of loss of friends, or the psychological danger of being emotionally hurt or disappointed. Each narrative was then coded for its predominant overall theme: vulnerability, pleasure, or equal presence of both vulnerability and pleasure. The narratives were double-blind coded; interrater reliability was high (Cohen's Kappa = .87).

To identify whether a girl had experienced sexual violation, we relied on how they answered the question, "Has anything bad ever happened to you that has to do with sex that you would like to tell me about?[9] The girls in this study reported various experiences of sexual abuse and sexual violence, including acquaintance rape and attempted rape, and molestation and rape by adult male family members and by teenage male baby-sitters, as well as by strangers. Because of the small number of reports of sexual harm within each category, we coded all instances as "reported sexual violation" for purposes of this analysis. Of the urban girls, seven did not report sexual violation, whereas eight did, and among the suburban girls, eight did not report sexual violation, whereas seven did. Notably, whether a girl lived in an urban or a suburban social location was not significantly related to whether she had reported an experience of sexual violation (Likelihood Ratio chi-square statistic [LRχ^2] .114, df 1, p = .705), nor was there any difference in numbers of desire narratives told by girls who did versus did not report sexual abuse or violence (see Table 1).

Results

In order to explore the differences in urban and suburban girls' associations of pleasure and vulnerability with their own sexual desire, we began examining the frequencies with which the girls told desire narratives that were predominantly about pleasure or vulnerability or in which both pleasure and vulnerability were equally present. Of these 128 narratives, 60 (46.9%) were predominantly about

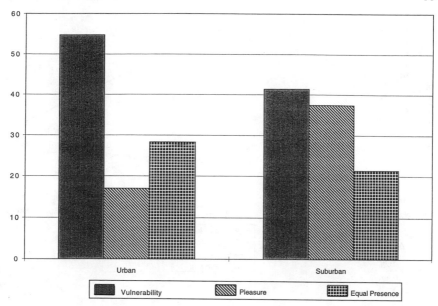

FIGURE 1.   Percentages of narratives stratified by predominant theme and social
location (*N* = 128).

vulnerability, 37 (28.9%) were about pleasure, and 31 (24.2%) included both pleasure and vulnerability themes equally. The proportions of the urban and suburban
girls' narratives that had vulnerability as their predominant theme were somewhat
different, with 54.7% of urban girls' narratives focusing on vulnerability, whereas
41% of suburban girls' narratives did so. The difference between percentage of
narratives in which vulnerability and pleasure were equally present was also small,
with 28% of urban girls' narratives versus 21% of suburban girls' narratives falling
in this category (see Figure 1).

A striking difference emerged between these two groups of girls, however, when
we examined the frequency of a predominant theme of pleasure in their narratives.
Suburban girls told many more narratives about pleasure than did urban girls.
37.3% of suburban girls' narratives were about pleasure as compared to 17% of
urban girls' narratives (see Figure 1). Contingency table analyses support this
observed difference (Likelihood Ratio chi-square statistic [LRχ^2] 6.54, df 2, $p <$
.04). Specifically, suburban girls tell equal numbers of narratives expressing pleasure
and vulnerability, whereas urban girls tell 3.2 times more narratives about vulnerability than about pleasure. These patterns suggest that although urban and suburban
girls all associate their experiences of sexual desire with vulnerability and, to a
lesser extent, a mix of vulnerability and pleasure in comparable proportions, the
place of pleasure in their experiences differs.

In examining what kind of narratives were told by urban and suburban girls who
had and had not reported sexual violation, we expanded our understanding of how
pleasure and vulnerability figure in the desire experiences of these girls. Figures

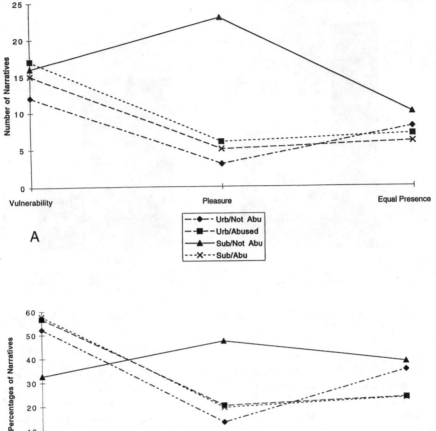

A

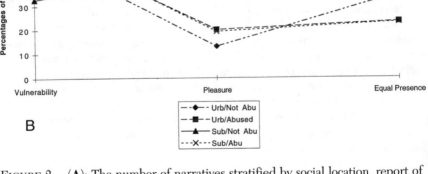

B

FIGURE 2. (**A**): The number of narratives stratified by social location, report of sexual violence and predominant theme ($N = 128$). (**B**): The percentage of narratives stratified by social location, report of sexual violence and predominant theme ($N = 128$).

2a and 2b display the number and percentages of desire narratives told by the girls, stratified by social location, report of sexual violation, and predominant theme. Three groups of girls—one of suburban girls who reported sexual violation and two of urban girls (those who did and did not report sexual violation)—display a similar pattern in predominant themes: They all tell many more vulnerability narratives than narratives about pleasure or narratives in which vulnerability and pleasure figure equally. There is almost no difference in the numbers or proportions of narratives about pleasure versus vulnerability told by urban girls who had and had not reported sexual violation. The group that stands out is the suburban girls who did not report sexual violation. They tell more narratives about pleasure and fewer narratives in which vulnerability and pleasure were balanced than did the other three groups of girls. In addition, a higher percentage of their narratives had a predominant theme of pleasure than narratives that included vulnerability. These findings suggest a further elucidation of the relationship between social location and experience of sexual desire—that, for suburban girls, sexual violation is related to an increased association of vulnerability and diminished association of pleasure with their experiences of sexual desire.

Contingency table analyses support these observations. We found that there was a relationship between a suburban girl's location, her exposure to sexual violence, and the predominant theme of her narratives ($LR\chi^2$ statistic 6.41, df 2, $p < .04$). Specifically, suburban girls who *had* reported sexual violation told 4.3 times more narratives that expressed vulnerability versus pleasure than those told by suburban girls who *had not* reported sexual violation. Furthermore, the narratives told by the girls in the other three groups expressed vulnerability versus pleasure or both pleasure and vulnerability nearly three times (2.8) more than those of suburban girls who had not reported sexual violation.

In order to determine whether these relationships were statistically significant, we fit three fixed-effects logistic regression models: for narratives with a predominance of pleasure, narratives with a predominance of vulnerability, and narratives with an equal balance between vulnerability and pleasure. By including dummy variables to estimate each girl's effect, we were able to address the potential problems associated with the lack of independence of each narrative and not overestimate the independent degrees of freedom (Green, 1993; Hanushek, 1990).

The regression models confirmed our earlier findings associating an interaction between a suburban social location and absence of sexual violation with telling more pleasure narratives. The estimated odds[10] that a suburban girl who had not reported sexual violation would relate a narrative expressing pleasure was 5.89 times that of urban girls who had not reported sexual violation (Wald chi-square $= 6.7679$, $p < .0093$). Furthermore, suburban girls who did report sexual violation told narratives with a predominant theme of pleasure only a quarter of the time (.269), as compared with suburban girls who had not reported such abuses.[11] A girl's social location, report of sexual violation, or an interaction between the two were not significant indicators of narratives with a predominant theme of vulnerability or of narratives with equally expressed themes of vulnerability and pleasure (Wald chi-squares $= 5.21$, $p = .390$ and $= 4.45$, $p = .485$, respectively).

This quantitative analysis enables us to elucidate further our understanding of how these urban and suburban girls experience their own sexual desire. We are able to describe specifically the magnitude of the difference we noted qualitatively between urban and suburban girls' experiences of desire. We are also able to highlight that an interplay between these girls' social locations and personal histories of sexual violation figures significantly in how they experience and give meaning to their own desire, specifically pinpointing how they are limited and supported in the possibility of associating their own sexual desire with pleasure. This analysis allows us to retain and extend the complexity of our understanding that vulnerability is a key aspect of sexual desire for all of these girls.

DATA ANALYSIS AND RESULTS: QUESTION 3

Question 3: How Do Descriptions and Narratives of Sexual Desire Offered by Suburban Girls Who Have Not Reported Sexual Violence or Abuse Compare with the Descriptions and Narratives Offered by Urban Girls Who Have and Have Not Reported Sexual Violence and Abuse and Suburban Girls Who Have Reported Sexual Violence and Abuse?

Our statistical analysis suggested that sexual violation can be a dimension of desire. The quantitative approach indicated that there were differences in how sexual violation shaped urban and suburban girls' experiences of desire. Our finding of a significant interactive effect between social location and report of sexual violation for suburban but not urban girls suggests the need to understand more about the comparative quality of their experiences of sexual desire. To pursue this lead, we chose to focus on how the girls spoke about their bodies in a second qualitative analysis, because, as the site of both vulnerability and pleasure (Vance, 1984), the specific context of bodily experience offers a theoretically compelling focal point for deepening our understanding of this dimension of desire.

Data Analysis
To explore this question, we returned to the original transcripts of the interviews and examined the complete text of each interview, an expansion on the original in-depth analysis of a single desire narrative. Using the same analytic method as described for answering Question 1, we tracked how the girls talked about their bodies and also tracked specific descriptions of how they related their bodies to their minds and their emotions (often referred to by the girls as their "selves"). Using The Listening Guide method, we marked all parts of each transcript where the girls mentioned their bodies for a voice of the body. We then listened for the self voice in each of these transcripts. This second time through the transcripts enabled us to determine how each girl related her experience of her body in her experiences of sexual desire and pleasure with her self, that is, how she related or integrated her mind and her emotions with her bodily experience. After completing a worksheet reflecting our interpretations of the girls' words, we organized these interpretations into a conceptually clustered matrix that would allow us to explore further and characterize the differences we had identified in the previous statistical analyses between the suburban girls who had not been sexually violated or abused and the other three groups of girls. We provide a section of this matrix to illustrate how this method makes it possible to identify similarities and differences within and between categories (see Table 2).

Results
In returning to the voices of urban and suburban girls who did and did not report experiences of sexual abuse or violence, we were able to investigate further the

Table 2

Partial Conceptually Clustered Matrix of the Voice of the Body,
Relationship Between Body and Self, and Girl Stratified by Social Location
and Report of Sexual Violence

Suburban Girls—No Report of Sexual Violation

Girl	Voice of the Body	Relationship Between Body and Self
Zoe (White)	Sexual desire and pleasure described in specific physical terms: "tingling," "shivering"	Desire as interplay between mind and body: interplay between "mental" and "physical" feelings
	Specific knowledge of pleasure: varying intensity and depth of feeling observed: "sometimes I kinda feel it's more deeper"	Linking physical feelings with mental feelings through relationship: "I don't know if you can feel it (desire) if you did it with someone who you didn't really love"
	Desire identified through embodied feeling	
Eugenia (White)	Sexual desire and pleasure described in specific physical terms: "strong," "wet," "between my legs," "throbbing," "burn," "waves," "your body's excited"	Desire as interplay between mind and body: interplay between strong emotions and strong physical/sexual feelings, response, excitement and pleasure; mind used to soothe and quiet body when required; specific pathway relating emotional and physical feelings (mind and then body); link between focus of mind and experience of body; interplay of expressing self in relationship and increasing sexual feelings: "when there's emotions behind it, it makes it like that much more exciting"
	Specific knowledge of pleasure: orgasm as loss of "control" that is positive and pleasurable, linked to "comfort" in a relationship; explicit detailed knowledge of how body does and does not respond	
	Desire identified through embodied feeling; strength of physical pleasure as motivation to continue behavior	Exploration of her relationship to own body: question about lack of sense of entitlement to self-pleasure through masturbation
		Knowledge of benefits of knowing own sexual, physical responses and bringing information into relationships
		Link of self-confidence to self-pleasure through masturbation

Table 2

Continued

Suburban Girls—No Report of Sexual Violation

Girl	Voice of the Body	Relationship Between Body and Self
Jane (White)	Embodied feeling described in nonspecific terms: "good," "expectant," "demanding," a "need," "jumpy," "excited" Link of physical pleasure to feeling of "happiness" and "being intimate" Desire linked to being touched physically: mouth, neck, skin, hair, "everywhere" Intimate knowledge of sexual pleasure as interplay of intensity and physical stimulation	Sense of entitlement to own body and its pleasures yet masturbation not sexually exciting or "natural" Link of pleasure and intensity of feeling to emotional anticipation Desire as interplay between mind and body Chooses to act on physical feelings only if they occur in the context of a relationship Enjoyment in experiencing embodied pleasure

---

Urban Girls—No Report of Sexual Violation

Girl	Voice of the Body	Relationship Between Body and Self
Beverly (African American)	Specific body parts associated with vulnerability to pleasure: "weak spot" on neck Descriptions of pleasure and desire suggest dissociation: "numb" Different descriptions of sexual pleasure and desire: as both numbness of body and body "saying yes"	Prohibition on action if absence of own embodied feeling: "If you want to do it, do it. If you don't want to, don't do it" Mind acts as vigilant guardian of responsive body: mind censors body "My body was saying yes, but my mouth was saying no" Body difficult to control, body as rogue: "my whole body is just going"
Charlene (White)	Sexual desire and pleasure described in specific physical terms: "having the shakes," "butterflies," "getting wet" Disembodied descriptions of desire: "felt like Jello," "in a daze," "I go to sleep" Specific knowledge of presence and absence of sex-	Sense of entitlement to satisfaction Mind acts as vigilant guardian of responsive body: mind censors and silences body: "the more I like feel myself getting wet or something, it's like, just change my mind and think about something else"

Table 2

Continued

Urban Girls—No Report of Sexual Violation

Girl	Voice of the Body	Relationship Between Body and Self
Charlene (continued)	ual satisfaction: "I think I get satisfied just by like hugs and kisses"; "sometimes he stops before like, you know, I am done" Specific knowledge of pleasure: "We have like different spots, you know, he touches you, that just makes you go in a daze or whatever"	Experience of desire associated with mistrust of self and fear of pregnancy
Rochelle (African American)	Specific knowledge of pleasure: enjoys sex intermittently ("once in a while" vs. "all the time") Specific knowledge of desire: moderate sex associated with more desire Desire expressed in specific physical terms: a "tingle," "like a fever or drugs" Embodied feeling described in nonspecific language: "this feeling, to get rid of" Desire experienced more when alone than being touched Connection between desire for thinness and desire to explore sexuality (discomfort with body, and with "being looked at")	Distanced from own body: intimidated by idea of masturbation Fear of pregnancy interferes with embodied feeling: "I don't really think I have any type of sexual pleasure . . . cause like I always have in the back of my mind, I'm gonna get pregnant . . . it's like, when I'm having sex, I just think about that" Fear of voicing own desire: "I just find it hard to come out and say . . . I would sort of like him to do it (cunnilingus)" Mind quiets body: "I just, you know, just be quiet and just go away by myself, I just be calm, and like they'll (sexual feelings) go away" Internalized cultural norms of femininity shortcircuit sexual curiosity: "I just sorta have in my mind that a woman's not supposed to be like aggressive doing stuff like that (being "on top")"

(continued)

Table 2

Continued

Suburban Girls—Reported Sexual Violation

Girl	Voice of the Body	Relationship Between Body and Self
Alexandra (White, bisexual, raped by boyfriend)	Distinction between physical arousal and pleasure Pleasure and desire described in specific physical terms: "makes me tingle," "feel giddy and tingly," "physically turned on" Specific knowledge of pleasure: soft things vs. "classically sexual acts, such as feeling up"; on top of the vagina, not inside Sexual stimulation associated with pain and discomfort as it intensifies: "a very sore sensation, a sort of nauseous feeling in my stomach" (associated with experiences with males) Describes having physical needs (in association with her girlfriend)	Response to desire and pleasure is to close body down, "refuse to let myself go" Resists cultural norms of femininity about female sexuality Equal importance of "physical, mental, social and emotional parts" of desire, although no clear relationship between them identified Mind as consultant for body: body as censor for self when mind is not vigilant enough Specific pathway relating emotional and physical feelings (mind and then body): "You meet a guy, you like him, you want to have sex with him, it's all in your mind . . . and then when he touches you, you get pleasure from it"
Nikki (White, hit repeatedly by boyfriend)	Absence of embodied feeling or desire: "I don't really feel anything" Disembodied desire for sex associated with wish to get it over with and avoid pain when drunk	Sexual pleasure and desire associated primarily with the mind, in thoughts Specific pathway relating ideas and physical feelings (mind and then body) Mind as eraser: "If you think about it long enough, you just forget"

Table 2

Continued

Suburban Girls—Reported Sexual Violation

Girl	Voice of the Body	Relationship Between Body and Self
Nikki (continued)		Dissociation of mind and body: "I know I want him but it doesn't make me feel anything"
Liz (White, molested by adult male, rape averted by circumstances, single occurrence)	Embodied feeling described in nonspecific language: "satisfaction," "tiring," "exhausted," "really tense and then I rest, it melts" Physical pleasure associated with specific behavior Absence of knowledge of body-part names yet knowledge of bodily response and pleasure Specific knowledge of what is pleasurable and not pleasurable Desire described in specific physical terms: "hot," "a burning sensation," "feeling sweaty" Distinguish between feelings of love and lust	Sexual desire includes desire for physical closeness in a relationship Discomfort with own body (self-conscious about weight) Desire emerges out of interactions that are not specific "sexual" behaviors Mind as a distraction to embodied response: concern about being found out doing something taboo Idea of a behavior can be pleasurable even when physical experience itself is not: "it makes me feel good, I think, just thinking about it being there (boy's erect penis), it just seemed so like sexual, so neat, it wasn't like I was getting excited, I was just doing it (fellatio) for him"

Urban Girls—Reported Sexual Violation

Girl	Voice of the Body	Relationship Between Body and Self
Laura (African American, repeatedly molested and raped by male babysitter in childhood)	"Not sure" about having experienced sexual pleasure or desire Embodied feeling described in nonspecific language: "jumpy," "like taking drugs," "hyper," "strange," "feel it all over," "want to do something"	Desire is something that happens to her: desire is an "unwanted visitor" Pleasure located in mind rather than in body Pleasure begins in the mind, leads to desire (not clear if that is associated with the body) and behavior, though sometimes it "just happens"

(continued)

Table 2

Continued

Urban Girls—Reported Sexual Violation		
Girl	Voice of the Body	Relationship Between Body and Self
Laura (continued)		Lack of clarity about whether desire occurs in mind and/or body; "I just felt different"
		Relationship of mind and body is one of control; mind as a controllable part of self vs. body, which eludes control, things "just happen"
Barbara (White, molested regularly between ages of 5–9 by adult male)	Sexual pleasure described in specific physical terms: body is "sensitive," "whole body can feel good," "gets your whole body turned on," "pressure in (chest)"	Interplay between mind and body: "when you concentrate, it brings more pleasure"
	Specific knowledge of pleasure and desire: "they (boys) can manipulate the clitoris and that drives any girl crazy"; "overwhelming"; "good if you can get it fulfilled," if not, "an annoyance"; orgasm "totally blew my mind"	Tries to avert mind's tendency to function as censor
		Desire needs to be communicated to other person to have pleasure
	Specific knowledge of what she wants: "not just backrubs, do the whole body"	Pleasure is physical and can be associated with emotional feelings too; physical desire is associated with emotional and mental knowledge
		Mind acts as guardian and censor of responsive body (refers to body and mind as "we"); mind speaks to body
		Express wish to feel pleasure and sexual desire led to "working upon [feeling desire] myself a lot"
Lily (Latina, attempted rape averted)	Intense sexual pleasure experienced when drunk and asleep: "best, funniest, most incredible time"	Emotional rather than physical pleasure "counts" and is "fun"
	Sexual pleasure is not experienced in her body (with the above exception) but described as emotional, being touched sexually is associated with disembodied "happiness"	Physical pleasure outside of emotionally meaningful context is "disgusting"
		When physical pleasure is experienced, it is because of what boyfriend does—not responsible for physical pleasure and "do[es] not care" if it occurs

Table 2

Continued

Urban Girls—Reported Sexual Violation

Girl	Voice of the Body	Relationship Between Body and Self
Lily (continued)	Disembodied perspective on pleasure of sex (pits relationship against physical experience) Disembodied experience of desire: feels it "in heart not body"; "tickling your heart"; "just a feeling inside, not a physical feeling at all" Experienced orgasms but not very important to her vs. emotional aspects of physical intimacy First experience of sex: no desire, "didn't know what was going on," "never thought about it"	Logic of emotions and desire: could only feel desire in a relationship, so has not felt desire for someone she hasn't loved

relative predominance of pleasure narratives spoken by suburban girls who have not experienced sexual abuse or violence as compared to the other groups of girls. We observed marked differences in how suburban girls who did not report sexual violation voice their bodies and speak about the relationship between their bodies and their psyches as compared with the other three groups.

These suburban girls speak about their desire as an embodied experience that they associate with intense feelings of pleasure and also with self-knowledge. Both sexual desire and sexual pleasure are known to them as profoundly physical experiences—as feelings that they perceive in their own bodies. They are able to describe these experiences in specific terms, reflecting their clear acquaintance with these feelings: Zoe called it a "tingling or a shivering," Eugenia explained that it is "a burn, a throbbing down there, in between my legs . . . sometimes I get wet . . . it was just like my body wanted to just be like touched and explored." They describe sexual feelings in the way that a naturalist might make observations, noting the specifics of how their pleasure and desire occur and unfold, as Jane reported:

> I want to be with him and touch him and have him touch me, in your fingers, in your mouth, like your neck and like everywhere, just on your skin . . . when you are finally alone, then it is like that much better, because you've waited so long that it's like the feelings are so strong inside you that they're just like ready to burst, and it's sort of like you've both been waiting so that when you're finally together, it's that much more exciting or special.

Jane, like the other suburban girls who did not report sexual violation, voiced a sense of entitlement to her own desire and pleasure, as well as an intimate knowledge of how her desire "works" (see Table 2).

There is a consistency in how these girls describe the relationship between their bodies and their selves when they talk about their desire.[12] They all explain that both emotional and physical feelings contribute to their overall experience of sexual desire. That is, they describe an equitable interplay of mind and body, working in collaboration to generate what they call sexual desire. For instance, Eugenia explicated the difference that she understood between having "really strong emotions towards him" and "hav[ing] sex" with someone who is attractive:

> I think I would enjoy it so much more than having a one-night stand, even if it was something really like you just like saw each other and just wanted to get together and so it was kinda sexy, but I just feel like when there's like emotions behind it, it makes it like that much more exciting.

She continued to elaborate her experience of having feelings in her mind and in her body engaged in an interplay of pleasure:

> I think part of it was in my mind and then part of it was just that physical thing, just knowing you're doing something that you want to physically want somebody like that, sexual pleasure's something that's like so intensely emotional and so intensely physical.

These girls appear to be taking on and succeeding in working out the unarticulated and ostensibly insurmountable task that society has set up for young women, to figure out how to unite their sexual feelings with their emotional feelings in a cultural context that generally splits emotions from embodied experience along the lines of gender, distributing emotions to girls and sexual desire to boys.

This integration of emotions and body in voicing desire is unique to the suburban girls who did not report sexual violation and serves as an explication of our observation in the quantitative analysis that this group of girls told relatively more desire narratives about pleasure than did the other three groups. This description of desire suggests a connection between mind and body that is present for the group of girls who have relatively little violence to negotiate in their lives, in their general sociocultural situation, their relational landscapes, or in their personal histories. These girls speak about having feeling bodies and about knowing that their bodies and sexuality can be a source of physical, emotional, and relational pleasure and even strength. The multiple privileges of a safer suburban community and the absence of oppressive violence means that these girls have the freedom to associate their own desire more with pleasure than with vulnerability.

This qualitative analysis also enables further understanding of the findings of the quantitative analysis that the remaining three groups of girls—suburban girls who reported sexual violation, urban girls who did and did not report sexual violation—told more narratives about vulnerability than about pleasure. Distinct from the embodied and integrated voices of body and desire that are audible among the suburban girls who did not report sexual violation, the other three groups of girls are similar to each other in how they talk about their bodies and how they articulate the relationship between their bodies and their selves. We discern a general pattern of dissociation and disconnection in how these girls voice their bodies, ranging from reports of dissociation in specific situations to consistent absence of physical feelings. For instance, although Rochelle, an urban girl who does not report sexual violation, says that "I don't really have no pleasure," she also reports that "just like certain times I really really enjoy it [sex] but not a majority of the time, it's only sometimes, once in a while." Ellen, another urban girl who did not report sexual violation, said of desire, "I don't feel it very much in my body." Alexandra, a suburban girl who was raped, explains, "I can enjoy it, but I'm always you know just sorta like looking at it." And Lily, an urban girl who reported narrowly escaping a rape, said, "Nothing really happens with my body." In addition, some of these girls associate the experience of desire with physical discomfort, nausea, or tension.

There are also interesting differences between and within these groups that this analysis makes visible. The suburban girls who had experienced sexual abuse or violence are in fact the most different from the suburban girls who have not reported these experiences. When they talked about their desire, their descriptions reflect the *idea* of desire and pleasure more than or as often as the actual embodied experience of it. Nikki said that "if you like someone, then you know that's sexual pleasure but you have to think about it." And Liz explained the pleasure she associates with fellatio, "It wasn't so much that it makes me feel good, I think that just thinking about it being there, it just seemed so sexual, like so neat." They described an out-of-sync relationship between their selves and their bodies, such as Alexandra's recollection that "when you're in a situation and your body's saying one thing, you don't really consult your mind all the time. And that's another reason that I think I get tense." For Nikki, her mind and her body sound like separate entities, "It's all in my head, I think about it, but my body has nothing to do with it. You know, sure my body feels desire if someone touches me or feels pleasure, but pretty much it's in what you're thinking about." In describing having sex with a boy who was more inexperienced than she, Liz said, "It wasn't even like pleasurable, I don't think" but went on to explain that she enjoyed the feeling of power she experienced "in my mind."

The two groups of urban girls sound quite similar, more so than the two groups of suburban girls, and very similar to the suburban girls who reported abuse or violence. This qualitative similarity explains the weakness of the interaction effect from our quantitative analysis, which distinguishes suburban but not urban girls who have and have not been abused or sexually violated. All of the urban girls are subjected to daily doses of frightening violence that appear to contribute to a kind of dissociation from one's own body and a conflictual relationship between the mind and the body when it comes to sexuality. Among the urban girls, there was a distinct split between their minds and bodies reflected in their narratives and descriptions. They described how their minds offer a type of control over their responsive bodies, associated with fear of trouble and negative consequences. Laura, an urban girl who described years of molestation at the hands of a male babysitter, said, "But, I mean your body doesn't always listen to your mind, so sometimes, you might not want your body to react that way but it might anyway," whereas Ellen, who did not report sexual violation, said, "Your mind might say 'no' and your body will say 'yes.' Like if you see a guy and you think he's cute or something, your body might send out different signals but, you know, your mind might say, 'well no, not really.'" She went on to explain why her mind and body may "send out different signals": "Once I'm in that mood, I know like I don't know, I don't really trust myself. I always think I'm gonna end up pregnant."

The urban girls who reported sexual violence or abuse includes a subset of girls who sound quite distinct from the other girls in these three groups and somewhat similar to the suburban girls who did not report sexual violation. They are girls who voice a clear resilience and a conscious articulated resistance to being dissociated from their own bodies in the wake of their experiences with abuse and violence. Exemplified by Barbara, their voices echo the suburban girls who did not report sexual violation in the kind of vitality, integrity, and sense of entitlement to their own bodies inscribed in their desire narratives. Barbara explained that, although she had been repeatedly molested as a young child, she "wanted to be able to feel pleasure . . . cause in the back of my mind, I knew that I couldn't just go on being this way, cause if I got married, I was never going to enjoy it. And I wanted to be able to enjoy it. And so I worked upon it myself a lot." They are girls who described sexual pleasure in specific physical terms and demonstrated a detailed knowledge of their own pleasure and desire. Barbara offered these descriptions of her experience and embodied knowledge of desire, "Most of my friends and me, our bodies are very sensitive, you're making out and your whole body can feel good . . . [boys] have this thing they can do with their hands, they can manipulate the clitoris and that drives any girl crazy, I know it does, it comes somewhere between being pleasure and pain, it's very overwhelming . . . your whole body gets turned on." There is an important complexity in how they voice the relationship between their selves, voicing a split yet also some sense of mind and body working together in the experience of desire and pleasure. Barbara explained that when "you're just concentrating on the pleasure, then it brings more pleasure than when you're thinking about something else." She also described her mind as a kind of chaperone for her body in risky situations, "I'll just tell myself, 'no, not today, we can wait, no need to rush it.' . . . I'm telling my body that I can wait." This small group of urban girls who reported sexual violation weave in and work for pleasure from within social locations and personal histories that highlight vulnerability—living in selves and bodies that have been harmed. This qualitative analysis reveals an important caveat to the general quantitative group finding that urban girls who had reported sexual violation associated their own desire more with vulnerability than with pleasure.

DISCUSSION

Together, the results of these three analyses contour a multidimensional understanding of adolescent girls' experiences of sexual desire. Grounded in a method of data collection that gave girls an opportunity to interrupt the usual silence about their sexuality and using qualitative and quantitative methods to analyze these data, we learned far more about this aspect of female adolescent development than forcing a choice between qualitative and quantitative methods would have afforded. This triangulation of analyses reinforces the basic finding that the dimensions of pleasure and vulnerability scaffold some pointed differences between urban and suburban girls in their experiences of desire.

In the first analysis, we found that urban and suburban girls described their experiences of sexual desire in both similar and distinct ways. They described the feeling of desire in comparable terms and spoke of desire as an embodied experience. There were discernable differences, however, in how they interpreted or understood their desire and in how they dealt with and managed their own sexual feelings. We interpreted these differences to be associated with the social locations in which their development and desire experiences occurred. We know that urban girls are subject to overt, constant violence and heightened chances of sexual experiences resulting in devastating consequences in a resource-constrained environment, whereas suburban girls live in a safer environment, at least in terms of the palpability of violence in their community, in which they have access to social and financial safety nets that can soften the blow of negative consequences of sexual exploration.

We expanded our understanding of this difference first by determining its magnitude, which was substantively and statistically significant. We refined our knowledge of pleasure and vulnerability as dimensions of desire by examining the effect of reported sexual violation. Our discovery that suburban girls who had not reported sexual violation told relatively more narratives about pleasure than the other three groups of girls offers insight into both urban and suburban girls' experiences of their sexual desire. Entering this dimension into our inquiry enabled us to fine-tune our understanding of how exposure to violence, sexual as well as environmental, is a significant factor in these girls' ability to know their own sexual desire as pleasurable.

Returning to our data with a third question and a new qualitative analysis refined and complicated this understanding further. We learned that suburban girls who had not reported sexual violation experienced their own desire as deeply grounded in their bodies and told narratives in which their desire integrated their emotional and physical feelings. The girls who had experienced sexual violence or were exposed to general violence in the community in which they lived sounded more dissociated from their own bodily feelings, an important source of self and relational knowledge (Debold, Wilson, & Malave, 1994) and voiced a split between their selves and their bodies. Suburban location brings the impact of sexual violation into high relief. Here, the blighting effects of sexual violence emphasize the vulnerability and eradicate the pleasure that girls can associate with their own sexuality. We also learned that within the group of urban girls who had experienced sexual violation, some had engaged in an active practice of resistance to being cut off from the pleasure and power that their bodies and sexuality could afford them. Despite having been sexually violated, they were still able to express pleasure in some of their narratives.

This study inscribes key shortcomings and suggests new challenges in expanding what we know about female adolescent sexuality. Although the urban sample was racially and ethnically diverse, it was too small to examine these crucial differences in female experiences of sexuality (Collins, 1991; Espin, 1984; Tolman, 1996), and the suburban sample lacked this variation. The same shortcoming applies to differences in religious backgrounds and religiosity. In addition, the small numbers of bisexual and lesbian girls did not allow us to examine how sexual orientation may be incorporated into this analysis of how vulnerability and pleasure figure in girls' experiences of sexual desire. Collecting and analyzing more desire narratives from these girls' perspectives is an important next step in learning about female adolescent sexual desire.

The findings of this study support and extend feminist theory that has asserted that sexual violence is a form of patriarchal oppression, disabling women by dividing them from the pleasure and power of their own bodies and of their erotic connections with other people (Lorde, 1984). The reality that female sexuality incorporates both pleasure and vulnerability for all women living in a society under the constraints of patriarchy suggests an important caveat in response to these findings. All of these girls demonstrated some capacity to balance both vulnerability and pleasure in their desire narratives. These two contradictory aspects are associated with female sexual desire in a world of AIDS, vibrators, insufficient access to and development of contraception, mass-mediated representations of sex, and powerful emotional and physical connections with other people. Knowing about and developing such a balance may be a crucial element of the healthy development of women's sexuality at this moment in history.

CONCLUSIONS

This study offers an illustration of one way to combine qualitative and quantitative methods to develop a comprehensive understanding of adolescent girls' experiences of sexual desire. Asking a series of questions informed by feminist theory, analysis, and methods, this study fills a research gap in girls' development left by conventional developmental psychology. We wish to emphasize that this study represents a feminist approach to bridging qualitative and quantitative methods of data analysis. A key component of our study was to begin with the voices of girls. As feminist psychologists, our central goals are to ask and answer questions that illuminate and challenge patriarchal assumptions about and negative effects on the lives of women and girls and to identify complexities in women's and girls' experiences and potential that have been difficult to know within the traditional practice of psychology. The use of a feminist eclectic approach to methods of data analysis in this study provides one way around the split that has tended to exist among feminist psychologists along epistemological and political lines, a split that may serve to diminish the impact that feminist psychologists can and need to have on the discipline.

Initial submission: November 29, 1996
Initial acceptance: November 22, 1997
Final acceptance: May 22, 1997

NOTES

1. In more recent years, the use of focus groups has increased. This approach has been used more to identify barriers to contraceptive and condom use (i.e., Kisker, 1985; Stanton, Aronson, Borgatti, & Galbraith, 1993)—to fulfill the agenda of preventing pregnancy and disease among adolescents—than as part of an inquiry into their experiences and the meanings they make of sexuality.

2. Maxwell (in Maxwell & Lincoln, 1990) contends that the debate rests, by and large, on an invalid assumption of paradigmatic unity; that is, that each paradigm constitutes a uniquely

integrated and consistent whole that cannot be disaggregated and recombined with parts of other paradigms without creating philosophical and practical contradictions. This uniformity, according to Maxwell, is largely illusory and there are not, therefore, any generic qualitative or quantitative research paradigms. If we abandon the notion that the components of each paradigm are inseparable parts of larger methodological and epistemological wholes, we have removed any objection to the integration of approaches as pursued by Patton (1990a, 1990b).

3. Reinharz (1990) suggested that the dominance of one method over the other—primarily of quantitative methods over qualitative ones, with some exceptions (e.g., see Fine, 1992)—is a not-accidental reflection of larger patterns of dominance and powerlessness in our society.

4. Tolman performed a clustered random sampling based on membership in White, Black, Latina, Asian and "other" racial/ethnic groupings for each social location. The proportions of girls in each group in the sample from each site represent the proportion they represent of the school population, with the exception of Asian girls (see note 7). There was a 45% refusal rate in the urban school and a 33% refusal rate in the suburban school.

5. This sampling approach represents an important compromise in the overall study design. One argument would have been to select a purposive sample of girls who had sexual experience or who could say definitively that sexual desire was something they had experienced. Part of the inquiry of the study, though, was to develop a sense of whether sexual desire was something that girls said they knew about or experienced. Balancing this open question with the power of a random sample for exploring differences quantitatively led to the decision to take this approach.

6. In addition, Tolman approached a gay and lesbian youth group to include self-identified lesbian and bisexual girls in this sample. Two girls were included in the sample from this group; based on their description of their social environments, one was added to the suburban sample and one was added to the urban sample.

7. No Asian girls from either school chose to participate. Asian colleagues explained that it was countercultural for Asian girls to talk about sexuality with a White woman in school. This study in some ways thus leaves open the question of how race is incorporated into girls' experiences of sexual desire. Feminist and cultural studies scholarship suggests that race may be crucial and further research in this direction is warranted.

8. Both the t-test statistics and the χ^2 statistics need to be interpreted cautiously as there is a violation of independence of the narratives. Note, however, that our purposes here are exploratory, and we address this in further analyses.

9. This question was suggested to the first author by Mary Belenky.

10. The reported estimated odds ratios are the antilogs of the estimated slope coefficients from the fitted fixed-effects logistic regression models.

11. This pattern arises in the group of girls who tell far fewer pleasure versus vulnerability narratives than do suburban girls who did not report sexual abuse or violence, but more pleasure narratives than the two groups of girls who did report abuse.

12. See Tolman (1994a) for a qualitative analysis of how a heterosexual, bisexual, and lesbian girl described their experiences of sexual desire in this study.

REFERENCES

Andersen, K., Armitage, S., Jack, D., & Wittner, J. (1990). Beginning where we are: Feminist methodology in oral history. In J. Nielson (Ed.), *Feminist research methods* (pp. 94–114). Boulder, CO: Westview Press.

Becker, H. (1986). *Writing for social scientists: How to start and finish your thesis, book, or article.* Chicago: University of Chicago Press.

Belenky, M., Clinchy, B., Goldberger, N., & Tarule, J. (1986). *Women's ways of knowing.* New York: Basic Books.

Benjamin, J. (1988). *The bonds of love.* New York: Pantheon.

Brown, L., Debold, E., Gilligan, C., & Tappan, M. (1991). Reading narratives of conflict for self and moral voice: A relational method. In W. Kurtines & J. Gewirtz (Eds.), *Handbook of* moral behavior and development: Theory, research and application. Hillsdale, NJ: Lawrence Erlbaum.

Brown, L., & Gilligan, C. (1992). Meeting at the crossroads. Cambridge: Harvard University Press.

Brown, L., Tappan, M., Gilligan, C., Miller, B., & Argyris, P. (1989). Reading for self and moral voice: A method for interpreting narratives of real-life, moral conflict and choice. In M. Packer & R. Addison (Eds.), Entering the circle: Hermeneutic investigation in psychology (pp. 141–164). Albany: State University of New York Press.

Carlson, R. (1996). Attitudes toward needle "sharing" among injection drug users: Combining qualitative and quantitative research methods. Human Organization, 55, 361–370.

Collins, P. H. (1991). Black feminist thought. New York: Routledge.

Cook, T., & Reichardt, C. (Eds.). (1979). Qualitative and quantitative methods in evaluation research. Beverly Hills, CA: Sage.

Cowie, L., & Lees, S. (1987). Slags or drags? In Feminist Review (Ed.), Sexuality: A reader (pp. 105–122). London: Virago Press.

Crawford, M., & Marecek, J. (1989). Feminist theory, feminist psychology. Psychology of Women Quarterly, 13, 477–491.

Debats, D. (1995). Experiences of meaning in life: A combined qualitative and quantitative approach. British Journal of Psychology, 86, 359–376.

Debold, E., Tolman, D., & Brown, L. (1996). Embodying knowledge, knowing desire: Authority and split subjectivities in girls' epistemological development. In N. Goldberger, J. Tarule, B. Clinchy, & M. Belenky (Eds.), Knowledge, difference and power: Essays inspired by women's ways of knowing. New York: Basic Books.

Debold, E., Wilson, M., & Malave, I. (1994). Mother–daughter revolution. Boston: Addison-Wesley.

Delameter, J., & MacCorquodale, M. (1979). Premarital sexuality: Attitudes, relationships, behaviors. Madison, WI: University of Wisconsin Press.

Denzin, N., & Lincoln, Y. (1994). Handbook of qualitative methods. Thousand Oaks, CA: Sage.

Espin, O. (1984). Cultural and historical influences on sexuality in Hispanic/Latin women: Implications for psychotherapy. In C. Vance (Ed.), Pleasure and danger: Exploring female sexuality (pp. 149–164). Boston: Routledge and Kegan Paul.

Fine, M. (1988). Sexuality, schooling and adolescent girls: The missing discourse of desire. Harvard Educational Review, 58, 33–53.

Fine, M. (1992). Disruptive voices: The possibilities of feminist research. Ann Arbor, MI: University of Michigan Press.

Fine, M., & Gordon, S. (1989). Feminist transformations of/despite psychology. In M. Crawford & M. Gentry (Eds.), Gender and thought: Psychological perspectives (pp. 45–65). New York: Springer-Verlag.

Firestone, W. (1993). Accommodation: Toward a paradigm-praxis dialectic. In E. Guba (Ed.), The paradigm dialog (pp. 105–124). Newbury Park, CA: Sage.

Freud, S. (1905). The transformations of puberty. In S. Freud (Ed.), Three essays on the theory of sexuality (pp. 73–96). New York: Basic Books.

Gilligan, C. (1982). In a different voice. Cambridge: Harvard University Press.

Gilligan, C., Brown, L., & Rogers, A. (1989). Soundings into development. In C. Gilligan, N. Lyons, & T. Hanmer (Eds.), Making connections: The relational worlds of adolescent girls at Emma Willard School (pp. 58–88). Cambridge: Harvard University Press.

Gladue, B. (1991). Qualitative and quantitative sex differences in self-reported aggressive behavioral characteristics. Psychological Reports, 68, 675–685.

Goldfarb, E. (1995). Gender and race in the sexuality education classroom: Learning from the experiences of students and teachers. SIECUS Report, 24(1), 2–6.

Green, W. (1993). Econometric analyses (2nd ed). Englewood Cliffs, NJ: Prentice-Hall.

Greene, J. (1994). Qualitative program evaluation: Practice and promise. In N. Denzin & Y. Lincoln (Eds.), Handbook of qualitative methods (pp. 530–544). Thousand Oaks, CA: Sage.

Guba, E., & Lincoln, Y. (1989). Fourth generation evaluation. Thousand Oaks, CA: Sage.

Hanushek, A. (1990). Diversity and complexity in feminist therapy. New York: Haworth.

Healy, J., Jr., & Sewart, A. (1991). On the compatibility of quantitative and qualitative methods for studying individual lives. In A. Sewart, J. Healy, Jr., & D. Ozer (Eds.), *Perspectives on personality: Theory, research and interpersonal dynamics* (Vol. 3). Greenwich, CT: JAI Press.

Hines, A. (1993). Linking qualitative and quantitative methods in cross-cultural survey research: Techniques from cognitive science. *American Journal of Community Psychology, 21,* 729–746.

House, E. (1994). Integrating the qualitative and quantitative. Speech to the American Evaluation Asssociation, Seattle, WA. In C. Reichardt & S. Rallis (Eds.), *The quantitative-qualitative debate: New perspectives, new directions in program evaluation* (pp. 13–22). San Francisco: Jossey-Bass.

Irigaray, L. (1981). This sex which is not one. In E. Marks & I. De Courtivron (Eds.), *New French feminisms* (pp. 3–37). New York: Schocken.

Jayaratne, T., & Stewart, A. (1991). Qualitative and quantitative methods in the social sciences: Current feminist issues and practical strategies. In M. Fonow & J. Cook (Eds.), *Beyond methodology: Feminist scholarship as lived research* (pp. 85–106). Bloomington, IN: Indiana University Press.

Jordan, J. (1987). Clarity in connection: Empathic knowing, desire and sexuality. *Work in progress/ Stone Center for Developmental Services and Studies; 29.* Wellesley, MA: Stone Center for Developmental Services and Studies, Wellesley College.

Kaplan, A. (1964). *The conduct of inquiry.* San Francisco: Chandler.

Keenan, D. (1996). Use of qualitative and quantitative methods to define behavioral fat-reduction strategies and their relationship to dietary fat reduction in the patterns of dietary change study. *Journal of the American Dietetic Association, 96,* 1245–1251.

Kidder, L., & Fine, M. (1987). Qualitative and quantitative methods: When stories converge. In M. M. Mark & R. L. Shotland (Eds.), *Multiple methods in program evaluation. New directions for program evaluation, 35* (pp. 57–75). San Francisco: Jossey-Bass.

Kisker, E. (1985). Teenagers talk about sex, pregnancy, and contraception. *Family Planning Perspectives, 17,* 83–90.

Lees, S. (1986). *Losing out: Sexuality and adolescent girls.* London: Dover.

Levinson, R. (1986). Contraceptive self-efficacy: A perspective on teenage girls' contraceptive behavior. *Journal of Sex Research 22,* 347–369.

Lorde, A. (1984). *Sister outsider: Essays and speeches.* The Crossing Press feminist series. Trumansburg, NY: Crossing Press.

Lykes, B., & Stewart, A. (1986). Evaluating the feminist challenge to research in personality and social psychology: 1963–1983. *Psychology of Women Quarterly, 10,* 393–412.

Marecek, J. (1989). Introduction [Special Issue on Feminist Research Methods]. *Psychology of Women Quarterly, 13,* 367–377.

Maxwell, J. (1996). *Qualitative research design: An interactive approach.* Thousand Oaks, CA: Sage.

Maxwell, J., & Lincoln, Y. (1990). Methodology and epistemology: A dialogue. *Harvard Educational Review, 60,* 497–512.

Miles, M., & Huberman, A. (1984). *Qualitative data analysis: A sourcebook of new methods.* Beverly Hills, CA: Sage Publications.

Mishler, E. (1986). *Research interviewing: Context and narrative.* Cambridge: Harvard University Press.

Morowski, J. (1994). *Practicing feminisms, restructuring psychology.* Ann Arbor, MI: University of Michigan Press.

Nava, M. (1987). "Everybody's views were just broadened"; A girls' project and some responses to lesbianism. In Feminist Review (Eds.), *Sexuality: A reader* (pp. 245–276). London: Virago Press.

Nielsen, J. (Ed.). (1990). *Feminist research methods.* Boulder, CO: Westview Press.

Oakley, A. (1981). Interviewing women: A contradiction in terms. In H. Roberts (Ed.), *Doing feminist research* (pp. 30–61). Boston: Routledge & Kegan Paul.

Omolade, B. (1983). Hearts of darkness. In A. Snitow, C. Stansell, & S. Thompson (Eds.), *Powers of desire: The politics of sexuality.* New York: Monthly Review Press.

Packer, M., & Addison, A. (1989). *Entering the circle: Hermeneutic investigation in psychology.* Albany, NY: State University of New York Press.

Patton, M. (1990a). *Debates on evaluation.* Newbury Park, CA: Sage.

Patton, M. (1990b). *Qualitative evaluation and research methods* (2nd ed.). Newbury Park, CA: Sage.

Reichardt, C., & Rallis, S. (Eds.). (1994). *The quantitative-qualitative debate: New perspectives, new directions in program evaluation.* San Francisco: Jossey-Bass.

Reinharz, S. (1990). So-called training in the so-called alternative paradigm. In E. Guba (Ed.), *The paradigm dialog* (pp. 290–302). Thousand Oaks, CA: Sage.

Rich, A. (1980). Compulsory heterosexuality and lesbian existence. *Signs: Journal of Women in Culture and Society, 5,* 31–62.

Riger, S. (1992). Epistemological debates, feminist voices: Science, social values and the study of women. *American Psychologist, 47,* 730–740.

Rogers, A., & Gilligan, C. (1988). *Translating girls' voices: Two languages of development.* Unpublished manuscript, Harvard University Graduate School of Education, Project on women's psychology and girls' development, Cambridge, MA.

Rubin, G. (1985). The traffic in women: Notes on the political economy of sex. In R. R. Reiter (Ed.), *Toward an anthropology of women* (pp. 157–210). New York: Monthly Review Press.

Schulman, L. (1986). Paradigms and programs. In M. C. Whitrock (Ed.), *Handbook of research on teaching* (3rd ed., pp. 35–60). Riverside, NJ: Macmillan Reference.

Scott-Jones, D., & Turner, S. L. (1988). Sex education, contraceptive and reproductive knowledge and contraceptive use among Black adolescent females. *Journal of Adolescent Research, 3,* 171–187.

Sechrest, L., & Sidani, S. (1995). Quantitative and qualitative methods: Is there an alternative? *Evaluation and Program Planning, 18,* 77–87.

Shadish, W. (1995). The quantitative-qualitative debates: "DeKuhnifying" the conceptual context. *Evaluation and Program Planning, 18,* 47–49.

Sktric, T. (1990). Social accommodation: Toward a dialogical discourse in educational inquiry. In E. Guba (Ed.), *The paradigm dialog* (pp. 125–135). Newbury Park, CA: Sage.

Snitow, A., Stansell, C., & Thompson, S. (Eds.). (1983). *Powers of desire: The politics of sexuality.* New York: Monthly Review Press.

Stanton, B. F., Aronson, R., Borgatti, S., & Galbraith, J. (1993). Urban adolescent high-risk sexual behavior: Corroboration of focus group discussions through pile-sorting. *AIDS Education and Prevention, 5,* 162–174.

Strauss, A. (1987). *Qualitative analysis for social scientists.* New York: Cambridge University Press.

Tashakkori, A., & Teddlie, C. (1998). *Mixed methodology: Combining qualitative and quantitative approaches.* Thousand Oaks, CA: Sage Publications.

Taylor, J., Gilligan, C., & Sullivan, A. (1996). *Between voice and silence.* Cambridge: Harvard University Press.

Thompson, S. (1984). Search for tomorrow: On feminism and the reconstruction of teen romance. In C. Vance (Ed.), *Pleasure and danger: Exploring female sexuality.* Boston: Routledge & Kegan Paul.

Thompson, S. (1995). *Going all the way: Teenage girls' tales of sex, romance and pregnancy.* New York: Hill and Wang.

Tolman, D. (1992). Listening for crises of connection: Some implications of research with adolescent girls for feminist psychotherapy. *Women & Therapy, 15,* 85–100.

Tolman, D. (1994a). Doing desire: Adolescent girls' struggles for/with sexuality. *Gender and Society, 8,* 324–342.

Tolman, D. (1994b). Daring to desire: Culture in the bodies of adolescent girls. In J. Irvine (Ed.), *Sexual cultures and the construction of adolescent identities* (pp. 250–284). Philadelphia: Temple University Press.

Tolman, D. (1996). Adolescent girls' sexuality: Debunking the myth of the urban girl. In B.

Leadbeater & N. Way (Eds.), *Urban girls: Resisting stereotypes, creating identities* (pp. 255–271). New York: New York University Press.

Tolman, D. (in press). Female adolescent sexuality in relational contexts: Beyond sexual decision making. In N. Johnson, M. Roberts, & J. Worell (Eds.), *Beyond appearances: A new look at adolescent girls*. Washington, DC: American Psychological Association.

Tolman, D., & Higgins, T. (1996). How being a good girl can be bad for girls. In N. Maglin & D. Perry (Eds.), *Bad girls/good girls: Women, sex and power in the nineties* (pp. 205–225). New Brunswick, NJ: Rutgers University Press.

Vance, C. (1984). *Pleasure and danger: Exploring female sexuality*. Boston, MA: Routledge & Kegan Paul.

Way, N. (1995). Can't you hear the courage, the strength that I have: Listening to urban adolescents speak about their relationships. *Psychology of Women Quarterly, 19,* 107–128.

Way, N., Stauber, H., & Nakkula, M. (1994). Depression and substance use in two divergent high school cultures: A quantitative and qualitative analysis. *Journal of Youth and Adolescence, 23,* 331–358.

Weedon, C. (1987). *Feminist practice and poststructuralist theory*. Oxford: Blackwell.

Whitbourne, S., & Powers, C. B. (1994). Older women's constructs of their lives: A quantitative and qualitative exploration. *International Journal of Aging & Human Development, 38,* 293–306.

Young, L. (1992). Sexual abuse and the problem of embodiment. *Child Abuse and Neglect, 16,* 89–100.

ECLECTICISM AND METHODOLOGICAL PLURALISM

The Way Forward for Feminist Research

Jane M. Ussher
University of Western Sydney

Within the annals of science, the subject of human sexuality has traditionally been studied within a narrow reductionist framework, in which sex is almost solely conceptualized as a physical behavior or bodily response. Equally, "sex" is almost unquestionably assumed to refer to heterosexual intercourse (or to a heterosexual encounter); man is positioned as naturally active or sexually driven, whereas woman is primarily described or studied in terms of sexual response; and the socially constructed nature of sex or sexuality is negated or ignored (Ussher, 1997a).

The gaze of psychologists who have entered the arena of sex research has historically been focused within a similarly narrow vein. The dictates of positivism and realism that still dominate our discipline mean that experimental studies of biology, behavior, or bodily response are deemed the most legitimate form of inquiry, with theoretical development being minimal or absent and research framed within a narrow hypothetical-deductive mold.

This perhaps explains why the subject of women's sexuality has long been neglected or ignored, for to date, the majority of sex research has focused on (the bodies of) men. This may be because, in contrast to the experimentally accessible penis, female sexual response is not very easily measured or observed within the permissible methods of legitimate scientific scrutiny (analyses of vaginal pulse amplitude being the one way that experimentalists have overcome this particular problem). Alternatively, this negation of the sexuality of women may result from the hitherto unquestioned dominance of phallocentric theory and practice within psychology, which perhaps provides an explanation for why this previously silent subject is currently being addressed. For it is not too extreme to say that a revolution in sex research is now potentially underway (in the Kuhnian sense of a paradigm shift at the very least). The proliferation of feminist theory and methodology and

Address correspondence and reprint requests to: Jane M. Ussher, Centre for Critical Psychology, University of Western Sydney, P.O. Box 10, Kingswood, NSW 2747, Australia. E-mail: j.ussher@nepean.uws.edu.au the development of alternative epistemological standpoints to that of the constricted closet of positivism/realism may act to overturn much of that which has been taken for granted as true in the field of sexuality research. This process is not only acting to illuminate our understanding of the sexuality of women, it threatens to dethrone hegemonic phallocentric notions of sex and also acts in a much broader sense to provide an alternative framework for researching the whole field of sexuality. The article by Deborah Tolman and Laura Szalacha stands as an exemplar of this new critical trend.

I have started this commentary on the article by Deborah Tolman and Laura Szalacha with a general statement on the current status of research on sexuality for a very good reason: to draw attention to the reactionary nature of this particular field (see Segal, 1994; Tiefer, 1991; Ussher, 1997a; Weeks, 1989 for further discussion of these issues) and to outline the background context in which Tolman and Szalacha's research must be viewed. For although realist/positivist approaches and hypothetical-deductive methods have been seriously questioned in other areas of psychology, they have not been successfully overturned to date in mainstream sex research. As Leonore Tiefer (1991) has argued, the majority of sex researchers still cling to the most narrow models of scientific inquiry. This is partly perhaps to prove themselves "real scientists" and thus to escape any questioning of their personal motivations in studying the seemingly seedy subject of sex. Yet Tolman and Szalacha clearly have no such fear. They know there is nothing seedy here. They confidently step outside of the experimental arena. They focus entirely on women (not merely adding women in as comparisons or controls), and to add to it all they commit what to many sex researchers is still a cardinal sin, asking their participants about their own subjective experiences of sexuality and desire.

Tolman and Szalacha begin their article with a brief analysis of the qualitative–quantitative debate within feminist psychology, a debate that is also ongoing in many parts of the wider discipline. Situating themselves within these often warring camps, they describe themselves as engaging in "sequential integration" of qualitative and quantitative methods and put forward what they claim to be a radical feminist perspective. Within a triangulated approach, rather than use different methods of data collection to answer a series of specific research questions about the nature of adolescent girls' sexual desire, they adopt three different forms of analysis of the text of 30 narrative interviews.

This is an interesting collection of methodological approaches. The listening to women's voices through in-depth narrative analysis allows for a sensitive reading of the texts and an identification from a grounded approach of the often contradictory voices women use in describing desire. Coming from a context in which discourse analysis is more commonly used for such detailed textual analysis, I was struck by the similarity in these two approaches, which appears to stem from their shared aim of conducting in-depth readings of women's subjective accounts. Greater integration or cross-fertilization of these different methods of analysis and increased dialogue between those trained in different analytic approaches could produce fruitful insight at both a theoretical and a methodological level for feminist researchers working in a number of different spheres. Equally, those working in arenas other than sexuality research could learn much from the way in which Tolman and Szalacha used thematic coding and the "conceptually clustered matrix" both to answer their specific research questions and cope with the problem of "too much data," which besets those conducting qualitative research.

The fact that Tolman and Szalacha adopt this eclectic or pluralistic stance, addressing their interrelated research questions from a number of different methodological standpoints, is to my mind the most powerful and thought-provoking aspect of this piece of research. It demonstrates the limitations of taking a unilinear approach, be it qualitative or quantitative, as it is only when we put the different pieces of the jigsaw puzzle together that we see a broader picture and gain some insight into the complexity of female sexuality, desire, or of what it means to be a woman. This methodological stance also demonstrates the nonsense of conceptualizing women as a homogeneous group, where generalized statements can be made about the nature of "female sexual desire." The in-depth narrative analysis and the conceptually clustered matrix provide a rich demonstration of the myriad different ways in which women describe both sexuality and themselves. At the same time, the reductive thematic coding of the data and again, the matrix, draws our attention to the commonalities *among* women, which reminds us that sexuality is not simply idiosyncratic or individualistic. We must clearly hold on to the multifaceted complexity of the sexuality of individual women, while acknowledging the power of being positioned as woman in a phallocentric sexual sphere.

In mainstream sex-research terms, the examination of this subject matter, women's sexual desire, the specific approach adopted, and the findings presented are undoubtedly innovative. As was noted previously, concepts such as desire, which are not easily subjected to a positivist gaze, have been notably absent from psychological investigations of sexuality to date (the exception being clinical descriptions of sexual problems, where absence of desire features as a diagnostic criterion worthy of medical treatment [see Ussher, 1997a]). From a feminist point of view, this research may be evaluated in a slightly different way. Taking women's subjective accounts of desire as the focus of their research fits easily within most definitions of feminist research. The adoption of a triangulated approach, however, resulting in the use of both qualitative and quantitative methods of analysis, is more contentious within feminism. As Tolman and Szalacha rightly point out, many avowedly feminist researchers define themselves as such because of their sole adoption of qualitative techniques, and those who stray from this particular party line are often castigated as advocates of a phallocentric creed. I question whether "radical feminist" is the term that best describes such a position; to my mind radical feminism refers to a specific genre of feminist theorizing and political activity that has specific ideological implications, not necessarily associated with the adoption of qualitative research strategies. Qualitative research has arguably become the taken-for-granted option for the majority of those doing feminist research regardless of the ideological stance they individually adopt (indeed few would define themselves as radical feminists today). This may be a cultural difference, but the use of the label "radical feminist" may lead to a misinterpretation of Tolman and Szalacha's particular position or stance and may in some ways open them to unwarranted criticism of their research or their findings for not fitting criteria adopted by others who would ascribe such a label to their own political stance or work.

Yet, paradoxically, although they describe themselves as being informed by a radical-feminist perspective, Tolman and Szalacha demonstrate in their research that qualitative methods are not necessarily more intrinsically feminist than quantitative methods. This is an important demonstration for feminist psychology and one that in my own view is too infrequently aired. Indeed, one could go further than adopting Tolman and Szalacha's integrated approach in questioning the purist no-numbers position, for qualitative research *could* be used to defend a misogynistic standpoint. Sympathetic analysis of interviews with pedophiles that position child–adult sex as beneficial for children or analyses of domestic violence that defend a victimology standpoint, in which women are positioned as to blame, are obvious examples. At the same time, as we see here, quantitative research can be a powerful tool in arguing for feminist principles: Experimental research which demonstrates that menstruation has no detrimental effect on women's performance, quantitative analysis of the magnitude of the long-term effects of sexual violence, or research that demonstrates the absence of difference between boys and girls in mathematical ability are other examples that spring to mind. It is naive to see counting as a bad thing per se. As Tolman and Szalacha demonstrate, the method of analysis chosen by researchers should be the one most appropriate to the research question at hand. If the questions concern the existence or extent of difference between individuals or groups, quantification may be the most appropriate path to tread. If the question concerns the *nature* of that difference or the nature of a phenomenon itself, qualitative approaches may be the most useful course to follow. Using both approaches together provides a multifaceted picture that can be used to powerful effect in illuminating a series of interlinked research questions, as is the case with Tolman and Szalacha's research. The crux of the matter is the status ascribed to the results, which brings us back to the issue of epistemology with which I began.

Feminist researchers can appear at times to be obsessed with the issue of methods. Yet, is it not epistemology that is actually at stake? The one surprise in Tolman and Szalacha's article was the absence of an explicit discussion of their own epistemological stance and the slight contradictions in some of the comments they made. On the one hand they clearly reject the assumptions of positivism/ realism, as demonstrated through the methodology they adopt and the conclusions they draw from what they found. Yet at the same time, they talk of the issue of "bias" in reading women's accounts (p. 16), which could imply a dichotomy between the real and discursive or constructivist influences, and their statistical analysis is reported in a very traditional manner or style, which could lead to realist conclusions. Arguably, these are contradictions that beset all those who attempt to straddle the gap between feminist theory or methodology and mainstream psychology, the latter being the arena within which most of us earn our daily bread (and have to achieve certain standards within, in order to meet promotional or tenure criteria or, in these increasingly competitive times, to keep our jobs). The conflicts in the life of the average feminist psychologist attempting to do good feminist research and yet still attain legitimacy within psychology as it is narrowly defined are not to be envied. But, in my mind, it is the adoption of a feminist epistemological standpoint that is the answer to the problem. This moves us away from the simple qualitative–quantitative divide and renders many of the criticisms or the need for defensive analysis of qualitative research redundant (see Henwood & Pigeon, 1994).

So I will end this commentary by taking the liberty of defining a particular epistemological standpoint that both reconciles the apparent contradictions in the research described here, and, in my view, offers the most positive way forward for the perennial quantitative–qualitative debate. In many ways the research described by Tolman and Szalacha could be categorized as falling within the boundaries of a critical realist epistemological standpoint, as critical realism facilitates reconciliation of both the material and discursive aspects of experience, as well as acknowledges the cultural and historical context in which individual women are positioned and in which meaning about experience is created (see Ussher 1996, 1997b). Briefly, critical realism (Bhaskar, 1989) affirms the existence of reality, both physical and environmental, as a legitimate field of inquiry, but at the same time recognizes that its representations are characterized and mediated by culture, language, and political interests rooted in factors such as race, gender, or social class (Pilgrim & Rogers, 1997). Critical realism does not limit methodological inquiry to the hypothetical-deductive methods used by positivist/realist researchers or the qualitative methods used by discursive researchers. A variety of skeptical approaches are suggested (Bhaskar, 1989), meaning that multiple methods can potentially be used, either simultaneously or in succession. Thus, the whole spectrum of methods from experimentation, to questionnaires, qualitative interviews, or participant observation might be used, if they were appropriate to the research question being asked. This approach implicitly accepts as legitimate all the questions that researchers might set out to answer, rather than limiting the research questions because of epistemological or methodological constraints. Critical realism explicitly rejects what have been described as the predictive pretensions of natural science, because it is argued that the complexity and fluidity of human agency and the influence of continuously shifting cultural and historical contexts excludes any possibility of accurate prediction in the social sciences (Pilgrim & Rogers, 1997). The final and perhaps most radical premise behind a critical-realist approach is the acceptance of the legitimacy of lay knowledge, which is viewed as having equal, although not superior, status to expert knowledge (Bhaskar, 1989; Pilgrim & Rogers, 1997). This allows for the voice and views of women to enter the arena, which is arguably the essence of a feminist approach.

Focusing specifically on gender, feminist standpoint theory is arguably a subtype of the critical-realist approach, as it follows many of the assumptions outlined in critical realism. Feminist standpoint theorists assume that knowledge is grounded in social reality; emphasize the importance of lay knowledge; reject methodological naturalism, the emphasis on observation and prediction, and the separation of facts from values; emphasize reflexivity; and position the body within a social constructionist perspective, while recognizing material aspects of bodily experience (Harding, 1991, 1993; Smith, 1987). Tolman and Szalacha could equally be categorized in such a way.

So, to conclude, Tolman and Szalacha have described an analysis of women's sexual desire that not only increases our understanding of the complexity of this important sphere, but, the way in which they have addressed their research questions and structured their research, provides a useful model for not only other researchers in the field of sexuality, but feminist researchers in other more disparate fields. Their confident adoption of a creative combination of methods is both refreshing and innovative, moving us away from the straitjacket of either traditional psychological approaches, or new-paradigm purism. I hope that this is part of an increasing trend in feminist research, suggesting that we have finally moved away from dogma and doctrine, allowing us to relegate the often bitter discussions of what constitutes legitimate feminist research to past history. Through embracing intellectual eclecticism and methodological pluralism we can only increase our understanding of the psychology of women, which is surely what feminist psychology is supposed to be about.

REFERENCES

Bhaskar, R. (1989). *Reclaiming reality: A critical introduction to contemporary philosophy*. London: Verso.

Harding, S. (1991). *Whose science? Whose knowledge? Thinking from women's lives*. Ithaca, NY: Cornell University Press.

Harding, S. (1993). Rethinking standpoint epistemology: "What is strong objectivity?" In L. Alcoff & E. Potter (Eds.), *Feminist epistemologies* (pp. 35–47). London: Routledge.

Henwood, K., & Pigeon, N. (1994). Beyond the qualitative paradigm: A framework for introducing diversity within qualitative psychology. *Journal of Community and Applied Psychology, 4*, 225–238.

Pilgrim, D., & Rogers, A. (1997). Mental health, critical realism and lay knowledge. In J. M. Ussher (Ed.), *Body talk: The material and discursive regulation of sexuality, madness and reproduction* (pp. 67–82). London: Routledge.

Segal, L. (1994). *Straight sex*. London: Virago.

Smith, D. (1987). *The everyday world as problematic: A feminist sociology*. Toronto: University of Toronto Press.

Tiefer, L. (1991). Commentary on the status of sex research: Feminism sexuality and sexology. *Journal of Psychology and Human Sexuality, 43*(3), 5–42.

Ussher, J. M. (1996). Premenstrual syndrome: Reconciling disciplinary divides through the adoption of a material-discursive epistemological standpoint. *Annual Review of Sex Research, 7*, 218–251.

Ussher, J. M. (1997a). *Fantasies of femininity: Reframing the boundaries of sex*. London: Penguin.

Ussher, J. M. (1997b). *Body talk: The material and discursive regulation of sexuality, madness and reproduction*. London: Routledge.

Weeks, J. (1989). *Sex, politics and society: The regulation of sexuality since 1800*. London: Longman.

"LIKE CHEWING GRAVEL"

On the Experience of Analyzing Qualitative Research Findings Using a Feminist Epistemology

Elizabeth Merrick
New York University

The researcher's role in creating knowledge and interpretations is of critical concern as new research methods are developed. Recent attention has been given to the "implications of difference" on the research process; however, the processes of analysis/interpretation and presentation of research remain to be illuminated. Seeking to address this, I present my experiences as a White researcher of middle socioeconomic status (SES) conducting qualitative research about childbearing with several pregnant Black American adolescents of lower SES. Although the research process was consistent with qualitative research methods, initial analyses of the data led to findings that seemed far afield from the participants' worlds. I subsequently reanalyzed the data with the principles of a feminist epistemology (Harding, 1991) in mind. The impact of using this epistemology on the processes of analysis and interpretation and my presentation of the data are presented. The results support the importance of developing feminist methodology and epistemology and provide new direction for further work.

As feminist researchers develop and apply principles for a feminist methodology and epistemology, concerns have been raised about the researcher's role in creating knowledge and interpretations. Scholars of feminist psychology (Fine, 1992; Franz & Stewart, 1994) have emphasized the need to attend to the role of the researcher

The author thanks Suzanne Gabriele and Lisa Simon for their helpful comments on drafts of this article and Mary Sue Richardson for her insightful questions about the research process.

Address correspondence and research requests to: Elizabeth Merrick, Department of Applied Psychology, New York University, 239 Greene Street, New York, NY, 10003. E-mail: emerrick@obox.com as we seek to study diversity among women. Although feminist scholars have argued that good qualitative research may be conducted by researchers whose standpoints differ from those of the people they study (Collins, 1991; Fine, 1992; Harding, 1991), this endeavor presents a variety of challenges.

In a recent treatment of the "implications of difference" for conducting research, Wilkinson (1996) and others explored several of the difficulties inherent in what they termed "representing the 'Other.'" These challenges included questions about who should presume to speak for whom (Richardson, 1996; Russell, 1996), issues related to "speaking for" women in more marginal social positions (Griffin, 1996), and difficulties of a "White woman researcher" relating with "Black women subjects" (Edwards, 1996). Missing from this exploration was a treatment of the "implications of difference" for the processes of analysis/interpretation and presentation of research.

Seeking to address this lack, I present my experiences as a white researcher of middle socioeconomic status (SES) conducting qualitative research about childbearing with several lower SES pregnant Black American adolescents. Although the research process was consistent with established methods of qualitative research (Lincoln & Guba, 1985; Strauss & Corbin, 1990), through the process of data analysis I realized that my interpretations did not reflect accurately the participants' meanings. I focus here on the impact that methods derived from a feminist epistemology (Harding, 1991) had on the processes of analysis and interpretation of the data as well as on my presentation of the research.

THE STUDY

In conducting my doctoral research on adolescent childbearing, I focused on six Black American[1] participants in an urban prenatal-care program. The participants ranged from 16 to 18 years of age. All were in their second trimester of pregnancy. Initially, my research questions centered on how these young women viewed their pregnancies. I anticipated that our interviews would focus on their sexual and birth-control histories, decision making about the pregnancy, and parents' and peers' views of the pregnancy. Because of the nature of qualitative research, I anticipated that my focus would change in response to what I learned from the participants. Indeed, my original focus later widened to include learning about their life histories and views, including their philosophies about life.

I undertook this research having been trained in the ethnographic principles of grounded theory (Glaser & Strauss, 1967; Strauss & Corbin, 1990) and naturalistic inquiry (Lincoln & Guba, 1985). I conducted open-ended, in-depth interviews and analyzed the data according to principles of ethnographic research. I typically interviewed each young woman three or four times for about an hour each time. These interviews were audiotaped and transcribed. I analyzed the interview data during and after the data collection, coding the data to develop categories reflective of the content. During the course of the study, I kept a field log in which I wrote about my evolving understanding as well as reflections about the analysis Throughout the research process, I met with two other researchers who were trained in qualitative methods who were conducting dissertation research. Thi group functioned to further my understanding of what I was studying and how I was studying it, as well as to challenge my findings and assumptions.

INITIAL ANALYSIS

In intensive qualitative research, the processes of data collection and analysis happen concurrently and inform each other (Tesch, 1990). I analyzed the interview data inductively to formulate categories and themes to describe or explain the phenomenon under study. In my analysis, I used a process of open coding to identify and label basic units of concepts in the data (Strauss & Corbin, 1990). This coding process led to the development of questions, hunches, and tentative directions for subsequent interviews. It also resulted in some 30 labels of units of data including mothers, fathers of the babies, self-esteem, and connection.

Once I had collected and done preliminary analyses of the data, I then sorted the data into provisional categories on the basis of look-alike characteristics (Lincoln & Guba, 1985). Using a computer, I created eight major provisional files into which I sorted the data. These initial categories were: Pregnancy, Mothers, Fathers of the Babies, Sex/Birth Control, Abortion, Education/Career, Future, and Marriage. Each file contained any data related to the particular topic. Data were put into one or more files as needed. For example, text in which a participant described her mother's feelings about the participant's relationship with the father of the baby was placed in both "mother" and "father of the baby" files.

Working with the sorted data, I then considered propositional statements to describe the data in each. For example, I tentatively proposed that "Mothers seem important." I similarly detected themes that, as Ely, Anzul, Friedman, Garner, and Steinmetz (1991) summarized, are statements of meaning that (a) occur frequently or (b) infrequently but carry heavy emotional or factual impact. (For a summary of the initial categories and themes see Table 1.) In identifying these themes, I relied on methods described by Ely et al. (1991). In addition, I employed several techniques suggested by Guba and Lincoln (1989) toward ensuring that credible findings would be produced. These techniques included prolonged engagement, reflexivity, peer debriefing, negative case analysis, and member checking. (For a description of how these were achieved see Merrick, 1995.)

I then divided the data within each category into segments that occurred to me logically and then summarized the content. For example, in addressing Fathers of the Babies, I selected and summarized interview material on the participants' descriptions of their partners. My original treatment included a summary of the partner's age, his occupation and/or education, and a history of their relationship. I also addressed his reaction to the pregnancy, whether the risk of pregnancy had been discussed, and any plans for the future.

REALIZATION AND REANALYSIS

On completing my initial analysis and summary of the thematic findings, I was challenged to consider that I had made meaning in a way that missed the participants' meanings. Important questions came from the members of my qualitative

Table 1

Comparison of Categories and Themes

After First Analysis	*After Reanalysis*

Theme about Pregnancy
  Pregnancy was sought
	Themes about Pregnancy
	  It happened/I wanted it
	  Life is hard
	  This baby will give me something I need
	  Deal with it!
	  Once you're pregnant, you have to think about future/I'm just living day-to-day

Themes about Mothers
  Mothers seem important
  Pregnancy as reaction against, or connection to, mother
	Themes about Mothers
	  My mother wasn't there for me
	  I'm not like my mother

Theme about Fathers of the Babies
  Relationship with the baby's father was important to becoming pregnant but not important in decision to maintain pregnancy
	Themes about Fathers of the Babies
	  I want the baby's father's support/ I could do without it
	  Something about him just attracted me
	  He's a knucklehead
	  He don't want no stupid baby mother
	  Our relationship's not the way I thought it would be

Theme about Birth Control
  Birth control methods were known about, but not used
Theme about Abortion
  Abortion wasn't really an option
Theme about Education/Career
  At the time of pregnancy, not doing well in school
Theme about Future
  At the time of pregnancy, uncertain about future
Theme about Marriage
  Marriage may be desired in the future but is not attractive now
	Theme about Race
	  Because I'm darker, is my heart different?

research group and colleagues with whom I shared my work. In addition, as I considered the findings in light of my original questions and the interview data as a whole, my own reflections prompted reconsideration. For example, my original analysis of the Fathers of the Babies category had focused on finding similarities and differences within the data such as education/employment. This treatment did not seem to capture the essence of the material when compared to the interview data, however. As this quote from Kim about her boyfriend, Colin, reveals, the issues were more complex: "I started to think I could have his baby. I mean with guys before I would always think I couldn't have a baby from them because they was knuckleheads. But with Colin, it was different" (Merrick, 1995, p. 75).

Although I had devoted much time and thought to creating these abstract systems and describing the data within them and despite using a method consistent with the ethnographic method, I subsequently realized I was far afield from the participants' perspectives of what was important to them about their pregnancies. In hindsight, I see my initial attempts at summarizing the results as essentially "top-down" models in which I described aspects that I or a reader might find interesting. At the time, I had been focused on the accuracy within my own interpretation of my coding and descriptions—a case of "not seeing the forest for the trees." Now, I was forced to realize that the participants were expressing issues more complex than my original analysis allowed.

My learning of the ethnographic method had emphasized trying to see the world through the eyes of the participants (Spradley, 1979) and I had attended to this goal during my data collection. Now, I was faced with the realization that this goal was somehow eluding me in my analyses and presentation of the data. On reflection, I realized these preliminary findings reflected neither the participants' lives and realities, nor the meanings of their pregnancies. It became apparent that I needed to return to the data to come from the "bottom-up." The tool for such a reanalysis came out of Harding's (1991) feminist epistemology.

AWARENESS OF FEMINIST EPISTEMOLOGY ON (RE)ANALYSIS

Harding's (1991) description of standpoint theories provided the direction for my reanalysis. Briefly, standpoint theorists argue that knowledge must be socially located and that social locations are determined in part by gender, race, and class. Rejecting any ideal of absolute truth, Harding endorsed an ideal of less partial and less distorting thought. This knowledge starts from life situations that have been considered "other" by mainstream perspectives.

I was particularly moved by Harding's (1991) call to—somehow—"reinvent" myself as "other." I was similarly motivated by her command to "begin thinking from their lives." Both statements were inspiring but ambiguous. Without any formal guide, I attempted to achieve these aims in the following ways.

Reimmersion in Data

I first reimmersed myself in the words and worlds of the participants by listening again to their audiotaped interviews as I reread the transcripts. I strove really to hear the participants. I contrasted the question, "What are they really saying?" with my own query, "What am I hearing?" In doing so, I challenged myself to take in and understand the participants' words while reminding myself that their meanings were different from mine. My goal was to avoid leaping to conclusions or overlaying my own meanings. For example, during one interview, Edouine first commented about her pregnancy, "It just happened." After encouragement that she wouldn't be judged, Edouine continued, "To tell you the honest truth, I wanted to have his child." In the next breath, she restated that pregnancy "just happened" (Merrick, 1995, p. 85). In my original analysis, I had interpreted saying "it happened" as a cover for her intention and agency in getting pregnant. This assessment had been guided by Dash's (1989) data from a similar population. In the relistening, however, I heard that pregnancy could be both intended and out of control. I subsequently detected other complex themes that suggested beliefs that appeared to oppose each other although these were not presented as conflictual by the participants. (See Table 1 for the resulting categories and themes.)

Through this reanalysis, I also realized that my original categories themselves were oriented to an outsider and were not reflective of the participants' views of the phenomenon or their world. For example, my original focus on topics like birth control, abortion, and marriage were not relevant to understanding their perspectives about their pregnancies. Although I had asked about participants' birth-control histories, and they had responded, the amount and quality of data suggested this was not an important issue in their perspective and should not be construed as a major category or theme.

The difficulty of the reanalysis process, the need to take in and work with the participants' words without changing their essence or meanings to my own, prompted me to describe it with the metaphor "chewing gravel." For example, when a participant talked about her "plans for the future," I struggled to conceive that I had no idea what plans or future might mean to her, in spite of my understanding of these words in my life and context. As Kim said about her mother's support, "You can't plan what another person is going to do. . . . That's why I'm not planning on what my mother may or may not do. If it happens, it will make my life easier" (Merrick, 1995, p. 159). The endeavor of sticking to the participants' words without imposing the researcher's meanings is difficult, and it is unclear by what indicator one should judge whether it has been achieved. The strategy of checking interpretations with the participants (Lincoln & Guba, 1985) was not possible because at this point I no longer had contact with them. I believe it is possible, however, to achieve a considered internal sense of truthfulness about one's representation of Other when review by participants is not feasible or desirable.

Exposure to Participants' World

I also sought exposure to the participants' worlds through other media. For example, my reading of Bell-Scott et al.'s (1993) *Double Stitch: Black Women Write About Mothers and Daughters* led me to consider the special qualities, often borne of hardship, of Black American mother–daughter relationships. This was useful in addressing themes which, through reanalysis, I detected in the participants' relationships with their mothers. For example, the theme, "My mother wasn't there for me," reflected participants' statements of love and conflict about their relationships with their mothers, which included an appreciation of their mothers' difficult circumstances. As Edouine said about her mother, "I try to do things for myself . . . . I've felt that way ever since I realized what my mother's all about. Since I realized that she didn't. . . . My mother loved me, but in a little way she don't love me because of being alcoholic" (Merrick, 1995, p. 86).

This step was particularly important because I no longer had contact with the participants and I sought feedback about my analyses from several other sources. In particular, I used the members of my research support group and others—including Black American colleagues and friends—to challenge my emerging perspective.

These people were especially helpful in encouraging me to risk revealing my involvement in the meaning-making process while simultaneously challenging my assumptions. For example, I was hesitant to discuss my findings of the participants' limited relationships with their babies' fathers (in part because of the stereotype of unwed Black American adolescent mothers). Colleagues encouraged me to face this finding, however, state what I made of it, and then challenged my perspective. Through this process, I came to a more thoughtful and explicit treatment of the findings. In this case, I noted that the participants' belief in their partners' eventual support in spite of their current frustrations might be a way to protect themselves from disappointment. I also acknowledged the possibility for strong, if not legal, ties between parents in lower SES Black communities (Furstenberg, Brooks-Gunn, & Morgan, 1987).

Dealing with Differences in Social Location Between Researcher and Participants

The metaphor of gravel also suggests my feelings about the material. Although I believe that dealing with difference need not necessarily be painful, I found it difficult to take in the experiences and realities of the participants whose lives had been marked by hardship and poverty. As an interviewer, it had been hard to listen to their struggles without intervening. I had wanted to take care of the participants while at the same time I experienced a desire to withdraw from them. Perhaps my early efforts at analysis, which resulted in abstract summaries, reflected my desire to flee that pain.

Throughout the process of interviewing, analyzing, interpreting, and presenting my research, I questioned, "Who am I to do this research?" My awareness of the differences between myself and the participants in terms of race, SES, context, experience, and perspective seemed to suggest a certain hubris in undertaking this endeavor. In questioning what right or reason I had conducting this research, I occasionally doubted what benefit, if any, there might be to it.

Eventually, my conflict about this issue abated as I realized that I could not change my standpoint, but could only acknowledge and take responsibility for it. In considering these issues, I was challenged and subsequently encouraged by reading Harding (1991) and Collins (1991). Harding (1991) discussed working from a different racial and social location, "I can be only a white who intends to take responsibility for her social location" (p. 283). After reflecting on Harding's (1991) arguments about the possibility of male feminists, I came to believe that one can do good research about others' lives, even those we have not lived, nor experienced. In addition, I think that the differences between oneself and those from whom one is learning may afford a unique and valuable perspective. Given this possibility, it is most important to acknowledge one's standpoint(s) and to be as honest and explicit as one can about its influence on the research. A continuing struggle with these issues is an integral part of the research process.

Looking for Who Said What to Whom, When

I used my understanding of Harding's (1991) feminist epistemology to develop a framework that emphasizes the importance of social location in interpretation. It seemed I needed to engage the complexity that what I learned about must include who said what to whom and when (Harding, 1991), while attempting to make claims that might be valid independent of who makes them. In thinking about the meaning of my findings, including the seeming contradictions, I considered what has been addressed as the "split subjectivities" of women (Fine & Zane, 1991, p. 86).

My interpretation also included an examination of the potential influence of my social location. For example, I had to consider the possibility that a thematic finding about race may have emerged as a result of my being White. I also discussed the fact that, developmentally, the participants might struggle with tasks of racial identity. In addition, I identified the pervasiveness of racism and discrimination as integral to the participants' experiences and perspectives. I discussed these thoughts in light of ethnographic works about Black Americans' life experiences (e.g., Gwaltney, 1980; Ladner, 1971).

Allowing for Uncertainty

Granting myself permission not to fully understand what I was finding was an implicit, essential component of this reanalysis process. This freedom allowed the process and findings to unfold. Similarly, uncertainty about what the findings would mean or how they would be received or interpreted by others was important. A tentativeness in approaching this work was in order along with an effort to make my process explicit.

INFLUENCE OF THE REANALYSIS PROCESS ON PRESENTATION OF FINDINGS

The principles of Harding's (1991) feminist epistemology suggest the importance of developing new ways to present findings that convey the realities of the participants. My struggle with issues of difference led me to question the extent to which, and how I should integrate these standpoint issues into the research report. I felt I risked either (a) overvaluing or interjecting my perspective into the process or (b) denying or dismissing my part in this research. Although it is important to be honest about the researcher's involvement, it is unclear how and how much to share this aspect of the research with readers. After all, a reader is presumably interested in the research topic or question, not the researcher's personal journey during the study. Both must be described in order to acknowledge the role of the researcher and to provide a context for the research, however. I attempted to present both—neither focusing on nor ignoring—my role and reactions as researcher. This included writing a "Stance of the Researcher" section in which I introduced myself, what had led me to undertake the study, and the assumptions or beliefs that informed my approach to the study.

Another difficulty occurred when I attempted to discuss the findings in relation to my original research questions. At that time, I began to question whether I *should* return to the original questions. The discovery that the participants' experiences of pregnancy were so intertwined with their life experiences and beliefs led me to feel that viewing them through the "adolescent pregnancy lens" was reducing the data, and them, to a group identity. Obviously, these young women were more than "adolescent childbearers," and the breadth and depth of their experiences were important. I realized that I needed to consider the original questions/label as well as the subsequent broader findings. I decided to discuss this tension and to include the larger frame in my discussion of the findings.

PRESENTATION OF FINDINGS

I presented the research in ways that I believe approach the aim to convey the realities of the participants while acknowledging the context of the research and identifying the researcher's role in the presentation. I presented the findings about the participants in two ways. First, I presented each participant's story as a first-person narrative. I did this in order to convey her context and the individual themes I detected. The first-person narratives are shaped to convey each participant's story. In writing these, relying on transcript material, I was guided by the question, "What would a reader need to know about this young woman, her life, and situation, to know her as I have through the research process?" In addition to the narratives, I included thematic findings that emerged as shared or significant from my analysis of the data. Second, I presented the main themes that emerged across participants along with the supporting evidence from each participant's transcript data. Wherever a theme did not "hold" for a participant or participants, I noted the difference in experiences. In writing both formats, I attempted to keep as close as possible to the data. In doing so, I was challenged to communicate the participants' meanings effectively. Often, I found this was difficult because of the nature of the interview: the sequential questions, responses, and comments seemed stilted. In my presentation of the narratives and the thematic findings, I described my role in influencing their final form. I included actual transcript data, alongside of which I placed the final narrative form, so that a reader could compare the two. I am not convinced that this is the "best" form through which to present findings. I believe much work remains to be done in this arena. However, the adoption of this form addresses Fine's (1992) statement that "the problem is not that we [qualitative researchers] tailor but that so few researchers reveal *how* we do this work" (p. 218).

In using these formats, I relied on the words of the participants as much as possible. In using other formats, I presented the findings by using my own—personal, less scholarly—words. Instead of a traditional "Discussion" section, I wrote "Reflections" about each theme or groups of themes. I intended these first-person "educated musings" as an opportunity to make connections with related literature while being explicit that they represented my perspective and meaning-making. In writing these reflections, wherever relevant, I noted the potential influence of my social location on my interpretations.

In addition to findings about the participants, I included my experience of the research process as a finding. Here I described my reactions, social location, and my own development during the study. The latter included considering my own pregnancy and its influence on my analysis and interpretation of the research. These reflections also included personal reactions to the differences in social location between myself and the participants. Here, I noted my experience of wondering to what extent I had used the participants for my own purposes and my questions about what they had received in return.

SUMMARY AND RECOMMENDATIONS

The analysis of one's role and position as it affects one's understanding and the research process has been identified as an important strategy in conducting feminist research (Stewart, 1994). In this study, the use of a feminist epistemology (Harding, 1991) was essential to the analysis, interpretation, and presentation of the research. The resulting thematic analysis led to what I see as valuable findings that are more complex and are closer to the participant's perspectives, representing their meanings and words. These unique, complex findings suggest the benefit of using a feminist epistemology within qualitative research. The complexity of the findings also indicates the importance of accounting for the researcher's and the participants' social locations as well as the interactions between them. The findings include conclusions about the research method and about myself as researcher. In sum, this study suggests several directions for qualitative feminist research as it embraces new methods.

The importance of these endeavors for feminist scholarship and for feminism cannot be overemphasized. Developing new ways of conducting and producing research to include the realities of a greater collection of women is essential to redefining feminism and to related efforts toward change. What is needed now are more models of how this may be achieved and more descriptions of the process of analysis and interpretation as well as presentation.

Initial submission: December 7, 1996
Initial acceptance: March 27, 1997
Final acceptance: July 2, 1997

NOTE

1. Participants' backgrounds included mixed race and varied ethnic identification (e.g., Caribbean). The descriptor "Black American" reflects the participant's self-identification of her race/ethnicity.

REFERENCES

Bell-Scott, P., Guy-Sheftall, B., Royster, J. J., Sims-Wood, J., DeCosta-Willis, M., & Fultz, L. P. (1993). *Double stitch: Black women write about mothers and daughters*. New York: Harper Perennial.

Collins, P. H. (1991). *Black feminist thought: Knowledge, consciousness and the politics of empowerment*. New York: Routledge, Chapman and Hall.

Dash, L. (1989). *When children want children: The urban crisis of teenage childbearing*. New York: William Morrow.

Edwards, R. (1996). White woman researcher—Black women subjects. *Feminism & Psychology, 6*, 169–175.

Ely, M., with Anzul, M., Friedman, T., Garner, D., & Steinmetz, A. M. (1991). *Doing qualitative research: Circles within circles*. New York: Falmer.

Fine, M. (1992). *Disruptive voices: The possibilities of feminist research*. Ann Arbor, MI: University of Michigan Press.

Fine, M., & Zane, N. (1991). Bein' wrapped too tight: When low-income women drop out of high school. *Women's Studies Quarterly, 19* (1&2), 77–99.

Franz, C. E., & Stewart, A. J. (1994). *Women creating lives: Identities, resilience, and resistance.* Boulder, CO: Westview.

Furstenberg, F., Brooks-Gunn, J., & Morgan, J. P. (1987). *Adolescent mothers in later life.* New York: Cambridge University Press.

Glaser, B. G., & Strauss, A. L. (1967). *The discovery of grounded theory: Strategies for qualitative research.* Hawthorne, NY: Aldine deGruyter.

Griffin, C. (1996). "See whose face it wears": Difference, otherness and power. *Feminism & Psychology, 6,* 185–191.

Guba, E. G., & Lincoln, Y. S. (1989). *Fourth generation evaluation.* Newbury Park, CA: Sage.

Gwaltney, J. L. (1980). *Drylongso: A self portrait of black America.* New York: Random House.

Harding, S. (1991). *Whose knowledge? Whose science? Thinking from women's lives.* Ithaca, NY: Cornell University Press.

Ladner, J. A. (1971). *Tomorrow's tomorrow: The Black woman.* New York: Doubleday.

Lincoln, Y. S., & Guba, E. G. (1985). *Naturalistic inquiry.* Newbury Park, CA: Sage.

Merrick, E. N. (1995). *Negotiating the currents: Childbearing experiences of six lower socioeconomic status black adolescents.* Ann Arbor, MI: University of Michigan Press.

Richardson, D. (1996). Representing other feminists. *Feminism & Psychology, 6,* 192–196.

Russell, D. E. H. (1996). Between a rock and a hard place: The politics of white feminists conducting research on black women in South Africa. *Feminism & Psychology, 6,* 176–180.

Spradley, J. P. (1979). *The ethnographic interview.* New York: Holt, Rinehart & Winston.

Stewart, A. J. (1994). Toward a feminist strategy for studying women's lives. In C. E. Franz & A. J. Stewart (Eds.), *Women creating lives: Identities, resilience, and resistance* (pp. 11–35). Boulder, CO: Westview.

Strauss, A., & Corbin, J. (1990). *Basics of qualitative research: Grounded theory procedures and techniques.* Newbury Park, CA: Sage.

Tesch, R. (1990). *Qualitative research: Analysis types and software tools.* New York: Falmer.

Wilkinson, S. (1996). Editor's introduction. *Feminism & Psychology, 6,* 167–168.

RECONSTRUCTING MOUNTAINS FROM GRAVEL

Remembering Context in Feminist Research

Natalie Porter
California School of Professional Psychology—Alameda

For 10 years I sat down almost weekly with young women at a high school for pregnant teens and teen mothers. They were referred to me for consultation for a combination of social and psychological reasons. During those 10 years, I found most of the theories and research about adolescent pregnancy or adolescent mothers of limited use in understanding or aiding the real people with real situations I faced. I had been raised on a lot of theories. From various psychodynamic perspectives I had learned of the multiple ways that the unconscious motivations of both mothers and daughters influence teen pregnancy. From a family perspective I had learned of the intergenerational repetition of a myriad of family patterns that could lead to adolescent pregnancy. From feminist theory, I learned to apply decision-making models about birth control, abortion, pregnancy, and parenting rather than pathology or deficiency-oriented models. Other strands of the feminist literature emphasized the exploitation of adolescent girls by older males, by family members, or via the sexual politics of socialized gender roles. From sociology and anthropology, I learned the role of race, class, culture, and economics on when, how, and why teenagers get pregnant. I am sure that somewhere along the line I was presented with a plethora of low-self-esteem theories as well. Of course, I was also exposed to prevailing societal views, including the "Newt Gingrich" White, middle-class perspective, shared through the mainstream media, that these girls (non-White) are reckless, promiscuous, or using helpless babies to collect welfare.

Each theoretical or research perspective did contribute some understanding to the construct *adolescent mothers* but provided little assistance in understanding the behavior, thoughts, motivations, or context of a particular individual. The totality of the young woman or her experience typically seemed lost. These "factoids" and

Address correspondence and reprint requests to: Natalie Porter, Ph.D., California School of Professional Psychology, 1005 Atlantic Avenue, Alameda, CA 94501. E-mail: nporter@mail. cspp.edu "theoroids" were often more useful, or at least more interesting, sometime later when I was trying to make sense of *my* experience with a particular person. At the time I was talking to the adolescent, her view of her world was the most useful information, and my feminist-informed clinical skills, which emphasized attention to context, were my most useful tools.

What did I learn about teen pregnancy from the young women themselves? I learned that some girls get pregnant because they want to have babies; some are involved in significant relationships and want to have children for the same reasons that older women want to have children. For many, they were becoming mothers at the same age as did their mothers and grandmothers. Rather than this pattern reflecting a family history of pathology, it reflected the historical and cultural continuity of girls raised in rural areas, or with specific working-class values, or from cultures where late adolescence was the natural age to begin a family. I also learned that some girls get pregnant in spite of the best decision-making skills, that some get pregnant because they want to "hook" their boyfriends, that some have been raped by their boyfriends, or by strangers, fathers, stepfathers, uncles, or neighbors. Some have been battered and continue to be violently battered during and after the pregnancy. Some have been severely abused or neglected by their mothers and fathers; others have stable, consistent, and caring relationships with their families. Sometimes the prevailing therapy theories applied, for example, when the mother of the adolescent does appear to want to undo her parenting failure by reparenting her daughter's baby. Frequently these theories did not apply, or they oversimplified the person and the situation. The images of the mainstream media or politicians did not apply. Few adolescents, where I lived, were having babies to leave home or collect welfare, and if they were, it was usually because of the severe sexual or physical abuse they had experienced.

Mainly, I learned from the young women that a complex web of intra- and interpersonal, community, school, familial, developmental, health, and psychological issues were always embedded in an equally complex economic, political, and social structure. The multiple cultures of these young women, experienced as a result of their gender, class, ethnicity, whether they adhered to traditional aspects of their culture, whether and how recently they immigrated to the United States, whether they reflected rural or urban ways of living, how they were socialized to relate to men and boys, whether they were persons of color, physically or learning disabled, able to speak English, lesbian, fat, too pretty/not pretty enough were not, and could never be, distinct from the identities of these young women or from their being teen mothers. And I learned that one could not understand them as teen mothers without attempting to understand them in all of these contexts.

During those 10 years I also learned how my relationship to them affected what I "knew" about them. My position as a White, middle-aged, middle-class (rich to some of them) professional woman brought in by the school hierarchy, intersected with their beliefs, assumptions, expectations, and experiences with people like me to influence why, how, when, and what they disclosed to me. Their decision making about disclosure was complex. They had their survival to consider and needed to make sure that I did not screw up their family life, friendships, relationships with boyfriends, friends, or teachers, ability to attend school, financial well-being, or even their residency in the United States. They often began by telling me what they thought I wanted to hear to avoid further negative judgment about their lives.

What I learned from these experiences was that any epistemological attempts to discover the worlds of these young women would need to be as complex as their lives. Being pregnant teens was a circumstance that did not unite them into a homogenous group. They were heterogenous in many ways, even when hailing from the same ethnic or socioeconomic backgrounds. I also believed that I could have constructed research to support any particular theory about teen pregnancy that I favored, using either quantitative or qualitative research methodologies. There were enough kernels of truth in each of the theoretical positions that I could have designed "neutral," "objective" research from the standpoint of any of the theories. By this statement, I do not mean that I would have consciously manipulated data, but that in knowing about a theory, I would be able to know how best to design a study to reflect my beliefs, values, and attitudes including which questions to ask, how to ask them, and how to interpret them. Just as Merrick (1999) describes, I could have constructed a methodology to "hear what I wanted to hear" rather than to "hear what they were saying" (p. 53). I realized that if I wanted to hear their themes and not mine, I would need to begin with an awareness of what my beliefs and values were, how they affected the methods I used, and how I would understand and represent any findings as a partial, inaccurate picture.

Merrick's article exemplifies both the feminist critique of many epistemological approaches in which the voice of the researcher drowns out the voices of the "researched" and the attempt to recover these voices when the researcher has the insight and courage to recognize this misunderstanding. In *Engendered Lives,* Kaschak (1992) described how the dominant societal group can both construct the knowledge or science about the "other" while appearing objective and neutral, because the mainstream values "coincide perfectly with what appears to be society in some generic, universal form" (p. 10). This allegedly value-free, universal knowledge of American, if not Western, psychology reflects "white, middle class, North American, married, Christian, able-bodied, heterosexual" (Brown, 1989, p. 447) norms that ignore the perspectives or realities of women generally (Fine, 1992; Harding, 1987; Kaschak, 1992), of women of color (Adelman & Enguidanos, 1995), poor women (Reid, 1993), gays and lesbians (Brown, 1989), and persons with disabilities (Kaschak, 1992). Merrick's initial understanding and interpretation of her research findings illustrates the pervasiveness of mainstream values in even the research of the well-intended and aware. Merrick showed the integrity of reexamining her results and interpretations when she realized that the meanings she had constructed from the interviewees might not represent *their* meanings. As she renewed her search to discover their voices, her position as researcher also changed to one in which she recognized and acknowledged her role in the process of making meaning rather than considering herself merely the conduit for the meaning of others.

In describing her research process, Merrick revealed the pitfalls inherent in all of our work: the ways in which our beliefs, attitudes, and values influence the process of research from the questions one asks; the language one uses; the methodology one selects, and the interpretations one makes. Merrick's process illustrated several themes found in the feminist critiques of the epistemological approaches in psychology: the overemphasis on the individual and the separation of the person from context, the imposition of meaning by way of the questions one asks or the categories derived, and the ways in which the interviewer affects the self-disclosure of the research participant.

Merrick's research shared a flaw common to current psychological research, even feminist psychology. It focused on the internal experiences of the adolescents at the expense of the broader context, an approach described by Prilleltensky (1989) as a major limitation of contemporary psychological research. Prilleltensky maintained that aiming the lens of research or therapy only at the individual ignored the contribution of sociocultural/historical factors in shaping human beings. He accused psychology of promoting the status quo by depreciating the importance of the social order in both understanding the roots or contexts of behavior or in developing solutions that went beyond the individual. Kahn and Yoder (1989) have added their voices in declaring that the field of psychology of women has abandoned its original sociocultural emphasis in favor of individually based, including "blame the victim" explanations.

In Merrick's original study, more attention to context would have altered the questions asked of the adolescent girls. As Kaschak (1992) reminded us, epistemology begins with the questions, not the answers. Merrick's questions centered on the individual adolescent, such as each one's birth-control regimen or attitudes about abortion; some questions attended to interpersonal issues but without the broader context of ethnicity, gender, class, and so on. Nonetheless, the adolescents addressed these broader issues even when the interviewer did not. Perhaps this was one reason why Merrick missed their meanings initially. In framing her questions one way, she may not have perceived the multiple levels and issues embedded in the responses. For example, when Merrick asked about mother/daughter relationships, she did not anticipate that the participants would frame them in the context of being Black and poor in U.S. society. Merrick anticipated commentary about relationships; instead she received accounts about relationships embedded in commentary about race relations and economic conditions. These answers appeared contradictory, confusing, and perhaps tangential. In the case of this study, Merrick could only reexamine the data she had already gathered. In future work, she could formulate different questions, questions that would embed the individual in her own, rather than the researcher's, context from the beginning.

On the surface, the initial categories developed by the author were logical and derived from the current research in the field. Nevertheless, they reflected more the beliefs, expectations, and assumptions of the researcher than of those being studied. Of course, from an interpretive viewpoint, this was to be expected (Benner, 1994). For instance, Gavey (1989) wrote that the understanding of our data is really the constitution of our data. In this article, Merrick revealed how her cultural frame of reference affected her interpretations. By doing so, she helps us see how this happens continually, not only in her work, but in everyone's work. Merrick's work demonstrates that even conscientious application of qualitative methods does not free us from the eye-of-the-beholder phenomenon.

The responses of the adolescents did not fit neatly into the categories developed by the researcher. This incongruence seemed to be caused in part by the researcher's expectation that the adolescents would draw the same boundaries around their experiences as she did. For these young women, however, views about pregnancy or relationships with one's boyfriend or mother could not be extricated from the rest of their lives, for example, themes that are more historical or sociocultural in nature. For the adolescents, context was central to their stories. For the researcher, context created confusion; it added contradiction and a certain messiness to the data. For example, rather than offer one opinion about their relationship to the fathers of their babies, the adolescents made statements such as: "I want the baby's father's support but I could do without it" (Merrick, 1999, p. 52). To the researcher, these apparent contradictions muddied the waters or even pathologized the participants. From a White, middle-class, mainstream psychology frame this response evoked for the researcher the negative connotations of the external-locus-of-control research rather than perhaps a concept of determined survivorship, an equally plausible interpretation. One meaning emphasizes values more salient for groups with social and economic power, such as the ability to exercise control in their lives. These values stem from a privileged position and, in general, from the dominant American ideology of self-contained individualism, where action is related to efficacy. For the adolescents of this study, action and efficacy are frequently unrelated: Making the best of a situation might reflect a realistic, if not adaptive, response to the contexts of their lives. A statement that appeared indecisive and contradictory emerges as a complex statement signifying both what the adolescent would like to occur (supportive relationship with boyfriend) and what she might have to live with (solo caretaking of child).

Merrick came to realize the importance of knowing one's social location in developing and conducting research. She provided a clear example of how her own work changed once she challenged herself to understand the impact of her beliefs and values on interpreting the statements of the adolescents regarding their pregnancies. Her ability to confront the world of her participants helped her confront her world—the biases and prejudices that constituted her vision. As a result she was able to see herself, her work, and finally her participants from a slightly shifted perspective. At that moment new data, new meaning, and new categories began to emerge (Cushman, 1995). Her shifted perspective helped a new category materialize: the meaning of being Black. This category represented some of the contextual elements crucial to the understanding of the lives and the pregnancies of these adolescents. This was the kind of creative, transcendent moment researchers live for—when something genuinely new appears.

Two other aspects of the researcher's social location remain less explored: the impact of the researcher as a stimulus on the responses of the persons being studied, and the need to understand the social location of the other prior to planning the research. How did the physical and relational qualities of the researcher affect the type, level, amount, and quality of disclosure of the participants? How would this study have been different if it had been more informed by the work of researchers with expertise in the areas of language and sexuality among women of color, such as the work of Oliva Espin (1993) or Gail Wyatt (1994)?

Not only does Merrick's article underscore the difficulties that arise when one does not begin by examining one's own role in influencing the outcome of research, it highlights the difficulties that occur even when one does. Merrick grappled with the question, "Once one has socially located oneself, how does one deal with this information?" First, the researcher must understand the difference between what the researcher is hearing and what the participants are saying, the impact of how one is viewed by the participants on their level of participation and responses, and the centrality of context in designing, conducting, or interpreting any research. As Merrick pointed out, once this process has been achieved, new dilemmas arise. The researcher must develop new ways to present the information—ways that replace reductionistic, fragmented, or distorted findings—with narratives that better fit the participants or situations being studied. The Merrick article captures the intricacy of attending to common themes while maintaining the complexity of the participants' narratives. Epistemological questions arise: What role does and should psychology play in feminist epistemology? What does feminist psychological epistemology have to offer that is different than feminist-oriented research in sociology or anthropology? If psychology becomes all narrative, what does it have to offer that is different from historical research, literary criticism, or literature itself?

Merrick's article has contributed significantly to research that seeks new and richer, fuller models of research more fitting for the study of humans. Most of us engaged in psychological study, whether by qualitative or quantitative means, have faced the same issues as Merrick. Psychology research would be more useful and relevant to our lives if more of us challenged ourselves or our findings as Merrick has.

REFERENCES

Adelman, J., & Enguidanos, G. (1995). *Racism in the lives of women: Testimony, theory, and guides to antiracist practice*. New York: Harrington Park Press.

Benner, P. (Ed.). (1994). *Embodiment, care, and ethics in health and illness*. Thousand Oaks, CA: Sage.

Brown, L. S. (1989). New voices, new visions: Toward a lesbian/gay paradigm for psychology. *Psychology of Women Quarterly, 13*, 445–458.

Cushman, P. (1995). *Constructing the self, constructing America: A cultural history of psychotherapy*. Reading, MA: Addison-Wesley.

Espin, O. (1993). Giving voice to the silence: The psychologist as witness. *American Psychologist, 48*, 408–414.

Fine, M. (1992). *Disruptive voices*. Ann Arbor, MI: University of Michigan Press.

Gavey, N. (1989). Feminist past structuralism and discourse analysis: Contributions to feminist psychology. *Psychology of Women Quarterly, 13*, 459–475.

Harding, S. (1987). *Feminism and methodology*. Bloomington, IN: Indiana University Press.

Kahn, A. S., & Yoder, J. D. (1989). The psychology of women and conservatism: Rediscovering social change. *Psychology of Women Quarterly, 13*, 417–432.

Kaschak, E. (1992). *Engendered lives*. New York: Basic Books.

Merrick, E. (1999). "Like chewing gravel:" On the experience of analyzing qualitative research findings using a feminist epistemology. *Psychology of Women Quarterly, 23*, 49–59.

Prilleltensky, I. (1989). Psychology and the status quo. *American Psychologist, 44*, 795–802.

Reid, P. T. (1993). Poor women in psychological research. *Psychology of Women Quarterly, 17*, 133–150.

Wyatt, G. E. (1994). The sociocultural relevance of sex research: Challenges for the 1990s and beyond. *American Psychologist, 49*, 748–754.

CONCEPT MAPPING AS A FEMINIST RESEARCH METHOD

Examining the Community Response to Rape

Rebecca Campbell
University of Illinois at Chicago

Deborah A. Salem
Michigan State University

A method used in program evaluation and public health research called concept mapping is examined in this article for its usefulness in feminist research. This method embodies several defining characteristics of feminist social science. Concept mapping is a single method that integrates qualitative and quantitative approaches, provides an opportunity for participants to work together as a group to develop an understanding of a concept, and places the participants in control of interpretation. Over the course of a six-step process, a group of people are assembled to discuss an issue or concept, moving toward a group understanding of that concept, which is then represented in a visual picture, or map. Concept mapping was used in the current study to examine how community resources for sexual-assault victims could be improved. A national random sample of 168 rape-victim advocates provided ideas as to how the legal, medical, and mental health systems could better serve victims. A subgroup of advocates then constructed and interpreted a concept map. The map suggested that rape victims still face many problems in seeking community help. Twelve clusters of broad-based and specific system changes were identified (e.g., fighting

We thank Karla Fischer and Cheryl Sutherland for their helpful comments on previous drafts of this article; the members of the Community Response to Rape Project for their assistance collecting the data; and the rape-victim advocates who participated in this study for their time, expertise, and feedback on this manuscript.

Address correspondence and reprint requests to: Rebecca Campbell, Department of Psychology (M/C 285), University of Illinois at Chicago, 1007 West Harrison, Chicago, IL 60607-7137. E-mail: rmc@uic.edu victim blaming, community education, sensitizing medical staff, legal reform). Implications for research on sexual assault and feminist research methodology are discussed.

Over the past 20 years, feminist philosophers and social scientists have examined the process of scientific inquiry, and presented a persuasive case that women's voices have been largely unheard in social science research (Acker, Barry & Esseveld, 1983; Cook & Fonow, 1990; Harding, 1986, 1987, 1991; Keller, 1990; Mies, 1983, 1991; Nielsen, 1990; Reinharz, 1992; Stanley & Wise, 1983, 1990; Westkott, 1990). Some writers have pointed to very literal aspects of this silence. Women are not included as research participants, generalizations about women are based on data collected from men, and female participants have been removed from samples because they were considered to be error variance (Denmark, Russo, Frieze, & Sechzer, 1988; Grady, 1981; Levy, 1988; McHugh, Koeske, & Frieze, 1986; Peplau & Conrad, 1989). Others have explored more subtle contributions to this silence, questioning the epistemological foundations of social science. Logical positivism, the epistemological framework of most research, is based on the assumption that researchers formulate ideas about the world, and then seek verification of those ideas. As most social scientists have been male, what is of interest to women has had less opportunity for verification (Allen & Baber, 1992; Mies, 1991). One of the challenges facing feminist scholars, therefore, is the development of research techniques that articulate women's experiences. In this article we describe a research method, concept mapping, that can be a useful tool for capturing women's voices. First, a brief review of the literature on feminist methodology and methods is presented, locating concept mapping within this framework. An example of concept mapping is then presented from our research on rape and efforts to change the social system response to sexual assault.

A FEMINIST ANALYSIS OF METHODOLOGY AND METHODS

Defining a feminist approach to social research has not been an easy task. Two issues central to this discussion are the examination of the appropriate methodological framework for researching women's lives, and the specific methods that could be used to that end. First, feminist researchers have debated the merits of qualitative versus quantitative methodologies. Some researchers have advocated for a qualitative approach to research, arguing that women's emotions, perceptions, and cognitions must be explored in those women's own terms (Mies, 1983; Oakley, 1988; Scott, 1985; Smith, 1987). This passion for qualitative approaches was driven by "a deep suspicion of quantitative methods as having concealed women's real experiences" (Jayaratne & Stewart, 1991, p. 89), and the belief that women must be allowed to describe the world as they experience it (Smith, 1987). Concerns about safeguards against researcher biases in qualitative approaches have led some to remain wed to primarily quantitative approaches (Cook & Fonow, 1990; DuBois, 1983). Others have noted that the recruiting method for volunteer participants in qualitative research often excludes women of color and working-class women (Cannon, Higginbotham, & Leung, 1991). These issues of bias aside, several researchers have noted that the abandonment of all aspects of traditional methodology may carry expensive political and scholarly costs (DuBois, 1983; Reinharz, 1979; Stanley & Wise, 1979). As this literature has evolved, this debate between qualitative and quantitative approaches has tempered. In fact, Jayaratne and Stewart (1991) refer to it as a "false polarization," and others have argued that an integrated methodological framework may be appropriate (Jayaratne, 1983; Wittig, 1985; Yllö, 1988).

Feminist scholars have also called for a closer examination of the methods of social science—the techniques for gathering evidence (e.g., questionnaires, interviews) (Fonow & Cook, 1991; Harding, 1987; Nielsen, 1990; Oakley, 1988). Several researchers have suggested that the goal should be to develop methods, either quantitative or qualitative, that can best answer a particular research question, *and* do so in ways that are consistent with feminist ideology (Jayaratne & Stewart, 1991; Stanley & Wise, 1983; Yllö, 1988).

Two approaches have been common in this reanalysis of social science methods. First, some writers have demonstrated how to rethink techniques with which we are already familiar. For instance, Oakley (1988) presented an alternative approach to semi-structured interviewing, which reduced the hierarchical relationship between the researcher and the participant. In her interview work with new mothers, the interviewers shared their own experiences and feelings about motherhood, and provided advice, feedback, and practical suggestions. The interview was reconceptualized as a two-way conversation, rather than a one-way interrogation (Oakley, 1988; Stanley & Wise, 1983, 1990).

A second approach has been to develop new methods designed to provide a medium through which women can describe their experiences. Reinharz (1992) reviewed a number of approaches in the humanities and social sciences introduced by feminist scholars—consciousness raising as a method of inquiry, group diaries, genealogy and network tracing, experiential analysis, multiple person stream-of-consciousness narratives, associative writing, structured conceptualization. Reinharz (1992) pointed out that many of these methods are not entirely new. They are new in the sense that their application is new to our academic fields, which have traditionally relied on experimental designs, questionnaires, traditional interviews, standard qualitative content analysis, and so on. These "new" methods often create ways of bringing women together as a group and collecting data within those groups. They ask women to do what they normally do—write, talk with each other, challenge each other—and capture those normalities for analysis.

Integrating these discussions about methodology and methods, we can begin to see a picture of what defines a feminist approach to social science. To capture women's voices, our methodologies and methods should provide a medium for direct documentation of women's experiences as they perceive them. The use of nonhierarchical group settings for data collection have been proposed as promising methods because many scholars believe that describing women's experiences is a group task (MacKinnon, 1989; Oakley, 1988). Furthermore, women must be in the driver's seat of research—they must be active participants, active interpreters, and active creators in the research process. The final documentation of women's experiences should be expressed in pure form with minimal interpretation by the researchers. These characteristics by no means set definitive boundaries to what does and does not constitute feminist research, but rather, they suggest several features raised over years of literature debates that can guide future efforts.

The goal of this article is to continue on this path of identifying feminist approaches to social science research by considering a specific method, concept mapping. Concept mapping is a technique that has been used primarily in program evaluation and public health research. Although it was not conceived as a feminist research tool, and consequently is not a "new" method (Reinharz, 1992), concept mapping can be effectively applied within a feminist framework. This method embodies several defining characteristics of feminist approaches to social science. Concept mapping is a single method that integrates qualitative and quantitative methodologies, provides an opportunity for women to work as a group to develop an understanding of a concept, and places the participants in the driver's seat.

OVERVIEW OF CONCEPT-MAPPING METHODOLOGY

Concept mapping is a methodological tool developed by Trochim (1985, 1989a, 1989b, 1989c) that can be used by groups to develop a conceptual framework. Initially, it has been used to guide program planning and evaluation. For example, concept mapping has been used to help a steering committee for rape crisis centers develop a 5-year strategic plan for outreach services to women of color (Campbell, 1994). This method can also be used to examine specific research questions for theory and measurement development. In both applied and research applications of concept mapping, the underlying approach is the same: a group of people are identified to discuss and "unpack" an issue or concept, moving toward a group understanding of that concept. The group discusses the steps that would be needed to implement a new program, or the domains that should be included in theory or measurement. This collective understanding is then represented in an actual picture, or map.

Figure 1 outlines this six-step process. In the first step, Preparation, two issues must be decided by the researchers: What is the idea or concept to be examined (i.e., what is the research question to be examined)?; and, Who should be involved in these discussions? Once a research question has been defined, an appropriate sample must be identified. The researchers must decide whose voices they want to capture. The goal is to maximize the diversity of perspectives so that the final map is more likely to reflect the expanse of the particular conceptual domain. To that end, some researchers have randomly selected participants from a larger defined population. If random sampling is not feasible, purposive sampling can be useful to recruit members from different groups that can speak to the topic. In contrast to many methods, there is no strict lower or upper limit on the number of participants that are needed to conduct concept mapping. Because of the fact that the second step of the process is often done in a group setting, the number of participants is often relatively small. Trochim (1989a) noted that a group of 10–20 participants is common, but working with groups of 75–80 has also been

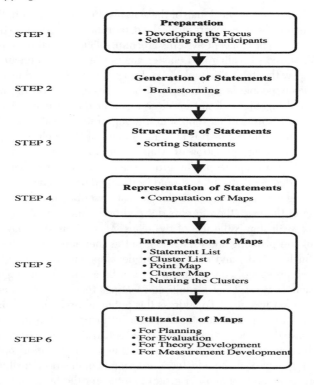

STEP 1	**Preparation** • Developing the Focus • Selecting the Participants
STEP 2	**Generation of Statements** • Brainstorming
STEP 3	**Structuring of Statements** • Sorting Statements
STEP 4	**Representation of Statements** • Computation of Maps
STEP 5	**Interpretation of Maps** • Statement List • Cluster List • Point Map • Cluster Map • Naming the Clusters
STEP 6	**Utilization of Maps** • For Planning • For Evaluation • For Theory Development • For Measurement Development

FIGURE 1. Overview of concept-mapping methodology (adapted from Trochim [1989a]).

possible. After the researchers have finalized the research question and sampling procedures, the participants are in the driver's seat; the researchers go along for the ride.

In the second step, Generation of Statements, the participants are asked to brainstorm answers to the research question, which are recorded either by a note taker, or through audio or videotaping. In most applications of concept mapping, this second step is done in a group setting (i.e., all of the participants are brought together in one setting), but if this is impractical, each participant can be interviewed separately. Generating ideas, therefore, can be done independently or in a group setting. At the conclusion of the second step, a list of items is generated with each response recorded as a separate item.

In the third step, Structuring of Statements, the list is edited to remove duplicate ideas and to check the clarity of the items. Each participant is then given a set of 3 × 5 cards, each of which contains one item, and instructed to sort the items into piles in a way that makes sense to them. Each person does this sorting task independently. It can be done in a group setting, but discussion while sorting is not permitted.

In these first three steps, the focus is on the generation and sorting of these individual items. In the final three steps, the focus shifts to developing and understanding a collective conceptual map of these items. In the fourth step, Representation of Statements, the researchers enter the data from these sorts into the concept-mapping software (The Concept System; Trochim, 1989d), and the maps are generated. Multidimensional scaling and cluster analysis are used to create a series of maps that display the items in visual space. Items that were placed together/sorted together by many people in the group will be close together on the maps. Items not often sorted together will not be close together on the maps. The items are then grouped into clusters that represent a group of items that were often placed together. The final concept map is an arrangement of these clusters.

In the fifth step, Interpretation of Maps, a group of participants is asked to interpret the final concept map. The group examines the items that were placed in each cluster, decides if any items should be dropped or moved to another cluster, and then provides a name for each cluster that describes its content and ideas. The meaning of the map, therefore, is decided on by the group.

Finally, the sixth step is the use of the maps. Most often, they have been used to guide program planning and evaluation, but as mentioned previously, can also be used to further theory and measurement development.

This six-step process of concept mapping can be a time-consuming process for the participants as it can involve multiple meetings (e.g., brainstorming meeting, final-interpretation meeting). To address this potential problem, Trochim (1989a) described several acceptable variations of concept mapping. For instance, it is not necessary to have the same participants involved across all of these steps. A subgroup of participants can be selected for the sorting and interpretation tasks. In fact, three *different* groups could be selected: one group to brainstorm the items, another group to sort them, and yet another group to interpret the final map. In addition, the brainstorming can be done individually rather than in a group setting. Fischer, Berger, Campbell, and Rose (1995) provided yet another example of this methodology. In a study of battered women's definitions of abuse, it was not feasible to involve the participants in the final stage of interpretation of the map so as to maintain their anonymity. In this modified procedure, the naming of the clusters was conducted by the research team, but in the presentation of the findings, the extensive use of narrative data provided a medium for participants' voices. The methodology is flexible in accommodating practical concerns and participants' schedules so as to maximize the number of perspectives that can be captured.

CONCEPT MAPPING AND A FEMINIST APPROACH TO RESEARCH

Concept mapping is a method that can be used in a manner consistent with feminist ideology to illuminate women's voices. First, it blends qualitative and quantitative approaches into a single method. Qualitative data, which describe women's own ideas about an identified concept, are collected in the brainstorming and interpretation steps. Quantitative analysis is then used to construct the maps in order to understand these ideas. Second, concept mapping usually brings participants together in a group setting to generate and/or interpret ideas. As noted previously, connecting women and providing opportunities for group discussion and consciousness raising has been proposed as an ideal setting for collecting information about women's lives. Such groups have a synergistic potential that is difficult to capture in even the most nonhierarchical interviews. Concept mapping differs from other methods of group data collection, such as focus groups. In focus-group research, the meaning of the group discussion is interpreted by the research team. By contrast, the participants in concept mapping are typically actively involved in constructing the meaning and outcomes. As noted previously, the final interpretation of the map is a collective exercise for the participants, and the "final product" can remain in the language of the participants. Concept mapping offers a method for examining women's lives that incorporates several aspects of a feminist approach to social science.

THE CURRENT STUDY

This article presents an example of concept mapping. The substantive topic of interest in our research was how the community systems that provide assistance to rape victims (e.g., the legal, medical, and mental health systems) could be more responsive to victims' needs. Previous research on sexual assault has suggested that rape victims are often denied help by their communities, and what help they do receive often leaves them feeling revictimized (Caringella-MacDonald, 1985; Estrich, 1987; Galvin & Polk, 1983; King & Webb, 1981; Koss, Koss, & Woodruff, 1991; LaFree, 1980; MacKinnon, 1987; Madigan & Gamble, 1991; Matoesian, 1993; McCahill, Meyer, & Fischman, 1979; National Victim Center, 1992; Warshaw, 1988). The focus of much of this research has been on the legal system and its response to sexual-assault cases (e.g., Estrich, 1987; Kerstetter, 1990). This study sought to expand this literature in two ways: (a) to explore ways to improve how victims are being treated by the community systems from which they seek help; and (b) to broaden the scope of this literature by considering not only the legal system, but also the medical and mental health systems as well.

To examine these issues, we wanted to capture the voices of rape-victim advocates. We chose this sample as opposed to a sample of rape victims for three reasons. First, we were interested in examining the multiple systems with which victims have contact (e.g., legal, medical, and mental health). Most communities in the United States have a rape-crisis center with staff to help victims negotiate these formal community systems (Webster, 1989). Advocates help victims understand the legal system, accompany them through the process of legal prosecution, and find emergency and follow-up medical care, as well as any counseling services they may desire. Rape-victim advocates, therefore, are in a unique position to be able to reflect on the working of multiple systems (Campbell, 1996, 1998). Rape victims themselves, by contrast, may not have contact with multiple systems.

Second, rape-victim advocates are in a unique position to observe how social systems respond to different types of victims in different types of assault situations. Over the course of their jobs, advocates work with multiple victims, so they can reflect on several cases, whereas victims can tell only their individual stories. Based on these experiences with multiple systems and multiple victims, we hypothesized that rape-victim advocates may have a great deal of valuable insight into how to improve services for rape victims.

Finally, although concept mapping can be used to identify local needs, we were interested in identifying issues that were relevant across localities. Although it was possible to recruit rape-victim advocates from across the United States, it would have been impossible to identify and recruit a national sample of rape victims. The geographical diversity of the rape-victim advocate sample allows us to identify problems in service delivery across the country.

METHOD

Sample

Following one of Trochim's (1989a) suggestions for modified concept-mapping methods, three samples were used in this study: the national random sample of advocates who brainstormed the items ($n = 168$), a subgroup of advocates from this national sample who sorted the items ($n = 20$), and the staff from our local rape-crisis center who interpreted the map ($n = 20$).

A two-step process was used to select the national random sample of rape-victim advocates. First, using a national directory of services for sexual-assault victims (Webster, 1989), 759 agencies that provide advocacy services to rape victims were identified: 390 free-standing rape-crisis centers and 369 combined rape crisis–domestic violence programs. A random sample of 213 agencies was selected, stratifying for agency type.[1]

In the second step of sample selection, the directors from the randomly selected agencies were contacted by phone. They were asked if they had paid or volunteer staff who provide community-based advocacy services to adult rape victims. The directors were then asked to provide the name of the advocate who provides the *most* direct advocacy work at that agency. If the director stated that no one provides these services, the agency was removed from the list of target agencies and a randomly selected replacement from the same type of agency was drawn. Of the 213 agencies contacted, 177 were eligible for participation in the study. Of the 36 centers that were not eligible for the study, 8 were no longer in existence, 19 had changed their services since the publication of the directory and now provided only therapy (no advocacy) for victims, 2 had not had a sexual-assault case in the past 3 years, 5 now worked only with domestic-assault victims (i.e., they had no sexual-assault program), and 1 now worked only with victims of child sexual abuse. From this pool of 177 eligible centers, 168 advocates participated in the interview (95% response rate).

A random subsample of 20 advocates were recontacted by phone and asked to participate in the sorting task; all agreed to participate yielding a 100% response rate. Finally, because it was not possible to bring the advocates who completed the sorting task together for the interpretation meeting, we asked the staff members from our local rape-crisis centers to interpret the map ($N = 20$). All staff agreed to participate (100% response rate).

The characteristics of these three groups can be found in Table 1. The groups were remarkably similar as most of the advocates were White women with education beyond the high school level. Almost half of each group were also survivors of

Table 1

Characteristics of Study Participants

Characteristics	Brainstorm Group (National Sample of Rape-Victim Advocates) (n = 168)	Sorting Group (Subsample of National Sample of Rape-Victim Advocates) (n = 20)	Interpretation Group (Local Rape-Crisis Center Rape-Victim Advocates) (n − 20)
Gender (Female) (%)	100	100	100
Age	37	34	32
Race (%)			
White	88	80	75
African American	5	10	10
Latina	4	4	10
Native American	2	1	5
Asian American	1	5	0
Arabic American	1	0	0
Education (%)			
Some high school	1	0	0
High school graduate	6	0	0
Some college	17	25	30
Associate's degree	6	10	5
Bachelor's degree	44	25	40
Some graduate school	8	25	10
Graduate degree	18	15	15
Survivor of sexual assault (%)	43	45	40
Years worked as advocate	5	4	4

sexual assault. The three groups did not significantly differ in their work experience as the average time worked as an advocate was 5 years in the national sample, and 4 years in the subsample and local group.

Procedure

This research was part of a larger study of system response to rape victims. Each advocate participated in a phone interview that included the concept-mapping question ("What would you like to see done differently to improve how rape victims are being treated by community systems, such as the legal, medical, and mental health systems?"). The advocates' answers to this question were written down verbatim, and then repeated back to the advocates to check the accuracy of the transcription. The interviews lasted on average 1.34 hours ($SD = 26.69$ minutes). For the sorting task, a subsample of 20 advocates were mailed the items, a postage-paid return envelope, and the following instructions:

Sort these items into piles in a way that makes sense to you. Sort them however you like, in whatever way you like, following whatever rules or ideas you like. You can have as many piles as you like, but there are a few guidelines you should follow:

1. Each item can be in one and only one pile.
2. You cannot put all of the items into one big pile.
3. You cannot put each item into its own pile.
4. It is okay to have a few piles with only one item in them.

It is important that you do this task independently.

The maps were generated using the Concept System software (Trochim, 1989d). The Concept System arranges the data into a matrix that has as many rows and columns as there are statements ($N = 91$ statements).[2] A matrix of this configuration is created for each participant. Each cell has either a 1.00 (statements for that row and column were placed together in a pile by that person) or 0.0 (not placed together in a pile). These individual sort matrices are combined to create a group similarity matrix. This time, each cell has the number of people who placed that pair of statements together in a pile. A high value means many participants placed those items together, and implies that the statements are conceptually similar. A low value indicates the items were not placed together very often, and those two items are more conceptually distinct.

Three steps are taken to create the concept maps from this group similarity matrix. First, a *point map* is constructed, which locates each statement as a separate point on a map. Statements closer together on the map were likely to have been sorted together more frequently. This point map is produced through two-dimensional nonmetric multidimensional scaling of the group-similarity matrix. In the second step, the individual statements (now represented as points on a map) are grouped or partitioned into clusters to create the *cluster map*. Hierarchical clustering is used in this step to create clusters of statements that should reflect similar concepts. Finally, *bridging values* are computed for each item and cluster. The bridging index is a value between 0.00 and 1.00 where lower values indicate that the statement was frequently sorted with the statements that are closer to it on the map, and higher numbers mean the statement was frequently sorted with statements farther away on the map. In general, the lower the bridging value, the more central the statement is to the meaning of the cluster. The bridging values of each item in a cluster are then averaged for a cluster index. Clusters with higher average bridgings indicate that there was disagreement among the sorters as to where the items in that cluster belonged.

The advocates from our local rape-crisis center interpreted the map in a group meeting that lasted 3.5 hours. The discussion in this meeting was audio recorded and transcribed. Although we did not specify how they should proceed in this meeting beyond stating that they should name each cluster and consider the overall structure of the map, the group worked under a consensual decision-making process. When there was disagreement as to the meaning of the map, the group continued to talk until consensus was reached. The director of the agency noted that this process was typical for the center as a consensus model is employed for all policy and program decisions. Differing opinions were discussed until these different points of view had been addressed to the satisfaction of the dissenting staff members. It did not appear to be the case that strongly held minority opinions were ignored in the interpretation of the map.[3]

RESULTS

Clusters in the Map

Eighteen clusters emerged in the advocates' map. Table 2 lists each cluster and its items with the individual and average cluster bridging values. Figure 2 represents these clusters in a visual map, which was generated by the concept-mapping software.[4] This map and Table were presented to the staff of our local rape-crisis center to discuss and interpret. The first task was to name each cluster—what was the idea conveyed by the cluster? Some clusters were quite easy to label. For example, Cluster 5 (Medical Services) concentrated on specific service changes for emergency medical care for rape victims, such as increasing the number of women doctors available in the emergency room and distributing "comfort packs" to victims with soap, toothbrush and toothpaste, mouthwash, and a change of clothes. The average bridging value for this cluster was rather low (.21), which indicates that many of the advocates grouped these items together. Cluster 3 (Community Education) was also quite easy to identify and had the lowest bridging value (.02). Almost all of these statements mentioned community education, targeting different groups in the community.

Some clusters reflected more abstract ideas. For example, Cluster 1 (The Big Goals) took quite a while to understand. The bridging value for this cluster was .40, which is high considering there are only four items in this group. Thus, there was more disagreement among the advocates as to how to sort and combine these items. The staff debated what these items represent, and after a period of silence, one advocate offered this interpretation, which was immediately and widely agreed on by the group:

> What unites all of these items is that they're the big goals we strive for in everything we do. In pretty much everything we do, we emphasize education, training, and prevention as we try to get women to work together on this issue and clear up how rape is different from sex.

Cluster 17 (Rape Is Not A Mental Illness) also eluded immediate interpretation. It likewise had a relatively high bridging value (.51), indicating that there was disagreement among the sorters as to where these items belonged. Some advocates were surprised these items were not in Cluster 9 (Policies for Rape Crisis Centers and Mental Health Workers), but over time, the group decided that these items were distinct because they spoke to a deeper change needed in the mental health system that went beyond individual policies. The advocates shared stories of frustrating experiences they had had with counselors, trying to explain that rape victims

Table 2

Items by Cluster With Bridging Values

Items	Bridging Value
Cluster 1: The Big Goals (cluster average)	.40
More education and sensitivity training for all professionals who work with rape victims	.47
We need to be more open about sex—as there is such a taboo about sex, there is a taboo about rape. Even though rape is not sex, it gets silenced because of its apparent "similarity" to sex	.39
Prevention—enough said	.17
Women need to be better organized as a group around this issue; we need to come together and work together	.56
Cluster 2: Victims (cluster average)	.24
Women need to stop being "victims"; they need to fight back and start pressing charges	.25
Victims need to report more	.25
Women need assertiveness training—say "no" and mean it	.23
Cluster 3: Community Education (cluster average)	.02
More public education on rape myths versus realities	.02
More community education specifically on date rape and acquaintance rape	.02
Sensitizing churches and school about this issue may be a more effective route than concentrating on the legal, medical, and mental health systems	.10
Sexual-harassment education in high schools so women are not portrayed by only their sexuality	.03
More college campus efforts to address rape	.01
Business community needs a great deal of education on this	.01
Get education on this issue started very early in the schools	.00
Faculty in universities should also be targeted for education because sometimes they are who students turn to for help. And because they are sometimes perpetrators too	.00
Need to figure out a way to get into private schools for education (i.e., don't just target public schools)	.00
Cluster 4: Sensitizing Police (cluster average)	.58
Police need to be more sensitive to victims' needs and understand victims' reactions (e.g., why some are calm, some cry). They need to believe victims regardless of their reactions	.51
More women in all positions of the criminal-justice system	.65
Cluster 5: Medical Services (cluster average)	.21
Hospital staff need more observation by supervisory staff through the process of the exam and then get feedback to improve their techniques	.08
More Sexual Assault Response Teams (SART) in hospitals	.37
Every ER doctor needs to know how to perform the rape kit, so we don't have to wait for the "one" who knows how to do it	.07
Shorten the waiting time in the ER	.14
The exam does not need to be done in the ER; it can be done in a clinic setting	.33
Women doctors in the emergency room are sorely needed	.21

Table 2

Continued

Items	Bridging Value
Nurses should be allowed to do the rape kit, so victims don't have another male looking at them again	.14
Hospital staff need to distribute more complete information to victims—about sexually transmitted diseases (STDs), about pregnancy, about physical and psychological health	.06
Women should not be asked a lot of questions during the actual exam; one thing at a time	.20
"Comfort packs" for all victims—soap, sweatshirt and sweatpants, new pair of underwear, toothbrush and toothpaste, mouthwash	.38
Medical staff needs to do the exam even if there has been some delay between the assault and the exam; there is often still evidence that could be obtained and used in the prosecution. They shouldn't make this decision for the victim	.06
Hospital staff needs to be more informed about STDs and victims' concerns about them	.06
Hospitals need to let go of the "turf" war with advocates and let the advocates help more	.42
The Morning After Pill needs to be more accessible	.22
Need to work out a better system for the payment of the rape exam—women do not need to be hassled by the hospitals or credit agencies for payment	.44
Cluster 6: Sensitizing Medical Staff (cluster average)	.22
Nurses need to be more aware of and more sensitive to the physical and psychological state of the victim—they are too abrupt	.23
Doctors should not belittle the nurses in front of the victim (or really ever at all); when they do this it's just showing the victim again how little women matter	.17
Doctors need more training on the rape kit so they don't have to read along with the papers as they do it	.33
Doctors need to talk directly to the victim, not around her, because this further depersonalizes the woman	.15
Cluster 7: Fighting Victim Blaming (cluster average)	.46
Less victim blaming by police and prosecutors	.41
Sanctions for police, doctors, nurses, and others for inappropriate and insensitive service—we need to make it not OK for this kind of service to go on	.56
Need to drop the standard of resistance—whether she fought back should not be an issue	.39
Need to provide more support to victims through the trial process to minimize the revictimization	.41
Polygraph tests for victims must be abolished	.48
Get rid of the phrase "alleged victim"	.49
The blame must be on the assailant, not the victim	.51
Cluster 8: Policy Changes (cluster average)	.53
Institute a protocol for police, prosecutors, and hospitals	.56

(*continued*)

Table 2

Continued

Items	Bridging Value
Institute a policy that makes it mandatory for police and hospitals to call for an advocate	.46
More cooperation between the various agencies that work on sexual-assault cases	.79
Advocates should be allowed to ride along with police to respond to sexual-assault calls	.33
Let advocates be present for the police interviews	.31
Every system should know what services the other systems provide (e.g., police should know about counseling services). If we can improve referrals, we can improve service	.84
Police need to have a pro-arrest policy for sexual assault	.36
Need a police sexual-assault unit	.30
Police reports should be taken by an officer with special training on rape, not by regular beat officer	.39
Rape is a multidisciplinary problem, so there needs to be a trained team to respond 24/7	.85
Would like to see a task force specifically for sexual assault pulling together all groups that work with rape victims	.42
Cluster 9: Policies & Services for Rape-Crisis Centers & Mental Health Workers (cluster average)	.51
More immediate availability of counseling	.48
Would like to have an "all purpose" center where a nurse practitioner can do the exam, where counseling would be available, the police would go there, legal advocates would be on hand. Pull all the community personnel together so the victim doesn't have to run around	.65
More availability of sliding scale therapy	.42
More funding for rape-crisis centers; we spend so much time in direct service that we cannot get out there to do the community education and social change work that we want to do	.55
A safe house or shelter for rape victims	.48
Mental health workers need to be a more integrated part of SART	.60
Cluster 10: Improvements for Court (cluster average)	.37
Speed up the process of criminal prosecution—attrition becomes a real problem and victims are worn down	.29
Closed courtrooms—this is not a freak show	.43
Need special court setups for children and adolescents	.39
The investigators need to keep the victim more informed about what's going on in her case	.37
Cluster 11: Tips for Prosecutors (cluster average)	.14
More date and acquaintance rapes need to be prosecuted	.16
Prosecutors need to be more aggressive about pursuing these cases and not just taking the "cut and dried" cases	.12
Prosecutors need to explain the process of legal prosecution to victims	.10
Prosecutors need more money so they will have the resources to prosecute	.21
Prosecutors should not plea bargain so often	.14

Table 2

Continued

Items	Bridging Value
Need two or three prosecutors who work on nothing but sexual assault cases	.18
Prosecutors need to prepare victims more for trial	.10
Cluster 12: Tips for Juries (cluster average)	.33
Need to spend more time on jury selection so we don't wind up with older retired people—it needs to truly be jury of your peers	.26
More information about Rape Trauma Syndrome needs to get to the juries, which takes more education of the judges	.39
Jury needs to be aware of the assailants' prior assaults. They need to know the history of the defendant	.34
Cluster 13: Training on Sexual Assault (cluster average)	.56
Cross-trainings with ALL parts of the criminal-justice system, including private attorneys—this training needs to be consistent and comprehensive; this across-the-board training must permeate the *entire* legal system	.48
More *time* when get to do professional trainings; for example, talking to police during shift change is not enough time	.52
We need to infiltrate the systems where professionals get their training—we need to be in the police academies, in medical schools, in psychology and social work programs; we need to train where professionals get their credentials	.50
Need to address the racism present in many rape myths—make people understand that rape is not the assault of White women by Black men; and that Black women can be raped	.62
Need institutional/societal changes—must change women's status in this society, which goes much deeper than changing a protocol	.66
Cluster 14: Legal Reform (cluster average)	.34
Reevaluate the rape laws and make them stricter—too many cases are still falling through the cracks	.27
Marital rape laws are a mess; we need to understand the intersections of domestic violence and sexual assault	.49
Pass legislation that allows for more plea bargains in rape cases, so assailants don't get to plead to nonsex-offense crimes	.31
Work with Native American groups to get stronger punishment for rapists in the Tribal courts	.30
Cluster 15: Punishment for Rapists (cluster average)	.22
The judges really need to condemn the rapists; send the message that rape is not OK	.21
Court-watch programs need to expand; we need more people in the courtroom	.34
Need real ramifications for men for committing these crimes; probation is not the answer	.18
Rapists are not getting enough time in jail	.21
If a rapist violates parole, he needs to be held accountable for that	.18
Cluster 16: Multicultural Issues (cluster average)	.36

(*continued*)

Table 2

Continued

Items	Bridging Value
As much as possible, match the victim and advocate on race/ethnicity; to better serve women of color, they need work with other women of color	.30
Rape-crisis centers need to do more outreach to diverse racial and ethnic groups; we cannot expect them to come to an all-White center for help	.29
More therapy services for women of color	.44
All system personnel need multicultural education as well as training on rape; their racist treatment of many women of color is probably related to why many of these women never follow through with prosecution	.40
Cluster 17: Rape Is Not A Mental Illness (cluster average)	.51
Mental health workers need to stop blaming sexual assault on alcohol or on provocation or on loss of control by the assailant	.66
Mental health workers need to understand the difference between rape victims and people with serious mental health problems	.36
Cluster 18: The Media (cluster average)	.32
Media is far too graphic and far too invasive in reporting about rape cases	.40
Media needs to report how often this is happening—not just report the "sensational" cases	.28
More media coverage of what services are available to rape victims	.28

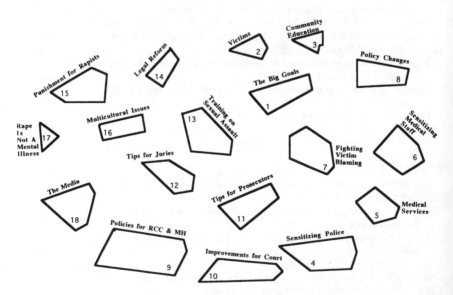

FIGURE 2.   Final concept map for improving the community response to rape.

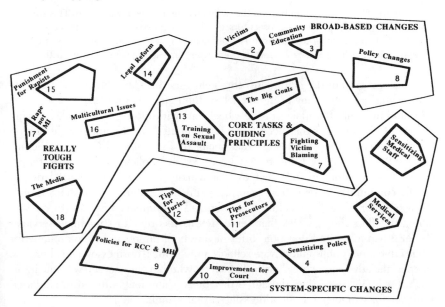

FIGURE 3.   Meta-interpretation of final concept map.

are not experiencing a mental illness—they are having a normal reaction to a traumatic event. As one advocate summarized,

> Counselors need to stop looking for the convenient excuse—she's mentally ill, she's experiencing disorder X from the DSM whatever, she was drinking, and so on. Their training really doesn't get them to think about why this is happening. It's about power and patriarchy, not mental illness and treatment plans.

Meta-Interpretation of the Map

After the group was satisfied with the name for each cluster, the analysis shifted to examining the structure of the map as a whole—what did this configuration mean? What was being conveyed through the *spatial placement* and arrangement of these clusters? Figure 3 reveals the group's meta-interpretation of the map. Over the course of the discussion concerning the spatial placement of the clusters, the advocates began drawing lines around groups of clusters, and naming these larger regions to explain why clusters were placed next to each other. Figure 3 represents their final drawing, their final grouping and meta-interpretation of the clusters, which they suggested resembled a wheel.

In the center of the map (the hub of the wheel) is a collection of clusters speaking to Core Tasks, the Guiding Principles driving other changes: The Big Goals (Cluster 1), Fighting Victim Blaming (Cluster 7), and Training on Sexual Assault (Cluster 13). As one advocate stated:

These are the things that go beyond the individual agencies we work with. This stuff is important for the police, the prosecutors, the doctors, everyone. Training is necessary to fight victim blaming and achieve the big goals we set for ourselves. This is our center, this is what we take with us in every case, for each person we work with.

This center region of the map unites three clusters that describe key components of advocates' jobs that they bring to each of their specific projects.

Around this hub, the spokes of the wheel start with more general tasks, moving to very specific changes that need to be implemented. In the upper right section of the map is a group of clusters that speak to Broad-Based Changes: Victims (Cluster 2), Community Education (Cluster 3), and Policy Changes (Cluster 8). These clusters offer general changes that usually transcend the boundaries of specific community systems. For example, many of the items in Cluster 8 (Policy Changes) offer ideas for creating a coordinated community response to rape by pulling together the agencies that serve victims in order to streamline services. Cluster 3 (Community Education) offers a variety of targets in the community for public education: public and private schools, universities, businesses, and churches. Whereas the advocates were sharply divided on whether they agreed with the items in Cluster 2 (Victims), they did agree that these statements offered broad-based strategies for women's role in addressing sexual assault.

After the group had decided what this region of the map represented, discussion turned to examining how this section (Broad-Based Changes) was different from the hub of the wheel (Core Tasks & Guiding Principles). Two advocates offered an interpretation that was agreed on by the group:

The ideas in this area (Broad-Based Changes) are more specific than those in the center. We start to get into specific tasks, specific policies we want to implement. We take our tools from the center [of the wheel] and bring those with us for this kind of broad-based work.

When you're trying to figure out if and how women should be educated about rape, where to target your community education, and what kind of policy changes you want to make, the underlying issues are prevention, training programs, and addressing victim blaming. This section (Broad-Based Changes) shows some of the most general ways we apply our guiding principles in the center of the wheel.

In this region of the map, we see examples of general applications of the key principles held by these advocates. Their core tasks of training and fighting victim blaming are introduced into community-education programs and general policy recommendations.

Moving clockwise around the wheel reveals a large grouping of clusters that suggest System-Specific Changes: Sensitizing Medical Staff (Cluster 6), Medical Services (Cluster 5), Sensitizing Police (Cluster 4), Tips for Prosecutors (Cluster 11), Improvements for Court (Cluster 10), Tips for Juries (Cluster 12), and Policies for Rape-Crisis Centers and Mental Health (Cluster 9). The focus had shifted from broad-based strategies to individual tasks unique to the different systems with which rape victims may have contact. It includes changes directed at juries, prosecutors, police, medical staff, mental health workers, and rape-crisis centers. For instance, some advocates stated:

These items read like the lessons learned from the worst cases in your careers. These are specific things you may not think of until you encounter them with a specific woman. You never think about how much a new pair of underwear means to a woman after she's been raped until you've seen the expression on one woman's face when she has to put back on the dirty pair.

These are lessons from the trenches. This is almost everything that can and does go wrong. Every doctor needs to know how to do the rape kit. I can believe an advocate mentioned that. Haven't we all waited forever in the ER with a victim who's dying to go home while the nurses round up somebody who might know something about how to collect the kit evidence?

This reads like a how-to manual for treating victims better. If these little changes could be implemented, we'd be so much better off. It's our collective wisdom.

This region of the map, therefore, illustrates specific implementations of the advocates' core guiding principles. This region summarizes concrete changes for all of the major social systems with which victims have contact.

Completing this wheel are the clusters in the upper left corner of the map, which the advocates labeled Really Tough Fights: The Media (Cluster 18), Multicultural Issues (Cluster 16), Rape Is Not A Mental Illness (Cluster 17), Punishment for Rapists (Cluster 15), and Legal Reform (Cluster 14). Several advocates noted that these clusters also spoke to fairly specific changes. But how did they end up close together? What was the significance of their location? As the advocates discussed each cluster and their items, a common theme emerged: These were changes about which they felt less optimistic. These were changes they wanted, but were unclear about how to work to achieve them and if they could be changed at all. For example, some advocates stated:

Changing the media? Getting a rape law that could actually mean something, do something? Getting a rapist locked up? Getting White folks to address their racism? Getting therapists to think about rape differently? You've got to be kidding. This battle is so uphill it might as well be perpendicular.

As we talk about these items, I feel completely overwhelmed. I don't know where to start. I don't know if it would do any good. That's not to say the rest of the items are a piece of cake, but they seem almost doable compared to these.

It's items like these that make a 24-hour response team look like an easy thing to pull off. Sorely needed, but I don't have much hope here. Let's go back to the center of the wheel and talk about our core tasks and guiding lights!

This region combines both general and specific strategies (note how its location touches both general Broad-Based changes and System-Specific Changes). Its salient feature is that it represents changes that may be much more difficult to implement.

This Concept Map represents the experiences and emotions of the workers in the front lines in the battle against sexual assault. Rape-victim advocates did indeed have many ideas as to how to improve services to rape victims, both general and specific, optimistic and pessimistic.

DISCUSSION

In this article we described how concept mapping can be a useful tool for feminist researchers. Its emphasis on both qualitative and quantitative approaches in both group and individual settings incorporates several characteristics that are consistent with feminist approaches to social science. This method was used to explore how to improve community services for rape victims. Rape-victim advocates described both general and specific changes for the legal, medical, and mental health systems that could be beneficial for rape survivors. As one advocate stated, the concept map is their "collective wisdom." It represents the lessons learned over hundreds of cases.

The concept map suggests that rape victims' experiences with social systems are still quite problem laden. Advocates reported that victims are not receiving the services they want, and are often revictimized by the process of seeking help. Victims' cases are dropped from the criminal justice system, the steps of legal prosecution are not explained to them, they are not kept informed on the status of their cases, they wait for hours in the emergency room, they are examined by doctors who have no experience with rape cases, they are stripped of their clothes and sent home in hospital scrubs, they cannot find counseling services, their experiences are splashed through the media, their stories are doubted, and their credibility is questioned.

Rape-victim advocates suggested both general and specific changes to address these problems. Some solutions targeted societal-level changes, addressing sexism, racism, and other forms of oppression. The advocates felt less optimistic about the likelihood of success for these changes. But other ideas for improvement were more specific and delineate tangible changes that could feasibly be implemented. For example, several advocates made concrete suggestions for improving emergency medical services for rape victims—provide more information to victims about pregnancy and sexually transmitted diseases, refrain from asking questions during the medical exam, provide victims with a change of clothes, and so on. These strategies begin to form a protocol for hospitals to follow in sexual-assault cases. Such ideas emerged not only for the medical system, but for the legal and mental health systems as well.

The maps generated by this study have been used to guide program development and policy-reform efforts for community help systems. We distributed this map to the participating rape-crisis centers and other state and national victim-advocacy groups. Although we do not know how every center has used this map, we are aware of some local applications. For example, a rape-crisis center in a rural northwest community has distributed this map to other social service agencies as part of its efforts to develop a coordinated system response to sexual-assault cases. Another center in the Midwest has used the map to rebuild its community-education curriculum as these findings suggested new target audiences and messages. One agency in the northeast now includes the map in its training materials for rape-victim advocates to illustrate the breadth of issues that arise in this type of community service work.

Turning to the methodological implications of this study, these results raise an important question: What, if anything, is different about the results obtained with concept mapping as compared to the findings we might have obtained with a more traditional method? What did concept mapping add to our understanding of improving the community response to rape? The interpretation of one of the meta-regions of the map—"Really Tough Fights"—addresses this issue. The meaning of this region was not clear to the researchers. In fact, we considered whether this grouping was a statistical artifact of the sorting and multi-dimensional scaling procedures. What we saw as a mistake made sense to the advocates. This region spoke to the emotions of their jobs—the changes they wanted, but did not think were likely. The region outlines some of the toughest battles to be fought to improve community treatment of rape victims.

The interpretation of this area of the map underscores two critical features of concept mapping. First, group discussion can facilitate understanding. What may elude each person individually may become clear through group interaction when people share their experiences. This aspect, however, may not be unique to concept mapping. Other group settings for data collection, such as focus groups, may also foster this collaborative interpretation. What distinguishes concept mapping from focus groups is the second critical feature of this method: the direct expression of participants' voices with minimal interpretation by the researchers. In focus-group research, the meaning of the discussion is interpreted by the researchers, which may or may not, as this case illustrates, be consistent with the participants' visions.

These methodological features of concept mapping are consistent with the developing vision of feminist research. If a primary goal of feminist research is to capture and understand women's voices, then their voices should be allowed to guide the research process. Our experience with this method illustrates how the researcher's perspective may be radically different from the participant's perspective. In concept mapping, the group discussion becomes the data, and remains in the language of the participants through the interpretation of the results. Allowing participants the opportunity to express their perspectives may enable us to uncover ideas that have been untapped by research.

A few words of caution about concept mapping in general and this study in particular are important. First, as with any method, the researcher's agenda is not completely absent. The choice of topic is dictated by the researcher, so it is possible to convene a group to examine an issue that is of interest to the researcher, but has little meaning to the participants. Therefore, it is worthwhile to examine the salience of the topic with the group to be sure that other, more pressing issues are not overlooked.

Second, care also needs to be paid to the selection of the participants. A researcher could create a vision that is entirely consistent with her own or his own perspective if she selects similarly minded people for the project. Alternative views cannot be presented if those holding such opinions are not included. Even efforts to include a diverse sample may yield a biased perspective. We selected participants based on their level of involvement with community help systems (i.e., we interviewed the advocate with the most direct advocacy experience), which resulted in a primarily White, educated sample. This sample may well be typical of women who work as rape-victim advocates. Alternatively, it may reflect other issues that determine how much direct service work advocates are involved in (e.g., full time versus part time, paid staff or volunteer status). Regardless of how well this sample represents the population of advocates, it is important to remember that their thoughts on victims and social systems reflect their societal standing and privileges. Advocates who are women of color may have different perceptions of how systems function and what changes are needed. A concept-mapping study targeting women of color would help address this issue.

Third, although several variations of concept mapping can be performed, the trade-offs of such modifications must be considered. In the interest of gaining national-level data to reflect system response across multiple states and geographic regions, we were unable to have a group meeting for the initial brainstorming. In selecting our approach, we had to choose between the increased diversity of a national sample versus the opportunity to bring a less geographically diverse group (e.g., advocates from our state) together for a meeting. It is possible that such a meeting may have created a more detailed, albeit more locally relevant item pool.

Finally, it is important to note that the use of concept mapping does not assure a feminist approach to research. Its use does not guarantee against hierarchy, promise diversity of responses, nor offer a vision completely untainted by the researcher's agenda. At each step in the process, the researcher must challenge herself or himself to implement this method in a manner consistent with a feminist vision of research.

Concept mapping can be a useful tool for feminist researchers. It is a single method that can address several key issues that have been defined in the feminist methodology literature as necessary to capture women's lives. Concept mapping can be used to further measurement and theory development, but can also be used to address policy and applied issues. The results of this study provided rape-crisis centers with several ideas for broad-based and specific system changes that could be targeted to improve the community response to rape victims.

Initial submission: April 2, 1996
Initial acceptance: June 28, 1996
Final acceptance: February 14, 1997

NOTES

1. This sample size was selected based on a power analysis for other statistical analyses in this project.
2. The Concept System version 1.0 was available when we conducted this study (Trochim, 1989d), and it had a limit of 91 statements, which must be remembered for the brainstorming meeting.
3. Other researchers interested in using concept mapping in their research should consider how to address dissenting opinions in the interpretation of the map. The group we worked with in this research was well-practiced in consensus decision making, and strived to address dissenting opinions so that the interpretation would reflect the beliefs of the entire group.
4. The size, shape, and position of the clusters in the map were determined by a complex set of factors, including the number of items in each cluster and the bridging values for the clusters. In general, clusters with a large number of items and high bridging values are often represented as large, spread-out shapes. Clusters with fewer items and low bridging values often have smaller, more compact shapes. For the interpretation of the map, the advocates were instructed to pay attention to the *position* of the clusters, but were not instructed to pay attention to their *size* or *shape*.

REFERENCES

Acker, J., Barry, K., & Esseveld, J. (1983). Objectivity and truth: Problems in doing feminist research. *Women's Studies International Forum, 6,* 423–435.

Allen, K. R., & Baber, K. M. (1992). Ethical and epistemological tensions in applying a postmodern perspective to feminist research. *Psychology of Women Quarterly, 16,* 1–15.

Campbell, R. (1994). *Expanding services to women of color: Five-year strategic plan for Midwestern rape crisis centers.* Unpublished report.

Campbell, R. (1996). *The community response to rape: An ecological conception of victims' experiences.* Unpublished doctoral dissertation, Michigan State University, East Lansing, MI.

Campbell, R. (1998). The community response to rape: Victims' experiences with legal, medical, and mental health systems. *American Journal of Community Psychology, 26,* 355–379.

Cannon, L., Higginbotham, E., & Leung, M. (1991). Race and class bias in qualitative research on women. In M. M. Fonow & J. A. Cook (Eds.), *Beyond methodology: Feminist scholarship as lived research* (pp. 107–118). Bloomington, IN: Indiana University Press.

Caringella-MacDonald, S. (1985). The comparability in sexual and nonsexual assault case treatment: Did statute change meet objective? *Crime and Delinquency, 31,* 206–222.

Cook, J. A., & Fonow, M. M. (1990). Knowledge and women's interests: Issues of epistemology and methodology in feminist sociological research. In J. M. Nielsen (Ed.), *Feminist research methods: Exemplary readings in the social sciences* (pp. 69–93). Boulder, CO: Westview Press.

Denmark, F., Russo, N. F., Frieze, I. H., & Sechzer, J. A. (1988). Guidelines for avoiding sexism in psychological research. *American Psychologist, 43,* 582–585.

DuBois, B. (1983). Passionate scholarship: Notes on values, knowing and method in feminist social science. In G. Bowles & R. Duelli Klein (Eds.), *Theories of women's studies* (pp. 105–116). London: Routledge & Kegan Paul.

Estrich, S. (1987). *Real rape: How the legal system victimizes women who say no.* Cambridge: Harvard University Press.

Fischer, K., Berger, A., Campbell, R., & Rose, M. (1995). *Battered women's definitions of abuse: A cluster analysis of narrative data.* Manuscript submitted for publication.

Fonow, M. M., & Cook, J. A. (1991). Back to the future: A look at the second wave of feminist epistemology and methodology. In M. M. Fonow & J. A. Cook (Eds.), *Beyond methodology: Feminist scholarship as lived research* (pp. 1–15). Bloomington, IN: Indiana University Press.

Galvin, J., & Polk, K. (1983). Attrition in case processing: Is rape unique? *Journal of Research in Crime and Delinquency, 20,* 126–154.

Grady, K. E. (1981). Sex bias in research design. *Psychology of Women Quarterly, 5,* 628–636.

Harding, S. (1986). *The science question in feminism.* Ithaca, NY: Cornell University Press.

Harding, S. (1987). Conclusion: Epistemological questions. In S. Harding (Ed.), *Feminism and methodology* (pp. 181–190). Bloomington, IN: Indiana University Press.

Harding, S. (1991). *Whose science? Whose knowledge?: Thinking from women's lives.* Ithaca, NY: Cornell University Press.

Jayaratne, T. E. (1983). The value of quantitative methodology for feminist research. In G. Bowles & R. Duelli Klein (Eds.), *Theories of women's studies* (pp. 140–161). London: Routledge & Kegan Paul.

Jayaratne, T. E., & Stewart, A. J. (1991). Quantitative and qualitative methods in social sciences: Current feminist issues and practical strategies. In M. M. Fonow & J. A. Cook (Eds.), *Beyond methodology: Feminist scholarship as lived research* (pp. 85–106). Bloomington, IN: Indiana University Press.

Keller, E. F. (1990). Gender and science. In J. M. Nielsen (Ed)., *Feminist research methods: Exemplary readings in the social sciences* (pp. 41–57). Boulder, CO: Westview Press.

Kerstetter, W. A. (1990). Gateway to justice: Police and prosecutorial response to sexual assaults against women. *Journal of Criminal Law and Criminology, 81,* 267–313.

King, F. H., & Webb, C. (1981). Rape crisis centers: Progress and problems. *Journal of Social Issues, 37,* 93–104.

Koss, M. P., Koss, P. G., & Woodruff, W. J. (1991). Deleterious effects of criminal victimization on women's health and medical utilization. *Archives of Internal Medicine, 151,* 342–347.

LaFree, G. D. (1980). Variables affecting guilty pleas and convictions in rape cases: Toward a social theory of rape processing. *Social Forces, 58,* 833–850.

Levy, J. A. (1988). Gender bias as a threat to construct validity in research design. In Nebraska

Sociological Feminist Collective (Eds.), *A feminist ethic for social science research* (pp. 139–157). Lewiston, NY: Edwin Mellen Press.

MacKinnon, C. A. (1987). *Feminism unmodified: Discourses on life and law.* Cambridge: Harvard University Press.

MacKinnon, C. A. (1989). *Toward a feminist theory of the state.* Cambridge: Harvard University Press.

Madigan, L., & Gamble, N. (1991). *The second rape: Society's continued betrayal of the victim.* New York: Lexington Books.

Matoesian, G. M. (1993). *Reproducing rape: Domination through talk in the courtroom.* Chicago: University of Chicago Press.

McCahill, T. W., Meyer, L. C., & Fischman, A. M. (1979). *The aftermath of rape.* Lexington, MA: Lexington Books.

McHugh, M. C., Koeske, R. D., & Frieze, I. H. (1986). Issues to consider in conducting nonsexist psychological research: A guide for researchers. *American Psychologist, 41,* 879–890.

Mies, M. (1983). Toward a methodology for feminist research. In G. Bowles & R. Duelli Klein (Eds.), *Theories of women's studies* (pp. 117–139). London: Routledge & Kegan Paul.

Mies, M. (1991). Women's research or feminist research: The debate surrounding feminist science and methodology. In M. M. Fonow & J. A. Cook (Eds.), *Beyond methodology: Feminist scholarship as lived research* (pp. 60–84). Bloomington, IN: Indiana University Press.

National Victim Center. (1992). *Rape in America: A report to the nation.* Arlington, VA: Author.

Nielsen, J. M. (1990). *Feminist research methods: Exemplary readings in the social sciences.* Boulder, CO: Westview Press.

Oakley, A. (1988). Interviewing women: A contradiction in terms. In H. Roberts (Ed.), *Doing feminist research* (pp. 30–61). New York: Routledge.

Peplau, L. A., & Conrad, E. (1989). Beyond non-sexist research: The perils of feminist methods in psychology. *Psychology of Women Quarterly, 13,* 379–400.

Reinharz, S. (1979). *On becoming a social scientist.* San Francisco: Jossey-Bass.

Reinharz, S. (1992). *Feminist methods in social research.* New York: Oxford University Press.

Scott, S. (1985). Feminist research and qualitative methods: A discussion of some issues. In R. G. Burgess (Ed.), *Issues in educational research: Qualitative methods* (pp. 67–85). Philadelphia: Falmer Press.

Smith, D. E. (1987). Women's perspective as a radical critique of sociology. In S. Harding (Ed.), *Feminism and methodology* (pp. 84–96). Bloomington, IN: Indiana University Press.

Stanley, L., & Wise, S. (1979). Feminist research, feminist consciousness, and experiences of sexism. *Women's Studies International Quarterly, 2,* 359–374.

Stanley, L., & Wise, S. (1983). *Breaking out: Feminist consciousness and feminist research.* London: Routledge & Kegan Paul.

Stanley, L., & Wise, S. (1990). Method, methodology, and epistemology in feminist research process. In L. Stanley (Ed.), *Feminist praxis: Research, theory, and epistemology in feminist sociology* (pp. 20–60). London: Routledge.

Trochim, W. M. K. (1985). Pattern matching, validity, and conceptualization in program evaluation. *Evaluation Review, 9,* 575–604.

Trochim, W. M. K. (1989a). An introduction to concept mapping for planning and evaluation. *Evaluation and Program Planning, 12,* 1–16.

Trochim, W. M. K. (1989b). Concept mapping: Soft science or hard art? *Evaluation and Program Planning, 12,* 87–110.

Trochim, W. M. K. (1989c). Outcome pattern matching and program theory. *Evaluation and Program Planning, 12,* 355–366.

Trochim, W. M. K. (1989d). *The Concept System.* Ithaca, NY: Concept Systems.

Warshaw, R. (1988). *I never called it rape: The Ms. report on recognizing, fighting, and surviving date and acquaintance rape.* New York: Harper & Row.

Webster, L. (1989). *Sexual assault and child sexual abuse: A national directory of victim/survivor services and prevention programs*. Phoenix, AZ: Oryx Press.

Westkott, M. (1990). Feminist criticism of the social sciences. In J. M. Nielsen (Ed)., *Feminist research methods: Exemplary readings in the social sciences* (pp. 58–67). Boulder, CO: Westview Press.

Wittig, M. (1985). Metatheoretical dilemmas in the psychology of gender. *American Psychologist, 40*, 800–812.

Ylló, K. (1988). Political and methodological debates in wife abuse research. In K. Ylló (Ed.), *Feminist perspectives on wife abuse* (pp. 28–50). Newbury Park, CA: Sage.

MEASURING SUBJECTIVITIES

"Concept Mapping As a Feminist Research Method: Examining the Community Response to Rape"

Stephanie Riger
University of Illinois at Chicago

Over 25 years ago, Kenneth Gergen (1973) radically challenged traditional understandings of knowledge in psychology. To him, knowledge, scientific or otherwise, was not an objective search for laws of behavior that held across time and place but rather a construction created by human beings that was intimately tied to culture and history. People—including scientists—actively construct meanings, interpreting their experience and the action of others rather than uncovering objective reality (Watzlawick, 1984). Social constructionism, as this viewpoint is known in psychology, has a long history in such fields as sociology. Yet it created an uproar among psychologists, many of whom believe that the aim of social science is to find timeless laws of behavior rather than to investigate subjectivities.

Gergen (1985) challenged not only the content of psychological research, but also its methods, disputing claims of "objectivity." To him, research produces not "facts" but rather "objectifications" or illustrations, similar to vivid photographs, that make an argument persuasive rather than provide proof of truth claims. Others are more restrained in their criticisms. Rhoda Unger (1983), for example, admonished feminists that abandoning the tools of empiricism would mean that our insights are likely to be ignored by the rest of psychology.

Many feminists find social constructionism to be the most useful perspective from which to understand gender (for a discussion, see Bohan, 1993; Hare-Mustin & Marecek, 1988). How, then to study gender—or indeed, any topic—from a social-constructionist perspective?

Hope Landrine and her colleagues (Landrine, Klonoff, & Brown, 1992) provide a creative example in their research contrasting White and non-White women's

Address correspondence and reprint requests to: Stephanie Riger, Women's Studies Program (M/C 360), University of Illinois at Chicago, 1022 Behavioral Sciences Building, 1007 W. Harrison St., Chicago, IL 60607-7137. E-mail: sriger@uic.edu responses to items from the Bem Sex Role Inventory (Bem, 1974). First, women rated themselves on gender-stereotypic items. Then they indicated their interpretation of the terms used in the items. Although overall scores were similar, White and non-White women differed sharply in how they had defined and understood the terms while rating themselves. For example, Latin and Asian women defined "assertive" as "say whatever's on my mind," whereas White women interpreted the same term a "standing up for myself." Black women chose "say whatever's on my mind" or "aggressive" as their definition of "assertive."

Celia Kitzinger's (1986) use of Q-sort methodology to study views of lesbianism is another example of the use of empirical methods to study subjectivity. Kitzinger sought not to assess the truthfulness or validity of accounts of lesbianism but rather "to describe the different ways that people construct their realities" (p. 152). She identified five accounts of lesbianism, ranging from seeing it as a source of self-fulfillment and true happiness to a traditional account of lesbianism as a personal failing or sin. Kitzinger emphasized that these five accounts are not inclusive. Rather, they represent only some of the possible ways to account for lesbianism. Nor are they necessarily fixed views, because people's accounts may change over time.

Q-sort methodology has become increasingly valued by feminist researchers (see Snelling, next issue). To increase its usefulness, Kitzinger (1986) advocated collective construction and sorting of items by a group in order to put control of the research in the hands of participants. From a feminist perspective, this would accomplish two goals. First, it would seek to equalize the power relations between scientists and those they study. Second, it would enhance the likelihood that the emergent findings would reflect the participants', not the scientists', worldviews.

Campbell and Salem's (this issue) research adopts these strategies. Grounding their study in a public-health tradition, they have extended participants' roles in the research process beyond that of simply being subjects. Following techniques developed by Trochim (1989) that are similar to the Q-sort, they included participants in the construction, sorting, and interpretation of clusters of items. Their research looks not at individuals' subjectivities but rather at the collective viewpoint of rape-victim advocates—as they put it, the collective "lessons learned over hundreds of cases" (p. 86). Their study presents a useful map of the domains of importance to rape-victim advocates, providing valuable directions for policy change.

Use of the concept-mapping technique raises some issues relevant not only to this study, but to measurement of subjectivity in general. Perhaps the most important consideration is the link between individuals' (or groups') subjectivities and their position in a social structure. Campbell and Salem studied rape-victim advocates' views. Would rape victims have produced the same conceptual map?

Stakeholder analysis assumes that points of view will vary with people's position in a social structure (Mark & Shotland, 1985). Adding the notion of power, Becker (1967) argues that there is a hierarchy of credibility: those at the top of the hierarchy can impose their worldviews on others. Concept mapping offers a way to examine the relationship of social structure to people's perspectives. Nonetheless, as Campbell and Salem acknowledge, concept mapping does not guarantee against hierarchy. Rape-victim advocates, defense attorneys, judges, and rape victims might differ in their conceptualizations of what constitutes rape, but the views of those higher in the legal system will prevail in court. Understanding the conceptualizations of those in power, and how those conceptualizations differ from others in a social system, might enhance the success of rape prosecutions and antirape policies.

Furthermore, knowing how the conceptual maps of rape victims differ from those of prosecutors and defense attorneys might be useful in attempts to change the legal system. Karla Fischer and her colleagues (Fischer, Berger, Campbell, & Rose, 1995) use concept mapping to identify battered women's definitions of abuse. To victims, abuse is multifaceted, including several dimensions that are generally not acknowledged by the legal system or others as abuse. In their view, abuse includes not only physical harm, but also the intent to harm, constraints on personal freedom, derogation, and degredation of self-esteem. Fischer et al. assert that using narrow definitions of abuse that include only physical harm prevents many women from seeking help because their experiences do not fit the common stereotype of severe and frequent beatings. Like Smith, Smith, and Earp (this issue), they recognize that experiential approaches to violence against women can provide vital insights for program and policy development.

Although it offers intriguing possibilities for research, concept mapping is not without problems. Concept mapping appeals to feminists because it permits participants to exercise control over key aspects of the research. Allowing participants not just to sort items but also to construct and interpret them helps to ensure that issues of concern to participants are included in the research. This assumes a high degree of awareness on the part of participants, however. Shulamit Reinharz (1992) points out that feminist interviewing methods work best with self-aware, articulate people. Concept mapping might have some of the same limitations.

Another concern is whether subgroup differences can emerge from concept-mapping methods. A technique designed to find a composite viewpoint risks obscuring minority views. This is a particular risk when item development and interpretation are done in groups. As Campbell and Salem point out, group discussion can facilitate understanding. Nonetheless, groups may suppress dissenting views. Feminists have long been aware of the "tyranny of structurelessness" in which the absence of a formal structure in groups permits domination by those who are more articulate or forceful or who have more supporters in the group (Joreen, 1973, p. 285). Those using concept mapping as a technique should be sensitive to this possibility.

Concept mapping also raises intriguing questions about reliability and validity (see Trochim, 1989). If maps differ over time, is this because the method is unreliable or because people's conceptualizations change? If people in the same social location produce different maps, is it because of lack of reliability or because of differences among individuals? Traditional ideas about reliability require reexamination when subjectivities are the focus of research.

Similarly, issues of validity are problematic. Trochim suggests several ways to measure validity, for example, by asking people to identify the computed concept map from a set of maps, thereby identifying the map that represents their thinking. But how are we to determine if such maps are a valid representation of reality, if the "reality" in question is a subjective one, which can change? Indeed, does the concept of validity apply in this case?

Kitzinger (1986) questions whether focusing on subjectivities leads to a radical relativism, in which various accounts are all given equal weight. She advocates assessing the accounts relative to how helpful they are toward achieving a certain goal. Hence, utility might be another criteria by which to evaluate maps. Campbell and Salem's study, and Fischer et al.'s (1995) research on battered women's portrayals of abuse provide excellent examples of how maps might be useful.

Concept mapping offers feminists an effective technique to measure subjectivities. Expanding our scope to include social structural factors associated with various conceptual maps will make this technique especially helpful for developing social-change strategies that benefit women.

REFERENCES

Becker, H. (1967). Whose side are we on? *Social Problems, 14,* 239–247.
Bem, S. L. (1974). The measurment of psychological androgyny. *Journal of Consulting and Clinical Psychology, 42,* 155–162.
Bohan, J. S. (1993). Regarding gender: Essentialism, constructionism, and feminist psychology. *Psychology of Women Quarterly, 17,* 5–21.
Campbell, R., & Salem, D. (1999). Concept mapping as a feminist research method: Examining the community response to rape. *Psychology of Women Quarterly, 23,* 67–91.
Fischer, K., Berger, A., Campbell, R., & Rose, M. R. (1995). *Battered women's definitions of abuse: A cluster analysis of narrative data.* Unpublished manuscript.
Gergen, K. J. (1973). Social psychology as history. *Journal of Personality & Social Psychology, 26,* 309–320.
Gergen, K. J. (1985). The social constructionist movement in modern psychology. *American Psychologists, 40,* 266–275.
Hare-Mustin, R. T., & Marecek, J. (1988). The meaning of difference: Gender theory, postmodernism, and psychology. *American Psychologist, 43,* 355–464.
Joreen. (1973). The tyranny of structurelessness. In A. Koedt, E. Levine, & A. Rapone (Eds.), *Radical feminism* (pp. 285–299). New York: Quadrangle.
Kitzinger, C. (1986). Introducing and developing Q as a feminist methodology: A study of accounts of lesbianism. In S. Wilkinson (Ed.), *Feminist social psychology: Developing theory and practice* (pp. 151–172). Stony Stratford, UK: Keynes.
Landrine, H., Klonoff, E. A., & Brown, C. A. (1992). Cultural diversity and methodology in feminist psychology: Critique, proposal, empirical example. *Psychology of Women Quarterly, 16,* 145–163.
Mark, M. M., & Shotland, R. L. (1985). Stakeholder-based evaluation and value judgments. *Evaluation Review, 9,* 605–626.
Reinharz, S. (1992). *Feminist methods in social research.* New York: Oxford University Press.
Smith, P. H., Smith, J. B., & Earp, J. L. (1999). Beyond the measurement trap: A reconstructed conceptualization and measurement of women battering. *Psychology of Women Quarterly, 23,* 179–198.
Snelling, S. J. (in press). Women's perspectives on feminism: A Q-methodological study. *Psychology of Women Quarterly.*
Trochim, W. M. K. (1989). Concept mapping: Soft science or hard art? *Evaluation and Program Planning, 12,* 87–110.
Unger, R. K. (1983). Through the looking glass: No wonderland yet! (The reciprocal relationship between methodology and models of reality). *Psychology of Women Quarterly, 8,* 9–32.
Watzlawick, P. (Ed.), (1984). *The invented reality: Contributions to constructivism.* New York: Norton.

FOSTERING RELATIONALITY WHEN IMPLEMENTING AND EVALUATING A COLLECTIVE-DRAMA APPROACH TO PREVENTING VIOLENCE AGAINST WOMEN

Community Education Team
Wilfrid Laurier University

The authors, the Community Education Team, implemented an intervention in schools in southwestern Ontario to prevent violence against women. Using collective drama as the medium to effect social change, we engaged students in high school and grades 7 and 8 in critical dialogue about issues of violence in their lives. We discuss how we fostered the feminist principle of relationality in our relationships with the students, their educators, and ourselves as a team when we practiced collective drama and evaluated its impact. We illustrate our reflections on doing feminist work with selected portions of our evaluation findings and excerpts from a formal dialogue among the authors.

This article illustrates how the implementation and evaluation of collective drama can reflect feminist principles and processes of gathering knowledge to prevent violence against women. We begin by describing a collective-intervention model and its accompanying evaluation. The heart of the article consists of an analysis of how the feminist concept of relationality was central to how we enacted our

The members of the Community Education Team for the Prevention of Violence against Women were Tammie Brunk, Judy Gould, Holt Sivak, Darlene Spencer, and Richard Walsh-Bowers. We are grateful to the students, parents, and school staff for their participation in the evaluations, and to our community advisory committee for their support. The Ontario Ministry of Education and Training provided the funding through the Interministerial Violence against Women Initiative. Judy Gould received partial funding from a Social Sciences and Humanities Research Council doctoral fellowship.

Address correspondence and reprint requests to: Richard Walsh-Bowers, Department of Psychology, Wilfrid Laurier University, Waterloo, Ontario N2L 3C5, Canada. E-mail: rwalshb@mach1.wlu.ca relationships with our participants and among ourselves as well as to how a collective-drama modality works to facilitate social change.

Feminist authors have argued for new parameters in research and scholarship that reflect feminist values. For example, Shulamit Reinharz (1992), Sandra Kirby and Kate McKenna (1989), and Jeri Wine (1989) purport that researchers and citizens should join in an egalitarian, democratic research relationship. An egalitarian approach to research is based on intersubjectivity, wherein all participants are knowers and have the capacity to equally contribute to the process of investigation (Kirby & McKenna, 1989). Additionally, the Task Force on Issues in Research in the Psychology of Women (1977) defined feminist scholarship as participatory, nonhierarchical, and oriented to social action. These notions were echoed by Maureen McHugh, Randi Koeske, and Irene Frieze (1986). These feminist values and principles, subsumed by the term "relationality," guided and shaped our day-to-day work. Jeri Wine (1989) defines relationality as:

> consciousness of the necessary interdependence of human beings, to a sense of connectedness to others, to awareness of one's embeddedness in human, social and historical contexts, to the maximization of well-being for all persons, and to commitment to non-violence. (p. 78)

By describing the overriding importance of relationality within the project, we hope to provide an integrated, holistic picture of how the process of collective drama enabled us to build social connections and work toward social change.

We have woven our individual and collective reflections on the enactment of feminist values with quotes from the young women, men, and teachers who worked with us to illustrate the interconnectedness of various aspects of the projects. We believe that our attention to different voices and to the process and context of the projects authentically reflects how this type of work evolves. Inspired by Laurel Richardson's (1994) metaphor for the construction of postmodern texts—the crystal, which exemplifies multiple, partial realities—we also include excerpts from a dialogue among team members (a complete manuscript of this dialogue is available on request). Furthermore, how we composed and revised this article collectively exemplifies the principle of relationality. In keeping with the feminist spirit of contextualized report-writing (Walsh, 1989; Walsh-Bowers, 1999), we personalize our involvement in this work, use the language of feelings, and reference the full names of authors cited.[1] We believe that experimentation with new styles of research reporting can help break away from mainstream dictates and aid in setting new standards that resonate with feminist principles.

In this article we attempt to give expression, in a two-dimensional form, to our multidimensional experience. To accomplish this task, first we briefly describe the projects, the intervention, and our evaluation research methods. Then we discuss how we fostered relationality: (a) in the relationships developed among all participants, and (b) when we used collective drama as a tool for social change to prevent violence against women.

IMPLEMENTING AND EVALUATING COLLECTIVE DRAMA

Background of the Projects

The collective-drama projects described in the text that follows were part of a larger program, funded by the Ontario Ministry of Education and Training, that was directed at preventing violence toward women in the Waterloo region of southwestern Ontario. The intention of the collective-drama intervention was to help young men and women challenge attitudes and behaviors that might lead to violence within their relationships. Students in grades 7 through 13 participated in projects at five different school settings. The project staff (i.e., the Community Education Team) included two drama facilitators: Darlene Spencer, a professional actor and director, who practiced and taught collective drama at the University of Waterloo; and Holt Sivak, also trained and experienced in acting and directing, who completed an M.A. thesis in community psychology on another type of social drama (Sivak, 1996). There were also two evaluation team members, Tammie Brunk, who completed her M.A. thesis on young men's experiences within our projects (Brunk, 1996), and Judy Gould, whose M.A. thesis research concerned a stakeholder approach to sexual-assault-prevention programming (Gould, 1994). Tammie and Judy did not have formal training in drama, but while working on the projects they gained experience in drama activities and have evaluated the collective-drama initiative since its inception. The academic consultant was Richard Walsh-Bowers, community psychologist, theater director, and actor at Wilfrid Laurier University, who has done research on applications of drama (e.g., Walsh-Bowers, 1992) and supervised Judy's, Holt's, and Tammie's theses. A community committee, including representatives from sexual-assault support centers, women's shelters, male batterers' treatment programs, universities, and school boards, advised the team.

This article is focused on process rather than on specific findings about how well the collective-drama approach works. Interested readers should correspond with the authors concerning outcomes.

The Collective-Drama Intervention

Collective drama has the potential for encouraging adolescents' growth in self-awareness and peer relations, in empathic understanding of differing viewpoints, and the ability to evoke emotional, as well as cognitive responses to problematic issues (Courtney, 1989; Gray & Mager, 1973). Drawing from Paulo Freire's (1990) critical pedagogy, Judy Gould (1994) argued that peer-based, collaborative education, in which young male and female students are encouraged to reflect on or critically challenge information, can provide a more meaningful and durable experience than a lecture format. Specialists in collective drama know experientially that live performance is more influential for audiences than lectures, texts, or even videos or films. Moreover, interactive drama promotes spontaneous discussions with audiences and can diminish attitudes supporting rape (e.g., Frazier, Valtinson, & Candell, 1994). Given the salience of peer groups during adolescence, drama activities and drama performances based on the participants' own ideas for characters, plot, and staging are well-suited to promoting change in adolescent attitudes.

The team used collective drama as a tool to increase the awareness and critical capacity of students regarding violence against women. In collective drama, a troupe of actors generates a script for performance in collaboration with drama facilitators based on research done by the troupe members themselves.

Each drama project consisted of four different stages. First, at schools where auditions could be conducted, Holt and Darlene selected drama-troupe participants based primarily on diversity. People were sought out who had not only different physical features, ethnic/cultural/social backgrounds and peer groups, but different thoughts on issues of gender relations. Additionally, the drama facilitators looked for people with enthusiasm, some affinity for drama (though not necessarily the "best" performers), and a willingness to contribute to and learn from the group. There was an introductory period during which students in the drama troupes and the facilitators became acquainted. During this time, the troupe members practiced basic drama skills and participated in discussions on violence in preparation for the workshops that followed.

Second, the workshops consisted of drama games that evolved into discussions on various aspects of violence in relationships and were held in a variety of classes at each school. The workshops allowed the troupe members to interact with their schoolmates to learn about their peers' views and experiences related to violence. The topics and ideas shared during workshops were subsequently used to inform the scripts.

Third, during script writing and rehearsals, the students decided which topics would be covered in the play. They then divided into small groups to work on the topic that interested them most. The script for each topic was written collectively by the students in each small group and was based on improvisational acting to keep the language and situations close to real life. Troupes at all schools chose to focus on quite similar topics: date rape, gender discrimination, physical violence, verbal and emotional abuse within intimate relationships, and peer pressure.

Fourth, the students in the troupes staged the play for their peers at host schools and often took the show to other high schools or junior high schools. Following the performances, the students in the drama troupes took part in discussion periods either with the whole audience or with smaller groups in classroom settings. At the last two school sites the drama presentations involved audience participation. Students watching the show were invited to complete scenarios by enacting their own ideas for conflict resolution.

Evaluation Approach

In order to assess the process and content of the drama activities at each school, Tammie and Judy employed some combination of the following evaluation methods: individual interviews with drama-troupe members, school staff, and drama facilitators; focus groups with troupe members, workshop participants, and audience participants; and surveys with workshop participants and audience members. Additionally, during each of the projects, all team members acted as participant-observers, writing reflection notes that described day-to-day activities, personal thoughts, and reactions. Keeping reflection notes helps to account for investigators' social locations and personal subjectivity (Kirby & McKenna, 1989). The reflection notes were used as a basis for informal discussion among team members to enhance the emergent quality of the intervention. As well, the notes informed our analysis about the systemic aspects in our work to prevent violence against women.

At each project setting, Judy and Tammie invited a sample of students and teachers to participate in evaluation activities. The choices of method were dependent on the needs of the drama facilitators and the individuals at each school. But for the purposes of this article our focus is on the experience of the drama-troupe members and the team, not on the student audiences.

All evaluation participants were informed of their rights as research participants both verbally and in writing (i.e., voluntary participation, right to withdraw, right to omit questions, right to anonymity/confidentiality, and feedback). The evaluators obtained signed consent forms from all participants. Students under age 18 also obtained parental consent to take part in evaluation activities. Over the course of 2 years, 4282 students and staff participated in some dimension of the collective-drama projects and 789 students and staff participated in the evaluation.

RELATIONALITY IN PRACTICE

Relationality was manifested in our egalitarian, collaborative approach, and our emphasis on reflecting multiple perspectives and social context. Judith Jordan (1991) describes the mutuality and fluid state of relationships:

> In a mutual exchange one is both affecting the other and being affected by the other; one extends oneself out to the other and is also receptive to the impact of the other. There is an openness to influence, emotional availability, and a constantly changing pattern or responding to and affecting the other's state. (p. 82)

Throughout the course of our project, we viewed the development and maintenance of relationships with students and teachers within each setting and relationships within the team and with advisory committee members as essential to our work. While trying to construct egalitarian relationships, we discovered that barriers such as acknowledging our institutional and personal power, as well as working within a hierarchical organization, affected our work.

Relationships Within the Project Settings

Within the drama process, Darlene and Holt modeled and encouraged egalitarian, collaborative interactions both among the troupe members and the students and themselves. Relationships were based on mutual respect and empathy for others' viewpoints. Rather than playing an authoritarian or "expert" role, the facilitators supported the students in critically reflecting on information and in making choices for themselves related to their roles, the script, and the performances. During a group interview, students in the drama troupe at one school commented on Darlene and Holt's relationship: "you guys work, like, really well together. You have . . . good personalities [that] go together . . . two people who were like . . . yin and yang." Concerning the mutual respect fostered between the drama facilitators and the drama troupe, one troupe member remarked that Darlene and Holt, "did a really good job of trying to understand our point of view and helping us to understand theirs."

Relationality was also central to how the evaluators gathered and interpreted evaluation data from each school setting. When possible, Tammie and Judy asked students for input regarding evaluation questions and procedures. At some settings, they asked students to keep journals of their experiences in the project. Of course, some students chose not to take part in the evaluation and others were unable to follow through with their commitment to participate.

The evaluation interviews became more fluid over time, with holistic, open-ended questions that encouraged dialogue between researchers and participants. Judy and Tammie believed that the interview guide should be loosely structured and flexible, able to shift with the changing needs of participants. Judy expresses these concepts in the following observation:

> I never ever found in an interview that we went through the questions, boom, boom, boom, boom [first question, then second question]. We'd ask one question. They might answer three. . . . They didn't answer in categories and I think we responded by not asking them in categories.

Tammie and Judy collected information from various constituencies (i.e., troupe members, workshop and performance participants, teachers and administrators, team members) in an attempt to fully represent the multiple perspectives within the projects. Finally, to place the findings in a sociopolitical context, the evaluators collected information on teachers' perspectives regarding gender relations and attitudes toward violence at each setting. The following dialogue excerpt elaborates on the principle of truthfully reflecting participants' perspectives and owning one's own social location in egalitarian research:

Darlene:	I always appreciated when you [the evaluators] made your quotes. . . . You would put all their "like's" and "as's" and all of that. I've just seen some . . . researchers change that sort of stuff and make it sound more articulate than it really was at the time.
Judy:	We can't discount . . . [their's or] our own presence and that's always a hard balance.
Holt:	How do you [Judy] fit in there?
Judy:	Well, reflection notes are one big way.
Darlene:	It seems like your voices were very sensitive to the . . . like, you were so serving of them [the participants] . . . and sometimes to the point of paranoia though. But I appreciated, as I look back, I appreciate that . . . . The one thing I really took from Shulamit [Reinharz, 1992] when I did that reading was to take into perspective the fact that your perspective is going to be totally different. And everyone has this different

makeup of who they are and so they're looking out from those eyes. Which is such a theatrical concept, such a huge part of theatre that it was obvious. . . . Well, good for you guys [evaluation team] to jump on this band wagon and see that. . . . You oftentimes would say "Well, I'm probably too sensitive here because I came from this situation."

Richard: You appreciated the fact that both Judy and Tammie were as much as possible owning their own locations and how their personal locations affected what they were perceiving.

Darlene: Yeah, or at least that you wanted to. It was something that you were working toward.

Tammie and Judy also tried to be conscious of their subjectivity, personal histories, and personal power when analyzing evaluation information and writing reports. They found they always needed to balance their perspective and their words with those of the participants. In presentations and reports about the collective drama projects, Judy and Tammie believed that it was imperative to express the findings in the participants' words and then introduce their own perspectives under a "team reflections" section. At the first two schools, the evaluators used category names based on the team's jargon to describe their findings (e.g., "consciousness-raising" and "empowerment"). Tammie and Judy felt these labels made the information less accessible to participants, however. Therefore, for the third and fourth schools, they decided to use labels that were based on the participants' words (e.g., "real-life situations," "created by peers").

Feedback to participants also played a significant role in establishing egalitarian research relationships as well as providing for confirmation of data and an opportunity for collecting additional information (Kirby & McKenna, 1989; Reinharz, 1992; Serrano-Garcia, 1990; Walsh, 1989). The evaluation team provided feedback to schools and participants in various forms (i.e., summaries of interview quotes for editing and validation, feedback sessions, feedback letters to parents, summary and comprehensive reports to individual schools and the school board).

Negotiating entry to each setting was another area in which a collaborative approach was evident. The drama facilitators and evaluators made a concerted effort to respond to the unique needs within each school. This approach required flexibility and responsiveness. In the following dialogue, Darlene and Richard draw a parallel between the mutual responsivity that was necessary in evaluation activities and that was needed for the collective drama process:

Darlene: Be reactive in the moment instead of going in with an agenda. Like when you're memorizing lines or doing a play. There's this voice in your head that says the line should be read *this* way. But as soon as you have an acting partner, that completely changes if you're listening to them.

Richard: So the analogy to theater is listening to or reacting to the persons who are on stage. You [evaluators] were really responsive to what was going on around you. That is the hallmark of high-quality acting and the hallmark of high-quality researching.

Relationships Outside the Settings

Working collaboratively and attending to relationality was also central to the team's own group processes. All team members offered suggestions during the development of both the drama process and evaluation plan. The team worked on an egalitarian basis with crossover and sharing of tasks. For example, Judy and Tammie suggested ideas during script writing or led rehearsals when needed, and Darlene and Holt helped with evaluation activities when appropriate. The following comments made by Tammie illustrate how the team practiced feminist principles during interactions:

> I read an article on feminist discourse (Chambers, 1995) and it helped me reflect on our team process . . . how we came together and talked about this stuff. And it had to affect each of our understandings. It [the article] talked about making feminine qualities valid and using them in this type of discourse: like reaching out to others, cooperation, emotional and intuitive sensitivity, respecting others' perspectives, looking for common understandings. And I feel like that [feminine qualities] was a big part of our team discussions . . . and I think that's an important part of our research methods.

Our commitment to a feminist approach was also reflected in how we linked the evaluation activities to the collective-drama process. Rather than trying to exert control over the research situation, the evaluators planned evaluation activities with respect for participants' busy schedules and to minimize disruption to the drama process. Tammie recalled how she and Judy felt challenged to remain sensitive to the drama participants' and facilitators' needs by using open-ended qualitative methods rather than quantifying the participants' perceptions:

> We don't want to go in there and hand out these scales and force them to sit down and talk about "Attitudes Toward Women" on paper and circle little numbers. We want to tag along and watch what's happening and ask them a question every now and then. . . . And sometimes that's disruptive. And I feel like it's up to us to balance that. I've also had feedback from people in interviews that having to do the interview really helped them consolidate . . . [their experiences].

Additionally, Judy and Tammie gave anonymous feedback from evaluation participants to Darlene and Holt as quickly as possible so that lessons learned from the students could reshape the intervention almost immediately.

Finally, egalitarian, collaborative relationships were fostered between the project team and advisory committee members. Members of the advisory committee not only heard and commented on updates from the team but were also actively involved in envisioning future directions for the initiative and in personally providing support to students in audiences, or in leading discussions with students following drama presentations.

Barriers to Enacting Our Feminist Ideals

As evaluators and activists, we felt that it was imperative to be ethical in our practice when implementing an intervention to prevent violence. While we strove to enact egalitarian, collaborative relationships, we had to acknowledge the external and internal barriers to this ideal. In the following section, Judy talks about the importance of reflecting ethical, nonviolent principles in our interactions with project participants:

> If you aren't an ethical person, yet you come in with . . . institutional ethics saying we have to do this and this and this [ethical procedures], well, probably the work that you're doing is going to be unethical anyway. And same with feminist methods. If you're not living it, then you're going to do a shoddy job . . . especially when we're doing this kind of work: violence against women. . . . [We] can't be abusive in the way we do our methodology . . . because we're supposed to be also role-modeling nonviolence. . . . [We] can't do violent research.

The project team struggled with how to come to terms with abstract ethical regulations that were intended to protect participants but seemed to disrupt the day-to-day relationships we hoped to develop. Although the team was sensitive to participants' frustration and confusion regarding our information letters and consent forms, we realized the positive intent of ethics guidelines. In fact, we felt that submitting our evaluation protocol for ethics review by the university committee heightened our sensitivity to the complexity of ethical issues.

Judy: I felt the parents and students didn't always understand ethics requirements, it felt like the university was covering its butt . . . because the words were strange to them . . . although I think it's important for people to be totally informed and all that stuff, obviously. It just felt at cross-purposes.

Tammie: I think the bureaucratic guidelines get in the way, because we [the project team] all go in there with good intentions: caring, wanting to connect with these kids, wanting to support them if they're having troubles, wanting to make sure that they're not doing anything that they don't want to, making sure they're fully informed. All the stuff that the university guidelines are based on and trying to protect, but then in my role as evaluator, I feel like I'm playing cop. . . . My running up to someone and saying, "Do you have your consent form?" does nothing for them as far as making sure that they're there voluntarily. Because half the time the time line is so rushed that they haven't read our information letter, or the information letter is so onerous that they don't want to read it. And they're probably on a gut level reacting to who we are and thinking "Yeah, so I'll give them consent because they need it, and I feel good with the relationship that we have."

Richard: The institutionalized approach to ethics, it seems to me, is abstracted from the nature of the relationship you have with the persons with whom you are immediately working, for whom the social-change orientation of this whole [intervention] was intended.

Holt: The consent forms wind up getting in the way of that relationship. They put it in people's faces again that these are institutional researchers who are representing a cold monolith. I have a sense of that dynamic in that I feel like we're going along just great and we're having a wonderful, personal relationship, and I'm talking and they're talking, and we're dialoguing and everything's wonderful. And, then I have to do this official thing that suddenly separates us again.

Tammie: I feel like there's a balancing act . . . there are some benefits. Having to
            do an ethics review, which feels like a pain in the butt while you're
            doing it, makes you really think about stuff. Think about, what are the
            benefits and risks for the participants? Just in a more formal way. Then,
            hopefully, you take that in with you, into the process and live it.

Andrea Fontana and James Frey (1994) assert that there has been a shift in
research to create "a closer relation between interviewer and respondent, attempting
to minimize status differences and [do] away with the traditional hierarchical
situation in interviewing" (p. 370). In this spirit, Judy and Tammie, as project
evaluators, attempted to demystify their presence with the students and staff by
sharing tasks with the drama coordinators and developing relationships with participants. Still, their personal and institutional power impacted negatively on their
relationships with participants. As Judy noted, "I don't think we ever achieve an
entirely egalitarian relationship. . . . Like, we're doing Master's degrees and Ph.Ds
and there's power that goes along with that whether we like it or not."

The team found it challenging to diminish power differentials between students
and themselves when working within the hierarchical structure of a school. The
drama facilitators emphasized the difficulties of nurturing participant control and
responsibility for a school-based project because students expect those in authority
to tell them what to do. Darlene and Holt also worried that course grading might
negatively affect the trust they tried to develop with students. Finally, they were
faced with balancing the representation of students' voices in the performance with
our agenda of prevention of violence against women. The facilitators gave students
equal opportunity to voice diverse opinions, but Darlene and Holt also challenged
beliefs that supported the status quo and encouraged critical reflection.

The project evaluators must acknowledge that the research relationship they
established at the schools were not fully participatory. Students were already very
busy with the drama activities associated with the project. Asking them to also
shape and inform the evaluation plan seemed onerous given the timelines given
by the school for project completion. The following dialogue underscores the
complex reality that the team faced in trying to live up to feminist ideals:

Tammie: The conclusion for me is, we have to go into that school, face the reality
            of working in a hierarchical situation, bring our histories and our training
            with us, and to the best of our abilities respond to the situation with
            our values there as much as we can. Like, come in with the intention
            of being positive and fair and equal . . . but sometimes it's not going to
            fit with feminist research literature. The one where I always felt that
            we fell short was the participatory research thing. Like, we're supposed
            to be getting our students to write our questions and do some interviews
            and analyze the interviews and ideally that would be so perfect. But I
            finally read Kirkup [1986, *The Feminist Evaluator*]. She said the invitation
            has to be there, *and* the participants need to be totally free *not* to get
            involved. They're busy people . . . you have to do that balancing act. You
            have to look at the reality, you have to respond to the audience.
Holt: It would actually be a positivist or modernist process to think, "Okay,
            we have a feminist method here. It has to be this way!" "You're going

to participate, damn it!" And, "You're going to participate now!" [P]art
of authentic dialogue is giving the other participant permission to say,
"Fuck you, I don't want to participate in this." And unless you're willing
to accept that you're not having a dialogue.

Darlene: And it's hard for them to say, "Fuck you" because of the structure that
we have.

Judy: So it's sort of the difference between doing feminist methods and living
feminist methods.

Despite the barriers inherent in practicing relationality, the values of relationality—recognizing the interdependence of humans and being committed to nonviolence (Wine, 1989)—fostered our relationships with all participants and enabled us to evaluate and implement the collective drama intervention. We would not have been able to effect social change, to prevent violence against women, however, unless we were using the tool of collective drama, our chosen liberatory modality.

Liberatory Modality: Collective Drama for Social Change

The feminist movement in psychology explicitly committed its scholarship to serve social action—that is, feminist research should contribute to eradicating social conditions that oppress girls and women. In the projects described within this article, a collective-drama modality was instrumental in this type of political education process. As Darlene put it, "If we're going to effect social change, you can't just stimulate someone intellectually. You can't just have them reflect in words. They have to take it to their core. . . . They have to feel and not just think it." The visceral impact of the collective drama on the performers and, to some degree, on the audience facilitates internalization.

When we use the phrase "liberatory modality," we refer to the potential for collective drama to facilitate the liberation of oppressed peoples, in this instance, women. Much of our drama work, particularly our later efforts involving audience participation, is based on the work of Augusto Boal (1979, 1992), which closely parallels Paulo Freire's (1990) writings (Sivak, 1996).

Freire's liberatory approach involves helping people to become aware of the subtle and not so subtle aspects of their own oppression. Such awareness can be achieved through a problem-posing methodology in which members of a community are presented with real examples of their life situations relevant to the oppression being enacted. The examples, derived through dialogue among researchers, community research partners, and other community members, are then deconstructed and an image of an emancipatory alternative and a plan on how to get there are developed.

Freire (1990) conceptualizes oppression as a dehumanizing process for both the oppressor and the oppressed. He states:

> As the oppressors dehumanize others and violate their rights, they themselves also become dehumanized. As the oppressed, fighting to be human, take away the oppressor's power to dominate and suppress, they restore to the oppressors the humanity they had lost in the exercise of oppression. (p. 42)

The collective-drama projects paralleled Freire's process. The drama-troupe members, themselves community members of the school population, became our allies in working for social change. The students and intervention team worked with members of the general school population to develop through dialogue real examples of violence against women within relationships from their community. The students codified these examples into dramatic presentations that were re-presented to the community as "problems" needing resolution. At this point, in our early work, we facilitated discussions intended to raise students' consciousness about issues of violence against women (deconstruction). More recently, we have asked student audiences to not only understand these issues, but to develop concrete action plans to mitigate the re-presented problems (i.e., create an image of an emancipatory alternative). For example, in the interactive model we encouraged the audience to complete the scenario by enacting their own ideas as directors or actors (i.e., taking the place of cast members).

In asking students to engage in the active process of deconstructing the oppression of women and planning how to end that oppression, we avoid the passivity inherent in traditional lecture formats. The issues become personal and solvable, not just by university "experts" but by local citizens embedded in their individual communities. Of course, there is a risk of dominant personalities and views hi-jacking the discussion and representational action. It is the responsibility of the intervention team members to "level the playing field," however, (while showing respect for all participants) and ensure that issues are resolved using criteria of justice, fairness, and respect. In this way, we found that we could, in ways limited by our situations, achieve Freire's ideal of liberation for both the oppressors and the oppressed.

The drama facilitators, supported by the evaluators and team discussions, endeavored to make the personal political in the students' drama activities. Students in the troupes commented on how they had "changed" because of the project. Some mentioned improved acting skills and increased self-confidence. Others reported that they thought more carefully about things they said and did to others. One troupe member confided, "It made me feel how other people feel, like, when I yell at them. . . . So now I'm going to start trying to stop doing that." Another troupe participant stated, "I just use the fact that I'm bigger than them to get what I want . . . I'm going to try and watch what I'm doing now because, like, I do have a bad temper." One young man talked about purposefully talking less when he was with his girlfriend so he would not dominate the conversation. Teachers at some of the schools also talked about changes in the troupe members. For example, one teacher commented:

> The project . . . made them even more aware. It made them even more, I think, less tolerant of what goes on in the hallways and that, and, you know, it does become a way of life sometimes. . . . There's pushing and shoving going on.

How those effects are developed comes in large part, our data indicate, from the ownership that troupe members develop for the process. Additionally, in our perception, the degree to which we were able to foster such project ownership and demonstrate genuine personal respect for all students was directly related to the degree to which we were able to counteract the personal and institutional power differentials previously discussed. School staff and troupe members made several comments that reflected on students' ownership of the project. Specifically, troupe members liked the independence and control they had over the work and felt good working on an important topic. One troupe member stated:

> I like the fact that everything came from us. . . . We started from scratch and built it . . . we had the chance to create something instead of being handed a bunch of papers . . . . We got to say how we felt and we weren't judged for how we, like, what our beliefs were, personal feelings, or backgrounds.

The student ownership dimension was also remarked on by workshop participants. One participant commented, "Normally it's the teacher talking. Now it's the students talking, which is kind of interesting because . . . you learn other peoples' perspective . . . makes you think of where you stand." Staff felt the peer-based approach was a strength of the project: "The kids themselves came up with the script. I think that's key. It's not as if anybody was leading them or feeding them. They were directing it, and I think that was a crucial part of it."

In an interview with Holt following our work at the first school he commented on the importance of respecting the direction that students wanted to take in the project:

> I think they develop a sense that they can tell us to go get stuffed. That they could say, "I don't agree with that" or "we don't like that" or "that's not how a 16-year-old would see it." But again that all comes from the value base. That comes from respecting their voice. That comes from being willing to hear them and give away our own power.

Perhaps the most important lesson we learned with regard to empowering troupe participants and facilitating personal change (and, subsequently, social change) was sensitivity to perspectives divergent from our own. We aspired to respect multiple perspectives when engaging both in the collective drama and evaluation activities and when considering how the culture of each setting contributed to our findings. The following dilemma illustrates this point.

On the one hand, as a team, we made an emotional investment in being explicit about naming men as the principle perpetrators of violence against women, to be fair to women survivors of violence, to women in general, and to ourselves. Naming the problem is the first step toward eliminating it. On the other hand, we found that respecting young men's (and women's) personal beliefs on the issues served to maintain dialogue and discussion in the collective-drama activities. By avoiding polemical dichotomies, in which we appeared unwilling to entertain perspectives other than our own, we were able to develop a respectful dialogue.

One such dialogue involved a cast debate at our first school around how the date-rape plot should conclude: whether or not the plot should end with the antagonist "looking bad." Darlene and Holt facilitated a discussion about the scene and about date rape, but the cast could not immediately come to a decision about how the scene should finish. The young man playing the date rapist was the primary advocate for an ending that he perceived would be sympathetic to the male character (e.g., he was confused, he misunderstood, he received mixed signals). Because the troupe could not make a decision, the decision was put off for another day so that more exploration around the topic could happen. In the end, the actor playing the antagonist decided that a sympathetic ending was not appropriate. Had Darlene and Holt made the choice to portray the date rapist as clearly responsible for his actions, we do not believe the young actor would have come to the same conclusion. It was sensitivity to the performer's need to engage in his own process and to be respected for what he believed that enabled him to make a critical shift. Although a conclusion creating sympathy for the date rapist would not have been acceptable for us, we were able to work within a range of other possibilities that allowed for personal exploration and evaluation on the part of our participants. At the conclusion of our work with this school, Judy and Tammie asked the drama troupe if the project team had imposed a message on them. One student replied:

> No, because . . . we picked what we wanted to do. We said like . . . "I want to do a scene involving this. Let's not do that." . . . Before you made any decisions, you both consulted us. . . . You imposed limits upon us, but at the same time you gave us the liberty to make our own limits for ourselves which was kind of good.

CONCLUSIONS

In developing a dialogical climate that raised issues of violence against women and exploring those issues within a collective-drama modality, we found that troupe participants were willing to critically examine their own perceptions and biases and, in several cases, make significant shifts in their own personal perceptions and beliefs. By presenting their dramatic vignettes on stage, troupe participants became quite visible to their peers and had the potential to sustain their influence long after our departure from their setting. In this way, the social change can live on beyond the limited duration of our intervention. We also had some influence on the citizens of the larger community in which we worked: through our discussions with teachers and principals; appearing with students in local news articles, radio, and television; and, by simply being visible ambassadors in the schools for a social message of prevention of violence against women. But our most critical social-change effect was always within the drama troupe itself. There, we affected and were affected.

Fostering the principle of relationality in our actual practice, then, enabled us to build relationships of mutuality, fluidity, and responsivity to produce intersubjectively meaningful evaluation findings and to contribute to liberatory social change. In the process, we as a team experienced the joy of tasting the fruits that collective creativity produced. This rich experience, in turn, strengthened our commitment to do the work of justice for women by practicing a feminist psychology that unites word and deed.

Initial submission: December 15, 1996
Initial acceptance: August 20, 1997
Final acceptance: October 15, 1997

NOTE

1. These can be found on the Innovative Methods Web site, at http://www.public.asu.edu/~atnfr.

REFERENCES

Boal, A. (1979). *Theatre of the oppressed* (A. Charles & M.-O. Leal McBride, Trans.). New York: Theatre Communications Group.

Boal, A. (1992). *Games for actors and non-actors* (A. Jackson, Trans.). London: Routledge.

Brunk, T. (1996). *The use of drama to explore violence within relationships: A study of young men's experiences.* Unpublished master's thesis, Wilfrid Laurier University, Waterloo, Ontario, Canada.

Chambers, S. (1995). Feminist discourse/Practical discourse. In J. Meehan (Ed.), *Feminists read Habermas: Gendering the subject of discourse* (pp. 164–178). New York: Routledge.

Courtney, R. (1989). *Play, drama, and thought.* Toronto: Simon & Pierre.

Fontana, A., & Frey, J. (1994). Interviewing: The art of science. In N. K. Denzin, & Y. S. Lincoln (Eds.), *Handbook of qualitative research* (pp. 361–376). London: Sage.

Frazier, P., Valtinson, G., & Candell, S. (1994). Evaluation of a coeducational interactive rape prevention program. *Journal of Counseling and Development, 73,* 153–158.

Freire, P. (1990). *Pedagogy of the oppressed* (M. Bergman Ramos, Trans.). New York: Continuum.

Gould, J. (1994). *A stakeholder approach to sexual assault programming in the Halton Board of Education.* Unpublished masters thesis, Wilfrid Laurier University, Waterloo, Ontario, Canada.

Gray, F., & Mager, G. C. (1973). *Liberating education: Psychological learning through improvisational drama.* Berkeley, CA: McCutchan Publishing.

Jordan, J. (1991). The meaning of mutuality. In J. Jordan, A. Kaplan, J. B. Miller, I. Stiver, & J. Surrey (Eds.), *Women's growth in connection: Writings from the Stone Center* (pp. 81–96). New York: Guilford Press.

Kirby, S., & McKenna, K. (1989). *Experience, research, social change: Methods from the margins.* Toronto: Garamond Press.

Kirkup, G. (1986). The feminist evaluator. In E. R. House (Ed.), *New directions in educational evaluation* (pp. 68–84). Philadelphia: Salmer Press.

McHugh, M. C., Koeske, R. D., & Frieze, I. H. (1986). Issues to consider in conducting nonsexist psychological research. *American Psychologist, 41,* 879–890.

Reinharz, S. (1992). *Feminist methods in social research.* New York: Oxford University Press.

Richardson, L. (1994). Writing: A method of inquiry. In N. K. Denzin & Y. S. Lincoln (Eds.), *Handbook of qualitative research* (pp. 516–529). Thousand Oaks, CA: Sage.

Serrano-Garcia, I. (1990). Implementing research: Putting our values to work. In P. Tolan, C. Keys, F. Chertok, & J. Leonard (Eds.), *Researching community psychology* (pp. 171–182). Washington, DC: American Psychological Association.

Sivak, H. (1996). *Forum theatre from a community psychology perspective.* Unpublished master's thesis, Wilfrid Laurier University, Waterloo, Ontario, Canada.

Task Force on Issues in Research in the Psychology of Women. (1977, October). Final Report. *Division 35 Newsletter, 4*(4), 3–6.

Walsh, R. T. (1989). Do research reports in mainstream feminist psychology journals reflect feminist values? *Psychology of Women Quarterly, 13,* 435–446.

Walsh-Bowers, R. (1992). A creative drama prevention program for easing early adolescents' adjustment to school transitions. *Journal of Primary Prevention, 13,* 131–147.

Walsh-Bowers, R. (in press). Fundamentalism in psychological science: The APA *Publication Manual* as bible. *Psychology of Women Quarterly, 23*(2).

Wine, J. D. (1989). Gynocentric values and feminist psychology. In A. Miles & G. Finn (Eds.), *Feminism: From pressure to politics* (pp. 77–98). Montreal: Black Rose Books.

POWER, SOCIAL CHANGE, AND THE PROCESS OF FEMINIST RESEARCH

Deborah Mahlstedt
West Chester University

The dismantling of a male-dominated "power-over" social structure and its manifestations in human activities and relationships lies at the center of feminist thought. For many feminist psychologists, this has meant challenging the privileged, all-knowing, objective position of the researcher; viewing the "naive subject" of study as a participant in the process of creating knowledge; and using research methods aimed at transforming an oppressive culture (Burman, 1992; Crawford & Marecek, 1989; Hollway, 1989). These goals are at the center of the Community Education Team's (this issue) article: "Fostering Relationality When Implementing and Evaluating a Collective-Drama Approach to Preventing Violence Against Women." The authors use the concept of relationality to describe the process of developing interdependence and an "egalitarian, democratic research relationship" among those involved in the study. Although "sharing power" is a goal of feminist research and pedagogy, detailed accounts of the process of incorporating feminist ideas regarding power relations in U.S. psychological research are rare. The Community Education Team reminds us that those ideas most central to feminist thought—power, process, and social change—are often the very ideas that still elude U.S. feminist psychological research.

SOCIAL CHANGE: TRADITION AND INNOVATION

I applaud violence-prevention research that expands its focus from changing individuals to changing systems that promote violence against women. Fifty years ago Kurt Lewin (1948), the "practical theorist" first introduced the idea of *action-research*.

I wish to thank Stacey Schlau and Ellen Wert for their helpful feedback on this commentary.

Address correspondence and reprint requests to: Deborah Mahlstedt, Department of Psychology, West Chester University, West Chester, PA 19383. E-mail: dmahlstedt@wcupa.edu

111

The research needed for social practice can best be characterized as research for social management or social engineering. It is a type of action-research, a comparative research on the conditions and effects of various forms of social action and research leading to social action. Research that produces nothing but books will not suffice. (p. 203)

Today we continue to celebrate Lewin's commitment to social change through the efforts of the Society for the Psychological Study of Social Issues. Yet, published research focusing on direct intervention in social problems in real-life situations continues to be surprisingly rare. Some of this research now falls under the rubric of applied and/or evaluation research, in contrast to "basic" psychological research, which focuses on the development of theory. Unfortunately, however, basic research often holds more status than applied research.

With the rise of feminist research in the 1970s came a renewed commitment to social change and a new focus on changing systems rather than individuals. Action-research took on new life as an "innovative" approach. The Community Education Team has made an important contribution to both the *tradition* of conducting socially responsible research and the *innovation* of achieving the feminist goal of ending violence against women. Labeling the authors' study as evaluation research risks losing valuable information about the "basic" processes involved in promoting social change in real-life situations—in this case, effective sexual-violence prevention efforts. Most sexual-violence prevention research translates into attitudinal outcome research that asks, "How can we change individuals' negative attitudes toward women or rape myths?" And although we know we can change peoples' attitudes in workshops, the changes are often temporary and narrow in scope (Lonsway, 1996; Mahlstedt, Falcone, & Rice-Spring, 1993). Research on effecting lasting change in male sexist behavior is limited. Also, Lonsway (1996) notes that we know absolutely nothing about the processes of change associated with sexual-violence prevention efforts. Knowledge about how individuals and groups experience the process of change is critical to developing effective prevention strategies. The work of the Community Education Team has provided an important step in that direction.

POWER AND PROCESS IN RELATIONALITY

Questions about power relations emerge from "Fostering Relationality." First, there is the perplexing problem of relationality, power, and equality among people of clearly different status and power positions. Is equality an achievable goal in hierarchically defined relationships? Can relationality occur without equality? How are these questions addressed by the Community Education Team? Second, I have concerns about the potential to universalize relationality while overlooking privilege. Would relationality look different within and among diverse groups based on race, social class, or sexuality?

Relationality, a conceptual framework designed to challenge the control typically held strictly by the primary researcher, is broadly defined to include interdependence, intersubjectivity, connectedness, mutuality, nonviolence, and social location. Embedded in this framework is the vexing problem of power and how to deal with "real" power differentials between people. In the beginning of their article, the authors discuss their expectations of "egalitarian, democratic research relationships" (p. 98). They later explain the difficulties of maintaining equality in research relationships. Although *relationality* is not the same as equality, the authors seem to suggest that relationality can *result* in equality. Is this possible where explicit and/or implicit power differentials exist? Probably not. What does feminist psychology offer regarding concepts of power within a context of power differentials? Feminist inquiry into the dynamics of power has focused largely on uncovering the dynamics of male privilege and systems of domination. But what about the processes that occur when feminists design studies and consequently bring their multiple, intersecting positions of privilege to the role of researcher? We have only begun to understand what is required of us. Brinton Lykes' (1989) groundbreaking research with Guatemalan Indian women stands as a model of participatory research which the author calls "engaged collaboration" (p. 180). Through collaboration—ongoing dialogue, self-disclosure, and shared decision making—the research process reflected the interests of the researchers, participants, and each individual participant's community. Other feminist psychologists have addressed the subtle, complex ways power and privilege enter into the research process of information exchange and making meaning between interviewer and interviewee (Burman, 1991, 1992; Fine, 1992, 1994). These researchers challenge us to risk being vulnerable. Relinquishing control demands no less.

Concepts such as shared power, consensual decision making, and empowerment are central feminist discourses of power. Most feminists would likely agree that the goal of empowerment defined as "a process in which each participant enhances the other's feelings of competence and/or power" (Miller & Cummins, 1992, p. 417), guides their teaching and research, yet there is limited research that examines these processes. What does empowerment look like? How do we know when empowerment has been achieved? Is empowerment different from relationality? The classroom has been one of the primary contexts for discussions and documentation about feminist efforts to empower others (e.g., Maher & Tetreault, 1994). Similarly, within the context of a feminist research team, what does it mean to share power? What about the "primary" investigator who has more power or the team member who acquires more status within an empowerment model? Ironically, the concept of power, which lies at the core of feminist thought, has not been the primary focus of much research. This may be partly because this type of research requires methodologies that examine interactions between people and document processes, whereas psychology has primarily focused on measuring attributes of individuals.

The Community Education Team's analysis of the process of change reported by troupe members provides important insight into the concept of relationality and its impact on power differentials in a context of learning. Troupe members reported that "everything came from us. . . . We started from scratch and built it." Their experience of ownership was an active expression of their power. The quality of the dialogue also gave troupe members an experience of their power in the situation, for example, in the decision about how to end the date-rape scene. The authors note that "sensitivity to perspectives divergent from our own" and "avoiding polemical dichotomies" allowed them to develop a dialogue in which the actor in question could "engage his own process and to be respected for what he believed," which led to a shift in his thinking. They admit though that they would not have accepted a script that was sympathetic to the date rapist. That is, they would have asserted their power. (At this point, I become confused. The authors acknowledge their "greater" power, yet still use the language of equality to explain this dimension of their research relationships.) The words of troupe members reflect their simultaneous knowledge that the facilitators "imposed limits" and at the same time gave the actors "the liberty to make our own limits for ourselves." Is that equality? Obviously not. The process meets the broader criteria of relationality and empowerment, however. Troupe members could accept the difference in power while at the same time maintaining a sense of their own control in the situation. "Fostering Relationality" contributes to and allows for necessary dialogue about the complexities of power. Their analysis of processes among people provides a means to begin understanding the negotiation of power relations.

PRIVILEGE AND RELATIONALITY

Many factors that the authors explain as facilitating relationality—use of participants' own words, feedback to participants, participants giving meaning to the data, participants setting the agenda—have long been core principles of conducting qualitative research (Glaser & Strauss, 1967; Reason & Rowan, 1981). Feminist qualitative research adds the dimension of recognizing the concepts of race, class, and heterosexual privilege. On the broadest theoretical level, I wonder about the role of privilege in determining the definition and behavioral characteristics of relationality. Does relationality require direct, verbal communication? Would relationality look the same among all people? Is relationality inclusive? Griscom (1992) notes that relational psychology in its original conception by Miller (1976/1986) did not deal with race and class distinctions. Although later developments addressed issues of race, Griscom explains that the basic theory still struggles with conceptualizing power inequalities related to difference and "has had difficulty in dealing with social structures" (p. 404).

The authors' definition of relationality addresses the individual's embeddedness in "human, social and historical contexts," as, for instance, "keeping reflection notes helps to account for investigators' social locations and personal subjectivity" (p. 101). Although the researchers accounted for their subjectivity with regard to its potential effects on the interpretation of information they collected, it is less clear that they closely analyzed the microlevel process of information exchange. That is, while the Community Education Team explained that participants influenced the direction of the interview and thereby exercised some structural control, an analysis of the language, through which power relations are partly constructed and negotiated, would provide additional understanding. This, of course, involves such methodologies as psycholinguistic and/or discourse analysis. Certainly, the collaborative approach used by the Community Education Team demonstrates the essential role of dialogue among researchers, and researchers and participants as one essential element in addressing power and privilege.

The Community Education Team has reminded us of the importance of closely examining the *process* of doing research, along with many dimensions: as a collaborative effort, as a means of social change, and as a way to understand power relations within a hierarchical structure. More important, this reminder challenges us to demand that journals regularly support *innovative* feminist research through publication, and not only in special issues.

REFERENCES

Burman, E. (1991). Power, gender, and developmental psychology. *Feminism & Psychology, 1,* 141–153.

Burman, E. (1992). Feminism and discourse in developmental psychology: Power, subjectivity, and interpretation. *Feminism & Psychology, 2,* 45–59.

Community Education Team (1999). Fostering relationality when implementing and evaluating a collective drama approach to preventing violence against women. *Psychology of Women Quarterly, 23,* 97–111.

Crawford, M., & Marecek, J. (1989). Psychology reconstructs the female, 1968–1988. *Psychology of Women Quarterly, 13,* 147–165.

Fine, M. (1992). *Disruptive voices.* Ann Arbor, MI: University of Michigan Press.

Fine, M. (1994). Working the hyphens: Reinventing self and other in qualitative research. In N. Denzin & Y. Lincoln (Eds.), *Handbook of qualitative research* (pp. 70–82). London: Sage.

Griscom, J. (1992). Women and power: Definition, dualism, and difference. *Psychology of Women Quarterly, 16,* 389–414.

Glaser, B., & Strauss, A. (1967). *The discovery of grounded theory.* Chicago: Aldine.

Hollway, W. (1989). *Subjectivity and method in psychology: Gender, meaning, and science.* London: Sage.

Lewin, K. (1948). *Resolving social conflict.* New York: Harper Bros.

Lonsway, K. (1996). Preventing acquaintance rape through education: What do we know? *Psychology of Women Quarterly, 20,* 229–265.

Lykes, B. (1989). Dialogue with Guatemalan Indian women: Critical perspectives on constructing collaborative research. In R. Unger (Ed.), *Representations: Social constructions of gender* (pp. 167–181). New York: Baywood.

Maher, F. A., & Tetreault, M. K. (1994). *The feminist classroom: An inside look at how professors and students are transforming higher education for a diverse society.* New York: Basic Books.

Mahlstedt, D., Falcone, D., & Rice-Spring, L. (1993). Dating violence education: What do students learn? *Journal of Human Justice, 4,* 101–117.

Miller, C. L., & Cummins, A. G. (1992). An examination of women's perspectives on power. *Psychology of Women Quarterly, 13,* 415–428.

Miller, J. B. (1986). *Toward a new psychology of women.* Boston: Beacon Press. (Original work published 1976)

Reason, P., & Rowan, R. (1981). *Human inquiry: A sourcebook of new paradigm research.* Chichester, UK: Wiley.

REFLECTIONS ON A FEMINIST RESEARCH PROJECT

Subjectivity and the Wish for Intimacy and Equality

Frances K. Grossman and Lou-Marie Kruger
Boston University

Roslin P. Moore
The Trauma Center at the Human Relations Institute

This article describes the group process in a feminist research project on resiliency in adult women survivors of childhood sexual abuse. Memos written by members of the research team that were content analyzed independently provided the major source of data. Researchers' subjectivity, members' expectations for intimacy, and the role of power were examined. We describe how group members learned that taking the researcher's subjectivity into account affected our understanding of participant stories. The longing for intimacy created frustrations that needed to be acknowledged and processed by the group. Further tensions revolved around the feminist ideal of egalitarian relationships, which at times conflicted with the need for efficient decision making. We conclude with suggestions to aid feminist researchers in negotiating process issues.

We want to acknowledge the following individuals who, in addition to the authors, were members of the research group at one point or another: Cheryl Barosi, Ruth Bell, Antonia Bookbinder, Katharine Culhane, Alexandra Cook, Colleen Gregory, Karen Curto, Judith Jordan, Selin Kepkep, Jodi Kilgannon, Judy Lam, Stephanie Marcy, Rhea Paneisin, Debra Reuben, Liesl Rockhart, Nurit Scheinberg, Etay Shilony, Sharon Thrasher, Bradford Stolback, and Anne Watkins. We also want to thank Deborah Belle, Alexandra Cook, Katharine Culhane, Kerry Gruber, Selin Kepkep, Karestan Koenon, Rhea Paneisin, and Catherine Riessman for their helpful comments on the manuscript.
Address correspondence and reprint requests to: Frances K. Grossman, Department of Psychology, Boston University, 64 Cummington Street, Boston, MA 02215. E-mail: frang@bu.edu

117

This is a description of an ongoing feminist research project that is studying the resiliency of female adult survivors of serious childhood sexual abuse (e.g., Bookbinder & Grossman, 1995; Grossman, Cook, Kepkep, & Koenen, 1999; Grossman & Moore, 1994, 1995; Grossman, Moore, & Watkins, 1994; Lam, Grossman, & Moore, 1994; Moore, Grossman, & Cook, 1993). It must be emphasized at the outset that this is *a* description, not *the* description. Despite significant input from the larger group in the form of memos, conversations, and comments on drafts of this article, the contents of this report constitute our view. The authors of this article (the "we") are a subgroup of the research group ("the group"). In this article, we consider the dynamics of the research group, focusing primarily on how the emphasis on shared subjectivity and increased self-disclosure led to changed expectations about intimacy and power. We discuss how ideals of equality and intimacy can facilitate the research process and also create very complex dynamics within the research group. Thus we will be emphasizing three topics: (a) the researchers' subjectivity, (b) intimacy, and (c) the role of power within the group.

Some general case studies of feminist research projects have been reported in the literature (e.g., Acker, Barry, & Esseveld, 1991; Belle, 1982, 1994; Brown & Gilligan, 1992; Hollway, 1989; Ladner, 1987; Riessman, 1990; Wasser & Bresler, 1996). Like the descriptions of Belle (1982), Hollway (1989), and Riessman (1990), ours is not a discussion of how principles of feminist research were applied in a systematic way. It is rather an attempt to describe how, while the group was doing research, it was simultaneously grappling with its understanding of what feminism is and experiencing some of the complexities of attempting to apply feminist principles. We present this account, then, not as a shining example of a successful feminist research process, but rather as an illustration of how a group of researchers struggled, bumbled, learned, and changed in the course of carrying out this project on resilient survivors of childhood sexual abuse. We are therefore consciously choosing to reflect on typically hidden aspects of the research process (Alderfer, 1988; Fonow & Cook, 1991).

We begin our account with a short narrative of the history of the group. In this narrative we introduce the cast of characters, sketch the time frame and describe what we consider to be the major developments in the group. With this overview of the process as a context, we then continue by exploring in detail how issues of subjectivity, intimacy, and power became important and were dealt with (or not dealt with) in the group. We conclude with suggestions for feminist researchers on how to negotiate process issues in research.

The major source of data for this study was memos, solicited by the authors from all members of the group who were currently active, asking them to reflect back on their experiences in the group. To obtain those memos, we first described in detail to the research group what we planned to do with the memos, which was to analyze them to understand the group process and then to use them in the article (which they knew we were writing) to describe aspects of that process. We told them that they would see a draft of the article before it was published and have an opportunity to edit their own comments, and also to decide if they wanted their name associated with their comments. For the first memo, in early 1994, we asked them each to write the story of the research project in their own words.

All 12 then-current members of the group, including the authors of this article, wrote memos. Four of those writing memos were from the original group, which began in late spring of 1989; one joined in the fall of 1989, one in 1991, four in 1992, and two in 1993. All quotes in this article are from those memos. Group members have given permission to use their quotes and their real names for this article.

Each of the authors read the first set of memos impressionistically for themes. From those readings and subsequent discussions among the authors, the three themes of subjectivity, intimacy, and power emerged. At that point we developed a questionnaire that included 11 specific questions about members' experiences in the group related to these themes. Examples of the questions are "How do you perceive decisions being made in the research group? How do you feel about this?" and "How would you describe the manner in which personal experience is processed in the group? How do you feel about it?"

The authors then met a number of times to discuss our impressions and understandings from the two sets of memos. These discussions were intense and sometimes difficult because we were talking about our own research group and at times our own behavior. The three of us had quite different perspectives, at least in part because of our different roles and statuses. When we had arrived at a consensus, we each took one of the themes and pulled together a draft of what we might say in the article. After reading these drafts, we met again—and again!—to make suggestions, reconcile differences, and so on and then usually a different one of us would rewrite the section. This process took many months. When we had a good complete draft of the article, we distributed it to all members of the research group, and received comments individually in person or in writing, and also in a research-group discussion. Not all of these communications were comfortable or easy, but, everyone eventually expressed satisfaction with the manuscript.

A BRIEF NARRATIVE HISTORY OF THE RESEARCH GROUP

In the spring of 1989, Fran Grossman, a professor in the Clinical Psychology Doctoral Program at Boston University and six graduate students (five female and one male) began a research project on resiliency in women who had survived histories of serious childhood sexual abuse. Our initial goal was to produce a book on resilient survivors (Grossman et al., 1999). From that first summer of 1989 until February 1995 the group met every second Tuesday at Fran's home in an upper middle-class neighborhood of a nearby suburb. The group had a very stable core membership. From the beginning there were also many entries and exits, however. Some students joined to fulfill a research requirement for the clinical doctoral program; others joined purely out of interest in the topic. Leaving was often more complex than joining. Members left for many reasons: when they completed their studies, moved out of the area, or became too busy. Some members left because they were dissatisfied with the project. To set the authors in context, Lou-Marie joined the group as a first-year graduate student in the clinical doctoral program in 1992, and Ros, as a senior clinician in the community, accepted Fran's invitation to join the group later in 1992.

From the beginning, there was a strong commitment to a research population that was diverse in ethnicity and social class, however, there was somewhat less awareness of the importance of diversity within the research group. Over time, the group has been diverse in terms of sexual orientation, age, social class, education, and country of origin, but much less so in terms of gender and race. During that first fall, the sole African American member of the group left. Although she said relatively little about it, it appeared as if issues of ethnicity and social class played a major role in her decision to leave. Relatively early in the process, one of the two male group members decided to do his dissertation on another population and left the group. It now seems clear that diversity of the research group was an issue.

During the first summer, the group began reading the literature on the aftereffects of childhood trauma and discussing the question of what constitutes resiliency. The struggle to arrive at a satisfactory and mutually agreeable definition of resiliency has continued from that time to the present. Despite difficulty defining the concept, the project moved ahead. By February 1990, the group had defined variables and located and/or designed measures for a quantitative research study. It was also at this time, however, that Fran became more interested in qualitative research. Others (primarily doctoral students beginning to think about dissertations) were intent on doing more traditional quantitative work, work that they thought would be more acceptable for dissertation purposes. When Fran decided that she would like this particular phase of the project to be a qualitative one, the group accepted this decision. Not all members were equally happy with the change in direction, however.

Although the group had been reactive to the traumatic nature of the material from the literature review, the move to qualitative research with intensive interviews very much exacerbated that reactivity. Early in the life of the group, members began to articulate the need to process personal issues that arose from working with the stories of trauma survivors. The group began to talk about the reasons that brought each person to the project. These reasons, in some cases, included personal histories of trauma. These conversations would inform the process of developing a methodology. At this time, the group established a rule of confidentiality for any information revealed in the group. Perhaps surprisingly, through all the ups and downs of the project, and despite the number of outside contexts in which group members had interactions, there were no known violations in which group members revealed information to others learned in these personal discussions.

During this same early period, a subgroup of about four or five members began congregating to talk about their reactions to the meetings and to process. These "after-meetings" first occurred in the street outside of Fran's house where the meeting occurred, and then moved to the apartment of a project member who lived nearby. Although the membership of these after-meetings was somewhat variable, it was relatively consistent. No member was explicitly excluded, but a few chose not to go. These meetings continued until around January 1993.

The first participant was interviewed in the fall of 1990. Those interviews, which lasted 10 hours over three meetings, were tape-recorded and transcribed. The group spent the entire next year going over the interview transcripts line by line, trying to develop a method of processing the interview material and to learn about resiliency. On the basis of that work, the interview format was modified and more interviews were conducted. Almost half of the research meeting time, beginning in early 1991 and continuing until the time the article was written in 1995, was spent analyzing transcripts. Between 1991 and 1994, nine more participants were interviewed, representing significant diversity in ethnicity, social class, sexual orientation, age, and type of serious sexual abuse. Sometime during 1991, the group began to set aside regular time in each meeting to talk about individuals' reactions to the participants discussed that day, as well as reactions to our discussion of the transcript. Also during 1991, members of the group began presenting the research at various forums.

In early 1994, three groups were formed to begin writing chapters for the book. Work on the book began in earnest in September 1994. Fran and Ros invited Alex Cook, one of the student members who was completing her dissertation on resiliency, to work with them as coauthor on the book. The announcement of this development about authorship led to the most frank—and painful—discussions about power that the group had yet held.

SUBJECTIVITY: BECOMING VISIBLE AS RESEARCHERS

This research study was started at a time when postmodern ideas were becoming more influential in the social sciences, including psychology (Harding, 1991; Hollway, 1989), and were strongly influencing many feminist researchers. Postmodern theories of knowledge question the possibility of objective research and posit the undesirability of an ideal of objectivity in research. The role of the researcher in the research process is emphasized. This means that instead of focusing on remaining neutral, the researcher has to become acutely self-reflective and self-aware (Berg & Smith, 1988; Grossman et al., 1997; Kram, 1988; Ladner, 1987; Smith, 1987; Stewart, 1994). Not only does she or he have to view the research participants in the full context of their lives, she or he also has to continually take into account her or his own personal, political, and academic worlds. She or he must see both the research participant and herself or himself as real individuals, each located in a time, place, and context. This perspective locates the inquirer in the same critical plane as those who are being studied (Harding, 1987; Landrine, Klonoff, & Brown-Collins, 1992; Smith, 1987). The premises, questions, motives, ideas, purposes, and even feelings of the researcher must become and remain open to the scrutiny of the researchers as well as their critics (Acker et al., 1991; Brown & Gilligan, 1992; Charmaz, 1990; Grossman et al., 1997; Kleinman & Copp, 1993; Stanley & Wise, 1991).

Despite the fact that these ideas about research and subjectivity were available and influential at the time that the research group was launched, they did not at first directly influence the way in which the research group structured itself. Despite the earlier absence of discussions concerning the theoretical underpinnings of this approach, however, it was clear from the beginning that the researchers in this study would not attempt to be objective and invisible. For example, all group members were aware that the choice to join the group was related to some important aspect of their view of themselves and/or of others in their lives. In a memo, Kate wrote, "Personal meaning making has lured many of us to the study."

Although it is true that in any research project the "baggage" of the researcher inevitably influences the research, this particular project had another set of issues imposed by the content of the research itself—inevitable reactivity to that content. In recent years many clinicians have discussed what McCann and Pearlman (1990, 1994) call "vicarious traumatization," the process by which individuals listening to and working with the traumatic experiences of others begin to experience the effects of trauma themselves. Although that literature refers primarily to individuals providing services to people who have been traumatized, McCann and Pearlman (1990) do discuss how groups providing such services can become traumatized.

Despite (varying degrees of) awareness of the significance of personal histories and personal issues in their involvement in the project, group members for a long time failed to address how these histories and issues affected the research. There was still the pretense that the research could be objective and that neutrality and objectivity were desirable. There was significant denial of the powerful reactions that the experiences, thoughts, and feelings of participants evoked in group members.

There were some conversations about personal histories during the first 2 years, but those were infrequent and largely disconnected from the rest of the research process. As early as the fall of 1989, the group began to acknowledge that they did need to find a way to talk about their feelings and needs as these were evoked by the reading and discussion of the interview transcripts. Members began to see that these very complex needs and feelings were also influencing their views of the material.

Rhea wrote:

> . . . we did, after a year or so, realize that talking about our experiences contributed significantly to our ability to do the work of the group . . .

Fran wrote:

> Judy, Alex, and Rhea were particularly helpful in insisting that the group not avoid some direct discussion of our histories, and ways those histories and our relative silence about them were influencing the research process. We understood that our disinclination to talk about difficult personal experiences was entirely typical of most research contexts . . . we were becoming more cognizant of the role of such silence in maintaining what we came to believe was the fiction of objective researchers looking at events in the world, as told by "subjects" who had the information. As long as we kept our stories to ourselves, we could pretend that we did not have a personal—and political—stake in these issues of trauma and resilience. . . . However, we were less and less inclined to such pretending, and in fact were heartily sick of pretense about how things really were.

During that early period, the way the discussions about personal issues were structured was chosen by Fran on the basis of her clinical expertise, but she felt quite in the dark about how they should occur in a group whose primary goal was to produce research. It is interesting that while reflexivity is valued in both feminist and postmodern research, it is seldom operationalized in the literature. Despite the fact that the notion of the invisible and neutral researcher is questioned, there is very little discussion about how researchers can become visible without getting lost in this often painful process, or without the personal issues co-opting the time and energy of the researchers so that no research actually gets accomplished. Further, little is known about how recognizing researcher subjectivity might affect the research outcomes in terms of shaping the "data" and conclusions.

Thus, a way to talk about all of this evolved slowly and painfully. In one striking instance, the group was discussing a section of an interview in which the participant was mocking her own sister (who also had a history of trauma) for the sister's awkwardness about physical contact—hugging, in this instance. The group began to speak derisively about the participant. At that point, Judy said, "Of course, this issue doesn't have anything to do with us." There was a long silence, and then with great reluctance several individuals began to talk about their own difficulties touching and being touched, and how much shame they felt about that usually hidden aspect of themselves. After a few minutes of this, the group went back to the discussion about the participant, and the tone was entirely different. The group was now able to see and feel from the participant's perspective. They no longer had to blame and accuse her. Judy stated in her reflections on the group:

> As we started to analyze the transcripts, it became more clear to me that we need, as a group and as individuals, to be aware of the possibly distorting influence of our own histories. I think distortions in either the positive or negative direction.

Even while members of the research group remained reluctant to process and talk about their own reactions to the research, a small group of members started to meet regularly after the formal meeting. In this "after-meeting," where there was no research work to be done and the focus could be on the sharing, there was ample opportunity to talk freely and openly about reactions to the material and the process in the larger group. It is clear that there was a serious need for such discussions. When these conversations could not become the focus in the larger group, an alternative forum spontaneously evolved. Alex writes about the "after-meetings":

> There were a few years when . . . meetings afterwards for a beer were a regular occurrence . . . I believe that was a useful and productive facet of the group in that it fostered comfort and ease with each other.

Despite the fact that participants in the "after-meetings" wrote about this aspect of the group with fond memories, emphasizing how close they grew to feel toward each other, the arrangement was not a satisfactory solution to the problem. Some members were excluded and felt increasingly isolated—even if they were unaware of the powerful processing and bonding that was happening in the subgroup.

The second time that group members formally shared their stories with other members in the larger group (July 1990), it was decided that members would have an opportunity to say as much or as little as they chose to about their histories. Fran emphasized that it was important to share only what felt safe. It was also decided that the group would not engage any member in a dialogue about what they said. The rationale was that such dialogues create the possibility of significant harm. Fran wrote in her memo about that difficult meeting:

> That meeting was painful and heavy. Individuals' histories ranged from no abuse to uncertainty about whether there had been abuse to extremely serious physical, sexual, and emotional abuse. Some people told a great deal; others told very little. We all left shaken and moved. . . . We were clear that we were continuing to develop a

method that felt safe, and that we needed to be aware and self-conscious about it. We also felt clear that it was useful that we had attempted to tell something about ourselves, because we now had the freedom to use that information in discussions of research.

It was evident, however, from many people's reactions to that meeting that its structure was not satisfactory. Kate commented in her notes:

> After our first personal revelations, I said that I felt as if I had made a declaration at an AA meeting, but there had been no, "Hello, Kate" (no response!)—that it (my history) felt as if it was "just laying there on the coffee table."

After this first meeting the group agreed that some kind of supportive response to members' stories was needed. In subsequent sharing meetings, members were explicitly asked whether there was something they needed from the group, but only supportive and limited reactions from the group members were encouraged.

The structured sharing of personal stories as they related to the group focus gradually became an annual event on the calendar of the group. It was still very difficult to maintain clarity about what was safe and appropriate in a research group, and how to prevent the group from simply becoming a support group or therapy group. Despite the difficulty of the process, the group slowly developed a deeper appreciation for what researchers bring to the research. The annual formal acknowledgment of the relevance of our histories made it possible—although never easy—for individuals to refer to, or describe, some aspect of their personal experiences when it seemed relevant in the ongoing research discussions. The increasing awareness of individual researchers' own active role in the different phases of the research ("data collection" or interviewing and "data analysis" or interpretation) led to more self-scrutiny and self-awareness.

One aspect of the personal reactions that was particularly difficult to express, or once expressed, to be accepted, was individual members' reactions to particular participants. The group desperately wanted to like all of the participants, who after all were victims and survivors. Yet inevitably, as Ribbens (1989), and Kleinman and Copp (1993) point out, group members did not like all of the participants, and some participants elicited particularly strong positive or negative reactions from different members of the research team. These reactions could not help but influence interpretations of the material from the participants. As the group matured and became more able to express personal reactions, members became more able to tolerate expressions of dislike for a participant. This was, however, never comfortable or easy to do.

As it became clear that personal reactions and feelings are not simply "distortions," but constitute a crucial aspect of the data, the group became more careful to document these reactions and feelings. In January 1993 it was decided that the last part of all meetings would be set aside for a discussion of personal reactions to the material in the transcripts and to the participant we were discussing, and how we felt these reactions influenced our judgments or perceptions. Although this was done because it was realized that the affective components of the process are crucial for the research, it also had important consequences for group members as individuals. Lou-Marie commented:

The group made it possible and necessary for me to constantly be aware of myself, the researcher, and the other members of the research group, my fellow-researchers. Who were we and what were we doing, listening to and reading the stories of women who had suffered so much? What do we as readers and listeners bring and contribute to the stories? How often do we recognize or discover ourselves or others in the stories of our participants? And how are we ourselves touched and moved and changed by these stories? These questions were central to the project. In taking these questions seriously it became possible to appreciate the stories of survivors in unique ways, but also, and perhaps as important, to understand ourselves and our fellow-researchers in new ways.

It is perhaps not coincidental that it was at around this time that the "after-meetings" stopped, at least in part because they were no longer necessary.

In this almost trial-and-error way, members of the group slowly and painstakingly learned to take themselves seriously as researchers. Group members increasingly tried to stay acutely aware of their personal thoughts, reactions, feelings, and insights as part of the knowledge that they were generating. In familiarizing themselves more with feminist and postmodern notions of research, they also developed a more solid understanding of the theoretical underpinnings of such an approach to research.

THE IDEAL OF INTIMACY AND CLOSENESS

The considerable emphasis on the personal and the subjective meant that group members made themselves more visible to each other. The close feelings thus generated led to varying levels of conscious or unconscious expectations that group members could and would relate to each other as intimate colleagues and friends. McCann and Pearlman (1990) comment, "As we have grown to trust each other and to allow ourselves to be vulnerable with one another, we have found time together powerful and meaningful" (p. 145). As group members gradually started to share more about themselves and got to know more about their fellow researchers, it seemed that they wanted more from each other. In a memo quoted earlier a group member described how she felt as if her history "was just lying there on the coffee table." Kate needed something more from the group after having shared so much. As she commented:

> Rhea said that in her community women would hug one another as an acknowledge-
> ment in such a situation. I then hugged Rhea (after she told her story). This scenario
> illustrates our need for script or structure for such a vulnerable sharing. (Yes, we all
> understand that this isn't group therapy!) Hugs aren't necessary—words would suffice.

Although Kate expressed her personal need most directly, it seems safe to say that the need or wish for some greater intimacy among (at least some) members of the group was present in others. The "after-meeting" satisfied this need for some members for a period of time, but others had no way of addressing it.

Although, as pointed out previously, the nature of the topic researched by this group made members unusually vulnerable to wanting more from each other than would be the case in most research projects, these high expectations can also be seen as a side effect of women working together. The work of feminist theorists at the Stone Center has focused on what they consider women's unique capacity and desire for relatedness, connection, and empathy (e.g., Miller, 1976; Surrey, 1985). Flax (1993) writes about "the recurrent power of our desire for a benign force or agent out there in the world looking out for us, attending to our needs, and ensuring their satisfaction" (p. 153). Feminist psychologists such as Miller and Surrey suggest that women often expect other women to be this "benign force." This might also have led to group members having expectations for greater intimacy with each other.

The group could not provide an experience of mutual empathy to all of its members at all times. This has much to do with the fact that even while members were becoming more visible in the research process, the group was still primarily a research group with work that needed to be done. Second, although members were encouraged to share what felt safe and what about themselves pertained to the research, this group could not pretend to provide the safety that, for instance, therapy groups can sometimes provide. Outside the group, members had to relate to each other as teachers and students, supervisors and supervisees, advisors and advisees, and classmates and colleagues.

Third, the ideal of mutual empathy is undoubtedly very difficult to attain, even in the most intimate of relationships. It is an ideal that is more and more questioned by feminist authors. Flax (1993) wonders if that ideal is ever attainable:

> We want to be caught and held securely in an idealized mother's gaze; we ask her to assure us that someone is really still there, to protect and catch us when we fall. . . . But whose voice can we really hear? An echo, a delusion, a fantasy of childhood always already past and yet disabling still. (p. 154)

For all these reasons, then, there was inevitable frustration for at least some group members between the wishes evoked by the process and the limited ability of the research process to satisfy those needs.

THE "PECKING ORDER": ISSUES OF POWER

In the previous sections we attempted to show how changing ideas and values about researcher subjectivity affected research group members' expectations of each other in terms of intimacy. These expectations were reflected in wishes that members could and would relate to each other as equal colleagues and friends. In other words, group members had the unspoken wish that the group could function without the power differences that exist in most research groups, as well as in virtually all other aspects of professional life.

There were also other reasons for the development of this egalitarian ideal in the group. The research group began at a time when increasing numbers of psychologists, in particular feminist psychologists (e.g., Flax, 1990), had become troubled by the effect of sharp power differentials not only on psychotherapy (e.g., Jordan, Kaplan, Miller, Stiver, & Surrey, 1991) but also on research (e.g., Grossman et al., 1997; Kahn & Yoder, 1992; Worell & Etaugh, 1994). A few feminist psychologists (e.g., Kitzinger, 1991) were writing about power from a more sophisticated perspective, emphasizing the central importance of feminists considering issues of power and the complexity of the concept itself.

When she established the research group, a concern with power and its distribution was central to Fran's thinking about all kinds of human interactions. She understood power as the ability to influence or control decisions. Because of this concern, she was committed to running a (relatively) egalitarian/democratic group. She was also aware of the difficulties and complexities of doing research. What was not so clear was the inevitable tension between those two. Her commitment to a cooperative and collaborative model was undoubtedly a factor in drawing others to the group. Lou-Marie wrote:

> I think at this stage it was the philosophy of the group that attracted me most of all. I understood it to be a feminist group of only women doing collective or collaborative qualitative research about women.

The ideal was very present but was difficult to fully realize. It was even difficult to discuss what it meant to different people and how it could or should be applied in practice. Selin said:

> I think the group professed a more egalitarian philosophy or idea early (regardless of what people felt but did not say) and maybe there were discrepancies among what different group members held as an ideal but these were hard to talk about.

Alex also wrote in her memo that she had been conscious from the beginning of the group of "the unspoken but felt pecking order within the group in terms of status and responsibility." The silence around these issues was perhaps best illustrated by the fact that even in 1994, when group members were asked to write memos about how they saw the story of the group, only Alex (who by that time was clearly a more senior group member) mentioned issues of hierarchy. It became clear that both the more and the less powerful members of the group felt frustrated, but their positions silenced them in very particular ways.

Perhaps the fact that the feminist egalitarian ideal existed in the context of substantial power differences made it very hard to address the issue of power within the group. Somehow it seemed embarrassing to admit that a hierarchy could exist in a feminist group. It felt unacceptable to talk about feeling too powerless or too powerful in the group.

From the authors' perspectives, it seemed clear that the major sources of power in the group were academic and professional status, and research experience and expertise. In addition, perceived wisdom—a combination of personality factors and thoughtfulness—was also accorded great respect.

Power was perceived by group members as being determined by many factors. Selin, in her reflections on power within the group, provided a whole list of such factors:

> Several factors contribute to power in the group. . . . These factors include age, clinical and research experience (or seniority in the field), association with the clinical program,

seniority in the group, productivity and contribution—which is already influenced/limited/facilitated by the above-mentioned factors.

Selin's remarks allude to the fact that the power differences were the result of both contextual factors and intergroup factors. Despite their ideals, the group operated in a context where very real power differences existed. Perhaps the most important contextual factor to affect the group was its close connection to two major institutions, the university and the profession of clinical psychology.

The university as an institution is characterized by very clear and steep hierarchies. Although Fran as a feminist professor takes her students seriously as people, as a tenured full professor she still is an advisor and teacher who has to assign grades, write references, make recommendations, advise, and sometimes even discipline. In this specific group, for example, there were many students who were in her classes, who wrote their dissertations with her, and/or who were her advisees. In other words, a substantial number of the group members were very dependent on Fran's continuing good will and therefore did not feel free to disagree with her. Perhaps this is the single most important reason that Fran was able to change the basic design of the study from quantitative to qualitative with the change barely discussed in the group. In this regard Antonia may have been understating the case when she said: "I have noticed over the years that the senior members of the group can subtly encourage or discourage lines of enquiry."

Conversely, Fran felt the burden of this particular power differential in the form of an acute sense of responsibility for those who were her students and advisees. She wrote:

> I have the responsibility to take care of members of the group and facilitate each member's development, although within certain limits and more for some members than for others . . . I tend to take on the responsibility not to be hurtful to anyone in the group, even when plain talk might be more useful. My sense of protectiveness towards the group members often feels to me as though it prevents me from taking care of myself very well.

This very real power difference between Fran and her students led to Fran asking a colleague, another senior clinician, Ros, to join the group.
Fran wrote:

> I was beginning to feel acutely that I needed a peer, a "playmate" who would not leave, as students do, and who could share the parenting of the group. I felt acutely alone as the one person on whose energies and constancy the group depended, and it felt burdensome.

Ros wrote as follows about her power in the group:

> I wasn't a faculty member at B.U. so didn't have other contacts with the students. I had no power "over" students like a dissertation advisor or a teacher does. In one sense I feel I have clear relationships with the members of the research group.

Perhaps because of the intimacy and the egalitarian ideal that accompanied it, some group members had difficulty with Fran's need to have a peer in the research group.

Alex wrote:

> I felt I had a choice about how much of a role I wanted to take. It doesn't feel like a struggle now—but it did particularly when Fran was looking for a "colleague." I felt like "What am I, chopped liver?" But I also understand that more now.

Kate said:

> While I understand Fran's need for a co-leader at her professional level, the changes in that role have been unsettling, perhaps unavoidable. There has been an imbalance in decision-making in this project. Some issues have been agonizingly debated within the group; others, such as the co-leadership, were made arbitrarily and independently.

Although Ros's power in the group was not related to the institution of the university, her experience and seniority in the profession of clinical psychology did make her more powerful than most other members of the group, who were students. Given her previous close collegial relationship with Fran, she had power by association as well. Because Ros joined the group so clearly as coleader, her entrance into the group highlighted the hierarchy and so sparked discussion, for the first time, about the power differences that existed among group members. Ros's entry into the group was accompanied by many group and individual discussions about power and collective work in the group.

Rhea commented:

> I remember Ros having to work *hard* to gain acknowledgement of her place in the pecking order and just generally to win us over.

Somehow, however, it was still easier to pretend that the only existing power differences were those imposed by an external world. Much more difficult to address were the power differences that were generated by the internal dynamics of the group.

Some of these power dynamics revolved around differences among members of the group. The group had been mindful from the beginning of the need for diversity among research participants as well as among members of the research team. We were also aware of the difficulty obtaining such diversity, as has been described by numerous others (e.g. Brown, 1990; Cannon, Higgenbotham, & Leung, 1991; Landrine et al., 1992; Reid & Kelly, 1994). The one African American member of the group had said enough to Fran about her reasons for leaving to suggest that she felt isolated and uncomfortable, and thus unheard. When individuals feel unheard for any reason, their own comfort is greatly affected. Furthermore, when a group is unable to make space for an individual's voice, that person's potential contribution is lost to the group. There was significant diversity in socioeconomic backgrounds of members. There were, at different times, three men (who appeared to feel quite comfortable in the group) although some women members were less comfortable with their presence. The group also included, at different times, a Chinese American, a South African, a Latina, and an Israeli, for all of whom English was a second language. There were also major differences in histories of trauma. All of these factors influenced individuals' experiences of power in the group. There is much more to say about diversity in this project, as well as the relationship of diversity to power, but it justifies an article in its own right. It is worth noting that it was easier—although still not easy—to obtain diversity among the research participants than among members of the research team.

Other major factors influencing power included seniority in the group and the actual contributions of members to the group. There were various ways of contributing: conducting interviews, writing memos, participating in discussions, attending meetings. It seems that more involvement led to more responsibility and eventually to more power. It also seems that certain types of involvement led to more power than others.

Alex wrote:

> Last year I began writing with the two most senior members in professional experience terms and I loved it. I was aware that it felt to me like this put some distance between myself and the other non-senior members, but the rewards of the challenging task and collegial atmosphere made it worthwhile to me.

Fran also remarked on how members who are willing to commit themselves, take responsibility, and do the hard work do become more powerful in the group:

> I would happily give up some power in exchange for more people (with the capacity to do the work) taking a more equal role. This would involve people being as committed as I am to getting it done, keeping an eye on the overall process, being willing and able to spend as much time on the project as I do, etc. I am not willing, and do not think it is appropriate, to give up power to people who are not as involved, committed, or contributing as much in a variety of ways. That seems neither helpful nor fair.

Fran's remark about people's capacities to do work raises perhaps the most difficult and painful of all the issues related to power: even if everyone were equally committed, energetic, involved and hard-working, all members would still not be equal. Personality and talent are also factors that affect power relationships. As can happen in any group, members worried about what they perceived as favoritism on the part of the leaders. Those issues are the hardest to discuss, especially in a group that aspires to collective and egalitarian ways of working together. At the point where issues of authorship were discussed, the topic of individual members' capacities became salient and exquisitely sensitive. Ros wrote about this tension:

> We reflected on the problem of different abilities within the group, both in terms of talent, time and motivation to do the writing. How on the surface we wanted to honor feminist principles of cooperation and collaboration and yet we seemed to need a structure to get things done.

For Fran, as leader of the group, this was a particularly difficult issue to deal with:

> For example, I would be more inclined to let everybody have a say in how something should be written, even though I feel perfectly clear that not everyone has something useful to say, and it would be a better project if the quality issue overrode the egalitarian commitment.

Kitzinger (1991), in a sophisticated analysis of the meaning of power, says power is central to how we define ourselves. It determines the language available to us for those definitions, and "privilege(s) some identities at the expense of others . . . . Power and knowledge, then, are inextricably connected" (p. 124). Some individuals in the group had some understanding of this more complex view of power (in part from Hollway, 1989), and particularly of the way it supports certain discourses and self-definitions but not others. Greater articulation of these issues would have helped the group steer its way through these complex relational issues.

CONCLUSIONS: THE LESSONS WE LEARNED

We have described aspects of the group process of a feminist research project. We emphasized how increased focus on the subjectivity of the researchers led to increasing expectations for intimacy and equality among members of the group. As we have noted, feminist research approaches bring with them some particular tensions or difficulties. There are good and compelling reasons to make room for the researchers' subjective experiences, and also for reducing the usual power hierarchies between members of a research group. These changes have the potential to create complications, however. Expectations for increased intimacy and equality may conflict with efficiency in getting research done. They also can conflict with the reality of relationships within many organizations or systems that research groups inhabit. Although relatively more equality among members of the team can greatly enhance involvement and the satisfaction individual members obtain from their participation, the commitment to egalitarianism among researchers can lead to a denial of the reality of power differences as they operate in such groups. Denying the existence of real power differences both inside and outside the research group is probably always destructive. Finally, there are potentials for harm around violations of confidentiality that need to be considered.

Given, then, what we see as the inevitability of tensions among members of a research group sharing aspects of their thoughts and feelings, and the consequent development of wishes for intimacy and for egalitarian relationships, we have arrived at some suggestions for feminist researchers.

Suggestion #1: Feminists establishing or in charge of research projects need to think clearly and explicitly about the needs of the project and the (current or anticipated) needs of the researchers, at any given point in the project's life, and make decisions that attempt to optimize the balance between these sometimes conflicting needs. This means being clearly aware that emphasizing the subjectivity of the researchers and sharing those self-reflections can greatly enhance the richness of the research, but will also lead to increased tensions around longings for greater intimacy and a more egalitarian structure of decision making. To the extent that the decision goes in the direction of emphasizing researcher subjectivity, these issues and the inevitable accompanying tension need to be discussed openly and often in the research group. For example, group members should regularly discuss the concrete and immediate goals of the project, and also on a regular basis assess their progress towards reaching these stated goals and evaluate the efficiency of the methods employed. One strategy for this might include having all research team members regularly write memos about their experience and use them to facilitate ongoing discussions. This continuous assessment can help to keep the group focused even while negotiating increased levels of intimacy and equality. Further, we suggest that new people entering the group be informed about the nature of the group and its stresses.

Suggestion #2: Whatever the nature of the research and the relationships among researchers, issues of power need to be thought about clearly. At the beginning, and periodically throughout the project, group discussions about power and how it relates to authority to make decisions about the project need to occur. Issues of power and authority include who controls entrance into the research group, who makes major design decisions, and who gets credit for authorship. Egalitarian arrangements may not be inevitably better (or worse), but they are certainly different, and have to be considered in all of their complexities. Whatever the nature of power relationships in general, authorship decisions need to be explicitly discussed at or near the beginning, and then reconsidered as the project and individuals' involvement evolve. (Fine & Kurdek [1993] explore the importance of such discussions when faculty and students work together on research.)

Suggestion #3: In any research project that is complex and/or extends over a year or more, all of these negotiations have to be reworked periodically. (Kram [1988] also makes this point.) As the project develops, what it asks of and what it gives back to individual research team members changes. Further, individual research team members' own lives continue to change and develop. These changes are more apparent if some of the members are students. Conscious awareness of the potential pitfalls can go a long way toward preventing the project or individual members from becoming casualties.

Suggestion #4: When participants in a research team share personal information with one another, there are potential problems of confidentiality. When these same individuals occupy various roles in a hierarchical system, such as a university, the hazards are greater that some information conveyed in the research context will be used destructively in the other system. Our experience was that promises to honor confidentiality of information revealed in the research group were sufficient to protect all individuals involved. We heard no reports of violations. Clearly, this issue needs to be addressed explicitly when self-revelation is invited in the research group.

Suggestion #5: One implication of the previous four suggestions, as well as the experiences leading up to them, is the inseparability of the process and the content of a research project. In our view, as in that of others (e.g., Brown & Gilligan, 1992; Wasser & Bresler, 1996), the two are never separable. All research is greatly shaped and determined by the thoughts, feelings, aspirations, and experiences of the researcher(s), as well as by the interactions among research team members, when there is more than one individual involved. Given this inseparability, we think that naming these various influences and attempting to understand the role they are playing in shaping all aspects of the project is necessary to ensure that the research remains grounded in reality. This requirement imposes on feminist researchers the burden of staying mindful of the multiple influences on their projects. The development of systematic procedures for regularly assessing how these individual and group processes are influencing the research seems essential. Finally, the role of these individual and interpersonal processes needs to be articulated in the final product, in order to allow readers to understand and evaluate the context and bias.

Further research about subjectivity, power, and intimacy, and their roles in traditional as well as in feminist research projects could yield important new understanding about how research gets done, and how these group and relationship issues influence individuals' experiences in research groups and the outcomes of the projects.

Initial submission: June 9, 1996
Initial acceptance: August 6, 1996
Final acceptance: September 30, 1996

REFERENCES

Acker, J., Barry, K., & Esseveld, J. (1991). Objectivity and truth: Problems in doing feminist research. In M. M. Fonow & J. A. Cook (Eds.), *Beyond methodology: Feminist scholarship as lived research* (pp. 133–153). Bloomington, IN: Indiana University Press.

Alderfer, C. P. (1988). Taking ourselves seriously as researchers. In D. N. Berg & K. K. Smith (Eds.), *The self in social inquiry: Researching methods* (pp. 35–70). Newbury Park, CA: Sage.

Belle, D. (Ed.) (1982). *Lives in stress: Women and depression*. Beverly Hills, CA: Sage.

Belle, D. (1994). Attempting to comprehend the lives of low-income women. In C. E. Franz & A. J. Stewart (Eds.), *Women creating lives: Identities, resilience, and resistance* (pp. 37–50). Boulder, CO: Westview.

Berg, D. N., & Smith, K. K. (Eds.). (1988). *The self in social inquiry: Researching methods.* Newbury Park, CA: Sage.

Bookbinder, A., & Grossman, F. K. (1995, August). *Religion: A good resource for women survivors of childhood sexual abuse*. Poster presented at the annual meeting of the American Psychological Association, New York, NY.

Brown, L. S. (1990). The meaning of a multicultural perspective for theory-building in feminist therapy. *Women and Therapy, 9*(1/2), 1–22.

Brown, L. S., & Gilligan, C. (1992). *Meeting at the crossroads*. New York: Ballentine Books.

Cannon, L. W., Higgenbotham, E., & Leung, M. L. A. (1991). Race and class bias in qualitative research on women. In M. M. Fonow & J. A. Cook. (Eds.), *Beyond methodology: Feminist scholarship as lived research* (pp. 107–118). Bloomington, IN: Indiana University Press.

Charmatz, K. (1990). "Discovering chronic illness": Using grounded theory. *Social Science & Medicine, 30*, 1161–1172.

Fine, M. A., & Kurdek, L. A. (1993). Reflections on determining authorship credit and authorship order on faculty-student collaborations. *American Psychologist, 48*, 1141–1147.

Flax, J. (1990). *Thinking fragments: Psychoanalysis, feminism, and postmodernism in the contemporary west*. Los Angeles: University of California Press.

Flax, J. (1993). Mothers and daughters revisited. In J. Zon Mens-Verhulst, K. Schrevrs, & L. Woertman (Eds.), *Daughtering and mothering: Female subjectivity reanalyzed* (pp. 142–165). London: Routledge.

Fonow, M. M., & Cook, J. A. (1991). Back to the future: A look at the second wave of feminist epistemology and methodology. In M. M. Fonow & J. A. Cooke (Eds.), *Beyond methodology: Feminist scholarship as lived research* (pp. 1–15). Bloomington, IN: Indiana University Press.

Grossman, F. K., Cook, A. B., Kepkep, S. K., & Koenen, K. C. (1999). *With the Phoenix rising: Lessons from 10 resilient women survivors of childhood sexual abuse*. San Francisco: Jossey-Bass.

Grossman, F. K., Gilbert, L., Genero, N. P., Hawes, S. E., Hyde, J. S., Marecek, J., & Johnson, L. (1997). Feminist research: Practice, problems, and prophecies. In J. Worell & N. Johnson (Eds.), *Feminist visions: New directions for education and practice*. Washington, DC: American Psychological Association.

Grossman, F. K., & Moore, R. P. (1994). Against the odds: Resiliency in an adult survivor of childhood sexual abuse. In C. E. Franz & A. J. Stewart (Eds.), *Women creating lives: Identities, resilience, and resistance* (pp. 71–82). Boulder, CO: Westview.

Grossman, F. K., & Moore, R. P. (1995, August). *Against the odds: Resiliency in an adult survivor of childhood sexual abuse*. Paper presented at the annual meeting of the American Psychological Association, New York, NY.

Grossman, F. K., Moore, R. P., & Watkins, A. (1994, November). *Resiliency in adult survivors of childhood sexual abuse*. Poster presented at the annual meeting of the International Society for Tramatic Stress Studies, Chicago, IL.

Harding, S. (1987). Introduction: Is there a feminist method. In S. Harding (Ed.), *Feminism and methodology* (pp. 1–14). Bloomington, IN: Indiana University Press.

Harding, S. (1991). *Whose science? Whose knowledge? Thinking from women's lives*. Ithaca, NY: Cornell University Press.

Hollway, W. (1989). *Subjectivity and method in psychology: Gender, meaning and science*. London: Sage.

Jordan, J. V., Kaplan, A. G., Miller, J. B., Stiver, I. P., & Surrey, J. L. (Eds.). (1991). *Women's growth in connection*. New York: Guilford Press.

Kahn, A., & Yoder, J. (Eds.). (1992). Women and power. *Psychology of Women Quarterly, 16,* 381–388.

Kitzinger, C. (1991). Feminism, psychology, and the paradox of power. *Feminism and Psychology, 1,* 111–129.

Kleinman, S., & Copp, M. A. (1993). *Emotions and fieldwork. Qualitative Research Methods Series No. 28.* London: Sage.

Kram, K. E. (1988). On the researcher's group memberships. In D. N. Berg & K. K. Smith (Eds.), *The self in social inquiry: Researching methods* (pp. 247–265). Newbury Park, CA: Sage.

Ladner, J. (1987). Introduction to tomorrow's tomorrow: The black woman. In S. Harding (Ed.), *Feminism and methodology* (pp. 74–83). Bloomington, IN: Indiana University Press.

Lam, J., Grossman, F. K., & Moore, R. P. (1994, November). *Resiliency and adaptation in female survivors of childhood sexual abuse*. Poster presented at the annual meeting of the International Society of Traumatic Stress Studies, Chicago, IL.

Landrine, H., Klonoff, E. A., & Brown-Collins, A. (1992). Cultural diversity and methodology in feminist psychology. *Psychology of Women Quarterly, 16,* 145–163.

McCann, I. L., & Pearlman, L .A. (1990). Vicarious traumatization: A framework for understanding the psychological effects of working with victims. *Journal of Traumatic Stress Studies, 3,* 131–149.

McCann, I. L., & Pearlman, L. A. (1994). *Therapists and vicarious traumatization*. New York: Guilford Press.

Miller, J. B. (1976). *Toward a new psychology of women*. New York: Beacon Press.

Moore, R. P., Grossman, F. K., & Cook, A. (1993, November). *A qualitative analysis of resilient survivors: A case illustration*. Poster presented at annual meeting of the International Society for Traumatic Stress Studies, San Antonio, TX.

Ribbens, J. (1989). Interviewing—An "unnatural situation"? *Women's Studies International, 12,* 579–592.

Reid, P. T., & Kelly, E. (1994). Research on women of color: From ignorance to awareness. *Psychology of Women Quarterly, 18,* 477–486.

Riessman, C. K. (1990). *Divorce talk: Women and men make sense of personal relationships*. New Brunswick, NJ: Rutgers University Press.

Smith, D. E. (1987). Women's perspective as a radical critique of sociology. In S. Harding (Ed.), *Feminism and methodology* (pp. 84–96). Bloomington, IN: Indiana University Press.

Stanley, L., & Wise, S. (1991). Feminist research, feminist consciousness, and experiences of sexism. In M. M. Fonow & J. A. Cook (Eds.), *Beyond methodology: Feminist scholarship as lived research* (pp. 265–283). Bloomington, IN: Indiana University Press.

Stewart, A. J. (1994). Toward a feminist strategy for studying women's lives. In C. E. Franz & A. J. Stewart (Eds.), *Women creating lives: Identities, resilience, and resistance* (pp. 11–35). Boulder, CO: Westview.

Surrey, J. L. (1985). The "self-in-relation": A theory of women's development. In J. V. Jordan, A. G. Kaplan, J. B. Miller, I. P. Stiver, & J. L. Surrey (Eds.), *Women's growth in connection* (pp. 51–66). New York: Guilford Press.

Wasser, J. D., & Bresler, L. (1996). Working in the interpretive zone: Conceptualizing collaboration in qualitative research teams. *Educational Researcher, 25*(5), 5–15.

Worell, J., & Etaugh, C. (1994). Transforming theory and research with women: Themes and variation. *Psychology of Women Quarterly, 18,* 443–450.

COMMENTS ON "FEMINIST RESEARCH PROCESS"

Abigail J. Stewart and Alyssa N. Zucker
University of Michigan

There are many strengths in Grossman, Kruger, and Moore's (this issue) article, "Reflections on a Feminist Research Project: Subjectivity and the Wish for Intimacy and Equality." The article is filled with rich examples of the life of the research group, and explores important dimensions of topics that are rarely discussed in accounts of studies. Grossman et al. do their colleagues a favor by sharing their own stories about the process of doing research—the times when it is rewarding and exciting, as well as when it becomes difficult. The article provides the research community an excellent starting point for greater consciousness and reflection about our own research processes. Even more, we found it provided a catalyst for conversations about our own experiences working together (with others) on two research projects.We suspect the article could help other researchers begin or deepen conversations with their colleagues about the work they share.

At the same time, we fear that some readers might find the account detailed in this article a bit alarming! Its focus is exclusively on the interpersonal process in the group, but surely a great deal of time must have been spent on the mundane tasks of all research projects, including making decisions about recruitment and sampling; scheduling participants; creating research materials; assigning interviewers; conducting, then transcribing interviews and checking transcripts. Without that context, some might conclude from this account that bringing a feminist perspective into research will only add taxing, even risky, interpersonal labor—labor that may not be interesting to all researchers. Although the potential costs of feminist research practices are indeed evident in this article, we are inclined to try to identify ways to maximize the potential benefits. We are drawn to this task both by the compelling evidence of the benefits evident in the article, and from our own experience.

DISCLOSING STANDPOINTS

A particular strength of this article is the authors' explicit use of standpoint theory to think through their position as researchers. Although this is often recom-

Address correspondence and reprint requests to: Abigail Stewart, Institute for Research on Women and Gender, University of Michigan, 460 West Hall, Ann Arbor, MI 48109-1092. E-mail: abbystew@a.imap.itd.umich.edu

mended—and probably practiced—how research groups actually do this "on the ground" is rather mysterious. It is refreshing to have some information! The authors note that using this perspective, the researcher "must see both the research participant and herself or himself as real individuals, each located in time, place, and context" (p. 123). Grossman et al. are quite honest and open about the fact that although they were generally persuaded by these notions, they were reluctant to apply them to their own work process. At the same time, they realized that it might be helpful to acknowledge their own histories with abuse and to discuss how their histories might affect their perspectives, even though such personal revelations crossed the boundaries of what one might traditionally consider an appropriate level of intimacy for a research group. The story of how they negotiated the rules for such sharing, including spelling out of times to share personal information versus do more day-to-day research work, is instructive. We found ourselves wondering, though, what features of their experience were particular to the fact that they were studying abuse, or that they were clinicians, or that all members of their group seemed to be working on precisely the same data. To begin to address these questions, we thought about our own experiences as members of the same feminist research groups, one of us as a graduate student, the other as a faculty member.

We have collaborated on two major projects: a collaborative/comparative study of college-educated women at midlife, and a cross-sectional study of differences in women's relationships to feminism by birth cohort. In the midlife study, we worked with a large research group both at our own university and in collaboration with a group at another university. The cross-sectional study emerged out of a larger collaborative group, but we have become an independent small group of two, with undergraduate research assistants, and colleagues doing parallel, related studies on their own. We considered how the issues of standpoint, disclosure, intimacy, and power operated in these two settings, as well as in other research-collaboration experiences we each have had independently.

The issue of our standpoint(s) as individuals within the group had become open for discussion in both groups. Yet the discussions were not quite so fraught as they seemed in the Grossman et al. group, perhaps because they did not have so powerful a connection with disclosure issues. In the midlife group, one reason disclosure may have been less relevant is that different group members were exploring different topics: stress and social support; personality and political activism; psychological significance of social class; agency, communion, and well-being; generativity. No single focus unified the group except a broad interest in "midlife women"; perhaps this protected the group from an extended examination of all members' relationship to any single topic.

On the other hand, an important issue in the midlife group—which involved collecting data from both African American and White women—was our own racial backgrounds. One of our collaborators, Sandra Tangri, has written about some of our experiences in struggling with the different standpoints both of our participants and of research group members. As she writes,

> the item [from a questionnaire previously used with White women] asking for a description of the family of origin was felt by the African American women [in the research team] to not describe the extended families they grew up in and was expanded

to allow fuller description of this history. The item "why did your mother work?" did not make any sense to these women. Everyone did; it was not a matter of choice. Conversely, the importance of the father's ability to work continuously was an issue. (Tangri, 1996, p. 132)

This kind of discussion occurred frequently in the course of designing and coding the questionnaire. It continues as we interpret results. We all felt that it was critical that we be able to discuss the different standpoints of African American and White women, and, in fact, found it to be extraordinarily useful and important to the research process, despite the fact that doing so takes time and sometimes requires rethinking issues thought to be already resolved or settled. In this sense, our experience was much like Grossman et al.'s.

On the other hand, there were some differences. Some of our discussions have certainly been intense, or heated, and African American women in the group have expressed discomfort when they were sometimes "solo" representatives at a meeting of a supposedly interracial research group (because White women usually outnumbered African American women in our research group, and the relevant faculty member at our university was White). Nevertheless, our discussions generally did not have the charged quality surrounding painful disclosures of private information that is evident—and seems entirely reasonable—in the context of the study of women's experiences of abuse. This may be because race is so explicitly "marked" in our culture generally and within our research group, or because everyone in the group knew at the outset that discussion of racial difference was part of the research agenda, or because neither the issues we were studying nor our own disciplinary training were frankly "clinical."

In the study of different generations' relationships to feminism, we have had mostly similar experiences. Because we ourselves are of different generations (one a "70s feminist" and one a "90s feminist"), we have often used our own experience and beliefs (sometimes unfounded!) about our own and other generations' feminisms to help us think about our project. Again, we began the project with the intention of exploring a topic on which we knew we had interestingly different "standpoints." And we are both "out" feminists and have discussed feminist theory and research in lots of contexts, so there was nothing private to disclose (though we have sometimes told each other during this research about experiences with feminism that we had never mentioned before). It may be, too, that the fact that we are not clinical psychologists has kept our focus on different issues.

For whatever reasons, our experiences with these two very different groups suggest that one thing that may be "generalizable" in the account of Grossman et al.'s research group is the value of explicit exploration of group members' different standpoints in relation to the project. On the other hand, emotionally charged issues of disclosure may not automatically follow from addressing standpoint issues.

FINDING INTIMACY IN THE GROUP

We engaged in a similar comparative process in thinking about the issue of intimacy. We both find deep satisfaction in the process of working closely with a group on research. For both of us, the research group can and often does provide a powerful sense of "belonging," as well as a potential for affirming a shared worldview. It includes moments of high silliness, giddy exhaustion, collective excitement about findings, anxious anticipation about presentations, wrenching empathy with nervous "practice talks," and much more! We have not often read accounts of the ways in which the research process provides these kinds of satisfactions and feel grateful to have some of them described here. At the same time, it seemed to us that the desire for intimacy, as well as the need for boundaries around it, were probably heightened in a group in which disclosure was both necessary and painful. Other research groups focusing on issues likely to heighten these needs might find it useful to adopt explicit rules about confidentiality, as Grossman et al. did. It isn't clear whether the creation of a secondary group that met after the research group is a necessary practice, but it points to the value of considering creation of multiple contexts for intimacy within the project.

STRUGGLING WITH POWER

Finally, the authors rightly indicate the tension that exists between the wish for intimacy and the fact of power differences. We both found the account of the group members' struggles with power differences poignant, but wondered if it was inevitable that power differences must always feel as bad as they clearly sometimes did in this account. For example, it seems right to us that in faculty–student research groups there always is a power difference (at least that one), and it is helpful for it to be acknowledged, as it was in this group. We wondered, though, whether power was the only issue at work in some of the tension. For example, we both felt that the faculty member had a "right" to bring in another nonstudent colleague to the group, and that it was in some sense "inappropriate" for students to question her decision (because she provided the continuity over time, and her needs for colleagueship deserved attention, just as students' needs for mentorship always do). Perhaps part of the problem (which felt arbitrary and unilateral to some group members) was that it wasn't talked about enough. The student group members might not like the fact that the continuing faculty member had a right to make this change, but they might have accepted it with less distress if they had felt they had a right to hear more about the reasons for it.

We wondered, too, whether the power issues in the group were exacerbated not only by the hierarchical division between faculty and students (which is, after all, both very explicitly marked and intended eventually to end), but also by an implicit hierarchy among the students (particularly when one student became coauthor of the book). It seems to us that in the groups we've worked in (where we think there has been less trouble with power issues), there has been both greater and lesser hierarchy among the students. Greater in that some students have been explicitly assigned "responsibility" (power) for certain aspects of the research project (for example, managing the questionnaire process, or creating the database). Lesser in that different students take on different powerful roles both over time and at the same time. So there was not exactly a simple "hierarchy"; power was distributed along multiple axes, and the distribution was unstable over time. Perhaps an approach like this underscores every group member's dependence on other members

Division of the project into "spheres of influence," and fluid power relations, like the "jigsaw classroom" (where each child has a piece of the crucial information to solve a problem, but no one has it all; see Aronson, 1982; Aronson & Patnoe, 1997) may actually encourage collaboration!

PROCESSING FEMINIST RESEARCH

No one said it would be easy to do feminist research, and these authors show us some of the reasons why it isn't. But they also offer us material for thinking through what we gain and what we lose when we work at it. They provide a backstage tour of one feminist research group's process, and they focus on absolutely central issues: figuring out how to use our standpoints to strengthen our work rather than endanger it; fostering healthy intimacy in our research group relationships; and creating as much equality as we can within shifting power differences. We suspect that instead of a "handbook of feminist research practices," we need more of this—more backstage tours, more discussions of how practices work on the ground, and more accounts of how we do what we do, in different contexts, with different research questions, group compositions, and structures.

REFERENCES

Aronson, E. (1982). Modifying the environment of the desegregated classroom. In A. J. Stewart (Ed.), *Motivation and society* (pp. 319–336). San Francisco: Jossey-Bass.

Aronson, E., & Patnoe, S. (1997). *The jigsaw classroom* (2nd ed.). Beverly Hills, CA: Sage.

Grossman, F. K., Kruger, L. M., & Moore, R. P. (1999). Reflections on a feminist research project: Subjectivity and the wish for intimacy and equality. *Psychology of Women Quarterly, 23,* 119–137.

Tangri, S. S. (1996). Living with anomalies: Sojourns of a White American Jew. In K. F. Wyche & F. J. Crosby (Eds.), *Women's ethnicities: Journeys through psychology* (pp. 129–143). Boulder, CO: Westview.

BATTERERS' EXPERIENCES OF BEING VIOLENT

A Phenomenological Study

Ronda Redden Reitz
University of Tennessee—Knoxville

Nine male batterers were interviewed about their experiences of being violent in domestic relationships. Interviews were analyzed using a phenomenological method to uncover themes in the structure of violent experiences. Results indicated two levels of themes: Contextual themes that described comparisons of self with other, forming the relational setting for violence, and focal themes that described experiences of being violent. Results were discussed in terms of social learning theory and gender-role attitudes, concluding that, for some men, being violent in domestic relationships is a failed attempt to assert a preferred identity and avoid a devalued one. The violence ultimately reproduces the relational context of perceived polarized identities from which it emerges. Implications of findings for the victim were discussed and suggestions made to expand treatment interventions to focus on the polarized and unstable terms by which the men in this study framed their identities in domestic relationships.

In 1983 I began working in a court of law where, as part of my duties, I interviewed women seeking warrants of arrest against their partners for domestic violence. Sometime during the interview nearly all the women asked, "Why does he do this to me?" Although it seemed a good question, I had no answer for it and could find no satisfactory answer in the social science research literature, which, at that time, was focused primarily on the victim, rather than the perpetrator, of domestic violence.

This article is based on data collected for doctoral dissertation research. A previous version was presented at the annual conference of the Southeastern Psychological Association, Norfolk, Virginia, March 1996. The author wishes to acknowledge the cooperation of Child and Family, Inc. of Knoxville, TN and the assistance of the Wednesday Evening Phenomenology Group.

Address correspondence and reprint requests to: Ronda Redden Reitz, Department of Psychology, 227 Austin Peay Bldg., University of Tennessee, Knoxville, TN 37996-0900.

There have been a number of changes in social policy on domestic violence since 1983. For example, warrantless arrest laws now remove the onus for lodging a domestic violence complaint from the victim who may well be subject to intimidation or retaliation. Also, the final report of the Attorney General's Task Force on Family Violence (U.S. Department of Justice, 1984) encouraged courts to mandate treatment programs for perpetrators in addition to, or instead of, incarceration, and there are now psychoeducational programs for batterers in cities and towns across the United States.

Despite these and other changes in social policy, however, domestic violence against women remains an entrenched social problem. According to the most recent National Crime Victimization Survey, in the United States, "Women aged twelve and older annually sustained almost 5 million violent victimizations in 1992 and 1993. . . . In 29% of all violence against women by a lone offender, the perpetrator was an intimate (husband, ex-husband, boyfriend, or ex-boyfriend)" (U.S. Department of Justice, 1995, p. 1). According to the Uniform Crime Reports, collected by the Federal Bureau of Investigation, of the 62% of homicides for which the perpetrator had been identified in 1992, approximately 28% of female homicide victims were known to have been killed by their husband, ex-husband, or boyfriend. This is compared to 3% of male victims known to have been killed by an intimate (U.S. Department of Justice, 1995).

In addition to changes in social policy in the past 15 years, the focus of domestic violence research has also changed, with the perpetrator now scrutinized nearly as often as the victim. In this decade alone, researchers conducting quantitative studies have observed and measured domestically violent men, among other things documenting their *personality characteristics* (e.g., Barnett & Hamberger, 1992; Beasley & Stoltenberg, 1992; Bersani, Chen, Pendleton, & Denton, 1992; Dutton & Starzomski, 1993; Flournoy & Wilson, 1991; Murphy, Meyer & O'Leary, 1994), their *attitudes* (e.g., Holtzworth-Monroe & Hutchinson, 1993; Smith, 1990; Stith & Farley, 1993), their *learning histories* (e.g., Cappel & Heiner, 1990; Doumas, Margolin, & John, 1994; Murphy, Meyer, & O'Leary, 1993), and their *conflict-interaction styles* (e.g., Babcock, Waltz, Jacobron, & Gottman, 1992; Holtzworth-Monroe & Anglin, 1991).

Although Dobash and Dobash's (1979) seminal qualitative inquiry into the experiences of battered women is credited with sparking much of the interest in the phenomenon of domestic violence, no such study has yet been identified that explores the experience of violence from the perspective of the batterer. In fact, following the work of Arias and Beach (1987), who found that domestically violent men chronically underreport both the quantity and severity of their abuse, researchers seem to have been reluctant to talk at all with batterers about their violent and abusive behavior. Instead, battered wives are routinely asked to report on their spouse's violent episodes. Although victim reports increase the validity of quantitative accounts of domestic violence, they cannot substitute for systematic documentation of the experience of being violent from the perspective of those who are so. Without such documentation our understanding of the phenomenon of domestic violence is incomplete. We are missing a potentially crucial piece of the "why he does this" puzzle and our attempts to ameliorate the violence may be missing their mark. This study is intended to help fill the gap in our information—the missing first-person perspective of the experience of being domestically violent—against which our efforts at amelioration can be assessed.

METHOD

Pollio, Henley, and Thompson (1997) remind us that the word "method" is derived from the roots "hodos," meaning "path" or "way," and "meta," meaning "across" or "beyond." Addison (1989) suggested that the choice of a method of investigation depends, in part, on the problem being investigated and the goal of the investigation. The path we take across the uncharted terrain of a research problem, then, depends on what we want to see and where we hope to end up: the goal of the journey.

Historically, psychology has attempted to ally itself with the natural sciences, adopting their research methods, with the paradigmatic method being the controlled laboratory experiment. The natural-science approach is well suited to those problems in which a third-person perspective is desirable: in the observation of overt behavior, for example, or in the measurement of the body as a material or organic object (Polkinghorne, 1988). It has been criticized as less well suited to the study of human experience where what is desired is a first-person description of the meanings present in conscious awareness (Colaizzi, 1978; Polkinghorne, 1989; Romanyshyn & Whalen, 1989).

Existential phenomenology offers an alternative to the natural-science approach to psychological phenomena. As its name implies, it draws from two philosophical traditions. *Existentialism* can be traced to the thinking of Kierkegaard, for whom it was important to make intelligible those themes with which human beings invariably seem to struggle. *Phenomenology* derives from that body of thought that, along with the Gestalt psychology of perception, is associated in the Western world with Kant. As a philosophy, it was first explicated by Husserl who saw phenomenology as the "rigorous and unbiased study of things as they appear so that one might come to an essential understanding of human consciousness and experience" (Valle, King, & Halling, 1989, p. 6). To existential phenomenologists, "understanding experience merely as a mental projection onto the world (the idealistic fallacy) or as a reflection of the world (the realistic fallacy) misses the necessity of the person–world relationship in the constituting of experience" (Polkinghorne, 1989, p. 42).

First brought together as a coherent approach to thinking about human beings by Heidegger (1927/1962) and cast into psychological insight by Merleau-Ponty (1962/1989), existential-phenomenological psychology concerns itself with those themes that are present to consciousness as human beings experience themselves in their everyday world. Existential-phenomenological research seeks to describe human experience as it is lived in the interrelationship of the person and his or her world (Thompson, Locander, & Pollio, 1989; Valle et al., 1989). As grounded as existential phenomenology is in human experience and the first-person perspective, it seemed a path especially well suited to an exploration of the batterer's experience of being violent.

Research methods based on existential-phenomenological principles render a set of general guidelines (Giorgi, 1975a) rather than a specific sequence of steps and "researchers are expected to develop plans of study specially suited to understanding the particular experiential phenomenon that is the object of their study" (Polkinghorne, 1989, p. 44). For this study, that plan included choices of participant selection, data collection, and data analysis. It also included implementing several "bracketing" procedures by which the researcher sought to ensure that the study's findings resulted not from her own preconceptions or biases regarding domestic violence, but from the batterers' descriptions of their experiences (Valle et al., 1989).

Participants

Colaizzi (1978) succinctly described the criteria for selecting participants in a phenomenological study stating that "experience with the investigated topic and articulateness suffice" (p. 58). In contrast to a natural-science method that seeks enough participants to meet statistical requirements for generalizing from samples to populations, phenomenological research seeks enough participants to "generate a full range of variation in the set of descriptions to be used for analyzing a phenomenon" (Polkinghorne, 1989, p. 48).

Participants for this study were drawn from the 60 or so members of a group program for domestic violence offenders. The researcher attended group meetings and explained her research interest and the method by which data would be collected. Group members were given a copy of the information and consent form and asked to contact the researcher if they wished to participate in the study. Initially 12 men volunteered to participate.

Because of the sensitive nature of the topic, anonymity was a condition of participation in the study. Two volunteers hoped to use the data that they provided as favorable evidence in court hearings and were dropped from participation by mutual agreement when they learned that this would not be possible. A third volunteer was unable to schedule a time to provide data that was convenient to both himself and the researcher.

The final group of participants consisted of 9 men, aged 28 to 51 years. Six of the men had been court-ordered to the domestic violence offenders program; the remaining three participants had joined voluntarily. Three of the participants (one program volunteer, two initially court-ordered) had completed the 24-week domestic violence offender program but continued to attend meetings because they wished to do so. These three men had been in the domestic violence program between 1 and 2 years at the time data were collected for this study. The remaining six participants had been in the program from 4 to 20 weeks at the time data were collected.

Four participants were divorced, four were separated, and one was married and living with his wife. Seven participants had high-school diplomas, one had dropped out of high school, and one had completed college. Eight of the participants were White, one was African American. Two of the men identified themselves as verbal abusers, although it became clear in their descriptions of abuse that they hit, kicked, slammed, and tore up objects other than humans, and that they knowingly used this activity both as an alternative to physical battering and as a way of intimidating their partners.

Data Collection

Data for the study of experience have been gathered from literary sources (Halling, 1979; Jager, 1979), from narratives written in response to an interviewer's question (Beier & Pollio, 1994; W. F. Fischer, 1989; Giorgi, 1989; Golledge & Pollio, 1995), and from interviews conducted over the telephone (C. T. Fischer & Wertz, 1979). Pollio et al. (1997), however, suggest that the face-to-face dialogic interview is the "almost inevitable procedure" for obtaining precise and systematic descriptions of experience:

> Since experience is personal, the problem of other minds can be bridged only with the help of some specific other whose experiences are at issue. The method, or path, that seems natural to attain a proper description of human experience is that of dialogue in which one member of the dialogic pair, normally called the investigator, assumes a respectful position *vis-à-vis* the real expert, the subject or, more appropriately, the co-researcher. (Pollio et al., 1997, p. 29)

Although it seeks a description of first-person experience, the dialogic interview is actually a second-person procedure in which the first person "I," who has experienced the phenomenon in question, seeks to describe it to, and clarify its meaning with a second person "you" and "perhaps even to realize [the meaning] for the first time during the conversation, itself" (Pollio et al., 1997, p. 29). Such an interview was used to collect the data for this study, the batterers' descriptions of their experience of being violent.

Interviews took place on the premises of the agency that sponsored the domestic violence offenders program and during times when participants might be expected to be in the building, usually just after a group meeting. Each interview was audiotaped for later transcription.

Open ended and unstructured, interviews began with the question, "Could you think of a time or times when you've been violent in a domestic relationship and describe that in as much detail as possible?" Subsequent questions arose from the context of the interview itself, and were intended to assist participants in focusing on the experiences they were describing (Kvale, 1983; Polkinghorne, 1989). Following the recommendations of Thompson et al. (1989), as well as Polkinghorne (1989), "why" questions and "what happened" questions were avoided as they tend to lead participants away from description of experience. Instead, the interviewer asked such questions as "What was that like for you?" and "What were you experiencing?," as well as framing questions in participants' own words (Pollio et al., 1997), that is, "You said you treated her like a child?" Participants were free to tell about as many or as few incidents of violence as they wished. Descriptions of experience that were unclear to the interviewer were queried until both interviewer and participant were satisfied that the experience had been communicated as fully as possible.

An interview began coming to a close when the participant indicated that there were no more incidents of violence he wished to describe. At that point, the interviewer described back to him, as completely as she could, her understanding of his experience of being violent in a domestic relationship. The participant clarified any misunderstanding, and the interview ended when the participant indicated that his experience had been accurately described. Interviews usually lasted about 1½ hours, although one lasted 3 hours. Each interview was transcribed and edited, removing names of people and places, dates, and other data that might serve to identify the participant or his victim. The transcribed and edited interviews provided the data for the analysis.

Bracketing

As mentioned, bracketing involves steps to ensure that the findings of a phenomenological study result from descriptions of experience rendered by research participants rather than from the researcher's own preconceptions and biases. This process is called "bracketing" because, ideally, it allows the researcher to become aware of and set aside her or his own biases, as if putting brackets around them. As an example, it is customary to begin a phenomenological investigation with an examination of the investigator's preconceptions of the phenomenon in question. This initial bracketing procedure may involve self-reflection on the part of the researcher (Colaizzi, 1973) or more interpersonal possibilities, such as writing down one's experiences of the phenomenon of interest, then discussing them with other members of the research team (C. T. Fischer & Wertz, 1979).

The initial bracketing procedure used in this study was an interview in which the investigator, before conducting any participant interviews, first discussed her own experiences of being violent. Ideally, the researcher would be asked the same question as the participants, but in this instance, because partner abuse was not part of her specific experience, she was asked to describe her experiences of being violent in any relationship. The text of this interview was then analyzed in the same manner as eventually would be used for individual participant interviews, rendering themes in the investigator's experience of being violent.

The bracketing interview, like other bracketing procedures, is not intended to eliminate completely a researcher's preconceptions of the phenomenon in question; such would be impossible (Gadamer, 1976; Merleau-Ponty, 1962/1989). Rather, it is intended to alert the researcher to their existence so that she or he may take steps to minimize the limiting effect such biases might have on descriptions rendered by study participants in their interviews (Polkinghorne, 1989). Two such steps, already discussed, are the choice of open, rather than leading, interview questions and questions using the participants' own words.

Themes in the investigator's experience of being violent that were identified in the analysis of the bracketing interview were not included in the thematic descriptions of the batterer's experience of being violent. Rather, they marked the starting point in the researcher's understanding of the experience of being violent from which more complex understandings of the phenomenon were expected to emerge over the course of the research (Guba & Lincoln, 1989; Pollio et al., 1997).

In addition to the bracketing interview, a second bracketing procedure implemented in this study was the use of an interpretive research group (C. T. Fischer &

Wertz, 1979; Pollio et al., 1997; Thompson et al., 1989). This group, comprised of several researchers experienced in phenomenological work with whom the researcher met on a regular basis, served the bracketing function in three main ways. First, because they analyzed the bracketing interview, they were aware of themes in the researcher's preunderstanding of the experience of being violent, placing them in a good position to point out failures of bracketing in participant interviews, most of which they also helped analyze. Second, they were able to point out failures of bracketing in the researcher's emerging understanding of the phenomenon of being violent. Third, group members provided challenges to any interpretation of the data, from the initial analysis of individual interviews, through the process of uncovering themes common to all interviews, to the proffering of a structure for the batterer's experience of being violent. At each juncture, group members functioned in a critical capacity, challenging the researcher and one another to point to specific evidence in the text of the interviews to support an interpretation. "While the ability of an interpretive group to see support for an interpretation does not guarantee its adequacy, failure to see such support serves as good evidence of its lack of adequacy" (Pollio et al., 1997).

Similarly, although the ability of study participants to see themselves in an interpretation of their experience does not guarantee its adequacy, the failure of participants to see themselves serves as evidence that the goal of the phenomenological research study—the description of experience from the perspective of the experiencer—has not been met. As an additional step in bracketing, Colaizzi (1978) proposes that final descriptions of experience be negotiated with research participants. Presenting preliminary results of the study to participants in a follow-up interview, the researcher asks how the results compare with participants' experiences and whether or not aspects of their experience have been omitted. Final descriptions of experience take into account new data garnered from the follow-up interviews.

The condition of participant anonymity prevented doing follow-up interviews with participants in this study. Because of this, the interviewer took extra care at the end of each interview to provide a detailed description of her understanding of the participant's experience and invite his clarification. In addition, results of the study were presented to a group of batterers who were willing to discuss the results in light of their own experience. Group members agreed that, although one theme or another might seem more salient to any particular man, their experiences of being violent had been adequately captured by the thematic descriptions as presented. Despite trying, they could come up with no experiences that were not encompassed by the study themes.

Finally, bracketing was also accomplished in this study by rendering themes uncovered in the descriptions of being violent not in the abstract and specialized language of the social sciences, but in the experience-near language used by participants (Pollio et al., 1997).

Analysis of Interviews

Given that phenomenology offers guidelines rather than specific rules for doing research, it should not be surprising that phenomenological researchers list slightly different steps in the process of analyzing their data (e.g., Colaizzi, 1978; C. T.

Fischer & Wertz, 1979; Giorgi, 1975a, 1975b; van Kaam, 1969). Common to all of them, however, is the use of the hermeneutic circle for data interpretation, the process of attending to the emergence of the meaning of experience in the constant interplay of partial to whole texts (Bleicher, 1980).

The first step in interpretation of the data in this study was analysis of each of the nine research protocols, seven of them by the interpretive research group working together, and two by the researcher working alone. For group interpretation, each group member was provided with an interview transcript from which to read along, while two group members read aloud the words of the interviewer and the participant.

"Because a whole protocol or a collection of protocols cannot be analyzed simultaneously, they have to be broken down into manageable units" (Polkinghorne, 1989, p. 51). In other words, one cannot attend to the interplay between parts and wholes without making a decision about what constitutes a useful part. Following the suggestions of Giorgi (1975a, 1975b), "meaning units" for protocols in this study were determined by a change in subject matter. Longer passages were divided at natural stopping points in the text, for example, at a change in speaker. The group discussed the portion of the interview just read with each member contributing his or her thoughts about the meaning or meanings of the events described. Alternative renderings and challenges to those already offered were encouraged. Disputes were resolved and consensus reached only when supporting evidence could be cited from the text of the protocol about the meaning of a particular passage to the research participant who had provided it (Pollio et al., 1997). A similar process was followed for the two protocols analyzed by the researcher working alone: Protocols were divided into meaning units that were examined for their dominant meaning as given by the research participant in his description of his experience of being violent (Colaizzi, 1978; Giorgi, 1975a, 1975b).

Following analysis of all nine interviews, the next step was to identify all of the varieties of meaningful experience described in each protocol in order to render a summary description of the meaning of being violent for each research participant. Pollio et al. (1997, p. 51) refer to this as the "idiographic interpretation," the interplay of meaning between the specific incidents and episodes described in an individual protocol and the meaning of the experience under investigation for the participant as revealed in the protocol as a whole. Giorgi (1975a, 1975b), too, includes this step in order to retain a sense of the situated context of the experience before moving to the transsituational or general thematic description.

To generate a set of themes common to all protocols (Colaizzi, 1978; Giorgi, 1975a, 1975b; Thompson et al., 1989), meaning units were identified that best exemplified all the various experiences of being violent described by all participants. These meaning units were categorized according to their likeness to one another as revealed in the words of the participants. Care was taken to ensure that all participants were represented in each preliminary theme.

Preliminary themes were presented to the interpretive research group for their consideration and assistance in synthesizing them into a smaller number of general themes. The interpretive research group then evaluated whether or not thematic descriptions were supported by the data presented in the original protocols and whether or not the data were represented by the themes. This comparison between themes and protocols, the process of "nomothetic interpretation" (Pollio et al.,

1997, p. 51), continued until it was agreed by all group members that the general themes fully encompassed the meaning and experience of being violent as presented across all protocols. Although some phenomenological researchers render themes in the language of their particular discipline (e.g., Colaizzi, 1978; Giorgi, 1975a, 1975b), the titles of themes in this study were drawn from the actual words used by participants so that the thematic description would represent as clearly as possible the batterers' experience of being violent (Pollio et al., 1997).

The final step in the data analysis of the experience of being violent was examining the general themes for evidence of the structural relationships between and among them—the Gestalt of the experience of being violent in a domestic relationship (Colaizzi, 1978; Polkinghorne, 1989; Pollio et al., 1997; Thompson et al., 1989). Results of this thematic analysis are presented in both text and diagrammatic form. The diagrams attempt to represent structural relationships between themes, whereas the text attempts to describe and explicate each theme in the batterers' experience of being violent.

RESULTS

During thematic analysis it became evident that participants had described two levels of themes in their interviews: *Contextual* themes, which described their experience of self in relation to other, and the setting in which their violence took place; and *focal* themes that described the experience of the violence itself.

Contextual Themes

The contextual themes described by study participants are located within the ground of self–other relationships, placing participants' experiences of being violent in the realm of identity-in-relationship. What this means is that participants reported specific dualities, which they used to compare themselves with their partners and by which they framed opposing identities for themselves and their partners. These opposed identities were always contested, and there seemed to be little room for either similarity of identity or negotiation. In the words of one participant, "There wasn't, it wasn't equality. It was either, 'I win and you lose, or you win and I lose.'"

The dualities encompassed by contextual themes concerned experiences of being Big or Little, Good or Bad, and Winning or Losing. Related experiences were grouped together under these titles chosen from the text of the interviews to reflect the dominant meaning of each theme. For example, Big or Little also included experiences that were described as "up or down," "adult or child," or "strong or weak." Table 1 presents each of the contextual and related themes.

It is important to note that these themes are not independent of one another. Rather, they form an overall pattern in which there is considerable overlap, both of language and meaning. For instance, when a participant said, "I am all messed up," it was coded under "normal or abnormal" for the dominant meaning of the statement in the context of the interview. This statement, however, also contains language about "neat or messy" (from the same theme of Good or Bad) and "up or down" (from the theme of Big or Little). Arguably, one who feels "all messed

Table 1

Contextual and Related Themes in the Experience of Being Violent

Big/Little	Good/Bad	Winning/Losing
Up/down	Good/evil	Matter/doesn't matter
Adult/child	Right/wrong	Controlling/controlled
Strong/weak	Neat/messy	Getting/giving
	Smart/stupid	
	Trustworthy/untrustworthy	
	Normal/abnormal	

up" also feels like a loser, and the context of the interview indicated losing was, indeed, a particular concern for this participant as he related to other people:

> When I am around a man, now—not a woman, believe it or not, but a man—who's taller than I am I feel inferior . . . and I can't tell you why, except that I just feel uncomfortable around men that are taller than I am. But women . . . of course, there aren't many women who are taller than I am.

And in his relationship with his wife, he appeared to keep score as the following comment illustrates:

> It was like she knew I'd never cooked a pot of beans and so she was trying to make a point, which was a good point, but I thought my comeback was good, too.

The one statement, "I am all messed up," represented all three themes, although one theme, Good or Bad, seemed to predominate. Participants presented the dualities encompassed by the contextual themes as polarized opposites. Although they were aware of identifying themselves as one or the other member of these polarities, their experienced identity was changeable. Further, the members of each pair were not equally valued. Instead, Big was a more desirable identity than Little, Good a more desirable identity than Bad, and Winning a more desirable identity than Losing. Participants reported their violence as often coinciding with their wish to assert themselves as the more desirable member of each pair.

For example, participants often reported feeling small, helpless, childlike, or childish in their relationships with their partners:

> I can't even remember how I dealt with it, with [my wife], but it was like, "Well, I'm sorry, but I'm old enough." You know? And I get these crazy, stupid thoughts like that. You know, "I don't need your permission," and "I'm old enough," and "I don't have to ask," and stuff like that. I guess I felt like a little kid that was being reprimanded for something that he hadn't done. I, I, I can kind of liken it to that. . . . I can imagine a little kid . . . knowing that he's innocent, being reprimanded by a teacher, or a parent, or any adult, and the kid trying to say, you know, "But I'm innocent. I didn't do it. Why are you treating me like this?" I could, you know, that's kind of the way I felt.

Alongside the experience of being little, however, participants also were aware that they were physically bigger than their partners and that their physical size could be used to reassert themselves as big:

There was one occasion where she walked away from me, and I drove down the road and picked her up. No, I ran down the road, and uh, picked her up, and smacked her on the rear end while carrying her back to my truck.

I'm very intimidating because I'm very big, and I don't like that, either. I, I really don't like being big. It's sort of like it's a controlling behavior for me because when I start raging . . .

The latter participant went on to describe a time when women in a therapy group had been frightened to the point of cowering by his display of anger, although his display was directed not at the women but at a chair cushion. He judged that his large size made his angry display more intimidating than it would otherwise have been. He also described a time when his physical strength and size allowed him, in frustration, to throw a screwdriver through the steel firewall of a car. He concluded these stories of strength and size by relating that displays of anger were the only way he had ever known to "control circumstances or people."

That physical abuse is used as a display of bigness or dominance is hardly surprising. Verbal abuse, however, was used for a similar purpose, to assert metaphorical bigness. As one participant said, "I think a lot of the insults I gave was just to bring [my girlfriends] down a little bit lower than I felt."

All participants in this study reported a general alertness to goodness and badness and a desire to identify themselves with the good. Those who reported being violent outside of domestic relationships saw themselves as using their violence in the service of the good:

But I always, in a way, I always been for right and wrong, you know, and, uh, I never went against the cops unless I felt like they was wrong in what they was doin'. But, hey, if I felt like they was right, and I was in the wrong, then everything was all right. But if I seen 'em hasslin' somebody else that I seen the whole thing from the beginning, and I knowed that the other person was in the right, I'd back 'em up regardless of how many cops was there, you know.

But crooks should be scared of me, you know? I'm going to get rid of them. Try my best, you know? But my friends, all my good friends, they should be happy because I'll always, I've got friends I've had for twenty years, you know? They'll be my friends to the end. I'd never draw my, you know, weapons against, or my hands against, you know, I've never gone against my friends.

Similarly, and without exception, all participants reported that their incidents of violence took place when they judged their partner was doing something bad or wrong:

I was on the edge of insanity, and she lied to me. She set me off. I mean, that set me off. I saw her as being untrustworthy.

Just because the Hamburger Helper wasn't done right, wasn't done to perfection, I'd just bounce it up over her.

We were livin' in a trash dumpster, and I didn't want to live that way. I can't live that way. So, I go in the house and I feel this rage comin' on, you know?

If [the women in my life] are doing what they're supposed to be doing then, you know, I like 'em. But if they're not, then I think maybe—I can't remember real far, exactly—but if they're acting stupid or doing something stupid, then I don't like 'em, and I treat 'em, you know, hateful and mean.

Some participants explicitly acknowledged that, in these instances of judging their partners wrong or bad, they assumed the role of an adult attempting to punish or correct their partners, who were placed in the role of a child. As mentioned previously, participants reported that at various times they experienced themselves on either side of the adult–child pair, although during those times when they were feeling like the adult, violence and abuse were assumed to be part of the role:

[If] I considered that she was doing something wrong, uh, then I had, uh, I had spanked her. . . . [It] would be just like a child. I had turned her over my knee and spanked her until she, until she would cry.

Sometimes it'd be because she done some little thing wrong, and uh . . . it would start out as tryin', wantin' to say somethin', but at the same time, the anger was there while I was tryin' to show her the right, and all of a sudden it would skip, you know, and there [the violence] would be.

Participants reported instances of violence and abuse when they perceived their partner's wishes to be in some way at odds with their own. These instances could deal with issues as large as how affection would be shown in the marriage or as small as who would determine how much salt should go in the soup. The underlying issue, however, always seemed to be a question of whose wishes would prevail. These themes were grouped under the heading Winning or Losing. Although each of the contextual themes was presented by participants in terms of opposites—Big or Little, Good or Bad—the theme of Winning or Losing dealt explicitly with participants' perceptions of domestic relationships as adversarial. Participants reported feeling not just opposed by their partners, but thwarted and deprived by them:

The first week we were married I realized there'd be problems and, of course, my dream was I wanted to be together. I wanted to love this woman and I wanted to be her love. I wanted all these things that go with marriage, to be her protector, her supporter, and blah, blah, blah, and all I really got was an adversary. And she plays the part of an adversary real well.

She was just not seeing my point of view at all and more or less telling me that I didn't have a point of view. I didn't matter.

I'm an affectionate-type person. I enjoy showing a person how I feel. I feel like I deserve that for myself. I don't get it, but it bothers me.

Figure 1 illustrates one possible configuration of participants' experiences of these polarized contextual themes in their domestic relationships. Each theme is surrounded by a broken line to indicate the instability of the experience—the sense that one is at times big while the other is little, at times little while the other is big; sometimes good while the other is bad, sometimes bad while the other is good; either a winner while the other loses, or a loser while the other wins. For participants in this study, using violence in domestic relationships was an attempt to assert their

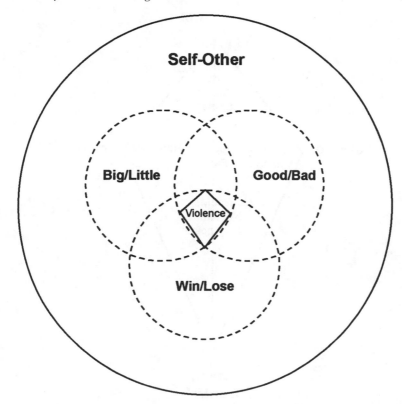

FIGURE 1.   Contextual themes in the structure of the batterer's experience of being violent.

identities as big, good, and winning in relation to partners who could then be
identified as small, bad, and losing.

Focal Themes

The kite-shaped area at the center of Figure 1 is meant to represent participants'
experiences of the moment of violence itself. Figure 2 presents an enlarged and
detailed view of this kite-shaped area. Participants in this study described their
experience of being violent as bounded by four focal themes: being In Control,
being Out of Control, experiencing a sense of Pressure, and Exploding. Pressure
and Exploding also were characterized as "tension" and "snapping," respectively,
although the text of the interviews made it clear the same phenomena were being
addressed:

> I could control myself very well and quite charmingly at the onset of a relationship,
> but at a point tension would build up and I would hit something, or I would scream
> at them.

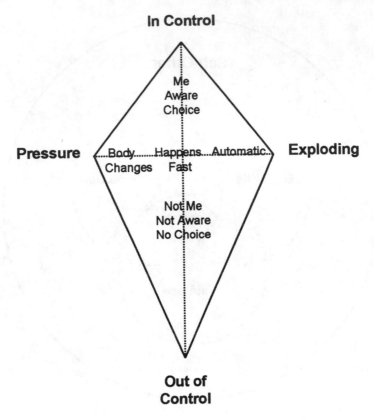

FIGURE 2.   Focal themes in the structure of the batterer's experience of being violent.

Everything that happened just brought on more tension and more rage. More and
more and more.
    All of the ingredients were there: very hot, drugs, methamphetamine at the time,
she lied to me, and I had a really, really stressful . . . you know, I had a death in the
family. My brother had died and I snapped one day.

As Figure 2 attempts to illustrate, these four themes can be envisioned as
pairs, In Control–Out of Control and Pressure–Exploding. It may be helpful in
understanding the experience of being violent to think of these pairs as the endpoints
of intersecting continua of axes as shown in Figure 2. Along these axes, within the
field defined by the major focal themes, subthemes express participants' reported
perceptions of change in aspects of themselves or their experience. Some of these
perceptions of change were reported as a series of contrasts: Me and Not Me,
Aware and Not Aware, Choice and No Choice. In addition, participants reported
experiencing changes in their bodies:

My heart would feel like it would jump up slap out of my chest.

You know, everything gets blurry at that time. My heart's racing and I might start twitching. I lose my focus.

Maybe it's endorphins or something because, because it was almost a high. It was almost a high. I would get dizzy from it, it would just be so intense.

In the most graphic terms, one participant described his sense of being overcome by the changes in his body:

P: I stay away from people that really piss me off until I can cool off, you know, to . . . I get to a point where I will explode . . . on them.

I: What's that experience of exploding like?

P: To me it's like sticking a, a needle in your arm of pure adrenaline. That's, that's an analogy that I use. I don't know what it's like to stick a needle in your arm of pure adrenaline, but I imagine.

I: What do you imagine?

P: That's, that's it, you know. Just coming through your whole body, just, you know, faster and faster, and focused, and energy, uncontrolled, but focused-on-the-target energy. You know, sometimes I even see, you know, everything turns red, you know, 'cause blood is pumping throughout my veins. My veins . . . everything just opens up. I feel it as a chemical change in my body. I don't know what everyone's adrenaline feels like, but I feel my adrenaline, and it feels so hard and so fast, and it over-, it just overtakes me, you know? . . . There's a change that's so dramatic and so intense that I feel like I'm powerless over it.

As this participant and others described, central to the perception of change was that it happened fast and that it culminated in some level of violent activity that felt as if it was automatic, "From the time she asked me to leave to the time she hit the ground was (snaps fingers) just like that." Happens Fast and Automatic also were subthemes within the field formed by the four focal themes of In Control, Out of Control, Pressure, and Exploding.

Again, it is important to remember that these themes and subthemes are not discrete, but form a Gestalt in which there is considerable overlap among themes. For example, Automatic seems to include elements both of choice and quickness, but was described by some participants as a separate experience along the (brief) continuum from Pressure to Exploding. This automatic quality to violent experience was also described as "programmed," "a habit," and "knee-jerk":

You know, I don't, "The person stepped on the brakes. Oh, gosh, I've got to cuss and rant and rave to get this pressure off my chest." You know, it's just they stomp on the brakes and, "AAAAAHH! Why the hell do you stomp on your . . . ?" It's not a thought. It's more a knee-jerk reaction.

Participants described some of their experiences of Pressure and Exploding as occurring when they were In Control. Their sense of being In Control was characterized by a greater awareness, in the moment, of themselves, their partners, and their own potential for violent behavior. A sense of choice about where and how to vent Pressure and Exploding also characterized the theme of In Control. When feeling In Control, participants reported being more able to choose a less severe form of violence or violence against something other than their partners. For example, one participant said, "If I had any control at all on the situation, I would tear up something else without hurting her, you know, or somebody else, but most of the time, I didn't have any control." Another participant told the story of a time he came home angry and, recognizing that he might take it out on his wife, drove through the back wall of the garage instead.

Of course, this is all relative. Grabbing a knife, holding it in someone's face, and shouting for her to "Sit the fuck down and leave me alone" would seem severely violent. To the participant who reported having done this, however, it seemed less severely violent than the possibility of killing the victim with his bare hands, which was what he was aware of as an alternative and what he was afraid he would do. The verbal abusers in this study reported much the same experience: There were times of Pressure and Exploding that they described as In Control. During these times they were aware of choosing less hurtful things to say or of ending their tirades sooner.

For experiences described by the themes Out of Control, Pressure, and Exploding, participants reported having no sense of choice about their behavior. They also reported decreasing awareness of self and other. Said one participant, "The night I hit her, I was so out of control that I don't even remember hitting her." Another said, "I'd forgotten what she meant to me, who she was, and what she meant to me." A third participant stated, "I wasn't even aware of where my hand was on her. You know, it was like I lost conscience [sic], and was actually . . . doing somethin', but I didn't realize what I was doing."

All participants described varying levels of "not me" experience when they reported being Out of Control. For some, this "not me" experience involved an almost total lack of recall for their own violent behavior and its consequences for the victims:

> At the time I about broke [my wife's] neck, it took me three days to actually believe that I did it, with her settin' there, practically 24 hours a day, telling me that I did it.
>
> The night that I hit her, I was so out of control I don't remember hitting her. I just know that's what happened with my left hand because there was a mark on her cheek, very small.
>
> So, a lot of times I, when I would get angry, I would black out and not know what was happenin' until somebody else tell me. I mean I could be sittin' there, talkin' to somebody, get into an argument, and if it become violent, I wouldn't know about it, or if it got into a hostility, the conversation, then I wouldn't, sometimes I wouldn't know about what was said. People's come back and told me what I've said and done, and I would not know a remembrance of it.

When this latter participant did come to some realization of his behavior and its consequences for his victim, he judged himself so evil that he tried to commit suicide:

But anyway, I took an overdose of pills, and it wasn't because [my wife] was gone. It was because it woke me up. You see, this friend of hers told me some of the conversations my wife had had with her about the violence and the abuse and the way things was. But it wasn't, it was more, it wasn't a lot like she was harpin' on the violence so much. It was included in the things. But that's what woke me up, and when it woke me up then I saw how evil I was, how wicked I was, and uh, that's what I done. That's why I took the overdose.

This man's report of his attempted suicide is strangely consistent with the previously noted finding that participants sought to identify themselves as good by using violence against the evil they identified in others, especially their partners. When this man perceived evil in himself, he tried to destroy himself. The participant further reported that during the coma induced by his overdose he experienced a vision in which God called him to be an evangelist. In this man's worldview, such a calling is perhaps the ultimate identification as good.

For most of the men in this study, the "not me" experience was less complete, although still present. Although they could remember their violent behavior it seemed inconsistent with who they believed themselves to be. Some used different epithets to describe themselves along the In Control and Out of Control dimension, with one man invoking the quintessential Dr. Jekyll/Mr. Hyde: "I lose any composure that I might have and I turn into Mr. Hyde." Another identified himself as Mr. Wonderful most of the time and a "crazed animal" when out of control. Even those who did not rename themselves described a different self when feeling Out of Control, a self who did not feel like the one they ordinarily knew themselves to be:

[When I'm in a rage] it's like it's not me, you know?
When I'm not like that, when I'm not angry, I'm a totally different, I'm a pretty okay guy to be around.
And that one instant I was different, hurting her.
I go back to being whoever it was I was before that and it's like [the violent episode] didn't even exist at that time.

Perhaps the most important finding of this study is the way in which domestic violence reproduces the context from which it arose. In their interviews participants described their judgments of themselves and their violent behavior:

Losing control is childish.
I don't think normal men act like I have. I don't think normal men use the kind of language and body language.
You have to really guard yourself. It just kind of sucks, that's basically what I'm trying to say. If you don't trust yourself, who's going to trust you?
I mean I lose things from [being violent]. I lose jobs. I lose friends. Stuff like that.

These statements suggest that in the aftermath of their violence, participants continued to experience themselves in the polarized terms of the contextual themes. Further, the statements suggest that the violence was unsuccessful in establishing for participants their identities as big, good, and winning. As a result of using violence against their partners, the men participating in this study experienced themselves on the devalued side of the polarities: They were little, they were bad, they were losing—experiences they had previously found intolerable. Should they continue to find them intolerable, the contextual stage from which to use violence to assert themselves as big, good, and winning will have once again been set.

DISCUSSION

What has been learned about "why he does this"? Participants in this study described their experience of being violent as a feeling of pressure building to explosion that is characterized by a change in their bodies, a sense that it all happens fast, and feels automatic. The pressure and exploding could take place while they were in control or out of control. If it took place while they were in control they were themselves, they were aware of self and other, and could make choices about where and how to vent their explosion. In contrast, if they were out of control they were not themselves, not aware of self and other, and had no sense of choice about what they did. Participants revealed that their experiences of being violent took place in relational settings in which they were concerned with identifying their partners as little, bad, and losing and themselves as good, big, and winning. They used violence, both physical and verbal, to assert their preferred identity.

If I were reporting these summarized results to the women I interviewed at court, I would also tell them that the results reveal that, for some men at least, the violence ultimately fails to achieve for them their goal. When they reflected on their use of violence, the men in this study found themselves back on the devalued side of the polarities: They judged themselves childish; they judged themselves evil; they recounted the wives, friends, jobs, and reputations they had lost because of their violent behavior. What, then, prompts violence against women to continue, or alternatively, fails to make it stop?

Dobash and Dobash (1979) have suggested that the social construction of wives makes them "appropriate victims" for domestic aggression. Where wives are constructed as victims, husbands must be constructed as victimizers. Social learning theory (Bandura, 1979) suggests that traditional male gender-role socialization may contribute to the rewards of domestic violence by prompting men to feel as though they must regain control and dominance over their wives, leading them to feel satisfied when they do (Dutton, 1988). The men in this study construed dominance as possible in any or all of three overlapping categories: bigness, goodness, and winning in a contested situation. They construed many marital encounters as contests in which there could be only one winner. This is consistent with Stith and Farley's (1993) data suggesting a direct link between nonegalitarian gender-role attitudes and wife abuse.

In contrast to another Stith and Farley (1993) finding—that wife abuse is directly linked to approval of marital violence—a conflict existed for the men in this study between their desire to dominate and their use of violence to achieve domination over their partners. Paradoxically, although they used violence to achieve dominance, the use of violence was in some ways inconsistent with their view of dominance. Specifically, they seemed unable to justify violence as "good." Dutton (1988) proposes that batterers use the process of "cognitive restructuring" to cope with such conflicts—constructing their understanding of their violent behavior in such a way that guilt is lessened and moral conflict relieved.

All of the men in this study noted that their violence took place when they were "out of control." Hallmarks of being out of control were that they felt unlike themselves ("not me"), as if they were unaware of what was happening and had no choice of alternative behaviors. One or two of the participants gave descriptions of the severity of their victims' injuries and their inability to recall having inflicted the injuries, which were consistent with deindividuated violence (Zimbardo, 1969) in which the batterer's behavior may neither be coded nor stored in memory (Dutton, 1988). Most of the violence participants described was not consistent with deindividuated violence, however. The experience of being out of control may also be a way in which the men constructed their understanding of their violent behavior to relieve felt conflict.

Granting the claim of these men, which valued being dominant (good, big, winning) but also did not condone the use of violence as "good," they would be expected to feel some level of moral conflict. One way to relieve the conflict is to construct goodness and dominance as mutually exclusive so that the choice between them is not a free one, but forced. If the choice were forced, the men would be less accountable. If they had no choice, or were unaware of what they were doing, or could not control what was happening, they could not be held accountable at all. These are exactly the descriptions of the moments of violence given by the men—they were unaware of what they were doing, they felt as if they had no choice, and they were out of control.

Of course, there are many situations in which we all experience restricted choice, and a few in which we experience no choice. There are some situations over which we have no control or in which we are unaware of what we are doing. In these latter situations usually we will not be held accountable by others even if our actions were wrong. We may still hold ourselves accountable, however, and feel guilty. An additional way for the men to relieve guilt would be to find some way to reclaim goodness for themselves, or rather, to reclaim themselves as good.

If the men in this study valued both dominance and goodness, but judged that by using violence they had chosen dominance rather than goodness, one guilt-reducing way for them to construct their understanding of their behavior would be to claim both dominance and goodness for themselves, but disavow themselves as violent. To be violent, then, would be a "not me" activity, exactly as the men described it.

Cognitive restructuring—constructing situations in such a way as to relieve moral guilt and conflict—is a largely unreflected process. It is one that probably everyone uses (Bandura, 1973) and one that may even be beneficial when unnecessary self-punishment impedes desired change. In the case of domestic violence, however, neutralizing self-punishment may prevent violent men from feeling the impetus to learn new behaviors and thus reclaim goodness for themselves by doing good.

If I had a chance to talk to the battered women I interviewed in the past, indeed, I would tell them that, based on this study, their partners' violent attempts to assert themselves as bigger, better, winners ultimately fails. I would caution the women, however, against taking from this finding any sort of solace or satisfaction. Lenore Walker (1979), in her work with battered women, has documented what she calls the "cycle of violence." From the perspective of the victim, following an episode of violence, her batterer is contrite and apologetic about his behavior, he is cooperative and treats her well, and the two enter a "honeymoon phase." The danger of this phase for the victim is that it persuades her to stay in the relationship with the batterer, who is suddenly behaving toward her as she always hoped he would. The victim becomes convinced that the violence was an aberration that will never happen again.

This study shows that, from the perspective of those committing it, the violence emerges in and from this phase of the cycle when the batterer feels not so much regretful as powerless—little, bad, and losing—while wanting desperately to feel otherwise. From this perspective, the violence almost certainly will happen again unless something intervenes to change the batterer's ongoing experiences of Big or Little, Good or Bad, and Winning or Losing.

The group programs that currently dominate treatment of domestic violence offenders often address the issues presented as focal themes in this study: In and Out of Control, Pressure, and Exploding. Using the diagram presented in Figure 2, the line from Pressure to Exploding is the one treatment programs most often attempt to change. The line is "moved down" when men are confronted about the ways that they construct their understanding of their behavior and are asked to stop minimizing and justifying it, denying aspects of it, or blaming their victim. It is moved down when the men are asked to take responsibility for their violence— owning it, and owning up to it. The line is also moved down when domestically violent men are taught to verbalize their feelings, thereby increasing the repertoire of behavioral choices available to them when they feel angry. These moves "enlarge" the upper triangle, moving more of the relevant pre-Explosion experience into the realm of "me," where the men reported feeling more in control of themselves.

The line from Pressure to Exploding also may be expanded horizontally—that is, attempts may be made to help domestic violence offenders increase the length of time from one state to the other, or defuse the explosion altogether. All of the men in this study spoke of changes in their bodies associated with the buildup of pressure or tension. They reported feeling muscle tension in their chests, shoulders, arms, or stomachs. Some experienced twitching facial muscles or changes in vision that produced narrowly focused or blurry content. A number of participants reported what they called an "adrenaline rush" in which it felt as though their veins were opening up and their hearts were pounding as though about to leave their chests. Although these changes were associated with a buildup of tension or pressure, they also contributed to the feeling of being out of control.

Treatment programs encourage men to note such changes and use them as a signal that they are fast approaching a critical point. They are advised to take a "time out," that is, to leave the vicinity for an hour or so to keep their partners safe, to cool down, and to think about constructive ways to work with their partners to resolve the conflict at hand. If taken and acted on, this encouragement and advice increases men's awareness (and their choices) by further "enlarging" the upper triangle. At the same time, this action increases the time between Pressure and Exploding. As such, it addresses the participants' reports that their violent explosions happened fast and were automatic—"knee-jerk reactions," as one of the men called them. In effect, present techniques ask potentially violent men to take the time (and space) to bind their own tensions rather than act them out on their partners.

More often, however, treatment programs do not question what it is that makes this tension so great in the first place. The physical changes the men report are consistent with defensive reactions to perceived threats to the self. How is it that these men feel so often and so greatly threatened in their domestic relationships? This study suggests the answer lies in the relational experiences of Big or Little, Good or Bad, and Winning or Losing. In a worldview where there is no equality, where identities are always polarized, always contested, and nonnegotiable, a person is constantly under threat of subjugation or annihilation unless he or she can first subjugate or annihilate the other.

This is not to suggest that interventions that focus on the moment of violence—the experiences of Out of Control, Pressure, and Exploding—should somehow be dropped or replaced in treatment curricula. It is to suggest, however, that the effectiveness of treatment interventions might be increased if the remedial focus were expanded to include the context from which violence arises, the context of identity-in-relationship from which violence is inexorably reproduced.

The number of batterers who volunteered to participate in this study was small. Each of the men acknowledged some level of moral conflict over his violent behavior. Each of them, sometime during the interview, expressed that he had volunteered for altruistic reasons. It is probably safe to assume that the men in this study are not representative of the entire range of domestically violent men. For example, they were probably not from the group of antisocial abusers who have little capacity to feel guilt (Hart, Dutton, & Newlove, 1993). The majority of men who are domestically violent do experience moral conflict, however, and examination of the experiences of the men in this study may have important implications for stopping the violence in this segment of the population.

Initial submission: January 15, 1997
Initial acceptance: March 10, 1997
Final acceptance: May 19, 1997

REFERENCES

Addison, R. B. (1989). Evaluating an interpretive account. In M. J. Packer & R. B. Addison (Eds.), *Entering the circle: Hermeneutic investigation in psychology* (pp. 39–59). Albany, NY: State University of New York Press.

Arias, I., & Beach, R. H. (1987). Validity of self-reports of marital violence. *Journal of Family Violence, 2,* 139–149.

Babcock, J. C., Waltz, J., Jacobson, N. S., & Gottman, J. M. (1992). Power and violence: The relation between communication patterns, power discrepancies, and domestic violence. *Journal of Consulting and Clinical Psychology, 61,* 40–50.

Bandura, A. (1973) *Aggression: A social learning analysis.* Englewood Cliffs, NJ: Prentice-Hall.

Bandura, A. (1979). The social learning perspective: Mechanisms of aggression. In H. Toch (Ed.), *Psychology of crime and criminal justice* (pp. 01 125). New York: Holt, Rinehart & Winston.

Barnett, O. W., & Hamberger, L. K. (1992). The assessment of maritally violent men on the California Personality Inventory. *Violence and Victims, 7,* 15–28.

Beasley, R., & Stoltenberg, C. D. (1992). Personality characteristics of male spouse abusers. *Professional Psychology, 13,* 310–317.

Beier, B. F., & Pollio, H. R. (1994). A thematic analysis of the experience of being in a role. *Sociological Spectrum, 14,* 257–272.

Bersani, C. A., Chen, H. T., Pendleton, B. F., & Denton, R. (1992). Personality traits of convicted male batterers. *Journal of Family Violence, 7,* 123–134.

Bleicher, J. (1980). *Contemporary hermeneutics as method, philosophy and critique.* London: Routledge & Kegan Paul.

Cappel, C., & Heiner, R. B. (1990). The intergenerational transmission of family aggression. *Journal of Family Violence, 9,* 157–175.

Colaizzi, P. F. (1973). *Reflections and research in psychology.* Dubuque, IA: Kendall Hunt.

Colaizzi, P. F. (1978). Psychological research as the phenomenologist views it. In R. S. Valle & M. King (Eds.), *Existential-phenomenological alternatives for psychology* (pp. 48–71). New York: Oxford University Press.

Dobash, R. E., & Dobash, R. (1979). *Violence against wives: A case against the patriarchy.* New York: Free Press.

Doumas, D., Margolin, G., & John, R. S. (1994). The intergenerational transmission of aggression across three generations. *Journal of Family Violence, 9,* 157–175.

Dutton, D. G. (1988). *Domestic assault of women.* Boston: Allyn and Bacon.

Dutton, D. G., & Starzomski, A. J. (1993). Borderline personality in perpetrators of psychological and physical abuse. *Violence and Victims, 8,* 327–337.

Fischer, C. T., & Wertz, F. J. (1979). Empirical phenomenological analyses of being criminally victimized. In A. Giorgi, R. Knowles, & D. L. Smith (Eds.), *Duquesne studies in phenomenological psychology* (Vol. 3, pp. 135–158). Pittsburgh, PA: Duquesne University Press.

Fischer, W. F. (1989). An empirical-phenomenological investigation of being anxious: An example of the phenomenological approach to emotion. In R. S. Valle & S. Halling (Eds.), *Existential-phenomenological perspectives in psychology: Exploring the breadth of human experience* (pp. 99–112). New York: Plenum Press.

Flournoy, P. S., & Wilson, G. L. (1991). Assessment of MMPI profiles of male batterers. *Violence and Victims, 6,* 309–320.

Gadamer, H. (1976). *Philosophical hermeneutics.* Berkeley, CA: University of California Press.

Giorgi, A. (1975a). An application of phenomenological method in psychology. In A. Giorgi, C. Fischer, & E. Murray (Eds.), *Duquesne studies in phenomenological psychology* (Vol. 2, pp. 82–103). Pittsburgh, PA: Duquesne University Press.

Giorgi, A. (1975b). Convergence and divergence of qualitative and quantitative methods in psychology. In A. Giorgi, C. Fischer, & E. Murray (Eds.), *Duquesne studies in phenomenological psychology* (vol. 2, pp. 72–79). Pittsburgh, PA: Duquesne University Press.

Giorgi, A. (1989). Learning and memory from the perspective of phenomenological psychology. In R. S. Valle & S. Halling (Eds.), *Existential–phenomenological perspectives in psychology: Exploring the breadth of human experience* (pp. 99–112). New York: Plenum.

Golledge, C. P., & Pollio, H. R. (1995). Themes in the experience of language. *Journal of Psycholinguistic Research, 24,* 79–100.

Guba, E. G., & Lincoln, Y. S. (1989). *Fourth generation evaluation.* Newbury Park, CA: Sage.

Halling, S. (1979). Eugene O'Neill's understanding of forgiveness. In A. Giorgi, R. Knowles, & D. L. Smith (Eds.), *Duquesne studies in phenomenological psychology* (Vol. 3, pp. 193–208). Pittsburgh, PA: Duquesne University Press.

Hart, S. D., Dutton, D. G., & Newlove, T. (1993). The prevalence of personality disorder amongst wife assaulters. *Journal of Personality Disorders, 7,* 329–341.

Heidegger, M. (1962). *Being and time* (J. Macquarrie & E. Robinson, Trans.). New York: Harper & Row. (Original work published 1927)

Holtzworth-Monroe, A., & Anglin, K. (1991). The competency of responses given by maritally violent versus non-violent men to problematic marital situations. *Violence and Victims, 6,* 257–269.

Holtzworth-Monroe, A., & Hutchinson, G. (1993). Attributing negative intent to wife behavior: The attributions of maritally violent versus non-violent men. *Journal of Abnormal Psychology, 102,* 206–211.

Jager, B. (1979). Dionysos and the world of passion. In A. Giorgi, R. Knowles, & D. L. Smith (Eds.), *Duquesne studies in phenomenological psychology* (Vol. 3, pp. 209–226). Pittsburgh, PA: Duquesne University Press.

Kvale, S. (1983). The qualitative research interview. *Journal of Phenomenological Psychology, 14,* 171–196.

Merleau-Ponty, M. (1989). *Phenomenology of perception* (C. Smith, Trans.). London: Routledge Press. (Original work published 1962)

Murphy, C. M., Meyer, S., & O'Leary, K. D. (1993). Family of origin violence and MCMI-II psychopathology among partner assaultive men. *Violence and Victims, 8,* 165–176.

Murphy, C. M., Meyer, S., & O'Leary, K. D. (1994). Dependency characteristics of partner assaultive men. *Journal of Abnormal Psychology, 103,* 729–735.

Polkinghorne, D. E. (1988). *Narrative knowing and the human sciences.* New York: State University of New York Press.

Polkinghorne, D. E. (1989). Phenomenological research methods. In R. S. Valle & S. Halling (Eds.), *Existential phenomenological perspectives in psychology: Exploring the breadth of human experience* (pp. 41–60). New York: Plenum Press.

Pollio, H. R., Henley, T., & Thompson, C. (1997). *The phenomenology of everyday life.* Cambridge: Cambridge University Press.

Romanyshyn, R. D., & Whalen, B. J. (1989). Psychology and the attitude of science. In R. S. Valle & S. Halling (Eds.), *Existential phenomenological perspectives in psychology: Exploring the breadth of human experience* (pp. 17–39). New York: Plenum Press.

Smith, M. D. (1990). Patriarchal ideology and wife beating: A test of a feminist hypothesis. *Violence and Victims, 5,* 257–273.

Stith, S. M., & Farley, S. C. (1993). A predictive model of male spousal violence. *Journal of Family Violence, 8,* 183–201.

Thompson, C., Locander, W., & Pollio, H. R. (1989). Putting consumer experience back in consumer research: The philosophy and method of existential-phenomenology. *Journal of Consumer Research, 16,* 133–147.

U.S. Department of Justice. (1984). *Attorney General's Task Force on Family Violence.* Washington, DC: U.S. Government Printing Office.

U.S. Department of Justice. (1995). *National crime victimization survey.* Washington, DC: U.S. Government Printing Office.

Valle, R. S., King, M., & Halling, S. (1989). An introduction to existential-phenomenological thought in psychology. In R. S. Valle & S. Halling (Eds.), *Existential phenomenological perspectives in psychology: Exploring the breadth of human experience* (pp. 3–16). New York: Plenum Press.

van Kaam, A. (1969). *Existential foundations of psychology.* New York: Image Books.

Walker, L. E. (1979). *The battered woman.* New York: Harper & Row.

Zimbardo, P. G. (1969). The human choice: Individuation, reason, and order versus deindividuation, impulse, and chaos. In W. J. Arnold & D. Levine (Eds.), *Nebraska symposium on motivation* (Vol. 17). Lincoln: University of Nebraska Press.

EXISTENTIAL PHENOMENOLOGY AND FEMINIST RESEARCH

The Exploration and Exposition of Women's Lived Experiences

Michael G. Garko
Tampa, Florida

The literature on feminist research methods is passionate and scrappy. When reading or participating in the dialogue on the content and conduct of feminist research, one cannot help being intellectually and emotionally energized. Yet, mixed in with this fervent and lively debate is a substantial amount of conceptual disarray on what should be the presuppositions, principles, and practices of feminist empirical research.

Writers have attempted to clear up the inconsistencies and misunderstandings surrounding the theory and practice of feminist research by addressing methodological issues. Ironically, when answers are given for methodological questions they are often too general, abstract, and limiting to be either theoretically useful or easily converted into feminist research practices (Jayaratne & Stewart, 1991). Feminist scholars believe that methodological discussions should be less esoteric and more concrete in connecting theoretical principles to pragmatic issues and recommendations supporting a feminist praxis to empirical research (see essays in Maynard & Purvis, 1994).

In the hope of not being recondite and adding to the conceptual confusion often characterizing the dialogue on feminist research methods, the purpose of this commentary is to show how existential phenomenology is methodologically compatible with some important feminist values and principles underpinning feminist research and how Reitz's piece, "Batterers' Experiences of Being Violent," is an exemplar of a feminist empirical study using existential phenomenology as a theoretical framework and empirical method to explore violence against women.

Address correspondence and reprint requests to: Michael Garko, 2534 Ranch Lake Circle, Lutz, FL 33549. E-mail: garko@ix.netcom.com

LINES OF COMPATIBILITY BETWEEN A FEMINIST RESEARCH
PERSPECTIVE AND EXISTENTIAL PHENOMENOLOGY

The discussion that follows sketches five lines of comparison between a feminist approach to research and existential phenomenology and shows how the existential-phenomenological features of Reitz's study fulfills some of the more important paradigmatic criteria of a feminist research perspective.

Women's Everyday Experiences

Investigating and understanding the everyday world of women's experiences is paramount to feminism and feminist research (e.g., Stanley & Wise, 1993). Stanley and Wise (1993) reflected the prevailing view of feminists when they contended that what is needed is "a woman's language, a language of experience. And this must come from our exploration of the personal, the everyday, and what we experience—women's lived experiences" (p. 146).

Exploration and Exposition of the Life-World
Existential phenomenology is well suited to satisfy the lived-experience criterion of a feminist approach to researching women's lives. Synthesizing existentialism's focus on concrete existence and phenomenology's quest to develop a method for examining existence, existential phenomenology attempts to explore and expose the meaning of phenomena in the life-world, the realm of day-to-day lived experiences prereflectively encountered in consciousness (i.e., consciousness unaware of itself).

Just as lived experiences are fundamental to feminism, so are they similarly crucial to existential phenomenology. "The life-world is the foundation upon which existential-phenomenological thought is built" (Valle & Halling, 1989, p. 9). Everyday lived experience is the beginning and ending point of understanding existential-phenomenological thought and research (Valle & Halling, 1989).

Misinterpretation and Concealment of Women's Experiences

The feminist critique of social science charges that women's lives have been studied from a positivistic, patriarchal paradigm, which has no existential connection to the personal, that is, the world of lived experiences (e.g., Stanley & Wise, 1993). For feminists, displacing the personal with the positivistic has contributed to women's everyday experiences being misconstrued or concealed. A chorus of feminist voices calls for openness and the use of descriptive methods to explore women's experiences. Among the reasons given in arguing for descriptive methods is that they give women the opportunity to talk about their experiences in their own voices; they are understanding based and not explanatory based; and they "do not break living connections in the way that quantitative methods do" (Mies, 1991, p. 67). Thus, in attempting to overcome the misinterpretation and concealment of women's experiences, a feminist research perspective advocates a commitment to openness, description, and understanding, qualities that characterize existential phenomenology.

Description and Understanding

Existential phenomenology is conducive to investigating unexplored and misinterpreted experiences because its methods and procedures are intended to describe and understand phenomena rather than to explain experiences in order to predict and control them. Existential phenomenologists rely on description "to let that which shows itself be seen from itself in the very way in which it shows itself from itself" (Heidegger, 1962, p. 58). They support Heidegger's assertion that a natural scientific explanation is no existential match for a human scientific description of what it means to be human. Moreover, existential phenomenologists uphold Heidegger's belief that abandoning description for scientific reductionism to get "to the things themselves" runs the risk of a person's existence becoming "hidden," "concealed," "disguised, " or "covered up." This captures precisely what feminist scholars say has happened to women's lives and experiences.

Openness and Objectivity

Gaining understanding through descriptive means requires openness and objectivity (in the phenomenological sense). Existential phenomenology is open because it studies phenomena from the perspective of those being researched. Existential phenomenologists do not pack up a research toolbox filled with ready-made interpretive categories based on conventional theories or studies to go off and discover the meaning of phenomena. Instead, they explore what lived experiences mean from the existential vantage point and in the language of the experiencing person. Relatedly, existential phenomenology is objective because it describes human experience on its own terms and not in operationally defined terms. From a phenomenological perspective, "*objectivity is fidelity to phenomena*. It is a refusal to tell the phenomenon what it is, but a respectful listening to what the phenomenon speaks of itself" (Colaizzi, 1978, p. 52).

To sum up, what makes existential phenomenology useful in studying the misinterpreted and concealed experiences of women is its devotion to description and understanding, its openness to the life-world, and its celebration of experience and the experiencing person, letting both speak so as to let the existential chips of meaning fall where they may.

Feminist Consciousness

The concept of consciousness is foundational to the feminist movement in that it is deeply implicated in feminist thinking about women's experiences and lives, how women perceive and make sense of the world, and research methods unique to the study of women. "What is essential to 'being feminist' is the possession of 'feminist consciousness'" (Stanley & Wise, 1993, p. 32).

Bartky (1077) contended that becoming a feminist involves a profound personal transformation in behavior and consciousness. For Bartky and other feminists, becoming a feminist is to have a "radically altered consciousness" about oneself, others, and the world. "Feminists themselves have a name for the struggle to clarify and to hold fast to this way of apprehending things: they call it 'consciousness-raising'" (Bartky, 1977, p. 23), considered to be a goal of feminist research and a feminist research method in and of itself (e.g., Kelly, Burton, & Regan, 1994).

Intentional Consciousness

From an existential-phenomenological perspective, consciousness is what connects humans to existence. It is how they relate to and intentionally give meaning to phenomena. "Whatever falls outside of consciousness . . . falls outside the bounds of our possible lived experience" (Van Manen, 1990, p. 9). Hence, existential phenomenology can be defined as "the reflective study and explication of the operative and thematic structures of consciousness, i.e., primarily a philosophical method of explicating the meaning of the phenomena of consciousness" (von Eckartsberg, 1986, p. 4).

It is not just existential phenomenology's interest in consciousness but also its construal of consciousness as intentional that further aligns it with a feminist research perspective. Consciousness being intentional implies that it is always directed toward some object. For example, when we perceive or touch, we perceive or touch someone or something. Hence, existential phenomenology conceives of an indissoluble link between one's conscious mind and that of which one is conscious. In other words, the subject–object dichotomy, assumed in positivistic social science, is not part of existential-phenomenological thought. Nor is it part of a feminist research perspective. It will be seen that the feminist critique of social science rejects the assumption that the individual and the world, generally, and the subject and object of research, specifically, are independent of one another.

Relationship Between the Subject and Object of Research

The feminist critique of social science denounces the assumption that there is an objective reality that sits in wait to be discovered by the knower and the assumption that the knower is separated from the known, a to-be-discovered objective reality (e.g., Nielsen, 1990). The intent of these assumptions is to have the researcher become a neutral observer who studies detachedly the objects of research with "antiseptic," scientific, distancing procedures so as not to "infect" the objective truth with the "contaminant" of subjectivity.

In contrast, feminists define research as a dialogue between the researcher and research participant. "Both are assumed to be individuals who reflect upon their experience and who can communicate those reflections" (Acker, Barry, & Esseveld, 1983, p. 427). Moreover, feminists recognize that in the dialogue between the subject and object of research there is reciprocal influence and the mutual exchange of knowledge and experience (e.g., Shields & Dervin, 1993). That is, the researcher and the researched are dialogical collaborators who are intersubjectively and dialectically linked.

Coconstitutionality

Just as feminism denounces the objectivity assumption and the subject–object dichotomy assumption so too does existential phenomenology. Based on the notion that consciousness is intentional, existential phenomenology sees the relationship between the individual and the world as being interdependent and dialogically coconstituted (Merleau-Ponty, 1945/1962, p. 410). It is through communication that the individual and the world become inextricably and "meaning-fully" united.

When the principle of coconstitutionality is applied to a research setting, existential-phenomenological research emerges as dialogical research and the vocabulary of "subject" and "object" is no longer operative. Existential-phenomenological research takes place between "coresearchers" who communicatively cocreate their relationship. According to Colaizzi (1978), dialogical research lets coresearchers reveal the existential and personal dimensions and conditions of their lives, which could not previously be easily examined but now can be interrogated and interpreted. This reinforces the earlier argument on the ability of phenomenological methods to help reveal the concealed and misinterpreted experiences of women.

Hence, existential phenomenology and a feminist research perspective are compatible in the way they conceive the relationship between the subject and object of research. Both assume the researcher and researched are interdependently and humanly linked and not individualistically and mechanically separated, that existential truth and meaning are gained through the intersubjectivity of the subject and object and that the relationship between the subject and object is a dialectical and dialogical relationship (e.g., Lopman, 1988).

Suspending the Taken for Granted

One of the principal assumptions underpinning the debate on the theory and practice of feminism and feminist research is that in order for women to overcome the social forces of a male-oriented culture they must change the accepted value systems of societies' institutions, especially those of science. The primary reason for transforming societies' patriarchal values is that the meaning women attribute to their experiences finds its genesis in women's consciousness, which is influenced by the cultural values of men (Lopman, 1988).

Bracketing

Feminist researchers believe that, if they are to challenge the taken-for-granted male-oriented values of society and transform societies' institutions, themselves, and other women, they must suspend their own taken-for-granted beliefs and presuppositions about the world as they attempt to explore and expose the meaning of women's lived experiences. In phenomenological terms, they must bracket their natural attitude so that they can connect with women's consciousness.

The natural attitude is bracketed because it biases and distorts researchers' perceptions as to what to see and how to see it. Failing to suspend one's taken-for-granted presuppositions represents the existential kiss of death in researching lived experiences. Hence, the natural attitude is put into abeyance "in order to launch the [existential-phenomenological] study as far as possible free of preconceptions, beliefs, and knowledge of the phenomenon from prior experience and professional studies—to be completely open, receptive, and naive in listening to and hearing research participants describe their experience of the phenomenon being investigated" (Moustakas, 1994, p. 22).

In terms of a feminist research orientation, bracketing the natural attitude allows researchers to describe and understand women's lives from the coresearchers' viewpoint, to perceive women's lived experiences with greater existential depth and breadth, and to see hidden sides and meanings of women's lived experiences made obscure by idiosyncratic and conventional ways of viewing the world. Du-

Bois (1983) advised feminist researchers to see what is there and not what they have been taught is there or what they might desire to be there so they can discover and uncover the facts of women's lived experiences.

AN EXISTENTIAL-PHENOMENOLOGICAL
EXEMPLAR OF FEMINIST RESEARCH

Reitz's study exemplifies how existential phenomenology can serve as a methodological framework to examine women's lives and experiences. The rationale for Reitz's investigation; her selection of the research participants; her relationship to the participants; the procedures she used to collect, analyze, and interpret the data; and her findings reflect an existential-phenomenological approach to exploring and exposing one of the most disturbing and dehumanizing experiences in the lives of women, the battering of women by men.

Rationale for the Study

Reitz's investigation deviates from the traditional approach of asking women to report on the male batterer's experience of being violent. Instead, she attempts "to supply the missing information" of what it means to be domestically violent from the batterer's perspective. As an existential phenomenologist, Reitz knows that in order to understand fully the meaning structure of a phenomenon such as domestic violence a researcher must remain open to all of the existential dimensions of a phenomenon and to the perspective of those who experience it.

Selecting Research Participants

In choosing research participants, Reitz did not use the positivistic criterion of randomly selecting the "right" number of subjects so that she could generalize from her sample to the general population. "Phenomenology does not allow for empirical generalizations, the production of law-like statements, or the establishment of functional relationships. The only generalization allowed by phenomenology is this: "'Never generalize!'" (Van Manen, 1990, p. 82).

Reitz chose the participants in her study on the basis of their having experience with the phenomenon of domestic violence and the ability to talk about it from their perspective. The starting point for an existential-phenomenological study is the coresearchers' personal experience with the phenomenon being investigated and not the adequate number of randomly chosen subjects to conduct statistical tests of significance to confirm or disconfirm hypotheses and make generalizations.

Relationship to the Researched

Reitz identified the participants in her study as coresearchers and the real experts of her investigation. She considers the relationship between the researcher and the researched to be a dialogic one that is coconstituted. Therefore, in keeping with the principle of coconstitutionality and the view that dialogue is the most natural way to obtain a proper description of human experience, Reitz conducted open-ended and unstructured interviews.

Collecting, Analyzing, and Interpreting the Data

Reitz's approach to collecting, analyzing, and interpreting the data reflects existential-phenomenology's belief that "the task of the researcher is to let the world of the describer . . . reveal itself through . . . description" (Giorgi, 1975, p. 74). According to Giorgi (1975), this task can be accomplished by the processes of bracketing, intuiting, and describing, which Reitz performs in her study.

Attempting to set aside her own presuppositions regarding domestic violence, Reitz invoked four bracketing procedures: (a) Conducting a bracketing interview with the researcher, (b) using an interpretative research group, (c) negotiating the description of the phenomenon with coresearchers, and (d) rendering themes in the experience-near language of the coresearchers.

Intuiting involves delineating protocols into their constituent meaning units and assessing their dominant meanings. The goal is to transform a *phenomenal description* of the meaning units into a *phenomenological understanding* of the meaning of the phenomenon (Aanstoos, 1985).

Describing engages the researcher in an idiographic and nomothetic interpretation of the data. With the former, protocols are analyzed for their situated structure and thematized. With the latter, the goal is to see if the generated themes are supported by the data and if the data are represented by the themes.

Summarizing, Reitz performed bracketing procedures to suspend the taken for granted in order to illuminate the phenomenon of domestic violence from the batterer's perspective. More specifically, she used bracketing in order to reach a phenomenological understanding of the violence perpetrated against women as it is prereflectively experienced in the consciousness of male batterers.

Findings

As an existential-phenomenological study, Reitz's findings are not meant to solve the problem of domestic violence. Instead, they are intended to clarify the lived meaning of the male batterers' experience of being violent against women. What is posed in an existential-phenomenological study are meaning questions and not problem-solving questions (Van Manen, 1990). This is not to say that Reitz's phenomenological findings do not contribute to improving the human condition or provide insight into what social or therapeutic action to take for domestic violence. For example, her findings suggest that treatment interventions might be more effective if more attention were given to the kinds of dualities (e.g., good or bad, winning or losing) batterers used to compare themselves with their partners and to form unequal and opposing identities, which seem to be at the existential core of batterers' experience of being violent. In short, Reitz' findings help illuminate the perplexing nature of the lived experience of men being violent against women.

CONCLUSIONS

I have attempted to illustrate how existential phenomenology is harmonious with a feminist approach to empirical research. Although the five feminist themes featured in this commentary are not the only ones in feminist scholarship, they represent some of the more defining and enduring issues surrounding feminism and a feminist approach to research. Shields and Dervin (1993) assert that methodologies used in feminist empirical work must strive to incorporate "the overarching themes that run through feminist theory" (p. 65). The evidence provided in this commentary strongly supports the view that existential phenomenology embraces feminist theory and a feminist perspective on the content and conduct of research. Moreover, it demonstrates that existential phenomenology is axiologically in tune with the single most important criterion of a feminist approach to research—valuing women's lived experiences.

Reitz's investigation of domestic violence is an exemplar of how existential phenomenology can be used to examine feminist issues. It shows the extent to which the various features of existential phenomenology complement and enhance the practice of feminist research and how those features are actually implemented in a study. Finally, Reitz's research demonstrates that feminist researchers can acquire an enriched understanding of the life-world of women by adopting an existential-phenomenological perspective.

REFERENCES

Aanstoos, C. M. (1985). The structure of thinking in chess. In A. Giorgi (Ed.), *Phenomenology and psychological research* (pp. 86–117). Pittsburgh, PA: Duquesne University Press.

Acker, J., Barry, K., & Esseveld, J. (1983). Objectivity and truth: Problems in doing feminist research. *Women's Studies Forum, 6,* 423–435.

Bartky, S. (1977). Toward a phenomenolgy of feminist consciousness. In M. V. Braggin, F. Elliston, & J. English (Eds.), *Feminism and philosophy* (pp. 23–47). Totowa, NJ: Littlefield, Adams.

Colaizzi, P. F. (1978). Psychological research as the phenomenologist views it. In R. S. Valle & M. King (Eds.), *Existential-phenomenological alternatives for psychology* (pp. 48–71). New York: Simon & Schuster.

DuBois, B. (1983). Passionate scholarship: Notes on values, knowing and method in social science. In G. Bowles & R. D. Klein (Eds.), *Theories of women's studies* (pp. 105–116). Boston: Routledge & Kegan Paul.

Giorgi, A. (1975). Convergence and divergence of qualitative and quantitative methods in psychology. In A. Giorgi, C. Fischer, & E. Murray (Eds.), *Duquesne studies in phenomenological psychology* (Vol. 2, pp. 72–79). Pittsburgh, PA: Duquesne University Press.

Heidegger, M. (1962). *Being and time.* New York: Harper & Row.

Jayaratne, T. E., & Stewart, A. (1991). Quantitative and qualitative methods in the social sciences: Current feminist issues and practical strategies. In M. M. Fonow & J. A. Cook (Eds.), *Beyond methodology: Feminist scholarship as lived research* (pp. 85–106). Bloomington, IN: Indiana University Press.

Kelly, L., Burton, S., & Regan L. (1994). Researching women's lives or studying women's oppression? Reflections on what constitutes feminist research. In M. Maynard & J. Purvis (Eds.), *Researching women's lives from a feminist perspective* (pp. 27–48). Bristol, PA: Taylor & Francis.

Lopman, L. L. (1988). *Claiming reality: Phenomenology and women's experiences.* Totowa, NJ: Rowman & Littlefield.

Maynard, M., & Purvis, J. (Eds.). (1994). *Researching women's lives from a feminist perspective.* London: Taylor & Francis.

Merleau-Ponty, M. (1962). *Phenomenology and perception* (C. Smith, Trans.). London: Routledge & Kegan Paul. (Original work published 1945)

Mies, M. (1991). Women's research or feminist research? The debate surrounding feminist science and methodology. In M. M. Fonow & J. A. Cook (Eds.), *Beyond methodology: Feminist scholarship as lived research* (pp. 60–84). Bloomington, IN: Indiana University Press.

Moustakas, C. (1994). *Phenomenological research methods*. Thousand Oaks, CA: Sage.

Nielsen, J. (Ed.). (1990). *Feminist research methods: Exemplary readings in the social sciences.* San Francisco: Westview Press.

Shields, V. R., & Dervin, B. (1993). Sense-making in feminist social science research: A call to enlarge the methodological options of feminist studies. *Women's Studies Forum, 16,* 65–81.

Stanley, L., & Wise, S. (1993). *Breaking out again.* London: Routledge.

Valle, R. S., & Halling, S. (1989). *Existential-phenomenological perspectives in psychology: Exploring the breadth of human experience.* New York: Plenum Press.

Van Manen, M. (1990). *Researching lived experience: Human science for an action sensitive pedagogy.* Albany, NY: State University of New York Press.

von Eckartsberg, R. (1986). *Life-world experience: Existential-phenomenological research approaches in psychology.* Washington, DC: Center for Advanced Research in Phenomenology & University Press of America.

BEYOND THE MEASUREMENT TRAP

A Reconstructed Conceptualization and Measurement of Woman Battering

Paige Hall Smith
University of North Carolina at Greensboro

Jason B. Smith
Family Health International

Jo Anne L. Earp
University of North Carolina at Chapel Hill

Many areas of women's health, including battering, suffer from conceptual and methodological deficits. This article uses the "measurement trap" (Graham & Campbell, 1991), a set of conditions defined by lack of information resulting from a narrow conceptualization of the problem, poor existing data sources, inappropriate outcome indicators, and limited measurement techniques, as a framework for describing how current approaches to conceptualizing and measuring battering hamper research and program efforts in the field of domestic violence. We then describe an alternative conceptualization-and-measurement approach that is based on battered women's experiences. We argue that an experiential approach, which grounds measurement in women's lived experiences, improves our ability to conduct research that correctly identifies, monitors, and explains the epidemiology of this phenomenon and provides a solid basis for policy and program development.

An earlier version of this article was presented at the annual conference of the National Council for International Health, June 1995. Partial funding for the research described in this article was provided by the Agency for Health Care Policy and Research (Dissertation Grant Award) and the University of North Carolina at Chapel Hill.

We would like to thank Robert DeVellis and Irene Tessaro for their contributions to this work and Anne Menkens for her editorial assistance.

Address correspondence and reprint requests to: Paige Hall Smith, Public Health, UNCG, P.O. Box 26169, Greensboro, NC 27402-6169. E-mail: Paige_Smith@uncg.edu, jbsmith@fhi.org, or Joanne_Earp@unc.edu

177

Violence against women by their male partners affects millions of women worldwide. Research in the United States indicates that each year an estimated 2 to 4 million women are battered by their husbands or boyfriends and that between 21% and 34% of all American women will be physically assaulted by a male partner at least once in their lifetime (Louis Harris & Associates, 1993). Research in developing countries suggests that the percentages of women battered globally is certainly no lower than this and perhaps is even higher in some countries (Heise, Pitanguy, & Germain, 1994). Today, private violence is increasingly recognized around the world as a major public health problem in light of growing evidence that the physical, psychological, and often sexual violence inflicted on battered women contributes to the development of many acute and chronic health problems (Heise et al., 1994; Koss et al., 1994). Battering also inflicts a social and financial burden on society including increased health care usage and costs, lost work productivity, increased poverty, and retarded social and economic development. The World Bank (1993) estimates that the global health burden from gender-based victimization among women aged 15–44 is comparable to that posed by other risk factors and diseases such as HIV/AIDS, tuberculosis, sepsis during childbirth, cancer, and cardiovascular disease.

To monitor accurately the epidemiology of male violence against women and develop effective prevention and intervention programs, available data must portray this phenomenon correctly and completely. Unfortunately, domestic violence, like some other women's health issues, suffers from conceptual and methodological problems (Dobash, Dobash, Wilson, & Daly, 1992; Koss et al., 1994; Skogan, 1981; Smith, Earp, & DeVellis, 1995). In describing the conditions that constrain research on women's health, Wendy Campbell and Oona Graham, with the Maternal and Child Epidemiology Unit of the London School of Hygiene and Tropical Medicine, outlined a set of conditions known as the "measurement trap" (Graham & Campbell, 1991). This "trap" is sprung when a narrow conceptualization of the problem combines with poor data sources, inappropriate outcome indicators, and limited measurement techniques in a cycle that leads to distorted information and neglect, hampering both programmatic and further research efforts.

The issue of battering is a specific example of how the measurement trap constrains women's health research. Using the measurement trap as a framework, this article describes the current approach to measuring battering that constrains research in the field and then offers an alternative conceptualization and measurement approach. The alternative approach draws on research we have conducted with battered women in the United States to derive a qualitative conceptual framework and quantitative measurement instrument that reflect the experiences of battered women from their own perspectives (Smith, Earp et al., 1995; Smith, Tessaro, & Earp, 1995).

CURRENT APPROACHES TO CONCEPTUALIZING AND MEASURING BATTERING

Conceptualization is the prime component of the measurement trap. It refers generally to the process of defining the essential characteristics of a phenomenon and formulating ideas on the topic for the construction of theory and testing of

Table 1

Conceptualizing and Measuring Battering: A Framework for Analysis

	Measurement Trap	*Untrapping Measurement*
Battering Conceptualization		
• Events orientation	Discrete events	Continuous process
• Treatment of gender	Neglect of gender	Gendered experience
• Time interval	Bounded by occurrence of assaults	Exposure to victimization and exercise of power
Measurement techniques	Emphasis on events	Emphasis on experience
	Emphasis on physical assault	Contextualized
	Acute condition	Chronic condition
Outcome indicators	Fatal injury	Fatal injury
	Nonfatal injury	Nonfatal injury
		Physical health
		Mental health
		Social health
Data sources	Injury surveillance	Multiple sources of surveillance

hypotheses. Graham and Campbell's (1991) research revealed that a weak conceptual framework lies at the center of the measurement trap hampering women's health research. Although the other three components have their own problems independent of conceptualization, an incorrect conceptualization will necessarily constrain the development of appropriate outcome measures, useful data sources, and valid measurement techniques (Graham & Campbell, 1991). Outcome indicators both influence and are influenced by conceptualizations and definitions, whereas conceptual approaches provide validity for the use of particular measurement instruments and data sources.

Graham and Campbell (1991) outlined three factors that shape a weak conceptualization: events orientation, the treatment of gender, and a narrow time interval. In their discussion of women's health generally, Graham and Campbell (1991) noted that the field has tended to conceptualize women's health as a discrete, negative state characterized by physical rather than social or mental manifestations. It has focused on the maternal role and, in the process, reduced an analytic span to the narrow time intervals shaped by pregnancy, delivery, and postpartum. Current approaches to measuring battering can be analyzed in terms of these three factors (see Table 1).

Events orientation refers generally to framing a health problem in terms of easily observable events. Researchers have a long history of equating battering with the events of physical assault (Dobash et al., 1992; Hudson & McIntosh, 1981; Shepard & Campbell, 1992; Straus, 1979), which predisposes them to measure battering by focusing on male behavior. This behavioral approach has three implications for our conceptualization of battering. First, it drives researchers to pay attention to events, not to people. Second, it allows us to consider and evaluate these events exclusive of their meaning to the victim or perpetrator; and, third, it removes them from the social context within which they occurred (Agudelo, 1992; Dobash et al., 1992; Skogan, 1981).

The second of Graham and Campbell's (1991) factors that shape a narrow conceptualization of the problem is the treatment of gender. They argue that researchers of women's health overuse gender as a conceptual frame, thus overemphasizing reproductive health and neglecting other important health concerns of women (e.g., cardiovascular disease) and men's roles in such reproductive health issues as family planning, contraception, and infertility. In contrast, the conventional approach to the conceptualization and measurement of battering neglects gender. The prevailing focus on events rather than people encourages a gender-neutral analysis of assaultive events and the erroneous conclusion that the conditions of women's lives are the same as those of men or that any differences are not germane to an understanding of the issues (Browne & Williams, 1993).

The third factor influencing conceptualization, according to Graham and Campbell (1991), is a *narrow time interval*. The time frame of interest in the conventional conceptualization of battering is the time during which the assault occurs. Thus, battering becomes equated with the time period defined by the beginning and ending of the assault, or set of assaults, be it a minute, an hour, or a day. This sharp bounding of battering in time and space (Skogan, 1981) implies that battering does not exist outside or between these intervals and furthers the expectation that we can analyze acts of assault or aggression outside the social context in which the aggression occurs and separate it from the interpretations applied by those directly affected (Skogan, 1981).

The current conceptual emphasis on episodes of physical assault leads naturally to a proliferation of measurement instruments that focus on the incidence and frequency of discrete events such as hitting, slapping, kicking, and beating (McFarlane, Parker, Soeken, & Bullock, 1992; Shepard & Campbell, 1992; Straus, 1979). Although a few instruments measure psychological abuse, these are not widely used or are used in tandem with measures of physical assault (Hudson & McIntosh, 1981; Shepard & Campbell, 1992). Following from this, outcome indicators, and hence the data sources required, typically reflect fatal and nonfatal injury (Centers for Disease Control and Prevention, 1997; Rosenberg & Finley, 1991). The focus on physical injury, or consequences assessed, as the critical outcome indicator by which changes in incidence are monitored persists despite the burgeoning literature on the traumatic and social effects of battering (Heise et al., 1994; Koss et al., 1994; World Bank, 1993).

ARGUMENTS FOR AN ALTERNATIVE APPROACH

In the authors' view, the current approaches hamper, constrain, or otherwise distort research and intervention efforts in the field. Regarding events orientation, some researchers have argued that domestic violence may be better characterized as a continuous process than as a series of discrete events (see Table 1) (Avni, 1991; Ferraro & Johnson, 1993; Landenburger, 1989; Skogan, 1981; Smith, Earp et al., 1995). Skogan illustrated this point:

> Consider a family in which the father comes home drunk every night, regularly beats his wife and threatens his children, who may in turn be protodelinquents in their own

right. Occasionally the family may generate an official statistic, as when the wife defends herself with a kitchen knife, or when the collective noise level reaches such heights that the neighbors call the police. When a crime survey interviewer enters the scene, a different set of statistics might be generated. Neither recordkeeping system adequately captures the situation; each samples ongoing activities in select slices of time. (pp. 7–8)

The focus on events as opposed to the chronic condition leads researchers, as Agudelo (1992) put it, "to pay attention only to the level of appearances, or force, rather than to that 'essential something' that exists underneath force . . . [which] is merely the instrument or physical expression of what is really at stake, which is power" (p. 366). Agudelo further reasoned that a power imbalance is a prerequisite for violence and that, in theory, a greater imbalance is accompanied by a greater potential for violence. By remaining at the level of discrete events, researchers choose to ignore power imbalances that predate or follow the use of observable force by men or women in intimate relationships.

This lack of attention to power issues relates to the second factor, neglect of gender, and the trap it creates for researchers. This trap is revealed in the long-standing controversy over the "battered husband syndrome" and debates over women's roles as perpetrators of domestic violence (Dobash et al., 1992; Steinmetz, 1977–1978; Straus, Gelles, & Steinmetz, 1980). Because domestic violence assault data indicate a similarity in the frequency with which men and women assault each other (Straus, 1980; Straus et al., 1980; Sorenson & Telles, 1991; Sorenson, Upchurch, & Shen, 1996), gender-neutral analyses indicate that the violence is "mutual," that men and women have an equal tendency toward violence, and that women and men both participate in their own victimization (Dobash et al., 1992; Straus, 1980). This view confuses assocation with causality. It further assumes, as Browne and Williams (1993) articulated, that the conditions of women's lives are either similar to those of men's or are irrelevant to how each uses violence, implying that preexisting power imbalances and structural inequalities are not relevant to the analysis of the use of force.

If conditions of gender discrimination and power imbalances do shape the use of force, however, then gender colors the social meaning of assaults by women and men, just as social meanings are known to differentiate many objectively similar events. As Skogan (1981) illustrated,

> When civilians kill policemen it is a crime but when policemen kill civilians it is not; parents who strike their children "discipline" them, while children who strike their parents are committing a crime (in common sense terms) only if they are grown up. Teachers, on the other hand, cannot strike anyone—but a decade ago many kept paddles on their desks. (p. 9)

Some feminist researchers respond to explanations of "mutual combat" by arguing that researchers should view battered women's aggressive behavior within a victim-precipitation framework wherein women's violence is viewed as defensive in nature (Koss et al., 1994; Saunders & Browne, 1991). This perspective, however, is inadequate because it continues to analyze battering within an events-specific conceptualization in which the use of force remains isolated from social context. This approach

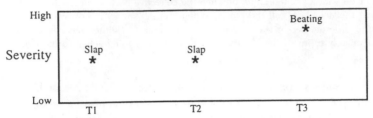

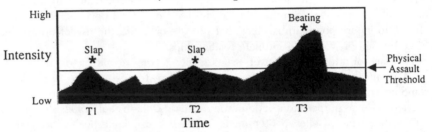

FIGURE 1. Two epidemiological views of battering.

still fails to capture the conditions, or issues of power, that give rise to the events, regardless of precipitation.

The third factor, a narrow time interval, also helps explain why the victim-precipitation framework fails to capture the social context. Once the connection between force and the underlying continuous experience of power imbalance has been severed, the only context one act of force has is another act of force. Hence, the defensiveness or offensiveness of one act of force is judged solely on its proximity to another act; those that occur in the absence of another act of force are assumed to be offensive, whereas those that follow are assumed to be defensive. Relating two distinct events whose association may be spurious or linked only by their relationship to a third unidentified factor violates one of the principle conditions of causality, that is, the elimination of rival causes—in this case, the underlying continuous condition of a gender power imbalance and inequality.

Taken together, the focus on discrete events, the exclusion of gender, and the use of a narrow time interval traps us into an acute epidemiological view of battering that makes for a weak conceptualization of the phenomenon (Figure 1). This conceptualization, in turn, affects, and is reinforced by, measurement techniques, outcome indicators, and data sources.

The means we use to generate or measure a phenomenon greatly affect our understanding of that phenomenon (DeVellis, Alfieri, & Ahluwalia, 1995). Researchers of battering who use conventional measurement instruments identify only the injurious events, an approach that fails to capture the chronicity of women's experience with battering. Consequently, the more we use discrete-event, assault-based measurement instruments to research domestic violence, the more convinced we become, from the body of knowledge available, that the narrow conceptualization is correct and independent (DeVellis et al., 1995).

The focus on injurious outcomes shapes even the framework some have used to provide a gendered analysis of domestic violence data. As Sorensen and colleagues (1996) write, "The validity and significance of gender symmetry in spousal violence are subjects of heated debate, yet parties on each side acknowledge that equal rates of perpetration, regardless of motivation, may not translate into equal rates of injury" (p. 35). This perspective suggests that the problem with the gender-neutral analysis is that it equates unarmed men's and women's potentials to harm and that a gendered analysis is found in the focus on outcomes (Koss et al., 1994; Sorenson et al., 1996). The reliance on discrete *injurious outcomes* as the frame for a gendered analysis, however, fails to capture the full range of empirically documented outcomes and how those differ by gender. It also fails to capture the gendered nature of the social context that gives rise to men's and women's use of assault.

UNTRAPPING MEASUREMENT

Grounding Conceptualization in Women's Experiences

The lesson of the measurement trap is that the development of a broader conceptual base is a prerequisite to good measurement. One approach to broadening the conceptualization of battering is to define it in the context of women's lives and to focus on battered women's experiences rather than on the discrete events of male behavior (Skogan, 1981; Smith, Earp et al., 1995; Smith, Tessaro et al., 1995). This continuous-process approach provides a way to incorporate into our measurement the meanings people attach to the events and the social context of the events (Skogan, 1981). Also, this approach opens up the time interval to reflect the victimization experience rather than the timing and duration of specific events, recognizing that the conditions of a battering relationship exist outside and between episodes of physical assault. This approach requires that the link between conceptualization and measurement be seamless and that the integrity of women's experiences be maintained from data collection through qualification.

In our own work on reconceptualizing battering according to battered women's experiences, we began by holding six focus groups in which battered women described their own experiences with abuse and what life was like for them. Because this first part of the study concerned understanding how battered women see their own world, the data were collected and initially analyzed from the perspective of empirical phenomenology (Fischer & Wertz, 1979; Smith, Tessaro et al., 1995). Two questions raised by Loeske (1992) in her research on the social construction of battering influenced this stage of the analysis: (a) what must be subjectively apprehended about an individual experience in order to classify it as one of battering; and (b) what must be subjectively apprehended about an individual woman in order to classify her as battered?

The coding process began with reading the 400 pages of transcribed data while simultaneously listening to the audiotapes of the focus groups in order to check the accuracy of the transcripts and make notes on the hard copy about the feelings expressed by the participants that could potentially be lost during transcription. The data were demarcated into units distinguishable as particular moments in the overall experience, resulting initially in 150 categories. Next, the experiences were revised by combining, separating, and recombining the categories into larger organizational clusters, with multiple different schema organizing the data.

The final organizing schema consisted of six domains representing the multidimensional nature of women's experiences with battering: perceived threat, managing, altered identity, yearning, entrapment, and disempowerment. These domains are interrelated and can be interpreted as a clustering of experiences around a common theme. Taken together, these six domains comprise a framework we called the Women's Experiences with Battering (WEB) Framework (Smith, Tessaro, et al., 1995). The WEB framework, by focusing on women's experiences, supplements knowledge of battering that has heretofore been shaped largely by its behavioral feature of physical assault.

The first domain, called perceived threat, reflects women's emotional (fear) and cognitive (danger) reactions to their environment. It reflects women's subjective perception of: susceptibility to future harm; the severity, distribution, and controllability of the risk; the controllability of their emotions in response to the event; and feelings of dread invoked by the risk. This domain combines the two concepts of perceived risk (susceptibility) and perceived severity integral to many social psychological theories, including the health belief model (Becker, 1974), theory of unique invulnerability (Perloff, 1983), protection motivation theory (Rogers, 1975), and the cognitive theory of stress and coping (Lazarus, 1966). The following words by a focus-group participant illustrate the domain of perceived threat:

> But each day I lived in fear. I was afraid he was gonna come in while I was taking . . . I would wait to take a shower. I would hurry up and wash up. I mean, I know I wasn't getting clean enough, under my arms, between my legs but that was it, because I had to make it a minute and a half, whatever you could do in that time because I was afraid he was gonna come in and just, you know, go off.

"Managing" follows from women's assessments of the danger of their situations. Once these women perceive their environment as stressful and assess the extent of the environment's harm or loss, threat or challenge, they take some form of direct action, inhibition of action, or intrapsychic coping behavior. This domain reflects Lazarus' (1966) cognitive theory of stress and coping and the concept of unique invulnerability, as well as women's outcome and efficacy expectations for their behavior. To avoid violence, women engage in behavior they think will be acceptable to their partners, trying to keep peace in the family and avoid giving men cause to be angry. The women's efforts fail to stop the violence, however, because it is the men who control the violence. Consequently, women in these situations spend an increasing amount of energy and take on increasing responsibility for suppressing the violent behavior. The following quotation reflects this experience:

> There was no way to tell [what was going to happen] because most of our arguments were not about anything serious . . . it was like "you got the wrong kind of bread" or

"I don't like that kinda candy bar." "Oh, you got the wrong beer!" And then I'd get beat for that and all night long, so I got to the point when I would go to the grocery store, if I wasn't sure about what to get him I would call home, "Now what kinda coffee was that you wanted?" Or, especially if they didn't have what he asked for, and you had to pick something else. I was like this—my hands are still shaking.

The third domain, "altered identity," reflects battered women's changing self-concept and loss of identity that follow from the images batterers reflect back to them, or demand of them, and which generally become increasingly negative over time. This aspect of battered women's experience illustrates Cooley's concept of the "looking glass self" (Mead, 1934).

It was always something for him, because when he was happy, I was happy. I knew I could breathe that night. But it was never do what I wanted to do. . . . I was always pleasing him to make me happy. And that's what I worked on, pleasing him. If he said I was a bitch, honey, I believed I was a bitch.

Woman 1: Just took away your identity. Who you are and what you want to be.
Woman 2: Yeah, absolutely. I had no, when I left he would say "So how do you feel about this?" What do you mean, how do I feel about this?
Woman 3: Of course. What are feelings? You gave up feelings.
Woman 2: Yeah, what kind of question is that? I don't feel. I just react.
Woman 1: You just react. I didn't even know who I was, you know?

"Yearning," the fourth domain, represents some battered women's largely futile efforts to establish intimacy with their partners. These women's efforts are not unlike those of women in nonabusive relationships, but battered women's efforts take on an aura of desperation as they persevere in spite of their partners' lack of reciprocity and violent behavior. This yearning for closeness and love is not necessarily fulfilled by sexual intimacy and, in fact, yearning can coexist with sexual intimacy. The words in brackets represent a different speaker.

That's what we as women do, we don't love ourselves. [We don't know how.] We don't think we deserve to be loved. You know, any morsel they give us. You know, they can kick the shit out of us and verbally abuse us. [Umhum . . . I can take it] . . . and then they'll give us a crumb. . . . I remember one time I went to this party and this guy was being friendly to me, and my husband got jealous, and I . . . I was, that made me feel good, I mean he showed he cared that . . . [yeah, something] . . . he was jealous! I mean, any morsel, I would just grab it.

"Entrapment" represents women's perceptions of being trapped in the relationship, which seems to result from the batterers' efforts to keep women in the relationship, the privacy of the violence, and the belief that no help or support is available.

Mine was fear and misery cause everyday he'd put fear in me cause he'd always threaten me saying that if I decided to ever leave that he'd hunt me down like a dog and shoot me and the girls. And he knew I had nowhere to go, so I just had to stay there and put up with it.

The sixth domain, "disempowerment," addresses the loss of power that occurs with the woman's sustained exposure to violence and abuse as her thoughts and behaviors become habitually modified in accordance with the batterer's desires. The concept of disempowerment is identified in Finkelhor and Browne's (1985) framework conceptualizing four traumatic ramifications of child sexual abuse. Although they use the word "powerlessness," they conceptualize the construct as disempowerment, or the "process in which the child's will, desires, and sense of efficacy are continually contravened" (p. 532). In the case of battered women the word "disempowerment" is preferred to "powerlessness" because disempowerment implies a process, whereas powerlessness implies a state of being. Although women may enter battering relationships in different degrees of powerfulness, this domain implies that battering itself may begin, or continue, a process of declining personal power. As in the case of sexually abused children, many different aspects of the battered woman's experience, highlighted in the WEB framework, contribute to her disempowerment: feeling trapped and afraid, being afraid to disclose the violence, feeling responsible for the violence, and feeling worthless. The following women's words illustrate this domain (the words in brackets represent a different speaker):

> Woman 1: Mine, he programmed me over a long, long, period of time, cause I saw him going through a divorce with his first wife, and I can look back now saying that was the beginning of his programming "If you do this, I'll kill you" . . . [Right] . . . And it was a constant thing, but you don't, at first you don't know what it is. I mean, you are taking their words, but the words . . . [They don't mean anything] . . . still he starts connecting the violence with it . . . [He starts connecting the violence with it.] . . . The violence gets, the violence gets really bad, and then you say, I mean, when I looked down the end of the gun barrel, um . . . [Yeah, I did that.]. . . . I knew at that point that he could kill me.
> Woman 2: Yeah. . . . Because he has a part you don't want to believe that he will do it. But you know he can do it.
> Woman 1: He can do it. Because he's already told you a 150 times. . . . [That he will.] That, that he will, and so then when you . . . [I know.] when he does that and he doesn't kill you, but you know he can. . . . [That's right] You know he will. And it's like a long process.

Our research revealed battering to be an enduring, traumatic, and multidimensional experience conceptually distinct from episodic physical assault (Smith, Tessaro et al., 1995). We found that battering in women's lives continuously shapes their behavior, views of self, and beliefs in the controllability of their own lives. We also found that battered women are actively engaged in this experience; they want to improve their situation and, as the managing domain in particular indicates, they are continuously engaged in both intrapsychic and active coping. Many of these efforts focus inward, however, and over time may enhance their feelings of personal responsibility for the violence. Based on this, we derived the following definition of battering: A process whereby one member of an intimate relationship experiences vulnerability, loss of power and control, and entrapment as a consequence of the other member's exercise of power through the patterned use of physical, sexual, psychological, and/or moral force.

The WEB framework is not, however, intended to reflect all possible behaviors or reactions that battered women have or that result from exposure to their partners' psychologically and physically violent and controlling behaviors. Because of its focus on the cognitive and affective experience of battering, it does not address battered women's coping and help seeking that are outwardly focused; it does not, for example, explicitly include anger or attempts at escape and resistance. The process of data collection and analysis was designed to derive battered women's perspectives on what it meant to them to be battered, rather than to explore the full range of their feelings or coping strategies. As such, the WEB framework works largely at the psychological or intrapsychic level: It represents the meanings that battered women give to the experiences and circumstances of their lives. Furthermore, calling for reconnecting the relationship between force and the underlying condition of power imbalance and inequity should not be perceived as an attempt to justify all violence used by women. Both women and men may engage, at times, in violence that is morally or legally justified by its social context and violence that is not.

Experiential Basis for Measurement

Women's experiences with battering point to a reconceptualization of battering as a chronic phenomenon, hence, a chronic epidemiology (see Figure 1). In this view, assaults are not isolated events but outcroppings from an underlying condition of continuous abuse and psychological vulnerability that occasionally break through a physical-assault threshold. Consequently, the time interval needed to define battering and within which assaults are analyzed is linked to the battered victim's exposure to, and the batterers' involvement in, the victimization. A gendered perspective seeks to evaluate the condition of women's and men's lives as they are played out in the victimization process and analyze their behavior within the framework of a chronic exposure.

This chronic epidemiology perspective has implications for measurement techniques, selection of outcome indicators, and data sources. Although some research may require techniques that measure the frequency and severity of physical assault, other research may need to discriminate battered (as opposed to assaulted) from nonbattered individuals and reflect the continuous and gendered nature of the battering experience. Consequently, we wanted to build on the conceptualization provided by the WEB framework to develop a measurement instrument that quantified the experience of battered women. This research, described elsewhere (Smith, Earp et al., 1995), required us to take a continuous-process approach to measurement, that is, to operationalize the *enduring condition* of battering rather than *discrete events*.

The first step in measurement is to define the construct of interest. Nunnally (1978) referred to the process of construct explication or the process of making an abstract word explicit in terms of observable variables. In our research, the construct of battering was composed in terms of psychological vulnerability (Smith, Earp et al., 1995). This construct is theoretically derived and was defined as women's continuous perceptions of susceptibility to physical and psychological danger, loss of power, and loss of control in a relationship with a male partner. To return to

Table 2

An Illustration of the Analytic Process Generating Items Operationalizing
Psychological Vulnerability: Scale Item, Original Text, and Supporting Text

Scale item
He has a look that goes straight through me and terrifies me.
Original text
And I saw the fire. And I saw the red-eye. I saw the look, um, and um, and um, he
turned around and pushed me. I don't remember the push like I remember the look.
[Oh, I know just what you are saying.] And after, and after when he, after that point,
all he would have to do was give me the look. The words, the words would not hurt
to the point that the look can. And at that point, I don't think that I really didn't
understand that. It was the night before, the night before he left, um, I left, I mean,
I left in a panic, I—I left in, um another fear. But I didn't realize until a week later
why I was so scared. The look. I mean, I knew the look, my soul knew the look. I mean,
I couldn't paint it for you, it's not something you can see, it is something that goes
straight through you.
Supporting text
• Well, I think if he could have gotten his hand on that gun, I would not be here today
  . . . . I had never seen him that angry in my whole life. And, I, I could just see, I
  mean, the fire of hell burning in his eyes, when he was lookin' at me "You just die
  bitch."
• Well, the look in my case, I called it when he got red in his eyes. He would get this
  look, he has brown, no he has blue eyes, I don't even remember. But he would get
  this look. His jaw would set and his eyes would just get this stare, but he would see
  red, and when he would see red, then things would go flying or there would be
  definite physical violence.

the language of the measurement trap, this approach discards an orientation toward
events and adopts an orientation toward the victimization. In addition, it opens up
the time interval under consideration so that the interpretative frame is the individual's subjective interpretation of her situation.

We began explicating the construct of psychological vulnerability by returning
to the focus-group data, examining the transcripts for fragments or clusters of text
that reflected the cognitive, affective, and/or behavioral expressions of susceptibility
to physical and psychological danger, loss of power, and loss of control in their
relationships. These pieces of text were then developed into items retaining the
women's exact words or the meaning of the words. Table 2 provides an illustration
of the data-analysis process, from uncoded text to item development.

We initially developed 153 items and reduced these to a set of 40, representing
all six of the domains in the WEB framework. Through a combination of expert
review and known-groups survey method, we determined a final set of 10 items
comprising the Women's Experience with Battering Scale (see Table 3) and determined the Scale's reliability and validity.

The WEB Scale exhibited high internal consistency reliability ($\alpha = .99$) and
correlated highly with known-group status and other constructs used in testing the
Scale's convergent and discriminant validity (Smith, Earp et al., 1995). The WEB
Scale, for example, was significantly correlated in the expected directions with
physical assault, psychological abuse, self-esteem, beliefs in a just world, depression,

Table 3

Women's Experience with Battering (WEB) Scale Items

1. He makes me feel unsafe even in my own home.
2. I feel ashamed of the things he does to me.
3. I try not to rock the boat because I am afraid of what he might do.
4. I feel like I am programmed to react a certain way to him.
5. I feel like he keeps me prisoner.
6. He makes me feel like I have no control over my life, no power, no protection.
7. I hide the truth from others because I am afraid not to.
8. I feel owned and controlled by him.
9. He can scare me without laying a hand on me.
10. He has a look that goes straight through me and terrifies me.

anxiety, marital satisfaction, locus of control, injury, perceived health status, chronic pain, physician visits, and hospital visits. The WEB Scale is scored using a 6-point Likert-type scale ranging from *agree strongly* to *disagree strongly*.

The Scale's 10 items represent five of the six WEB framework domains. They do not represent the domain of yearning because the results indicated that although the ideas represented by this domain are part of the battering experience for many battered women, they are not *unique* to battered women. For this reason, these items were less useful than items representing other domains for distinguishing battered from nonbattered women.

This shifting of the focus away from events and toward people has implications for outcomes and data sources. The WEB Scale, as a measure of the magnitude of the problem, is a measure of prevalence, not incidence (Skogan, 1981). Additionally, battering involves a complex exposure that places women in prolonged stress because of physical, psychological, and/or sexual abuse. This abuse, coupled with women's attempts to manage the stress and violence, has been shown to result in many different health and behavior outcomes. Hence, indicators need to reflect this range of outcomes, which might include not only injury but chronic pain, substance abuse, recurrent gynecological disorders, increased health care use, delayed prenatal care, reduced control over fertility, and reduced participation in economic development projects or other events of community life.

This variability in outcomes indicates the need to use multiple sources of data that broaden our ability to understand battering in its complexity and that give voice to women's perspectives. This includes the need for monitoring and evaluation systems that are qualitative as well as quantitative, that are developed and monitored by the battered women's movement as well as by social services and researchers, and that are derived from the sociocultural experiences of battered women.

DISCUSSION

Feminist research often calls for an increasing use of nonquantitative research methods (Fonow & Cook, 1991). This article supports this view by demonstrating one way of using both qualitative methods and a feminist perspective to inform quantitative methods. A critical feminist concept that informed our research process was that battered women are the experts of their own lives: They provided the only data source for our conceptualization of battering and the WEB Scale items. Battered women also acted as expert reviewers of the survey instrument and potential scale items and as respondents for the known-groups survey. Additionally, although the battered women did not perform the data analysis, the techniques we selected for analysis called for us to remain as true as possible to the battered women's own experiences and words. Our research methods were not new or radical or inherently feminist. Rather they can be considered classic scale-development methods (DeVellis, 1991; Nunnally, 1978). We believe that grounding these methods in women's experiences accounted for the strong preliminary findings on the WEB Scale's validity, however.

Good conceptualization and measurement are essential to good research. It is impossible to investigate the prevalence of battering, its health or social costs, or the effectiveness of interventions designed to reduce battering if the condition is incorrectly understood and its measures are invalid, impractical, or unreliable. Additionally, often a measurement instrument or approach becomes difficult to replace once it becomes established (DeVellis et al., 1995). For this reason, feminist scholars must continue developing, validating, and critiquing quantitative measures of social phenomena and, equally important, deconstructing the conceptual basis for the measures. As Graham and Campbell (1991) argued, and as our work suggests, measurement instruments derived from weak conceptual frameworks can hamper women's health research by distorting the knowledge base from which our policies and interventions are derived.

Future research will indicate whether, and in what ways, research using the WEB Scale yields findings different from those of other research. Given the WEB Scale's stronger correlation with known-group status than either the Conflict Tactics Scale or the Index of Spouse Abuse (Smith, Earp et al., 1995), we anticipate that the WEB Scale will produce less misclassification of study participants and, thus, more accurate findings. Second, as is the case with other types of serial incidents, it may be difficult for victims of domestic abuse to disentangle them for a survey (e.g., disentangle a push from a hit) and remember the specific months in which they occurred. Consequently, data on discrete events do not always accurately assess frequency (Skogan, 1981). Because the WEB Scale does not require respondents to recall all violent events they encountered or the number of times during each "episode" they were actually pushed, hit, kicked, and so on, use of this scale could reduce respondent burden and make collecting retrospective data more reliable.

The WEB Scale, potentially, can also make it easier to study the relationship between battering and some women's health problems and behaviors. The WEB Scale is a continuous variable that may allow us to examine associations between battering and other continuous measures of health (e.g., depression, anxiety, self-esteem) more clearly. Additionally, the WEB Scale may make studying the relationship between battering and pregnancy more accurate. Research investigating whether pregnancy is a high-risk time for abuse suffers from methodological problems (Gazmararian et al., 1996) including, but not limited to, the difficulty of determining when battering starts and ends. Although incidence-based measures, such as the Conflict Tactics Scale, may provide researchers with an accurate timing of assaultive episodes in relationship to pregnancy, they ignore the fact that the exposure of interest is chronic and prevalent in some women's lives independent of the occurrence of assault, making it difficult to determine precisely whether a woman is battered prior to pregnancy. Researchers interested in studying these relationships might want to investigate both the prevalence of battering in women's lives as well as the timing and incidence of assaults in battered and nonbattered women. This approach could reduce the misclassification of women as battered or not prior to pregnancy, indicate the intensity of women's perceptions of their vulnerability and whether it changes during pregnancy, and provide information on the frequency and severity of assaults battered women are exposed to before, during, and after pregnancy.

The WEB Scale could also prove useful in evaluating the effectiveness of intervention programs. For example, evaluations of batterer treatment programs suffer from poorly conceptualized and measured outcome indicators. The literature indicates that measuring change in men's use of assaultive behaviors insufficiently determines whether men in treatment have reduced their battering behaviors. Gondolf (1987) wrote that "the acts in themselves may not be as significant as the constellation of behaviors that create a subjective state of terror for the woman. Even when a battered woman is not hit, the possibility of being hit sustains a high degree of fear and uncertainty" (p. 103). He concurred with Edelson (1985) that battered women's experience of terror must inform the definition of battering. The WEB Scale could be used, alone or in combination with other measures of physical assault and psychological abuse, to investigate from the women's perspective whether their experience of psychological vulnerability differs after their partners complete batterer treatment programs. In sum, as an instrument explicitly situated in the lives of battered women, the WEB Scale ideally could provide a starting point for the development of knowledge that validates and reflects battered women's actual experiences of life.

Initial submission: December 19, 1996
Initial acceptance: March 4, 1997
Final acceptance: July 7, 1997

REFERENCES

Agudelo, S. F. (1992). Violence and health: Preliminary elements for thought and action. *International Journal of Health Services, 22*, 365–376.
Avni, N. (1991). Battered wives: The home as a total institution. *Violence and Victims, 2*, 137–149.
Becker, M. H. (Ed.). (1974). Health belief model and personal health behavior [Special Edition]. *Health Education Monographs, 2*, 324–473.
Browne, A., & Williams, K. R. (1993). Gender, intimacy, and lethal violence: Trends from 1976–1987. *Gender and Society, 7*, 78–98.
Centers for Disease Control and Prevention. (1997). *Grants for intimate partner violence prevention research. Notice of availability of funds for fiscal year, 1997.* (Announcement number 723). Atlanta, GA: Author.
DeVellis, R. F. (1991). *Scale development: Theory and applications.* Newbury Park, CA: Sage.
DeVellis, R. F., Alfieri, W. S., & Ahluwalia, I. B. (1995). The importance of careful measurement in health education research, theory and practice. *Health Education Research, Theory and Practice, 10*(1), i–vii.
Dobash, R. P., Dobash, R. E., Wilson, M., & Daly, M. (1992). The myth of marital symmetry in marital violence. *Social Problems, 39*(1), 71–91.
Edelson, J. (1985). Men who batter women: A critical review of the evidence. *Journal of Family Issues, 6*, 229–247.

Ferraro, K. J., & Johnson, J. M. (1993). How women experience battering: The process of victimization. *Social Problems, 30*, 325–339.

Finkelhor, D., & Browne, A. (1985). The traumatic impact of child sexual abuse: A conceptualization. *American Journal of Orthopsychiatry, 55*, 530–540.

Fischer, C. T., & Wertz, F. J. (1979). Empirical phenomenological analyses of being criminally victimized. In A. Giorgi, R. Knowles, & D. L. Smith (Eds.), *Duquesne studies in phenomenological psychology* (Vol. 3, pp. 135–158). Pittsburgh, PA: Duquesne University Press.

Fonow, M. M., & Cook, J. A. (Eds.) (1991). *Beyond methodology: Feminist scholarship as lived research*. Bloomington, IN: Indiana University Press.

Gazmarian, J. A., Lazorick S., Spitz, A., Ballard, T. J., Saltzman, L. E., & Marks, J. S. (1996). Prevalence of violence against pregnant women: A review of the literature. *Journal of the American Medical Association, 276*, 1915–1920.

Gondolf, E. (1987). Evaluating programs for men who batter: Problems and prospects. *Journal of Family Violence, 1*(2), 95–108.

Graham, W., & Campbell O. (1991). *Measuring maternal health: Defining the issues*. London: London School of Hygiene and Tropical Medicine.

Heise, L. L., Pitanguy, J., & Germain, A. (1994). *Violence against women: The hidden health burden. World Bank Discussion Papers*. Washington, DC: World Bank.

Hudson, W. W., & McIntosh, S. R. (1981). The assessment of spouse abuse: Two quantifiable dimensions. *Journal of Marriage and Family, 43*, 873–885.

Koss, M. P., Goodman, L. A., Browne, A., Fitzgerald, L., Keita, G. P., & Russo, N. F. (1994). *No safe haven: Male violence against women at home, at work, and in the community*. Washington, DC: American Psychological Association.

Landenburger, K. (1989). A process of entrapment in and recovery from an abusive relationship. *Issues in Mental Health Nursing, 10*, 209–227.

Lazarus, R. (1966). *Psychological stress and the coping process*. New York: McGraw Hill.

Loeske, D. R. (1992). *The battered woman and shelters: The social construction of wife abuse*. Albany, NY: State University of New York Press.

Louis Harris & Associates, Inc. (1993). *The Commonwealth Fund Survey of Women's Health*. New York: Commonwealth Fund.

McFarlane, J., Parker, B., Soeken, K., & Bullock, L. (1992). Assessing for abuse during pregnancy: Severity and frequency of injuries and associated entry into prenatal care. *Journal of the American Medical Association, 267*, 3176–3178.

Mead, G. H. (Ed.). (1934). *Mind, self and society*. Chicago: University of Chicago Press.

Nunnally, J. (1978). *Psychometric theory* (2nd ed.). New York: McGraw Hill.

Perloff, L. S. (1983). Perceptions of vulnerability to victimization. *Journal of Social Issues, 39*(2), 41–61.

Rogers, R. W. (1975). A protection motivation theory of fear appeals and attitude change. *Journal of Psychology, 91*, 93–114.

Rosenberg, M. L., & Finley, M. A. (1991). *Violence in America: A public health approach*. New York: Oxford University Press.

Saunders, D., & Browne, A. (1991). Domestic homicide. In R. T. Ammerman & H. Herson (Eds.), *Case studies in family violence* (pp. 379–402). New York: Plenum Press.

Shepard, M. F., & Campbell, J. A. (1992). The Abusive Behavior Inventory: A measure of psychological and physical abuse. *Journal of Interpersonal Violence, 7*, 291–306.

Skogan, W. (1981). *Issues in the measurement of victimization* (Bureau of Justice Statistics, NCJ-74682). Washington, DC: U.S. Department of Justice.

Smith, P. H., Earp, J., & DeVellis, R. (1995). Measuring battering: Development of the Women's Experience with Battering (WEB) Scale. *Women's Health: Research on Gender, Behavior and Policy, 1*, 273–288.

Smith, P. H., Tessaro, I., & Earp, J. (1995). Women's experiences with battering: A conceptualization from qualitative research. *Women's Health Issues, 5*, 173–182.

Sorenson, S. B., & Telles, C. A. (1991). Self-reports of spousal violence in a Mexican American and non-Hispanic white population. *Violence and Victims, 6*(3), 3–16.

Sorenson, S. B., Upchurch, D., & Shen, H. (1996). Violence and injury in marital arguments: Risk patterns and gender differences. *American Journal of Public Health, 86*(1), 35–40.

Steinmeitz, S. K. (1977–1978). The battered husband syndrome. *Victimology: An International Journal, 2,* 499–509.

Straus, M. (1979). Measuring intrafamily conflict and violence: The Conflict Tactics (CT) Scale. *Journal of Marriage and Family, 41,* 74–85.

Straus, M. (1980). Victims and aggressors in marital violence. *American Behavioral Scientist, 23,* 681–704.

Straus, M., Gelles, R., & Steinmeitz, S. K. (1980). *Behind closed doors: Violence in the American family.* New York: Doubleday/Anchor.

World Bank. (1993). *World Bank development report 1993: Investing in health.* New York: Oxford University Press.

MULTIDIMENSIONAL ASSESSMENT OF WOMAN BATTERING

Commentary on Smith, Smith, and Earp

Mary Ann Dutton
George Washington University

Based on my experience as a domestic violence researcher, clinician, and forensic consultant, current methods of measurement are inadequate to capture a full understanding of the phenomena of battered women's experience. The reconceptualization of woman battering offered by Smith, Smith, and Earp (this volume) begins to fill a gap in research-and-assessment approaches to the problem of domestic violence. This commentary to Smith et al. addresses three major issues: (a) the importance of reconceptualizing battering as defined only by a series of discrete events, (b) the importance of a multidimensional assessment that includes measurement of discrete events along with an evaluation of battered women's experience, and (c) the continuity or developmental progression of battered victims' experience over time.

BATTERING IS MORE THAN A SERIES OF DISCRETE EVENTS

Smith et al. have correctly identified an important problem in the measurement of woman battering: It is more than a series of discrete events. It is a pattern of ongoing, continuous or continual, sometimes escalating, coercive control (Ganley, 1991) that may include acute episodes of physical or sexual assault, as well as more diffuse psychologically abusive behaviors. Defining battering as discrete behavior alone decontextualizes it. Thus, as Smith et al. note, the problem of neglecting gender in the analysis of domestic violence follows from defining battering as a discrete event. If battering is merely the occurrence of a defined set of behaviors, then gender becomes irrelevant. Some data suggest that the problem is similar for men and women (cf. Straus, 1990), however, other data indicate that women are much more likely than men to become victims of violence by intimates (Zawitz,

Address correspondence and reprint requests to: Mary Ann Dutton, 5507 Spruce Tree Avenue, Bethesda, MD 20814. E-mail: Mad@gwis2.circ.gwu.edu

1994). In either case, "injuries must be measured separately from the acts that produce those injuries" (Straus, 1990, p. 79) as these data reflect very different patterns across gender than do data on violent acts. Women are injured at a rate 7.5 times greater than are men (Straus, 1990). Among the 1994 emergency department violence-related injuries from a spouse/ex-spouse, rates for women (88,400) were 5.7 times greater than rates for men (15,400), whereas injuries to women from a boy/girlfriend (116,000) were 4.9 times greater than for men (23,600) (Rand, 1997).

Smith et al.'s criticism that assessing battering as discrete events necessarily places emphasis on a narrow time frame is not necessarily true. For example, a focus on the chronology of discrete events over time—even over 30 years of an abusive marriage—can still involve a focus on discrete events. The discrete-events approach does create a related problem of how to define the endpoints of battering, however. The onset of physical beating by one partner in the relationship may occur as an escalation of months or years of intimidation, emotional abuse, or other types of psychological abuse. Alternatively, the first physical blow with an object by one partner may follow a period of extreme controlling behaviors by the other partner. In both cases, the onset of battering or domestic violence actually began long before the first discrete act of physical violence. Likewise, implicit or explicit verbal and nonverbal threats continuing long after the last discrete episode of physical assault often keeps the threat of danger and, thus, the battered person's fear a reality. Even though an actual physical assault may not have recently occurred, the less discretely defined acts of control and intimidation maintain the threat value of physical assaults. Thus, the definition of battering as discrete acts of violence by the batterer precludes examination of the battered victim's experience as developed over time and as defined by threats, intimidation, and control, as well as discrete physical and sexual assaults.

BATTERING IS ALSO A SERIES OF DISCRETE EVENTS

The approach to "reconstructing the conceptualization" of battering, and therefore its measurement, taken by Smith et al. appears to be dichotomous: It *is* about battered victims' experience and it is *not* about events or behavior. In this section, I make the argument that battering is indeed about both and, further, that we need to measure both (and more) in order to fully capture battered women's experience in our measurement approaches.

For purposes of research, clinical intervention, criminal prosecution, civil litigation, and policymaking, we need to consider a range of dimensions related to battering, not simply shift the focus from the perpetrator's behavior to the victim's experience. We not only need to develop measures for multiple dimensions of the battering phenomena, but to do so using multiple methods from varying perspectives (Dutton, 1992; Gondolf, 1998).

Relevant dimensions of victims' experience include perceptions and other cognitions about the violence and abuse; strategies for attempting to resist, avoid, protect from, and stop the violence; and the psychological effects, health consequences, economic outcomes, and social consequences of violence (Dutton, 1993). Shifting the focus of measurement of battering solely to victims' experience, however, risks failing to recognize the actor in the battering scenario as accountable for his/her actions in whatever context they occur. It is necessary to understand the nature of the violence and abusive behavior along with the victim's experience of it.

But what are the relevant dimensions of battering that are important to measure? Dimensions of battering that are routinely measured include the nature or type of abuse, for example, physical, sexual, psychological, and abuse to property or pets (Ganley, 1981); the frequency or pervasiveness of violent and abusive conduct; the level of severity of the act; the severity of injury; and the context in which the violence or abusive behavior occurred (e.g., in front of others, in the home vs. in public, when the victim is otherwise vulnerable such as soon following childbirth or when injured) (Dutton, 1992). The batterer's behavior and the victim's experience of it are both essential dimensions for understanding the overall phenomenon of domestic violence: Alone, each provides an incomplete picture. The Women's Experience with Battering Scale (WEB) provides a new approach for capturing battered victims' experience, but it should not be used to the exclusion of information about the battering behavior. Without information about features of the battering behavior, the battered victims' experience as measured using the WEB cannot be considered in the context of the various dimensions of the events leading to their experiences (e.g., duration of violence in the relationship, developmental stage of relationship in which the battering occurred, potential life threat of the violent behavior). This perspective is necessary for understanding the factors that determine individual differences in battered victims' experience.

THE CONTINUITY OR DEVELOPMENTAL PROGRESSION OF BATTERED VICTIMS' EXPERIENCE

The WEB Scale provides an approach to measurement of battered victims' experience that taps several important dimensions: perceived threat, managing, altered identity, entrapment, and disempowerment. These dimensions reflect a battered victim's self-reported perceptions of her own experience at a given point in time, and in this way the WEB will make an important contribution. We need to recognize the static nature of most measurement tools, however, including the WEB. What the WEB cannot do, as presented, is to provide an understanding of the development of the battered woman's experience over time.

The transtheoretical model of behavioral change applied to battered women posits that attempts to overcome the abuse in their lives reflects a process of change defined by cognitive, emotional, and behavioral components (Brown, 1997). Battered women's perceptions of their battering experience, as well as their efforts to resist, avoid, escape, and stop the violence and abuse change over time, as do batterers' behaviors (and other concurrent nonviolent behaviors of batterers). Based on this approach (Brown, 1997) battered victims' experience will vary as they move, for example, from attempts to "help" the batterer stop his violence through counseling or other means to contemplating an end to an abusive relationship to actively seeking separation or divorce. Similarly, as the batterer's behavior escalates from slapping and pushing to choking and use of a weapon, no doubt, the battered woman's experience of the violence changes accordingly. As new methods of assessing battered women's experience are developed, we need to keep in mind that their experience continues to be shaped not only by the batterer's behavior, but also by the economic and tangible resources available to them, the social and cultural context in which the violence and abuse occurs, the response of others within the battered victim's social network, and by the individual characteristics of battered women (Dutton, 1997).

In sum, the WEB offers an important new direction for assessing battered women's experience of battering. It should complement, not replace, other assessment methods that focus on batterer behavior—both discrete and diffuse—as well as the social context in which the battering occurs. Finally, it is imperative to recognize that battered women's experience is not static and to strive for the development of measures of that experience that reflect the process of change over time.

REFERENCES

Brown, J. (1997). Working toward freedom from violence: The process of change in battered women. *Violence Against Women, 3*(1), 5–26.

Dutton, M. A. (1992). *Empowering and healing the battered woman.* New York: Springer.

Dutton, M. A. (1993). Understanding women's response to domestic violence: Redefinition of battered woman syndrome. *Hofstra Law Review, 21,* 1191–1242.

Dutton, M. A. (1997). Battered women's strategic response to violence: The role of context. In J. L. Edleson & Zvi C. Eisikovits (Eds.), *Future interventions with battered women and their families* (pp. 105–125).Thousand Oaks, CA: Sage.

Ganley, A. (1981). *Court mandated treatment for men who batter.* Washington, DC: Center for Women Policy Studies.

Ganley, A. (1991). The impact of domestic violence on the defendant and the victim in the courtroom. In J. Carter, C. Heisler, & N. K. D. Lemon (Eds.), *Domestic violence: The crucial role of the judge in the criminal court cases* (pp. 17–45). San Francisco: Family Violence Prevention Fund.

Gondolf, E. W. (1998). *Assessing woman battering in mental health services.* Thousand Oaks, CA: Sage.

Rand, M. D. (1997). *Violence-related injuries treated in hospital emergency departments* (NCJ-156921). Washington, DC: U.S. Department of Justice.

Smith, P. H., Smith, J. B., & Earp, J. L. (1999). Beyond the measurement trap: A reconstructed conceptualization and measurement of woman battering. *Psychology of Women Quarterly, 23,* 179–195.

Straus, M. A. (1990). Injury and frequency of assault and the "representative sample fallacy" in measuring wife beating and child abuse. In M. A. Straus & R. J. Gelles (Eds.), *Physical violence in American families* (pp. 95–112). New Brunswick: Transaction Books.

Zawitz, M. W. (1994). *Violence between intimates* (NCJ-149259). Washington, DC: U.S. Department of Justice.

EXPLORING A TEACHING/ RESEARCH NEXUS AS A POSSIBLE SITE FOR FEMINIST METHODOLOGICAL INNOVATION IN PSYCHOLOGY

Ann Weatherall
Victoria University of Wellington

In this article the links between feminist pedagogy and feminist research are used as a basis for exploring the potential that teaching about women and gender has a methodological resource for feminist research in psychology. Inspiration for this article stemmed from the author's experience of teaching a postgraduate class in Gender Issues in Psychology in New Zealand. An assessed task for the course required students to interview two women. The interviews were transcribed and the content summarized in a written report and an oral presentation. All parties involved with the project reported finding it an educational experience. The exercise is evaluated as an example of feminist research. The advantages and limitations of using the classroom as a resource for research by feminist psychologists are discussed.

In traditional Western models of education, teachers are seen as neutral transmitters of information, students as passive receivers of it, and knowledge as a body of immutable material that needs to flow from instructor to pupil. A feminist pedagogy refutes the independence of teacher, student, and knowledge—instead, teachers and students are seen as active and interdependent agents in the production and

The author would like to thank Natilene Bowker, Sue D'Ath, Kristy Davies, Penny Dean, Susie Malcolm, Meredith Mora, Siann Nathan, Ann O'Sullivan, Wendy Sheddan, and Jo White. The success of the interviews was a result of their hard work and their enthusiasm motivated me to write this article. I would also like to thank Marsha Walton with whom I enjoyed many interesting discussions about feminist research and pedagogy in psychology.

Address correspondence and reprint requests to: Ann Weatherall, School of Psychology, Victoria University of Wellington, P.O. Box 600, Wellington, New Zealand. E-mail: Ann.Weatherall@ vuw.ac.nz.

legitimization of knowledge (Luke & Gore, 1992). Feminist pedagogy and feminist research share a number of critical strands, one of which is the crucial recognition that knowledge can never be entirely objective and value free. In addition, both feminist educators and feminist researchers disrupt the binary oppositions that have traditionally organized their endeavor. Feminist pedagogy disrupts the teacher/ student dualism by highlighting the interactive productivity of the instructive act (Orner, 1992). Similarly, feminist research disrupts the autonomy of the knower and the known by emphasizing a reciprocal relationship between investigator and investigated (Worell & Etaugh, 1994). In this article, the links between feminist pedagogy and feminist research are considered in order to explore the potential that experiences and practices of teaching about the psychology of women have as a methodological resource for feminist research in psychology.[1]

For feminist educators researching pedagogical strategy, the classroom is both a site of practice and a source of data. Teaching and researching processes inform each other and have the potential for producing useful methodological insights. An example of the possibilities of a teaching/research dialectic is Lather's (1988) work on student resistance to a liberatory classroom. Pupils of Lather's Introduction to Women's Studies course were participants in her study. Interviews and surveys, repeated at intervals over 3 academic years, were used to investigate the changes that students perceived within themselves as a result of the course. The students were also asked to comment on the impact of participating in the research process on their experience in class. The empirical work was used by Lather not only to report the change in consciousness that the students experienced but also to address methodological questions concerning interpretative strategy, narrative authority, and critical perspectives (Lather, 1991). A crucial insight that she reported gaining from her work was how her own efforts to use empowering teaching strategies could be understood as reproducing the authoritarian nature of the teacher/student relationship. Thus Lather's teaching and research became a reciprocally educative encounter. Her reflective analysis became a methodological resource for examining her data and informing her about how to conduct more empowering teaching and research.

Psychologists have a long history of involving students in their research. Unlike Lather's (1988) work, however, traditional use of students in psychological research has been for the sake of convenience. Stark contrasts exist between Lather's (1991) praxis-oriented research (which aims to both produce emancipatory knowledge and empower the researched) and conventional psychological research processes that function to maintain the status quo (Prilleltensky, 1989). In the latter, the researcher/ subject binary remains very much intact, with the experimental context manipulated to make the participant as object or rock-like as possible (Wallston & Grady, 1985). A consequence of the depersonalizing, decontextualizing features of laboratory-based social-psychological research has been to reproduce, in the research encounter, the nonegalitarian hierarchies of power found in society. A powerful, all-knowing researcher instructs, observes, and sometimes deceives a supposedly naive subject—whose personal contribution to the study is largely unacknowledged. The pervasive focus on the individual, combined with a reluctance to admit subjective influences on the research process, results in the production of knowledge that promotes conservatism and hinders social change (Kahn & Yoder, 1989).

In addition to pointing out problems of context stripping and the influence of power differentials between investigator and investigated, feminists have criticized mainstream psychological research for its dependence on college students as research participants and called for an expansion of the range of people studied (Peplau & Conrad, 1989). Avoiding an overreliance on White, able-bodied, heterosexual, male college students as research participants is clearly an important move. Lather's (1988) work illustrated, however, that research with students should not be dismissed out of hand. Involving students in research need not be exploitive or restricting but can be a mutually educative encounter. Such work has the potential to inform discussions of power, subjectivity, and political commitment, which are issues considered central both to feminist research and feminist psychology (Bannister, Burman, Parker, Taylor, & Tindall, 1994; Stanley & Wise, 1990). My experience of developing and teaching a course entitled "Gender Issues in Psychology" reported here supports the idea that research with students (rather than research on students) has the potential to make a valuable contribution to feminist psychology.[2]

TEACHING GENDER ISSUES IN PSYCHOLOGY

The work that I describe here involved 10 students who constituted the Gender Issues in Psychology class of 1996. The students (all female) were in their fourth year of university study and final year of an honors degree in psychology. Admission into the honors program is determined on the basis of grades so students are generally bright and motivated. All students taking the course had completed a 3-year bachelor's degree in psychology within which a conventional, positivist paradigm had been promoted as the legitimate methodological approach in psychological research. In order to introduce students to alternative perspectives, a course objective was to encourage the students to be reflective about the values, assumptions, and normative practices of psychology and, in particular, how those forces have influenced the study of women.

The first part of the course involved "foundations for feminist psychology." Lectures and readings covered material focusing on the feminist critiques of psychology (e.g., Bohan, 1992), as well as addressing feminists' more general critical intellectual engagement with epistemological issues (e.g., Harding, 1986). Readings were assigned before class, and students were encouraged to share their responses to the readings in class discussions. The next part of the course consisted of student-led seminars on key topics in the psychology of women (e.g., the development of gender roles, motherhood, and violence against women). For their seminars, students were encouraged to think about the relevant research in light of what they had learned in the foundations section. Next, issues of feminist methodology were explored in detail (e.g., Stanley & Wise, 1993). In the final part of the course I talked with the students about my own research in the general area of gender and language.

To have students "walk the talk" of what they had been learning, a practical activity was assigned toward the end of the course to enable students to directly experience the ethos of feminist research. The aims of the project were based on Worell and Etaugh's (1994) themes of what constitutes feminist research. The five goals of the exercise were to: (a) focus on the lives and experiences of New Zealand women, (b) consider how appropriate the category "woman" was across individual women, (c) identify research questions grounded in the personal experiences of the interviewees, (d) attend to women's strengths and capabilities, and (e) reflect on how personal experiences influence the research process. Each student was responsible for recruiting and interviewing two women who were different from each other and from the student in terms of demographic variables such as age, class, education, and ethnicity. The interview questions were selected on the basis of a class discussion of what might be important psychological influences on women's lives. The interview items related to personal identity, significant life experiences, influential people, and the impact of feminism. Each interview was transcribed by the student, the content summarized, and the results shared in an oral presentation to the class as well as a written paper to me.

A concern that the students expressed about the exercise was a lack of knowledge and experience on how to conduct interviews. Their concern confirmed my perception that the range of research methods they had been exposed to in other psychology courses was narrow. I tried to address their concern about interviewing by directing them to some readings (e.g., Breakwell, 1990) and suggesting that they practice with each other.

An ethics application was submitted for the practical exercise because it was a teaching activity that involved interviewing human participants. Approval was granted on the basis that the students satisfied three conditions. Each of their interviewees was provided with an information sheet that outlined the aims of the interview; the anonymity of the participants was assured, and it was explained how material resulting from the interview would be used (this included the possibility that the interviews from the whole class could be collated and submitted for publication). Each interviewee was asked to sign a consent form which demonstrated that they had read and understood the nature and purpose of the interview.

FEMINIST TEACHING/RESEARCH

Given that there is no intrinsically feminist method or methodology (Harding, 1987; Peplau & Conrad, 1989), the feminist teaching/research dialectic that I am describing was evaluated by assessing whether it achieved what was intended. What I will argue is that it was more than successful—the goals of the exercise were surpassed because the educative encounter encompassed not only the students, but also myself (the teacher) and in some cases seemed to be consciousness raising for the interviewees.

Thinking About Women

The first two aims of the assessment were to focus on New Zealand women's lives and consider the category "woman." These aims were largely evaluated by considering the characteristics of the participants that the students recruited. Table 1 summarizes information about the 20 women interviewed; the pseudonyms they chose, their age, their relationship to the student, and the reasons given by the students for their selection. One of the interview questions related to age so it was recorded for all the interviewees. The average age was 44.5 years old with a range of 78 years (from 14 to 92 years old). There were no questions directly relating to

Table 1

Characteristics of the Interviewees

Interviewee (Pseudonym)	Relationship to Student	Characteristics Guiding Choice of Interviewee	Age	Family Relationships
Sheena	Work colleague	Ethnicity (Maltese)	40	Married, 2 children
Lisa	Work colleague	Ethnicity (Scottish descent)	24	Living with parents, youngest of 2 children
Joan	Family friend	Occupation (housewife)	48	Married, 2 children
C.B.	Family friend	Occupation (paid work)	36	De facto, 2 children
Julia	Distant acquaintance	Ethnicity (Hungarian)	61	Widowed, 1 child
Elizabeth	Work colleague, Personal friend	Able-bodiedness (disabled)	27	Single
Agnes	Family friend	Age	92	Single, youngest of 7 children
Edith	Family friend	Age	70	Married, 1 child
Edith	Extended family member	Age	66	Divorced, 2 children
Meg	Extended family member	Age	71	Married, 4 children, 10 grandchildren
Vicki	Sister-in-law	Views on feminism (anti)	33	Married, 3 children
Sandra	Stranger, contacted via a feminist organization	Views on feminism (pro), Sexual orientation (lesbian)	32	Single, oldest of 2 children
Maggie	Mother	Age and family relationship	66	Widowed, 5 children
Linda	Niece	Age and family relationship	14	Oldest of 3 children
Winnie	Relative	Age	86	Widowed, mother and grandmother
Tallulah	Close friend	Sexual orientation (lesbian)	24	Single, youngest of 2
Mona	Karate trainer	Views on feminism (pro)	26	Single
Megan	Employer	Career (hotel manager)	27	De facto, 1 child
	Sister	Education (university), Overseas experience (none)	23	"Undecided" marital status
	Sister	Education (polytechnic), Overseas experience (substantial)	25	Single "but looking"

family relationships; however, these emerged from the interviews as a dominant theme in response to questions about identity ("If you were introducing yourself to a stranger how would you describe yourself?") and influential people ("Could you describe people in your life who have been very important or influential to you?"). The information that each woman volunteered about family is also presented in Table 1.

Asking students to select and interview women proved to be an effective means of recruiting a wide variety of participants, thus responding to feminist calls to expand the range of people studied in psychological research beyond that of college students (Peplau & Conrad, 1989). Individuals within the sample differed in terms of age, ethnicity, occupation, able-bodiedness, and sexual orientation. The interviews with the oldest women (Agnes and Winnie) were particularly special because those specific individuals led such private and isolated lives that it would be unlikely that they would be recruited for other kinds of research projects.

A social category that was not well represented in the sample selected by the students was socioeconomic status. All women interviewed were economically, educationally, and socially privileged. Walkerdine (1996) suggested that social class has become increasingly important to a feminist agenda, yet it did not feature as a significant characteristic influencing the content of the present interview. On reflection, the invisibility of class as a site of difference among women in the students' interviews led me to question how an exercise framed as feminist may at some levels perpetuate class-based relations of dominance. It seemed to me that a solution to this dilemma was that as a teacher and a researcher I need to be more explicit about my "classification"[3] and more sensitive to how it functions to perpetuate a socially privileged feminism, while disguising other forms of women's experiences. Apart from social class, however, the interviews were successful in meeting the first aim, which was to focus on the lives of a diverse sample of New Zealand women. It was additionally successful because it prompted me to become more cognizant of how the sin of silencing could occur under the guise of "giving voice."

The appropriateness of the category "woman" to describe the interview participants was considered by each student when summarizing the content of her two interviews, as well as by the class after listening to all the oral presentations. There was unanimous agreement among the students that the different demographic characteristics, combined with the divergent life experiences, belied assigning any single, meaningful label across all of them. Susan Malcolm, a student in the course, aptly summarized this view when she wrote:

> The most valuable insight gained in conducting this type of qualitative analysis was the recognition of women as an extremely diverse and heterogeneous group. In the choice of my participants I revealed my own belief of a generic group of women in that I believed that if I wish to obtain contrast in my responses then I needed to choose women from different categories such as age and sexuality. Obviously in doing this I was able to obtain this contrast, however[,] in conducting the research it also made me aware of the fact that even if I had chosen two 86 year old, heterosexual, Anglican widows chances are that I still would have obtained a degree of contrast in their responses due to the fact that every individual woman has unique experiences

that influence the person she is, the knowledge she possesses and the opinions she holds.

Another example that demonstrated the differences disguised by the category label "woman" was the student who interviewed her two sisters. Despite similarities of age, ethnicity, and family background, the female siblings' different educational backgrounds and levels of overseas experience resulted in substantial differences in their outlooks on life. Natilene Bowker, another student in the class, took questioning the category of "woman" a step further by doubting the universal usefulness of focusing on gender. Her interview with Elizabeth suggested to her that gender may not be the most salient characteristic for identifying and understanding an individual. In the case of Elizabeth, disability and not gender was the most significant factor impacting on her identity, ambitions, experiences, and opinions.

A difficulty with deconstructing "woman" as a group is that it may undermine any sense of collective identity around which social and political action can be mobilized. Indeed, the students initially reported a sense of helplessness about the ease with which they could dismiss any validity in the category of woman. They felt if they couldn't identify a common thread of experiences among their small group of interviewees, there was little use in focusing on women or analyzing causes of their disadvantage. Given that a commitment to political and social activism is a characteristic of feminist research, the students response challenged me to explain why emphasizing the diversity among women could possibly be a profitable activity for feminist researchers. Lather (1991) suggested that part of the process of deconstruction involves creating a more fluid and less coercive conceptualization of a term (or binary), which transcends both its unity and diversity. By applying this to the label "woman," it can be argued that it is a valid label category because it makes visible an underresearched group of people with a common experience of oppression. In addition, Stanley and Wise (1990) pointed out:

> to say that women share experiences of oppression is not to say that women share the *same* experiences. The social contexts within which different kinds of women live, work, struggle and make sense of the world differ widely across the world and between different groupings of women . . . the experience of women is ontologically fractured and complex because we do not share one single and unseamed material reality. (pp. 20–21)

Hence, the differences among women do not necessarily mean that the category label has no meaning. Rather it functions to demonstrate that the way women experience disadvantage varies depending on the particular social historical moment that the individual inhabits. The contextual specificity of experiences of oppression was made particularly salient through the analyses of some of the older women's stories. Sue D'Ath, another student, pointed out that when interpreting the experiences of older women, it is critical to consider the social context in which their lives were formed—a time before legislation in New Zealand on equal pay or matrimonial property. So women's experiences of oppression today will be quite different from that experienced by adult women in the 1950s. A final motive for being critical of the category "woman" is to avoid the experiences and analyses of oppression made by academic feminists being generalized to all women.

Generating Research Questions Relevant to Women

The third objective of the task was generating ideas for research grounded in women's experiences. As hoped, the exercise stimulated the production of several interesting possibilities for future research. What had not been anticipated was the variety of sources from which the research questions sprung. As expected, the accounts that the women gave of themselves, their experiences, and their opinions about feminism were used directly by students to formulate potential topics for future research. Examples of experiences that the interviewees talked about and the students recognized as being issues worthy of further research included experiences of sexism in the tourist industry in New Zealand, the feelings of loss women experience as a result of separation from female relatives and friends, and experiences resulting from having atypical career aspirations (e.g., a girl wanting to be an electrician).

The content of the interviews, however, was not the only source of research questions. The students also used the interpretative process of the interview material as a resource for suggesting questions that they thought were worthy of more detailed analysis. Here, the research questions were not so much grounded in the experiences of the women being interviewed, but rather were grounded in the experiences of women interviewing other women. A major issue raised by the students about understanding and interpreting the content of the interviews was that their feminist perspective caused them to wonder why the interviewees were unable to recognize the constraints that being a woman places on their lives. Related to this was the concern of some students that their feminist-based interpretations of the interviewees' experiences may have been somewhat at odds with how the interviewees themselves understood their own experiences.

The class presentations of the interview material were a further source of inspiration for research questions. Here, the students were able to consider others' interviews and compare them to their own experiences and interpretations of interviewing women. Aspects of women's lives that became salient in the oral presentations were factors that linked different women's experiences. For example, it became clear that the meaning and impact of feminism varied across generations of women. Older women (e.g., Edith) saw feminism as widening the range of prospects they had in their lives by promoting equal job opportunities. In comparison some of the younger women (e.g., Nicki) understood feminism as narrowing women's choices because they believed that feminism invalidated some women's choice to be a wife and mother. The comparison of women of different ages led the students to recognize the need for longitudinal studies of women's lives. The oral presentations highlighted the differences apart from age that were worthy of exploration; the women differed greatly in who and when they considered others to be significant in their lives. The variability led students to wonder about the nature and function of personal relationships during women's lives.

The exercise was successful in its aim to generate research questions grounded in women's experiences. The sources of experience were far more complex than had been anticipated originally. Instead of questions only being generated from the experiences of the women being interviewed, they emerged as a result of the interview/interviewer relationship and in the context of a feminist teaching/research activity. The exercise provoked both the students and myself to identify relevant areas of investigation on women and feminism that have remained largely untouched by psychological inquiry.

Representing Women As Strong and Capable

The fourth objective of the task was to attend to women's strengths and capabilities. Three themes emerged from the interviews regarding this objective: the capacity and resilience the women used in coping with difficult circumstances, the ability to maintain a sense of optimism despite experiencing personal inequities, and the crucial role the women played in maintaining the family structure. Parents' alcohol problems, physical disabilities resulting from accidents, rural isolation, and being deserted by a spouse were among the problems with which the interviewees reported coping. One student suggested that a potential research topic would be an investigation into how women developed such successful coping strategies despite difficult circumstances.

Personal inequities reported included being barred from an education in science, being paid less than a man for the same work, and being excluded from the "old boys' network." Instead of becoming resentful about such discrimination the women strove to overcome it, however. For example, the interviewee who had been barred by her father from receiving a science scholarship went on to become a highly successful musician—her second choice of career. The woman who was paid less than men doing the equivalent job signed her job under her husband's name and so got paid more. Exclusion from the old boy's network just motivated the interviewee to work harder to become the company manager.

The final theme that emerged from the interviews that related to the fourth objective was the crucial role that women played in maintaining the family structure. That role involved both practical and emotional elements. Among the practical aspects of keeping the family functioning were earning money, putting food on the table, providing clothing, and organizing family occasions. The emotional contributions that the women made included maintaining a sense of normality in times of adversity and maintaining support networks in the community. In class, the students expressed their surprise that the enormous contribution made by their interviewees to maintaining familial relationships was not only unacknowledged as being valuable by the interviewees but also received no formal recognition. Appreciating women's practical and emotional contributions was an important outcome of the exercise for both the students and myself. Some feedback from one participant indicated that describing her work at home made her realize how central her role was to the successful running of the family—hence, it seemed that the educational web had spread beyond the teacher/student to the interviewees.

The Role of Subjectivity in the Research Process

The final goal of the assessment exercise was to encourage the students to reflect on their role in the research process. The students reported finding this part of the task quite alien, especially in the written reports. In the oral presentations, questions from the class seemed to make it easier for the students to report their personal involvement in the research process. In the more formal context of writing a research report, however, they seemed to find it difficult to drop the objective and make the research process seem more subjective.

Dominant themes that emerged from their analyses were: the influence they had on formulating the interview questions, their motivation behind their choice of participants, how their previous relationships and knowledge about the interviewees affected what questions were asked, how the personal dynamics varied across interviews, and the biases involved in what they chose to present in their reports. An important outcome of the reflective process was a class discussion on how the interview questions were constructed. The students came to realize that the original questions had been driven from their perspective of what was important. On reflection they proposed that the interview schedule should allow enough flexibility to drop items that did not seem relevant to a particular participant and pursue issues that arose as important in the context of the interview. The feedback on the process and nature of constructing the interview schedule was important for the teaching/research nexus as it functions as a resource for future development of the project. The iterative process in which all involved parties (teacher/student, researcher/researched) contribute to future development highlights the fluidity of the research endeavor and illustrates how the teaching/research nexus empowers participants.

The student who chose to interview her two sisters had quite a complex story of her experience that only emerged during a conversation with me sometime after the written report had been graded and returned. She admitted that she had chosen her two sisters because she thought it would be a convenient and easy way to complete the exercise. Her sisters proved very awkward during the interview, however, refusing to cooperate with thoughtful replies to the questions. She pointed out that in the case of her interviews, she was the one who was exploited rather than the interviewees (one of her sisters demanded cups of tea and biscuits before cooperating). A difficulty for her had been to make what seemed like disastrous interviews into material reasonable enough to present to the class and write up in a research report. This student's admission that she selected what she thought were going to be "safe" interviews hinted at one reason why socioeconomic status failed to be represented in the students' choice of interviewees. It is possible that they considered interviewing women who were less socially privileged than themselves to be too risky. Instead, students may have been selecting participants whom they felt would be less risky. In future years I will encourage students to reflect on the level of risk they were prepared to make in their choice of interviewees.

A theme that was conspicuous in its absence was the fact that conducting the interviews was a course requirement for the students. This fact encouraged me to reflect how I influenced their experience of the research process and how I had failed to make the students feel comfortable enough to state my influence explicitly.

End-of-year anonymous evaluations of the course as a whole suggested that the students found me approachable and that my attitude toward students was good. No specific evaluations of the practical exercise were measured, however, making it difficult to ascend the level of coercion the students may have felt.

THE TEACHING/RESEARCH NEXUS AS FEMINIST METHODOLOGY

The assessment exercise that I have just described demonstrates the potential that teaching about gender issues in psychology has for feminist research and praxis. The class seemed to unanimously agree on the success of the exercise. One of the most important aspects of the task was that it was a mutually educative encounter. The students reported themselves being better able to understand and relate to ideas about the feminist critique of psychology. Feedback from the interviewees suggested that it had been a consciousness-raising experience for them (some had never thought about feminism or the pivotal role they played in families), and I was given insight into some women's lives that I would not have been exposed to otherwise.

An important aspect of the exercise was that it prompted me to think more critically about my role as a teacher and researcher in the production of knowledge. Despite my best intentions, the way in which I set up the project reduced the chance that some social classes of women would be included in the research—this emphasized to me how important it is to consider the perspectives I privilege in my teaching and research activities. Prilleltensky (1989), among others, has pointed out how the process of conducting research in psychology functions to perpetuate the status quo. It seems that Prilleltensky's point is equally relevant to the process of teaching about psychology. A lack of reflexivity about the role of subjectivity in how psychological knowledge is taught may also contribute to the reproduction of knowledge that supports dominant social values.

The teaching/research dialectic described in this article did encourage critical reflection on issues of power. Feminist theory about teaching and research usually considers the power relationships between two subjects, instructor/instructed and researcher/researched, respectively. The usually distinctive subject positions of instructor, instructed, researcher, and researched become less clear in a teaching/research nexus, providing an opportunity to reconsider and challenge the dynamics that have traditionally organized those relationships. The power of teacher over student was disrupted in the present exercise by emphasizing their shared roles as researchers. Both teacher and student were active participants in the production of knowledge, so the teacher as well as the student learned from the experience.

In the present exercise, the interviewees were not only participants in a research exercise but were also contributing to an instructive act. Hence issues of power can be considered in light of their participation in an educative encounter. At one level their involvement had an instructive element; students approached participants with the goal of gaining knowledge. The teaching aspect of the interviewee's role in the teaching/research nexus can be viewed as empowering insofar as the students became dependent on the participants' cooperation for the success of the exercise. At another level their involvement was as a student. The exercise offered an opportunity for the interviewees to gain new insights into themselves. The interviewees in our study reported enjoying the opportunity to reflect on their lives. It seems then, that research with students may be considered feminist insofar as it disrupts the traditional hierarchies of power between the all-knowing researcher/teacher and the "naive" subject/student.

In addition to disrupting the traditional power hierarchies, a further advantage of the teaching/research nexus was that it encouraged both the students and me to think critically about our roles in the research process. For the students, the reflexivity was a prescribed part of the assessment exercise. Nevertheless their analyses produced some interesting observations. For me, the reflexive insights were specifically a product of the teaching/research dialectic. The exercise led me to consider more closely how my "class-ification" influenced student's choice of interviewees. Despite intentions to the contrary, my supposedly liberatory approach failed to encourage the students to become interested in some sorts of women's experiences. This realization has reinforced the need to reflect constantly on how feminist teaching and research activities can exclude and silence, just as any other approach to teaching and research can. What is clear from the example I have described is that when a teaching/research nexus is approached from a feminist perspective, it has the potential for informing discussions of power and subjectivity.

Ethical Considerations

Any research involving human participants raises ethical concerns about voluntary involvement, informed consent, confidentiality, and so on. However, a specific ethical question raised when involving students in research is, "Who benefits from their participation?" Traditionally within psychology, participation in research has been seen as an essential aspect of undergraduate training. It is quite usual for published articles to refer to the fact that college students participated for course credit (e.g., Campbell, Schellenberg, & Senn, 1997). The assumption underlying such references is that the educational benefits from participation outweigh any problem about coercion of students by the teacher/researcher. The obvious gain for the researchers is that they are provided with data.

Over the last few years there has been increasing concern that student participation in research, for course credit or as an obligatory element of a psychology course, involves a level of coercion that is unacceptable. Increasingly, the arrangement is seen as profiting the teacher/researcher more than the students. Currently, at my university, a psychological research project that proposes to recruit undergraduate students will not get ethical approval unless there is absolutely no hint that participation is anything other than voluntary. Even asking students to fill out questionnaires in class is seen as being too coercive (in class, students may feel peer pressure to conform).

Gaining research experience is clearly an important aspect of training in psychology. It seems that confining the students' role to that of research subjects is becoming increasingly untenable, as evidenced by mounting concerns about compulsion to participate. When a research exercise involves more than just data collection, however, the links between the task and the pedagogical objective (to gain research experience) are more apparent. The central ethical issue is still that students benefit from their involvement in the research and their efforts are not exploited by the teacher/researcher. I would like to think that if the teaching/research nexus is informed by feminist principles then ethical problems will be avoided. For the protection of students and for the good of psychology as a discipline, however, it is important that the ethical issues of student involvement in research be openly debated and discussed.

The Benefits of a Teaching/Research Nexus

To conclude, I would like to explore more fully the advantages and problems of using the teaching/research dialectic as a feminist method. The first advantage is that feminist pedagogy and feminist research share similar theoretical positions, wedding them philosophically and practically and making them compatible for psychologists who wish to challenge traditional relations of dominance. The aim of a feminist pedagogy is to promote teaching practices that are empowering for the students. Two important aspects of feminist pedagogical theory are that both teachers and students are seen as active and interdependent agents in the production of knowledge and the consideration of how emancipatory teaching efforts may disguise teacher imposition of particular kinds of knowledge on students (Lather, 1991). Similar concerns exist for feminist researchers about the relationship between the investigator and the investigated (e.g., Oakley, 1981). Lather's (1988) work on student resistance to a supposedly emancipatory curriculum demonstrated the potential of the classroom as a site for both feminist teaching and feminist research practices. My experience of using teaching about women and gender as a methodological resource for feminist research in psychology verifies that potential.

Many feminist psychologists have a joint commitment to teaching and researching gender issues (e.g., Paludi, 1990; Unger & Crawford, 1996). Thus, a practical advantage of using teaching as a resource for research is that it can be used as a strategy for increasing research output. Criticisms about using students as research participants (e.g., Wallston & Grady, 1985) may have discouraged thinking about how student participation in research could be considered feminist. The experience reported in this article suggests that feminist psychologists should reconsider how their teaching activities can be used as a methodological resource capable of informing our work.

Getting students to recruit and conduct in-depth interviews is an example of a teaching/research exercise that worked well with a small class of advanced students. Such an exercise may not be appropriate with larger classes, where the quantity of material generated may be too great to promote insightful comparisons and discussion. In addition, less advanced students may not be mature enough to conduct interviews responsibly and sensitively. Interviews are not the only activity that can be used in a teaching/research exercise, however. Any research project that has links with the content of a course may be adapted so that it fulfills both pedagogical and research goals.

An example of a teaching/research nexus that was successful with a larger class of undergraduates ($N = 69$) involved asking students to listen for metaphors involving sex or sexual experiences as they pursued their daily activities. The examples that the students collected were used in a practical activity that had two pedagogical goals—to train the students how to develop coding schemes for qualitative data and to encourage the students to reflect how metaphors influence the way the world is experienced. The data collected also formed the basis for an article on the metaphorical construction of sex (Walton & Weatherall, 1997). In the research project the students were taking dual roles—on the one hand they were informants or participant observers reporting on their language communities, but at the same time they were research collaborators. Their interpretations of the metaphors were essential for our (the teachers/researchers) understanding of some of the examples.

Related to the idea that research with and for students may be a useful strategy to increase research activity is that using teaching as a research resource legitimizes a feminist pedagogical act as worthwhile. Encouraging students to become active agents in the production of knowledge involves a personal and political commitment on behalf of the teacher. The personal and political investment involved with feminist teaching practices may have payoffs, one being that it becomes a means of producing as well as disseminating knowledge.

A final strength of the teaching/research dialectic described in this article is that it was strongly focused on women. It was an interactive and contextualized method for conducting research. The interviews, as well as the reports of the interviews, involved talking and thinking about women. The interviewees' accounts and the interviewers' reports involved discussion that focused on exploring patterns of experiences. There was critical consideration of the multiple ways in which gender is implicated (or not) in the distribution of power and privilege at a personal level. The assessment exercise can be understood as a feminist method in that it was personal (for the students and the interviewees) and embedded in the everyday lives and experiences of women.

Disadvantages of a Teaching/Research Nexus

Despite the advantages of using a teaching/research dialectic as a feminist method, the approach has some limitations. One problem is that there is nothing specific to the merger of teaching and research practices that makes it feminist. As already mentioned, the use of students in psychological research has a long history, little of which could be described as feminist. Harding (1987) suggested that no method is intrinsically feminist; rather, what is crucial to conducting feminist research is the methodological approach (or underlying theory guiding how investigations proceed). With the exception of a few feminist-oriented psychology texts (e.g., Unger & Crawford, 1996), there seems to be little evidence of psychology being taught using critical pedagogical principles. It appears likely that as long as the educative encounter is perceived as merely being the transfer of knowledge from instructors to pupils, there is little chance that the teaching/research dialectic can be considered a feminist method. A methodological starting point for the teaching/research dialectic to be feminist is to acknowledge the interdependence of teaching and learning.

Insights that I gained from the exercise will influence how the assessment exercise will be approached with future classes. In particular, I will endeavor to make more explicit how I may unintentionally influence their choice of research participants and the way they report their experience of the task.Bonus points could be awarded to students for "giving voice" to someone I have "silenced." Also, I will provide the students an opportunity to be honest about the way they conducted the task and how they felt about it by inviting them to make anonymous evaluations. A further improvement to the exercise would be to work with the students on an interview schedule that is more likely to enhance the experience for the interviewees. In the present exercise, students appreciated the strength and resilience women showed in times of adversity. In future exercises I will encourage students to design questions that will encourage the interviewees themselves to come to a better appreciation of the value of their lives.

A limitation of using the teaching/research dialectic to produce knowledge for feminist psychologists is that the work does not lend itself to developing models of prediction and control. The result of the feminist research/teaching dialectic that I have described is a contextualized exploration of patterns of meaning—the process of the work being as important as the product. Given that models of prediction and control are highly valued in psychology, the type of interpretative account produced from a research/teaching dialectic may not be an attractive option for feminist psychologists seeking to establish themselves using conventional paradigms.

For approaches that view power as a fixed commodity, a disadvantage of using the teaching/research nexus as a means for conducting praxis-oriented inquiry is that it may be seen as diminishing the status that one gains from being a teacher and a researcher in an educational institution. Encouraging agency in students and seeking emancipatory knowledge could be construed as disempowering for academicians. An important theoretical aspect of some forms of feminist inquiry, however, is that power is construed as being exercised rather than possessed (Stanley & Wise, 1993). According to such thinking, power imbalances can be challenged and disrupted even by those who are advantaged by the status quo. A final disadvantage of using teaching as a methodological resource is that it is unlikely to be recognized as a valuable method for conducting research within fields of academic inquiry that subscribe to traditional models of education and research.

In conclusion, a teaching/research dialectic has the potential for being a feminist method. By disrupting the dualisms that have dominated thinking about teaching and research, we can conduct interactive and contextualized inquiry into women's lives.

Initial submission: November 26, 1996
Initial acceptance: February 27, 1997
Final acceptance: May 19, 1997

NOTES

1. I follow Harding's (1987) distinction between method as a research technique such as an experiment or a questionnaire and methodology as a perspective or theoretically informed framework of how research should proceed.
2. The proposed title of the course Feminist Psychology was rejected by the chairperson of the psychology department because of its political overtones. It is interesting to note that the same objection (of being too political) was made in response to the first proposal to establish a Psychology of Women section in the British Psychological Society in 1985 (see Wilkinson, 1991). The feminist orientation of the course is made explicit in the course description, which reads "In 1968, Weisstein argued that 'psychology has nothing to say about what women are really like, what they need and what they want, essentially because psychology does not want to know.'

Over the past 25 years there have been significant theoretical and methodological developments in feminist psychology. The present course will critically examine woman as an 'object of psychological inquiry' and also look at development within psychology as the result of the critique."

3. See Walkerdine (1996).

REFERENCES

Bannister, P., Burman, E., Parker, I., Taylor, M., & Tindall, C. (1994). *Qualitative methods in psychology: A research guide*. Buckingham, UK: Open University Press.

Bohan, J. S. (Ed.). (1992). *Seldom seen, rarely heard: Women's place in psychology*. Boulder, CO: Westview Press.

Breakwell, G. M. (1990). *Interviewing*. Leicester, UK: British Psychological Society.

Campbell, E., Schellenberg, G., & Senn, C.Y. (1997). Evaluating measures of contemporary sexism. *Psychology of Women Quarterly, 21,* 89–102.

Harding, S. (1986). *The science question in feminism*. Ithaca, NY: Cornell University Press.

Harding, S. (1987). *Feminism and methodology*. Ithaca, NY: Cornell University Press.

Kahn, A. S., & Yoder, J. D. (1989). The psychology of women and conservatism. Rediscovering social change. *Psychology of Women Quarterly, 13,* 417–432.

Lather, P. (1988). Feminist perspectives on empowering research methodologies. *Womens Studies International Forum, 11,* 569–581.

Lather, P. (1991). *Getting smart. Feminist research and pedagogy with/in the postmodern*. New York: Routledge.

Luke, C., & Gore, J. (Eds.). (1992). *Feminisms and critical pedagogy*. New York: Routledge.

Oakley, A. (1981). Interviewing women: A contradiction in terms. In H. Roberts (Ed.), *Doing feminist research* (pp. 30–61). Boston: Routledge, Chapman and Hall.

Orner, M. (1992). Interrupting the calls for student voice in 'liberatory' education: A feminist post structuralist perspective. In C. Luke & J. Gore (Eds.), *Feminisms and critical pedagogy* (pp. 74–89). New York: Routledge.

Paludi, M.A. (1990). *Exploring/Teaching the psychology of women*. Albany: State University of New York Press.

Peplau, L. A., & Conrad, E. (1989). Beyond nonsexist research. The perils of feminist methods in psychology. *Psychology of Women Quarterly, 13,* 379–400.

Prilleltensky, I. (1989). Psychology and the status quo. *American Psychologist, 44,* 795–802.

Stanley, L., & Wise, S. (1990). Method, methodology and epistemology in feminist research processes. In L. Stanley (Ed.), *Feminist praxis: Research, theory and feminist epistemology in sociology* (pp. 20–60). London: Routledge.

Stanley, L., & Wise, S. (1993). *Breaking out again. Feminist ontology and epistemology*. London: Routledge

Unger, R., & Crawford, M. (1996). *Women and gender. A feminist psychology* (2nd edition). New York: McGraw Hill.

Walkerdine, V. (1996). Subjectivity and social class: New directions for feminist psychology. *Feminism & Psychology, 6,* 355–360.

Wallston, B. S., & Grady, K. E. (1985). Integrating the feminist critique and the crisis in social psychology. Another look at research methods. In V. E. O'Leary, R. K. Unger, & B. S. Wallston (Eds.), *Women, gender and social psychology* (pp. 7–33). Hillsdale NJ: Lawrence Erlbaum.

Walton, M., & Weatherall, A. (1997). *The metaphorical construction of sexual experience in the speech community of New Zealand university students*. Unpublished manuscript, Wellington, New Zealand; Victoria University of Wellington.

Wilkinson, S. (1991). Why psychology (badly) needs feminism. In J. Aaron & S. Walby (Eds.), *Out of the margins: Womens studies in the nineties* (pp. 191–203). London: Falmer Press.

Worell, J., & Etaugh, C. (1994). Transforming theory and research with women: Themes and variations. *Psychology of Women Quarterly, 4,* 443–450.

ISSUES OF POWER AND RISK AT THE HEART OF THE TEACHING/ RESEARCH NEXUS

Hilary M. Lips
Radford University

The use of the delicate interconnection between teaching and research to serve the dual purpose of illuminating feminist methodology and gathering data has much to recommend it. It is a way of forging a stronger bond between teacher and student, of empowering students and ensuring them more understanding of the research process, of keeping the teacher humble by reminding her or him that she or he cannot possibly anticipate everything that could go wrong. It exposes teacher and students to perspectives on the research that would have been missed without the collaborative effort, and provides for the generation of new ideas for exploration. It highlights and reinforces, for both the teacher and the students, two important principles that are shared by both feminist research and feminist pedagogy: that knowledge is sought and constructed in a social context, and that the teacher/ student or researcher/subject partnership is mutually influential. Thus, for many reasons, this endeavor might be labeled good feminist practice.

There are, however, some cautionary considerations. To some extent control is always an illusion in research; however, the teacher even more dramatically than usual "loses control" of the research process when she or he enlists the students as partners. In the current example, students did not recruit as broad a sample of interviewees as their instructor had envisioned, omitting women of lower socioeconomic status. Other departures from the instructor's plan are possible. Students may not follow the lines of investigation that their professor had in mind—and the lines that they do follow may end up appearing less interesting, or more interesting, than the instructor's original idea. By losing some control, the instructor may find herself or himself opened to new ways of looking at a research question. A more negative possibility is that students may simply flounder and gather data that have so little focus as to be useless. They may finish the enterprise by feeling that research is an uninteresting waste of time, and indeed, in such a case, it will have been just that.

Address correspondence and reprint requests to: Hilary Lips, Department of Psychology, Radford University, Radford, VA 24142. Email: hlips@runet.edu.

To ensure that the research will be coherent and useful, the instructor must obviously use her or his authority. She or he must insist on guidelines that help the students lay careful groundwork for the project. If an interview or questionnaire is to be used, the class must work together to develop and/or agree on the questions to be used, as occurred in this case example. If observation or participant observation is planned, the class must jointly develop their ideas of what is to be observed and how it is to be recorded. If the method is content analysis, coding categories should be discussed and agreed on. Then, in class, there should be at least some practice in using the methods that have been developed. In the current example, students had no interviewing experience and were simply urged to practice with each other outside of class. Because the class was a small and enthusiastic one, this strategy worked reasonably well, but a preferable approach would have been to have at least a day of role-playing the interviews.

Anyone who has done research knows that, regardless of the amount of preparation, there will be mistakes. However—and this is one lesson that ought to be reinforced to the student researchers—the "mistakes" can provide the most useful of all insights. For example, in the current study, reflections on the problems encountered in the research illuminated critical issues of power and risk in face-to-face research. Students had to recruit volunteers to be interviewed for their research. Because students had to complete the interviews as part of a course requirement, they needed the interviewees more than vice versa. The more desperate the student-researchers, the more power the interviewees could wield, as discovered by the student who sought to interview her two sisters. Thus, worry about "exploiting" research participants became worry about being exploited—about yielding too much power to the participants because they were so badly needed. This situation is not necessarily so different from that faced by investigators in all kinds of research who do not use "captive" populations such as students. Whenever a researcher ventures beyond the walls of academe she or he incurs a potential loss of control and then she or he is desperate to complete the research because of time commitments, tenure pressures, or grant requirements. People may refuse to talk to her or him, may make fun of or become irritated by her or his questions, or may ultimately try to take control of the information she or he gathers. If feminist researchers are to live up to the ideal of studying diverse populations of women, we must face up to the very real fear that this kind of situation engenders.

That fear is evident in the way students selected participants for the research described in this article. Students avoided selecting interviewees whom they thought would be "risky," thus inadvertently limiting their sample to members of middle and upper socioeconomic class groups. They were apparently unsure how to approach participants who did not share their class background and were afraid of being uncomfortable and awkward in their interactions with them. Their behavior mirrors behavior in which we have all engaged (but on which we may not have reflected) and reveals, at a very basic level, one of the chief reasons why psychology has spent so much time and energy studying such limited samples. These issues cut to the heart of our research practice. Who is included in our research and how are such decisions made? Are we honest with ourselves about the reasons for our choices? Do we try to maintain our power as researchers and our image as experts by focusing on "safe" participants? How do these choices affect what we "know" as a result of our research? If many researchers are inhibited by these same uncertainties, how does that affect the big picture of what psychology "knows"? What might be the implications for science in general? These are some of the questions that emerge from this particular research example. Such questions deserve to be reflected on jointly by the teacher/student research team as part of the self-critical process inherent in this methodology.

The teaching/research nexus takes place, of course, in a particular context: the educational institution that employs the teacher and accepts the tuition of the student. Consideration of this context raises a number of practical issues, as well as additional issues of power and risk. For example, instructors must ensure that the research project in question has been cleared through the institution's research ethics committees, and this imposes a level of formality and time constraints that must be incorporated into planning the course. For faculty who are under strong pressures to publish, the devotion of time and energy to this type of research may be risky, given that it may prove difficult to publish the findings. On the other hand, for such faculty, there may be a strong temptation to use their students' work as a way to get published—a power strategy that has a long, and sometimes bitter, history in academia.

The notion that instruction should involve joint productivity, that teachers and students should be partners in exploration and scholarship, is completely consistent with feminist approaches to scholarship. Yet it ought not be regarded as a new insight or as the special invention of feminist pedagogy or feminist methodology. Good educational practice has always implied teachers and students collaborating in creative ways, although that notion seems to have been buried under the recent popular rhetoric that turns teaching and research into opposing dualities. The formal adoption of the teaching/research nexus as a site for feminist methodological innovation may help to break down these oppositional categories and help academia to rediscover that, indeed, teaching and research are different faces of the same process.

FOCUS GROUPS

A Feminist Method

Sue Wilkinson
Loughborough University

Focus groups are little used in feminist psychology, despite their method-ological advantages. Following a brief introduction to the method, the article details three key ways in which the use of focus groups addresses the feminist critique of traditional methods in psychology. Focus groups are relatively naturalistic and so avoid the charge of artificiality; they offer social contexts for meaning-making and so avoid the charge of decontextualization; and they shift the balance of power away from the researcher toward the research participants and so avoid the charge of exploitation. The final section of the article, which evaluates the potential of focus groups for feminist research, identifies some other benefits of the method and also discusses some problems in the current use of focus groups. It concludes that the use—and development—of focus group methods offer feminist psychology an excellent opportunity for the future.

A family group, gathered around the TV in their living room, argues over a favorite soap opera; teenage girls sprawled over tables in a classroom swap stories about sexual harassment in high school; women waiting for appointments in a family planning clinic discuss methods of contraception—these are all potential focus group scenarios. A focus group is—at its simplest—"an informal discussion among selected individuals about specific topics" (Beck, Trombetta, & Share, 1986, p. 73). Researchers using focus groups typically organize and run a series of small, focused, group discussions and analyze the resulting data using a range of conventional qualitative techniques. As a research method, focus groups are similar to one-to-one interviews, except that they involve more than one participant per data collection

The author thanks Hannah Frith for the data extract quoted and for enthusiastic discussion of focus group method.

Address correspondence and reprint requests to: Sue Wilkinson, Women's Studies Research Group, Department of Social Sciences, Loughborough University, Loughborough, Leicestershire LE11 3TU, UK. E-mail: S.Wilkinson@lboro.ac.uk.

session; indeed, they are sometimes described as focus group interviews, group interviews, or group depth interviews.

Although focus groups are widely used in some fields, particularly in applied areas—such as communication/media studies (e.g., Lunt & Livingstone, 1996), education (e.g., Vaughn, Schumm, & Sinagub, 1996), and health care (e.g., Brems & Griffiths, 1993)—few feminists (and even fewer feminist psychologists) use the method. This article makes the case for the value of focus groups in feminist psychology and in feminist research more generally. As such, it is a contribution to the continuing feminist debate on methodology, both within psychology (e.g., Marecek, 1989; Morawski, 1994; Peplau & Conrad, 1989; Wilkinson, 1986) and beyond it (e.g., Bowles & Klein, 1983; Fonow & Cook, 1991; Harding, 1987; Stanley & Wise, 1993; Westkott, 1979). This debate considers not only the pros and cons of different methods of data collection, but also the ways in which methodological issues are intrinsically conceptual ones (cf. Unger, 1983). The design and conduct of a research project, the questions that are asked, the methods of data collection, the type of analysis that takes place, the perceived implications or utility of that analysis—all of these necessarily incorporate particular assumptions, models, and values. As Jeanne Marecek (1989, p. 370) noted, "a method is an interpretation." The choice of one method over another is not simply a technical decision, but an epistemological and theoretical one. This means that, as feminists considering the use of innovative or unusual methods, we need (as much as with conventional methods) to be aware of the epistemological commitments and value assumptions they make (Riger, 1992). In this article, I introduce focus group method; I then highlight the particular advantages of focus group method for feminist researchers; finally, I evaluate the potential of focus group method for feminist research.

INTRODUCING FOCUS GROUPS

As the authors of a key text on focus groups pointed out, "what is known as a focus group today takes many different forms" (Stewart & Shamdasani, 1990, p. 9), but centrally it involves one or more group discussions in which participants focus collectively on a topic selected by the researcher and presented to them in the form of a film, a collection of advertisements, a vignette to discuss, a "game" to play, or simply a particular set of questions. The groups (rarely more than 12 people at a time and more commonly 6 to 8) can consist of either preexisting clusters of people (e.g., family members, Khan & Manderson, 1992; work colleagues, J. Kitzinger, 1994a, 1994b) or people drawn together specifically for the research. Many aspects of focus groups (e.g., the selection of participants, the setting in which they meet, the role of the moderator, the specific focus of the group, the structure of the discussion) are discussed in detail in the various "how to" books that address this method (e.g., Krueger, 1988; Morgan, 1988, 1993; Stewart & Shamdasani, 1990; Vaughn et al., 1996), and I will not rehearse such discussions here. Discussions between group participants, usually audiotaped (sometimes videotaped) and transcribed, constitute the data, and methods of qualitative analysis (ranging from conventional content analysis to rhetorical or discursive techniques) are generally employed. The method is distinctive not for its mode of analysis but for its data collection procedures. Crucially—and many commentators on the method make this point—focus groups involve the interaction of group participants with each other as well as with the researcher/moderator, and it is the collection of this kind of interactive data that distinguishes the focus group from the one-to-one interview (cf. J. Kitzinger, 1994a; Morgan, 1988).

In general, focus group method is well suited to exploratory, interpretive, multi-method, and phenomenological research questions (Frey & Fontana, 1993). In considering whether to use focus groups, two leading experts (Morgan & Krueger, 1993) suggested that the researcher should take into account not only the purpose of the study, but also the appropriateness of group discussion as a format, the match between researchers' and participants' interests, and the type of results required. In conducting a focus group study, the researcher must make critical decisions about the following key parameters, all of which fundamentally affect the design and analysis of the study: the type of participants and the number of groups to be conducted, the topic or activity on which the groups are to focus; the conduct of the sessions; recording and transcription issues; and the analytic frame to be employed (see Knodel, 1993, for a useful summary discussion of design issues).

Although social psychologist Emory Bogardus (1926) used group interviews in developing his social distance scale, the invention of the focus group is usually attributed to sociologist Robert Merton, who, along with his colleagues Patricia Kendall and Marjorie Fiske, developed a group approach ("the focussed group-interview") to elicit information from audiences about their responses to radio programs (Merton & Kendall, 1946; Merton, Fiske, & Kendall, 1956). The method is most widely used within the fields of business and marketing (Goldman & McDonald, 1987), and it is only in the past five years or so that it has been described as "gaining some popularity among social scientists" (Fontana & Frey, 1994, p. 364), so the current "resurgence of interest" (Lunt & Livingstone, 1996, p. 79) in focus groups is a recent phenomenon. Focus groups have not been widely used in psychology, in part because "they did not fit the positivist criteria extant in the dominant research paradigm" (Harrison & Barlow, 1995, p. 11). The method rarely appears in texts of psychological research methods (although for recent exceptions see Millward, 1995; Vaughn et al., 1996), nor is it often cited in feminist research methods texts. (For an exception see Reinharz, 1992. But even here there are only two paragraphs on focus groups, and the author cites just one focus group study by a feminist psychologist—and that in an unpublished dissertation.)

Despite half a century (or more) of focus group research, feminist psychologists' use of the method seems to have begun only during the 1990s. Such focus group research includes work on men talking about 'sex (Crawford, Kippax, & Waldby, 1994) and about unemployment (Willott & Griffin, 1997); immigrant/refugee women exploring sexuality and gender-related issues (Espin, 1995); and sorority women talking about the threat of sexual aggression (Norris, Nurius, & Dimeff, 1996). In particular, feminist psychologists at the beginning of their careers seem to be drawn to focus groups as a research method: under the heading of student "work in progress," see Barringer's (1992) work with incest survivors, Lampon's (1995) study of lesbians' perceptions of safer sex practices, and Raabe's (1993) research on young people's identities. There are, of course, other feminist psychologists who rely on conversations between groups of participants as a means of data collection but do not use the term "focus groups" or rely on the literature associated with this method. Michelle Fine's research with groups of girls (e.g., Fine, 1992; Fine & Addelston, 1996; Macpherson & Fine, 1995) is an example of such group work; others include Billinghurst (1996), Erkut, Fields, Sing, and Marx (1996), Kissling (1996), Lovering (1995), Walkerdine (1996), and Widdicombe (1995).

ADVANTAGES OF FOCUS GROUPS FOR FEMINIST RESEARCHERS

Feminist researchers have identified a range of problems inherent in traditional psychological methods (see, e.g., critiques by Jayaratne & Stewart, 1991; Reinharz, 1983). Central to such critiques are the artificiality of traditional psychological methods, their decontextualized nature, and the exploitative power relations between researcher and researched. These three problems are key to feminist critiques of traditional methods, and it is precisely these problems, I argue, that can be addressed through the use of focus groups.

Artificiality.   Many feminist psychologists have been critical of data generated via experimental methods (e.g., Parlee, 1979; Sherif, 1979/1992) and by tests and scales (e.g., Lewin & Wild, 1991; Tavris, 1992), urging "the abandonment of the experiment as contextually sterile and trivial in favor of more qualitative methods that are closer to actual experience" (Lott, 1985, p. 151). Feminist researchers have argued that feminist methods should be naturalistic in the sense that they should tap into the usual "modes of communication" (Maynard, 1990, p. 275) and the "everyday social processes" (Graham, 1984, p. 113) that constitute people's social lives.

Decontextualization.   From the beginning of second wave feminist psychology, researchers emphasized the importance of social context and insisted that feminist methods should be contextual: that is, they should avoid focusing on the individual devoid of social context or separate from interactions with others (e.g., Weisstein, 1968/1993). The "context-stripping" nature of experiments and surveys was criticized because, as Janis Bohan (1992, p. 13) stated, "the reality of human experience—namely that it always occurs in context— . . . is lost." Feminists (along with other critical social psychologists, e.g., Gergen, 1987; Prilleltensky, 1989; Sampson, 1988) have criticized psychology's individualism, proposing that the individual self may be characterized as "in connection" or "relational" (e.g., Jordan, Kaplan, Miller, Stiver, & Surrey, 1991; Taylor, Gilligan, & Sullivan, 1996) or seen primarily as a social construction, a cultural product of Western thought (e.g., C. Kitzinger, 1992; Lykes, 1985). "If you really want to know either of us," wrote Michelle Fine and Susan Gordon, then "do not put us in a laboratory, or hand us a survey, or even interview us separately alone in our homes. Watch me (MF) with women friends, my son, his father, my niece, or my mother and you will see what feels most authentic to me" (Fine & Gordon, 1989, p. 159). Other (social constructionist and postmodernist) critics have gone further in suggesting that human experience is constructed within specific social contexts. Collective sense is made, meanings negotiated, and identities elaborated through the processes of social interaction between people (e.g., Hare-Mustin & Marecek, 1990; Morawski & Agronick, 1991; West & Zimmerman, 1987).

Exploitation. Feminist psychologists have criticized the extent to which the interests and concerns of research participants are subordinated to those of the researcher and the way in which people are transformed into "object-like subjects" (Unger, 1983, p. 149) and have castigated the traditional hierarchy of power relations between researcher and researched (e.g., Campbell & Schram, 1995, p. 88; Peplau & Conrad, 1989, p. 386). In feminist research, "respecting the experience and perspective of the other" (Worell & Etaugh, 1994, p. 444) is key. Many feminist researchers express commitment to "realizing as fully as possible women's voices in data gathering and preparing an account that transmits those voices" (Olesen, 1994, p. 167), suggesting that feminist research is characterized by "non-hierarchical relations" (Seibold, Richards, & Simon, 1994, p. 395), and evaluating research methods (at least partly) in terms of their adequacy in enabling feminist researchers to engage in "a more equal and reciprocal relationship with their informants" (Graham, 1984, p. 113).

These three problems—artificiality, decontextualization, and exploitation—in conjunction have led feminist researchers frequently to advocate qualitative approaches, even to suggest that these are "quintessentially feminist" (Maynard & Purvis, 1994, p. 3). I will not rehearse here the arguments for the use—or particular merits—of qualitative methods in feminist research, as these have been well documented elsewhere (see, e.g., Griffin, 1985; Henwood & Pidgeon, 1995; Marshall, 1986; Reinharz, 1983). Rather, I will demonstrate the particular value of focus groups as a qualitative feminist method.

Avoiding Artificiality: Focus Groups are a Relatively "Naturalistic" Method

The claim that focus groups are "naturalistic" (or "ecologically valid") is commonplace in the focus group literature (e.g., Albrecht, Johnson, & Walther, 1993, p. 54; Liebes, 1984, p. 47). Focus groups avoid the artificiality of many psychological methods because they draw on people's normal, everyday experiences of talking and arguing with families, friends, and colleagues about events and issues in their everyday lives. It is exactly this ordinary social process that is tapped by focus group method. Everyday topics about which focus groups are invited to talk might include drinking behaviors (Beck et al., 1987), sexual decision making (Zeller, 1993), labor and birth experiences (DiMatteo, Kahn, & Berry, 1993), buying a new car (Stewart & Shamdasani, 1990), coping with marriage breakdown (Hamon & Thiessen, 1990), and experiences of friends' and acquaintances' heart attacks (Morgan & Spanish, 1984). As focus group textbook author Richard Krueger (1988, p. 44) noted, people are "social creatures who interact with others," who are "influenced by the comments of others," and who "make decisions after listening to the advice and counsel of people around them." Focus groups tap into the "natural" processes of communication, such as arguing, joking, boasting, teasing, persuasion, challenge, and disagreement. Robin Jarrett (1993, p. 194) described her focus groups with young women as having "the feel of rap sessions with friends. The atmosphere was exuberantly boisterous and sometimes frank in language."

Feminist researchers who have used focus groups have typically commented favorably on the extent to which they mirror everyday social interchange in a relatively naturalistic way. A study of female friends' talk about abortion involved groups of friends meeting to watch an episode of the TV program *Cagney & Lacey* in the home of one of their members, which "provided a fairly naturalistic environment for television viewing" (Press, 1991, p. 423). Feminist psychologist Kathryn Lovering (1995), in talking about menstruation with young people at school, found that group discussions provided a context for a "relatively naturalistic conversational exchange" (p. 16)—in this case characterized by a great deal of "embarrassment" and "giggling" (pp. 22–23). In discussing these topics, participants draw on the modes of interaction, communication, and expression common in their everyday lives.

Many focus groups use preexisting or naturally occurring social groups such as friendship groups (e.g., Liebes, 1984), work colleagues (e.g., J. Kitzinger, 1994a, 1994b), family members (e.g., Khan & Manderson, 1992), members of clubs (J. Kitzinger, 1994a, 1994b), or simply "people who have experienced the same problem, such as residents of a deteriorating neighborhood or women in a sexist organization" (Rubin & Rubin, 1995, p. 139). According to focus group researcher Jenny Kitzinger (1994a), in a study of the effects of media messages about AIDS:

> By using pre-existing groups we were sometimes able to tap into fragments of interactions which approximated to 'naturally-occurring' data. . . . The fact that research participants already knew each other had the additional advantage that friends and colleagues could relate each others' comments to actual incidents in their shared daily lives. (p. 105)

Feminist researchers have also drawn on people who already know each other in setting up their groups. Heterosexual college women from sorority houses at a large west coast university in the United States were invited (together with a friend) to attend group meetings to discuss the perceived threat of sexual aggression from fraternity acquaintances (Norris et al., 1996). In another project, the participants themselves decided to bring along their best friends, which worked well for the group: "The best friend pairings ensured that each girl had a familiar audience and, as it turned out, a critical one; challenges came only from the friend at first, uncritical questions came from the other girls" (Macpherson & Fine, 1995, p. 182). Participants who know each other may recall common experiences, share half-forgotten memories, or challenge each other on contradictions between what they are professing to believe in the group and what they might have said or done outside the group ("What about the other day when you . . . ?"; "But last night you said . . . !").

The value of having people who know each other as participants in a focus group is illustrated in the following exchange between Marlene and Rebecca, two members of a focus group asked to discuss a television drama dealing with abortion as a moral issue. In the following extract, the interviewer apparently misunderstands Marlene's initial response to a question (hearing "eloquent" as "awkward") and subsequently seeks clarification of her referent. Rebecca intervenes with a shared memory, which both she and Marlene understand as contradicting Marlene's earlier statement:

Interviewer:	So what did you think? In general.
Marlene:	Parts of it were kind of unrealistic. . . . I think the pro-life people. . . . They're not that eloquent and I don't think they're that knowledgeable.
Interviewer:	Not that awkward . . .
Marlene:	Eloquent . . . and not that knowledgeable and also every . . .
Interviewer:	The pro-life people?
Marlene:	Yeah . . . and everyone I've talked to basically told me a lie, so . . .
Rebecca:	But remember the um, the false clinic that we went to . . .
Marlene:	. . . that one woman . . .
Rebecca:	That one woman was so eloquent. (Press, 1991, p. 432)

In this extract, Rebecca contrasts the material in the TV drama with an actual experience, which Marlene shared, and their joint memories of this particular experience provoke a detailed discussion typical of what can occur when participants already know each other.

In sum, focus groups enable feminist research to be "naturalistic" insofar as they mirror the processes of communication in everyday social interaction. This is particularly the case when group members are friends or already acquainted and/ or when they are discussing topics or issues within the range of their everyday experiences. Focus groups themselves are not, of course, "natural" (in the sense of spontaneously arising). They are facilitated by a researcher for research purposes. There are debates within the literature about the extent to which they may be considered "naturalistic" (see, e.g., Morgan, 1993). However, the interactions that take place within focus groups are closer to everyday social processes than those afforded by most other research methods. The use of focus groups allows feminist researchers to better meet the feminist research objective of avoiding artificiality.

Avoiding Decontextualization: Focus Groups are Social Contexts for Meaning-Making

A focus group participant is not an individual acting in isolation. Rather, participants are members of a social group, all of whom interact with each other. In other words, the focus group is itself a social context. As David Morgan, a leading focus group researcher, emphasized: "The hallmark of focus groups is *the explicit use of group interaction to produce data and insights that would be less accessible without the interaction found in a group*" (Morgan, 1988, p. 12; his emphasis). These social interactions among participants constitute the primary data.

The interactive data generated by focus groups are based on the premise that "all talk through which people generate meaning is contextual" (Dahlgren, 1988, p. 292). The social context of the focus group provides an opportunity to examine how people engage in generating meaning, how opinions are formed, expressed, and (sometimes) modified within the context of discussion and debate with others.

As Jenny Kitzinger (1994b, pp. 170–171) pointed out, in focus group discussions, meanings are constantly negotiated and renegotiated:

> Participants do not just agree with each other, they also misunderstand one another, question one another, try to persuade each other of the justice of their own point of view and sometimes they vehemently disagree. . . . Such unexpected dissent [can lead] them to clarify why they thought as they did, often identifying aspects of their personal experience which had altered their opinions or specific occasions which had made them rethink their point of view. . . . People's different assumptions are thrown into relief by the way in which they challenge one another, the questions they ask, the sources they cite, and which explanations seem to sway the opinion of other members of the group.

In the focus group, people take differing individual experiences and attempt to make "collective sense" of them (Morgan & Spanish, 1984, p. 259). It is this process of collective sense-making that occurs through the interactions among focus group participants.

In individual interviews, the interaction is between the interviewer and a single interviewee; in focus groups, "a multitude of interpersonal dynamics occur," through interactions people change their views, and "the unit of analysis becomes the group" (Crabtree, Yanoshik, Miller, & O'Connor, 1993, p. 144). Focus groups not only provide a context for the collection of interactive data, but also offer "*the opportunity to observe directly the group process*. In the individual interview respondents *tell* how they would or did behave in a particular social situation. In the group interview, respondents react to each other, and their behavior is directly *observed*" (Goldman, 1962, p. 62, his emphasis). An example of the way in which group processes can become a key part of the analysis is found in Michael Billig's (1992) work on talk about the British Royal Family. One of Billig's concerns is the way people construct others as gullible and uncritical consumers of the media; they are used as "contrastive others" to illustrate the speaker's own critical powers and thereby enhance his or her own identity. Billig described a group discussion among four people, aged between 59 and 66 and all related, plus the mother of one of them, aged 87, whose "contributions to the conversation were often interruptions, as she told jokes or reminisced about poverty before the war. She even broke into song once: "I'm 'Enery the Eighth I am," she sang. For periods, she remained mute, while the not-so-elderly got on with their nimble conversational business" (Billig, 1992, p. 159). It is this woman who is constructed as the gullible other by her relatives. Billig analyzed the interactive mechanisms through which this othering (cf. Wilkinson & Kitzinger, 1996) is achieved. In his presentation of the data, one can see the process of othering at work and how the elaboration of the speaker's own identity depends on the interactive production of this contrastive other. (For a more extended discussion of the way in which Billig's analysis has made full use of the group interaction, see Wilkinson, 1998a.) Focus groups, then, offer the researcher the opportunity to observe directly the coconstruction of meaning in a social context via the interactions of group participants.

The few feminist researchers who have used focus groups (and other kinds of group work) have similarly taken advantage of the method to illustrate how arguments are developed and identities elaborated in a group context, typically through challenge and provocation from other members of the group. For example, after viewing a televised reconstruction of the rape and murder of a young female hitchhiker, one participant in Schlesinger, Dobash, Dobash, and Weaver's (1992, p. 146) research responds to another member of the focus group (who had expressed the opinion that the hitchhiker "was leading them on . . . the way she was dancing and her clothes as well . . . her top, her shirt") with the unequivocal statement: "Her clothes have got nothing to do with it." She adds, "I didn't want to say anything because my views are totally clear on this . . . ," and she then expounds them at some length. The provocation of the earlier speaker ensured that this woman's views were elicited and elaborated. Other examples of this include a (self-identified) "upper class" teenage girl, whose remarks imply that the behavior of the working class is responsible for the problems of the class system and who is challenged by other discussion group members to defend this view (Frazer, 1988, p. 349), and female students in an elite law school, who elaborate their experiences of profound alienation (and support each other in so doing) in the context of provocation from a male student who refers to "making a mountain out of a molehill" (Fine & Addelston, 1996, pp. 131–132).

The elaboration of meaning and identity through group interaction is also evident in an over-dinner group, in which "the text of conversation co-created by we six" (Macpherson & Fine, 1995, p. 181) is used to elaborate racial/ethnic differences among the participants. Janet (described by the authors as "Korean American") is challenged by Shermika, when she refers to African Americans at her school:

Shermika: I don't consider myself no African-American.
Janet: That's the acceptable politically correct . . .
Shermika: I'm full American, I've never been to Africa.
Janet: Are you black or wh[ite] . . . African-American? (Sorry.)
[Janet inadvertently repeated the "black or white" dichotomy that Shermika had announced was excluding Janet.]
Shermika: I'm neither one.
Michelle: What racial group do you consider yourself?
Shermika: Negro. Not black, not African-American. That's just like saying all white people come from Europe. Why don't you call 'em Europe-American? (Macpherson & Fine, 1995, pp. 188–189)

Here, Shermika is defending and elaborating her identity (as "full American" and as "Negro") in the context of a challenge from a group member. Janet's challenge also leads Shermika to explain her reasons for these identity label choices ("I've never been to Africa"). This exchange then prompts Janet to elaborate her own identity, creating her own differences from Shermika.

In sum, then, feminist focus group researchers have shown how the social context of the focus group offers the opportunity to observe the coconstruction of meaning and the elaboration of identities through interaction. The interactive nature of focus group data produces insights that would not be available outside the group context (although there is disappointingly little evidence of sophisticated analyses by feminists of such interactive data). This emphasis on the person in context makes the focus group an ideal method for feminist psychologists who see the self as relational or as socially constructed and who argue, therefore, that feminist methods should be contextual.

Avoiding Exploitation: Focus Groups Shift the Balance of Power

Focus groups inevitably reduce the researcher's power and control. Simply by virtue of the number of research participants simultaneously involved in the research interaction, the balance of power shifts away from the researcher. The researcher's influence is "diffused by the very fact of being in a group rather than a one-to-one situation" (Frey & Fontana, 1993, p. 26). As the aim of a focus group is to provide opportunities for a relatively free-flowing and interactive exchange of views, it is less amenable to the researcher's influence, compared with a one-to-one interview. Focus groups place "control over [the] interaction in the hands of the participants rather than the researcher" (Morgan, 1988, p. 18).

In direct contrast to the goals of most feminist researchers, the reduced power and control of the researcher is typically identified as a disadvantage of the method in the mainstream focus group literature. As Richard Krueger, a leading handbook author, lamented:

> the researcher has less control in the group interview as compared to the individual interview. The focus group interview allows the participants to influence and interact with each other, and, as a result, group members are able to influence the course of the discussion. This sharing of group control results in some inefficiencies such as detours in the discussion, and the raising of irrelevant issues. (Krueger, 1988, p. 46)

Similarly, other researchers have warned that the potential of groups to "usurp the moderator" (Watts & Ebbutt, 1987, p. 32) may lead to "relatively chaotic data collection" (Kvale, 1996, p. 101). The reassertion of control over focus group participants is seen as a management issue and is addressed by many of the "how to" books on focus groups, which offer advice for dealing with individual "problem" participants who do not behave in line with the researcher's requirements (e.g., Krueger, 1988; Stewart & Shamdasani, 1990; Vaughn et al., 1996). One focus group expert offered detailed instructions for maintaining power over participants in a section headed "Pest Control" (Wells, 1974). Moderator training is seen as essential and typically focuses around "leadership" issues. According to the handbooks, such training should enable the moderator to take "the role of nominal leader" (Stewart & Shamdasani, 1990, p. 70) and to exercise "a mild, unobtrusive control over the group" (Krueger, 1988, p. 73).

With this emphasis on the moderator's role, the issue of power and control in interactions among group members is rarely addressed, either as a feature of focus group method or even as a management issue for the moderator/researcher. A rare exception is a footnoted comment on the researcher's ethical obligation to deal with offensive comments, bullying, or intimidation directed at other group members (J. Kitzinger, 1994a, p. 118), also suggesting how this may be done (e.g., by considering group composition in advance, by using dissent within the group to challenge offensive remarks, or by direct intervention to silence or move on the discussion). In general, the more subtle exercise of power relations among group members (e.g., apparent collusion in constructing a particular argument or silencing a particular member) is rarely made explicit and is addressed in the focus group literature only insofar as it can be reduced to a "problem" generated by an individual group member and "solved" by direct intervention of the researcher. Billig's (1992, p. 159) demonstration of the process by which a family constructs its oldest member as the gullible other is therefore an unusual exception (although note that the researcher appears here only as recorder/analyst, not as a participant in the group interaction).

Some researchers do recognize that the reduction in the researcher's influence in focus groups can be seen as an advantage. David Morgan (1988, p. 18) pointed out that "participants' interaction among themselves replaces their interaction with the interviewer, leading to a greater emphasis on participants' points of view." Focus groups are sometimes presented as an opportunity for "listening to local voices" (Murray, Tapson, Turnbull, McCallum, & Little, 1994), for learning the participants' own language instead of imposing the researcher's language on them (Bers, 1987; Freimuth & Greenberg, 1986; Mays et al., 1992), and for gaining an insight into participants' conceptual worlds (Broom & Dozier, 1990). Focus groups can allow participants much greater opportunity to set the research agenda and to "develop the themes most important to them" (Cooper, Diamond, & High, 1993), which may diverge from those identified by the researcher. Compared with a one-to-one interview, it is much harder for the researcher to impose his or her own agenda in the group context.

The relative lack of power and control held by the researcher in the focus group allows the participants to challenge each other (Jarrett, 1993) and to challenge—or even to undermine—the researcher, insisting on their own interpretations and agendas being heard in place of the formal requirements of the research project. The following exchange is taken from the first few minutes of a focus group session in which the moderator (a 45-year-old man) attempts to set the agenda for the discussion. The participants are 18- and 19-year-old women:

Moderator:	The discussion is on sexual decision making and interpersonal relationships between those of the female and those of male arrangements. Tomorrow night, we are talking to the guys to see what their view of this thing is.
Participant:	I'd like to listen to that. [laughter]
Moderator:	There is every reason to believe that . . .
Participant:	[Like] Oprah Winfrey! [laughter]
Moderator:	There is every reason to believe that girls and guys see sex differently.
Participant:	I can tell you that right now. [laughter] (Zeller, 1993, pp. 174–175)

The interruptions, laughter, jokes, badinage, and cryptic comments of the participants cut across and over the formal introduction attempted by this moderator. The apparent attempt to set particular discussion topics is undermined by the young women, who frivolously compare his agenda to that of a popular TV program or who imply that his (rather pompously presented) hypotheses are simply self-evident ("I can tell you that right now"). In this extract the participants are—collaboratively—taking control over the process of context-setting and hence contributing to the determination of the subsequent course and nature of this discussion. (To be fair, this author does acknowledge the advantages of this process.)

Focus group researchers, then, are virtually unanimous that, compared with many other methods of data collection (especially the one-to-one interview), focus groups reduce the researcher's influence. For some (e.g., Krueger, 1988), this is a disadvantage that, although offset by the numerous advantages of the method, needs careful management. For others (e.g., Morgan, 1988), it is an advantage that enables participants to contribute to setting the research agenda, resulting in better access to their opinions and conceptual worlds. But, whether identified as a problem or a benefit, researchers concur on the relative lack of power held by the focus group researcher.

The few feminists who have used focus groups (and other kinds of group work) have similarly emphasized the shift in the balance of power—and particularly the extent to which the method enables research participants to speak in their own voice—to express their own thoughts and feelings and to determine their own agendas. In a recent article in the *Psychology of Women Quarterly*, Jeanette Norris et al. (1996, p. 129) claimed that: "Within feminist research, focus groups have been used to provide a 'voice' to the research participant by giving her an opportunity to define what is relevant and important to understand her experience." Feminist psychologist Oliva Espin (1995, p. 228), using focus groups in her exploration of immigrant/refugee women's understandings of sexuality and their internalization of cultural norms, commented that the method's "open-ended narratives allow for the expression of thoughts and feelings while inviting participants to introduce their own themes and concepts." Similarly, in a study of women's reactions to violent episodes on television, Schlesinger et al. (1992, p. 29) saw the group discussions as an opportunity for women to "determine their own agendas as much as possible." (See also Griffin (1986) and Frazer (1988) for examples of how group discussions led the researcher to change the research questions to address participants' concerns better.)

The following exchange arises in response to a (young, female) researcher's request to her focus group participants for examples of the excuses they use to avoid sex. Three young, heterosexual women (Lara, Cath, and Helen), challenge the researcher's implication that young women have to find excuses to avoid having sex with their male partners:

Cath:	Do you mean like really naff excuses?
Researcher:	Well, anything that you would use.
Lara:	But I mean. . . .
Cath:	But it depends how far you've got because that can go completely . . .
Helen:	No, but . . . no, but that just gives you a few days respite doesn't it?—and then I think that after a few days you'd just feel so shitty that you had to rely on that.
Lara:	That's horrible, why should you have to lie on an issue that is just perfectly right and you feel strongly about, why do you have to come up with excuses?
Cath:	That's right.
Lara:	I mean, I would much rather, it would be so nice just to be able to say no, for no particular reason. I don't really know, I haven't felt the need to think about it, I just don't particularly fancy it.

Helen: I just don't feel like it at the moment.
Lara: Wouldn't that be nice! (Frith, 1997)

Although these young women are evidently able to generate excuses to avoid sex, they reject the idea that this is an appropriate question for the researcher to be asking or a desirable action in which to be engaged.

In sum, feminist focus group researchers recognize that focus groups shift the balance of power and control toward the research participants, enabling them to assert their own interpretations and agendas. Despite the disadvantages of this in some contexts (particularly when researching powerful—e.g., male—groups; cf. Green, Barbour, Bernard, & Kitzinger, 1993), this reduction in the relative power of the researcher also allows the researcher to access better, understand, and take account of the opinions and conceptual worlds of research participants, in line with the suggested principles of feminist research.

THE POTENTIAL OF FOCUS GROUPS FOR FEMINIST RESEARCH

As I have shown, the particular advantages of focus groups for feminist research are that they are relatively "naturalistic," that they offer a social context for meaning-making; and that they shift the balance of power away from the researcher toward the research participants. In this manner, focus groups meet the concerns of feminist researchers to avoid the problems of artificiality, decontextualization, and exploitative power relations. There are also other ways in which focus group method may benefit feminist research: for example, in the appropriateness of focus groups for use with underrepresented and severely disadvantaged social groups, their value for action research, and the role of focus groups in consciousness-raising.

Work with underrepresented social groups. Some focus group researchers have suggested that focus groups may be particularly useful for accessing the views of those who have been poorly served by traditional research:

> Social research has not done well in reaching people who are isolated by the daily exhausting struggles for survival, services and dignity—people who will not respond to surveys or whose experiences, insights and feelings lie outside the range of data survey methods. These people are also uncomfortable with individual interviews. We found that almost all elements in the community could be accessed in the safe and familiar context of their own turf, relations and organizations through focus groups. (Plaut, Landis, & Trevor, 1993, p. 216)

Focus group participants have included, for example, difficult-to-reach, high-risk families in an inner city (Lengua et al., 1992); Black gay men (Mays et al., 1992), the elderly (Chapman & Johnson, 1995), and village women in rural counties of China (Wong, Li, Burris, & Xiang, 1995). Such use of focus groups is in line with the proposal that feminist research should pay particular attention to the needs of "those who [have] little or no societal voice" (Rubin & Rubin, 1995, p. 36), and feminist focus group researchers have similarly used the method in researching the lives of immigrant/refugee women (Espin, 1995) and urban African American preadolescents and young adolescents living in poverty (Vera, Reese, Paikoff, & Jarrett, 1996).

Action research.   Some focus group researchers have suggested that the method "has promise in action research" (Vaughn et al., 1996, p. 32), that it can be used radically "to empower and to foster social change" (Johnson, 1996, p. 536). For example, Raymond Padilla (1993) described a project to overcome barriers to the success of Hispanic students in a U.S. community college, based on the work of Brazilian educator Paulo Friere. He used focus groups as a "dialogical method" to empower research subjects to change their own lives as part of "a larger project of political freedom, cultural autonomy, and liberation from oppressive economic and social conditions" (p. 154). It is the project's intent that

> By critically examining through dialogue the problematic aspects of their own lives, the subjects are able to gain the critical understanding that is necessary to identify viable alternatives to existing social arrangements and to take appropriate actions to change and improve their own lives. (Padilla, 1993, p. 154)

Some feminists have also wanted their research to have direct practical effects in women's lives and have used focus groups (and other kinds of group work) in action research projects. For example, Maria Mies (1983), in a project aiming to make practical provision for battered women, insisted that, in order to implement a nonhierarchical egalitarian research process, to ensure that research serves the interests of the oppressed, to develop political awareness, and to use her own relative power in the interests of other women, "interviews of individuals . . . must be shifted towards group discussions, if possible at repeated intervals" (p. 128). Mies' view is that "this collectivization of women's experience . . . helps women to overcome their structural isolation in their families and to understand that their individual sufferings have social causes" (p. 128). Similarly, Jean Orr's (1992) project on Well Women Clinics "encourages members to see that problems are often not caused by personal inadequacy but are based in current social structure" (p. 32), offering "support to members in changing aspects of their lives" and enabling them to "feel confident in asserting their needs to others" (p. 32) within the Community Health Movement and beyond. (Further examples of the use of focus groups in feminist action research on health issues may be found in de Koning & Martin's (1996) edited collection.)

Consciousness-raising.   The similarities between focus group discussions and the consciousness-raising sessions common in the early years of second wave feminism have fueled the interest of several feminist researchers. Noting that it was through consciousness raising that Lynn Farley (1978) came to identify and name the experience of "sexual harassment," feminist sociologist Carrie Herbert (1989) included group discussions in her work with young women on their experience of sexual harassment. Similarly, Michelle Fine (1992, p. 173), chronicling a set of group discussions with adolescent girls, claimed that "through a feminist methodology we call 'collective consciousness work,' we sculpted . . . a way to theorize consciousness, moving from stridently individualist feminism to a collective sense of women's solidarity among difference." Feminist researchers using focus group work in this way (cf. Mies, 1983; Orr, 1992) hope that, through meeting together with others and sharing experience and through realizing group commonalities in what had previously been considered individual and personal problems, women will develop a clearer sense of the social and political processes through which their experiences are constructed and perhaps also a desire to organize against them.It has to be said, however, that other researchers using focus groups are less sanguine about their consciousness raising potential. Jenny Kitzinger's (1994a) focus groups' discussions of HIV risk offer salutary counterexamples of the alleged consciousness raising benefit of group discussion. In several groups, she said, "any attempt to address the risks HIV poses to gay men were drowned out by a ritual period of outcry against homosexuality" (J. Kitzinger, 1994a, p. 108).

Given the advantages of focus groups, it is perhaps surprising that they are not more widely used by feminist researchers. Among the qualitative methods available to feminists, the one-to-one interview is the most commonly used technique; according to some researchers (Kelly, Burton, & Regan, 1994, p. 34), it has become "the paradigmatic 'feminist method'." Many of the classic qualitative studies in feminist psychology use the one-to-one interview as their only or primary research tool (e.g., Belenky, Clinchy, Goldberger, & Tarule, 1986; Chesler, 1972; Gilligan, 1982; Walker, 1979). Of the 77 empirical articles published in the first six volumes (1991–1996) of the international journal *Feminism & Psychology,* 43 (56%) used interviews, and no other qualitative method was used in more than 10% of studies. Over a similar period, *Psychology of Women Quarterly* published 25 studies using interviews, although these constituted a much smaller proportion of the total number of empirical articles (only 17%), with no other qualitative method used in more than 2% of studies. Focus groups were rarely used: in the same period, there were 8 focus group studies published in *F&P* and only 1 in *PWQ* (plus two studies that used group discussions).

I would suggest that there are many reported instances of the use of interviews in feminist research where focus groups could have met the researcher's aims better, provided fuller or more sophisticated answers to the research question, or addressed particular methodological concerns. For example, Niobe Way (1995) interviewed 12 girls individually to answer the question: "What are the various ways urban, poor, and working-class adolescent girls speak about themselves, their schools and their relationships to parents and peers over a three-year period?" (p. 109). Given the stated assumptions of this study, including that research is "inherently relational" (p. 109) and that "the words of adolescents cannot be separated from the cultural and societal context of which they are a part" (p. 109), it seems that focus groups might have been a better methodological choice. It is particularly surprising that the work of the Harvard Project on Women's Psychology and Girls' Development (e.g., Brown & Gilligan, 1983; Gilligan, 1982; Taylor et al., 1996), which theorizes the self as fundamentally "relational," relies almost exclusively on individual interviews with young women.

Finally, although it is a pity that there is not greater use of focus groups in feminist research, it is also a pity that there is not better use of focus groups, capitalizing on their particular advantages as a method. I will close by highlighting some of the main problems in the current use of focus groups (by feminists and others) and indicate the ways in which these could be overcome, in order to maximize the value of the method as a tool for feminist research. These problems are inappropriate use of focus groups, neglect of group interactions, and insufficient epistemological warranting. I will look briefly at each.

Inappropriate use of focus groups. Although the "how to" books include advice on "how not to" (and also "when not to") use focus groups (e.g., Morgan & Krueger, 1993; Vaughn et al., 1996), this advice is often disregarded, not least by feminist focus group researchers. For example, although the textbooks caution against using focus groups as a quick and easy way of increasing sample size, indicating that the method is unsuitable for conducting large-scale studies, it is not uncommon for researchers to present as their rationale for using focus groups that they are "effective and economical in terms of both time and money" (Espin, 1995, p. 228), or that they are "a means of gathering qualitative data from a relatively large sample" (Lampon, 1995, p. 171). Similarly, although the handbooks warn against inappropriate quantification of focus group data (cf. Morgan & Krueger, 1993, p. 14), this, too, is often apparent: for example, Geraghty (1980) offered a statistical profile of donors to a particular charity based on four focus groups, and Flexner, McLaughlin, and Littlefield (1977) presented a graph comparing three focus groups ("consumers," "potential consumers," and "providers" of abortion services) in terms of the average ranks given by members of each group to features of an abortion service. More recently, an article included in a special issue of *Qualitative Health Research* on "Issues and Applications of Focus Groups" (Carey, 1995) categorized the social service concerns of HIV-positive women and tabulated the number of responses coded under each category (Seals et al., 1995). This is despite at least two injunctions elsewhere in the special issue not to quantify focus group data.

Neglect of group interactions. Although interaction among group participants is supposed to be a defining characteristic of focus group methods, one review of over 40 published reports of focus group studies "could not find a single one concentrating on the conversation between participants and very few that even included any quotations from more than one participant at a time" (J. Kitzinger, 1994a, p. 104). For this article, I reviewed almost 200 focus group studies ranging in date of publication from 1946 to 1996, with the same result. Focus group data are most commonly presented as if they were one-to-one interview data, with interactions among group participants rarely reported, let alone analyzed. This is despite clear statements in the focus group literature that "researchers who use focus groups and do not attend to the impact of the group setting will incompletely or inappropriately analyze their data" (Carey & Smith, 1994, p. 125). The extracts quoted in this article are not, in fact, typical of the way in which focus group data are normally reported. I have deliberately sought out those rare published examples of interactive data in order to make the best possible case for the use of focus groups. In presenting these data extracts, I have often drawn attention to interactional features that are not commented on by the authors themselves. More commonly, the focus is on the content rather than the process of interaction. One wishes feminist focus group researchers were producing analyses of interactions approaching the sophistication of that offered by Billig (1992).

Insufficient epistemological warranting. In common with other types of qualitative data, data from focus groups are open to either essentialist or social constructionist interpretations (Guba & Lincoln, 1994; cf. also C. Kitzinger & Powell, 1995). For feminist researchers working within an essentialist frame, it may be the voices of individual women (speaking with, or in contradiction to, other women) that they wish to hear, and for them focus groups offer a valuable route to "the individual in social context" (Goldman, 1962; Rubin & Rubin, 1995, p. 95). These researchers may well argue that focus group data are more "authentic" or "closer to the essential meanings of women's lives" than data elicited by other methods. Within a social constructionist (or postmodernist or discursive) frame, however, focus group data are just as constructed—albeit differently—as, say, responses to an opinion poll or behavior in a laboratory setting. Viewed within this frame, the method offers access to "the patterns of talk and interaction through which the members of any group constitute a shared reality" (Devault, 1990, p. 97). The analytic emphasis is on the construction and negotiation of persons and events, the functions served by different discourses, and—for feminists—the ways in which social inequalities are produced and perpetuated through talk (cf. Wilkinson & Kitzinger, 1995, for further examples of this approach). However, focus group researchers rarely offer a clear epistemological warrant for the interpretation of their data, and there is a great deal of slippage between essentialist and social constructionist frames.

In conclusion, this article has argued that focus groups offer considerable potential for the future development of feminist research in and beyond psychology in ways congruent with feminist goals. I do not embrace the orthodoxy that qualitative methods are "quintessentially feminist" (Maynard & Purvis, 1994, p. 3), nor do I believe that any particular method can be designated feminist per se (cf. Wilkinson, 1986, p. 14). Indeed, as Peplau and Conrad (1989, p. 379) observed, "no method comes with a feminist guarantee." Following Peplau and Conrad (1989), I do not seek to define feminist research in psychology primarily at the methodological level but rather to evaluate a particular method—the focus group—in terms of its usefulness in the pursuit of feminist goals. Within this context, I have shown that focus groups are a valuable method for feminist research because they meet three key feminist goals: they enable relatively "naturalistic" research, give due account to social context, and shift the balance of power in research. They are also useful in work with underrepresented groups, in action research, and in consciousness-raising.

In order to realize the potential of focus groups as a research method, however, feminist researchers could develop a better awareness of the appropriate uses of focus groups and the functions they can—and cannot—serve. In general, focus group method is well suited to research questions involving the elicitation and clarification of perspectives, the construction and negotiation of meanings, the generation and elaboration of hypotheses, and a whole range of exploratory analyses. It is poorly suited to research questions involving the estimation of frequencies, the testing of causal relationships, generalizations to larger populations, comparisons between population groups, and most types of inferential analysis. It would also be useful for feminist researchers to pay more attention to the interactive nature of focus groups, reporting and analyzing interactions among group participants in ways that do justice to their role in meaning-making. Finally, feminist researchers could more clearly identify the epistemological frameworks that inform their interpretations of focus group data in order to warrant the particular analyses they present.

It is true that, at present, focus groups are not widely used by feminist psychologists, perhaps because, as Jill Morawski (1994, pp. 21–22) stated, "Attempts to study women's experiences that take seriously the transindividual, contextually embedded, or socially constructed nature of those experiences risk using methodologies that are appropriate to their mandate but that fail to meet orthodox standards of the science." We have, as psychologists, undergone training within a discipline that has "placed a high value on quantification and imbued us with suspicion of alternative methods and non-positivistic science" (Mednick, 1991, p. 618). If, however, as feminist psychologists we agree on "the need for more interactive, contextualized methods in the service of emancipatory goals" (Riger, 1992, p. 736), then feminist psychology needs to be bolder in its challenge to the orthodoxies of the discipline. It needs to harness "varied epistemological forces from empiricism and materialism to utopianism and postmodernism, in order to construct *feminist science*" (Morawski & Agronick, 1991, p. 575, my emphasis), and it needs to demonstrate a commitment to "developing and testing innovative concepts, methods and applications for understanding and empowering women" (Russo, 1995, p. 1). The continued use and further development of focus group method offer feminist psychology an excellent opportunity for the future.

Initial submission: November 17, 1996
Initial acceptance: January 22, 1997
Final acceptance: September 18, 1997

ENDNOTE

I am delighted to report that the field of focus group research has developed considerably since this article was accepted for publication. Second editions of several of the classic handbooks have appeared, as well as a number of new texts. There is now a growing body of feminist focus group research, and some of the researchers referenced in this article (e.g. Niobe Way, members of the Harvard Project) have moved from exclusive reliance on one-to-one interviews to include group discussions in their work. More up-to-date reviews of the field have also been published, including two of my own, on the use of focus groups in health research (Wilkinson, 1998b) and across the social sciences (Wilkinson, 1998c).

REFERENCES

Albrecht, T. L., Johnson, G. M., & Walther, J. B. (1993). Understanding communication processes in focus groups. In D. L. Morgan (Ed.), *Successful focus groups: Advancing the state of the art* (pp. 51–64). Newbury Park, CA: Sage.
Barringer, C. E. (1992). Speaking of incest: It's not enough to say the word. *Feminism & Psychology, 2*, 183–188.
Beck, L., Trombetta, W., & Share, S. (1986).Using focus group sessions before decisions are made. *North Carolina Medical Journal, 47*, 73–74.
Belenky, M., Clinchy, B., Goldberger, N., & Tarule, J. (1986). *Women's ways of knowing: The development of self, voice and mind.* New York: Basic Books.
Bers, T. H. (1987). Exploring institutional images through focus group interviews. In R. S. Lay & J. J. Endo (Eds.), *Designing and using market research* (pp. 19–29). San Francisco: Jossey-Bass.
Billig, M. (1992). *Talking of the royal family.* London: Routledge.
Billinghurst, B. (1996). Theorizing women's self-blame. *Feminism & Psychology, 6*, 569–573.
Bogardus, E. (1926). The group interview. *Journal of Applied Sociology, 10*, 372–382.
Bohan, J. S. (Ed.). (1992). Prologue: Re-viewing psychology, re-placing women—An end searching for a means. In J. S. Bohan (Ed.), *Seldom seen, rarely heard: Women's place in psychology* (pp. 9–53). Boulder, CO: Westview Press.

Bowles, G., & Klein, R. D. (Eds.) (1983). *Theories of women's studies*. London: Routledge & Kegan Paul.

Brems, S., & Griffiths, M. (1993). Health women's way: Learning to listen. In M. Koblinsky, J. Timyan, & J. Gay (Eds.), *The health of women: A global perspective* (pp. 255–273). Boulder, CO: Westview Press.

Broom, G. M., & Dozier, D. M. (1990). *Using research in public relations: Application to program management*. Englewood Cliffs, NJ: Prentice-Hall.

Brown, L. M., & Gilligan, C. (1993) Meeting at the crossroads: Women's psychology and girls' development. *Feminism & Psychology, 3,* 11–35.

Campbell, R., & Schram, P. J. (1995). Feminist research methods: A content analysis of psychology and social science textbooks. *Psychology of Women Quarterly, 19,* 85–106.

Carey, M. A. (Ed.). (1995). Issues and applications of focus groups [Special issue]. *Qualitative Health Research, 5* (4).

Carey, M. A., & Smith, M. W. (1994). Capturing the group effect in focus groups: A special concern in analysis. *Qualitative Health Research, 4,* 123–127.

Chapman, T., & Johnson, A. (1995). *Growing old and needing care: A health and social care needs audit*. London: Avebury.

Chesler, P. (1972). *Women and madness*. New York: Avon.

Cooper, P., Diamond, I., & High, S. (1993). Choosing and using contraceptives: Integrating qualitative and quantitative methods in family planning. *Journal of the Market Research Society, 35,* 325–339.

Crabtree, B. F., Yanoshik, M. K., Miller, W. L., & O'Connor, P. J. (1993). Selecting individual or group interviews. In D. L. Morgan (Ed.), *Successful focus groups: Advancing the state of the art* (pp. 137–149). Newbury Park, CA: Sage.

Crawford, J., Kippax, S., & Waldby, C. (1994). Women's sex talk and men's sex talk: Different worlds. *Feminism & Psychology, 4,* 571–588.

Dahlgren, P. (1988). What's the meaning of this? Viewers' plural sense-making of TV news. *Media, Culture and Society, 10,* 285–301.

de Koning, K., & Martin, M. (1996). *Participatory research in health: Issues and experiences*. London: Zed Books.

Devault, M. L. (1990). Talking and listening from women's standpoint: Feminist strategies for interviewing and analysis. *Social Problems, 37,* 96–116.

DiMatteo, M. R., Kahn, K. L., & Berry, S. H. (1993). Narratives of birth and the postpartum: Analysis of the focus group responses of new mothers. *Birth, 20,* 204–211.

Erkut, S., Fields, J. P., Sing, R., & Marx, F. (1996). Diversity in girls' experiences: Feeling good about who you are. In B. J. R. Leadbetter & N. Way (Eds.), *Urban girls: Resisting stereotypes, creating identities* (pp. 53–64). New York: New York University Press.

Espin, O. M. (1995). "Race," racism and sexuality in the life narratives of immigrant women. *Feminism & Psychology, 5,* 223–238.

Farley, L. (1978). *Sexual shakedown: The sexual harassment of women on the job*. New York: Warner Books.

Fine, M. (1992). *Disruptive voices: The possibilities of feminist research*. Ann Arbor: University of Michigan Press.

Fine, M., & Addelston, J. (1996). Containing questions of gender and power: The discursive limits of 'sameness' and 'difference'. In S. Wilkinson (Ed.), *Feminist social psychologies: International perspectives* (pp. 66–86). Buckingham: Open University Press.

Fine, M., & Gordon, S. M. (1989). Feminist transformations of/despite psychology. In M. Crawford & M. Gentry (Eds.), *Gender and thought: Psychological perspectives* (pp. 146–174). New York: Springer-Verlag.

Flexner, W. A., McLaughlin, C. P., & Littlefield, J. E. (1977). Discovering what the consumer really wants. *Health Care Management Review, 1,* 43–49.

Fonow, M. M., & Cook, J. A. (Eds.). (1991). *Beyond methodology: Feminist scholarship as lived research*. Bloomington: Indiana University Press.

Frazer, E. (1988). Teenage girls talking about class. *Sociology, 22,* 343–358.

Freimuth, V. S., & Greenberg, R. (1986). Pretesting television advertisements for family planning products in developing countries: A case study. *Health Education Research, 1,* 37–45.

Frey, J. H., & Fontana, A. (1993). The group interview in social research. In D. L. Morgan (Ed.), *Successful focus groups: Advancing the state of the art* (pp. 20–34). Newbury Park, CA: Sage.

Frith, H. (1997). *Young women refusing sex.* Unpublished doctoral dissertation, Department of Social Sciences, Loughborough University, England.

Geraghty, G. (1980). Social research in Asia using focus group discussions: A case study. *Media Asia, 7,* 205–211.

Gergen, K. (1987). Toward self as relationship. In K. Yardley & T. Honess (Eds.), *Self and identity: Psychosocial perspectives* (pp 52–67). Chichester: Wiley.

Goldman, A. E. (1962). The group depth interview. *Journal of Marketing, 26,* 61–68.

Goldman, A. E., & McDonald, S. S. (1987). *The group depth interview: Principles and practice.* Englewood Cliffs, NJ: Prentice-Hall.

Graham, H. (1984). Surveying through stories. In C. Bell & H. Roberts (Eds.), *Social researching, politics, problems, practice* (pp. 104–124). London: Routledge & Kegan Paul.

Green, G., Barbour, R. S., Bernard, M., & Kitzinger, J. (1993). "Who wears the trousers?" Sexual harassment in research settings. *Women's Studies International Forum, 16,* 627–637.

Gilligan, C. (1982). *In a different voice: Psychological theory and women's development.* Cambridge, MA: Harvard University Press.

Griffin, C. (1985). Qualitative methods and cultural analysis: Young women and the transition from school to un/employment. In R. Burgess (Ed.), *Field methods in the study of education.* London: Falmer Press.

Griffin, C. (1986). Qualitative methods and female experience: Young women from school to the job market. In S. Wilkinson (Ed.), *Feminist social psychology: Developing theory and practice* (pp. 173–191). Milton Keynes: Open University Press.

Guba, E. G., & Lincoln, Y. S. (1994). Competing paradigms in qualitative research. In N. K. Denzin & Y. S. Lincoln (Eds.), *Handbook of qualitative research* (pp. 105–117). Thousand Oaks, CA: Sage.

Hamon, R. R., & Thiessen, J. D. (1990). *Coping with the dissolution of an adult child's marriage* (Report No. CG-023-311). Seattle, WA: National Council on Family Relations. (ERIC Document Reproduction Service No. ED 330 968)

Harding, S. (1987). *Feminism and methodology.* Bloomington: Indiana University Press.

Hare-Mustin, R. T., & Marecek, J. (Eds.). (1990). *Making a difference: Psychology and the construction of gender.* New Haven, CT: Yale University Press.

Harrison, K., & Barlow, J. (1995). Focused group discussion: A "quality" method for health research? *Health Psychology Update, 20,* 11–13.

Henwood, K., & Pidgeon, N. (1995). Remaking the link: Qualitative research and feminist standpoint theory. *Feminism & Psychology, 5,* 7–30.

Herbert, C. M. H. (1989). *Talking of silence: The sexual harassment of schoolgirls.* London: Falmer Press.

Jarrett, R. L. (1993). Focus group interviewing with low-income minority populations: A research experience. In D. L. Morgan (Ed.), *Successful focus groups: Advancing the state of the art* (pp. 184–201). Newbury Park, CA: Sage.

Jayaratne, T. E., & Stewart, A. J. (1991). Quantitative and qualitative methods in the social sciences: Current feminist issues and practical strategies. In M. M. Fonow & J. A. Cook (Eds.), *Beyond methodology: Feminist scholarship as lived research* (pp. 85–106). Bloomington: Indiana University Press.

Johnson, A. (1996). "It's good to talk": The focus group and the sociological imagination. *Sociological Review, 44,* 517–538.

Jordan, J. V., Kaplan, A. G., Miller, J. B., Stiver, I. P., & Surrey, J. L. (1991). *Women's growth in connection: Writings from the Stone Center.* New York: Guilford Press.

Kelly, L., Burton, S., & Regan, L. (1994). Researching women's lives or studying women's oppression? Reflections on what constitutes feminist research. In M. Maynard & J. Purvis (Eds.), *Researching women's lives from a feminist perspective* (pp. 27–48). London: Taylor & Francis.

Khan, M. E., & Manderson, L. (1992). Focus groups in tropic diseases research. *Health Policy and Planning, 7,* 56–66.

Kissling, E. A. (1996). Bleeding out loud: Communication about menstruation. *Feminism & Psychology, 6,* 481–504.

Kitzinger, C. (1992). The individuated self concept: A critical analysis of social-constructionist writing on individualism. In G. M. Breakwell (Ed.), *Social psychology of identity and the self concept* (pp. 221–250). London: Surrey University Press, in association with Academic Press.

Kitzinger, C., & Powell, D. (1995). Engendering infidelity: Essentialist and social constructionist readings of a story completion task. *Feminism & Psychology, 5,* 345–372.

Kitzinger, J. (1994a). The methodology of focus groups: The importance of interaction between research participants. *Sociology of Health and Illness, 16,* 103–121.

Kitzinger, J. (1994b). Focus groups: Method or madness? In M. Boulton (Ed.), *Challenge and innovation: Methodological advances in social research on HIV/AIDS* (pp. 159–175). London: Taylor & Francis.

Knodel, J. (1993). The design and analysis of focus group studies. In D. L. Morgan (Ed.), *Successful focus groups: Advancing the state of the art* (pp. 35–50). Newbury Park, CA: Sage.

Krueger, R. A. (1988). *Focus groups: A practical guide for applied research.* Newbury Park, CA: Sage.

Kvale, S. (1996). *InterViews: An introduction to qualitative research interviewing.* Thousand Oaks, CA: Sage.

Lampon, D. (1995). Lesbians and safer sex practices. *Feminism & Psychology, 5,* 170–176.

Lengua, L. J., Roosa, M. W., Schupak-Neuberg, E., Michaels, M. L., Berg, C. N., & Weschler, L. F. (1992). Using focus groups to guide the development of a parenting program for difficult-to-reach, high-risk families. *Family Relations, 41,* 163–168.

Lewin, M., & Wild, C. L. (1991). The impact of the feminist critique on tests, assessment and methodology. *Psychology of Women Quarterly, 15,* 581–596.

Liebes, T. (1984). Ethnocriticism: Israelis of Moroccan ethnicity negotiate the meaning of "Dallas." *Studies in Visual Communication, 10,* 46–72.

Lott, B. (1985). The potential enrichment of social/personality psychology through feminist research and vice versa. *American Psychologist, 40,* 155–164.

Lovering, K. M. (1995). The bleeding body: Adolescents talk about menstruation. In S. Wilkinson & C. Kitzinger (Eds.), *Feminism and discourse: Psychological perspectives* (pp. 10–31). London: Sage.

Lunt, P., & Livingstone, S. (1996). Focus groups in communication and media research. *Journal of Communication, 42,* 78–87.

Lykes, M. B. (1985). Gender and individualistic versus collectivist biases for notions about the self. *Journal of Personality, 53,* 356–383.

Macpherson, P., & Fine, M. (1995). Hungry for an us: Adolescent girls and adult women negotiating territories of race, gender, class and difference. *Feminism & Psychology, 5,* 181–200.

Marecek, J. (1989). Introduction. [Special Issue on Theory and Method in Feminist Psychology.] *Psychology of Women Quarterly, 13,* 367–377.

Marshall, J. (1986). Exploring the experiences of women managers: Towards rigour in qualitative research. In S. Wilkinson (Ed.), *Feminist social psychology: Developing theory and practice* (pp. 193–209). Milton Keynes: Open University Press.

Maynard, M. (1990). Trend report: The re-shaping of sociology? Trends in the study of gender. *Sociology, 24,* 269–290.

Maynard, M., & Purvis, J. (1994). Introduction: Doing feminist research. In M. Maynard & J. Purvis (Eds.), *Researching women's lives from a feminist perspective* (pp. 1–9). London: Taylor & Francis.

Mays, V. M., Cochran, S. D., Bellinger, G., Smith, R. G., Henley, N., Daniels, M., Tibbits, T., Victorianne, G. D., Osei, O. K., & Birt, D. K. (1992). The language of black gay men's sexual behavior: Implications for AIDS risk reduction. *Journal of Sex Research, 29,* 425–434.

Mednick, M. T. (1991). Currents and futures in American feminist psychology: State of the art revisited. *Psychology of Women Quarterly, 15,* 611–621.

Merton, R. K., & Kendall, P. L. (1946). The focused interview. *American Journal of Sociology,* *51,* 541–557.

Merton, R. K., Fiske, M., & Kendall, P. L. (1956). *The focused interview.* New York: Free Press.

Mies, M. (1983). Towards a methodology for feminist research. In G. Bowles & R. D. Klein (Eds.), *Theories of women's studies* (pp. 117–139). London: Routledge & Kegan Paul.

Millward, L. J. (1995). Focus groups. In G. M. Breakwell, S. Hammond, & C. Fife-Shaw (Eds.), *Research methods in psychology* (pp. 274–291). London: Sage.

Morawski, J. G. (1994). *Practicing feminisms, reconstructing psychology.* Ann Arbor: University of Michigan Press.

Morawski, J. G., & Agronick, G. (1991). A restive legacy: The history of feminist work in experimental and cognitive psychology. *Psychology of Women Quarterly, 15,* 567–579.

Morgan, D. (1988). *Focus groups as qualitative research.* (Sage University Papers, Qualitative Research Methods Series, No. 16.) London: Sage.

Morgan, D. L. (Ed.). (1993). *Successful focus groups: Advancing the state of the art.* Newbury Park, CA: Sage.

Morgan, D. L., & Krueger, R. A. (1993). When to use focus groups and why. In D. L. Morgan (Ed.), *Successful focus groups: Advancing the state of the art* (pp. 3–19). Newbury Park, CA: Sage.

Morgan, D. L., & Spanish, M. (1984). Focus groups: A new tool for qualitative research. *Qualitative Sociology, 7,* 253–270.

Murray, S. A., Tapson, J., Turnbull, L., McCallum, J., & Little, A. (1994). Listening to local voices: Adapting rapid appraisal to assess health and social needs in general practice. *British Medical Journal, 308,* 698–700.

Norris, J., Nurius, P. S., & Dimeff, L. A. (1996). Through her eyes: Factors affecting women's perception of and resistance to acquaintance sexual aggression threat. *Psychology of Women Quarterly, 20,* 123–145.

Olesen, V. (1994). Feminisms and models of qualitative research. In N. K. Denzin & Y. S. Lincoln (Eds.), *Handbook of qualitative research* (pp. 158–174). Thousand Oaks, CA: Sage.

Orr, J. (1992). Working with women's health groups. In P. Abbott & R. Sapsford (Eds.), *Research into practice: A reader for nurses and the caring professions* (pp. 23–38). Buckingham: Open University Press.

Padilla, R. V. (1993). Using dialogical research methods in group interviews. In D. L. Morgan (Ed.), *Successful focus groups: Advancing the state of the art* (pp. 153–166). Newbury Park, CA: Sage.

Parlee, M. B. (1979). Review essay: Psychology and women. *Signs, 5,* 121–129.

Peplau, L. A., & Conrad, E. (1989). Beyond nonsexist research: The perils of feminist methods in psychology. *Psychology of Women Quarterly, 13,* 379–400.

Plaut, T., Landis, S., & Trevor, J. (1993). Focus groups and community mobilization: A case study from rural North Carolina. In D. L. Morgan (Ed.), *Successful focus groups: Advancing the state of the art* (pp. 202–221). Newbury Park, CA: Sage.

Press, A. L. (1991). Working-class women in a middle-class world: The impact of television on modes of reasoning about abortion. *Critical Studies in Mass Communication, 8,* 421–441.

Prilleltensky, I. (1989). Psychology and the status quo. *American Psychologist, 44,* 795–802.

Raabe, B. (1993). Constructing identities: Young people's understandings of power and social relations. *Feminism & Psychology, 3,* 369–373.

Reinharz, S. (1983). Experiential analysis: A contribution to feminist research. In G. Bowles & R. D. Klein (Eds.), *Theories of women's studies* (pp. 162–191). London: Routledge & Kegan Paul.

Reinharz, S. (1992). *Feminist methods in social research.* New York: Oxford University Press.

Riger, S. (1992). Epistemological debates, feminist voices: Science, social values and the study of women. *American Psychologist, 47,* 730–740.

Rubin, H. J., & Rubin, I. S. (1995). *Qualitative interviewing: The art of hearing data.* Thousand Oaks, CA: Sage.

Russo, N. F. (1995). Editorial: PWQ: A scientific voice in feminist psychology. *Psychology of Women Quarterly, 19,* 1–3.

Sampson, E. E. (1988). The debate on individualism: Indigenous psychologies of the individual and their role in personal and societal functioning. *American Psychologist, 43,* 15–22.

Schlesinger, P., Dobash, R. E., Dobash, R. P., & Weaver, C. K. (1992). *Women viewing violence.* London: British Film Institute.

Seals, B. F., Sowell, R. L., Demi, A. S., Moneyham, L., Cohen, L., & Guillory, J. (1995). Falling through the cracks: Social service concerns of women infected with HIV. *Qualitative Health Research, 5,* 496–515.

Seibold, C., Richards, L., & Simon, D. (1994). Feminist method and qualitative research about midlife. *Journal of Advanced Nursing, 19,* 394–402.

Sherif, C. A. (1979/1992). Bias in psychology. Reprinted in J. S. Bohan (Ed.), *Seldom seen, rarely heard: Women's place in psychology* (pp. 107–146). Boulder, CO: Westview Press.

Stanley, L., & Wise, S. (1993). *Breaking out again: Feminist ontology and epistemology.* London: Routledge.

Stewart, D. W., & Shamdasani, P. N. (1990). *Focus groups: Theory and practice.* London: Sage.

Tavris, C. (1992). *The mismeasure of woman.* New York: Simon & Schuster.

Taylor, J. M., Gilligan, C., & Sullivan, A. M. (1996). Missing voices, changing meanings: Developing a voice-centred relational method and creating an interpretive community. In S. Wilkinson (Ed.), *Feminist social psychologies: International perspectives* (pp. 233–257). Buckingham: Open University Press.

Unger, R. K. (1983). Through the looking glass: No wonderland yet! (The reciprocal relationship between methodology and models of reality.) *Psychology of Women Quarterly, 8,* 9–32.

Vaughn, S., Schumm, J. S., & Sinagub, J. (1996). *Focus group interviews in education and psychology.* Thousand Oaks, CA: Sage.

Vera, E. M., Reese, L. E., Paikoff, R. L., & Jarrett, R. L. (1996). Contextual factors of sexual risk-taking in urban African American preadolescent children. In B. J. R. Leadbetter & N. Way (Eds.), *Urban girls: Resisting stereotypes, creating identities* (pp. 291–304). New York: New York University Press.

Walker, L. (1979). *The battered woman.* New York: Harper & Row.

Walkerdine, V. (1996). Working class women: Psychological and social aspects of survival. In S. Wilkinson (Ed.), *Feminist social psychologies: International perspectives* (pp. 145–162). Buckingham: Open University Press.

Watts, M., & Ebbutt, D. (1987). More than the sum of the parts: Research methods in group interviewing. *British Educational Research Journal, 13,* 25–34.

Way, N. (1995). "Can't you see the courage, the strength that I have?": Listening to urban adolescent girls speak about their relationships. *Psychology of Women Quarterly, 19,* 107–128.

Weisstein, N. (1968/1993). Psychology constructs the female; or, The fantasy life of the male psychologist (with some attention to the fantasies of his friends, the male biologist and the male anthropologist). Reprinted in *Feminism & Psychology, 3,* 195–210.

Wells, W. D. (1974). Group interviewing. In R. Ferber (Ed.), *Handbook of marketing research* (pp. 2-133–2-146). New York: McGraw-Hill.

West, C., & Zimmerman, D. H. (1991). Doing gender. In J. Lorber, S. A. Farrell et al (Eds.), *The social construction of gender* (pp. 13–37). Newbury Park, CA: Sage.

Westkott, M. (1979). Feminist criticism of the social sciences. *Harvard Educational Review, 49,* 422–430.

Widdicombe, S. (1995). Identity, politics and talk: A case for the mundane and the everyday. In S. Wilkinson & C. Kitzinger (Eds.), *Feminism and discourse: Psychological perspectives* (pp. 106–127). London: Sage.

Wilkinson, S. (1986). Sighting possibilities: Diversity and commonality in feminist research. In S. Wilkinson (Ed.), *Feminist social psychology: Developing theory and practice* (pp. 7–24). Milton Keynes: Open University Press.

Wilkinson, S. (1998a). Focus groups in feminist research: Power, interaction and the co-construction of meaning. *Women's Studies International Forum, 21,* 111–125.

Wilkinson, S. (1998b) Focus groups in health research: Exploring the meanings of health and illness. *Journal of Health Psychology, 3,* 329–348.

Wilkinson, S. (1998c). Focus group methodology: A review. *International Journal of Social Research Methodology, 1,* 181–203.

Wilkinson, S., & Kitzinger, C. (Eds.). (1995). *Feminism and discourse: Psychological perspectives.* London: Sage.

Wilkinson, S., & Kitzinger, C. (Eds.). (1996). *Representing the other: A "Feminism & Psychology" reader.* London: Sage.

Willott, S., & Griffin, C. (1997) Wham bam, am I a man? Unemployed men talk about masculinities. *Feminism & Psychology, 7,* 107–128.

Wong, G. C., Li, V. C., Burris, M. A., & Xiang, Y. (1995). Seeking women's voices: Setting the context for women's health interventions in two rural counties in Yunnan, China. *Social Science and Medicine, 41,* 1147–1157.

Worell, J., & Etaugh, C. (1994). Transforming theory and research with women: Themes and variations. *Psychology of Women Quarterly, 18,* 433–450

Zeller, R. A. (1993). Focus group research on sensitive topics: Setting the agenda without setting the agenda. In D. L. Morgan (Ed.), *Successful focus groups: Advancing the state of the art* (pp. 167–183). Newbury Park, CA: Sage.

COMMENTS ON "FOCUS GROUPS"

Rhoda K. Unger
Montclair State University

A number of years ago, Barbara Wallston (1981) wrote an article entitled, "What Are the Questions in the Psychology of Women?: A Feminist Approach to Research." In that article (which was also her presidential address to Division 35) she pointed out that psychologists are much more highly trained to evaluate research critically than to generate critical questions. Since Barbara's untimely death, feminist psychologists have enlarged greatly our definition of acceptable methods (as this special issue demonstrates) as well as shown that the answers to most psychological questions are often partial, contingent, and temporary—in other words, socially constructed (Morawski, 1994).

This view that facts are relative and that subjective biases enter into every level of the research process puts feminist psychologists into conflict with mainstream "science" (Unger, 1996). Feminist psychologists may be excluded from the intellectual marketplace (cf. Buss & Malamuth, 1996) because we do not deal with the so-called facts, which are its basic commodity. We are, nevertheless, forced to deal in this marketplace because "bad science" has both major policy implications and personal consequences for those who have low power in society.

Feminist psychologists are placed in the paradoxical situation of being asked to disprove models and theories whose assumptive premises we reject. We know that the way we ask questions determines our answers. Thus, how may we question a determinist and positivist model of reality without being coopted by its tools and language?

Although she does not directly address this question in her interesting and informative article, I believe that Sue Wilkinson (1999) has provided us with one of its answers. Focus groups allow researchers to demonstrate the socially constructed nature of behavior. They may be used not only to analyze the ways meaning is socially negotiated, but also to demonstrate that meaning is socially negotiated. Thus, the major limitation of this method from a positivistic viewpoint (that the meanings negotiated by different groups are not the same) is its major strength from a feminist perspective.

Wilkinson points out that the analytic emphasis of focus group research is on "the construction and negotiation of persons and events, the functions served by different discourses, and—for feminists—the ways in which social inequalities are produced and perpetuated through talk" (p. 237). She suggests that these worthy

243

goals can be met by studying focus groups derived from already existing communities. She provides a number of fine examples of how such focus groups can further our understanding of the viewpoints of underrepresented populations.

It is also possible to manipulate the composition of focus groups. It is clear from Wilkinson's analysis that a group's negotiation of meaning may change when a particularly assertive individual with a strong viewpoint is present. The impact of such individuals might vary depending on his or her prior experience with the group or his or her ascribed status within the group or within the community. Of course, the researcher would not be able to conclude anything about the generation of meaning in "normal" discourse. Instead, the point of this exercise is to show how different meanings are negotiated by similar communities with differing participants.

Wilkinson argues that focus groups are particularly "well suited to research questions involving the elicitation and clarification of perspectives, the construction and negotiation of meanings, the generation and elaboration of hypotheses, and a whole range of exploratory analyses" (p. 237). I would add that they are also well suited for questioning that aspect of positivist epistemology that feminists sometimes share—the idea that there is indeed one answer to any of our questions.

REFERENCES

Buss, D., & Malamuth, N. (Eds.). (1996). *Sex, power, and conflict: Evolutionary and feminist perspectives*. New York: Oxford University Press.

Morawski, J. G. (1994). *Practicing feminisms, reconstructing psychology: Notes on a liminal science*. Ann Arbor: University of Michigan Press.

Unger, R. K. (1996). Using the master's tools: Epistemology and empiricism. In S. Wilkinson (Ed.), *Feminist social psychologies: International perspectives* (pp. 165–181). Milton Keynes: Open University Press.

Wallston, B. S. (1981). What are the questions in the psychology of women? A feminist approach to research. *Psychology of Women Quarterly, 5*, 597–617.

Wilkinson, S. (1999). Focus groups: A feminist method. *Psychology of Women Quarterly, 23*, 221–244.

WOMEN'S PERSPECTIVES ON FEMINISM

A Q-Methodological Study

Susan J. Snelling
Social Research Consulting

This Q-methodological study identified and described women's multiple perspectives on feminism. Fifty Q-sort items reflecting various perspectives represented in feminist theory were developed. These items were rated by 59 women along a "most agree"–"most disagree" dimension. Principal components analysis was used to identify groups of women who sorted the items in similar ways. Six distinct points of view were identified in the Q-sorts, five of which are discussed in detail. The five perspectives were interpreted and labeled based on the examination of the Q-sorts of the participants in each group. Follow-up interviews with selected participants also contributed to the understanding of these perspectives. The research demonstrates the multidimensional nature of the feminism construct. Future research on feminism should recognize the multiple ways of conceptualizing feminism in order to represent the construct as women experience it.

Although many women define themselves as feminists, it is apparent that the term "feminist" has different meanings among those people who claim the label. Similarly, many people who appear to hold feminist beliefs do not claim the label "feminist" for themselves. The definition of feminism is the central issue in the controversy over who is a feminist and what it means to be a feminist. Although psychologists have studied the relationship of feminist views to a number of variables, the actual meaning of "feminism" has been underresearched.

Feminist theorists have made many attempts to define feminism. One approach to this definitional question has been to identify different types of feminism. For

Thanks to Sandra Pyke, Erin Hewitt, Regina Schuller, and Charlene Senn for helpful comments on various versions of this manuscript.

Address correspondence and reprint requests to: Susan J. Snelling, Social Research Consulting, Site 1, Box 56, Mindemoya, Ontario P0P 1S0, Canada. E-mail: snelling@kanservu.ca.

example, in a popular feminist theory textbook, Jaggar and Rothenberg (1993) defined seven perspectives on feminism: conservatism, liberal feminism, classical Marxism, radical feminism, socialist feminism, multicultural feminism, and global feminism. Other feminist theorists identify a different set of perspectives (e.g., Code, 1988; Tong, 1989) or use different criteria for discriminating among perspectives (e.g., Black, 1989; McFadden, 1984). Some theorists include a "conservative" category as a perspective on feminism (e.g., Descarries-Belanger & Roy, 1988/1991; Jaggar & Rothenberg, 1993).

In contrast to feminist theorists, who have frequently recognized different types of feminism, the majority of psychological researchers have conceptualized feminism as a single ideology. Most of the psychological studies have used a standardized questionnaire measure of feminism that implicitly recognizes only one type of feminism. Most commonly, questionnaire measures of feminist attitudes or beliefs use a liberal feminist definition. For example, the Attitudes Toward Women Scale (Spence & Helmreich, 1972), a measure that is widely used to assess feminism, is described by the authors as covering "areas of activity in which men and women were, in principle, capable of being granted equal rights" (p. 3). If the Attitudes Toward Women Scale is a measure of feminism at all, it is assessing a liberal form of feminism, one focused on equal rights.

Although the most common approach to the study of feminism is through attitude questionnaires, some studies have taken different approaches. In one example, Linton (1989) used multidimensional scaling and cluster analysis to produce a "concept map" of feminism. The procedure involved asking self-identified U.S. feminists to brainstorm ideas about feminism in a mailed survey. Of the ideas provided, 150 were randomly selected to represent the concept "feminism." These ideas were printed on cards and were sorted by 34 feminists into piles that "made sense to them" (p. 26). Data analysis identified groups of items that were frequently sorted together into piles by the sorters. A concept map representing the results of the cluster analysis by grouping the items in two-dimensional space was examined to identify the thematic content of each cluster or group of items.

The clusters identified in Linton's (1989) research may be seen as groups of feminist issues that are connected or distant in the minds of the sorters. However, because the method produces a single representation of the way feminist issues are grouped, it excludes the possibility of competing or conflicting positions among the participants. It suggests that there is agreement on the grouping and proximity of the items but does not provide an indication of the extent to which such agreement existed in fact. As a survey of feminist theory reveals, there are differences among feminists as to the issues and connections that are considered to be important in feminism. Linton's method can reveal the areas of agreement but cannot reveal areas of difference among the participants.

One method that has been used to identify both similarities and differences in points of view is Q-methodology. As described by Stephenson (1953), Q-methodology is a reformulation of factor analysis that allows the correlation of persons instead of tests. In a Q-methodological study, participants explain their points of view through their sorting of items (a Q-sort), and the researcher, by using factor analysis, identifies groupings of these points of view. The groups are then labeled by the researcher, with reference to the Q-sorts provided by the members of each group. Q-methodology has been used effectively by feminist researchers to examine women's subjective points of view on such issues as pornography (Senn, 1991, 1993), lesbianism (Kitzinger, 1987; Kitzinger & Rogers, 1985), and, most relevant to the topic of the present research, women's responses to inequality (Breinlinger & Kelly, 1994).

Breinlinger and Kelly (1994) used Q-methodology to examine women's responses to discrimination and status inequality. Their Q-sort items reflected Tajfel and Turner's (1986) social identity theory. The theory proposes that there are three strategies for achieving a positive social identity when one is part of a low status group: individual mobility (dissociating oneself from the group), social creativity (viewing one's group positively), and social competition (taking steps to change the low status of the group). Breinlinger and Kelly (1994) explored the application of the theory to women's responses to being members of a low status group relative to men. Based on interviews with five women, research on women, and newspaper and magazine articles, statements that represented each of the three strategies in social identity theory were developed. Among the 50 women who completed the Q-sort, those women whose Q-sorts loaded on a single factor were interviewed subsequent to doing the Q-sort task. Four factors were identified, two of which matched strategies suggested by social identity theory and two of which were departures from what would be expected based on the theory.

As shown in Breinlinger and Kelly's (1994) Q-methodological study, multiple perspectives on an issue can be revealed through the use of this methodology, including perspectives that would not have been anticipated on theoretical grounds. Furthermore, Q-methodology allows similarities between factors to emerge, so that areas of agreement between people holding somewhat different views can be identified. For example, in Senn's (1991, 1993) research on pornography, there was some agreement among "radical feminist" and "conservative" women on the harmful effects of pornography, although opinions on the specific focus of the harm (women only vs. women and men) differed.

The present study provided a test of the contention in feminist theory that there are multiple feminisms and tested the adequacy of theoretical descriptions of feminism to account for the perspectives on feminism actually held by women.

METHOD

Participants

The aim of recruitment for Q-methodological research is not to achieve a sample that is representative of the population but to ensure that a wide range of relevant viewpoints are represented. Some women who were known to the researcher were asked to distribute packages to women whom they worked with or whom they know socially in order to achieve a broad distribution of the packages. Packages were also distributed to volunteers from day and evening students at a large Canadian university, members of the Women's Centre Collective at the University, members of the Women's Caucus of a union, and acquaintances of the researcher who were thought to represent particular views or backgrounds. In total, 143 packages were distributed; of these 59 packages were returned, for a response rate of 41%.

The ages of the participant group ranged from 17 to 73, with a median of 25 years. Approximately half the participants were students (college, university, high school, or professional training school) at the time they participated in the research. The majority of the participants were White (85%) and heterosexual (85%).

All women who returned the request for payment form were sent a letter thanking them for their participation and were paid $10 for their participation or had $10 directed to a charity.

Materials

A total of 190 one-sentence statements reflecting important issues from various perspectives on feminism were generated from relevant books and articles. From this initial set, 5 items were selected to represent the central tenets of each of 10 perspectives on feminism, resulting in a 50-item set (see Table 1). In order to check whether the items did indeed address the central issues for each of the 10 perspectives, the items were reviewed by three psychologists familiar with feminist theory. The items were found to be satisfactory in the breadth of issues covered, their intelligibility, and their accurate representation of key issues for the perspectives. The perspectives represented were: antifeminist, conservative, cultural, lesbian, liberal, marxist, postfeminist, radical, socialist, and women of color.

An alternative approach to item development would have been to begin with interviews to determine women's perspectives on feminism, with Q-sort items being developed based on the interview content. The advantage of basing the Q-sort items on written theory, as the present study did, was that representative sampling of diverse points of view on feminism could be more easily achieved. By identifying 10 perspectives and ensuring that each was represented by 5 items, we hoped to ensure that no area of the domain had been under- or oversampled.

The package the volunteers received contained a consent form, a set of instructions, a background information questionnaire, a deck of 50 Q-statement cards, a sorting template, three Q-sort record sheets (one for each of three conditions of instruction), a request for payment form, and two stamped envelopes.

Procedure

Q-sort
The set of 50 statements about feminism were sorted by women under three instructional conditions. Only the results from the first condition are described in this report. The statements were sorted on an 11-point Likert-type template from the woman's own perspective, indicating her beliefs about each of the statements. Participants were asked to sort four cards into each of the extreme positions on the distribution (the ±5, ±4, and ±3 positions), five cards into the middle positions (−2, −1, +1, +2), and six cards into the neutral (0) position.[1]

Participants recorded the sorting of each item by number on a record sheet, completed the background information questionnaire and request for payment form, and returned the materials by mail to the researcher in the envelopes provided. Payment forms were mailed separately to allow anonymity of the responses.

Table 1

Q-sort Items and Factor Arrays

	Factor					
Q-sort Item	1	2	3	4	5	6
1. We should work for and support "affirmative action" hiring programs for women in the workplace.	0	+3	+4	−1	0	+2
2. Working-class women are discriminated against in ways that upper-class women are not.	+4	0	+1	−2	0	0
3. A capitalist system discriminates against the working class as a whole and against women as a group.	+3	0	−1	+1	−2	0
4. We should celebrate the differences between men and women rather than having women try to be like men.	+1	−1	+4	+4	−2	+1
5. The ideal situation for a woman is to combine marriage to an egalitarian man with motherhood and a successful career.	−3	+1	0	0	+5	−2
6. Even though women have a lot in common with each other, differences associated with race mean that some women have rights others don't have.	+4	+2	−1	−1	+3	−3
7. Men and women have some reasons for conflict, but there are problems that affect both men and women that they should work on together.	0	+5	+5	+4	+2	−2
8. Men's need to dominate women can clearly be seen in what is considered "normal" male sexuality.	+3	0	−4	0	−4	−3
9. Women of color, as a group, have different problems than White women have.	+2	+2	−2	0	+4	−4
10. Men and women are basically very different.	+2	−4	0	+1	+1	0
11. Men and women will always be different; you can't fight nature.	−1	−3	0	+5	+3	−5
12. Women will never be free of male domination if they continue to have sexual relationships with men.	−1	−5	−5	−5	−5	−5
13. We don't have to have a society where everyone is equal; we just have to be sure everyone has an equal chance.	−1	0	+4	+5	0	−5
14. Lesbians can be completely devoted to feminism in a way that women who are sexually involved with men can never be.	+1	−3	−4	−5	−4	−4
15. The women's movement hasn't just focused on the needs of a group of White, middle-class women.	−3	+2	+3	−1	+2	+1
16. Women—especially mothers—have experiences and capabilities that lead them to hold life-affirming, peaceful, caring values.	+1	−3	−1	+3	−3	+2
17. In order to eliminate social inequality, we will need to get rid of capitalism, racism, and sexism.	+5	+2	+1	+2	+1	+5

(*continued*)

Table 1

Continued

Q-sort Item	Factor 1	2	3	4	5	6
18. Women's unpaid household work makes it possible for the rest of the economy to run.	+1	+1	−3	−3	−1	−2
19. Women and men can be equal in marriage even if the woman is financially dependent on the man.	−4	−2	+3	0	+5	−1
20. If I were going to join a political action group, I would rather the members were all women.	+4	−1	−5	−5	−3	−3
21. Our society is not structured to give men power and control over women.	−5	−4	−2	−4	+4	−4
22. Most of the goals of the women's movement have already been reached.	−4	−4	−5	−2	−1	−1
23. The ultimate goal of the feminist movement is equal opportunity for women.	0	+3	+2	+1	+3	+4
24. The main reason that women don't have much power in our society is that we have a capitalist system that exploits women's work.	0	+1	−1	−1	−2	+2
25. Everyone in society should take responsibility for childcare and housework.	+3	+5	+3	0	+4	+3
26. There is too much emphasis on a woman's right to have a career and not enough emphasis on her right to stay home and raise a family.	−2	−2	−2	+5	0	+1
27. We should change the traditional roles for men and women.	+2	+4	+2	+1	+1	+1
28. Women and men are basically very similar.	−4	+4	−4	−2	−3	−2
29. Women and men are equal in our society.	−5	−5	−3	−5	0	−4
30. The reason for many social problems is that women's values, which are so different from men's values, have not been taken into account.	+3	−1	+2	−2	−2	+3
31. Strengthening the family means strengthening society as a whole.	−2	+3	+5	+5	+5	−1
32. The fact that women are paid less than men is one reason that women have relatively little power.	+2	+4	0	+3	+2	+3
33. In some ways, women have it better than men.	0	0	−2	+3	−4	−5
34. Women don't have special qualities that make them better people than men.	−2	+1	+2	+3	+5	0
35. We need an active women's movement that will fight against male dominance.	+4	+3	+1	−3	0	+3
36. Even if a woman agrees with some of the goals of feminism, that doesn't mean she should be a part of the feminist movement.	−3	−2	+1	+2	+2	+4

(continued)

Table 1

Continued

Q-sort Item	Factor					
	1	2	3	4	5	6
37. Marriage and motherhood give a woman the opportunity for all-round fulfillment as a woman.	-2	-5	-2	0	-5	-2
38. If women were considered equal to men there would be no need of a women's movement.	-1	+2	0	+2	+1	+2
39. It isn't necessary for women who want to work against sexism to separate from men and create a woman-only culture.	-2	+4	+2	+4	+2	+4
40. Homosexuality threatens family values.	-4	-3	-5	+2	+4	-1
41. Lesbianism is the basis for a changed view of sexuality in which male domination is replaced by supportive relationships without domination.	+1	-2	-3	-4	-5	-3
42. By looking at the unequal relationships between women and men, we can understand a lot of other problems, like racism.	+2	-1	+1	-1	-4	+2
43. It isn't enough to understand sexism, we have to understand how sexism, racism, and class discrimination work together.	+5	+1	+5	+4	+1	+4
44. The best society would be one in which people didn't even notice a person's sex or race.	-3	-1	+4	-3	-1	+5
45. We need to work toward a society in which women have control over their own bodies, including access to birth control and abortion.	+5	+5	+3	+2	-1	+5
46. The traditional family, with a father who goes out to work and a mother who stays home, is the best setting for bringing up children.	-5	-5	-5	+1	-5	0
47. The structure of the family gives women equality with men.	-5	-4	-3	-4	-2	0
48. Things would be better for women if women weren't responsible for housework, and instead worked at jobs for which they were paid.	0	0	0	-2	-1	+1
49. There is no reason that mothers with young children shouldn't work outside the home.	-1	+5	+5	-3	+3	+5
50. Women should stop spending their energy on men and start spending it on themselves and other women.	+5	-2	-1	-4	-3	-1

Note: Factor array numbers (right side of table) represent the position on the -5 to +5 scale assigned for each Q-item in each factor array.

Interviews

On the background information questionnaire completed along with the Q-sort, participants had the option of indicating their willingness to participate in interviews about their responses by providing their names and telephone numbers. Of the 36 women who indicated a willingness to be interviewed, 17 women whose sorts loaded significantly on a single factor were identified as possible interview candidates; 9 women were contacted and agreed to be interviewed. An appointment was arranged at the convenience of the participant, and the researcher telephoned her at the prearranged time for an interview lasting approximately 30 minutes. Interviewees were asked to define feminism, asked whether they considered themselves to be feminists, and asked about the accuracy of the researcher's factor label for describing their personal perspectives on feminism. Additional follow-up questions were asked during the interview as necessary. Participants were asked for permission to audiotape the interviews and were given the guarantee that only the researcher would hear the tapes. Women who were interviewed were paid $10 for this phase of the research.

RESULTS

The data presented and discussed here are based on the Q-sorts and questionnaire responses of 59 women. Material from interviews with the 9 women is also presented where relevant.

Analysis and Interpretation of Q-sorts

A Q-sort is defined as the entire set of ratings assigned to the 50 statements. Thus, one person's Q-sort consists of 50 ratings from −5 to +5, one rating for each of the 50 statements. The data from the Q-sorts represent each participant's subjective representation of feminist issues. Patterns or similarities among these subjective representations are identified through factor analysis.[2]

The meanings of the identified patterns (or factors) are interpreted based on the content of the Q-sorts and the relationships among the statements in each factor, as well as on interview data, where available. Each of the factors identified represents a view of women's roles in society that is shared by the women whose Q-sorts loaded significantly on that factor. The women whose Q-sorts are grouped on one factor did not sort all the items in an identical way but merely in a way that is similar in substantial respects. The goal of interpretation is to determine which views or beliefs are held in common by people whose Q-sorts load on a given factor.

Principal component analysis (SPSS Inc., 1988) on a 59×59 correlation matrix of participants was used to determine the factors. The factors were then rotated orthogonally, using the Varimax method. Six factors were extracted. The factor solution accounted for 66% of the variance. The decision of how many factors to extract was based on meeting the following criteria: eigenvalues greater than 1 and at least one "pure" loading per factor. A pure loading on a factor refers to a Q-sort with a significant loading on that factor and on no other factors. To determine pure loadings, a significance level of $p < .01$ was established for the factor loadings. Q-sorts that had a factor loading above .36 on one and only one factor were selected as representative of that factor. In Q-methodological parlance, a pure loading is said to define a factor. In total, 26 Q-sorts had pure loadings on one of the six factors identified in the present research.

In order to determine the meaning of each factor, a "factor array" (McKeown & Thomas, 1988, p. 53) is created for each factor. The result is a new Q-sort that represents aspects of the factor that are similar among the Q-sorts that loaded purely on that factor. The factor array for each of the six factors is provided in Table 1.

Five[3] of the six factors identified in the analysis are described in turn, based on the factor array. The ranking of some of the items from the array for each factor are presented in the description. The number that precedes the statement is the item number; the number that follows the statement is the rating (from −5 to +5) assigned to this item in the factor array. Material from interviews with women whose Q-sorts were pure loadings on the factor, if available, is presented and discussed in order to expand on the meaning of the factor.

Factor 1

Factor 1, described as a radical, lesbian, antiracist feminist perspective, was defined by four Q-sorts with pure loadings. Nineteen women's Q-sorts loaded significantly on this factor but loaded significantly on other factors as well. The median age of the women whose Q-sorts loaded purely was 35 years, with a range of 34 to 43 years. Three women were lesbian. Three described themselves as White or Anglo-Saxon; the fourth was from an Eastern European background.

The society described in these women's Q-sorts was one based on inequality of the sexes, races, and classes. These women saw the women's movement as important and saw the necessity for activism to address many social issues. They considered feminism to be a very important part of who they are. An excerpt from an interview demonstrates the activism and personal significance of what it meant to this woman to be a radical feminist.

> K: Well, I guess for myself what that means is to be proactive rather than to be reactive, . . . having feminism be at the forefront of my consciousness rather than just something that I think about occasionally.

These women held an activist position that supported women working together politically. The women in this group were less convinced that working with men was a productive strategy. Sexism, male dominance, racism, and classism were all important concerns for the radical/lesbian/antiracist perspective. And items that linked discrimination based on race, sex, and class together were seen as some of the most important items in this perspective, indicating that the *connections* among these issues were central to this view. Some example items include the following:

2. Working class women are discriminated against in ways that upper class women are not. +4
6. Even though women have a lot in common with each other, differences associated with race mean that some women have rights others don't have. +4

21. Our society is not structured to give men power and control over women. −5
35. We need an active women's movement that will fight against male dominance. +4
17. In order to eliminate social inequality, we will need to get rid of capitalism, racism, and sexism. +5

The women whose Q-sorts loaded on this factor were opposed to traditional systems of family, marriage, and childrearing, and they did not see adding a career to marriage and motherhood as a more desirable option. For these women, the multiple problems in the current system meant that the status quo must be changed if we are to have a better society for women. Because their focus was more on understanding patriarchy and other forms of oppression, women's access to paid work and careers on a level with men was not very important in this factor. The women whose Q-sorts defined this factor saw themselves as radical, lesbian, and antiracist feminists whose focus was not on attaining equal rights to men but on achieving broad-based social changes, as demonstrated in the following quotation and items.

K: I was just trying to figure out what exactly I thought the differences between those two views [liberal feminism and radical feminism] were, and I guess one is whether equality for women can come within the current structure as opposed to that the structure has to change and I think that the structure has to change. . . . The whole system, which I consider a patriarchal system, has to change.

46. The traditional family, with a father who goes out to work and a mother who stays home, is the best setting for bringing up children. −5
5. The ideal situation for a woman is to combine marriage to an egalitarian man with motherhood and a successful career. −3

With respect to the similarity of this view to feminist theoretical perspectives, Factor 1 represented a radical feminist view, with the oppression of women being an important concern. The women whose Q-sorts defined this factor saw the fight against patriarchy as critical and wished to wrest control over women's bodies and women's sexuality from men.

The perspective represented by Factor 1 also had similarities to a lesbian separatist feminist perspective. The items concerning lesbianism were in the neutral range for this factor, so this perspective did not insist that lesbianism was the superior sexual orientation. In a broader sense, however, the Factor 1 perspective is not incompatible with a lesbian separatist view that critiques heterosexual institutions, patriarchy, and male dominance and supports women's separatism from men. In addition, one woman who was interviewed described herself as a lesbian feminist.

The perspective represented by Factor 1 integrated concern and activism regarding gender, race, and class and, therefore, had a similarity to the women of color perspective as defined by some feminist theorists (e.g., Jaggar & Rothenberg, 1993). The choice of the term "antiracist" was more appropriate than "women of color" to define this factor, because none of the women who defined this factor were women of color, although they did hold an antiracist view.

Factor 2

Six women's Q-sorts had pure loadings on Factor 2. Twenty-three Q-sorts also had significant loadings. The median age of women with pure loadings was 19 years, with one woman aged 38 and the rest under 22. All were heterosexual. Two were Jewish, two were White Catholics, one was French-Canadian, and one did not specify a cultural affiliation.

Factor 2 represented a liberal feminist view that sought to promote equality between men and women and to reform marriage and family while preserving them. Like the women whose Q-sorts defined Factor 1, the society described by the women whose Q-sorts defined Factor 2 was one of inequality, but for Factor 2 women, the inequality was specifically between men and women, with less emphasis placed on race and class inequalities than in Factor 1. Women and men were considered to be similar, and the goal of feminism was seen as promoting this essential equality through equal opportunity for women. However, this was not seen as requiring political work separate from men. Indeed, working with men was an important part of this perspective, as shown in the ratings given to these items:

28. Women and men are basically very similar. +4
23. The ultimate goal of the feminist movement is equal opportunity for women. +3
29. Women and men are equal in our society. −5
7. Men and women have some reasons for conflict, but there are problems that affect both men and women that they should work on together. +5

Both women who were interviewed appreciated the value of feminist activism and were aware that such activism existed and had positive aspects, but they did not see themselves as part of that activist group. This perspective was relatively apolitical and nonactivist.

M: I'm not a very political person, although I have friends who are more into, involved in political aspects of organizations, and sexual harassment activities and things like that, but ... I guess I can't invest a lot in anger.

D: I believe they [feminist activists] are fighting for a good cause, but I could never fight for the cause, but I would never, I could never see myself using my time that way, or fighting along with them, although in the future it would benefit me if I did, but, so I don't know, in that sense I differ from them because I wouldn't be actively involved.

An important part of the Factor 2 perspective was the need for reform of marriage, family, and work to allow women to be equal to men in the home and in the workplace. They wanted to retain marriage and family as social institutions but in a more egalitarian form.

25. Everyone in society should take responsibility for childcare and housework. +5
49. There is no reason that mothers with young children shouldn't work outside the home. +5
27. We should change the traditional roles for women. +4

The women whose Q-sorts define this factor were particularly clear about the need for equality between the genders. For M., being a feminist meant focusing on reducing inequalities or differences between men and women.

> M: I guess it just means, to me it means seeing myself, getting a perspective of myself, and my place in the world, as unfettered by my gender.

M's emphasis on the similarity and equality between men and women led her to reject gender as an important category.

Issues of racism and class discrimination or any combination of race, sex, and class issues were relatively unimportant in this perspective. All of the items that specifically concern race, class, and/or capitalism were scored between −2 and +2. So, although inequality was an important issue for the women, inequalities between the genders were most apparent to them, with other forms of social inequality being much less apparent or important.

The underlying assumption of the women whose Q-sorts loaded on this factor was that equality and fairness should be our guiding principles in society. In M's interview, she demonstrated the emphasis on equality that was apparent in this factor: "I have the type of personality that goes for equality, balance, and fairness, and I tend to cut to the bottom line of whether something is fair." Another important aspect of her view, which was consistent with a liberal feminist view, was evident in this comment: "I'm reminded how similar men are [to women]."

Factor 3
Seven women's Q-sorts loaded purely on Factor 3, and fourteen Q-sorts also had significant loadings. The median age of the seven women who had pure loading Q-sorts was 21, with one woman aged 61 and the remainder under 24 years of age. All were heterosexual. One was Afro-Canadian, one was Asian, and five were from Western European backgrounds.

This factor represented a humanist framework, defined by Oakley (1981) as the view that "men and women are both alienated from their human potential by being forced into masculine and feminine roles" (p. 336). Gender inequality was not a central concern for women whose Q-sorts defined this perspective. These women were not supporters of an active women's movement; items that addressed this issue were rated neutrally. They would have liked to see equal opportunities for everyone. A society in which race and gender did not matter was seen as desirable. The society that would be most desirable was one in which we did not focus on differences or "blame" certain groups for social problems. They did not consider men and women to be similar but viewed gender differences positively.

13. We don't have to have a society where everyone is equal, we just have to be sure everyone has an equal chance. +4
44. The best society would be one in which people didn't even notice a person's race or sex. +4
4. We should celebrate the differences between women and men rather than having women try to be like men. +4

Like the women whose Q-sorts loaded on the liberal feminist Factor 2 perspective, these women were not concerned about race or class issues, rating almost all of these items between −2 and +1. One woman who was interviewed placed a lot of emphasis on men's value and positive qualities, as shown in this quotation from the interview.

> H: A lot of my close friends are males, and, it's just, I feel kind of bad for them, because there is nice guys out there, but a lot of feminists won't give them a chance.
> I: Do you think that men are just as hurt by stereotyped roles as women are?
> H: Yeah, I think so. Like not all of them, but I know, like, do you know, you hear people, like when a guy, like this, uh, Paul Bernardo[4] and stuff like that, my boyfriend's so upset about it because you know, he just gets so mad when he finds out about guys doing that, like you know, it's "all males are rapists" and stuff like this, like it just really upsets him, like all my guy friends, they really get upset with stuff like that.

H viewed men positively and believed that it was unfair to implicate all men by the actions of a few. Her male friends, in particular, objected to the characterization of men as violent or sexually aggressive. In the discussion of Paul Bernardo, H's concern, and her account of the concerns of her male friends, was not primarily for the female victims of the violent crimes but for the impact of the publicity of Bernardo's crimes on general impressions of men. The humanist perspective seemed to represent a view that discrimination, victimization, and oppression can happen to all groups of people, and that paying particular attention to the ways in which women have been affected, as feminists are perceived to do, was unfair to men. The women interviewed as representatives of this factor were quite critical of feminism and feminists.

> H: Well, like, some of the aspects of feminism I agree with, but in some ways, like feminists are just way too pro-feminine, like a lot of them seem to be like man-haters to me, like a lot of women that I've come across that are feminists are real male-beaters, like, you know what I mean, like, "Oh, well men are no good." I like to see men and women on an equal level, like, I think we're both equal, just because we're different sexes doesn't mean anything, we're humans first. So many feminists see women as the first, as the top, you know like "Let's excel over the men instead of just becoming equal" and I mean, I just don't think that's right because I think it's defeating the purpose. Like, I mean, men were always the top ones, now women are coming up. Let's stay equal instead of the women going over and being the top ones and the men being you know, the minor or whatever.

Although this factor was not a feminist or an activist position, neither was it a perspective that strongly supported the traditional family. The women whose Q-sorts loaded on this factor did not believe that the traditional family is the best setting for children, although they perceived some value in the family as a social structure. This perspective was quite supportive of women's work outside the home, which probably reflected a desire for equal opportunity for everyone, male and female.

46. The traditional family, with a father who goes out to work and a mother who stays home, is the best setting for bringing up children. −5
31. Strengthening the family means strengthening society as a whole. +5

49. There is no reason that mothers with young children shouldn't work outside the home. +5

When asked if the label "humanist" fit her perspective, H responded:

> H: Humanist, it sounds like, as opposed to feminist, that's pro-feminine and that's it, but humanist is more like men and women, you know what I mean, like men and women together type of thing, like the equality thing again and equal opportunity, as opposed to "women are better than men" and that's the way a lot of feminists are, 'we're better than men so we have to prove it' type of thing. But I just think we're all good, you know, we've just got to, we each belong to different roles.
>
> I: So you feel pretty comfortable with that label then, that describes your views?
>
> H: Oh, yeah, I was afraid you were going to say feminist and I was going to say, "Oh, no, I hope I'm not that bad."

In contrast to the women who defined Factors 1 and 2, who perceived value in the feminist movement, this representative of the humanist factor perceived feminists as female supremacists who care only about women, and she strongly rejected any suggestion that her views might be "feminist."

Factor 4

Seven women's Q-sorts loaded purely on Factor 4, along with seven Q-sorts that loaded on both this and other factors. Their median age was 19 years, with a range of 19 to 41 years. All were heterosexual. Two described themselves as Canadian, and the other women described varying cultural backgrounds (Caribbean, Latvian, British, Italian, and German Iraqi).

The perspective defined by the Q-sorts on Factor 4 was a conservative position with some antifeminist elements. These Q-sorts described a society in which men and women were and always will be different. Gender differences were seen positively: the women whose sorts defined the factor acknowledged gender inequality but also saw benefits in this for women. With respect to gender differences, one said:

> B: Women are different, but I don't necessarily think that they're better. And if they're different, that's a good thing. We need that.

She did believe that men had more economic power than women, but she went on to add another side to that view.

> B: I see instances where the women actually have the power, in the family for instance, they just don't tell the men. A lot of it's kind of underhanded and not out in view, the power that women have.

The position reflected a view of men and women as different, even unequal, but complementary.

11. Men and women will always be different; you can't fight nature. +5
29. Women and men are equal in our society. −5
33. In some ways, women have it better than men. +3

This perspective was not antifeminist in the sense of promoting activism against feminism. The women whose Q-sorts loaded on this factor were relatively neutral about feminism but did not think a women's movement was necessary. Like Factor 3, Factor 4 did not represent an activist position. Their ideals were strong families, an end to overt discrimination, and a harmonious interaction between the genders. As demonstrated in the ratings given to the following items, equality was not an important concept in these Q-sorts.

35. We need an active women's movement that will fight against male dominance. −3
13. We don't have to have a society where everyone is equal; we just have to be sure everyone has an equal chance. +5

Like Factors 2 and 3, race and class items were rated between −2 and +2, indicating that these were not important issues for this perspective. This position saw homosexuality in a neutral to negative light and scored any item relating to lesbians in a strongly negative direction. The women who were interviewed expressed strong views about the feminist movement. In particular, B mentioned negative feelings about what she saw as a feminist challenge to heterosexuality and to the traditional family. If they were to be activist on any issue, it would be concerning women's right to stay in the home, especially for mothers with young children.

26. There is too much emphasis on a woman's right to have a career and not enough emphasis on her right to stay home and raise a family. +5
49. There is no reason that mothers with young children shouldn't work outside the home. −3

B: I think a lot of my negativism comes from the impact on the concept of sexuality, where, well, the gays and lesbians are, uh, what am I trying to say? It's a negative connotation for me. And that freedom seems to be imposed on me. Like, I don't agree with a lot of the changes that are happening, and it seems to me that the feminist movement has been associated very much with the lesbian movement, and very much against the mothers that wanted to stay home with their children.

The definition of conservatism presented in theoretical taxonomies describes many of the issues that are emphasized in Factor 4. The women whose Q-sorts defined this factor acknowledged inequalities between women and men but were not concerned about them and instead showed relative contentment with traditional public/private sphere divisions. They did not desire major social changes. They were accepting of traditional roles for women and viewed differences between men and women as natural and not as a source of concern. The two women who were interviewed from this perspective were proud to consider themselves conservative and traditional. These women were certainly aware of the challenges to their views posed by some aspects of the feminist movement. Nonetheless, they strongly defended the value of their choices and perceived their efforts to preserve and support traditional family structures as very important contributions that they made to their own families and to society.

B: I have never regretted staying home with my children, and I think my children are nice people, and part of that, a big part of that, is because I stayed home with them.

Factor 5

One woman's Q-sort loaded purely on this factor, with five Q-sorts loading on this and other factors. The woman whose Q-sort loaded purely on this factor was 18 years old, heterosexual, and Jewish. Because of reliability concerns, the interpretation of a factor on which there is only one pure loading must be considered tentative.

This factor represented a postfeminist view. The perspective was almost completely apolitical, certainly not feminist, but also not traditional. Society as conceptualized in this account did not have a lot of problems in need of change. In general, men were not seen as dominating women, and in many respects equality between the genders was portrayed as a given. Feminism was irrelevant in this Q-sort because, from this perspective, gender equality was established in society.

21. Our society is not structured to give men power and control over women. +4

35. We need an active women's movement that will fight against male dominance. 0

This position was very supportive of work outside the home for women and saw that the family, although indispensable, must adapt to allow women to have careers. In short, this woman's Q-sort described a society in which women could have it all, and she saw no barriers to women's integrating marriage, family, and career.

37. Marriage and motherhood give a woman the opportunity for all-round fulfillment as a woman. −5

5. The ideal situation for a woman is to combine marriage to an egalitarian man with motherhood and a successful career. +5

46. The traditional family, with a father who goes out to work and a mother who stays home, is the best setting for bringing up children. −5

The woman who defined Factor 5 did not indicate a willingness to be interviewed after completing the Q-sorts, so there is no supporting or disconfirming evidence from an interview regarding the interpretation of this factor.

DISCUSSION

There is a paucity of research that looks at feminism as a social phenomenon on which there are multiple points of view. In this project, multiple ways of thinking about feminist issues were demonstrated. Six factors were extracted representing six distinct points of view on feminism and women's roles in society. By comparing the representative sort for each factor to theoretical positions on feminism as described in the literature, and by considering the important issues for the women whose Q-sorts defined the factor, the factors were labeled as: (1) a combination of radical, lesbian, and antiracist feminist theoretical positions; (2) a liberal feminist viewpoint; (3) a humanist perspective; (4) a conservative position with some antifeminist elements; (5) a postfeminist point of view; and (6) a position that was not labeled. These perspectives differed not only in their agreement or disagreement with certain issues and ideas but also in the extent to which certain ideas were seen as central or peripheral to the perspectives. Thus, perspectives on feminism can be seen to differ not only in terms of opinion but also in terms of the boundaries of the views. Issues that are included as important parts of some perspectives are not important to others.

The radical/lesbian/antiracist feminist perspective would be expected based on taxonomies of feminist theory. Virtually every categorical system of feminist perspectives includes radical feminism or some variant of it. Definitions of this type of feminism vary in different sources, but references to the oppression of women as a group or class, the importance of reclaiming female sexuality and reproduction, and the need for broad social change are hallmarks of radical feminism, as described in feminist theory and as identified in Factor 1. The inclusion of antiracism as a part of this factor modified the perspective slightly from a pure radical feminist perspective, but antiracism is quite compatible with the radical feminist position against oppression. The lesbian aspect of this position is also highly compatible with radical feminism, as key features of radical feminism are women's control over their own sexuality and a critique of heterosexuality. This position may, in fact, be an updated radical feminist position,[5] which incorporates race, gender, and sexuality in an analysis of oppression (e.g., see Frye, 1992).

Liberal feminism is a category that appears in virtually all taxonomies of feminist perspectives and, therefore, would be expected to emerge as a factor in this study. An emphasis on similarity and equality between men and women and equal opportunities for women characterized the Factor 2 perspective. There was an acknowledgment of, and a focus on, discrimination against women but relatively little emphasis on racism, classism, or other forms of discrimination.

The humanist perspective described in Factor 3 was not one that is discussed in most taxonomies of feminist theory and was not one of the perspectives anticipated in this research. Nonetheless, the factor had the highest number of pure factor loadings of any of the factors and clearly represented a distinct viewpoint. The social changes desired by the women whose Q-sorts loaded on this factor seem small compared to Factors 1 and 2, but issues like support for women's work outside the home are still a considerable departure from traditional views.

The conservative theoretical view, as defined by Descarries-Belanger and Roy (1988/1991) and Jaggar and Rothenberg (1993), places emphasis on maintaining traditional family structures, and in this respect the Q-sorts that defined Factor 4 clearly represented a conservative view.

A postfeminist perspective (Stacey, 1990)—exemplified by an absence of feminist consciousness, a depoliticization of feminist issues, and the taking for granted of marriage, family, and work—was shown clearly in the Factor 5 perspective. Equality between the sexes was accepted, and sexism was not a concern. This was a "women can have it all" point of view, the expectation being that women would incorporate marriage, work, and family.

New directions for feminist theory are identified in this research, directions that are already present in the implicit feminist theories presented through the participants' Q-sorts. The identification of a radical/lesbian/antiracist feminist perspective, in particular, demonstrates that a perspective that unites a number of concerns is possible to envision, even if feminist theorists have not yet developed a label for it. The patterns or factors identified in this research are not considered to be the endpoint; rather, their identification suggests the need for further developments in feminist theory and suggests the need for a much more complex understanding of feminism in future psychological research on the topic. In particular, psychologists seeking to measure feminism will need alternatives to scales that measure only a liberal feminist dimension.

There are many women whose Q-sorts did not define a single factor in this research because their sorts had significant loadings on more than one factor. That not all Q-sorts fit into the six factors identified here should not be seen as a failure of the analysis to account for all the data. Rather, women whose Q-sorts have multiple high loadings make the complexity of views that has been the focus of the research even more apparent. Although their data have been included in the formulation of the factors, their individual Q-sorts do not conform to one single perspective as identified in the factor analysis. And yet there is no reason to believe that women with multiple high loadings experience their viewpoints as ambiguous, contradictory, confusing, or inconsistent. A view that is both liberal feminist and humanist, for example, does not fit the pattern identified in these factors, but the existence of such a view demonstrates that views of feminism are highly complex and can unify what may appear to be dissimilar or opposing ideas.

Clearly, perspectives on feminism cannot be described simply or in terms of absolute agreement or opposition. The perspectives represented among these factors are multifaceted, with blurred boundaries. Given this outcome, it is unlikely that any taxonomic system of feminist perspectives can truly capture the nature of the multiple viewpoints. Although labels, such as those applied to the factors in the present study, may be a necessary tool for the communication of concepts, these data suggest that the labels must be seen as ultimately inadequate for the task of representing viewpoints on feminism.

One of the objectives of this research project was to advance the possibilities for feminist research in psychology. As Kitzinger (1986) pointed out, Q-methodology is ideally suited for feminist psychology because it allows the researcher to "acknowledge and present the reality constructions of different women and men without prejudging or discrediting them, and without insisting on the superior (more 'objective') status of the researcher's own construction of reality" (p. 153). In this study, the use of Q-methodology, which has previously been used as a feminist research tool (e.g., Breinlinger & Kelly, 1994; Kitzinger, 1987; Kitzinger & Rogers, 1985; Senn, 1991, 1993), preserved the subjective nature of the participants' opinions on feminism. Their views were not compared to any "standard" determined by the researcher; nonetheless, patterns were still identifiable through the use of factor analysis.

By conducting post Q-sort interviews with a selected portion of the participants, I was able to obtain information from the women about the meaning of the data. In this way, I do not claim total responsibility for understanding and interpreting the data. Rather, the goal of making meaning out of the different Q-sorts was reached partially through a collaborative effort of the researcher and the participants. As part of a feminist approach to research that considers participants to be the "experts" on their own points of view, the interviews provided important information.

One limitation in the participant group concerns the lack of access to any antifeminist group of potential participants. Although some of the women who participated in the research may have been members of such a group, they were solicited through other avenues that did not specifically seek their participation as antifeminists. The inclusion of women from antifeminist organizations would not have affected the other factors that were identified but might have resulted in the identification of another, distinct antifeminist factor.

The Q-items are satisfactory with respect to their apparent intelligibility to the participants and in terms of the broad range of relevant issues covered by the items. However, the initial selection of perspectives identified in written feminist theory means that some of the items addressed ideas that are important in academic feminist thought but may have little or no importance to women who are not feminist academics. The inclusion of items that are perceived as irrelevant to some participants is not, in itself, a problem in a Q-methodological study. The "0" or neutral category is available for just this kind of irrelevant item. The use of feminist theory as the starting point for the items means that points of view that have been systematically excluded from feminist theory, or from publication in any field, may not be represented among the items. Points of view that are not well covered in the items may not emerge from the Q-sorts, and so views that are marginalized in feminist theory may continue to go unheard in this research. However, the appearance of the humanist factor, for example, suggests that, despite some limitations, it was possible to express a viewpoint that was not one of the original theories on which the Q-items were based.

As Morawski (1992) wrote, "Feminist psychologists have joined with feminist scholars in other disciplines . . . in a journey in feminist epistemology [that] suggests the future inappropriateness of thinking in gridlike terms. . . . Feminist psychologists are entering a new field—one that requires mobility in our theories and practices and promises innovations yet unthought" (p. 264). Although the research does not completely escape "gridlike" thinking, the project demonstrates that it is possible to include complexity and subjectivity within our taxonomies. The challenge for future research on feminism is to include an understanding of feminism as a multidimensional construct.

Initial submission: February 12, 1997
Initial acceptance: June 10, 1997
Final acceptance: July 17, 1997

NOTES

1. Although it is possible to allow sorters to place the items "freely" (i.e., without restrictions or requirements on the number of items to be placed under each category), under a free-sort condition there is little consistency across sorters in the task performed, because some sorters will independently try to use all categories and others will try to avoid making distinctions, putting most items in the neutral category. The "forced" sort requires that all sorters complete the same basic task in approximately the same way, ensuring that all the sorters approach the task fairly systematically, making fine distinctions among the items. Sorters who find the distribution too constraining can be allowed to deviate from it without an adverse impact on the statistical analysis of the data (McKeown & Thomas, 1988). In the present study, no women deviated from the distribution.
2. Brown (1980) and McKeown and Thomas (1988) both provided details on Q-methodological factor analysis.
3. Factor 6 is not described because it proved too difficult to interpret without a follow-up interview with the woman whose Q-sort had a pure loading for this factor, and she did not wish to be

interviewed. The factor array for Factor 6 is presented in Table 1 for readers interested in examining this woman's Q-sort.

4. At the time of the interview, Paul Bernardo had recently been arrested and charged with numerous violent assaults on women and with two counts of murder of women in Ontario.

5. Thanks to Charlene Senn for this insight regarding radical feminism.

REFERENCES

Black, N. (1989). *Social feminism.* Ithaca, NY: Cornell University Press.

Breinlinger, S., & Kelly, C. (1994). Women's responses to status inequality: A test of Social Identity Theory. *Psychology of Women Quarterly, 18,* 1–16.

Brown, S. R. (1980). *Political subjectivity: Applications of Q methodology in political science.* New Haven, CT: Yale University Press.

Code, L. (1988). Feminist theory. In S. Burt, L. Code, & L. Dorney (Eds.), *Changing patterns: Women in Canada* (pp. 18–49). Toronto: McClelland and Stewart.

Descarries-Belanger, F., & Roy, S. (1991). *The women's movement and its currents of thought: A typological essay* (J. Beeman, Trans.) Ottawa: CRIAW/ICREF. (Original work published 1988).

Frye, M. (1992). *Willful virgin: Essays in feminism.* Freedom, CA: Crossing.

Jaggar, A. M., & Rothenberg, P. S. (1993) (Eds.). *Feminist frameworks: Alternative theoretical accounts of the relations between women and men* (3rd ed.). New York: McGraw-Hill.

Kitzinger, C. (1986). Introducing and developing Q as a feminist methodology. In S. Wilkinson (Ed.), *Feminist social psychology* (pp. 151–172). Milton Keynes: Open University Press.

Kitzinger, C. (1987). *The social construction of lesbianism.* London: Sage.

Kitzinger, C., & Rogers, R. S. (1985). A Q-methodological study of lesbian identities. *European Journal of Social Psychology, 15,* 167–187.

Linton, R. (1989). Conceptualizing feminism: Clarifying social science concepts. *Evaluation and Program Planning, 12,* 25–29.

McFadden, M. (1984). Anatomy of a difference: Toward a classification of feminist theory. *Women's Studies International Forum, 7,* 495–504.

McKeown, B., & Thomas, D. (1988). *Q methodology.* (Sage University Papers: Quantitative Applications in the Social Sciences Series, No. 07-066). Beverly Hills, CA: Sage.

Morawski, J. (1992). Review of *Gender and thought: Psychological perspectives. Psychology of Women Quarterly, 16,* 261–264.

Oakley, A. (1981). *Subject women.* Oxford: Martin Robertson.

Senn, C. Y. (1991). *The impact of pornography in women's lives.* Unpublished doctoral dissertation, York University, North York, ON.

Senn, C. Y. (1993). Women's multiple perspectives and experiences with pornography. *Psychology of Women Quarterly, 17,* 319–341.

Spence, J. T., & Helmreich, R. (1972). The Attitudes Toward Women Scale: An objective instrument to measure attitudes toward the rights and roles of women in contemporary society. *JSAS Catalog of Selected Documents in Psychology, 2,* 66 (Ms. No. 153).

SPSS Inc. (1988). *SPSS-X user's guide* (3rd ed.). Chicago: SPSS Inc.

Stacey, J. (1990). Sexism by a subtler name? Postindustrial conditions and postfeminist consciousness in Silicon Valley. In K. V. Hansen & I. J. Philipson (Eds.), *Women, class, and the feminist imagination: A socialist feminist reader* (pp. 338–356). Philadelphia: Temple University Press.

Stephenson, W. (1953). *The study of behavior.* Chicago: University of Chicago Press.

Tajfel, H., & Turner, J. C. (1986). The social identity theory of intergroup behaviour. In W. G. Austin & S. Worchel (Eds.), *The psychology of intergroup relations* (2nd ed., pp. 7–24). Chicago: Nelson-Hall.

Tong, R. (1989). *Feminist thought: A comprehensive introduction.* Boulder, CO: Westview.

RESEARCHING SUBJECTIVITY AND DIVERSITY

Q-Methodology in Feminist Psychology

Celia Kitzinger
Loughborough University

Given the relative rarity of Q-methodology in feminist psychology, I am delighted to see it included in this Special Issue on Innovations in Feminist Research. Susan Snelling's article demonstrates a sophisticated understanding of Q-methodology, and her study provides an exemplary use of the method in researching people's subjective perspectives and in exploring a diversity of different viewpoints. In this commentary, I draw on her article to illustrate some of the key features of Q-methodology: in particular, its use in researching subjectivities and exploring diversity and the issues involved in factor interpretation. More broadly, I wish to use this opportunity to reflect on the advantages and disadvantages of Q-methodology for feminist psychology.

Q-methodology was invented by William Stephenson in the 1930s (Stephenson, 1935, 1936a, 1936b) during the time he was working as Spearman's research assistant when Spearman was formulating and refining factor analysis. Stephenson's Q-methodology involves two radical reformulations of Spearman's factor analytic approach. First, it considers the data in terms of what Stephenson called "self-reference" (i.e., subjective rankings as opposed to seeking objective definitions of tests); second, it treats these data in terms of each individual's whole pattern of response (rather than looking for patterns item by item or test by test across people). The method was first known as "the inverted factor technique" (Stephenson, 1936a)—factor analysis of a data matrix by rows, rather than columns, so that persons, instead of tests or test items, constitute the variables. Correlating items (the technique used in the vast bulk of factor analyses carried out by psychologists) is referred to as R-methodology. For a full discussion of the differences between Q- and R-methodology (as well as detailed guidance on how to carry out Q-methodological research), see Brown (1980). For discussion of the theoretical implications

Address correspondence and research requests to: Celia Kitzinger, Loughborough University, Loughborough, Leicestershire LE1 13TU, UK. E-mail: C.C.Kitzinger@lboro.ac.uk.

of Q-methodology specifically in relation to psychology, see Kitzinger (1987) and Curt (1994).

From the outset, Q-methodology was intended to research people's own subjective experiences, opinions, ideas, beliefs, and perspectives. As one of the leading British Q-methodologists, Wendy Stainton Rogers (1991), pointed out, Q-methodology "does not set out to 'measure' anything objectively" (p. 127). Q-methodology also assumes that people's subjective experiences are diverse, and it aims to explore and to chart that diversity. "Q-methodology is ideal for addressing the critical kinds of research questions which are concerned to hear 'many voices'" (R. Stainton Rogers, Stenner, Gleeson, & W. Stainton Rogers, 1995, pp. 250–251). Susan Snelling's article illustrates both of these key points: her focus is on women's own perspectives on feminism, and her method makes possible the emergence of a diverse range of different perspectives.

Q-methodology's focus on uncovering research participants' own perspectives, understandings and definitions, instead of simply measuring participants' understandings in relation to an operational definition imposed on them by the researcher, is one of the key features that should make this methodology attractive to feminist researchers. As Snelling points out, most psychologists engaged in quantitative research on women's attitudes toward feminism have used "a standardized questionnaire measure of feminism that implicitly recognizes only one type of feminism" (p. 248), and it is in relation to this one version of feminism (usually a liberal/equal rights version) that all women's attitudes and beliefs are measured. The effect is to dismiss as "unfeminist" or even "antifeminist" the beliefs of women with alternative feminist perspectives not shared by the researcher.

This is typical of attitude research generally. I have shown elsewhere, in relation to homophobia scales, the way in which the operational definition of "antilesbian/ gay" beliefs is rooted in liberal/humanistic values, such that radical lesbian feminists routinely find themselves diagnosed as suffering from "homophobia." We agree with items scored as indicating homophobia (such as "Lesbians pose a threat to the nuclear family and society as we know it") and disagree with items scored as indicating an unprejudiced attitude (e.g., "What people do in bed is their own business") (cf. Kitzinger, 1987). What is at issue here is not whether lesbian feminists are or are not suffering from homophobia. The point is that homophobia scales incorporate a particular political/ideological perspective on what counts as being in favor of, or prejudiced against, lesbians and gay men. This should not be read as a call for better or more objective scales, either. The operational definitions incorporated into attitude questionnaires can never be objective—they always reflect the ideological commitments of the researcher and the majority norms of the time, place, and culture in which the research is embedded (see also Condor, 1986; Kaye, 1947; Rosier, 1974, for graphic illustrations of this point for attitudes toward women, anti-Semitism, and racism, respectively).

People have different understandings and definitions of homophobia, racism, and sexism, and it is precisely these different understandings that are elicited and explored in Q-methodological research. In conventional attitude research these differences are resolved by definitional fiat and are not considered worthy of research in their own right. In Q-methodology these different perspectives constitute the research topic. A researcher may use her own understandings and definitions to structure her Q-sort (as Snelling does in deriving items that purportedly reflect 10 different perspectives of feminism), but the structuring of a Q-sort in this way does not mean that these (researcher-hypothesized) classifications necessarily map onto the participant perspectives that emerge from the data, nor does it prevent the emergence of alternative and unanticipated perspectives (such as the "humanist" perspective in Snelling's research). As one Q-methodologist has stated: "Those of us who use Q method in our research do so because it is the only technique that we have found which places the *participants in the study* in control of the classification process. A factor cannot emerge unless participants sort items in ways that enable it to do so" (W. Stainton Rogers, 1991, p. 130).

In sum, the key advantages of Q-methodology for feminist psychology are (a) its focus on subjective experiences, perspectives, and beliefs, which are permitted to emerge in their own right and not simply in relation to an objective operational definition imposed by the researcher, and (b) its focus on eliciting and describing a wide diversity of different subjective experiences, perspectives, and beliefs, none of which are defined a priori by the researcher.

INTERPRETING FACTOR ARRAYS

Compared with the large literature on the selection of items, the construction of Q-sorts, the choice of participants, and the mathematical procedures involved in factor analysis and in the calculation of factor arrays, there is relatively little about the interpretation of factor arrays (i.e., the process of working out the "meaning" of a factor based on the weighted average Q-sort distribution for that factor). Yet, this is the most subjective part of the entire process of Q-methodological research. It is in interpreting factor arrays that the researcher's own biases and limitations may be most apparent and may result in meanings being inadvertently imposed on research participants. It is for this reason that many Q-methodologists follow William Stephenson's (1972) advice to "go back to the original Ss, the Q-sorters, to find out what their interpretations are for the factors on which the factor-analysis has placed them" (p. 182). Many, like Susan Snelling, use follow-up interviews to assist them in interpreting factor arrays. Other aids to factor interpretation include asking participants to make comments on individual items at the time of completing the sort (e.g., R. Stainton Rogers & Kitzinger, 1995; W. Stainton Rogers, 1991) and preparing brief summaries of factor interpretations and feeding them back to participants for comment (R. Stainton Rogers & Kitzinger, 1995). The discerning reader of Q-methodological studies should bear in mind that labels for factors "are always contestable and are best reflected upon in the light of the factor exegesis" (R. Stainton Rogers & Kitzinger, 1995, p. 105). Moreover, as long as researchers present the full factor array and the set of Q-sort items (as in Snelling's Table 1), the adequacy of the researcher's factor interpretation is open to evaluation by the reader.

In interpreting a factor array, a researcher is telling a plausible story about the choices made by the research participants whose sorts load on that factor, seeking to explain the pattern of their rankings. This interpretation should include (obviously) a discussion of those items scored in the extreme positions indicative of strong agreement and strong disagreement (in Snelling's case, +4, +5, −4, −5). These items are relevant because, compared with other Q-sort items, they are those about which the participant feels particularly strongly. Their relevance in factor interpretation is enhanced when items that receive strong agreement on one factor receive strong disagreement on another (and vice versa) or for cases in which items scored neutrally across most of the factors are scored strongly positive or negative on one factor. Factor interpretation should involve inspection of item scores across as well as within factor arrays. An item that receives the same score across all factors (even if that score is a +5) is not useful in discriminating one factor from another. Comprehensive factor interpretation should also include discussion of (a) any apparent discrepancies in the Q-sort rankings, (b) apparent differences in word interpretation across different factors, and (c) items scored in the center of the Q-sort distribution. As these aspects of factor interpretation are often neglected, I will briefly outline the relevance of each in turn.

Apparent Discrepancies in the Q-sort Rankings

It is almost always the case that a researcher (or reader) inspecting a factor array will spot what seem to be discrepancies in the way items have been ranked: that is, scores that lead the researcher (or reader) to think, "How can she say she agrees with this, if she disagrees with that?" These apparent discrepancies can yield fruitful avenues for exploration. In Snelling's work, for example, it is surprising (to me, anyway) to find that the "humanist" perspective represented in the Factor 3 array includes strong support for affirmative action programs (item 1, +4) because the logic behind affirmative action is often represented in terms of precisely the "female supremacist" position of which humanists are so critical. It is very helpful to be able to draw on the written or verbal comments of participants in explaining these apparent discrepancies—to be able to ask the humanist, for example, what affirmative action means to her and how it fits in with her other views about the danger of "women going over and being the top ones." I have emphasized that these discrepancies are apparent because, of course, what I as reader or Snelling as researcher consider to be discrepancies derive from our own personal and political perspectives. What we might see as a discrepancy may not be experienced as such by research participants with other personal and political perspectives.

Apparent Differences in Item Interpretation Across
Different Factors

One reason for apparent discrepancies in sorting Q-items is that the same words mean different things to different people. At one level this is a self-evident fact, but it is routinely obscured in conventional R-methodological attitude testing. In attitude tests, item meanings are determined a priori and fixed by the researcher in the operational definition incorporated into the scale. In Q-methodology, by contrast, the meaning of an item is determined by how different participants understand it, as evidenced by the score they give it, relative to other items in their Q-sorts. In Q-methodology, the same item can mean different things to different participants in a single study. So, as I have argued elsewhere, in Q-methodology the meaning of an item like "Lesbians pose a threat to the nuclear family and society as we know it" is not fixed (as it is in homophobia scales) but is determined through the use participants make of it in the context of the overall Q-sort they complete. If it is scored +5 by someone who also scores as +5 items such as "Lesbians are sick" or "Lesbianism is against the word of God," then it would appear that the participant has understood this threat to the nuclear family and society as we know it in a negative light and that the item is an expression of concern about the implications of lesbianism for normal family life. If, on the other hand, it is scored as +5 by someone who also scores as +5 items such as "We need to work for the end of heteropatriarchy" or "Lesbians are in the vanguard of the feminist movement," then the item seems to have been understood as supportive of the radical potential of lesbianism for social and political change. Similarly, in Snelling's Q-sort, item 49 ("There is no reason that mothers with young children shouldn't work outside the home") seems to be interpreted differently by those participants whose Q-sorts define Factors 1 and 4. Both groups of participants disagree with the statement (i.e., believe there are reasons that prevent mothers with young children from working outside the home). For Factor 1, the "radical/ lesbian/antiracist" perspective, this presumably refers to the absence of 24-hour free childcare provided by the state (or something similar); for Factor 4, the "conservative" perspective, it presumably refers to the need young children have to be cared for by their mothers. In Q-methodology, meaning is always contextual.

Items Scored in the Center of the Q-sort Distribution

Items scored in central (+1, 0, −1) positions may be as salient to a factor interpretation as are items with extreme scores. It is particularly worth inspecting items that receive central scores when they are items that the researcher (or reader) might expect (on the basis of the ranking of other items) to receive extreme scores. For example, the "postfeminist" perspective of Factor 5 is described by Snelling as one in which "[f]eminism was irrelevant because . . . gender equality was established in society" (p. 262). Yet, item 22 ("most of the goals of the women's movement have already been reached") is given a central score (−1), indicating that this is not a particularly important statement. (Is there perhaps a distinction being made here between "gender equality" and "the goals of the women's movement"?) Centrally scored items may also be particularly salient in interpreting a factor when these same items are assigned extreme scores by other factors. Take, for example, item 8 in Snelling's factor array. This item ("Men's need to dominate women can clearly be seen in what is considered 'normal' male sexuality") is scored +3 on Factor 1; −4, −4, and −3 on Factors 3, 5 and 6, respectively; and 0 on Factors 2 and 4. This item is something about which participants whose sorts load on four of the factors express strong views (one way or the other) and about which participants whose sorts load on the remaining two factors are completely neutral. It might be interesting to explore the purpose and function of this careful neutrality of the heterosexual "liberal" (Factor 2) and "conservative" (Factor 4) women. Their reasons for not agreeing with it may be fairly easily deduced, but their reasons for not disagreeing with it may be worth further exploration.

Comprehensive interpretation and exegesis of factor arrays include the inspection of item scores within and across factors, at the center as well as at the extremes of the Q-sort distribution, and the exploration of apparently discrepant rankings. Published Q-sort studies should always (but often do not) include the full factor arrays and set of Q-sort items so that readers can assess for themselves the adequacy of particular factor interpretations.

Finally, it is common for authors to report (as Snelling does) that a factor or set of factors accounts for a given percentage of the total variance; but as Stephenson (1978b) pointed out, in Q-methodology this is more habitual than informative. In Q, the substantive or theoretical importance of a factor is not equivalent to factor size (as measured statistically, e.g., via the amount of variance it explains or via eigenvalues) (see Brown, 1980; Stephenson, 1978b). The reporting of factor size in Q-methodological studies is commonplace not because this information is of any relevance to Q-methodological research, but because most psychologists are familiar with R-methodological factor analysis (in the context of which such information is important), and, as Stephenson (1978b) put it, "It is sometimes necessary to toss a statistical bone to the mastiffs which guard the professional journals" (p. 124).

IS Q-METHODOLOGY A GOOD METHOD FOR FEMINISTS?

One aim of feminist research is to respect the diversity of people's own meanings and understandings without imposing a predetermined set of definitions on what they say. Compared with tests and scales (including those in common use among feminists, e.g., Bem Sex Role Inventory (BSRI) and Attitudes Toward Women Scale (ATWS), Q is certainly successful in doing this. There are no a priori operational definitions in Q-methodology, and research participants are not constrained by researchers' own prior theories or hypotheses. On the other hand, it is common for participants in Q-methodological studies to say that they feel constrained by the requirements imposed on them to rank order preselected items according to rules prescribed by the researcher, and the fact that item meanings are not prede- fined is rarely appreciated by research participants. Feminist researchers have expressed concern about how individual participants experience the process of data collection, and (although there are always participants who enjoy doing Q-sorts) my impression is that, in general, there is a preference for more open-ended approaches, such as interviews or focus groups, in which people feel freer to express themselves in their own language and on their own terms.

It is important to point out, however, that participants' feelings that they are constrained, categorized, or misrepresented by a particular research method do not necessarily map onto what actually happens. The sense of free self-expression that is part of participating in interview research with a skilled interviewer derives at least in part from the fact that the process of constraining, categorizing, and representing what participants say is invisible to them. It is not part of the data collection process but is carried out subsequently through the analytic procedures applied to the data by the researcher. Whatever methods of qualitative analysis are chosen (clinical insight, grounded theory, content or discourse analysis, voice- centered relational method), the analytic process involves decisions by the re- searcher about what are the most important views expressed by the participant and what they ("really") mean. In Q-methodology, as we have seen, the participant tells the researcher directly (via ranking items at the extreme ends of the distribution) which of her views are most important to her and (via the pattern of her sort and through her help in factor interpretation) provides information on the meaning of these views to her.

Used appropriately, to research the diverse range of subjective perspectives that people may hold on any given issue and with careful attention to appropriate factor interpretation, I consider Q-methodology to be a useful contribution to feminist research methods. I do, however, have some reservations in recommending its use. In particular, there are serious disadvantages for feminist psychologists in adopting a method that is rarely used and little understood within mainstream psychology (or within feminist psychology, for that matter). Whereas researchers using more familiar methods can usually rely on their colleagues' understanding of (if not agreement with) the basic principles on which these methods are based, Q-methodologists are forced to spend a lot of time and energy explaining and justifying their method to journal editors and referees and to conference audiences. Compared with the sometimes helpful and informed criticism I have received from such sources in relation to other research methods I have used, I have found criticism of my Q-methodological research usually misplaced and unhelpful—an experience shared by other Q-methodologists with whom I have discussed this problem. In many cases this is because Q-methodological research is judged by criteria appropriate for the evaluation of R-methodological work. The use of inappropriate criteria in assessing Q-methodological research often leads reviewers (chosen for their competence with conventional factor analytic procedures) to request unnecessary or irrelevant additional information (e.g., factor size), while failing to spot what are, to Q-methodologists, crucial omissions (e.g., factor arrays). This situation does not encourage the development of high quality Q-methodological research.

As a feminist, I want to communicate my research findings both to other feminist psychologists and, more generally, to other psychologists (and social scientists) working on related topics. As a Q-methodologist, I found it very hard to communicate about my research. When presenting my findings, I encountered a barrage of criticism about my method. This criticism was particularly frustrating because I was not being criticized for failing to do Q-methodology the way a good Q-methodologist should (which would be entirely legitimate) but for using Q-methodology at all—that is, for failing to do conventional R-methodological, or even conventional qualitative, research. Researchers should, of course, be able to defend the methods we choose to use. But to have to explain and justify the basic premises (at the expense of any informed discussion of one's application of them, let alone any discussion of one's results) is very tiresome.

Q-methodologists are generally criticized by both qualitative and quantitative researchers. Qualitative researchers typically view Q-methodology as sharing all the disadvantages of conventional quantitative methods: preselected items, a restricted response format, the use of complex statistical procedures, and "findings" that are often read as the production of "categories" into which the research participants are neatly slotted. It is the similarities rather than the differences between Q and conventional psychological measurement techniques that are most apparent to qualitative psychologists new to Q-methodology, and I have generally found that researchers committed to qualitative methods are usually not receptive to detailed explanations about these differences. In particular, qualitative researchers tend to insist on the inherent superiority of their own approaches in revealing and respecting the meanings of the research participants. As I have indicated, I do not think that this argument is defensible. Nonetheless, many qualitative researchers adopt this position and dismiss Q-methodology as no more than another mainstream quantitative technique.

Quantitative researchers, on the other hand, generally judge Q-methodology in relation to the conventional (R-methodological) techniques with which they are more familiar and then criticize Q-methodology for failing to meet the standards set for psychometric testing. It is common, for example, for Q-methodologists to be berated for not including a sufficient number of randomly selected participants in their studies, for failing to establish the content validity of their Q-sort structures, or for seeking to interpret factors with "insufficient" numbers of defining Q-sorts. Because Q-methodology begins from a set of assumptions that are very different from those of R-methodology, most of these concerns are simply misplaced.

In mainstream "scientific" psychology, there is, as Stephenson (1978a) noted, a rampant "ideology of objectivity" (p. 25), which means that quantitative researchers are rarely content to view Q-methodological findings as provisional, shifting confluences of subjectivity. One common move is to reify factor interpretations as representing fixed taxonomies of people. I have frequently found my own research (mis)represented as indicating (for example) that there are "five types of lesbians." These reified categories are then sometimes used to develop conventional measures, converting factors into scales. This would be akin to taking Snelling's five interpreted factors, using her Q-sort items to derive a questionnaire, and testing large numbers of participants in order to determine whether they are "conservatives," "humanists," "postfeminists," and so on. To do so is clearly against the spirit of Q-methodological research, yet it is not uncommon. For example, Wendy Stainton Rogers' (1991) Q-methodological research, which found eight different accounts of health and illness was criticized (e.g., for having "only" 83 participants) and "replicated" by Furnham (1994), who carried out a factor analysis of the initial Q-sort by items (rather than people) and converted it into a scale, thereby violating the Q-methodological precepts embodied in the original study, with (apparently) no awareness of the shift in methodological approach involved. This is a typical example of the extent to which Q-methodological research is "read" (and criticized) from within a conventional R-methodological framework.

The interpretation of Q-methodology in terms of the conventional approach of R-methodological testing has also led to a variety of misuses of the method, and these misuses (and theoretical justifications for them) are now part of the standard literature on Q-methodology. In the early days of Q-methodology, many quantitative researchers were unwilling to accept Q-methodology's principle of self-reference and adapted it for use as a supposedly objective measure of mental health and as a diagnostic tool in psychiatric research and personality assessment. Perhaps surprisingly, this approach was particularly common among devotees of Carl Rogers' "client-centered therapy" (e.g., Butler & Haigh, 1954). Jack Block's (1955, 1961) misrepresentation of Q as a measure of personality is now more widely known among psychologists than is Stephenson's original conception of the method, and it was (for example) Block's version of Q, not Stephenson's, that was used by Daryl Bem and his associates in the 1970s in experimental research (Bem & Funder,

1978; Bem & Lord, 1979). This widespread incorporation into the standard literature of (mis)uses of Q-methodology, which diverge dramatically from Stephenson's original conception, adds to the problem for novices seeking to develop a clear understanding of what the method has to offer and increases the difficulty of explaining Q-methodology to its critics.

It may now be apparent that I no longer use Q-methodology myself. I was initially enthusiastic about the method in carrying out my doctoral research (published as Kitzinger, 1987); I was excited by the opportunity it offered to avoid operational definitions of healthy lesbian identity and to explore the range and diversity of lesbians' own definitions. Using Q-methodology, I was able to show that the operational definitions routinely used in so-called lesbian and gay affirmative psychology were rooted in liberal/humanistic ideology and that they imposed the particular ideological perspective of the researcher on lesbians with a wide diversity of different perspectives. I also subsequently used Q-methodology when I was employed as a researcher studying the diversity of different conceptions of human rights (later published as R. Stainton Rogers & Kitzinger, 1995). I continue to think of Q as a valuable research method, but I became increasingly frustrated with having to argue about the method when what I wanted to discuss were my findings and their implications. At conference after conference, I found myself in earnest discussions about eigenvalues and varimax rotation instead of lesbian politics. I became weary of having to explain to quantitative researchers the differences between Q and R and to qualitative researchers the way in which Q enables the emergence of a diverse range of subjective perspectives not predefined by the researcher. It did not seem possible simply to pick up and use Q-methodology to research topics about which I was deeply concerned. Instead, I was forced into becoming an ambassador for the method. I experienced the need for all this justification and explanation as a deflection from my absorbing interests in lesbianism, feminism, and human rights and thought that I could avoid this intensive focus on method if I chose other approaches. I was right. In my subsequent research (using interviews, story completion, and discourse analysis) my methods have been recognized as part of established traditions with their own criteria of evaluation. In sum, my decision not to use Q-methodology is not an indictment of the method but rather of psychology's rigid and blinkered approach to factor analytic work.[1]

In conclusion, I have outlined what I see as some very positive aspects of Q-methodology and its potential in researching and documenting the range and diversity of subjective experiences, perspectives, and beliefs. My discussion of the problems of using Q-methodology in feminist psychology are not intended to deter potential Q-methodologists but simply to alert them to possible difficulties in communicating their research, which they might thereby be better able to address. I welcome Susan Snelling's contribution to this Special Issue, and I hope that more feminist psychologists will be inspired by her example to explore the use of Q-methodology in their own research.

NOTE

1. It is worth noting that, although Q is an excellent method for revealing a range and diversity of different perspectives, it does not enable exploration of how people actively construct and negotiate these different perspectives in interactions with others, and it is this constructive aspect in which I am currently more interested.

REFERENCES

Bem, D. J., & Funder, D. C. (1978). Predicting more of the people more of the time: Assessing the personality of situations. *Psychological Review, 84,* 485–501.

Bem, D. J., & Lord, C. G. (1979). Template matching: A proposal for probing the ecological validity of experimental settings in social psychology. *Journal of Personality and Social Psychology, 37,* 833–846.

Block, J. (1955). The difference between Q and R. *Psychological Review, 62,* 356–358.

Block, J. (1961). *The Q-sort method in personality assessment and psychiatric research.* Springfield, IL: Charles C Thomas.

Brown, S. R. (1980). *Political subjectivity: Applications of Q-methodology in political science.* New Haven, CT: Yale University Press.

Butler, R., & Haigh, T. (1954). Changes in the relation between self-concepts and ideal concepts consequent upon client-centered counseling. In C. R. Rogers & R. F. Dymond (Eds.), *Psychotherapy and personality change* (pp. 72–89). Chicago: University of Chicago Press.

Condor, S. (1986). Sex role beliefs and "traditional" women: Feminist and intergroup perspectives. In S. Wilkinson (Ed.), *Feminist social psychology* (pp.97–118). Milton Keynes: Open University Press.

Curt, B. (pseud.). (1994). *Textuality and techtonics: Troubling social and psychological science.* Milton Keynes: Open University Press.

Furnham, A. (1994). Explaining health and illness: Lay perceptions on current and future health, the causes of illness and the nature of recovery. *Social Science and Medicine, 39,* 715–725.

Kaye, L. W. (1947). Frames of reference in "pro" and "anti" evaluations of test items. *Journal of Social Psychology, 25,* 63–68.

Kitzinger, C. (1987). *The social construction of lesbianism.* London: Sage.

Roiser, M. (1974). Asking silly questions. In N. Armistead (Ed.), *Reconstructing social psychology* (pp. 75–92). Harmondsworth: Penguin.

Stainton Rogers, R., & Kitzinger, C. (1995). A decalogue of human rights: What happens when you let the people speak. *Social Science Information, 34,* 87–106.

Stainton Rogers, R., Stenner, P., Gleeson, K., & Stainton Rogers, W. (1995). *Social psychology: A critical agenda.* Cambridge: Polity.

Stainton Rogers, W. (1991). *Explaining health and illness: An exploration of diversity.* London: Harvester Wheatsheaf.

Stephenson, W. (1935). Techniques of factor analysis. *Nature, 136,* 297.

Stephenson, W. (1936a). The inverted factor technique. *British Journal of Psychology, 22,* 344–361.

Stephenson, W. (1936b). A new application of correlation to averages. *British Journal of Educational Psychology, 6,* 43–57.

Stephenson, W. (1972). Applications of communication theory: II—Interpretations of Keats' "Ode on a Grecian Urn." *Psychological Record, 22,* 177–192.

Stephenson, W. (1978a). The shame of science. *Ethics in Science and Medicine, 5,* 25–38.

Stephenson, W. (1978b). The importance of factors in Q-methodology: Statistical and theoretical considerations. *Operant Subjectivity, 1,* 117–124.

KEEPING AND CROSSING PROFESSIONAL AND RACIALIZED BOUNDARIES[1]

Implications for Feminist Practice

Gill Aitken
Mental Health Services of Salford

Erica Burman
The Manchester Metropolitan University

In this article we reflect on the process of a white woman researching a Black woman's experiences of engaging in clinical psychology services. This involved interviewing both a Black woman client and her white woman therapist four times over an 11-month therapy period. We discuss issues of identifications and relationships, the interface between research and therapy, and professional and ethical responsibilities of disclosures arising from this particular study in relation to general debates about feminist research. Rather than presuming that feminist research involves identifications between women or the aim of dissolving power relations, we highlight how issues of power and difference form a continuous topic and site of negotiation within the research relationship. We explore how this parallels and informs the therapy process. Despite differences in structural relations of privilege and power and reservations about feminist research practices around disclosure, we argue that fruitful consequences can follow from an explicit acknowledgment of the multiple identifications and institutional positions all participants occupy within research relationships. These include dimensions of difference between women structured around race, class, and professional–client relations.

Address correspondence and reprint requests to: Gill Aitken, Adult Forensic Psychology Services, Mental Health Services of Salford, Bury New Road, Prestwich, Manchester M25 3BL, United Kingdom.

This article reflects on the process of research conducted by one of us (GA) under the supervision of the other (EB) into Black[2] women's referrals to, and engagement in, clinical psychology services (Aitken, 1996a). The research involved semi-structured interviews with Black women recipients of clinical psychology therapy services, their (clinical psychology) therapists, and their general practitioner referrers before, during, and after therapy. As an example of feminist, qualitative action research,[3] its innovative character in terms of both method and topic has met with some resistance in "malestream" clinical psychology (Aitken, 1996b; Burman, 1996). In this article we revisit the process of this project from the perspective of the researcher's position and view of her interventions to explore how this work informs and extends debates within feminist psychological research.

In terms of the concerns of this Special Issue, the innovative character of this research relies less on its techniques (for action-oriented research and discursive or thematic analysis of semi-structured interviews are scarcely new) than on the ways a feminist consciousness has entered into and interacted with other researcher and professional positions. It is relevant to note that this approach was adopted as appropriate for this research without equating qualitative research with feminist research or indeed presuming that any method could be deemed intrinsically feminist or otherwise (Griffin & Phoenix, 1994; Harding, 1986).

What this qualitative approach afforded was the generation of material for analysis that was not prestructured according to a model of subjectivity that viewed categories of identities as separate and additive. This is the model of subjectivity that predominates within positivist empirical psychology. It has been soundly contested for its implicit androcentrism and denial of emotional investments (including those of passion, embodiment, and the implication of the researcher within the process and outcome of the research) (see Hollway, 1989). A precondition for our analysis, therefore, was the generation of material that would allow for the documentation of multiplicity, variability, and contradiction within the accounts. This seemed particularly appropriate for the dual character of this research, which documents therapeutic process and change (see also Heenan, 1995, 1996) and explores issues raised in working (in research and in therapy) across structural differences of "race"[4] and culture. In terms of interpretive resources, the research drew on feminist analyses, highlighting the race-specific character of gendered identities (e.g., Anthias & Yuval-Davis, 1993) as well as the historical complicity of second wave feminisms within racial/colonial practices (e.g., McClintock, 1995). Such accounts render problematic the notion of a common or generalizeable gendered identity as women, let alone as feminists. By taking a qualitative approach, the negotiation of commonalities and differences mobilized by gender could become a research topic rather than a premise.

The remit of a feminist commitment to the transformation of power relations includes attention to those enacted within the researcher–researched relation. Many feminists are calling for the development of more collaborative and empowering ways (for researcher and researched) of conducting feminist (psychological) research (Olesen, 1994). Furthermore, current debates highlight how identifying ourselves or our work as feminist may simply obscure the reenactment or reproduction of dominant representations and practices because of "the complexities of power relations and ideologies identified within the feminist researcher/researched relationship" (Opie, 1992, p. 53). This has particular relevance for research with women whose experiences may be structured around differently arranged but intersecting relations of race, class, sexuality, and age (Bhavnani, 1994; Harding, 1993; Lewis, 1996). Moreover, the feminist commitment to critical reflexivity inevitably involves acknowledging a particularity of context and intervention that limits claims to general application. Hence, we do not present our account here to make claims about models or to offer innovative techniques for feminist research. Rather, we reflect on and chronicle the conditions that made this research fulfill its aims of identifying and developing good practice.

Setting the Scene

In my (GA) identifications as a white, antiracist, feminist, trainee clinical psychologist, I am an "insider" in relation to clinical psychology as a profession and a discipline and to the workings of racism. But in my antiracist stance, I try to position myself as an "outsider" in relation to colluding with racism and reproducing dominant representations of Black women. I am an outsider to Black women's experiences of racism but an insider to oppression as a woman and in challenging institutional oppressive assumptions and practices. These positions and identifications framed the structure and process of the project in ways that were not only multiple, but also constantly changing. I needed to reflect continuously on how these could affect the researcher–researched and therapist–client relations in ways that might perpetuate dominant representations and distribution of resources. This article is an expression of that work of reflection so far.

Like Marshall (1996) we draw on a range of material to illustrate our arguments, including various accounts presented of the research, interview transcripts, and interpretations of the experience of conducting it. At the time of conducting the research project, I was aware of some of the implications of my actions and interpretations. However, the process of ongoing discussions with participants, with EB, and indeed our joint writing of this article clearly involved further levels of self-reflection. Hence, we move from writing as a "we" to "I" and back again as we shift between accounts of the research process and our interpretations of it. When we comment on interview extracts, we would want to frame the status of these comments as neither immanent to the moment of the interview, nor entirely a construction of our reflections on it. We say this because claims about intentionality (whether of authors or readers) bedevil analysis of textual material and often threaten to impose voluntarist and individualistic models of the conditions for, and constraints of, discursive positions.

Although we highlight a number of ambiguities in reading the texts, we also argue that such ambiguities cannot be resolved at the level of text except in relation to a broader context or frame of the research relationship. This acknowledgment of structures that enter into, but exist outside, specific texts has obvious links with debates over the relativizing tendencies of the "turn to the text" (Burman, 1993). We draw attention to ambiguities in the texts we present here to highlight the importance of contexts both of the production and the interpretation of texts. We see textual material as generated within research relationships that in themselves are institutional practices and also intersect with others. The focus of this article is on how negotiations between participants are constant, but shifting, as an evolving process between embodied individuals participating in a range of institutional practices.

NEGOTIATING IDENTIFICATIONS/RELATIONS WITH PARTICIPANTS THROUGHOUT THE RESEARCH PROCESS

Researcher Identifications in Engaging Participants

In common with many self-identified feminist researchers, we understand a feminist commitment to research with participants as being concerned with developing open and honest relations (transparency) with participants (Lather, 1988; Opie, 1992). However, our partiality in the identifications we communicate to potential participants in our attempts to engage them in (our) research is less often acknowledged. For us, such partiality illuminates the dilemmas and paradoxes which as feminist researchers we face in our commitment to transparency. How do we locate ourselves and lay claim to positions outside dominant institutions but at the same time acknowledge the power and privilege of being able to choose (at least to some extent) how to identify/position ourselves? And to what extent are these choices available in the same way to potential research participants?

In my (GA's) commitment to be open about the context and purpose of the research project and about my own positionings, I distributed the same three-paged letter to all participants prior to any interviews. Under the heading, "Who will be carrying out the project/ interviewing," I explicitly communicated my identifications as white, female trainee practitioner along with my age. This could be interpreted as making clear, how in relation to the topic of the research (the exploration of race and gender in clinical psychology service provision), how these identifications were both necessary and sufficient to communicate to all potential participants (doctors, therapists, and clients). That I suppressed my feminist identification implies that I constructed this as problematic for potentially engaging participants in the project. For example, I was aware of my (well-justified?) assumption that without meeting me I might be constructed as "too radical," or that the assumed aims of myself as a (white) feminist would not immediately be shared by professionals and/or Black women (e.g., Bhavnani & Coulson, 1986; Carby, 1982; Collins, 1990). When read in conjunction with a statement about my commitment to questioning and challenging prejudice and discrimination (although racism was not specifically named), one interpretation is that I presumed, first, some shared understandings of the relevance of such a project, and, second, that I would need to establish my credibility (i.e., construct my textual authority to conduct and author such a study [Smith, 1990]) to address this project with (potential) Black women clients and professionals.

Clearly, a participant's initial decision to engage in a study may be based on information provided about a researcher's explicit identifications. However, the assumptions that these identifications are (a) fixed, (b) invoked and evoked invariably across participants, and (c) fixed once and for all are, as we will show, contestable. Despite this, within the context of developing relatively secure research relationships we attempt to elaborate how the shifting relations between participants as mediated by these identifications can be used as a resource within and across interviews and therapy contexts.

From my perspective, how I (GA) identified, and was identified, within the interview contexts was neither consistent nor systematic. Variations occurred according to which participant I was interacting with and whether I (or she) was privileging a researcher/practitioner and/or interventionist/supportive role. This poses two issues for feminist research. First, the feminist research process may share more commonalities with other forms of institutional interactions (such as therapy) than may often be acknowledged. Second, the significance of asymmetrical disclosure within the research (and therapy) relationship must be explored. After commenting on these two issues, we then reflect on how both run counter to feminists' presumption (romanticization?) of egalitarian and reciprocal research relationships.

Disclosure, Negotiation, and Impact of Researcher Identifications/Relations

Whiteness and Professionalism in the Context of Interviewing a Black Woman
Looking back, it is striking how little I explicitly brought myself and my personal experiences into the context of Black–white relations with the client. As I listened to the client's accounts I became increasingly aware that she was talking about professionals (therapists, teachers, lecturers, general practitioners, members of government) and white people as being primarily outside of our interview situation, as "they." At the same time, I noticed how we shifted among the pronominal terms "you," "they," and "we" when speaking about white people. This could be read in a number of different ways: first, the social difficulty of the client either confronting or implicating me in racism without causing offense; second, an indication of the varieties of differentiations brought into play about white people, of which the research relationship was merely a token; or third, a marker of the ways in which our relationship was developing. At the time I privately interpreted the shifts as an effort to differentiate me from specific/"worst" instances of her experiences of racism.

How did I (wittingly or otherwise) manage the apparently contradictory and shifting positionings by the participant of myself as a white researcher and trainee practitioner? Although I wanted to be open about my own insider positionings in relation to structural power relations (as white, as a psychologist), I was concerned that if I did this I could be positioned as working against her interests as a Black woman. At the same time, I wanted to engage the participant in the research and work toward developing relations of trust and reciprocity that reflected my own felt commitments. The following exchanges indicate how there was no consistent way I could manage this. At times, on the basis of wider structural power relations, I could be seen to take responsibility for explicitly raising difficult and sensitive issues in the context of race and identifications in relation to our own research relationship, as well as those in the therapy relationship. I also recognized that it was easier and more important for me to raise these differences (and their implications for our relations) than it would be for her. At other times, I felt the responsibility to create a safe environment for her to raise issues of difference and the implications for not only myself as researcher and the therapist, but also for her as a Black woman client and/or research participant.

On reviewing the transcripts, I only twice explicitly raised issues about the ways in which I experienced the client as either including me in or excluding me from the category "white." The first occasion occurred three hours into our first interview (which lasted three and a half hours), when I referred to Black–white structural differences and acknowledged how such differences might have worked to silence her in the interview process.

> Interviewer: So . . . what you're saying is that you might have held back about some
>   of the things cos I am—I'm white?
> Client: Cos you're white, yeah—sorry to say that but yeah.

My comment arose from my privately drawing an analogy between myself and the therapist (based on our whiteness) with an earlier account by the client in which she described how she had held back from disclosing to her white therapist. Whereas the woman could be seen to indicate (nonspecific) difficulties in disclosing to me as a white person (and apologizes for this), at this moment I did not share with her my own concerns about being a white woman, with some awareness of my white cultural heritage in relation to Blackness, or talking to a Black woman who was relatively unknown to me about sensitive issues of race and racism. Nor did I acknowledge the possible power basis from which I was talking as a white researcher with her. If I had, perhaps we could have achieved a different form of relationship, whereby communicating my own uncertainties might have worked more clearly to subvert whiteness as a powerful category, at least in our relationship. Alternatively, had I raised these issues it might have been read by her as my asking her to assuage my "white guilt" or to educate me as to how to forge relationships across race differences (Ridley, 1995; Thomas, 1995). Did this reflect a sense of myself as a white researcher being caught between the imperative to talk about race and the need to deal with its consequences? At the very least these concerns underscore how what is said and not said in early moments shapes and constrains future possibilities for the research relationship. Shortly following this exchange, when I invited questions from the participant, she expressed surprise that she could ask me direct questions about myself. This perhaps indicates how roles within particular contexts (in this case interviewer/ee) may be understood to be structured (Acker, Barry, & Esseveld, 1983), even when as researchers we aim to make such role boundaries less rigid and more egalitarian. It also indicates the importance of creating conditions that are safe enough for participants to raise concerns.

Her concerns in this case related to my own relationship to whiteness: as the Black woman client asked me why I referred to (my) whiteness rather than to racism. Her questioning of me can be read as an implicit challenge to the notion that whiteness as a category can be differentiated from racism. This can also be read as the woman trying to understand or challenge whether I, by explicitly identifying as white, do not consider myself to be racist. In my response, although indicating that I do not differentiate between the two categories, I neither positioned myself personally as racist nor related racism to myself personally, but shifted the topic back to whiteness. Instead, I related how I came to "color" the category "white" (charles, 1992; Frankenberg, 1993), characteristically experienced by myself as a noncolored backdrop in relation to Blackness's visibility as a color. Here racism could be constructed as predominantly outside of myself, whereas whiteness had become a part of me or my identification. At no point did I personally identify with racism except by implication. Thus, the textual construction of the account of the development of my own relationship to racism moved from (a) noncoloring of white $\rightarrow$ coloring of white $\rightarrow$ white = self; (b) white $\rightarrow$ racist; so that (c) self = white = part of white racist practices (where $\rightarrow$ means implication and = means equation).

This covertly structural issue formed an explicit theme of the interviews. So it was not until the third interview that I felt the conditions (i.e., greater levels of trust) existed to reflect back explicitly to the client how she differentially included and excluded me as part of a white categorization and how this might impact on the research relationship or affect the therapy situation. I further attempted to communicate how I was trying to understand from her perspective (and drawing on my knowledge of the literature, as well as my own experiences) why she might do this (e.g., to "protect" me). She questioned whether this variability functioned to protect me (at an interpersonal level) or whether from her perspective it worked to protect her in the context of her experience of Black–white relations. We would argue that the conditions that made possible such an admission evolved from the context of the developing research relationship and my reflecting back my understandings of the differential inclusion/exclusion of myself as white.

Client: I'm not sparing your feelings out of—I suppose I could be actually—cos we were er conditioned to do that as Black people so I could be—could be a bit of both couldn't it? But I tend to think it out of my—saving my own neck . . .

Interviewer: I was just thinking about that power thing then—there seems to be an issue that I could then take—use my position to then, you know, I suppose, well what would it be, like punish you or I'd hurt you in some way . . .

This seemed to provide the context and conditions for me to discuss my personal and institutional power as a white person (irrespective of a researcher/therapist role). Significantly what I did not do was to reflect with her how I also at times included or excluded myself in the category of white and/or professional. Clearly it could be argued that by this I did not make myself accountable to her and, worse still, positioned her as accountable to me, which clearly would run counter to my antiracist feminist stance. As feminist researchers we often get paralyzed by such a sense of responsibility/guilt as to what we as researchers should, and can, raise— es pecially around sensitive issues such as racism—when researchers occupy different and multiple positions of power from their research participants.

An alternative reading could be that a split is being enacted between the research and therapy relationship, with the therapy situation as the primary forum in which issues of racism are played out and the interview as the place where they receive comment. It could be argued that in my position as a white researcher/professional

I was modeling ways to raise issues about race within therapy, as well as in research. Interestingly, for this interpretation of modeling to hold, the Black client would have both to see me as identifying with her and to identify with me. Both of these possibilities highlight the fluid and shifting character of identifications available within and across interviewing contexts.

The contested character of commonly presumed fixed identifications is highlighted in the next extract. Here, the client asked me to clarify my personal relationship to my membership in a range of social identifications that historically and contemporarily have not served Black people's interests. This also could be read as a strategy to check out whether I was consistent in my understandings of my positions or to remind me that I occupy powerful institutional positions. This exchange occurred at the end of the second interview (when again I asked her if she wanted to raise anything that we had not covered in the interview).

Client: ... and then I says to you about erm when has white people ever looked after us—you know cos of that feeling that I has—or our well being—how do you fit into that then?

Interviewer: I'm part of the profession that has a particular bias you know in my training—I'm part of erm the you know—as a white woman—as well I think I'm part of that—I'm part of erm I think among certain people who are trying to question and challenge my own privileges—erm but I don't—also don't think—and I think I've said this to you before—I don't think that everything will be solved by Black on Black ... it's part of my responsibility to work for change—not only within myself personally, but within my inverted commas group, as a white—as a white person—within my group as a clinical psychologist and that I need to use part of my power and my privilege to actually question that privilege and to work for change.

Here, I seem not only to acknowledge my multiple identifications and the different structural power privileges that accrue to me in occupying these positions, but also to convey my commitment to trying to redistribute these resources. Interestingly, I did not go beyond the categorizations (of clinician and white) she initially introduced to extend this to the role of researcher. I would argue that the reflections I made were ones I felt able to undertake in my role as interviewer rather than in the role of practitioner. I believe I would have felt obliged to silence or downplay my criticisms of the profession if discussing them in face-to-face contact with a client as a clinical psychologist.

The Influence of a Researcher's Disclosure of Other Identifications
We now reflect on another development in the nexus of identifications. Immediately following the exchange in which I gave an account of the development of my relationship to racism, I introduced a previously undisclosed nationality (German) identification (I have dual nationality, English–German). This was to highlight how my understandings and experiences of difference (based on white nationality relations) are markedly different from hers (based on Black–white relations). At that time my priority was to communicate my experience of how, in growing up with a German mother in Britain, we occupied the position of "other" in the context

of British–German historical relations, which could account for why I had not previously been aware of racism/whiteness as a color.

This disclosure about my German origins appeared to allow space for the client to question my identity as only English (and even, implicitly, as white). She immediately responded, "I was just gonna ask you that, you're not English are you?" This raises the broader question about whether, in a British context, there is a conflation of identification, whereby white is seen as synonymous with an English nationality. That the client also understood racism in the context of the history of European–African slavery and colonization also contested the stability of English = white identification in our relations. In the context of the client's later comment that she had thought I wasn't entirely white, I then disclosed my Jewish origins (interestingly, this never arose in my interviews with the [white] therapist), knowing that others may perceive (based on my looks) this aspect of my identification as relevant to my sense of self. Indeed, the interviewee then responded, "Yeah, I can tell." The possibilities mobilized by this perceived visible difference and minority cultural background in generating new varieties of identificatory positions within the interviews are the focus of discussion later in the article.

At other times the client privileged my identification as a person who was prepared to challenge white dominated institutions and my "atypical" researcher role (i.e., she later reflected back to me that I did not simply "take and run"). But, more important, it was the Jewish aspect of my identification that underpinned her increased acceptance of me. This appeared to position me as having the potential not to be oppressive/exploitative, although this was a continuously contested and unstable construction of me by her.

Thus, at times I experienced sharing commonalities (whiteness, professionalism) with her therapist, while at other times the Jewish aspects of my identification were used by the participant to differentiate me from the therapist. For example, in the third interview (six months after we first met) the client explicitly questioned my automatic or stable inclusion within the category "white."

> Client: I know you're you're—you're white—I don't—I don't know if I would say
> you was white to be honest. I'm not being funny I just don't, but like I would
> say like [therapist] then I know she's white.

Although up to that time we had never explicitly discussed in what ways I was (not) included in the categorization of white, at the time I could be understood to accept her statement without challenge. On her (implicit) recommendation, I read a text referenced by her in an earlier interview—*The Isis Papers* by Frances Cress-Welsing (1991)—in which people of Jewish origins are positioned as Black. Notwithstanding the ambivalence of my own identifications (as Jewish/German), my deference to her definition arose out of subscription to the feminist research convention that in the context of her social marginalization the participant's reality should hold sway.

Research Relations As a Resource in the Therapy Context

That the client could use my identifications and our relationship (researcher–researched) as a resource was also indicated by the accounts of the therapist. In this exchange (from the third interview) with the therapist, she reflected on how she understood the client to set up the conditions to raise issues of difference between them. It was reported that the client flagged for the therapist how institutional positions of power could silence or harm the client. It seemed that the client used her relationship with GA to highlight possibilities to the therapist of different ways the therapy could proceed.

Therapist: In allowing me access to her world as a white person—she said that she told you about this book—and she talked about the difference between talking to you and talking to me—that she could be sp-very spontaneous with you and she could swear, be herself—but—but within therapy relationship she watches what she says, she's careful in case I might respond in a hostile defensive way—and those are my words she wasn't using quite those words.

Interviewer: So that kind of layer then of the therapist–client—is that what's come out? I mean I'm still a white woman.

Therapist: But she sees you—she sees you differently in that, you know, it feels like she feels much safer in—in that relationship than within the therapy relationship.

Although I raised issues of commonality with the therapist (as we are both white), the relationship context of therapist–client was configured differently from that of researcher–client, and I was aware of the differences between us as experienced by the client.

Clearly, interviewing each partner in a therapist/client dyad across the period of their therapeutic involvement intervenes and impacts on their therapy process. Indeed, such matters warranted the close scrutiny to which this proposed research was subjected by three ethical committees (Aitken, 1996b). What I am attempting to illustrate here is more than the mere banal fact that the research has "affected" the therapy; rather I wish to explore the form and development of these "effects": that is, how the particular configurations of relationships and histories of relationships offered particular opportunities for challenge and the development of new practices.

RESEARCHER ACCOUNTABILITY TO PARTICIPANTS: SHARING RESOURCES/RECIPROCITY OF DISCLOSURE

The Influence of Researcher's Positionings As Researcher/Therapist

Feminist researchers have argued that feminist research practice involves reciprocity in disclosure and the sharing of information in order to develop empowering ways of working with participants. In this way a researcher may be understood as occupying dual positions as researcher and advocate. We argue that these positions are not without tensions. Next, we focus on the inscrutability/permeability of both information and role boundaries.

From the accounts presented and interpreted in the preceding section, GA arguably failed to demonstrate an empowering way of working, as there was a lack of reciprocity and a withholding of information from the participants. However, this assumption would fail to recognize particular features of these interview situations and the possible (adverse) impact of some disclosures and/or sharing of interpretive resources. As the client commented at the end of the project, it was not the volume of disclosure that mattered; rather it was the fact that she saw GA as willing to disclose and/or answer her questions about particular issues and in ways she experienced as sincere.

Clearly, both my researcher/practitioner positionings and antiracist feminist stance gave me access to a range of resources and institutional positions within the interviews. First, a practitioner base gave a working knowledge of clinical psychology, therapy models, and various organizational systems and procedures. Second, a researcher base gave access to information (concerns, hopes, and/or agendas) of both the client and the therapist. Third, an antiracist feminist stance provided access to a conceptual framework by which to evaluate existing assumptions, processes, and structures and to question the dominant, presumed universally applicable, psychological theory and practice. At the same time, these same positions constrained the extent to which I felt able to share these resources in ways that as feminist researchers we may not always openly acknowledge (either to ourselves or to participants). In the first place, my research practices were informed by ethical and practical understandings that originate from my therapist/practitioner positionings; yet, in my relations with the client I was not officially acting as her therapist. But, I had made a commitment to each participant to honor and maintain our relations of trust relating to the disclosures they made to me. The dilemmas I experienced were further heightened by the research context (taking place over time with participants who were engaging in a parallel therapy process).

Throughout, I made active choices about what and what not to disclose, although this was not without tensions. For example, I knew that the therapist was committed to, and engaged in, networks around antioppressive practices, of which the client was unaware. Yet, tempting though it was to allay the client's uncertainties about the therapist's commitments, I felt I would either betray the confidence of the therapist or set up expectations on the part of the client that might not necessarily be met if I decided to communicate this information. In addition, I understood the client to hold concerns about the differences between clinical psychology and counseling, but I did not share my views on this with her because they may not have been held by her therapist. Rather than discuss these and their consequences for how she (or her mental health) might be viewed, I attempted to access her understandings of counseling and therapy using the terms she herself had introduced.

Researcher As Interface Between Client and Therapist

At the outset I saw one of the distinctive features of the project design as being able to adopt an advocate role. My complex position, as a researcher engaged in research over time with the same participants and as one who could move between participants (who were engaged in a parallel therapy process), afforded me the opportunity of tracking through the client's concerns and in indirect ways feeding these back to the therapist to impact on the quality of their therapy relations. I introduced ways for the therapist to consider alternative ways to work and traced through how she went on to develop other ways of working that were of greater benefit to the client. Here, I focus on the process of researching and practicing across difference (e.g., along the dimensions of race and profession) and reflect on the client's continuous concerns, as I understood them, about psychology's implication in racism and about the therapist's perspective on racism.

Something that, from the client's perspective, differentiated the research relationship from the therapeutic relationship was that the client had no clear sense of the therapist's stance on racism. As illustrated earlier, the client felt able to ask me directly as the researcher about my own stance (probably reflecting the different conditions in which the project and the interview structure were set up). As a researcher I am perhaps less constrained by some of the debates around the importance of maintaining professional distance and detachment, which would limit self-disclosure, than is a therapist. Nevertheless, hesitations and restarts characterized how I talked with the client around issues of race and racism. Although these could be markers of my discomfort, they could also indicate my own uncertainty of how to talk about such issues without drawing on overly rehearsed responses. We hope that the client would have read them as issues that were being negotiated as well as worked through by me throughout the interviews with her.

This was different from the form of my discussions with the therapist. We talked more openly about racism as white people committed to antioppressive practices and as coprofessionals. I used my knowledge of professional issues, the therapist's commitment to antioppressive practices, and my understanding of the therapist's dilemmas (and the client's concerns) to encourage the therapist to question the limits and implications of such boundaries in working with clients. These could be introduced generally through exploring perceptions of clinical psychology as a profession. I understood from the therapist's accounts that she had not discussed with the client the latter's concerns about engaging in clinical psychology (of which I was aware). So, in subsequent interviews I ascertained whether this concern had been addressed with the therapist (and the client) and in what ways—but indirectly without compromising the confidentiality of either party.[5] For example, in the following exchange (the second interview with the therapist), I asked what had happened since the first interview. As indicated by my initial response, I was surprised to hear how the client had approached the session with the therapist (although the client had reported that the impact of the first interview with me had given her more confidence to raise issues with the therapist).

Therapist:	And she came in much more active kind of frame of mind erm—kicked off with erm why she'd been referred to me and not a counselor—or to somebody else.
Interviewer:	Oh right.
Therapist:	And started asking about the difference between counseling and psychology—and I always find it difficult to answer–because—I suppose because counseling is so—you know it can—it can be so many different things—and there's much less kind of regulation about it.

I then attempted to get the therapist to reflect on her own feelings and understandings of what could be happening in the therapy process.

Interviewer: So how were you feeling when she kind of kicked off with this?

Therapist: Erm well—o-okay with it cos quite a lot of people ask that—erm usually at another time—usually fairly early on—which she hadn't—erm—er you know it was only at this point that she felt confident enough to ask that or whatever—so we've—we talked a bit about that and I don't think I gave her a very good answer . . . cos I think the answer that I gave her in response to this counsellor and psychologist thing was mostly about the training I think—and erm—and the qualifications and—erm—and I think you know what—what I gave back to her was perceived as kind of hanging on to labels hanging on to sort of power thing I guess.

Interviewer: Right—what you thought she might think that of you?

Therapist: Yeah—well this is what kind of things led on to—in hindsight I think that was—well yeah—she was asking for information—she was wanting to empower herself in terms of what this was all about—about why she'd been sent to see me.

From the therapist's account, the impact of this power differentiation appeared to reinforce constructions of clinical psychologists/therapists as representing white, expert-dominated institutions. The therapist's "I think you know what I gave back to her" suggests how the therapist was highly aware of my movement as researcher between the therapist and client and of what the client may have reported back to me. This acknowledgment of power differentials may be experienced as a dilemma for practitioners, for as professionals we attempt to emphasize the collaborative and egalitarian quality of therapeutic interventions with clients. Yet, in attempting to explain the position of clinical psychology in relation to other professions, we may inadvertently emphasize our own power differentials in relation to clients.

In this research I could trace through the history of individual participant accounts and reflect back what I identified as the key themes implicated in maintaining power differentials in the therapy relationship. As the therapist discussed her difficulties and dilemmas as a white woman working with a Black woman client, I attempted to reflect back to the therapist the shifts in how she presented herself in relation to issues around race. I continuously attempted to explore with the therapist what it could mean as a professional, and for the therapy relationship, to share either personal information or her uncertainties with the client. In the third interview the therapist described how she chose to make a personal disclosure so that therapy could progress. Aware of her earlier concerns about making such disclosures, I asked her to reflect on her feelings about transgressing professional boundaries.

Interviewer: As a professional how do you feel about that?

Therapist: Well very threatened you know—I mean then you know I didn't feel comfortable and then—you know I don't—it's not something that I talk about a lot to anybody really but erm—so not comfortable but knowing that it—that was a necessary thing so feeling quite—I suppose like all this stuff about boundaries—was really very very there.

In undertaking an indirect advocate role on the part of the client and tracking through possible changes in the therapy relations, I was aware of the vulnerability of the therapist. Drawing on my own experiences of training, my difficulties and concerns about how to work with difference in practice, and my networking in related areas as well as the therapist's own accounts of the dilemmas she experienced, by the second interview I attempted to check with the therapist about the availability of supervisory support in relation to these issues and learned that none was available.

In my role as researcher and in the absence of supervisory support for the therapist, the interview context came to provide a forum to facilitate the practitioner's reflecting on alternative ways of working with a client. That is, the research helped to identify the needs of the service provider as well as the service user. This highlights three issues for feminist research. First, the practice of interviewing offers the potential to create a much needed space and forum to reflect on issues and may influence interviewees' future practices and relationships to others. Second, the practice of distributing transcripts between interviews (although demanding in different ways for all parties) may be useful as a marker of the development of more open ways of working (researcher–researched). And beyond this, participants can use this record in various beneficial ways. In the present example, the therapist claimed that the interview and transcript process served a metafunction for her—providing "internal" supervision. Third, over the interview period, the therapist reported her increased efforts to set up an interdisciplinary forum with peers, one committed to providing clinical supervision in a "safe" context and to exploring how they work with intercultural issues in therapy. Taking part in the project and reflecting on the issues it raised further highlighted the personal and professional limitations of existing supervisory support and precipitated new strategies for addressing these.

IMPLICATIONS FOR FEMINIST DEBATES

So far, we have identified a range of issues that have implications for feminist researchers conducting research across dimensions of difference, such as race and profession (both as academic researchers and psychological practitioners). Here we draw together four key issues that exemplify particular dilemmas and arenas for feminist psychological research. The first is the impact of the shifting and relational character of participants' professional and political identifications over the duration of the research. The second concerns professional and ethical responsibilities that constrain the feminist commitment to transparency and reciprocity. Third, although it is not without risks, we suggest that the carefully negotiated interface between research and therapy may function in fruitful ways: (a) to support the therapeutic as well as the research process, and (b) to move from researcher to advocate. And fourth, as a piece of action research, the relationships among participants have indeed changed and developed since the official end of the research and its proliferation into new projects.

Before developing these issues we reiterate three specific contexts and features of this research that distinguish this project from much of the other work conducted within the rubric of feminist (psychological) research, each of which has paved the way for our analysis. First, several interviews were conducted with each participant over an extended period of time. This process created the conditions for the development and exploration of a research relationship different from those evolving from the single interview paradigm and introduced its own dynamics and constraints in ways that became a vital resource for analysis. Second, a key factor in the conduct and interpretation of these relationships was GA's dual position as both researcher and (potential) practitioner. Third, GA's set of explicitly compromised (or structurally ambivalent) positions—as neither exclusively researcher nor practitioner, as neither independent nor complicit, as both inside and outside, and as white and professional but dedicated to antiracist and feminist practices—potentially increased the opportunities for exposure and exploitation of the client and, in a different way, of the therapist. We would argue that, notwithstanding these dangers, in this case these aspects interacted to facilitate the client's therapy as well as to enable GA to challenge features of its practice.

Impact of Shifting and Relational Character of Professional and Political Identifications

The present work highlights how participants' identifications are multiple, shifting, and intricately interwoven with a variety of structural power relations. These power relations may be organized, for example, along dimensions of researcher–researched, White–Black, therapist–client, and/or middle class–working class. The privileging of feminist identifications and/or research aims may obscure such differences and diminish the tensions arising from the negotiation of the meanings and power associated with structural differences in interpersonal and institutional relationships, of which the researcher–researched is just one. As described in this article, the structural relationships associated with GA as a white researcher parallel the Black woman's experiences across a range of other institutional (education, research, therapy) and daily settings (Black–white relations).

The challenge for us as feminists is to acknowledge our structural positions and to situate research relations within wider contexts of sociohistorical power relations. The onus is on us as researchers not to mask the privileges we accrue from these positionings, nor to be paralyzed by our guilt about the privileges that can lead us into inaction at personal or institutional levels. Instead, we suggest that such tensions can be used in productive ways. One clear example from the present study is how we can use our role as interviewer/therapist to take responsibility for creating safer conditions for participants to raise concerns about the meanings and effects of difference—whether at interpersonal, structural, or ideological levels. As the present study indicates, safety need not necessarily be premised on assumed similarity of identifications between researcher and researched. This has obvious implications for current feminist and/or antiracist debates about research and therapy practice, where some researchers/practitioners have promoted the validity of their work based on assumed commonalities with those with whom they work (Weekes & McDermott, 1995; Wilkinson & Kitzinger, 1996). Such assumptions appear to reflect a conception of identities as separate and additive and to presume shared meanings and understandings of such identifications. We would argue that, regardless of feminist or racial identifications, other identifications necessarily enter into interactions within researcher–researched or therapist–client relationships. Because identifications are unstable and contestable, it may be more important to highlight the conditions and contexts in which specific accounts are produced rather than to attempt to represent the generality of accounts (Griffin & Phoenix, 1994).

Within this framework we would want to pose another question about the usefulness of attempts to develop general sets of techniques or methods (whether feminist or antiracist). Aren't these practices that must be lived, explored, and negotiated by us as embodied individuals in particular contexts and situations rather than presumed to be resolved by methodological fixes? This point is developed in the next section, which explores the role of disclosure and reciprocation in the context of professional and ethical responsibilities.

Professional and Ethical Responsibilities

Self-disclosure on the part of a researcher is often emphasized in feminist research as promoting relations of trust and equality with the researched (Lather, 1988). By this account, self-disclosure on the part of the researcher is an attempt to break down the conventional power relations structured around the difference between the researcher and the researched. We raise two questions. First, are we deluding ourselves about the extent to which this is achievable, in view of obvious structural inequalities that typically characterize researcher–researched relationships? Second, how does an emphasis on the role of self-disclosure on the part of the researcher perpetuate and reproduce dominant power relations and further silence the voices of the researched who are characteristically marginalized? The position we take has ramifications for schools of feminist research that privilege the role of autobiography. Of course, all research is autobiographical, but we would argue it is important to tell more than our own story in the process of working toward personal and social transformations. The key issue here is the importance of ongoing reflection and self-questioning about whose needs are being met in self-disclosure on the part of the researcher/therapist.

We have argued that disclosures should be considered in the context of their usefulness; that is, as researchers, we must try to be accountable not only to the specific (emancipatory feminist, antiracist) aims of the research, but also to the participants. But to what extent are we as researchers necessarily aware of the effects of self-disclosure both within and beyond a particular research project? Notwithstanding the obvious asymmetry in the disclosures made within the research and therapy contexts in our study, there were specific and far reaching effects of those disclosures made by GA. In the present study, GA's awareness of these consequences arose in part from the unusual situation of being able to trace through the effects of the researcher–researched relationship in accounts that were produced over time and among participants.

Interface Between Research and Therapy

In our analysis we suggested that the interface between research and therapy functioned in fruitful ways to support the therapeutic as well as the research process; however, the exploitative potential of such an interface is ever present (e.g., Opie,

1992). We have suggested how research could provide an arena in which (a) the interviewee could raise issues of difference/power in other situations (therapy), (b) the white professional could be recognized as identifying in some respects with the position of the Black person (with obvious implications for therapy), (c) the therapist could raise issues of difference with her client, and (d) the therapist could come to question the conventional demarcation of boundaries within her professional role around particular disclosures of her (antiracist) commitment (with parallels for GA in the research process). These covert interventions via the research process into the therapy process were also supplemented by the therapist's use of the interviews with GA as a form of informal supervision. If such implications of a research project were helpful contributions to the therapeutic process (and we acknowledge that there are always some implications—whether experienced as beneficial or not), a number of general questions can be posed about the purposes of feminist research.

It is often presumed that members of socially marginalized groups gain some therapeutic benefit from participating in research, from being listened to or from their accounts being taken seriously and seen as having value. Setting aside for a moment the problems of appropriation of accounts and imposition of interpretations that this empowerment model can sometimes involve (cf. Opie, 1992; Reay, 1996), does this account imply that we as feminist researchers are also, in some ineffable way, therapists providing validation for, and conferring meaning on, a participant's account? Where does this account leave the uncomfortable feelings and experiences of research? Is this failed rapport or a strain in the therapeutic alliance? From this, and notwithstanding the interrelation between research and therapy that played a key role in the design of this study (or even perhaps because of this), we would caution against too close an equation between the processes of therapy and research and, correlatively, against too benign an interpretation of the process of therapy, which we see as revolving around moments of discontinuity and discomfort as much as continuity and safety.

Increasing congruence of views and amicability over the course of research (as is likely within any relationship over time) does not obscure the prevailing power relationships or structural differences among participants. We see the role of the researcher as one of using her position of privilege to raise issues of difference and power between herself and her interviewee(s). Here, the demands made of the researcher are not dissimilar to those of a therapist, as the researcher needs to be able to hear and contain the difficult feelings and responses that this evokes, for herself and for her participants.

Changing Relationships

If we return to the early accounts of feminist research that describe the process as an elaboration of continuing and increasingly amicable relationships with one-time interviewees, then when and where does our responsibility as researchers end? Are we not deluding ourselves to think that a relationship set up according to an inequitable power relationship can ever shed itself entirely of that history? This is not to say that relationships initially precipitated by a research project cannot develop into something much more than this. This, we argue, has happened in relation to the present study.

Following the official end of the project, GA attempted to move toward different ways of working, for which at the time she did not have (or, some might argue, make) the time or role. This included cowriting with the client (together with another client) and sharing GA's available resources (including knowledge of journals) to enable them to write independently of GA. GA met with the two client participants (independently and cojointly) and noticed a change in the formality of the relationships as they worked together to coconstruct the various understandings of the researcher–researched relationship and the influence of the different constructions held about each other in relation to race, class, and other positionings. Not only did the two Black women openly share their experiences of the process of having been interviewed, but they also expressed the commonalities (and differences) in their experiences and understandings of the impact and importance of race, gender, cultural, and class relations in their everyday experiences, in their experiences with GA, and in relation to statutory services, particularly clinical psychology. GA experienced the women as both supporting and challenging each other (as well as GA) and the work we did together.

It is important to acknowledge that, despite GA's understandings of increasing mutuality in our relations, the women still expressed concerns about the trajectory of future relationships. One of the women wondered whether GA would withdraw once her interest in these projects (or the women) moved on. While GA reflected on whether she was manipulating the friendships for her own ends, the women also reflected on whether they too would gain cultural capital (e.g., credibility, possible publication) from the changing relationships. We (GA and the two participants) have acknowledged that without this project it is unlikely that we would have met, particularly as our social worlds are geographically and, at times, classwise and culturally separate across a number of different dimensions. Nevertheless, we have all entered aspects of each other's social and personal spaces (e.g., visited each others' homes, cooked for each other, been introduced to friends/families). How permanent or temporary this will be is not clear. At the time of writing (nine months after the final official interviews), we made a commitment to support each other (it is important for me to acknowledge that I too receive support from these relationships) in those ways we want, can, and feel able to offer and accept. However, an awareness of GA as the researcher, with the assumed skills of knowing how to write and speak the language appropriate for an academic publication, is still evident and subject to ongoing debate.

Taking these changing relationships as an example, it is appropriate to reflect on how and whether such relationships can be regulated according to the rules and vicissitudes of friendship rather than those of professional responsibilities of research. Yet, if we take seriously those models that theorize commonality (of commitment, if not identity) as something that is forged rather than fixed (e.g., Yuval-Davis, 1993), then we would argue that the present study has generated many valuable future and changing relationships among its participants.

ADDRESSING POWER AND DIFFERENCE IN FEMINIST PRACTICE

We have focused our reflections on feminist research around this study to highlight what we see as some key issues for feminist researchers in psychology. The analysis of a therapy process in part turned into support/advocacy for the therapy and a resource for both client and therapist. Our discussion has focused primarily on the fruitful consequences that can follow from, as well as careful negotiation required by, an acknowledgment of the multiple identifications and multiple institutional positions all participants occupy within research relationships, which here included dimensions of difference structured around race, class, and professional–client relations. We have emphasized the importance of addressing and sometimes explicitly discussing the politics and ethics of these institutional identifications and positions. We see this process of connecting the personal and the structural as central to a feminist practice that is committed to challenging oppression and developing better practices.

As a jointly authored piece, we see the account of this study as working against the dominant "malestream" individualist ethos that portrays the creative scholar as isolated from support and deprived of a critical community of coworkers. We present it as a public record of valuable work we have done together. Finally, we present this work as innovative not because it exemplifies good practice, but because it works toward better practice. That is the best we can do. We see working toward change as a process, the results of which never can be entirely predicted or guaranteed or ensured by the application of particular techniques or methods. Rather, what has proven most important to us in designing and following through this project has been (a) being clear with ourselves and the participants about roles, role convergences and divergences, and corresponding responsibilities; (b) never presuming an immunity from the charges of methodological limitations we might level at others; and (c) knowing that there is no final limit to good practice. Rather, good practice involves a continuous commitment to critical reflection on the work.

Initial submission: December 10, 1996
Initial acceptance: March 27, 1997
Final acceptance: July 3, 1997

NOTES

1. We use the term "boundary" to denote dimensions of separation and difference structured by class, race, and different professional positionings. The term also carries other psychotherapeutic nuances around practice that figure later in the article.
2. The term "Black" as used by us is capitalized as a political category and as a marker of the exploitation of Black peoples by white British peoples. In this context, the term "white" is left uncapitalized. Our use of Black here embraces all peoples of African, Indian, and West Indian origins but is not intended to obscure the diversity, multiplicity, or dynamic aspects of Black (or white) peoples' own self-identifications or experiences.
3. The epistemological [theory of knowledge] and methodological [theory of methods] underpinnings of forms of action research and participatory (feminist/emancipatory) qualitative research share in common a commitment to challenge the separation of the "knower from the object of the study" (Acker et al., 1983, p. 427; see also Lincoln, 1995; Orford, 1992). Researchers in these traditions try to develop and engage in collaborative, participative, and empowering research with participants. For example, collaboration can occur throughout the interrelated phases of the research process: in choosing the research topic; in developing the design of the study; in the collection, analysis, and/or interpretation of the material and report writing/publication. "Emancipatory/action research" views research participants as partners in the research process. The extent to which this can be achieved may be moderated by the interpretations and understandings of researchers of what this means as well as the institutional/disciplinary contexts in

which the research is conducted (see, e.g., Punch, 1994), as evidenced in the debates about what constitutes collaborative and empowering research (Lather, 1988; Opie, 1992; Wilkinson & Kitzinger, 1996). What we as researchers intend and what is experienced by the participants may differ. An accessible account of the history of action research and action research applied in practice across a range of settings can be found in Hart and Bond (1995).

4. This term has been initially placed within quotation marks to alert readers that we do not subscribe to its association with biological essentialism, which can be found within (social) scientific and popular discourses.

5. The range of debates about confidentiality in the United Kingdom are likely to differ from those in an American context, particularly in relation to the different statutory legal obligations of psychology/therapy institutions (see, e.g., Bollas & Sundelson, 1995). We would view the level of "compromise" at issue here as being poles apart from the kind of legal and professional practices that predominate in the United States.

REFERENCES

Acker, J., Barry, K., & Esseveld, J. (1983). Objectivity and truth: Problems in doing feminist research. *Women's Studies International Forum, 6,* 423–435.

Aitken, G. (1996a). Exploring "race" and gender in referrals to, and engagement in, clinical psychology services. Unpublished dissertation, Department of Clinical Psychology, University of Manchester, U.K.

Aitken, G. (1996b). The covert disallowing/discrediting of qualitative research: Exploring Black women's referrals to, and engagement in, clinical psychology services. *Changes: An International Journal of Psychology and Psychotherapy, 14,* 192–198.

Anthias, F., & Yuval-Davis, N., with Cain, H. (1993). *Racialised boundaries: Race, nation, gender, color and class and the antiracist struggle.* London: Routledge.

Bhavnani, K-K. (1994). Feminist research and feminist objectivity. In H. Afshar & M. Maynard (Eds.), *The dynamics of race and gender: Some feminist interventions* (pp. 26–40). London: Taylor and Francis.

Bhavnani, K-K., & Coulson, M. (1986). Transforming socialist–feminism: The challenge of racism. *Feminist Review, 23,* 82–92.

Bollas, C., & Sundelson, D. (1995). *The new informants.* London: Karnac.

Burman, E. (1993). Beyond discursive relativism: Power and subjectivity in developmental psychology. In H. Stam, L. Mos, W. Thorngate, & B. Kaplan (Eds.), *Recent trends in theoretical psychology III* (pp. 433–440). New York: Springer Verlag.

Burman, E. (1996, April). *Psychologising "race" and gender.* Paper presented at the British Psychological Society Annual Conference, Brighton, U.K.

Carby, H. (1982). White woman listen! Black feminism and the boundaries of sisterhood. In Centre for Contemporary Cultural Studies, *The empire strikes back: Race and racism in 70s Britain* (pp. 212–235). London: Hutchinson.

(charles) Helen. (1992). Whiteness—The relevance of politically coloring the "non." In H. Hinds, A. Phoenix, & J. Stacey (Eds.), *Working out: New directions for women's studies* (pp. 29–35). London: Falmer Press.

Collins, P. (1990). *Black feminist thought: Knowledge, consciousness and the politics of empowerment.* London: Harper Collins.

Cress-Welsing, F. (1991). *The Isis papers: The keys to the colors.* Chicago: Third World Press.

Frankenberg, R. (1993). *The social construction of whiteness: White women, race matters.* London: Routledge.

Griffin, C., & Phoenix, A. (1994). The relationship between qualititative and quantitative research: Lessons from feminist psychology. *Journal of Community and Applied Social Psychology, 4,* 287–298.

Harding, S. (1986). Is there a feminist method? In S. Harding (Ed.), *Feminism and methodology* (pp. 1–14). Buckingham: Open University Press.

Harding, S. (1993). Rethinking standpoint epistemology: What is "strong objectivity"? In L. Alcott & E. Potter (Eds.), *Feminist epistemologies* (pp. 49–82). London: Routledge.

Hart, E., & Bond, M. (1995). *Action research for health and social care: A guide to practice.* Buckingham: Open University Press.

Heenan, C. (1995). Feminist psychotherapy—A contradiction in terms? *Feminism and Psychology, 5,* 112–117.

Heenan, C. (1996). Feminist therapy and its discontents. In E. Burman, G. Aitken, P. Alldred, R. Allwood, T. Billington, B. Goldberg, C. Heenan, A. Gordo Lopez, D. Marks, & S. Warner (Eds.), *Psychology, discourse, practice: From regulation to resistance* (pp. 55–71). London: Taylor and Francis.

Hollway, W. (1989). *Subjectivity and method in psychology: Gender, meaning and science.* London: Sage.

Lather, P. (1988). Feminist perspectives on empowering research methodologies. *Women's Studies International Forum, 11,* 569–581.

Lewis G. (1996). Situated voices: Black women's experience and social work. *Feminist Review, 53,* 24–56.

Lincoln, Y. (1995). Emerging qualitative criteria. *Qualitative Inquiry, 1,* 275–289.

Marshall, J. (1995). Heavy periods. In E. Burman, P. Alldred, C. Bewley, B. Goldberg, M. Heenan, D. Marks, J. Marshall, K. Taylor, R. Ullah, & S. Warner (Eds.), *Challenging women: Psychology's exclusions, feminist possibilities* (pp. 62–76). Buckingham: Open University Press.

McClintock, A. (1995). *Imperial leather: Race, gender and sexuality in the colonial context.* London: Routledge.

Olesen, V. (1994). Feminisms and models of qualitative research. In N. Denzin & Y. Lincoln (Eds.), *Handbook of qualitative research* (pp. 158–174). London: Sage.

Opie, A. (1992). Qualitative research, appropriation of the "other" and empowerment. *Feminist Review, 40,* 52–69.

Orford, J. (1992). *Community psychology: Theory and practice.* Chichester: Wiley.

Punch, M. (1994). Politics and ethics in qualitative research. In N. Denzin & Y. Lincoln (Eds.), *Handbook of qualitative research* (pp. 83–97). London: Sage.

Reay, D. (1996). Insider perspectives or stealing the words out of women's mouths: Interpretation in the research process. *Feminist Review, 53,* 57–73.

Ridley, C. (1995). *Overcoming unintentional racism in counseling and therapy.* Thousand Oaks, CA: Sage.

Smith, D. (1990). *Texts, facts and femininity: Exploring the relations of ruling.* London: Routledge.

Thomas, L. (1995). Psychotherapy in the context of race and culture: An intercultural therapeutic approach. In S. Fernando (Ed.), *Mental health in a multi-ethnic society: A multi-disciplinary handbook* (pp. 172–192). London: Routledge.

Weekes, D., & MacDermott, T. (1995). Conceptions of power of/between Black and white women. In G. Griffin (Ed.), *Feminist activism in the 1990s* (pp. 113–126). London: Taylor and Francis.

Wilkinson, S., & Kitzinger, C. (Eds.). (1996). *Representing the other: A feminism and psychology reader* (pp. 1–32). London: Sage.

Yuval-Davis, N. (1993). Gender and nation. *Ethnic and Racial Studies, 16,* 621–632.

COMMENTS ON "KEEPING AND CROSSING PROFESSIONAL AND RACIALIZED BOUNDARIES"

Christine Griffin
University of Birmingham

In their article, Gill Aitken and Erica Burman use a discourse analytic framework and a feminist perspective to explore issues of professional and racial boundaries in interviews with a Black woman client and her white woman therapist. The context for this piece is a study of Black women's experiences of contact with the clinical psychology services in Britain, which have a long history of racist and sexist treatment of Black women. Aitken and Burman employed a qualitative approach to examine "the negotiation of commonalities as well as differences" (p. 278) around race as well as gender. The article begins by questioning two common assumptions about feminist research: first, that qualitative methods (or indeed any method) can be inherently feminist; and, second, that feminist analyses need not necessarily concern themselves solely with gender and/or sexuality. Race, or the processes involved in racism, are placed firmly on the agenda of feminist research in psychology. What is unusual about this article, for me, is the way in which the social and psychological dimensions of race are explored in relation to the research process itself.

Aitken and Burman's piece devotes considerable attention to issues that some researchers—including some feminist psychologists—might not see as of immediate relevance to research methods in psychology. They discuss questions of research techniques (e.g., how and when interviews were conducted with the client and her therapist) alongside questions of methodology and epistemology (e.g., the impact of Gill Aitken's political perspective on the research process and choice of the research topic). As in most similar projects that adopt a critical discursive and feminist approach, that approach frequently informs *all* aspects of the research, from the choice of topic; the research design; recruitment of participants; methods of collecting, recording, and analyzing information; to what counts as knowledge or research-relevant information in such an endeavor. It is not possible to separate

Address correspondence aand reprint requests to: Christine Griffin, School of Psychology, University of Birmingham, Birmingham, B15 2TT, UK. E-mail: C.E.GRIFFIN@bham.ac.uk.

a discussion of one's theoretical/political perspective from debates about research methods in any straightforward manner.

Debates among feminist researchers and others using qualitative research methods frequently stress the importance of *reflexivity*, or as Banister, Burman, Parker, Taylor, and Tindall (1994) put it, "The ways in which we explore a problem will affect the ways we examine it, and the ways we explore a problem will affect the explanation we give" (p. 13). The notion of reflexivity places researchers as important elements in the social context of the total research process. Who we are and what we bring to the research process can never be put to one side under the guise of objectivity. Most feminist researchers using qualitative methods would advocate the explicit examination of the various aspects of reflexivity for each research project. Aitken and Burman's article is a good example of this process in practice, and most psychological studies would seldom address such issues in the standard reports of research findings found in traditional academic journals.

As a White, antiracist feminist based in the United Kingdom and working in (and against) psychology, I share something of Gill Aitken and Erica Burman's positioning on the issues raised in their article, although I do not work in the field of clinical psychology or the professional mental health services. I also share something of the interest expressed by the client/respondent quoted in their article about the reasons why this particular topic was chosen. It often appears that some explanation is required when researching across difference, but, as Aitken and Burman rightly point out, this is usually dependent on the political context in which the project is taking place and the power relations that are relevant to the boundaries of the difference in question. Detailed documentation of such debates is scarce, but Celia Kitzinger and Sue Wilkinson (1996) have collected articles on issues raised by the representations of others by feminist research in psychology.

In different contexts, lesbians have encountered suspicion on attempting to study the experiences of heterosexual women (e.g., Kitzinger & Wilkinson, 1996); women's research interest in girls and young women has been seen as inherently feminist—with positive or negative connotations depending on the perspective of the commentator (e.g., Griffin, 1989); and the role of Black researchers in studies that do not focus on issues of race and ethnicity is sometimes challenged (e.g., Bola, 1996). These are only a few of many possible examples, and it would be wrong to assume that all such research relationships across differences are automatically treated as controversial or even notable. The interest of almost exclusively male gynecologists and researchers in women's reproductive and sexual "problems" scarcely attracts comment—apart from among feminists (Greer, 1991). Nor do we as researchers blink an eye at the tendency for predominantly middle-class and middle-aged academics, policymakers, and practitioners to devote so much energy to their concern and interest in young people's experiences and activities (see Griffin, 1993, for critique). The disproportionate interest of White and middle-class researchers in individuals, groups, and communities that are working-class and/or comprised of people of color has also attracted minimal comment, apart from those critical researchers who see such studies as part of wider moral panics over constructed social problems such as teenage pregnancy, youth crime, or the decline of the nuclear family (Skeggs, 1997).

Aitken and Burman subject their own research to a scrutiny that is relatively unusual in psychology, as in other academic disciplines. They call their own choice of research topic into question, or, rather, they see their choice of research topic as a valid focus for examination. In so doing, they validate the client/respondent's questioning of the reasons for Gill Aitken's choice of research topic and consider this issue in political terms. Given the (none too happy) history of psychological research and therapy (including some feminist research and therapy) in their approaches to Black women in Britain and in the United States, there are good reasons for any Black woman client to wonder why a White woman trainee therapist should want to study Black women's experiences of clinical psychology. For this particular client/respondent, Gill Aitken's choice of research topic cannot be taken for granted as unproblematic: it is something that needs to be accounted for and explained. By presenting the client/respondent's critical approach to the research as emerging—like the project itself—from a particular historical and political context, Aitken and Burman refused to construct her as an unreasonable or uncooperative participant. As researchers, even if potential respondents do not query the rationale of our studies so explicitly, and regardless of the methodologies or theoretical perspectives that we employ, we all need to develop our own detailed and politically informed accounts of the reasons for each specific project, subjecting such accounts to at least the same degree of scrutiny that we might expect to receive from a potential funding agency.

Aitken and Burman discussed the issue of race in the relationship between client and therapist and particularly client/respondent and researcher (Aitken). It is refreshing to see a White researcher reflect on the part she/he has played in terms of the racial aspect of such encounters. It is more commonplace for White researchers (including feminists) to see race as only relevant to people of color, who are then constructed as Other: White people are seldom made aware of race (see Ware, 1992, for an exception). Psychology has played a crucial role in constructing and pathologizing Black people as deviant, deficient Others in the fields of education, therapy, and so on, but this practice is not inherent in psychology.

I have been unable to mention other, equally important issues raised by this article, including the complex relationship between research and therapy. I would see this question as relevant, to some degree, to *all* research projects that use intensive interview techniques, especially in longitudinal studies. The tendency for intensive one-to-one interviews to take on qualities of the confessional mode of therapeutic practice is unavoidable, but something that all researchers need to bear in mind. Aitken and Burman also discussed the multiple positioning of the researcher in this project, as practitioner, researcher, and antiracist feminist and the constraints on disclosure (to respondents) that such multiple positioning can impose. To me, this article provides an excellent example of the ways in which researchers are read and positioned by everyone involved in research situations, whether respondents, gatekeepers, observers, funders, audiences at academic conferences—or the readers of this Special Issue. Even if researchers approach the field as positivists, determined to maintain an objective stance and to disclose nothing about themselves that might contaminate the data, their attempts are bound to fail. Respondents will come to their own conclusions about what they think researchers are up to, even in postal questionnaire surveys or traditional laboratory experiments, and sometimes even before they have encountered a living, breathing, talking researcher (see Griffin, 1989). British sociologist Ann Oakley (1981) gave a good account of this in her interview study with women who were about to give birth for the first time. Oakley described her decision to discard traditional positivist instructions on the proper conduct of interviews from an objective stance, arguing that the latter made for bad research that showed little empathy for the respondents and was anathema to feminist research. Oakley's emotional involvement with her respondents was brought home to her when one of the women died in childbirth.

Aitken and Burman's piece provides eloquent testimony to the importance of reflexivity in research; to the complex relationship between academic research, practice (in this case therapy), and political engagement; and to the argument that all research involves intervention, but not necessarily full disclosure on the part of researchers. Feminist approaches to research have always paid considerable attention to methodological and epistemological issues alongside debates over research techniques (e.g., Harding, 1987). It is now commonplace in feminist debates on research for the perspective of the researcher to be the focus of analysis and interpretation to at least the same extent as that of the respondents, and that any analysis should enable the audience to locate the researcher(s) and the respondent(s) in the context of the research as a whole (Stanley, 1990; Stanley & Wise, 1983). Having said this, however, surprisingly few pieces of feminist research put this into practice to any significant degree, especially in the psychological domain. Aitken and Burman's piece does just this, and it also indicates that, in practice, such an approach is not necessarily an easy ride for researchers, given the complexity of the social and political contexts concerned and the variety of issues under investigation. Feminist debates on research do not assume an automatic sisterhood between (female) researchers and (female) respondents based on a commonality of shared experience, but unpacking the complexities of those commonalities and differences that exist in any given context is no easy task. Aitken and Burman's article demonstrates this, illustrating the importance of understanding the ways in which researching across difference (as well as commonality) can affect the research process itself.

REFERENCES

Banister, P., Burman, E., Parker, I., Taylor, M., & Tindall, C. (1994). *Qualitative methods in psychology: A research guide*. Buckingham: Open University Press.

Bola, M. (1996). Questions of legitimacy? The fit between researcher and researched. In S. Wilkinson & C. Kitzinger (Eds.), *Representing the other: A* Feminism and Psychology *reader* (pp. 125–128). London: Sage

Greer, G. (1991). *The change: Women, ageing and the menopause*. Harmondsworth, UK: Penguin.

Griffin, C. (1989). "I'm not a women's libber, but . . . ": Feminism, consciousness and identity. In D. Baker & S. Skevington (Eds.), *The social identity of women* (pp. 173–193). London: Sage.

Griffin, C. (1993). *Representations of youth: The study of youth and adolescence in Britain and America*. Cambridge: Polity Press.

Harding, S. (Ed). (1987). *Feminism and methodology: Social science issues*. Buckingham, UK: Open University/Indiana University Press.

Kitzinger, C., & Wilkinson, S. (1993). Theorizing heterosexuality. In S. Wilkinson & C. Kitzinger (Eds.), *Heterosexuality: A* Feminism and Psychology *reader* (pp. 1–32). London: Sage.

Oakley, A. (1981). Interviewing women: A contradiction in terms? In H. Roberts (Ed.), *Doing feminist research* (pp. 30–61). London: Routledge and Kegan Paul.

Skeggs, B. (1997). *Formations of class and gender: Becoming respectable.* London: Sage.

Stanley, L. (Ed.). (1990). *Feminist praxis.* London: Routledge.

Stanley, L., & Wise, S. (1983). *Breaking out: Feminist consciousness and feminist research.* London: Routledge and Kegan Paul.

Ware, V. (1992). *Beyond the pale: White women, racism and history.* London: Verso.

Wilkinson, S. & Kitzinger, C. (Eds.) (1996). *Representing the other: A* Feminism and Psychology *reader.*

COMMENTS ON "KEEPING AND CROSSING PROFESSIONAL AND RACIALIZED BOUNDARIES"

Faith H. McClure
California State University, San Bernardino

In Aitken and Burman's article, professional and racial boundaries are explored by a White female researcher (GA) using a discourse-analytic framework and a feminist perspective. The researcher interviewed Black female clients (participants) and the clients' White female therapist (therapist). A number of factors make this a useful case for exploring professional and racial issues in research with diverse clinical populations. These include the emphasis on feminist values, such as collaboration, advocacy, mutual empowerment, and the fact that the researcher was White, female, and a clinical psychology trainee.

Although the context (clinical practice) and the involved parties' identities (clinical trainee, female, White; clients, female, Black) were appropriate given the focus on professional and racial boundaries, these methodological features actually seemed in conflict with several of the feminist values espoused by Aitken and Burman in this article, as well as by other feminist researchers (e.g., Armstead, 1995; Lather, 1988). For these Black female clients, the research process could easily have reenacted their experience of "disempowerment" and "nonmutuality" in society based on their race, gender, profession (or social class), and their role as the ones having a need. Thus, the research process and the racial and professional differences accented the power inequity between GA and the participants.

The fact that the researcher was also a clinical trainee brought several potential dilemmas and conflicts to the fore. Here, GA interviews clients and the clients' therapist and takes on a supervisory role with the therapist, who is also a clinical trainee and thus a peer and colleague. In this context, GA as researcher, clinical trainee, and clinical supervisor, has to negotiate role boundaries with the therapist and the participants, manage issues related to confidentiality, and strike an appropriate balance between a research focus and clinical sensitivity.

For example, GA interviewed the participants and the therapist and was privy

Address correspondence and reprint requests to: Faith H. McClure, Department of Psychology, California State University, San Bernardino, 5500 University Parkway, San Bernardino, CA 92407. E-mail: fmcclure@wiley.csusb.edu.

to confidential information from both. The agreements about sharing information and GA's own feelings about what aspects were confidential and which were unrestricted would be at issue. She was in a position of having information that could be useful to the participants and the therapist, which could be seen as related to feminist and clinical psychology values of advocacy and empowerment. Limits on divulging confidential information are set by the clinical psychology profession, however. In addition, the development of trust among all involved and the extent to which each felt free to discuss issues openly was probably affected by how confidentiality was managed. Further, the clients/participants were faced with developing trust with a researcher *and* therapist who are both White clinicians. The mutual racial and professional identity between researcher and therapist likely enhanced reciprocity between them but highlighted further the participants' separateness and difference.

Confidentiality issues were further raised by GA's supervisory role and how she managed privileged information in that context. Her input and feedback to the therapist, although not necessarily divulging specific statements made by the participants, provided information about what was salient to the clients/participants. This challenges notions of what confidential information consists of and what it means to break confidentiality. That is, are attitudes, suggestions about managing certain issues, and so forth, which are informed in this case by GA's experience with the participants, privileged information or not? One can also question how GA's supervisory role affected the therapy process and in turn the research focus. These concerns are all clearly exacerbated by GA's identity as a clinician-in-training.

Another issue related to GA's identity as a clinician-in-training has to do with professional boundaries. In her relationship with the participants, GA has to address the extent to which she brings herself and her personal experiences into the dialogue. Beyond issues of race, the extent to which she talks about herself relative to focusing on the participants' experiences is influenced by her professional identification. As a feminist researcher, she is committed to developing trust and reciprocity in the relationships, which calls for self-involvement and transparency. As a clinical trainee, however, she has to take into consideration the limits the profession typically imposes on self-disclosure and clinical policies on appropriate self/other boundaries.

Further, self-disclosures have the potential of perpetuating differences if not made sensitively. Alternatively, they can promote a sense of safety and bonding by increasing identification between researcher and participants. Self-disclosures can also be useful modeling and can help the participants engage in this important activity with their therapist. In this case, one participant's ability to ask GA questions about herself probably "equalized" the relationship and provided greater safety and engagement on the part of the participant. GA's clinical background could thus be seen as a methodological strength, which increased her sensitivity and facilitated the client's ability to generalize the important activity of self-disclosure and of asking direct questions in the therapy setting.

With the therapist, GA had to balance her role as a supervisor with the fact that she and the therapist are peers and colleagues. This could become a "dual relationship," which would be seen as a problem in the clinical psychology profession.

One advantage of being a clinical trainee doing clinical research is that the researcher will have greater knowledge and insight into what are the salient issues.

GA was then faced, however, with balancing her role as researcher (i.e., gathering information), and her role as a clinical trainee (i.e., responding to emotions evoked by the issues raised). Her clinical training and ability to be empathic was probably useful as she was working with a population that had experienced oppression. For those who have been historically oppressed, interpersonal competence and the quality of the relationship often supersede the "task" aspects. Thus, from this perspective, the researcher–clinician match can be seen as a methodological strength.

Other challenges embedded in this study include the issue of constructing knowledge of others (especially if they have been disenfranchised) from a position of relative power. Large differences in life experience will affect the researcher's ability to construct reality or make accurate interpretations from the research participants' perspective. A good example of "misperception" in the preceding case was when GA thought the participant had excluded her (GA) from the "White" category to protect GA. Instead, the participant noted that it was for the participant's own protection. For the participant, not seeing the researcher as "White" helped her feel more equal, less disempowered, or in the one-down position vis-à-vis race as construed in society. This example illustrates how interpretations are often influenced by one's experiences and subjective worldview. It also highlights the importance of clarifying interpretations.

Examining the appropriateness of the methodologies we use is a very important activity. It is similarly important that we examine the conclusions we draw and the impact of the social context and dominant perspectives on these conclusions. Interpretations that fail to take into account each participant's subjective worldview (see McClure & Teyber, 1996) and/or are based on norms from other, differing, populations have the potential of perpetuating stereotypes and biases and will fail to capture the participants' reality.

REFERENCES

Armstead, C. (1995). Writing contradictions: Feminist research and feminist writing. *Women's Studies International Forum, 18,* 527–636.

Lather, P. (1988). Feminist perspectives on empowering methodologies. *Women's Studies International Forum, 11,* 569–581.

McClure, F. H., & Teyber, E. (1996). The multicultural-relational approach. In F. H. McClure & E. Teyber (Eds.), *Child and adolescent therapy: A multicultural-relational approach* (pp. 1–32). Fort Worth, TX: Harcourt Brace.

NEGOTIATING THE LIFE NARRATIVE

A Dialogue with an African American Social Worker

Rosario Ceballo
University of Michigan

This article explores two methodological issues that arise when research-ers involve the women they study in the construction of life narratives. These issues are examined in the context of an interview-derived, life-narrative study of an African American social worker. First, the tension between presenting a neatly unified identity in a written text and ac-knowledging the contradictions within any person's life story are dis-cussed from both the researcher's and participant's vantage point. The second issue addresses the dilemma that arises when the researcher and the research participant disagree about the meanings and interpretations garnered from the participant's life story. I contend that it is precisely at this moment that the research process has the potential to become a dialogue between theorists and that scholars can incorporate a woman's own theorizing about her life in the research. In concluding, several methodological suggestions are offered as broad guidelines for research-ers planning a life-narrative study.

Feminist psychologists have underscored the importance of involving the women they study as active participants in the research process (Belle, 1994; Cook & Fonow, 1990; Franz, 1994; Harding, 1987; Lykes, 1994; Nagata, 1994; Stewart, 1994). As simple as that may sound, it is a difficult and often complicated goal to achieve in practice, even when writing life narratives. This article examines two

The author is deeply appreciative of the many thoughtful and insightful comments provided by Matthew Countryman, Mary Crawford, Joan Ostrove, Abigail Stewart, and two reviewers on earlier drafts of this manuscript.

Address correspondence and reprint requests to: Rosario Ceballo, Department of Psychology, University of Michigan, 525 East University, Ann Arbor, MI 48109. E-mail: rosarioc@umich.edu.

methodological challenges that confront feminist researchers seeking to involve their "subjects" in the construction of life narratives. First, I discuss how the duality and contradictions of a person's life story may be overlooked in the quest to present a coherently unified identity and an integrated scholarly product. Second, I explore the tension between scholarly analysis and women's own interpretations of their lived experiences. I explore these issues by focusing on the research process I underwent in constructing a narrative about an African American social worker named Mary. My global interpretation of Mary's life differed from Mary's own memories of her daily life experiences in important ways. In fact, we disagreed about the overall meaning that others could garner from her life story. As we discussed her life and my writing of her life, Mary and I became two theorists engaged in a dialogue about the different meanings of her narrative. Thus, my differences with Mary reveal the methodological importance of listening to and respecting the interviewee's own theories about her life.

MARY'S LIFE JOURNEY

As background, I will present a brief, chronological sketch of Mary's life (Ceballo, 1994). My purpose here is to summarize certain key events that occurred in Mary's life in order to give the reader a sense of who Mary is as a person. I will caution, however, that this summary account of Mary's life is based on my initial interviews with her and consequently was influenced by what we focused on and gave primacy to during those initial meetings. It is thus only one possible representation of the chronological events in Mary's life; another researcher who attended to different issues or who did not share my friendship with Mary might choose to highlight different aspects of her life story.

Presently, Mary is a retired, 80-year-old woman living in North Carolina. Throughout her life, Mary has negotiated a series of difficult and emotionally traumatic life events. She was born in the Jim Crow South in 1915 and was only 3 years old when her mother died of tuberculosis. Mary described her childhood as a lonely period. She was the only female child in her nuclear family, which consisted of her father and five older brothers, in addition to herself. Mary remembered her father as a silent and undemonstrative man who somewhat ineptly single parented a household of children. When Mary was 10, her father moved the family from Durham, NC, to Washington, DC, where they lived in a series of boardinghouses. Mary explained, "We never established a home or anything. We had a room in somebody's house. That was the way we grew up." Although her father worked as an attorney, Mary's family always lived with financial hardship and economic uncertainty. Her father's career never flourished, in part because he did not enjoy or take part in the social obligations that accompany successful business practices. As a child, Mary confronted many incidents of racism and classism in school. She was embarrassed by her appearance and the clothes she had for school and described herself as a "little ragged kid who never had any decent anything." Most of Mary's teachers, who were all African American, visibly favored the wealthy, better dressed, lighter skinned African American children in their classes.

Health problems presented another area of difficulty in Mary's life. Mary contracted rheumatic fever while in high school and a complication of the illness caused a reactive arthritis to develop in her right hip. Although Mary's hip was treated surgically, she has slightly dragged one foot when walking ever since that time. During this period, Mary was hospitalized several times and missed many days of school. Despite the many hospitalizations, she was able to graduate with the rest of her high school class in 1934.

Mary talked about the 4 years after high school as the worst period of her life. Her oldest brother had become a widower, and Mary spent those years caring for his house and children. She did all of the housework and provided all of the child care. Those years greatly contributed to Mary's determination to establish her independence and self-sufficiency. At age 23, she enrolled herself at Howard University. She later received a master's degree from Smith College's School for Social Work and established a successful career in the field of social work. Mary's professional career flourished in Milwaukee and later in Philadelphia, where she served as the assistant director of a family-service agency.

Socially, Mary's romantic interests developed slowly, and she dated sporadically after high school. In 1943, during her senior year in college, Mary had an illegal abortion and described it as an emotionally dreadful experience. As a young adult, she had an intimate relationship with a man, off and on, for 20 years. She ended the relationship when she realized that there was little intimacy and communication between them. Mary has never been a wife or a mother, and although she does not regret her life decisions, she acknowledged the complicated nature of her feelings about them. She has mourned the absence of a partnership and also declared that "the new feminism has absolved me from much anxiety about the single state."

I first interviewed Mary in 1992 when we talked over a span of 3 days in the living room of her home. She allowed me to tape-record most of our conversations and has commented on everything I have written about her life, including this article. These initial interviews provided the basis for writing an interview-derived life narrative (Ceballo, 1994). I asked for the opportunity to do a second set of interviews with Mary in May of 1995. At that time, I simply hoped to gain more information about different periods in her life, to fill in some gaps. However, it is the disjuncture and points of incongruency between my theorizing after the initial interviews and our dialogue 3 years later that has led me to think about the methodological issues explored in this article.

DUALITY AND CONTRADICTIONS IN A LIFE STORY

As the research process unfolds, there is enormous pressure to uncover a unified and integrated narrative—perhaps because we are socialized to expect chronological and coherently consistent stories that present people in unambiguous terms. On finishing the first set of interviews with Mary, I did just that and wrote my interpretations and conclusions about her life into a cohesive narrative. Mary reviewed and commented on my writing, and we were both satisfied with the final product. In retrospect, I can see that I was perhaps a little too comfortable with my insights and ability to make empathic connections in sewing the pieces of her life story together for public consumption. Suffice it to say that I had not sufficiently heeded the feminist caution to avoid the search for unified and singular identities in studying women's lives. Stewart (1994) warns that:

> The women whose lives we study are unlikely to have more stable or monolithic identities than we do, but the effort to "tell a good story" and to summarize and define a person pushes us to represent them as unified persons and personalities. This effort to organize and structure the different voices and selves must be understood as an effort to control—literally to impose an order or unity on what is in fact multiple and even disorderly. (pp. 29–30)

By allowing for paradoxes in the lives of the women we study, feminist scholars can highlight the underlying strengths often embedded in the midst of women's positions of marginality or uncover previously hidden vulnerabilities in women's positions of agency and power.

Moreover, feminist scholars have emphasized the need to explore interconnections among gender, race, social class, and sexual orientation in understanding the identities of women of color and our experiences with oppression. Compelling arguments illustrate that our identities are not merely additive, gender plus race equaling an identity, but much more complicated and fluid in nature (Collins, 1990; Harding, 1987; King, 1988; Spelman, 1988). Certain aspects of our identities, for example, will be more salient in certain contexts, at different developmental time periods, and in varying combinations. Hence, it is only logical that the different parts of our identities will not always peacefully coexist; there will be contradictions and inconsistencies in women's words and actions. As Harding (1987) concludes, "these fragmented identities are a rich source of feminist insight" (p. 8).

Despite my awareness of such feminist paradigms, I came to grapple with the contradictions in Mary's stories and the inconsistencies in her character only after a second round of interviewing. When the initial interviews with Mary were done, the quest to reveal a neatly packaged life story was further strengthened by a desire to produce an integrated and cohesive scholarly product. All of this is, moreover, influenced by the interviewee's own desire to present a coherent self and a logical story. Thus, the interviewer and the interviewee share a desire for coherence. Nevertheless, the presence of duality and paradox in any woman's life mandates that researcher and interviewee forego the desire to present a unified identity with a logically cohesive academic narrative. Instead, the metaphor of African American women's quilting should help keep us open to the fluid, ever-changing, and complicated nature of life experiences. As Brown (1989) notes, "the essential lessons of the quilt (are) that people and actions do move in multiple directions at once" (p. 929). The challenge for feminist scholars then is to find methods that will facilitate the representation of dichotomies and contradictions in women's quilted stories.

In my initial narrative, I focused on Mary's resiliency and identified her ability to attract, nurture, and use relationships as a major source of strength. After his wife's death, Mary's father could not maintain a stable and supportive family unit. This led Mary to rely on surrogate family systems and relationships with people outside her nuclear family for care and nurturance. She developed a relational coping strategy that is in keeping with the psychological literature on resilient children. Stable relationships with adults can buffer children from a host of adverse and stressful life events (Rutter, 1979; Werner & Smith, 1982).

During her childhood summers, Mary sought and identified positive role models among the extended family she visited. Her maternal aunts were school teachers in their teens and early 20's who became important role models to her. Later, as a teenager restricted to a hospital room, Mary used a network of relationships with the hospital staff to facilitate her own emotional growth and self-awareness. She believed that the long stretches of time spent in the hospital cured her of her "dependency needs." She explained:

> I knew all of the residents, and everybody in the hospital knew me by then. I got a lot of attention. . . . I think I cured my dependency problem. . . . I mean I had all these needs that hadn't really been met. All the feelings I had about not being well taken care of, somehow were satisfied during this period.

The story of Mary's unconventional route to college also illustrated how her life was powerfully shaped by the ties she established with others and how her professional beliefs incorporated this understanding of the primary role relationships may play in people's lives. Mary told the story:

> Let me tell you how I happened to go to school. I came down here (Oxford, NC) that summer, and Beecher [a maternal aunt] always somehow, was kind of special. I was special to her. She said to me, "We should have kept you after your mother died. If we had kept you, you would be finishing college this year." And it was true. If I'd stayed, I would have gone to college. So I went back to Washington, I told my brother Buster that I wanted to go to school. And he said, "okay," and he said that, it was way late, "but I'll help you." And I went to Howard and applied, and they accepted me, and he paid my tuition all through. He was working at the post office. He sent me through school.

I said, "And that all came about . . . " and Mary finished:

> Because of what Beecher said. And you never know. This is one of the things in the helping profession. This is one of the things I've learned. You never know the effect you're going to have on people. You never know. Just a word, or a kindness, or something can mean a lot to a person in life. The whole pattern of my life was set from just this one comment that she made.

In the first interviews, Mary identified her search for close, familial relationships as a salient theme resonating throughout her life story. She concluded that, "Throughout all of this, lack of family, lack of stability, I gravitate to situations where I'm in a family." Therefore, in view of her search and desire for supportive family connections, "it seems natural in terms of working, you work in a family agency. . . . The first job I had was in a family agency. Basically, my whole professional experience was with families." Throughout her years of working in Milwaukee, a small group of Black professionals provided Mary with a supportive social network.

In fact, Mary lived with a middle class, Black family for 10 years, and to this day, they remain a surrogate family for her.

Although I believe that Mary's use of relationships and her ability to develop familial connections with others was an important source of her resilient functioning, the presence of an opposing construct, that of privacy and social isolation, emerged as equally prominent in her life story. During the second set of interviews, I was surprised to learn that Mary rarely spoke to *anyone* about difficult times in her life. One summer when Mary was visiting an aunt, this aunt told her father that Mary had no decent socks and he should send some immediately. I asked Mary how she coped with such painful experiences, like not having adequate clothes, and she replied, "The most painful part was the shame. (Silence) And what did I do about the shame? I don't know. Just live with it, I guess. Endure it. (Was there anyone you could talk to about it?) No, because if you exposed the shame, there it was again. I can't say I denied it. Couldn't deny it. I don't know. I just endured it, I guess." I commented that there seemed to be many painful times when she carried a lot inside, never sharing her thoughts and feelings with anyone. She responded, "Or putting it another way, there was no one to share it with. Or I didn't want to share it with anyone. Or I thought, well, this is my problem; I got myself into it, I have to figure it out for myself." Even after her mother died, Mary recalled that there was never anyone to help her with this loss or to talk to about her mother's death. My discussions with Mary broached personal topics and events in her life that she had never before shared with anyone despite the presence of many warm and caring people in her life. These topics included such things as a negative self-image, a sense of her body as damaged, an abortion, and an incident of sexual abuse as a young girl.

Yet another duality in Mary's life was that her own silence coexisted with her strong belief in the healing power of therapy and the power of discussing one's painful and joyous experiences with another, more objective person. When we talked about this, Mary concluded that "maybe this is the reason that I went into it (social work) in the first place. . . . I knew unconsciously that I never had anybody to talk to and it's important, so I want to be a person that people could talk to. And I could help myself." I believe that Mary's intelligence, professional training, and intuitive psychological mindedness allowed her to gain insights and understanding about herself and her life as they related to earlier relationships and childhood experiences.

With retrospective reflection, further contradictory themes in Mary's narrative emerged. There was tension between her descriptions of a neglected, lonely childhood and the enormous gratitude she feels toward her father. Mary described herself as a sad and lonely child who was often left at home by herself. She has painful memories of not being adequately dressed or prepared for school, and she believes that is why her father did not make his children go to church. "The reason he didn't is because he didn't see to it that we had decent clothes. And in those days, you had to dress up to go to church. He knew that we didn't have decent clothes, so he didn't insist (that we go), but he took himself," Mary explained. A particularly difficult memory of her father's neglect centered around Mary's experiences in the first grade. Mary's father failed to intervene or even inquire when her teacher decided that Mary would have to repeat the first grade. Mary recalled that her father "didn't do anything about it, and I held it against him, all of his life! And all of my life! Until about 3 weeks ago. . . . I never forgave my father for not going to school and seeing about that, but I have finally forgiven him."

These painful images of loneliness and neglect were coupled with enduring love, affection, and, more recently, forgiveness for her father. Her forgiveness was rooted in her appreciation of his determination to keep his family together following the death of his wife. It would have been commonplace for a widowed man to send his children to live with female relatives. Mary's affection and gratitude was also evident in her recollections of childhood. Mary remembered one incident when her father had gone away for business:

> He did all of the cooking for us, my father. And he had this, he wore this old apron that he put on, a denim apron. And it hung behind the door. As I can remember, it was always greasy, because I don't think he ever washed it, but you know, he just put it on whenever he was cooking. And I remember, I have no idea how old I was. I just knew my dad was away and I remember going and taking myself and standing behind this old, greasy apron 'cause I missed my dad. . . . I'm sure I didn't want to be any place other than with my dad and my two brothers. Even though I would have had a better life, in terms of material things and that sort of stuff, some of the sadness or maybe some of the misery. In spite of that, I have always felt that I was glad that he kept us and that he kept us together. Because I always knew that I belonged there. I belonged with him.

This quote, from the second round of interviews, epitomizes the strong, yet contradictory emotions Mary simultaneously holds toward her father. In this one brief memory, Mary vividly illustrates the competing tensions between her childhood loneliness and her potent familial sense of connection. The greasy apron that has never been washed poignantly symbolizes her father's simultaneous neglect and caretaking.

Contradictory pieces in women's stories also emerge in other research. For Honig (1997), this occurred when she and two colleagues returned to conduct a second round of interviews with Chicana garment workers who had been involved in a strike at the Farrah Manufacturing Company in El Paso, Texas. Honig posits that the present historical time influences people's narration of the past in complicated and contradictory ways. The women whom she interviewed tended to view their participation in the strike as a transformative experience. They described dramatic personal transformations from shy, timid factory workers to brave, fearless strikers. These dramatic claims of transformation were directly contradicted by subsequent recollections of themselves as nonconformist and assertive young adults. Honig stresses that the present historical moment, in the aftermath of the strike, most likely influenced what these women identified as salient from their pasts and which family anecdotes they chose to share. In this instance, the present historical moment "of fierce pride in their battle against political injustice and social conventions" (p. 148) changed and complicated their chronicled past histories. In sum, the Chicana garment workers were "not inventing nonexistent past experiences, but they are retelling them with the language, perceptions, and mandates of their present " (p. 154).

NARRATIVE INTERPRETATIONS VERSUS WOMEN'S LIVED
EXPERIENCES AND PERSONAL THEORIES

As previously noted, two basic tenets of feminist methodology assert that the "subject" should be a participant who, with the investigator, is engaged in the empirical process and that the researcher should identify his or her subjective role and how his or her own biases may shape the research process (Cook & Fonow, 1990; Harding, 1987; Stewart, 1994). Far less has been written on what should be done when the researcher and interviewee come to hold conflicting interpretations and differing conclusions. I encouraged Mary to provide me with feedback at all stages of this research endeavor. After writing my initial narrative of Mary's life story, I was sure that we had a mutual and stable understanding of the central themes in her life. It was only when I returned for more interviewing to bolster my initial impressions that I learned that Mary's memory of her daily experiences differed greatly from my overall conceptualization of her life story. She had, in fact, only ambivalently accepted my initial construction of her life's themes.

My interpretation of Mary's life as an African American "heroine" guided my focus on strength and resiliency throughout her life story. However, Mary did not see herself as a resilient person who overcame a barrage of obstacles to succeed despite them, and she identifies even less with the conceptualization of herself as an African American "heroine." In the second round of interviews, I asked Mary if she has always been a determined and strong-willed woman, a question obviously based on my own overall assessment of her identity. To my surprise, Mary replied:

> No, I don't think I'm that way. . . . When I think of strong-willed, I think of people who go out there and tackle it and get the job done and come what might, and fight all the battles and overcome all the struggles, and knock anybody down that gets in your way, and that's not me.

In fact, Mary went on, "I don't think I really accomplished anything that was very meaningful to many people. . . . I don't want you to admire me for any terrific contributions because I haven't made any."

Mary's perceptions about her life were enormously instructive to my understanding of resiliency. I viewed Mary's life course as the epitome of a resilient identity—an African American woman surmounting enormous obstacles in life and succeeding despite them. The obstacles were numerous and significant, including the early death of her mother, an early incident of sexual molestation, her family's limited financial resources, the discrimination of the Jim Crow South, the absence of family unity, a series of physical problems and hospitalizations, and an illegal abortion. When I read this list to her, however, Mary responded:

> But you see, when you read it off like that, it seems as if these are all things that are happening at the same time, and they're not that way. It's sequential. And you do whatever you have to do with what happens today. Day to day. In other words, I guess the word for me is "survival." . . . And I can see how from your vantage point—Oh my gosh, how could anybody overcome, how could anybody get through and do anything with all of this? And I do too. When you read it off to me, my God! (deep breath).

Hence, Mary never experienced her daily life as I interpreted it, as the emergence of a resilient identity. She views her life quite simply, as most of us do, as something we live day to day and manage as we go. When I returned to ask probing questions about how she had overcome obstacles in life, Mary replied:

> I guess what I'm hung up on is the word "overcome." As if it was a deliberate effort you made to solve a task, to solve the problem. I don't see it that way. It was just making do, you know, and living through it. . . . I dealt with life as it came. I did what had to be done or what you could do.

Mary modified and added subtlety to my conceptualization of resiliency in African American women. She understood how an observer, like myself, could focus on the underlying strength and self-empowerment in her story. She eloquently explained, however, why an observer's conclusions about another person's life can never match the person's own daily life experiences. In our daily lives, we are never entirely "resilient" or "strong." Moreover, as we all know experientially, there can be an enormous difference between how we feel and make sense of things internally versus how our lives are perceived by others. But Mary went beyond this difference in the actor–observer vantage point; she directly rejected my conceptualization of her as a "heroine" and resilient survivor. She finds this description of herself to be unsettling and uncomfortable, and she was steadfast in explaining why her life does not match this conceptualization. Mary would prefer to have herself characterized as a "coper," rather than as someone with a resilient identity. Additionally, my tendency as an observer may have been to uncover a finished "identity" for Mary, whereas Mary typically referred to her actions, her coping, and her engagement with the world. Thus, my dialogue with Mary helped me reframe my notions about psychological theories of resiliency, while continuing to disagree with her claim that she did not accomplish anything of value.

One of the major contributions of postmodern thought is the recognition that there are a multitude of meanings to a text and by extension, to a person's life. As Hare-Mustin and Marecek (1990) explain, postmodernists "challenge the idea of a single meaning of reality and a single truth. Rather than concerning themselves with a search for 'the truth,' they inquire instead about the way meanings are negotiated, the control over meanings by those in authority, and how meanings are represented in language" (pp. 24–25). If we believe in the construction of reality and many available interpretations to a text, then the conflict between Mary and me is not a crisis but rather a source of richness. "Constructivism asserts that we do not discover reality, we invent it (Watzlawick, 1984). Our experience does not directly reflect what is out there but is a selecting, ordering, and organizing of it" (Hare-Mustin & Marecek, 1990, p. 27). My own and Mary's selective organizing and overall interpretation of her life journey are both informative. Although she is, on the one hand, an impressively resilient, African American heroine, she is also someone who is simply living her life day by day. Although her daily experiences felt routine and uneventful, they are nonetheless, in the aggregate, quite remarkable to others. Finally, although her accomplishments will seem highly impressive to many, Mary would not let anyone forget the self-doubt and insecurity that pervaded much of her life.

My interest in the resilient aspects of Mary's story is based, in part, on the points of connection and similarities between us. Like Mary, I was raised in a poor, working-class family and acquired access to educational opportunities through a unique and unconventional surrogate family relationship. Mary and I also share commonalities of gender, race, social-class journeys, and professional careers in helping professions. Although I focused on sources of strength in her life, I did not romanticize Mary's experiences into the stereotypical image of a "strong" Black woman who can overcome any odds (hooks, 1981). Although different parts of Mary's life story will resonate more strongly to other researchers, the similarities between us inevitably drew me to the resilient aspects of her life story.

With the written narrative and with time for reflection, Mary and I both theorized further and considered new themes in her life story. When we talked again, I sought elaborative information to further support my theories and new evidence to fill in questions that had arisen since the initial interview. I wanted to develop a fuller understanding of Mary's emotional life. How did she *feel* when she was struggling with the isolation of a hospital bed as an adolescent? How did she make sense of her father's neglectfulness? Likewise, Mary seemed to have new thoughts and ideas about her experiences and a desire to complicate the story so that it would more accurately reflect her experiential memories.

During the second round of interviews, Mary and I were no longer confined to the "researcher" and "subject" positions; instead we became dialoguing theorists, conversing and debating about our different interpretations of her life. Ironically, this new relationship was facilitated by the creation of a shared text—the initial, cohesive narrative. The written narrative and time for reflection enabled each of us to theorize further about the themes in her life.

Indeed, the very act of interviewing transforms an interviewee's formulation and retelling of her life. After a day of interviewing, Mary proclaimed that she had been flooded by many old memories the next morning. She awoke thinking about "stuff that I haven't thought of for years, people that I haven't thought of for years . . . . I just began to remember. It's really strange." On yet another day, she began by saying, "I was thinking this morning that there are certain threads that run through my life and one is loss. Loss goes right on through. Loss of the mother, physical loss, handicap, loss of attractiveness." As the interview proceeded, it became clear that I was not the only one speculating and theorizing about Mary's life. Just as I was developing and testing conclusions about her life, so was she. Moreover, Mary's conceptualization of her life was influenced by our dialogue and her own personal process of thinking about, giving voice to, and sharing her story. As scholars, it is imperative that our methodology incorporate women's own theorizing about their lives. Further, we must accept that scholarly theories may be disrupted as women's theories about their own lives change.

Although most women may privately theorize and draw conclusions about their lives, not all women engage in a dialogue about their theories. Mary's therapeutic training may account, in part, for her openness and acceptance of our disagreeing on points of interpretation. As a trained psychotherapist, Mary is intimately aware of how the process of dialoguing with someone can cast new light on thoughts and perceptions about one's life. Hare-Mustin and Marecek (1990) call attention to the similarities between the process of therapy and deconstructionist methods. On listening to a client's narrative and reconstructed memories, a therapist proposes new meanings and ways of interpreting the client's material. Having access to alternative ways of understanding one's life events allows the client to activate change in her or his life. For example, a therapist may help a female client see that her actions fulfill her spouse's desire to have a mother figure who looks after his every need; the client may then try to reconstruct a marital contract with her spouse that allows for a more mutual sharing of goals and needs.

> The therapist's task of listening and responding to the client's narratives is akin to a deconstructive reading of a text. Both seek subtexts and multiple levels of meaning. Just as deconstructive readings disrupt the frame of reference that organizes conventional meanings of a text, so a therapist's interventions disrupt the frame of reference within which the client customarily sees the world. (Hare-Mustin & Marecek, 1990, p. 48)

In the midst of our conversations, Mary reviewed and reevaluated aspects of her own life story. It is not surprising therefore that she can acknowledge, understand, and respect our different interpretations and conclusions about her life.

At the same time, the interviewee's sense of the interviewer's audience must also influence the telling of her story. Mary's concern about the audience's impressions was evident when I explored the source of her resiliency in surmounting numerous obstacles. She said:

> I'm afraid that putting it all together like this might arouse this sense of poor self-pity, and I don't really feel that way about my life. Now there were times when I felt sorry for myself. I've always felt sorry that my mother died. . . . I just don't want to convey the idea of this poor thing.

Who did Mary envision as the audience for her narrative? White women? Well-educated women? Upper-class women? Any women like herself? Her awareness of an audience for her life narrative and the desire to present a logical story clearly influenced her warm acceptance and approval of the first written text. Her later willingness to add greater complexity to the narrative reveals ambivalence, on Mary's part, regarding how best to represent her life experiences.

CONCLUSIONS

My dialogue with Mary suggests several methodological recommendations for the planning of a life narrative. The following strategies are offered only as broad guidelines in an effort to help us use interviews to provide fuller representations of the people we study and to include them in the research endeavor in meaningful ways. I propose that researchers should consider the following strategies when constructing a life narrative:

1. Conduct interviews that respect the "subject" as a key participant in the research process and as someone who guides and shapes the interview.
2. Formulate a "first-draft narrative" that researcher and interviewee can read and react to; allow this written narrative to form a basis for further dialogue.
3. Let enough time pass for the researcher and interviewee to engage in private reflection about the narrative and the discussions that followed.

4. Return to do more interviewing.
5. Incorporate the interviewee's reactions to your written material and to the research endeavor in your thinking, interviewing, and future writing.
6. Do not avoid searching for and discussing conflicts, criticisms, and disagreements between yourself and the interviewee; remember that presenting a final "answer" or resolution to the differences and contradictions that emerge is not necessary.

As academics we must accept the indeterminate nature of narratives and the scholarly products based on them. Fully incorporating the interviewee in the research process entails making the analysis and scholarly product itself part of the discussion. In such a discussion, women's theorizing about their own lives must be identified and respected so that a dialogue between theorists can occur. This process requires flexibility and openness to dialogue, criticism, and disagreements. Both researcher and research participant share power and control over the research endeavor. Together, they can acknowledge that the outcomes are only a partial representation of what scholar and interviewee choose to share, and give salience to, at that particular moment in time.

Initial submission: November 27, 1996
Final acceptance: September 15, 1997

REFERENCES

Belle, D. (1994). Attempting to comprehend the lives of low-income women. In C. E. Franz & A. J. Stewart (Eds.), *Women creating lives: Identities, resilience, and resistance* (pp. 37–50). Boulder, CO: Westview Press.
Brown, E. B. (1989). African-American women's quilting: A framework for conceptualizing and teaching African-American women's history. *Signs, 14*, 921–929.
Ceballo, R. (1994). A word and a kindness: The journey of a black social worker. In C. E. Franz & A. J. Stewart (Eds.), *Women creating lives: Identities, resilience, and resistance* (pp. 83–95). Boulder, CO: Westview Press.
Collins, P. H. (1990). Women's studies: Reform or transformation? *Sojourner: The Women's Forum, 10*, 18–20.
Cook, J. A., & Fonow, M. M. (1990). Knowledge and women's interests: Issues of epistemology and methodology in feminist sociological research. In J. M. Nielsen (Ed.), *Feminist research methods: Exemplary readings in the social sciences* (pp. 69–93). Boulder, CO: Westview Press.
Franz, C. E. (1994). Reconstituting the self: The role of history, personality, and loss in one woman's life. In C. E. Franz & A. J. Stewart (Eds.), *Women creating lives: Identities, resilience, and resistance* (pp. 213–226). Boulder, CO: Westview Press.
Harding, S. (1987). Introduction: Is there a feminist method? In S. Harding (Ed.), *Feminism and methodology* (pp. 1–14). Bloomington, IN: Indiana University Press.
Hare-Mustin, R. T., & Marecek, J. (1990). Gender and the meaning of difference: Postmodernism and psychology. In R. T. Hare-Mustin & J. Marecek (Eds.), *Making a difference: Psychology and the construction of gender* (pp. 22–64). New Haven, CT: Yale University Press.
Honig, E. (1997). Striking lives: Oral history and the politics of memory. *Journal of Women's History, 9*, 139–157.
hooks, b. (1981). *Ain't I a woman: Black women and feminism.* Boston: South End Press.
King, D. K. (1988). Multiple jeopardy, multiple consciousness: The context of a black feminist ideology. *Signs, 14*, 42–72.
Lykes, M. B. (1994). Speaking against the silence: One Maya woman's exile and return. In C. E.

Franz & A. J. Stewart (Eds.), *Women creating lives: Identities, resilience, and resistance* (pp. 97–114). Boulder, CO: Westview Press.

Nagata, D. K. (1994). Coping with internment: A Nisei woman's perspective. In C. E. Franz & A. J. Stewart (Eds.), *Women creating lives: Identities, resilience, and resistance* (pp. 115–126). Boulder, CO: Westview Press.

Rutter, M. (1979). Protective factors in children's responses to stress and disadvantage. In M. W. Kent & J. E. Rolf (Eds.), *Primary prevention of psychopathology. Vol. 3: Social competence in children* (pp. 49–74). Hanover, NH: University Press of New England.

Spelman, E. V. (1988). *Inessential woman: Problems of exclusion in feminist thought.* Boston: Beacon Press.

Stewart, A. J. (1994). Toward a feminist strategy for studying women's lives. In C. E. Franz & A. J. Stewart (Eds.), *Women creating lives: Identities, resilience, and resistance* (pp. 11–35). Boulder, CO: Westview Press.

Werner, E. E., & Smith, R. S. (1982). *Vulnerable but invincible: A study of resilient children.* New York: McGraw-Hill.

INTERPRETING THE LIFE NARRATIVE

Race, Class, Gender, and Historical Context

Karen Fraser Wyche
New York University

Life narratives provide a technicolor view of a person's life, giving both historical and developmental context to the life journey. As a qualitative method it can elucidate themes that are not captured by quantitative methods. When women are the narrators, the social and personal meaning of their lives can unfold. For women of color the life narrative can contextualize the multiple jeopardy of being both female and a member of a minority in America.

Rosario Ceballo (1999) has written the life narrative of Mary's story, taking us on an 80-year journey. Although we are not told the questions that elicit the story, the parts that we are given are both interesting and compelling snapshots of her life. In multiple readings of this article I continue to be struck, as is Ceballo, by the richness of Mary's life, which, as do most lives lived this long, has joys and sadness, peaks and valleys. The interview becomes the stimulus that elicits Mary's reflection of her own life. She describes how the process of the interview and the subsequent reading of the article brought forth both old memories and new understandings. Rosario Ceballo's sharing of her written description about the interview with Mary and the incorporation of Mary's responses in the article increase the validity of the interview. As she suggests in her conclusions, providing the interviewer and the interviewee an opportunity to discuss the agreements, disagreements, and criticisms engages both women in a collaborative process furthering a dialogue about women's lives that can be incorporated into the research process. This is a feminist process that takes power away from the researcher and shares it with the participant.

Including the interviewee's assessment of the interview analysis is a strength of this feminist approach to qualitative research. But there are also limits and these

Address correspondence and reprint requests to: Karen Fraser Wyche, New York University, School of Social Work, One Washington Square North, New York, NY 10012.

321

are related to interpretation—the degree to which the researcher understands the experience of the participant. How is validity of that experience established? How do researchers incorporate participants' disagreements about that experience? Are participants honest in what they share with researchers? Do the researchers change their opinions about the interpretation of the life narrative once a participant has informed them of a disagreement in interpretation? These questions are difficult to answer. Those researchers who desire simpler explanations for complex problems may wish to adhere to quantitative research methods that allow for statistical manipulations of the data as opposed to this imprecise process.

The life narrative is an interpretative method. As with any interpretative method, researchers are concerned with improving the accuracy of interpretations about other people's lives. This is a question of internal validity—are the interpretations valid? Qualitative researchers use the technique of triangulation to reduce the likelihood of misinterpretation and bias (Huberman & Miles, 1994; Rizzo & Corsaro, 1992) by asking participants and researchers (who represent different perspectives—age, culture, gender, etc.) to clarify the meaning of the experiences being described in a life narrative. Because experience is bound by class, race, and time, it is important to have multiple readings of the narrative to identify the different ways the phenomena or experiences are being perceived. There is an attempt to obtain a convergence of meanings among the readers (e.g., the representation of the particular events in everyday life, the cultural significance of events, the communicative intent of the experience) (Huberman & Miles, 1994). The triangulation process keeps narrowing the interpretations by checking and rechecking the findings with researchers and participants (Rizzo & Corsaro, 1992). The goal is to increase internal validity. Of course "perfect" validity is impossible, but the triangulation process is a way of trying to achieve it. It does not mean that a final answer must be found, as in whether or not the null hypothesis is confirmed or rejected. It does mean that there are multiple checks on interpretation. Reliability, important for quantitative research, is addressed only indirectly. By discussion among readers, the interpretation of the life narrative becomes increasingly meaningful and accurate and hence more reliable as validity presupposes reliability (Rizzo & Corsaro, 1992). This process differs from the postmodern analysis of reading a text for multiple meanings rather than a single truth. As Ceballo points out in her article, there is a fundamental difference between the life narrative and an historical or fictive text. It is that the interviewee is able to provide feedback as opposed to reading a text that must be deconstructed for multiple meanings.

In this article Mary, our participant, does not agree with Ceballo's interpretation of her life. She directly rejects the conceptualization of herself as a heroine and a resilient survivor. Instead, Mary prefers to be characterized as a "coper" rather than someone with a resilient identity.

How did this disagreement of the interpretation of the life narrative happen? Ceballo describes how she and Mary discuss their differences of opinion. "With the written narrative and with time for reflection, Mary and I both theorized further and considered new themes in her life story" (Ceballo, 1999, p. 318).

It is understandable that Ceballo views Mary's life as being one of a resilient heroine, for Ceballo sees parallels in their lives—connections and similarities that she discusses as inevitably drawing her to the resilient aspect of Mary's story. The resilience theme continues throughout the article with acknowledgment of Mary's disagreement.

I wish Ceballo had told us why she did not change her interpretations based on what Mary said. What we have is a difference of opinion regarding identity—how the self is constructed. Is it a heroic and resilient self or a coping self?

I am interested in these differing interpretations, but I can only comment on what is written in the article. I too want to understand Mary's life narrative. What are the themes that influence the way Mary views herself and why is she steadfast in her distinction between coping and being a resilient heroine? How can I interpret her life? How do I triangulate the available data, and what biases do I bring to this interpretation? There are several. I am a middle-aged African American woman, and like Mary and Rosario I have advanced degrees in social work and psychology. I acknowledge any biases that come from these personal characteristics and that may influence my interpretation of Mary's life narrative. What are the interpretations and reinterpretations I make? I will address only a few points.

The first interpretations are based on the sociohistorical context and cultural norms that shape behaviors. Mary as an 80-year-old woman who views herself as a "coper." At her age it is culturally appropriate to live one's life in a way that never brings attention on oneself. She coped, but it was functional and done in a way so as not to disrupt the family and to keep the father's role as caretaker (albeit emotionally distant) intact. She did not divulge painful experiences or memories and kept things to herself. Age and cultural norms operate here for women. Age norms give messages of not sharing one's pain with others. For example, in a Psychology of Women course, I have assigned undergraduate women to interview their mothers and grandmothers (or women related from those generations) in order to assess how they coped with the stress in their lives. All of the students (of varying ethnicity) were amazed that the stories from the grandmothers' generation (Mary's age cohort) were devoid of any talk of problems, whereas their mothers talked about many problems and ways of coping. The point here is that it is not uncommon for an 80-year-old woman to not have self-disclosed problems to others. Furthermore, the cultural norm for Black women was to bear their burden and suffer in silence.

Social class is important in interpreting this narrative. Mary comes from an educated African American family. Her father had a law degree that he must have obtained in the late 1800s. He was better educated than most White men at the time. Her aunts were school teachers and were probably educated at a normal college. These highly educated family members would have prestige in the community because of these accomplishments. Her brother worked in the post office (an excellent job for African American men during that time) and paid for her to attend college, which was not typical of what happened to single women in her generation. She was supposed to get a husband, not an education, but the social roles for women in this family included advanced education. Mary graduated from an historically black college (Howard University) in 1943, and from Smith College School of Social Work, an elite White professional school. This is the legacy of the elite, upper class of the African American community during this period. She comes from a family of Black professionals—the educated elite—who held positions traditionally occupied by Whites during the 1930s–1940s. Her father's lack of economic success makes them poor within this elite African American community. This is her reference group. Her father's lack of money to buy presentable clothes or provide better housing resulted in an understandable sense of shame. If she had come from a family that was uneducated, like the overwhelming majority of African Americans during this time period, her lack of appropriate clothing would probably not have been so obvious or painful. So feeling poor within this context is different if your reference group is also poor. Thus the social and historic context is very important for clarifying and interpreting events. Her father's keeping of the children after his wife's death may be a result of his education and social-class norms. I wonder if a less educated man would have kept all of the children or would he have sent the youngest children and the only girl to live with relatives?

There is also the historical reality of Washington, DC, during the period that Mary was growing up. It was a city where Blacks segregated themselves by skin color. The elite classes of Blacks were university graduates and professionals. Skin-color discrimination among them was common. Mary talks about this, but is it explored further? She had the correct social status, but not money or the right (i.e., light) skin color. So knowing something about the social structure in Washington, DC, is important in understanding the story. How do these class and race issues relate to emotional pain and coping? We need Mary to validate this contextual interpretation.

As researchers, we need to be aware of how a person's unique experiences influence the manner in which she or he tells his or her life stories. We must integrate sociopolitical and community contexts, historical factors, race, and gender into the analysis. This is hard to do when participants and researchers can share both differences and similarities across various domains. By sharing of the text with others, however—both participants and researchers—we can begin to make sense of life experiences and to generate new awareness. As researchers we want to be honest in representing the lives of the people we study. The sharing of interpretations from participants of this process and from informed researchers helps us gain the objectivity we need. The life narrative is an excellent tool to provide new theories regarding the lives of women across class, race, and other distinguishing variables. Rosario and Mary have added their voices to this literature.

REFERENCES

Ceballo, R. (1999). Negotiating the life narrative: A dialogue with an African American social worker. *Psychology of Women Quarterly, 23,* 309–321.

Huberman, M. A., & Miles, M. B. (1994). Data management and analysis methods. In N. K. Denzin & Y. S. Lincoln (Eds.). *Handbook of qualitative research* (pp. 428–444). Newbury Park, CA: Sage.

Rizzo, T., & Corsaro, W. (1992). Ethnographic methods and interpretative analysis. Expanding the methodological opinions of psychologists. *Developmental Review, 12,* 101–123.

UNDERSTANDING GRADUATE WOMEN'S REENTRY EXPERIENCES

Case Studies of Four Psychology Doctoral Students in a Midwestern University

Marjorie A. Padula
University of Nebraska Medical Center

Dana L. Miller
Doane College

This multiple case study describes the experiences of reentry women in psychology doctoral programs at a major Midwestern research university and illustrates the usefulness of the qualitative case-study method in exploring women's experiences. Semistructured interviews were conducted with four women who were purposefully selected as information-rich participants. Observations and informal interviews were also conducted over a period of up to 2 1/2 years. Eight themes emerged from the data and have been labeled: the decision to return, expectations versus reality, measuring up, frustrations and difficulties, changing family relationships, the necessity of organization, "do it and get on with life," and rewards. This article illustrates that case-study research can be a powerful tool for feminist researchers to document women's experiences.

The purpose of this study was to describe the experiences of reentry women in psychology doctoral programs at a major Midwestern research university and to illustrate the usefulness of the qualitative case-study method in exploring women's experiences. The study describes the experiences of four married women who have children at home and who reentered the university as full-time students. We

Address correspondence and reprint requests to: Marjorie A. Padula, Department of Psychology, University of Nebraska Medical Center, 600 S. 42nd Street, Omaha, NE 68198-5577. E-mail: mpadula@unmc.edu.

identified our research focus through the use of grand-tour questions. The term "grand tour" is often used in ethnographic texts and is drawn from the experience of showing someone around—giving him or her a grand tour to highlight major features of a residence or business (Spradley, 1980). Applying this to developing research questions, Creswell (1994) suggested that "the grand tour question is a statement of the question being examined in the study in its most general form" (p. 70). This question, consistent with the emerging methodology of qualitative designs, is posed as a general issue so as not to limit the inquiry. One might ask, "What is the broadest question that can be asked in the study?" (p. 70). Three grand-tour questions guided this study: (a) How do women in a psychology doctoral program describe their decision to return to school? (b) How do women in a psychology doctoral program describe their reentry experiences? and (c) How does returning to graduate school change these women's lives?

Reentry women are usually defined as women reentering educational institutions or the labor force after an absence ranging from a few years to as many as 35 years (Lewis, 1988). Ranging in age from 25 to over 65 years, the majority of reentry women are between the ages of 25 and 54 (U.S. Department of Commerce, 1994). The need for research on reentry women is apparent when information issued by the Bureau of the Census on college enrollments is examined. At 13.1 million students, total college enrollment was higher in 1988 than in any previous year. Most of this growth in enrollment was among students aged 25 and older; from 1980–1988, women aged 25 and older constituted 48.6% of the total growth of college enrollment (U.S. Department of Commerce, 1990). A recent Bureau of the Census publication reported 1993 college enrollment at 13.9 million, with more women than men enrolled in 2-year colleges, 4-year colleges, and graduate schools (U.S. Department of Commerce, 1994). There are indicators that this reentry trend will continue. In addition, the U.S. Department of Education (1990) predicted women will earn more doctorates than men by the year 2001.

In order for psychologists, educators, and counselors to better meet the needs of this ever-growing group, an understanding of the experiences of these women is essential. The current body of research on reentry women is mainly limited to quantitative survey studies of undergraduate women (Padula, 1994). Although these studies have provided valuable information about reentry women, the depth of that information has been limited. We could not identify published studies specifically using reentry women doctoral students as participants. Therefore, this qualitative study adds significantly to the current body of research by providing an in-depth look at the reentry experiences of four married psychology doctoral students who have dependent children at home.

Qualitative studies are especially appropriate for defining important variables and developing new ideas (Borg & Gall, 1989), an area of critical need in our studies of women. The richness of the qualitative case-study method lies in its use of the words of the participants. Several terms have been used to describe qualitative research. Lincoln and Guba (1985) called the approach constructivist or naturalistic. Smith termed it interpretative, and Quantz associated it with the postpositivist or postmodern perspective (cited in Creswell, 1994). Important characteristics distinguish qualitative research from traditional quantitative designs, and each of these apply to this study. (a) Qualitative research occurs in natural settings. Researchers enter participants' worlds without purposefully manipulating or altering the context (Eisner, 1991; Lincoln & Guba, 1985; Merriam, 1988). (b) Qualitative research is inductive. Hypotheses are not established a priori and theory emerges from the data rather than testing or verifying preexisting theory (Creswell, 1994; Fraenkel & Wallen, 1990; Lincoln & Guba, 1985; Locke, Spirduso, & Silverman, 1987; Merriam, 1988). (c) The researchers are the primary data-collection instruments (Eisner, 1991; Lincoln & Guba, 1985; Merriam, 1988). Researchers interact with participants (Creswell, 1994) and cannot function apart from the context and participants. This adds sensitivity and responsiveness to the research process (Fraenkel & Wallen, 1990). (d) Qualitative data are descriptive in nature and are presented in words or pictures rather than numbers (Fraenkel & Wallen, 1990; Locke et al., 1987; Marshall & Rossman, 1989; Merriam, 1988). (e) The focus of qualitative research is participants' perceptions and experiences and the way they make sense of their lives (Fraenkel & Wallen, 1990; Locke et al., 1987; Merriam, 1988). Realities are constructed by participants in the research, and multiple realities exist (Creswell, 1994). Creswell suggested that researchers need to "report faithfully these realities and to rely on voices and interpretations of informants" (p. 6). (f) Process is of greater importance than product in qualitative inquiry. Qualitative researchers are interested in understanding how things occur, rather than simply identifying outcomes (Fraenkel & Wallen, 1990; Merriam, 1988). (g) Qualitative research is developing its own language. Creswell (1994) contended that words such as "understanding, discovery, and meaning [form] the glossary of emerging qualitative terms" (p. 6). He added that "the language of qualitative studies became personal, informal and based on definitions that evolved during a study" (p. 7).

METHOD

Participants

Purposeful sampling was used to select participants. This type of nonrandom sampling is "done to increase the utility of information obtained" in that participants are chosen "because they are likely to be knowledgeable and informative about the phenomenon" of interest (Schumacher & McMillan, 1993, p. 378).

The primary criteria used to select participants were: (a) the women were full-time students enrolled in one of several psychology programs at a major Midwestern research university; (b) all had reentered graduate school after absences due to career, child care, and homemaking responsibilities (from 6 to 20 years); (c) they were married with children (from 2 to 16 years of age); and (d) they were willing and able to articulate their reentry experiences. We specifically chose reentry women who were married with children because of the unique demands of juggling multiple roles and because the primary researcher was a graduate reentry student who met the preceding criteria and had access to women meeting this criteria at the time of data collection. The literature suggests that "growing numbers of women are moving back into school following marriage and motherhood" (Bradburn, Moen, & Dempster-McClain, 1995, p. 1518). Today's typical reentry woman is "juggling the demands of family, young children and full- or part-time employment" (Petersen, 1991, p. 42). Responsibilities include being a wife, mother, wage earner, community member, or a combination of several roles (Lewis, 1988). There is concern that these reentry women's "academic success is often curbed by the realities of uniquely stressful situations" (Rifenbary, 1995, p. 1). We believed that it was important to explore the complexity of these roles and purposefully chose women who fit these criteria.

The women in this study ranged in age from 32 to 48 years. One woman was African American, and three women were European American. All had middle-class socioeconomic backgrounds. The women were at varying stages in their doctoral programs, from the first to the third year. These sampling criteria provided a varied perspective to the study. All the participants were cooperative, articulate, and eager to describe their experiences.

Case-Study Method

The qualitative case-study method was used. In her book, *Feminist Methods in Social Research*, Reinharz (1992) suggested that "feminist interest in case studies stems from the desire to document aspects of women's lives and achievements" (p. 171) and that "case studies are essential for putting women on the map of social life" (p. 174). Reinharz contended that case-study research is a tool of feminist research and that "the power of the case study to convey vividly the dimensions of a social phenomenon or individual life is power that feminist researchers want to utilize" (p. 174). We believe that the case-study method has provided a powerful avenue to explore the experiences of female psychology doctoral students and give voice to those experiences.

The case-study design applies to this study for several reasons. (a) The goal of case-study research is to seek greater understanding of the case (Schumacher & McMillan, 1993; Stake, 1995). Our goal was to provide an understanding of the experiences women encountered when they chose to return to graduate school, after years of absence, to pursue a terminal degree. (b) Case studies focus on one specific phenomenon of interest (such as a specific individual, program, event, process, or institution) and study that phenomenon in depth (Merriam, 1988; Schumacher & McMillan, 1993). In this case, four women were selected to provide their perceptions of the phenomenon of interest: reentry experiences. (c) Yin (1989) suggested that "case studies are the preferred strategy when 'how' or 'why' questions are being posed, when the investigator has little control over events, and when the focus is on a contemporary phenomenon with some real-life context" (p. 13). We explored women's real-life experiences returning to graduate school, focusing on how they perceived and interpreted those experiences. (d) Merriam (1988) described the focus of case-study research as a "bounded system" (p. 9). Miles and Huberman (1994) explained that researchers often struggle with identifying "the case" (p. 25) and that "sometimes the 'phenomenon' may be an individual in a defined context" (p. 26). In this case, this study is bounded by the unit of analysis (the participants), the context (reentry experiences in psychology doctoral programs at a major Midwestern research university), and sampling criteria (graduate reentry women who were married with children).

In his text on case-study research, Yin (1989) delineated three types of case-study designs: exploratory, descriptive, and explanatory. This study is both exploratory and descriptive. Our goal was to investigate a relatively unexplored phenomenon (women psychology doctoral students' reentry experiences) and provide a description of those experiences so readers could better understand the phenomenon.

Data Collection

Three strategies dominate qualitative data collection: interviews, participant observation, and document collection (Glesne & Peshkin, 1992). A key characteristic of case-study research is the use of multiple sources of evidence (Yin, 1989). In this study, reentry women participated in interviews, were observed over a period of time, and provided relevant documentation for review by the primary researcher.

Interviews
Semistructured interviews were the primary data-collection tool in this study. Reinharz (1992) identified semistructured interviews as the primary data-collection strategy feminist researchers use to allow women the opportunity to construct data about their lives. Interviews allow researchers to access women's perceptions, feelings, ideas, and memories and rely on the language of participants in order to give voice to women's experiences that may have been ignored.

Bogdan and Biklen (1992) described interviews as purposeful conversations that allow researchers to gather descriptive data in participants' words in order to develop insights into some piece of participants' worlds. They suggested that "qualitative interviews vary in the degree to which they are structured" (p. 97). An interview protocol, consisting of eight open-ended questions, was used as an interview guide in this study (see Appendix). This protocol increases confidence that comparable data are being collected across participants (Bogdan & Biklen, 1992). Though semistructured interviews provide structure to the questions-and-interview format, there is flexibility to probe issues participants raise. Glesne and Peshkin (1992) described the qualitative interview as "an occasion for depth probes—for getting to the bottom of things . . . [in order to] do justice to the complexity of [the] topic" (p. 85). Then, during data collection, researchers take on a "special learner role," as a naive listener (Glesne & Peshkin, 1992, p. 80).

Initial interviews ranged from 60 to 90 minutes. Interviews were conducted privately in a university office and were audiotaped. Following the interviews, the audiotapes were transcribed verbatim and the notes taken during the interview were typed. Follow-up interviews of varying length were conducted to review the accuracy of the transcripts and to ensure that participants could add any information that would help us better understand their experiences.

Participant Observations
Participant observation is a data-collection technique with a long and established history in anthropology (Merriam, 1988; Spradley, 1980). Informal observations of the reentry women occurred during a period ranging from one semester to 2½ years. The women were observed both in and out of the classroom by the primary researcher, a married woman with a family, who at the time of the research was also a reentry student in a psychology doctoral program. Formal classroom observations were conducted weekly for 3-hour blocks of time for a minimum of

one semester (15 weeks) per participant. Informal observations included sharing meals and attending activities together. The observations corroborated much of what the participants discussed in their interviews, particularly the highly affective nature of the reentry experience.

Documents
The participants were asked to provide copies of their graduate-school applications and autobiographical and goal statements. These documents provided increased understanding of participants' goals for graduate school.

Data Analysis

All transcripts, interview notes, documents, and observation field notes were reviewed and coded continuously during data collection in order to identify themes. Data collection and data analysis are simultaneous activities (Creswell, 1994; Glesne & Peshkin, 1992; Schumacher & McMillan, 1993). Interviews were transcribed and data were analyzed throughout the research process as data analysis drives further data collection. Miles and Huberman's (1994) suggestions for text-based coding were used. Data were examined line by line or chunk by chunk, and one- to two-word codes were attached to each segment to represent, as closely as possible, participants' words. After initial coding was done, similar codes were grouped together and labeled to identify the broader themes those codes represented. The themes were reviewed by the participants in the study and by a colleague (peer reviewer) to verify their accuracy. The themes were named by using participants' words and the authors' interpretations. The themes were iterative, defined by Constas (1992) as created at various points in time during the research process. They were subject to revision, elaboration, or deletion throughout the course of the study.

Ethical Considerations

Participants were informed of the purposes and procedures of the study, that their participation was voluntary, and that they had the right to withdraw from the study at any time. They were assured that their right to remain anonymous would be protected by the use of pseudonyms and that information that might reveal their identities would not be reported. The women understood that the product of the study would be publication; however, those data would only be used for the purposes explained to them.

Verification Strategies

In qualitative studies, researchers are the primary data-collection instruments: it is impossible to conduct value-free inquiry. We were cognizant from the beginning of the study of the need to be aware of potential biases, particularly as the primary researcher was also a full-time graduate reentry student at the time of data collection.

Our goal was to represent participants' perceptions and experiences accurately. Locke et al. (1987) suggested that what researchers bring "to the setting can become a positive part of the process" (p. 93) but caution that the researcher's experiences become an integral part of the study. It is the creation of this awareness that is critical, "not the divestiture of self" (p. 93). Similarly, Marshall and Rossman (1989) cited as one of the strengths of qualitative research that researchers are better able to describe complex social systems because of their abilities to gain entry into participants' worlds. At the same time, they suggested that researchers "must provide controls for bias in interpretation" (p. 147). Therefore, we incorporated a number of verification strategies into our research design to address concerns about researcher subjectivity/bias.

There are a number of strategies used to assess the trustworthiness of the results of qualitative studies (Glesne & Peshkin, 1992; Lincoln & Guba, 1985; Merriam, 1988). Several of those strategies were employed in this project. Two forms of triangulation of data were used in this study: (a) multiple sources, that is, multiple participants; and (b) multiple methods, that is, interviews, observations, and corroborating documents. Triangulating the data is a major strength of case-study research (Merriam, 1988; Yin, 1989).

Other verification strategies included: (a) using member checks, that is, taking data and interpretations back to participants to check accuracy; (b) having a colleague and qualitative-methods instructor who played the role of a disinterested peer reviewer to comment on the findings, play devil's advocate, and challenge biases; (c) conducting observations over an extended period of time; (d) clarifying researcher bias (particularly with respect to the rewards and difficulties associated with being a full-time doctoral student while juggling the responsibilities of family and work); and (e) using thick, rich descriptions so that readers can make decisions on the transferability or comparability of the findings to other contexts.

RESULTS

Introducing the Participants

Jane is in her late 40's. She lives with her husband, two teenagers, and a preteen. She is a third-year doctoral student in psychology who worked both in and outside her home before returning to school.

Susan is in her mid-40's. She lives with her husband, two teenagers, and a preteen. She is a first-year doctoral student in psychology who described herself as "a housewife" before returning to school.

Laura is in her early 30's. She lives with her husband and preschool-aged child. She is a third-year doctoral student in psychology who worked full-time prior to returning to school.

Karen is in her early 40's. Like Jane and Susan, she lives with her husband, two teenagers, and a preteen. She is a second-year doctoral student in psychology who worked both in and outside of her home before returning to school.

Table 1

Themes Identified by Graduate Reentry Women and Related Key Concepts

Theme	Key concepts
Decision to return	Outside impetus: degree a necessity for career attainment Labored over decision for an extended time A conscious/intentional decision that became a commitment
Expectations versus reality	Not always challenged to learn Jumping through hoops Disappointment in relationships with faculty: • lack of support • difficulty connecting with faculty mentors • lack of understanding of nontraditional student needs
Measuring up	The importance of grades (versus learning) Competing and comparing with other (often younger) students
Frustrations and difficulties	Too little time Lack of understanding by friends, family High stress Exhaustion
Changing family relationships	Negative: • strain on relationships • difficulty maintaining intimacy Positive: promoted greater independence
Necessity of organization	Survival depended on organization A servant to the date book Every minute scheduled The "unexpected" interfered
Rewards	Anticipated career advancement Learning Developing camaraderie/relationships with other students Increased positive self-perception: more self-confident, assertive, articulate, knowledgeable

Themes

The data indicate that the participants shared many common experiences in their return to graduate school. As patterns in the data emerged, we identified eight themes that captured the essence of these women's experiences. The themes are presented in Table 1.

Decision to Return

The decision to return to school was fueled in part by an outside impetus for all the reentry women interviewed in this study. All believed that completion of their Ph.D. was necessary to their career goals or to their security in their desired career field. All four of the reentry women cited teaching as one of their goals following completion of a doctorate. Three of the women also anticipated conducting research. This theme supports previous research that indicates that vocational reasons are a primary motive for educational reentry (Badenhoop & Johansen, 1980; Clayton & Smith, 1987; MacKinnon-Slaney, Barber, & Slaney, 1988; Pickering & Galvin-Schaefers, 1988; Read, Elliott, Escobar, & Slaney, 1988; Sewall, 1984; Smart & Pascarella, 1987).

For two of the women, family problems that precipitated a desire to distance themselves from their home lives and to establish lives outside their families played a part in their decision to return to school. Jane explained that after she had spent years "raising kids, really intensely raising kids . . . I decided I needed to do something else." She added "I felt like I had done a lot for my children . . . and I could start developing some things for myself." Susan described her marital situation: "My husband and I have actually been having a lot of problems, and I returned because I have been staying home with my kids for . . . years and my skills were rusty . . . I just decided I was going to do something else." Consistent with previous studies, family variables have been reported as important reasons for reentry (Clayton & Smith, 1987; MacKinnon-Slaney et al., 1988; Pickering & Galvin-Schaefers, 1988; Sewall, 1984). For Laura, the opportunity for tuition reimbursement through her employer influenced her decision to return to school.

All of the participants reported that they considered returning to school for a period of at least 1 year prior to reentering as full-time students. They all said they had made conscious decisions to pursue their doctorates at some point before they reentered school and reconfirmed those decisions after entering school. Susan, the first-year student, was still in the process of deciding if she would continue to pursue her Ph.D.—if it was worth the sacrifice required.

Expectations versus Reality

None of the women experienced returning to school in a way they expected. All four expressed disappointment in one form or another about some aspect of their education. Three participants specifically discussed expecting to learn a lot and discovering that was not the reality in some of their classes. Susan expressed her frustration particularly succinctly: "Don't waste my time. Tell me something I don't know. I don't feel like I have a lot of time to waste on professors that don't know anything." Three of the participants were disappointed with what they perceived to be the necessity for "jumping through hoops." The fourth, Laura, expressed the same idea but described it as learning "how to get through the system." Jane prefaced her remarks with "Now this is awful," but added that "in some ways I see it (school) as a sort of prison term."

Participants were asked what role faculty had played in their reentry experience. The responses were varied but carried an underlying theme that faculty members could be very important, but often were not. Jane believed that faculty had not had much impact on her but had produced some occasional "pearls of wisdom." Susan and Laura mentioned their desire for mentors and disappointment that they did not really have one. Susan concluded that "the younger female professors are not supportive, which is pretty interesting. But the older faculty are very supportive." Susan described one older faculty member's encouragement, this person told her she could "do whatever I want" and that "age is totally immaterial." She also gave Susan permission to "let the kids cook dinner, you go study." Susan needed that kind of influence and spoke of the faculty member as someone who "really can set a head back on straight sometimes." Susan went on to say "the older faculty treats you like we're all in this together and we're gonna get you through this." Karen expressed a different concern, that the program she was enrolled in was geared for traditional students who had gone straight through school. She was distressed that faculty were not supportive of nontraditional students with families and jobs. Kirk and Dorfman (1983) concluded that faculty could play an important role in students' experiences, although sometimes they did not. That clearly seemed to be the experience of these women.

Measuring Up
Participants spontaneously raised the issue of grades or of comparing themselves to other, often younger, students. It bothered Susan and Laura to make "B's" rather than "A's." In fact, Laura indicated that she did not think B's represented someone who was doctoral material. Jane, on the other hand, had decided at the outset that she would not work for grades, but for knowledge, and that B's were "okay."

In addition to grades, the concern about whether or not the women "measured up" to others was implicit. These women struggled with comparing themselves to other students, especially the younger students. For example, Susan lamented, "I'm taking a stats class that requires me to study six times the norm because I don't get it and it's been 22 years since I've had math, and these kids, they pick it up and do it and they're done, and I'm still trying to turn the computer on."

Frustrations and Difficulties
Several areas were identified as frustrating or difficult for participants since returning to school, including little time, lack of understanding or support from family and friends, stress, and exhaustion. All experienced the frustration of not having enough time to do everything—juggling work, school, family, friends, and time for themselves. They were frustrated that no one really seemed to understand what they were "going through" except for the older, married women with children who were in school with them. Karen explained that, in addition to community members not understanding what she was experiencing, she felt the school staff also failed to understand: "There's very little consideration for the fact that older students like myself have families, have jobs, have real-life experiences, and when you talk about those kinds of things the response that you get is, well, we told you this was a full-time program." She added, "I'm sorry, but I don't know how an older person, particularly a woman, is going to get through school without having a job to help support herself."

All four participants discussed how exhausting the program was and how "crazy" and overburdened they felt at times. Susan believed "being in a Ph.D. program requires about 65 hours a week" and voiced her struggle: "I can't devote that kind of time. I have three children. I have a large house. I have laundry that's mounting. I have leaves to be raked. I have thousands of things to do."

Some of the negative emotions and attitudes observed and/or reported during the discussion of frustrations and difficulties included anger, depression, exhaustion, disappointment, confusion, and bitterness. Negative emotions were reported more frequently and were more affectively charged than positive emotions. All reported they were highly stressed by the experience of being back in school full time. When asked to describe what the experience of returning to school had been like, Susan reflected "If I had a dime for every tear I've cried, I'd be a millionaire. It's one of the most stressful things I've ever done." Though they persevered, several asked, "Why am I doing this to myself?"

Changing Family Relationships

All the participants expressed concern that they were not able to invest as much energy in their families and that being in school had put a strain on their family relationships in some ways. Karen acknowledged that school "really takes away from my family life, and everybody's frustrated with me, and everybody's mad, 'cause I'm not at home." Susan described her experience as "being a donkey and carrying baggage." She explained, "I get home and it's just total chaos . . . I've got four people that I'm carrying along kicking and screaming who don't want to go where I'm leading them. And it's very stressful, so it's a good thing God made humans with senses of humor." Susan illustrated the potential importance of seemingly insignificant things in affecting family relationships: "like this week, I've gotten in the shower and have no soap. My kids have taken my soap because they didn't have any, and so I have to get out of the shower." She went on, half-jokingly and half-seriously "it's just crazy little things like this . . . this is why people kill each other . . . just because that one time they got in the shower, there wasn't any soap and they were all wet." The struggle these women describe is no surprise. Several researchers have reported that reentry women experience problems as a result of family issues (Badenhoop & Johansen, 1980; Gilbert, Manning, & Ponder, 1980; Kinnier & Townley, 1986; Read et al., 1988). Priorities change, and the demands of school leave little time to invest in quality family life.

Jane and Laura initially identified some ways returning to school had positively changed their family lives. Jane said she "had to pull out of a lot of mothering things," and added, "I think in a sense it's made my family be less dependent on me." She perceived that as a "very good" experience for her family. Laura said returning to school had made her relationship with her husband "stronger." She explained that they had "gotten stronger and closer, because . . . the first year and a half . . . we didn't have a social life and so that's forced us to get closer and set priorities." After reviewing her interview transcript, however, Laura reflected, "I don't know who I thought I was kidding when I said that." She noted on the transcript about her marital relationship that "there is definitely a difference in our relationship. We don't have as much time to discuss issues in our daily life so we aren't as aware about each other's lives as we used to be. There are also times that arguments develop much more quickly than before. . . . It is much more difficult to maintain a level of intimacy."

Necessity of Organization

The necessity for being organized was clearly an issue for all participants. The sentiments for all the women seemed to be summed up in Karen's statement: "The only way a person like myself can survive in this program is to be really organized. I have a date book that has every minute of my day scheduled." Jane concurred that "every minute is filled with something to do" and admitted that "having a sick kid" would completely throw her schedule off. Susan noted "there are lots of times when I can only study between 9 and 1 in the morning and that's when I study," acknowledging that "at 45, it's just not very healthy." Becoming organized seemed to be a key strategy all of the participants used to survive the demands of graduate school and their multiple roles. To these women, however, organization meant reordering priorities and fitting things in when and where they could.

Do It and Get on with Life

The participants wanted to finish their graduate programs as quickly as possible. This was an issue raised spontaneously by all participants and often accompanied by strong emotion. The sense of urgency was especially salient for the three women in their 40's. Some of their comments reflect this theme poignantly. Jane said "I've got to get this finished and get on with my life." She had the sense that she was "getting old" and needed to "do it and move on." Susan believed the best approach was to "just do it and get out of here," and Karen agreed, "I don't want to be in school until I'm 52; I want to get out relatively quickly." Laura made a conscious decision that "it would probably be better if I stayed in (school) and did it and got it over with and then got on with my life after that." The emotions associated with this theme seem to be summed up by Laura: "This delayed gratification is really getting old." All of the participants talked about how their lives would be different, that is, better, after they finished school. All are in school, making sacrifices now, for long-term benefits.

Rewards

A number of rewards were identified by the participants and these were what made school worthwhile or exciting for them. Rewards included brighter career prospects, developing camaraderie with other women students, learning, and developing more positive self-perceptions. Some of the positive emotions or attitudes observed and/or reported included excitement, animation, affection, happiness, humor, dedication, perseverance, and commitment. All believed that they would be more likely to get the kind of job they wanted at the completion of their program. This is another illustration of delayed gratification or long-term benefits. All four participants described learning as something that made school worthwhile for them. Three of the participants mentioned the other students as making school worthwhile for them. Susan expressed, "One of the nicest things about (being in school) is that I'm meeting people who are somewhat more like me." Laura stated, "I'm really enjoying working with the other students. I've enjoyed the camaraderie that's been developing." Although Jane did not directly identify other students as helping make the program worthwhile, she did state that it was very helpful to have other students experience school with her. Without that, she stated, "I just felt so alone."

Laura, Jane, and Karen expressed positive self-perceptions of returning to school including increased self-confidence. Laura has "learned to become more articulate about certain things" and added that she has "become a little more assertive for myself than I've been before." Jane feels "more centered," and Karen feels "stronger in myself" as a result of being in school.

Only one participant expressed negative self-perceptions. Susan indicated she feels "really disorganized" and is experiencing "a lot of self-doubt." She added that she hoped she could finish the interview "without crying." Perhaps Susan's negative feelings are related in part to her first-year status; several of the other women also discussed feeling less sure of themselves when they first entered their programs. The gamut of emotions was observed in each of the participants both informally, while they attended school, and during the interview process.

DISCUSSION

This study adds new information to the growing body of literature on reentry women and illustrates the usefulness of the qualitative case-study method in studying women's issues. One obvious advantage of the case-study method in studying women is the opportunity it affords to use the words and behavior of those actually experiencing a situation to achieve a description of that experience. This is a much richer source of information than can be achieved through traditional quantitative methods. Identifying themes from these data provides a grounded basis for identifying areas of particular salience to women. This information is useful in developing greater understanding of women, in identifying the needs of women in different contexts, and in prioritizing research in women's issues. The persons experiencing the situations, rather than researchers, provide their view of reality. Researchers can then use these relatively unstructured data to generate themes of importance. Though there was some variation in responses among the four participants (i.e., individuals described some unique experiences), the focus of analysis was on the identification of common themes that emerged from the data. The description of similarities increases the likelihood that others may be able to relate to the findings and apply them to their particular contexts.

Most published studies of reentry women have been quantitative studies of undergraduates (Padula, 1994). This case study provides a description of issues and experiences of graduate reentry women who were living with husbands and children while attending school full time. These data suggest that reentry graduate women experience intense emotions about returning to school. In addition, the decision to return to school is difficult, often made over a long period of time after carefully considering potential ramifications. Both negative and positive self-perceptions and a myriad of difficulties for women living with spouses and children are experienced. The findings also suggest that, though faculty in graduate programs have the potential for playing a significant role in these women's lives, they frequently did not. In fact, the reentry women who desired mentors did not feel they had them. This could be attributed to the reentry women themselves, the educational institution, or the faculty with whom they studied. Perhaps faculty in a major research university have less time or inclination to mentor students. Perhaps reentry women, because of their age and life experiences, expect a greater level of faculty interaction than is reasonable. Further study will be necessary to determine whether other graduate reentry women share this frustration about the role of faculty.

This study deliberately focused on full-time graduate reentry women in heterosexual relationships who were living with their spouses and children. This is an advantage in providing an in-depth look at a specific population, but a disadvantage in providing generalizable information or more detailed information about other populations. We believe that the findings of this study can be applicable to both graduate and undergraduate reentry women. For instance, Klasek (1995) interviewed graduate and undergraduate women about their reentry experiences and found remarkably similar results. Klasek's participants agonized over the decision to return to school for as long as 3 to 4 years. They expressed fear about grades and competing with younger students. Klasek noted other findings similar to ours, including the frustration of too little time, a sense of urgency, the need to sacrifice, and the rewards of skill building, career growth, and increased self-confidence. In another qualitative case-study exploring adult learner perceptions of issues on the college reentry experience, Sookram (1997) identified controlling stress, finding and managing time, maintaining home and grades, dealing with unexpected life circumstances, and making sacrifices as the greatest challenges for the undergraduate women participants in her study.

A number of questions are raised by this study. (a) What makes women reentry students persist, especially when their educational and relational expectations are not met? To what degree do the rewards outweigh the frustrations? (b) How many and what kind of sacrifices do women reentry students make to return to school and at what price to their jobs, families, and health? (c) What survival skills do reentry women develop to assist them in getting through the system and in dealing with the stress of multiple demands/roles? (d) How can reentry women be better prepared for academic challenges and to deal with their fears associated with competition for grades, particularly with younger students? (e) How can institutions better serve reentry women and understand the unique demands placed on them by multiple roles? (f) In the end, what difference does the degree make in their career progression? These questions reflect the potential extent and variation of future research on reentry women's experiences.

This study has several implications for various audiences. Reentry women need to be given the opportunity to share their stories. Their experiences may inform women who are considering reentry and may develop greater support and collegiality among women students who have returned to school. Reentry women need to be clear about their goals in returning to school, realistic in their expectations (of themselves and school), and prepared for the sacrifices that completing an academic program will take. It is critical that reentry women find ways to manage the stress of multiple roles and demands. The reentry experience can be an important personal-growth opportunity, particularly in developing increased self-confidence.

Faculty who serve these students need to understand their fears, concerns, and special needs as nontraditional students. It is the role of faculty members to help reentry students be successful in their pursuit of academic goals. Faculty can have a positive impact on reentry women by providing a balance of challenge and support.

Institutions need to make the transition back to school as smooth as possible by having systems in place to welcome students, orient them, advise them, and track their progress. If institutions target reentry women as students, they must be prepared to assist them in meeting their academic goals.

This study underlines the importance of continuing to research women's reentry experiences. It also illustrates the advantages of using qualitative methods to better understand the experiences of reentry women. Given the increasing numbers of reentry women, additional research in this area is critical. Exploring the diverse experiences of reentry women is necessary in order to meet the psychological, personal, interpersonal, and professional needs of graduate reentry women. Additional qualitative studies of reentry women could include studies of women who are single, are single parents, are partnered but childless, live in nontraditional relationships, and have disabilities, to mention a few. An effective way to begin knowing these women is to hear their own descriptions of their experiences, as illustrated by this case-study, and then build on those descriptions. Using qualitative methods to refine those descriptions for additional quantitative study has the potential to produce more powerful and meaningful insight and understanding about women's lives and experiences.

Initial submission: November 27, 1996
Initial acceptance: April 3, 1997
Final acceptance: July 14, 1997

REFERENCES

Badenhoop, M. S., & Johansen, M. K. (1980). Do reentry women have special needs? *Psychology of Women Quarterly, 4,* 591–595.

Bogdan, R. C., & Biklen, S. K. (1992). *Qualitative research for education: An introduction to theory and methods.* Needham Heights, MA: Allyn & Bacon.

Borg, W., & Gall, M. D. (1989). *Educational research: An introduction.* New York: Longman.

Bradburn, E. M., Moen, P., & Dempster-McClain, D. (1995). Women's return to school following the transition to motherhood. *Social Forces, 73,* 1517–1551.

Clayton, D. E., & Smith, M. M. (1987). Motivational typology of reentry women. *Adult Education Quarterly, 37,* 90–104.

Constas, M. A. (1992). Qualitative analysis as a public event: The documentation of category development procedures. *American Educational Research Journal, 29,* 253–266.

Creswell, J. W. (1994). *Research design: Qualitative and quantitative approaches.* Thousand Oaks, CA: Sage.

Eisner, E. W. (1991). *The enlightened eye: Qualitative inquiry and the enhancement of educational practice.* New York: Macmillan.

Fraenkel, J. R., & Wallen, N. E. (1990). *How to design and evaluate research in education.* New York: McGraw-Hill.

Gilbert, L., Manning, L., & Ponder, M. (1980). Conflicts with the student role: A comparison of female and male reentry students. *Journal of the National Association for Women Deans, Administrators and Counselors, 44*(1), 26–32.

Glesne, C., & Peshkin, A. (1992). *Becoming qualitative researchers: An introduction.* White Plains, NY: Longman.

Kinnier, R., & Townley, J. (1986). Major values conflicts of young reentry graduate students. *Guidance and Counseling, 1*(3), 16–21.

Kirk, C. F., & Dorfman, L. T. (1983). Satisfaction and role strain among middle-age and older reentry women students. *Educational Gerontology, 9,* 15–29.

Klasek, A. O. (1995). *Experiences of reentry women in higher education: A multiple case study.* Unpublished master's thesis, Doane College, Lincoln, NE.

Lewis, L. H. (Ed.) (1988). *Addressing the needs of returning women.* San Francisco: Jossey-Bass.

Lincoln, Y. S., & Guba, E. G. (1985). *Naturalistic inquiry.* Newbury Park, CA: Sage.

Locke, L. F., Spirduso, W. W., & Silverman, S. J. (1987). *Proposals that work: A guide for planning dissertations and grant proposals.* Newbury Park, CA: Sage.

MacKinnon-Slaney, F., Barber, S. L., & Slaney, R. B. (1988). Marital status as a mediating factor on the career aspirations of re-entry female students. *Journal of College Student Development, 29,* 327–334.

Marshall, C., & Rossman, G. B. (1989). *Designing qualitative research.* Newbury Park, CA: Sage.

Merriam, S. B. (1988). *Case study research in education: A qualitative approach.* San Francisco: Jossey-Bass.

Miles, M. B., & Huberman, A. M. (1994). *An expanded source book: Qualitative data analysis.* Thousand Oaks, CA: Sage.

Padula, M. A. (1994). Reentry women: A literature review with recommendations for counseling and research. *Journal of Counseling and Development, 73,* 10–16.

Petersen, R. P. (1991, Spring). Reentry women: Implications for adult education. *Delta Kappa Gamma Bulletin, 57,* 41–52.

Pickering, G. S., & Galvin-Schaefers, K. (1988). An empirical study of reentry women. *Journal of Counseling Psychology, 35,* 298–303.

Read, N. O., Elliott, M. R., Escobar, M. D., & Slaney, R. B. (1988). The effects of marital status and motherhood on the career concerns of reentry women. *Career Development Quarterly, 37,* 46–55.

Reinharz, S. (1992). *Feminist methods in social research.* New York: Oxford University Press.

Rifenbary, D. (1995). Reentering the academy: The voices of returning women students. *Initiatives, 56*(4), 1–10.

Schumacher, S., & McMillan, J. H. (1993). *Research in education: A conceptual introduction.* New York: HarperCollins.

Sewall, T. J. (1984). A study of adult undergraduates: What causes them to seek a degree? *Journal of College Student Personnel, 25,* 309–314.

Smart, J. C., & Pascarella, E. T. (1987). Influences on the intention to reenter higher education. *Journal of Higher Education, 58,* 306–322.

Sookram, K. B. (1997). *Adult learner perceptions of issues related to the college reentry experience: A case study.* Unpublished doctoral dissertation, University of Nebraska at Lincoln.

Spradley, J. P. (1980). *Participant observation.* New York: Holt, Rinehart & Winston.

Stake, R. E. (1995). *The art of case study research.* Thousand Oaks, CA: Sage.

U.S. Department of Commerce, Bureau of the Census. (1990). *School enrollment—Social and economic characteristics of students: October 1988 and 1987* (Series P-20, No. 443). Washington, DC: U.S. Government Printing Office.

U.S. Department of Commerce, Bureau of the Census. (1994). *School enrollment—Social and economic characteristics of students: October 1993* (Series P-20, No. 479). Washington, DC: U.S. Government Printing Office.

U.S. Department of Education, Office of Educational Research and Improvement. (1990). *Projections of education statistics to 2001: An update* (NCES 91-683). Washington, DC: U.S. Government Printing Office.

Yin, R. K. (1989). *Case study research: Design and methods* (rev. ed.). Newbury Park, CA: Sage.

APPENDIX: INTERVIEW QUESTIONS

1. Tell me about your decision to return to school.
2. Tell me what the experience of returning to school has been like for you.
3. Could you tell me about aspects of this experience that have been frustrating or difficult for you?

4. Tell me about the kinds of things that really make school worthwhile or exciting for you.
5. How is the whole reentry experience impacting you?
6. What factors have contributed to your personal and professional development since returning to school?
7. What role has the faculty played in your experience?
8. Where are you going when you finish school?

COMMENTS ON "UNDERSTANDING GRADUATE WOMEN'S REENTRY EXPERIENCES"

Bernice Lott
University of Rhode Island

Psychologists have, once again, begun to pay attention to qualitative methods, to ways of gathering information that do not lend themselves easily to quantitative summaries or statistical analyses. For those of us who attended graduate school in the 1950s, however, case studies and field studies are familiar methods that were presented as respectable alternatives to experiments and systematic observations (correlational and survey methods) when circumstances or conditions were most appropriate for their use. We were taught the importance of distinguishing between idiographic and nomothetic data and both were considered valuable. Within feminist psychology, qualitative methods are regarded by some as being *most appropriate* to gaining knowledge about women's lives and by others as equal in respectability and acceptability to, and *just as useful* as, quantitative methods. This debate was well summarized by Peplau and Conrad (1989).

I place myself within the group that believes that feminist psychology is most distinguishable from other theoretical frameworks not by its methods, but by its assumptions, the questions it raises about the meaning and construction of gender, its investigation of the antecedents and consequences of gender, and a commitment to using the knowledge we gain to improve women's lives. The fine article by Padula and Miller (1999) offers us a good example of case-study use and provides an opportunity to discuss issues relevant to this and other qualitative methods.

One issue that this article raised for me was that, although the method used was interesting, rich, and certainly replicable, there seemed to be little in what the investigators found that would not have been predicted from the considerable research on reentry students that has used quantitative methods (e.g., Ballmer & Cozby, 1981; Gerson, 1985; Quina & Kanarian, 1988). Thus, although the case study yields far more complete and more personal information of greater depth, the conclusions drawn from the data, at least in this study, are not all that different from those drawn from more quantitative investigations. These conclusions are

Address correspondence and reprint requests to: Bernice Lott, Department of Psychology, University of Rhode Island, Kingston, RI 02881. E-mail: berlott@uriacc.uri.edu.

that reentry women with spouses and children, whether undergraduate or graduate, "experience intense emotions about returning to school . . . [experience] the decision to return to school . . . [as] difficult . . . [and must deal with] a myriad of difficulties . . . living with spouses and children" (Padula & Miller, p. 339). Does this in-depth investigation of a very small group of reentry women graduate students in psychology in one university raise questions for further research that have not been raised by previous quantitative studies with larger, more heterogeneous samples? The reader is invited to consider this question after examining the "questions . . . raised by this study" presented by Padula and Miller (p. 340).

Another issue that needs to be considered is one raised by Padula and Miller who note (p. 333) that in qualitative research there is a need "to address concerns about researcher subjectivity/bias." As many have now pointed out, this is necessary in quantitative research as well. Because most quantitative researchers ignore this while qualitative researchers invariably raise this point, we are led to expect that the latter will practice what they preach. In the Padula and Miller research, the primary investigator was a graduate student, and the case-study participants were her peers. She was thus doing what anthropologists call "participant observation." In what ways did her own experiences within the graduate department, as well as her personal relationship with each participant and her attitudes and beliefs about them, influence what participants said and how their statements were perceived and interpreted by the investigator?

There is considerable room for investigator bias in the process of taking what respondents have said and subjecting their words to "revision, elaboration, or deletion" (Padula & Miller, p. 332) in order to code the content and identify themes. This is not to say that investigator values, experience, expectations, and so on are not always factors to be considered in any research. But qualitative researchers face the special problem of not being able to give as clear and detailed a description of their procedures and analyses as other researchers, making replicability problematic.

An interesting paradox or irony raised for me by the Padula and Miller article is that, although qualitative research is best suited to studying the richness of individual experience, the first two drafts of the research report of their case studies ignored the issue of variation in responses among the four informants. The reader is told how many of the informants mentioned each of the themes identified by the investigators, but there are some important remaining questions. For example, were there differences in the salience or importance of themes? Were there "outlier" concerns, issues mentioned by just one participant? It appears as though it is still the "central tendency" that the researcher tends to look for—in both qualitative studies (as represented by the Padula and Miller research) and quantitative ones.

Finally, I want to raise the question of how feminist psychology regards, or might regard, reported personal experience as a source of information about women's lives. Elsewhere (Lott, 1997), I have noted that the results of studies illustrating the "eye of the beholder" phenomenon (e.g., Karraker, Vogel, & Lake, 1995; Rubin, Provensano, & Luria, 1974) reveal that parents of a newborn girl tend to "see" her as finer featured, less strong, more delicate, and more feminine than the parents of a newborn son "see" him. We have no reason to question the authenticity of the parents' reports. Yet, these data clearly illustrate how gender stereotypes affect our perceptions. That gender beliefs permeate and intersect with "experience" would seem to be an obvious proposition that most psychologists would accept; at the same time, however, it must give us pause to recognize that experience is "already an interpretation," that it cannot be taken "as a given" or located simply in the individual (Scott, 1992, as cited by Markens, 1996).

I raise this point not to question the validity of qualitative research but to suggest that each of the ways we have thus far devised of gaining knowledge about ourselves and the world around us presents important epistemological problems. Raising the questions and attempting to answer them should help us understand that a multimethod approach is the best strategy, and, indeed, a necessary one.

REFERENCES

Ballmer, H., & Cozby, P. C. (1981). Family environments of women who return to college. *Sex Roles*, *7*, 1019–1026.

Gerson, J. (1985). Women returning to school: The consequences of multiple roles. *Sex Roles*, *13*, 77–92.

Karraker, K. H., Vogel, D. A., & Lake, M. A. (1995). Parent's gender-stereotyped perceptions of newborns: The eye of the beholder revisited. *Sex Roles*, *33*, 687–701.

Lott, B. (1997). The personal and social correlates of a gender difference ideology. *Journal of Social Issues*, *53*, 279–297.

Markens, S. (1996). The problematic of "experience." A political and cultural critique of PMS. *Gender & Society*, *10*, 42–58.

Padula, M. A., & Miller, D. L. (1999). Understanding graduate women's reentry experiences: Case studies of four psychology doctoral students in a Midwestern university. *Psychology of Women Quarterly*, *23*, 327–343.

Peplau, L. A., & Conrad, E. (1989). Beyond nonsexist research: The perils of feminist methods in psychology. *Psychology of Women Quarterly*, *13*, 379–400.

Quina, K., & Kanarian (Zahm), M. A. (1988). Continuing education. In P. A. Bronstein & K. Quina (Eds.) *Teaching a psychology of people* (pp. 200–208). Washington, DC: American Psychological Association.

Rubin, J. Z., Provenzano, F. J., & Luria, Z. (1974). The eye of the beholder: Parents' views on sex of newborns. *American Journal of Orthopsychiatry*, *44*, 512–519.

SUBJECT TO ROMANCE

Heterosexual Passivity as an Obstacle to Women Initiating Condom Use

Nicola Gavey and Kathryn Mcphillips
University of Auckland

Safer sex campaigns directed at heterosexuals have increasingly targeted women to encourage them to take responsibility for condom use. It appears, however, that many women are unable or unwilling to accept this role. In this article we report on one particular kind of obstacle that some women face in initiating condom use. We draw on data from interviews with 14 women, aged 22 to 43 years, about their experiences with, and views of, condoms. There was considerable variability, as well as commonalities, among the women interviewed in the way they regarded condoms. Using a feminist poststructuralist form of discourse analysis, we explored two women's accounts of being unable to initiate condom use despite their stated intentions not to have intercourse without a condom and having condoms in their possession. We suggest that this particular dynamic results from the passivity women can experience through being positioned in a discourse of heterosexual feminine sexuality in general and a discourse of heterosexual romance in particular. We discuss how this passivity can be experienced by

Kathryn McPhillips is now Clinical Manager, Auckland HELP Foundation, P.O. Box 10345, Dominion Road, Auckland, New Zealand.

This research was supported, in part, by grants from the Health Research Council of New Zealand and the University of Auckland Research Committee. Parts of this research have been presented previously at the Annual Meeting of the Society for the Scientific Study of Sex, Miami, Florida, 1994; the New Zealand Psychological Society Conference, Wellington, 1993; the AIDS Committee of the Health Research Council of New Zealand, Wellington, 1993; and a Women in Health Research Network meeting, Auckland, 1993.

We thank members of the University of Auckland Psychology Discourse Research Unit (Alison Towns, Fiona Cram, Kate Paulin, Peter Adams, Ray Nairn, and Tim McCreanor) for support and critical feedback on an earlier draft of this article and our friend (nameless, to protect participants' anonymity) for help with recruitment of participants.

Address correspondence and reprint requests to: Nicola Gavey, Department of Psychology, University of Auckland, Private Bag 92019, Auckland, New Zealand. E-mail: n.gavey@auckland.ac.nz.

347

women who are otherwise assertive and committed to sexual equality, making it confusing and disconcerting for them and others.

With the heterosexual transmission of HIV well established (e.g., Gavey & McPhillips, 1997), women have become a prime new target for condom promotions. Social scientists have advocated that women should be encouraged to take responsibility for condom use, because it is perceived that women are less resistant to using condoms than are men (e.g., Barling & Moore, 1990; Chapman & Hodgson, 1988). Indeed, condom manufacturers have wasted no time in targeting their products to this new market (Gamson, 1990; Hoffman, 1987). Despite this attention, however, it has been consistently found around the world that many women, as well as men, resist using condoms.

The difficulties that women may face in taking on the responsibility for condom use have been acknowledged by many writers. However, these difficulties have generally been formulated in terms of the practical issues involved in persuading male partners to use a condom. The most frequently proffered solution is that of teaching willing women how to assertively negotiate the use of a condom with a reluctant male partner. But what if the woman is unwilling or if her inability to initiate condom use arises from constraints other than an apparent lack of assertiveness skills? Some feminist researchers have indicated that a simple call to assertiveness has its limitations. For example:

> Interventions such as, "If it's not on, it's not on," which target females to encourage them to take the initiative in condom use may be too cynical, and do not address young women's real concerns that such behavior leads to interference in the relationship with a partner. (Moore & Rosenthal, 1991, p. 223)

Nevertheless, even this recognition of some of the relational complexities involved leaves open the question of whether women themselves are willing, albeit not always successful, agents in the deployment of condoms. That is, are women's own relationships to condoms as unproblematic as is implied by the new targeting? We suggest there are at least four kinds of factors that can work against women wanting to or being able to initiate condom use with a male partner.

First, as has been recognized by many feminist writers, not all women have enough power and control in their heterosexual relationships to be able to determine whether or not their partner wears a condom (e.g., Gavey, McPhillips, & Doherty, 1999; see also Gavey, 1992). Second, there are various characteristics of condoms and the effects they have on sexual practice that women themselves do not like, leading them to reject condom use for reasons to do with their own pleasures and desires (Gavey et al., 1999). Third, condomless sexual intercourse can signify important meanings such as trust, commitment, and "true love" within relationships (Holland, Ramazanoglu, Scott, Sharpe, & Thomson, 1991; Kippax, Crawford, Waldby, & Benton, 1990; Willig, 1994; Worth, 1989; see also Hollway, 1989), which some women may regard as more important than seemingly remote health risks. In our research on women's experiences with and views about condoms, we identified a fourth kind of dynamic that seemed to render some women unwilling and/or unable to introduce a condom despite being in a situation in which they perceived health risks and were carrying condoms at the time. Although the constraints on these women were related to women's lack of control in heterosexual relationships, to women's own dislikes about condoms, and to the symbolic meanings of condoms, there was another level of resistance from these women which was not reducible to these factors alone. It took the form of an inexplicable inability to act—a sort of unchosen but inescapable passivity that paralyzed them at the necessary moment.

In this article we focus on this fourth sort of obstacle and explore some of the subtle discursive processes that can induce a passivity in some women leaving them unable or unwilling to act upon their own intentions or self-imposed rules to use a condom. First, we consider a typical model used to understand the rational decision making involved in people's health-risk and health-promotion behaviors. We then suggest that a limitation of this model and others like it lies in their assumption of a coherent rational self-contained individual. Instead, we adopt a poststructuralist concept of the discursively constituted subject. We argue that this concept allows us to better explain apparently contradictory behavior and to understand the ways in which it is socially produced. We will then present feminist poststructuralist discursive analyses that attempt to make sense of two women's narratives about not using a condom in situations in which they thought they should have.

THE SELF-CONTAINED INDIVIDUAL OR THE DISCURSIVELY CONSTITUTED SUBJECT?

In the field of health psychology, several models have been developed to predict people's decisions and actions related to reducing their health risks. The health belief model (see Janz & Becker, 1984) is typical of these and has been used to predict health protective behaviors like using condoms. According to the health belief model, a woman is more likely to insist that her male partner use a condom if (a) she believes herself to be personally susceptible to HIV exposure, (b) she believes the consequences of such exposure are severe, (c) she believes condom use is effective in preventing HIV transmission, and (d) she perceives few barriers to using condoms (Hingson, Strunin, Berlin, & Heren, 1990). From the perspective of this and similar models, once a woman has these beliefs and perceptions, all that is required is assertive behavior on her part if her partner shows a reluctance to use a condom. Such models of health-risk behavior give the impression that change can occur at the level of rational cognitive processes (in terms of beliefs and attitudes) and skills (such as assertiveness).

Imagine a woman who believes there is a risk of contracting HIV through having sexual intercourse without a condom with a particular man, who believes this would have severe consequences, and who believes condoms afford some protection. In a situation where her male partner does not produce a condom, rational decision-making models could account for her not insisting on a condom through proposing that she perceives barriers to condom use or that she is not sufficiently assertive to initiate condom use. Perceived barriers may relate to reduction of her own sexual pleasure or to the expectation that her partner will respond negatively.

However, are these factors sufficient to explain the complex and contradictory behavior of nonuse for a woman who expresses strong views about the importance of using condoms? On the other hand, postulating a lack of assertiveness (assuming the male partner is not abusive or coercive) implies that the woman unambivalently wants to use a condom, but simply lacks the skills to make this happen. Talking to women about condoms has led us to question whether decision making is always so straightforward.

We suggest that the explanatory value of such rational decision-making models is limited by assumptions of a rational self-contained individual whose desires, motivations, and interests are unitary and coherent. Instead, we propose that a poststructuralist concept of a discursively constituted subject may be helpful for making sense of how a woman could act against her intentions in ways that sacrifice her own health interests. The poststructuralist move clarifies how the rationality of decisions about health protection might be contained in ways that allow its impact on behavior to be overshadowed by less well understood and possibly unarticulated discursive factors.

In a Foucauldian sense, the subject is determined by multiple discourses, creating subjectivity that is rich and complex, yet fragmentary and contradictory. Here, discourse refers to "a system of statements which cohere around common meanings and values" that "are a product of social factors, of powers and practices, rather than an individual's set of ideas" (Hollway, 1983, p. 231). Although the term can be used in a way that is similar to a "set of assumptions" (Hollway, 1983, p. 231), the concept of discourse has radical implications beyond what this would suggest: "Discourses are more than ways of thinking and producing meaning. They constitute the 'nature' of the body, unconscious and conscious mind and emotional life of the subjects which they seek to govern" (Weedon, 1987, p. 108). While all discourses offer subject positions that suggest particular ways of being in and experiencing the world, they vary in their accessibility and power. Those discourses that are commensurate with widely shared commonsense understandings of the world are perhaps most powerful in constituting subjectivity, yet their influence can most easily remain hidden and difficult to identify and, therefore, to resist. At the same time, other discursive influences can generate different expectations, understandings, and so on, which may result in inconsistent, even contradictory, experiences.

We suggest that women and men are more likely to actively and self-consciously adopt positions in relation to oppositional discourses (such as feminism) and discourses that espouse new cultural ideals (such as the call to safer sex). For example, they may choose to adhere to or reject new norms or to express an explicit ambivalence about them. By comparison, the influence of more traditional cultural assumptions, patterns, and practices may be almost invisible. Such dominant discourses may position us in various ways without us even knowing it. For example, a woman's heterosexual identity could be largely comprised of ways of thinking about and experiencing herself in her sexual relationship that are consistent with dominant discourses on heterosexuality and women's sexuality, yet she may be unaware of how she has been socially produced in these ways because they exist at the level of taken-for-granted norms within a culture. Despite this, she may be very aware of those ways in which she attempts to carve an identity in opposition to those aspects of heterosexuality that she has identified and critiqued. For example, inspired by popularized feminist discourses about women's rights to sexual pleasure, she (and her partner) may deliberately strive for equality under the guise of mutuality and reciprocal (physical) pleasure. Nevertheless, it may be more difficult to recognize and resist other forms of normal(izing) practice—for example, the male sexual drive discourse (Hollway, 1984, 1989) and the coital imperative which together function to ensure that penis–vagina penetration is a necessary part of "real" sex for heterosexuals. Arguably, part of the reason for this is that critiques of the regulatory function of the coital imperative, in particular, are not yet well established or widely available.

This way of thinking about identity and social action differs in important ways from both commonsense Western notions of the individual and conventional psychological concepts of the self. It disposes with the assumption of a unique essential core self and deconstructs the social–individual dualism implicit in psychology. Poststructuralism holds that people are always already social and that the "individual" cannot be understood apart from social and cultural contexts (see Henriques, Hollway, Urwin, Venn, & Walkerdine, 1984). In these ways, it is different from humanist models which accept that an individual's actions may be incongruent with her or his "true" desires, for example.

In this article we use a form of discourse analysis which draws on feminist analyses of heterosexuality and Foucauldian theory to identify discursive forces that could be partially constitutive of a woman's ways of seeing and her choices for acting in the heterosexual moment. In doing so we are seeking to locate sociocultural determinants of apparently contradictory acts in relation to women's condom use.

THE ANALYTIC APPROACH

Discourse analysis refers to a wide range of analytic styles that are not always compatible. As Hollway (1989) noted, "the term has come to cover virtually any approach which analyzes text, from cognitive linguistics to deconstruction" (p. 53). Writers associated with the development of discourse analysis in social psychology have been careful to introduce it as a "method" quite different from the positivist methods of most psychological research (e.g., Hollway, 1989; Parker, 1992; Potter & Wetherell, 1987). It has been developed within psychology in conjunction with critiques of conventional research practice, with the exploration of new epistemological terrain, and with a critical political edge (although these features are not intrinsic to discourse analysis [Burman, 1991; Gill, 1995]). Consequently, there is often a wariness about presenting discourse analysis as a "value-free technology" (Parker & Burman, 1993, p. 162), which can be "absorbed by the discipline as just yet one more 'method' in its armoury" (Burman & Parker, 1993, p. 10). It is not surprising, therefore, that guidelines for how to do discourse analysis or how to identify discourses tend to be suggestive and open ended rather than prescriptive and formulaic (e.g., Parker, 1992; Potter & Wetherell, 1987).

As with all methods, the different approaches to discourse analysis are inextricably located within particular theoretical perspectives, such that the method of doing research cannot be explained in a way that is divorced from the theory. One important philosophical difference between the sort of methodology used here and conventional methodology in psychology is its epistemological starting point. Our research arises out of a postmodern acceptance of the impossibility of foundational knowledge (e.g., Gergen, 1990; Hare-Mustin & Marecek, 1988; Lather, 1991). It does not attempt to generate reliable new facts, but rather to generate new ways of making sense of the "ordinary but troubling." In this way, it is "a type of 'passionately interested inquiry'" (Gill, 1995, p. 175), which is fueled by a pragmatic (see Squire, 1995) or neopragmatic (see Polkinghorne, 1992) desire to produce knowledge that can contribute to social change.

The style of discourse analysis we use here is influenced by feminist poststructuralist theory and draws on the Foucauldian concepts of discourse and subjectivity briefly introduced earlier. In identifying discursive influences in a woman's narrative we aim to develop analyses that contextualize her experience and show how it may be constituted in relation to broader sociocultural patterns of meaning and practice (see Weedon, 1987). In doing so, we hope to disrupt taken-for-granted and normalizing assumptions about the way things are and thus highlight areas for potential resistance and change. This deconstructive impulse is another important feature of this style of analysis.

Our analyses pay attention both to the language of the women's narratives as a route into theorizing the discursive context which may shape choices a woman has, as well as to what we were told about the material context in which she was acting. We would argue that the material details of a woman's experience—such as the nature and history of a heterosexual relationship and the outcomes of previous sexual experiences—are also essential "data" for developing a feminist reading of these women's accounts. In some discourse analytic approaches, these extratextual factors are considered irrelevant or impossible to take into consideration given that the analyst has only mediated access to such material. However, although we recognize the impossibility of obtaining a "true account" of what happened, we contend that some appreciation of relevant aspects in the broader context of a woman's life is necessary for developing an analysis that takes gendered power seriously (see also Gill, 1995). Moreover, as Wetherell (1995) has suggested, to make "a strong ontological distinction between the discursive and the extradiscursive is a mistake, both methodologically and epistemologically" (p. 140). A feminist poststructuralist form of discourse analysis tends to accept that the text to be analyzed is broader and more diffuse than just the words of a transcript written on the page.

METHOD FOR THE STUDY

In-depth interviews were conducted by the first author with 14 predominantly Pakeha[1] women (two women had mixed ethnic backgrounds, but primarily identified as Pakeha). The women's ages ranged from 22 to 43 years; 12 of the women were between 27 and 37 years old. They all had experience of heterosexual relationships and at least some experience with condoms. The women were recruited through word of mouth and included five women known to the interviewer through work contacts, three women who were friends or family members of colleagues, and six women who were recruited by word of mouth by a friend we employed to find women interested in talking about this personal subject. All participants either chose or were given pseudonyms to protect their anonymity.

Interviews were semistructured to the extent that all women were questioned about the same broad range of topics, including: their past and current experiences with condoms, their heterosexual relationships and practices more generally (where relevant), their personal views of condoms, and how they thought others regarded condoms. An interview schedule was used as a guide, although the style of the interviews was more conversational than a question–answer format. The aim was to facilitate open, detailed, and reflexive discussion rather than circumscribed answers to predetermined questions. Discussion was allowed to flow on and develop according to interviewee responses, but was directed by the interviewer so that all areas of interest previously determined by the researchers were covered. Another feature of the interview style was that the interviewer sometimes shared her own observations and rudimentary analytic reflections with the participant during the interview process and sought the participant's response to these reflections. In general, we have found that giving participants the opportunity to respond to analytic ideas as they evolve during the research is useful in at least two ways. It can work as an interview technique to promote additional reflection by the interview participant and to generate productive discussion in areas that we might not otherwise have reached. It also helps to enrich and refine the process of our analysis and to strengthen our confidence in some thematic directions while dispensing with others. However, although we acknowledge that accounts are to some extent always constructed through the interview process, detailed exploration of participants' accounts of their experiences and views always takes precedence. Furthermore, we believe that the success of this interactive style of interviewing is dependent on creating an interview environment in which the participant is able to openly disagree with the interviewer.

Most interviews lasted between 1 and 1½ hours long. All interviews were fully transcribed.

We now present feminist discursive analyses of two case examples in an attempt to generate more nuanced understandings of the complexities that may exist for some women considering condom use.

ANALYSES

Despite our small and relatively homogenous sample (i.e., most participants were articulate, middle class, Pakeha, with tertiary education), there was considerable variability in the women's experiences and accounts. Clearly, this study will not provide findings that give a picture of how women in general regard condoms. Although some women appeared to have relatively unproblematic relationships to condoms, we were particularly interested in understanding more about some of the problems that some women do experience with them.

Woman's Passivity in a Discourse of Romance

In this section we will present a detailed exploration of one woman's experiences of being rendered unable to act out her explicit intentions to use a condom. We suggest that this example shows the power of a discourse of heterosexual romance to strongly influence the behavior of a woman who in many ways consciously rejected any appeal to romance.

Christine

Christine is a professional Pakeha woman who was in her mid to late thirties at the time of the interview. She had been in an 8-year long heterosexual relationship until 3 years prior to the interview, when this relationship had ended. She was therefore one of a number of women who had come out of a long-term relationship "post-AIDS," as she described it, which "changes everything" in terms of "safe sex stuff." (Although condoms have a dual role as barriers against disease and unwanted conception, Christine was typical of New Zealand women of her generation, for whom condoms have not been a popular method of contraception.) After her 8-year relationship Christine was single for 5 months and then started another heterosexual relationship which lasted 2 years and ended approximately 6 months prior to our interview.

Christine said she didn't like condoms and hadn't used them in the 2-year relationship with Rick or in a one-night stand she had had with another man, Craig, in recent months. During our interview, she frequently berated herself for being "bad" and "stupid" and it being "ridiculous," "dumb," "terrible," and "embarrassing" not to have used condoms in these circumstances. She said that her friend Donna "is vehement, you know, that this is really stupid. And, um, that I have to get my act together." Researchers using some strands of discourse analysis might be skeptical about the meaning of such statements, perhaps suggesting that they reflect nothing more than the implicit self-presentation demands of an interview about condoms (e.g., Widdicombe, 1995). We agree that a focus on the function of such statements in the specific interactional context of the interview is a necessary consideration. However, a person's ways of speaking in an interview are resources that are likely to be drawn on in other social situations, and are illustrative of how she or he is discursively positioned. We would argue that, even if the interview situation enhanced the strength of Christine's expressed opinion about condom use being sensible and necessary in these times, it was nevertheless a perspective that was a part of her identity (as was further supported by her reported action of obtaining condoms for the occasion under discussion). The fact that she could strongly endorse this position and yet have equally strong but unarticulated contradictory responses is not surprising given a poststructuralist understanding of subjectivity (e.g., Weedon, 1987).

Given the strength of Christine's feeling about the rightness of using condoms, what was preventing her from using them? She said that she had never liked them, but she hadn't actually used them since she was a teenager—approximately 20 years prior. As Christine said: "So I've got these antiquated attitudes from the seventies, and I've carried them through to the nineties." However, this hadn't stopped her from taking the issue of "safe sex" seriously at some rational level, discussing it with her friends, and obtaining a condom from one friend on the night that her 2-year relationship first started. What follows is the part of the interview in which Christine tells the story of that first night she had sexual intercourse with Rick:

> *Christine:* Well it was funny because (laughing), I went to his place for dinner- you
> know, we'd sort of met a few times and stuff like that, and he invited me

over for dinner. And I thought you know, I might end up staying the night. So I, I (laughing) got a condom from Donna, 'cause she's the expert on the things. And then I did stay the night and I didn't use it. And I didn't even raise the issue.

Nicola: So what happened?

Christine: So isn't that disgusting.

Nicola: So- . . . this was a guy that you knew, but you hadn't had any sort of sexual relationship with. But it was kind of obvious to you that there was some sort of mutual attraction or something?

Christine: Yeah, so I mean it was kind of like- it was almost like planned that we would spend the night together. It wasn't really planned, but it was obviously a possibility. It was a conscious possibility in my head. I mean I prepared for it. I went and got- you know, I got- . . . I had a condom. Which I just got from my (laughing) friend. And um-

Nicola: Why- What had actually led you to get the condoms? What- I mean what-

Christine: I guess that kind of whole AIDS thing and being aware of the fact that it wasn't- you know, it's not the same as it was in the old days.

Nicola: So you had this idea in your head that if you- since AIDS you should- when you-

Christine: That they think that was more important, yeah. That it sort of changes things in terms of safe sex stuff.- But you know I mean I basically think my attitude to condoms is sort of ah- because I'm a product of- a product of the sort of generation I come from.- I mean that's just sort of partly a kind of um- well not an attitude to condoms so much as that sort of inability to actually do it (laughing) when it came to it. It's tied up with kind of um not finding it easy to talk about sex anyway generally, you know. And not finding it easy to kind of just bring up the subject and be overt about it.

Although Christine's memory of the night was only somewhat clear, she did recall:

I do remember being um- (pause) being kind of shocked that Rick didn't think about it either. Or didn't bring it up either. And in fact we talked about it later and he had done more or less the same as I'd done. Like he'd thought about it and he did have condoms but neither of us had actually articulated it.

The next day they talked about the fact that they hadn't used condoms, and "I think we both agreed" that "that's pretty sort of stupid" and that "in this day and age . . . you know you shouldn't do that kind of thing." They never did use condoms in the relationship, however, which continued for 2 years. Christine later said:

Well it s ridiculous to take those kind of risks and be- but it is- it seems to me, it's just tied up with um (pause) kind of generational thing and kind of uptightness or you know, lack of openness about sex and- yeah.

Christine later said that she thought it would be easier to use condoms in a "one-night stand," because "maybe it is just much more overtly about sex or something." We then began to explore Christine's views on the possible differences between using a condom during a one-night stand and with a man she envisioned potentially having a relationship with:

Christine: You know . . . it seems to me, a lot of younger [people] can- are a lot more pragmatic about sex. There's less confusion. You know. Less of that kind of um- they've been- they've grown up with less of that kind of expect- or that kind of combination of love/romance/sex kind of thing. And it- suppose a condoms are very unromantic, aren't they. So that's probably the way I'd see it. Yeah. . . .

Nicola: So that for you . . . would mean, say in some imaginary scenario, with this kind of fantasy (laughing) man, for you to bring up the condom would be somehow um marring the kind of romantic um- kind of whole narrative of it- the sort of-

Christine: Yeah

Nicola: sense of- your vi- your kind of idea of . . . how things like that work-

Christine: Yeah

Nicola: -in a kind of ideal sense?

Christine: Yeah. I think that's what it is. (pause) How do I fight that one? (laughing) Just have to um- I mean I know (unclear) it's not like that.

She was then asked:

Nicola: . . . is there a kind of particular way that these things- that in your experience that sex happens? You know. When there's two people together for the first time.

Christine: It's really quite hard for me to answer that. . . . I guess that kind of experience where it wasn't really articulated but it's probably just kind of let it happen type of thing. That's probably my common feelings about it. Well, from what I can remember.

Nicola: Is that what happened with Rick?

Christine: Yeah, I guess so, yeah.

Nicola: So he would've sort of made some kind of-

Christine: Yeah

Nicola: -move?

Christine: 'Cause me being the passive female he would've made some kind of move, and I- that's what- yeah that would've been, and how it started. (ironic tone)

Nicola: And you would've kind of responded to that, in the (laughing) "appropriate" way? (laughter)

Christine: Yeah, that pretty well probably sums it up.

Nicola: So-

Christine: Terrible eh.

During this part of the interview an analysis of the power of a narrative or discourse of romance was co-constructed:

Nicola: So . . . if in your experience, it often is kind of- like a man being quite- taking initiative and all that,

Christine: Yeah

Nicola:	and you're kind of following that in some way, um- I mean if you think of a narrative that's structured like that,
Christine:	Yeah
Nicola:	it's hard then for you to-
Christine:	To actually initiate-
Nicola:	Yeah, anything.
Christine:	Yeah, yeah.
Nicola:	Particularly something as kind of um- that has to be quite direct.
Christine:	Yeah
Nicola:	-relatively, compared to just sort of a subtle sort of thing,
Christine:	Yeah, right.
Nicola:	I suppose.
Christine:	Yeah, 'cause that sort of ties in with the way I looked at it. Like my thing that he didn't do it, either, you know what I mean?
Nicola:	Yeah.

We went on to discuss Rick's attitudes toward contraception and her ongoing anger with his not taking any responsibility because he believed it was women's responsibility. Christine then said:

Christine:	. . . Oh dear. So yeah, so I think I probably- was probably- and if I felt pissed off with him, um then that kind of ties into that idea of this narrative where a man's in charge,
Nicola:	Yeah.
Christine:	too, doesn't it?
Nicola:	Yeah.
Christine:	And he failed to take charge,
Nicola:	Yeah.
Christine:	In a way that was um very proper.

Our analysis of the processes operating to constrain Christine from using a condom started to be developed during the interview, with the help of Christine's own reflections. The preceding passage illustrates our approach to interviewing where there is not always a strict boundary between "data collection" and analysis. Through seeking clarification and sharing tentative analytic ideas with Christine, we started to formulate and develop a particular line of analysis during the interview itself. In this case it was co-constructed to the extent that ideas about the possible relevance of romantic discourse arose for the interviewer in the process of exploring and clarifying Christine's own account with her, and they were further developed with her input during discussion of these ideas in the interview.

We read Christine's account to suggest that she was positioned within a fairly conventional discourse of romance, which constituted her feminine sexuality as passive and responsive to her male partner's leads. Within this traditional discourse of romance, the man's role is to be in control of the situation in a chivalrous manner so that the woman can entrust herself to his protection. Moreover, a woman should rely on her lover's knowledge and skill and not be too explicit in expressing her desires (see Waldby, Kippax, & Crawford, 1993) and, presumably, her preference for safer sex.

When a woman and a man are not situated within the same discursive space, their conscious and unconscious desires and expectations about responsibility for themselves and their partner may not be compatible. Thus when Rick "failed to take charge in an appropriate manner," Christine was "unable" to act in a way that took charge of the situation, because in the discursive context in which their relationship was embedded for her only the male partner was authorized to take on this role. Ironically, Jackson (1993) has suggested that men are generally not aware of the complex aspects of conventions of romance. It could be assumed that Rick was positioned instead within a liberal permissive discourse (Hollway, 1984, 1989) which promotes equal sexual rights and responsibilities for women and men, but which from a feminist perspective may ignore differences between women and men that make its justness more illusory than real (Ryan & Gavey, 1998). Christine also subscribed to values of equality, which probably led her to share responsibility for a condom not being used. Indeed, this sort of process is likely to be particularly problematic for women like Christine who in most areas of their lives are strong and assertive, with feminist beliefs and expectations of equality within relationships.

We suggest that romantic discourse can shape the subjectivity of women so that their taken-for-granted expectations for how to be within a heterosexual relationship are powerfully determined in ways that may be contradictory with other areas of their life—possibly due to the private and therefore comparatively unexamined nature of sexual relationships. As Christine had noted, she found it difficult to talk about sex. Her experience within the intimate heterosexual situation was of acting in ways she did not understand. At some level she handed over responsibility to Rick, but she was unaware of doing so because it was not a deliberate choice but a discursively constituted and unconscious act that was required, taken for granted, but not usually explicit within contemporary incarnations of romantic discourse. Thus, when Rick did not assume the responsibility that was properly his within a romantic narrative she was unable at that moment to see what was happening clearly enough to work out what else she could do.

We contend that the political value of this sort of analysis lies in its function as cultural critique in making the invisible visible. Understanding how particular discourses constrain and enable certain ways of being and choices for acting is, hopefully, one of the first steps to resisting their constitutive power. Although this may be easier said than done for individual women and men constituted through these powerful discourses, broader social change can be promoted through the exposure of such discursive effects and the mobilization of alternative discursive possibilities.

Passive Passion

This next example is related to the preceding discussion on the discourse of romance in its focus on the possibility of a paralyzing passivity for women in heterosexual encounters. It explores the ease with which a woman could repeat a potentially dangerous pattern of having condomless sexual intercourse on a one-night stand, despite both her assessment of it being high risk and her having had traumatic consequences to a previous experience of unprotected sexual intercourse.

Michelle

Michelle is a professional Pakeha woman who was in her early to mid thirties at the time of the interview. She described an experience a few years earlier in which she had accidentally become pregnant on the first night she had sexual intercourse with a man with whom she went on to have a relationship. They had not used a condom or any other form of contraception. She said it was a:

> . . . terrible tragic mistake that could've been otherwise prohib- stopped. And yes I did regret that instance because that further on resulted in a terrible emotional abortion and all the related trauma that goes with it, and it's not something I particularly wish to experience again. But, interesting to- enough, I'm not any more cautious than I was.

The consequences of that occasion of sexual intercourse were clearly extremely painful for her. She said the pregnancy, with which she would have continued if her partner had been supportive, "destroyed" their relationship, and of having the abortion she said, "I probably would've thrown myself off the harbour bridge really, than having to confront myself on a moral issue again."

Against a backdrop of this experience and her knowledge about health risks associated with not using condoms, Michelle stated right at the beginning of the interview that:

> I would prefer to remain celibate than to have to use condoms. . . . . It's you either play by the new rules or you don't play at all. And definitely I feel that it- the condom thing has become a rule and if you don't wish to use them then you can't play.

However, she went on to talk about an experience approximately 8 weeks prior to the interview in which she had broken this self-imposed rule and had sexual intercourse with a man in a casual situation without using a condom. She explained that after a night on the town drinking with friend, she and a male friend had ended up "crashing" on the floor of somebody else's house. As she said, "it was the result of a very drunken leering night, where we'd ended up in the bed together and more I felt to sleep." Later she elaborated:

> *Michelle:* . . . we awoke in unison and proceeded to become intimate with one an-other. And it resulted in the, (clicks her fingers) "damn maybe you should've worn a condom," statement at the end of it and that was probably all the thought I gave to the matter. But certainly the awareness that that's what I should've been doing was there. It was more that, no I wasn't gonna participate in it.
>
> *Nicola:* In?
>
> *Michelle:* Well in getting up, (*Nicola:* Right) digging around for the packet of condoms in my handbag and-
>
> *Nicola:* . . . do you still remember what was going through your head at the time, like whether it was sort of- like when you said you proceeded to become intimate, um-
>
> *Michelle:* You mean did I decide at that point that I should go and get the condoms just in case this progresses on further?

Nicola:	Or- or anything like that, yeah.
Michelle:	No. (*Nicola:* Or-) No didn't enter my mind.
Nicola:	Or did you think, I am going to end up having sexual intercourse with this man, or-, when you started becoming intimate?
Michelle:	No. No, I didn't actually think it would get that far.
Nicola:	So how did it get that far?
Michelle:	Um, very suddenly (laughing) actually. (*Nicola:* [laughter]) (laughter) A lot more sudden than I'd thought it was going to. Um, yeah it progressed a lot faster than I thought it was going to, more because *he* had been fairly inebriated and was (unclear). I had actually been curious as to whether it was going to get this far. But um it did and- and no the condom didn't feature in my mind at *all*. And I was quite surprised. It sort of- it's a bit hard to sort of describe it really. Is it believable to say that the whole thing just sort of happened so quickly that there really wasn't the opportunity to say, hey where's your condom, put your gumboot on, or whatever. Um, that didn't come into the discussion with either of us. (*Nicola:* Yeah.) And we're both of the same age group, so yeah, I'd say we both have that mental point where condoms don't really feature very greatly in our minds. And it was only afterwards that I made a reference to it. And more that that's what should've happened.
Nicola:	So you- you said that? (*Michelle:* Yes.) Um, what did he say?
Michelle:	"Ohh, well I didn't have any." I said, "Well probably I have some." Which I had, but I only had some because I'd been to the Family Planning Clinic to have my IUD removed, ... and so they had given me a packet of condoms . . .

After Michelle explained why she had condoms and where they were kept, I asked:

Nicola:	So what was your thought, like when you said that, "Ohh you know maybe we should've used a condom," um, do you remember having any sort of thoughts about that?
Michelle:	Um, yes I do. Simply because the person who I was in bed with at the time is somebody who I would probably have considered to have been in a high-risk group. On further consideration, yes I would've said that he could've been considered to have been in a high-risk group. But then I also know that he's tested fairly regularly, because of his high-risk group, that he is tested fairly frequently.
Nicola:	And in the- in the sort of um the time, the very quick time that it happened, that didn't enter your head at all?
Michelle:	No.
Nicola:	That- yeah you didn't think about-
Michelle:	No, didn't think about it at all. No, well you see it's the passion thing really gets you and mmm, are you able to make those decisions, in the hot throes of passion? No, I don't think you can. I mean I got caught out and got pregnant through doing exactly the same thing.

Michelle had strongly expressed numerous reasons why she disliked condoms, including their feel, smell, and taste. She found them physically uncomfortable, like "having a bit of sandpaper rubbed around inside you," and said that they detract from the "spontaneity" and "instant pleasure" of sex and that their unpleasant taste limits "afterplay" and "foreplay." However, she had also demonstrated several strong reasons why, in her own assessment, she and her partner should have used a condom on this occasion. First, she was not using any other form of contraception, and she had had a previous traumatic experience of an accidental pregnancy and abortion as a result of having sexual intercourse in similar circumstances without using a condom or diaphragm. Second, she now regarded it as a rule that condoms should be used with sexual intercourse to protect against a range of sexually transmitted diseases including HIV. Third, in her own assessment this particular man was in a high-risk category for HIV, and he was regularly tested for HIV. Nevertheless, she did have sexual intercourse without using a condom (see Holland et al., 1991, for discussion of a young woman's similar story). We are interested in trying to understand how this could happen.

It has been widely noted that both women and men report that one reason for not liking condoms is that putting them on can be perceived to interrupt and potentially disrupt an intensely stimulating and pleasurable interaction that neither partner wishes to stop (e.g., Browne & Minichiello, 1994; Chapman & Hodgson, 1988; Hodges, 1992). At the end of Michelle's account she indirectly referred to her own "hot throes of passion" at the time, but elsewhere she reported on the event as though it was something that happened *to* her. Indeed it was striking that in Michelle's recounting of this sexual experience she talked about what happened as though she was playing a role in someone else's script. Michelle did not infer any coercion on the part of her partner, nor did she imply that the sex was unwanted by her but, from her account, it would seem that she had little or no control over determining if and when they had sexual intercourse: "I didn't actually think it would get that far," it was "a lot more sudden than I'd thought it was going to be." The actions she attributed to herself at the time were to do with spectating on what was going on, as if regarding herself as a passive object of the sequence of events: "I had actually been curious as to whether it was going to get this far," "I was quite surprised."

Michelle explained that she had been using alcohol on this occasion, and it is of course possible that she was not usually as passive as she portrayed. Indeed, she presented herself as frank and forthright in the interview. It is interesting, however, that she could tell us about a sexual encounter in which so little of her own agency was present, and yet this aspect of the dynamic could go unremarked upon by her and by the interviewer. Presumably, this is because female passivity is not out of the ordinary within discourses of heterosexuality.

The New Pragmatics?

It may be a coincidence that the two youngest women interviewed for this study both emphasized what they believed to be the importance of using condoms, and both described situations in which they had had to act very assertively to ensure a casual partner wore a condom (Gavey et al., 1999). In contrast to Michelle, Rose (early twenties) gave the impression of being more actively involved in the decision to have intercourse and to use a condom. (Although she also used a passive voice to speculate about whether or not she was going to have intercourse, she clearly showed an awareness of the agentic function of offering a condom.) She explicitly related this to her not subscribing to a "romantic view" and described how this had unfolded on another occasion, a "one-night stand."

> Nicola: In that situation who raised the issue of the condom?
> Rose: Um, I think me. Because it was my place and I have some beside the bed. And it was sort of like- like it- it wasn't a matter of not using one, it was just shall we get that far. (*Nicola:* Right.) Is this just a sort of kissing game or are we gonna go that far and it's- I guess I- just when things seemed to be getting to that point I just said you know, "Would you like a condom now?", and then- because it sort of- in a way I suppose it's like instead of saying um, "Do you want to have sex (laughing) with me?" it's- you just say, "Would [you] like a condom?" And it's the same question really. Yeah I mean some people don't actually like to ask and expect it all to happen, and I suppose that's fair enough, that's quite a romantic view but I'm pretty down to earth I think when it comes to matters like that. I sort of like to know what's going to happen. How far it's going to go.

Thus, in Rose's narrative, her active rejection of aspects of romantic discourse enabled her to be more pragmatic in arranging for a condom to be used by her partner. It should also be noted that her reported experiences of condoms were less negative than Christine's and Michelle's, which probably also rendered her less ambivalent about using them.

DISCUSSION

Heterosexual women are increasingly the preferred target of condom promotions designed to encourage safer sex among heterosexuals. Encouraging women to take responsibility for condom use seems to assume that, compared to men, women find condoms relatively unproblematic. In this study we set out to interrogate this assumption, by exploring in more detail some of the difficulties women may experience in relation to condoms. Even in our small and relatively homogeneous sample of 14 women we found considerable differences in how condoms were regarded. As noted, some women had a pragmatic attitude toward condoms and seemed to find using them reasonably straightforward. While this is an important point to emphasize, our focus in this article has been to explore a particular dynamic that some women experienced, whereby at the critical moment they disregarded their own prior "rational" decision not to have intercourse without a condom.

Previous work has often inferred that women are more favorably disposed toward condoms than are men and has concluded that women may need to be more "assertive" and gain more skills in "negotiating" with their male partners to persuade them to use a condom. The implication is that women need to take advantage of their stereotypical heterosexual role of restricting male sexual access, and that they should bargain with the requirement that "sex is conditional on condoms being worn" (Chapman & Hodgson, 1988, p. 104). Such advice, sloganized in forms such as "If it's not on, it's not on" or "no glove, no love," ironically relies on women being both (a) traditional feminine subjects who are comparatively asexual (i.e., whose sexual desires are more subservient to reason) and the gatekeepers of hetero-sex and (b) strong and staunch women who are not afraid to speak openly and explicitly about aspects of their sexual requirements. Although it has been suggested that some women may need help in being able to master the interpersonal demands involved in this form of communication, it is implicitly presented as a realistic goal within each woman's control, with little consideration of the ways in which men can facilitate or impede assertiveness (see Crawford, 1995). In this article we have attempted to show how the practical effect of these contradictory embodiments of femininity can be a paralyzing inability to act on this simple message.

Discourses of conventional heterosexuality constitute the male as the active, leading partner and the female as the passive, responsive partner. When men actively take control in heterosexual practice—be it in a chivalrous or overtly abusive way—women's agency can be restricted. Women's abilities to instigate condom use can also be compromised in more subtle ways, that is, even in the apparent absence of a man's control. Some feminists have observed, for example, that "tradi-tional sex roles may hinder women in asserting themselves to say what they expect or want from sex" (Tamsma, 1990, p. 191). We would argue, however, that the effects of a discursive production of subjectivity are more profound than this sex roles analysis might suggest. A poststructuralist analysis would propose, for instance, that a woman's expectations and desires are themselves constructed through the discursive possibilities available to her. In the discourse of heterosexual romance feminine sexuality is passive, with the implicit promise of a man's love and protection in return. For women, such as Christine, whose identities are at least partly consti-tuted through this discourse, taking control of a sexual situation—if only to the extent of introducing a condom—would involve actions that potentially disrupt her feminine sexual identity, her sense of who she is and how she should feel and act in the context of the heterosexual relationship. Moreover, the prospect of taking control in this way could threaten the potential rewards she may expect in the form of love, respect, and protection. Although the shadow of romance was not so clearly present in Michelle's account, the effects of passive feminine sexuality were illustrated through her narration of her own participation in a sexual encounter as a virtual object of some externally scripted interaction.

For Christine and Michelle, we can see how the act of introducing a condom would require balancing inconsistent desires and expectations of themselves. Given that the decision and action must happen in the pressure of a sexual moment, it is not surprising that these women were somehow unable to act in the way they had previously, "rationally" chosen to act. When it came to the time, health protec-tion was not the only thing on their minds. In contrast, Rose's explicit rejection of romance meant she did not have expectations inconsistent with her wish to use a condom.

In this article we have shown how forms of women's passivity, prescribed by traditional ideals of feminine heterosexuality, can be embodied in ways that constrain them both from deciding during sex to use a condom and from then making this happen. We contend that because feminine passivity is a commonsense position in conventional forms of heterosexuality, its influence may go largely unnoticed among women who identify with values of sexual equality. In drawing attention to the embodiment of this passivity and its social construction through discourses of romance and traditional heterosexuality, we hope we have identified sites for resistance and change.

Initial submission: December 20, 1996
Final acceptance: November 5, 1997

NOTE

1. Non-Maori New Zealanders of European descent.

REFERENCES

Barling, N. R., & Moore, S. A. (1990). Adolescents' attitudes towards AIDS precautions and intention to use condoms. *Psychological Reports, 67*, 883–890.

Browne, J., & Minichiello, V. (1994). The condom: Why more people don't put it on. *Sociology of Health & Illness, 16*, 229–251.

Burman, E. (1991). What discourse is not. *Philosophical Psychology 4*, 325–342.

Burman, E., & Parker, I. (1993). Introduction—Discourse analysis: The turn to the text. In E. Burman & I. Parker (Eds.), *Discourse analytic research: Repertoires and readings in action* (pp. 1–13). London: Routledge.

Crawford, M. (1995). *Talking difference: On gender and language.* London: Sage.

Chapman, S., & Hodgson, J. (1988). Showers in raincoats: Attitudinal barriers to condom-use in high-risk heterosexuals. *Community Health Studies, 12*, 97–105.

Gamson, J. (1990). Rubber wars: Struggles over the condom in the United States. *Journal of the History of Sexuality, 1*, 262–282.

Gavey, N. (1992). Technologies and effects of heterosexual coercion. *Feminism & Psychology, 2*, 325–351.

Gavey, N., & McPhillips, K. (1997). Women and the heterosexual transmission of HIV: Risks and prevention strategies. *Women & Health, 25*, 41–60.

Gavey, N., McPhillips, K., & Doherty, M. (1999). *"If it's not on, it's not on"—Or is it?: Discursive constraints on women's condom use.* Manuscript submitted for publication.

Gergen, K. J. (1990). Toward a post-modern psychology. *Humanistic Psychologist, 18*, 22–34.

Gill, R. (1995). Relativism, reflexivity, and politics: Interrogating discourse analysis from a feminist perspective. In S. Wilkinson & C. Kitzinger (Eds.), *Feminism and discourse: Psychological perspectives* (pp. 165–186). London: Sage.

Hare-Mustin, R. T., & Marecek, J. (1988). The meaning of difference: Gender theory, postmodernism, and psychology. *American Psychologist, 43*, 455–464.

Henriques, J., Hollway, W., Urwin, C., Venn, C., & Walkerdine, V. (1984). *Changing the subject: Psychology, social regulation and subjectivity.* London: Methuen.

Hingson, R. W., Strunin, L., Berlin, B. M., & Heren, T. (1990). Beliefs about AIDS, use of alcohol and drugs, and unprotected sex among Massachusetts adolescents. *American Journal of Public Health, 80*, 295–299.

Hodges, I. (1992). *Passionkillers: Issues relating to low condom use.* Wellington, New Zealand: Department of Health.

Hoffman, R. (1987). Women are new targets for condom advertising. *Advertising and Graphic Arts Techniques, 21*, 18–21.

Holland, J., Ramazanoglu, C., Scott, S., Sharpe, S., & Thomson, R. (1991). Between embarrassment and trust: Young women and the diversity of condom use. In P. Aggleton, G. Hart, & P. Davies (Eds.), *AIDS: Responses, interventions and care* (pp. 127–148). London: Falmer Press.

Hollway, W. (1983). Heterosexual sex: Power and desire for the other. In S. Cartledge & J. Ryan (Eds.), *Sex and love: New thoughts on old contradictions* (pp. 124–140, 230–231). London: Women's Press.

Hollway, W. (1984). Gender difference and the production of subjectivity. In J. Henriques, W. Hollway, C. Urwin, C. Venn, & V. Walkerdine (Eds.), *Changing the subject: Psychology, social regulation and subjectivity* (pp. 227–263). London: Methuen.

Hollway, W. (1989). *Subjectivity and method in psychology: Gender, meaning and science.* London: Sage.

Jackson, S. (1993). Even sociologists fall in love: An exploration in the sociology of emotions. *Sociology, 27,* 201–220.

Janz, N. K., & Becker, M. H. (1984). The health belief model: A decade later. *Health Education Quarterly, 11,* 1–47.

Kippax, S., Crawford, J., Waldby, C., & Benton, P. (1990). Women negotiating heterosex: Implications for AIDS prevention. *Women's Studies International Forum, 13,* 533–542.

Lather, P. (1991). *Getting smart: Feminist research and pedagogy with/in the postmodern.* New York: Routledge.

Moore, S. M., & Rosenthal, D. A. (1991). Condoms and coitus: Adolescents' attitudes to AIDS and safe sex behavior. *Journal of Adolescence, 14,* 211–227.

Parker, I. (1992). *Discourse dynamics: Critical analysis for social and individual psychology.* London: Routledge.

Parker, I., & Burman, E. (1993). Against discursive imperialism, empiricism and constructionism: Thirty-two problems with discourse analysis. In E. Burman & I. Parker (Eds.), *Discourse analytic research: Repertoires and readings in action* (pp. 155–172). London: Routledge.

Polkinghorne, D. E. (1992). Postmodern epistemology of practice. In S. Kvale (Ed.), *Psychology and postmodernism* (pp. 146–165). London: Sage.

Potter, J., & Wetherell, M. (1987). *Discourse and social psychology: Beyond attitudes and behaviour.* London: Sage.

Ryan, A., & Gavey, N. (1998). Women, sexual freedom, and the 'coital imperative'. In R. du Plessis & L. Alice (Eds.), *Feminist thought in Aotearoa/New Zealand: Connections and differences* (pp. 147–155). Auckland: Oxford University Press.

Squire, C. (1995). Pragmatism, extravagance and feminist discourse analysis. In S. Wilkinson & C. Kitzinger (Eds.), *Feminism and discourse: Psychological perspectives* (pp. 145–164). London: Sage.

Tamsma, N. (1990). Increasing awareness: Safer sex education for women. In M. Paalman (Ed.), *Promoting safer sex: Prevention of sexual transmission of AIDS and other STDs* (pp. 190–198). Amsterdam: Swets & Zeitlinger.

Waldby, C., Kippax, S., & Crawford, J. (1993). Research note: Heterosexual men and "safe sex" practice. *Sociology of Health & Illness, 15,* 246–256.

Weedon, C. (1987). *Feminist practice and poststructuralist theory.* Oxford: Basil Blackwell.

Wetherell, M. (1995). Romantic discourse and feminist analysis: Interrogating investment, power and desire. In S. Wilkinson & C. Kitzinger (Eds.), *Feminism and discourse: Psychological perspectives* (pp. 128–144). London: Sage.

Widdicombe, S. (1995). Identity, politics and talk: A case for the mundane and the everyday. In S. Wilkinson & C. Kitzinger (Eds.), *Feminism and discourse: Psychological perspectives* (pp. 106–127). London: Sage.

Willig, C. (1994, July). *"I wouldn't have married the guy if I'd have to do that." Heterosexual adults' constructions of condom use and their implications for sexual practice.* Paper presented at the 23rd International Congress of Applied Psychology, Madrid, Spain.

Worth, D. (1989). Sexual decision-making and AIDS: Why condom promotion among vulnerable women is likely to fail. *Studies in Family Planning, 20,* 297–307.

COMMENTS ON "SUBJECT TO ROMANCE"

Jeanne Marecek
Swarthmore College

The meanings of gender in contemporary feminist theory range far beyond psychology's preoccupation with gender as individual difference (Hare-Mustin & Marecek, 1994; Marecek, 1995). For most social scientists, the term "gender" refers to the ideational and normative system that regulates relationships within and between the sexes (Scott, 1988). This meaning of gender not only sets the agenda for feminist research but also provides an indispensable analytic tool. One can no more understand women's experiences without this tool than one can understand the experiences of workers and African Americans without the analytic categories of class and race. For psychologists, this meaning of gender demands a significant shift of focus. It requires that we relinquish the individual-centered ways of working that are hallmarks of the discipline in favor of approaches geared toward examining the patterns of cultural life within which individual action is embedded.

Discourse analysis focuses attention on the forms of everyday language, exposing the power of language to regulate people's identities and actions. Therefore, as "Subject to Romance" (Gavey & McPhillips, 1999) shows, discourse analysis is well suited to producing knowledge about the gender system. Yet, although discourse analysis is an established part of the repertoire of feminist psychologists outside the United States, discourse analyses have rarely appeared in *Psychology of Women Quarterly*. It was Nicola Gavey who first introduced *PWQ* readers to discourse analysis in a piece that appeared in the special issue on theory and method in feminist psychology nearly 10 years ago (Gavey, 1989).

"Subject to Romance" examines some of the language practices that regulate heterosexual intimacy. It is an important addition to the growing body of work by feminist psychologists concerned with the discursive constitution of heterosexuality (e.g., Crawford, 1995; Hollway, 1984, 1989; Tiefer, 1991). This work has brought

This article was prepared while I was a fellow at the Swedish Collegium for Advanced Studies in the Social Sciences, Uppsala, Sweden. I am grateful to SCASSS for its material support and collegiality.

Address correspondence and reprint requests to: Jeanne Marecek, Department of Psychology, Swarthmore College, 500 College Avenue, Swarthmore, PA 19081. E-mail: jmarece1@swarthmore. edu.

to light some of the language practices that reinscribe male–female inequality, so that men's sexual interests are given priority, coercion of women is normalized or confused with consent, and women's interests and sexual agency are made light of or erased.

This special issue of *PWQ* is about innovative methods, so I will focus my comments on questions about discourse analysis as a methodological approach. First I ask whether discourse analysis is indeed an "innovative method." Next, using "Subject to Romance" as a case in point, I ask what is distinctive about the knowledge that discourse analysis can produce. What does discourse analysis add to the feminist practice of psychology? Third, drawing once again on "Subject to Romance" as a case example, I revisit feminist debates about the utility of postmodern initiatives.

IS DISCOURSE ANALYSIS AN INNOVATIVE METHOD?

By this time, calling discourse analysis an innovative method is stretching the truth. It is a misnomer that understates the scope and significance of discourse analysis in contemporary psychology. Although discourse analysis may seem new to psychologists situated within the American tradition of scientific orthodoxy, it has a 20-year history in other countries (notably, the United Kingdom, Australia, New Zealand, and the Nordic countries). Jonathan Potter and Margaret Wetherell's *Discourse Analysis and Social Psychology: Beyond Attitudes and Behavior*, published in 1987, drew together the first wave of developments in discourse analysis. Today discourse analysis has propagated a number of different strains and variations (Potter, 1996). Some researchers focus on the processes internal to talk and texts that regulate the production of meaning. Others (Nicola Gavey and Kathryn McPhillips among them) direct their attention to interpretative repertoires that circulate in a culture. These interpretative repertoires are the resources available to members of the culture for constructing meaningful accounts of their actions and experiences. In short, discourse analysis, though it has had limited exposure in the United States, is by now a well-established way of producing psychological knowledge.

We must also query whether discourse analysis should be regarded as a "method," a description that some of its practitioners have pointedly refused. Discourse analysis is avowedly *not* a formally specified set of procedures or calculations, nor is it meant to be applied in rote fashion. To signify this, some workers prefer to call discourse analysis an approach or a way of working (Potter, 1996; Weedon, 1987).

Conventional psychology draws sharp boundaries between theory and method and between methods and results; the dictates of American Psychological Association style compel researchers to reinscribe these boundaries in their research reports. In the conventional view, methods are seen as no more than neutral technologies by which hypotheses are put to test and preexisting facts discovered. I argue, however, that a method is not a neutral tool at all. All so-called methods entail theoretical and epistemological commitments that determine not only what are taken as proper questions for psychological study but also what form the answers will take. What is distinctive about discourse analysis is not its investigative procedures but a metatheory that is strongly opposed to that of conventional psychology.

WHAT IS DISTINCTIVE ABOUT DISCOURSE ANALYSIS?

Discourse analysis is closely associated with social constructionism. For discourse analysts, language is the access route for learning about social processes; the forms of everyday discourse create pattens of cultural life. Terms and categories of language do not merely describe reality; they constitute what we know to be reality. Thus, language, rather than being a tool at a speaker's command, exerts restraining and regulating effects on what can be said and seen (Hare-Mustin & Marecek, 1990). Bringing to light language practices and examining their effects is the project of discourse analysis.

Many presumptions of conventional psychology—such as logical positivism, realism (in one or another of its inflections), biological foundationalism, and abstracted empiricism—are at odds with social construction and other postmodern initiatives. Shaking loose from these presumptions is not an easy matter for psychologists trained in the North American tradition. We were taught to swim in these waters without any recognition that we were wet. In our methods courses, we were taught "the scientific method," leading us to believe that the research practices we learned constituted the only means of producing scientific knowledge and that the category of "science" was neither historically situated nor culturally specific.

Conventional research technologies such as inventories, scales, closed-ended questionnaires, and contrived laboratory situations are of little use in investigating discourse. They force research participants to speak in the researcher's idiom, squeezing out the everyday language practices that are the focus of interest. Moreover, these data-generating technologies typically leave few avenues for participants to express vacillation, ambivalence, or confusion. Faced with the demand for data that can be categorized and quantified, researchers must employ techniques that impose coherence, consistency, and uniformity on research participants (Marecek, Fine, & Kidder, 1997). Discourse analysis proceeds along wholly different lines, as even a cursory reading of "Subject to Romance" reveals. It prizes the ragged, hesitant, self-contradictory, and even incoherent character of real-life talk. It embraces the indeterminacy and fluidity of people's efforts to explain themselves and to formulate intelligible accounts of their experiences.

Social construction involves another radical departure from conventional psychology. It reverses the commonsense idea that inner thoughts occur separate from and prior to expression in language, asserting instead that the terms and categories of language constrain what can be thought. Constructionism thus disputes the presumption that the individual is the origin of thought and action, what one theorist has dubbed the myth of the isolated mind. Consider Michelle and Christine, the women whose accounts of condom use are the focus of "Subject to Romance." Both women had made a firm resolve to use condoms during sexual encounters to the extent that each had obtained condoms in anticipation of having sexual intercourse. To their chagrin, however, both had failed to make use of those condoms. How can we explain their failure to act in accord with their intentions, a failure that might have had life-threatening consequences? Conventional psychologists might invoke explanations involving ambivalent attitudes, erroneous beliefs, weak motivation, or personality deficits. Gavey and McPhillips, however, set aside such person-centered explanations in favor of an exploration of culturally shared meanings of heterosexual intimacy. These shared meanings are encoded in and promulgated by linguistic constructs such as passion, romance, love, and spontaneity. By tracing the appearance of these constructs in Michelle's and Christine's narratives, the authors explore how language sets limits on the range of possible actions and shapes self-conceptions.

Gavey and McPhillips's approach to theorizing about condom use has advantages for feminist theory-building. It offers feminist psychologists a way out of the impasses created by what Mary Crawford and I (1989) have labeled the Woman-as-Problem approach. In that approach, women who do not use condoms in risky sexual encounters appear to have (or be) the problem; they may be seen as uneducated, lacking assertiveness, having low self-esteem, victims of sexist socialization, and so on. Fixing attention on such personal deficits limits the scope of available remedies to technologies of individual change, such as assertiveness training, counseling, or sex education.

Gavey and McPhillips's approach directs attention to the culturally sanctioned narratives of heterosexual intimacy that Michelle and Christine make use of, as well as the terms and categories they rely on. They take Michelle and Christine at their word, seeing them as active, self-conscious, and reflective agents who assemble elements of diverse narratives into their accounts of their actions and motives. Strategies for change that follow from a discourse analysis focus not on changing Michelle and Christine but on exposing and challenging the narratives that are available to them. Moreover, there is not just one all-encompassing narrative in the culture by which all women are relentlessly bombarded, but rather any number of crosscutting ones. This variety offers a multiplicity of possible alternate narratives.

FEMINISM, POSTMODERNISM, AND
THE PSYCHOLOGY OF GENDER

Among feminist scholars, the merits of social constructionism and other postmodern initiatives have been vehemently debated. Some feminist critics have called postmodernism patriarchy's last ruse, charging that it seeks to invalidate the category of women just when women have claimed their rights as speaking subjects (Fox-Genovese, 1991). Others have argued that the turn to language entails turning our backs on "real" women and the material reality of suffering, retreating from activism into intellectualized game-playing (Weisstein, 1993). Yet others have been concerned about the elitism of indulging in the intellectual pleasures of postmodern philosophy when those pleasures are not widely accessible even to other academics (Bohan, 1995). Moreover, among feminists who have counted on empirical facts as the grounds for demanding gender equality, postmodern ideas threaten to impose political paralysis (Allen & Baber, 1992).

We can assess these criticisms against a reading of "Subject to Romance." Embedded in the criticisms are a number of binary oppositions or dichotomies. One such dichotomy opposes postmodernism against feminism; in this view, a feminist postmodernism would be impossible. For me, the defining quality of feminist scholarship is that it is carried out from a subject position that advocates human equality. Without doubt, the work of Gavey and McPhillips fits this definition; its postmodern sensibilities are equally indubitable.

"Subject to Romance" explodes another dichotomy, that of language versus material reality. Gavey and McPhillips, though they study language practices, study "real women" in "real" situations. Their work is interventionist in its intent, aiming to expose and interrupt those discursive practices that sustain and naturalize material practices of heterosexuality that endanger women's lives.

The third dichotomy relegates postmodern thought to the realm of high theory and esoteric jargon and positions empiricism in the realm of the ordinary and accessible. But is postmodern work necessarily esoteric and jargon laden? And is the language of empirical psychology—replete with its abstracted language of variables, factors, and effects, as well as statistical argot—necessarily more accessible? To whom? One of the common complaints of women's studies scholars outside psychology is that psychologists' writings are hermetic and inaccessible to those outside the field. All disciplines devise a specialized language that demarcates those who are and are not counted among its members. Psychology is certainly not immune to this tendency.

Scrutiny of the discursive practices—whether in popular culture or in our own discipline—that maintain the gender system is long overdue in U.S. psychology. By now, the limitations of approaching gender as individual difference are well-rehearsed—essentialism, false universalism, and problematic assumptions regarding agency, among them (Bohan, 1993, Hare-Mustin & Marecek, 1994; Marecek, 1997; Spelman, 1988). It is time to catch up with our colleagues in women's studies and in many other disciplines—sociology, anthropology, history, philosophy, literary studies, cultural studies. And it is time to join up with feminist psychologists elsewhere in the world. Although feminist psychologists in the United States have created a space in the discipline for politically committed scholarship, we have managed to carve out only a tiny niche for methodological innovation. For *PWQ*, that niche seems to consist of special issues that appear roughly once per decade! Instead of occupying the disciplinary hinterland, innovations—such as discourse analysis—deserve to be placed at the center of attention.

REFERENCES

Allen, K., & Baber, K. M. (1992). Ethical and epistemological tensions in applying a postmodern perspective to feminist research. *Psychology of Women Quarterly, 16*, 1–16.
Bohan, J. (1995, August). *Every answer is a question*. Paper presented at the annual meeting of the American Psychological Association, Los Angeles, CA.
Bohan, J. S. (1993). Regarding gender: Essentialism, constructionism, and feminist psychology. *Psychology of Women Quarterly, 17*, 5–22.
Crawford, M. (1995). *Talking difference*. London: Sage.
Crawford, M., & Marecek, J. (1989). Psychology reconstructs the female, 1968–1988. *Psychology of Women Quarterly, 13*, 147–165.
Fox-Genovese, E. (1991). *Feminism without illusions: A critique of individualism*. Chapel Hill, NC: University of North Carolina Press.
Gavey, N. (1989). Feminist poststructuralism and discourse analysis: Contributions to a feminist psychology. *Psychology of Women Quarterly, 13*, 459–475.
Gavey, N., & McPhillips, K. (1999). Subject to romance: Heterosexual passivity as an obstacle to women initiating condom use. *Psychology of Women Quarterly, 23*, 349–367.

Hare-Mustin, R. T., & Marecek, J. (1990). *Making a difference: Psychology and the construction of gender*. New Haven, CT: Yale University Press.

Hare-Mustin, R. T., & Marecek, J. (1994). Asking the right questions: Feminist psychology and sex differences. *Feminism and Psychology, 4*, 531–537.

Hollway, W. (1984). Gender difference and the production of subjectivity. In J. Henriques, W. Hollway, C. Urwin, C. Venn, & V. Walkerdine (Eds.), *Changing the subject: Psychology, social regulation and subjectivity* (pp. 227–263). London: Methuen.

Hollway, W. (1989). *Subjectivity and method in psychology: Gender, meaning and science*. London: Sage.

Marecek, J. (1995). Gender, politics, and psychology's ways of knowing. *American Psychologist, 50*, 162–163.

Marecek, J. (1997). Feminist psychology at thirty-something. In D. Looser & E. A. Kaplan (Eds.), *Generations: Academic feminists in dialogue* (pp. 132–150). Minneapolis, MN: University of Minnesota Press.

Marecek, J., Fine, M., & Kidder, L. (1997). Working between worlds: Qualitative research and social psychology. *Journal of Social Issues, 53*, 631–664.

Potter, J. (1996). Discourse analysis and constructionist approaches: Theoretical background. In J. T. E. Richardson (Ed.), *Handbook of qualitative research methods* (pp. 125–140). Leicester, UK: BPS Books.

Potter, J., & Wetherell, M. (1987). *Discourse analysis and social psychology: Beyond attitudes and behavior*. London: Sage.

Scott, J. W. (1988). *Gender and the politics of history*. New York: Columbia University Press.

Spelman, E. V. (1988). *Inessential woman*. Boston: Beacon Press.

Tiefer, L. (1991). Historical, scientific, clinical, and feminist criticisms of "The Human Sexual Response Cycle" model. *Annual Review of Sex Research, 2*, 1–23.

Weedon, C. (1987). *Feminist practice and poststructural theory*. Oxford: Blackwell.

Weisstein, N. (1993). Response and afterword: A call for a revitalized feminist psychology. *Feminism and Psychology, 3*, 239–245.

FUNDAMENTALISM IN PSYCHOLOGICAL SCIENCE

The Publication Manual as "Bible"

Richard Walsh-Bowers
Wilfrid Laurier University

Drawing from social historical studies and critical feminist perspectives on psychological method and report writing, I analyze the content of the fourth edition of the *Publication Manual of the American Psychological Association* (APA, 1994) as if it were a biblical text. I focus on the correspondence between the espoused intention of sensitivity toward participants and the codes of investigative conduct made explicit and implicit in the manual. Specifically, I examine definitions of research, research roles, ethical standards, writing style, and gender issues. I then discuss the manual's function as a fundamentalist bible in relation to psychologists' culture, including socialization of psychology students and the production of research articles. I conclude with recommendations for investigative and compositional alternatives.

The growing literature on the social context of method in psychology indicates that both hierarchical investigative practice and depersonalized, decontextualized report writing have been the norms in North American psychology (Budge & Katz, 1995; Danziger, 1990; Morawski, 1988; Walsh-Bowers, 1995). Over the last 40 years, the explicit and implicit directives in successive editions of the *Publication Manual of the American Psychological Association* (APA, 1994) have been instrumental in shaping the nature of investigative practice and research report writing (Madigan, Johnson, & Linton, 1995). By design, the *Publication Manual* plays a central role in the quotidian life of the psychological scientist.

This article is a revised version of a paper presented at the Canadian Psychological Association meeting held in Charlottetown, P.E.I., in June 1995 and the American Psychological Association meeting held in Toronto, Ontario, in August 1996. The author is grateful to the members of the Laurier Critical Issues Seminar and to the reviewers for their comments.

Address correspondence and reprint requests to: Richard Walsh-Bowers, Department of Psychology, WLU, Waterloo, Ontario, Canada N2L 3C5. E-mail: rwalshb@mach1.wlu.ca.

In this article I argue that the *Publication Manual,* which some psychologists affectionately refer to as their "bible," serves to enculturate its adherents in a fundamentalist approach to codes of scientific conduct. Taking the biblical metaphor seriously and drawing from feminist recastings of psychological methodology, I examine the research relationships between the investigator and her or his assistants, on the one hand, and research participants, on the other hand, as these relationships are constructed in the *Publication Manual's* fourth edition. I focus on the contradictions between the *Publication Manual's* espoused intention of "sensitivity" toward participants and the codes of investigative conduct actually stipulated or implied, by examining definitions of research, research roles, ethical standards, writing style, and gender issues. After reflecting on the fundamentalism in the *Publication Manual* and its culture, I suggest alternative investigative and compositional practices, based on the belief that there is some capacity for reform within methodological traditions.

My personal investment in this project is considerable. As a social historian of psychological method, I have been focusing on the evolution of the research relationship in community psychology (Walsh, 1987), feminist psychology (Walsh, 1989), gay and lesbian research (Walsh-Bowers & Parlour, 1992), and the mainstream interpersonal areas of psychology (Walsh-Bowers, 1995). The general finding from these studies is that objectivistic report-writing conventions established early in the formation of a subdiscipline reflect investigators' actual constructions of research relationships and serve as templates for subsequent generations of authors and researchers.

As a teacher of the history of psychology to undergraduates and as thesis supervisor for B.A. and M.A. students in community psychology, many of whom are feminists, I usually encounter formidable anxiety about adhering to "APA style." That is, the students report intense feelings of apprehension about their attempts to conform with canonical forms of conducting research and writing about it. They scrupulously strive to "do the right thing" and fear any deviation from canon law. In short, they literally have been indoctrinated in disciplinary norms. As an educator, I am disturbed by this state of affairs.

My concerns about the apparently fundamentalist constraints on report writing also stem from practicing prevention of violence against women, using collective drama as the educational medium (Community Education Team, 1999). Traditional reporting norms in psychology were not helpful to us as we struggled to find an appropriate compositional form for our work, so, inspired by feminist recastings of academic writing (e.g., Richardson, 1994), we adapted the descriptive format of author dialogue to suit our purposes.

In light of these personal considerations, upon the 1994 publication of the fourth edition, I resolved to examine the crucial function that the *Publication Manual* serves in the discipline. Institutionalized in the 26 APA and 3 Canadian Psychological Association journals, the *Publication Manual* is now the standard for other U.S. and British, Continental European, and Australian psychology journals (Dzinas, 1996). Some historians argue that, although other scientific disciplines maintain their regimens for composing research articles, none has imposed its conventions so systemically and rigidly on its authors as the APA *Publication Manual* (Bazerman, 1988; Dzinas, 1996). But this current status has a social history. Dzinas has documented how the *Publication Manual* emerged in the context of the exponential increase in manuscripts submitted to APA journals after World War II. This was the social climate that produced the first edition of the *Publication Manual*. Concise writing and brevity of manuscripts were paramount criteria for publishable articles. Subsequent editions have perpetuated these criteria.

As to the question of the particular *form* that research articles should take, Bazerman's (1988) extensive analysis is helpful. His view is that the progressive codification of APA style from the original stylesheet of 1929 to the third edition of 1983 reflected the rhetoric of behaviorist psychology that has dominated contemporary psychology. The experimental lab report, with its four sections of introduction, method, results, and discussion, and the detached language chosen render the investigators and the human sources of data virtually invisible. This objectified rhetoric was intended to reflect the tenets of the hypothetico-deductive model of science that psychologists espoused, inasmuch as generalizable, universalized laws about behavior that transcend the persons producing the knowledge were—and are—the discipline's primary goal (Danziger, 1990). In fact, Budge and Katz's (1995) rhetorical and literary analyses show in specific detail the objectivistic characteristics of the *Publication Manual*'s third edition (APA, 1983). Furthermore, Madigan et al. (1995) indicate that this orientation prevails in the fourth edition.

Clearly, this continuity of traditions has been intentional. In the only rationale for the *Publication Manual* ever published in the *American Psychologist*, Madigan et al. (1995) stated:

> We propose that APA style is not just a collection of arbitrary stylistic conventions but also encapsulates the core values and epistemology of the discipline. APA style is itself a model for thinking about psychological phenomena and serves as an important socialization experience for psychologists. (p. 428)

Madigan et al. (1995), who came not to bury the *Publication Manual*'s codification of APA style but to praise it, confessed the faith of the discipline in a compositional form and writing style that match the "empirical" (i.e., experimental) paradigm. In their view, the canonical research article is a model for how psychologists should think about, conduct, and write about research. Although Madigan et al. noted that the reality behind logical, linear, impersonal research reports includes a "more complex human story" (1995, p. 430), they lauded psychologists' tradition of producing a "sanitized, rationalized account" (p. 430) of empirical investigations. Madigan et al. contended that APA style as a writing genre, with its subheadings, minimal footnotes and quotes, frequent citations, and disembodied "voice of the expert in the field" (p. 429), rightly distinguishes psychology as a deductive science from humanities disciplines.

In the overleaf of the jacket for the 1994 hardcover edition, the *Publication Manual*'s stated goals are "to encourage authors to write about their research with specificity and to guide them in their writing about their participants with sensitivity and accuracy." These goals are reiterated in the *Publication Manual*'s "Introduction":

> The revisions in the fourth edition were guided by two principles: specificity and sensitivity. The first principle is that researchers need to describe the details of what they did, with whom they did it, how they measured it, and what they found at an appropriate level of specificity—and one that enables others to replicate the research.

The second principle is that evaluative terms and language with pejorative implications are inappropriate in scientific writing. (p. xxvi)

How well do the authors of the *Publication Manual* achieve their purposes of encouraging psychologists to write about their research with specificity and sensitivity? One way to answer this question is to assess critically the correspondence between the *Publication Manual's* goals and the specific practices that its authors explicitly and implicitly recommend. In my view, a meaningful conceptual framework for this critical reflection is to consider the *Publication Manual* as a socially constructed text and a product of modernity. Briefly, modernity in science refers to the Enlightenment ideology of scientifically driven progress and detached objectivity, founded on the values of empirically based reason and hierarchical authority relations between scientists and the objects of their study. Feminist critical analyses have illuminated the patriarchal roots of this scientific ideology and of accepted methodological norms in psychology (e.g., Bohan, 1992; Morawski, 1992).

TOWARD A FEMINIST RECASTING OF REPORT WRITING

Some psychologists contend that science and its conceptions, procedures, and institutions are socially constituted within patriarchal values of hierarchical relations, linear thinking, and detached objectivity that rule the roost in the natural and social sciences (Bleier, 1986; Harding, 1987; Keller, 1984). That is, psychology's epistemological tenets of realism (including objectivism), determinism, and reductionism and its specific rules for playing the game of science reflect the social order of male privilege and the male worldview. Indeed, interdisciplinary, cultural analyses show the central role that androcentric myths have played in the conscious and unconscious lives of those who aspire to the Apollonian life of the scientific mind (e.g., Ruether, 1992, 1993; Smith, 1990). It would not be surprising, therefore, if the *Publication Manual* as a product of psychologists' culture reproduced the patriarchal values that have suffused the discipline from its inception.

A focal point for feminist approaches to the epistemological foundations of empirical psychology is the question of objectivity and subject–object relations (Wittig, 1985). One popular position is that those observers who are themselves members of a marginalized group (e.g., women) can attain objective vision about their own group, as long as they follow extant scientific procedures assiduously (e.g., McHugh, Koeske, & Frieze, 1986). But, as Morawski (1992) pointed out, both the idealized rules of scientific conduct and their actual implementation are socially constructed in terms of male-valued norms. Feminist objectivity becomes a process of mobile positioning, discovered through webs of connections and shared conversations with participants, rather than staunch belief in the possibility of total perspective, universality of vision, and the gaze of objectivity that are the privilege of the objective observer who presumably transcends the object (what Haraway, 1988, called "the God trick" p. 584). Thus, science transforms into a dialectic of accountable and responsible, "contested and contestable" interpretations—ultimately, "situated knowledges" rooted in and engaged with the marginalized (Haraway, 1988).

There are some important implications of this social-constructionist orientation for both the relationship between investigators and participants and the composing of empirical articles that dovetail with feminist epistemological desiderata for psychology (Wittig, 1985). First, feminist inquiry would incorporate an egalitarian research relationship of shared roles and responsibilities (Reinharz, 1992), although researcher–participant collaboration could vary from minimal involvement to joint contributions to all phases of an inquiry, depending on the nature of the project and each party's preferences. Second, because investigators' social locations influence the research question, tools for investigation, and interpretations (Harding, 1987; Reinharz, 1992), authors need to account for their own conscious and unconscious intersubjectivity. Third, reflexivity and flexibility in implementing an inquiry means being responsive to the participants' changing needs. Renegotiated consent and active feedback to participants are instrumental in nurturing egalitarian relationships as well as in providing for confirmation of data and an opportunity for additional information (Kirby & McKenna, 1989; Reinharz, 1992). Fourth, feminist psychologists explicitly committed their scholarship to serve social action. Thus, action strategies flow from research findings (Walsh, 1989); that is, feminist research could contribute to eradicating oppressive social conditions.

These principles suggest why, ideally, descriptions of methods and ethics should be integrated in feminist psychology research reports to produce humanized, contextualized articles focusing on the research relationship (Walsh, 1989). As Olesen (1994) noted, however, there is considerable tension between the feminist principle of working toward intersubjective understanding and the conventions of objectified reporting in which we have all been enculturated. The pressure to conform with the standards of report writing codified in the *Publication Manual* apparently affected the first decade of research published in this journal and in *Sex Roles* (1976–1987), such that there was little correspondence between espoused ideals of feminist research and actual practice (Walsh, 1989). But, if psychologists were to "get serious" about the research relationship, then both the form and style of empirical articles might fundamentally change, liberating writers' creativity from the bonds of the internalized censor of "APA style." In fact, feminist qualitative research, much of it in disciplines outside of mainstream psychology, has given birth to new means of reporting, such as narratives, dialogues, parallel voices of researcher and participant, poetry, researchers' personal stories, and even dramatic readings of text (for reviews, see Olesen, 1994; Richardson, 1994).

EXEGESIS OF THE *PUBLICATION MANUAL*

But just what concrete problems do the prescriptions of the discipline's epistemological standards, codified in the *Publication Manual*, pose for feminist psychologists? Closely related to the patriarchal nature of mainstream North American psychology and its *Publication Manual* is scientism, or the virtual religious belief that the only valid form of knowledge is scientific. An egregious form of scientism is found in the origins of positivism. Its founder, Auguste Comte (1798–1857), exalted science to the highest form of knowledge, while declaring positivism a "religion of humanity" (Leahey, 1992). Although more subtly than Comte, I would argue that psychologists in the late 20th century invest the *Publication Manual* with canonical authority for propagating the faith about required investigative conduct. The *Publication Manual* is written impersonally. Thus, the unknown authors cannot be held accountable for their views. It is as if the purely objective Voice of Authority is speaking, paternalistically addressing mortals. Accordingly, the scholarly method for reflecting critically on this quasi-bible in exegetical detail is hermeneutics, which, appropriately enough, originated in the textual interpretation of sacred scriptures.

Definitions of Research

Like constructions of methodology and the research relationship (Danziger, 1990), psychological "variables" (Danziger & Dzinas, 1997), and psychological theories (Danziger, 1997a), the *Publication Manual* and its prescriptions for APA style are products of social history. These social products hold an implicit, taken-for-granted status in the discipline, as if they were self-evident truths. One unquestioned article of faith is that psychological tools, like the *Publication Manual,* merely hold up a mirror to objective reality. For example, Madigan et al. (1995) asserted that when authors emulate APA style they employ "neutral" language that transparently communicates "objective information about a fixed external reality" (p. 434).

Perhaps the development of an objectivistic APA style reflects the traditional distinction in positivist philosophy of science between the "context of discovery" and the "context of justification" (Danziger, 1997b). The former term refers to the notion that irrational factors partly influence how science proceeds, but as they purportedly are not amenable to logical analysis, they should remain invisible in scientific articles. The notion of the context of justification, however, preserves the inviolability of rational methodological procedures when writers faithfully adopt APA style. Yet, as Danziger noted:

> [A]ny context of justification depends on a framework of beliefs, traditions, choices, cognitive styles, cultural preferences, and so on, which cannot itself be rationally justified. It is this framework which makes the process of discovery possible. I refer to it as the *context of construction* [underline in original]. . . . Half a century ago contexts of construction were largely invisible. But that has changed and modern studies of science are very much concerned with making such contexts the objects of scientific scrutiny. (pp. 15–16)

That the *Publication Manual* is an expression of the positivist position on epistemology can be discerned in the notion of science embedded in it, for example, in the phrase "the growth of a cumulative science" (APA, 1994, p. 11), presumably through the steady march of investigative progress. At another point, the *Publication Manual* authors proclaim that cumulative knowledge is "[l]ike a wall that is built one brick at a time" (APA, 1994, p. 291), a simile evidently constructed to evoke a comforting image of scientific solidity. But "cumulative science" as a linear conception of making scientific knowledge has been a contested notion in the philosophy of science for several decades. An alternative view is that science proceeds through cycles of consensual acceptance and rejection between clashing scientific paradigms (Kuhn, 1970).

In their modernist vision of science, the *Publication Manual*'s authors explicitly distinguish thinking and believing from *feeling*, which is proscribed in a "scientific style" (APA, 1994, p. 28) that ought to be characterized by precision and clarity of language. Consequently, those of us who think with our hearts are marginalized, because, in modernist science, reason and emotion are separate functions. Ironically, Damasio's (1994) research shows that emotions are fundamental to reasoning and sound "cognitive" decision making. Besides, the literature on scientists' creative work clearly shows the interdependence of intuition and emotion with reasoning, problem solving, and careful attention to sensory detail (e.g., Mitroff, 1974; Wertheimer, 1945).

In psychologists' bible (and in Madigan et al.'s 1995 apologia), definitions of investigative features are narrow in scope. Specifically, the generic term "empirical" typically refers to one specific research method, namely, the quantitative experiment; "manuscript" means experimental lab report; and "data" are numbers, almost never words. Here are several examples of the *Publication Manual*'s orientation in the crucial opening chapter, "Content and Organization of a Manuscript."

1. In item 1.01, "Designing and Reporting Research," the authors state, "Editors find in submitted articles the following kinds of defects in the design and reporting of research: failure to build in needed controls, often for a subtle but important aspect of the study (p. 3). In item 1.02, "Evaluating Content," the authors provide a checklist that "may also help in assessing the quality of content and in deciding whether the research is likely to merit publication. . . . Are the outcome measures clearly related to the variables with which the investigation is concerned?" (p. 3). At first glance, this discussion of common defects of submitted manuscripts is appropriate. On closer examination, however, the commentary is framed almost entirely in terms of quantitative experiments, as if there are no other types of submissions.

2. In item 1.04, "Types of Articles," after stating, "Journal articles are usually reports of empirical [*sic*] studies, review articles, or theoretical articles" (p. 4), the authors stipulate the "distinct sections" for the empirical article "that reflect the stages in the research process and that appear in the sequence of these stages" (p. 4). Then the traditional experimental lab-report sections of introduction, method, results, and discussion follow. The impression created is that no other reporting format is possible, which is highly problematic for those researchers who use empirical methods other than the experiment.

Later in this item (pp. 4–5) the authors acknowledge reviews and theory statements as other possible manuscripts, but they clearly privilege "empirical work" over mere theory and argument, which they later identify in item 1.13 (p. 20), "References," as "nonempirical" and less worthy of emulation.

3. In item 1.07, "The Abstract," the prescribed content of any empirical study presumes quantitative experiments and "should describe, . . . the subjects, specifying pertinent characteristics . . . the experimental method, including the apparatus . . . and the findings, including statistical significance levels" (p. 10).

4. In the concluding section (pp. 21–22), "Quality of Presentation," the authors

provide key questions for writers about "the content and organization of the manuscript," for example, "Is the research question clearly identified, and is the hypothesis explicit?" "Is the method clearly and adequately described?" "Are the results and conclusions unambiguous, valid, and meaningful?" Although these questions are helpful, again, the impression is that just one type of manuscript, the report of a statistically based experiment, is permissible.

5. In Chapter 4, the only model articles provided on "Manuscript Preparation," namely, a "one-experiment" and a "two-experiment" article, buttress the message that the statistically based experiment is *the* method that the faithful should employ. Then, well toward the end of the *Publication Manual* in item 6.15 (pp. 306–316), "Policy Statements on [APA] Journal Coverage," the statements of individual journals in several cases include reference to other empirical methods than the experiment. For instance, under the *Personality Processes and Individual Differences* section of the *Journal of Personality and Social Psychology*, the editors state, "All methodological approaches will be considered" (p. 313). This invitation stands in stark contrast to the monolithic presence of the experiment everywhere else in the *Publication Manual*.

Research Roles

Over the last three decades several psychologists have taken a critical look at the traditional research relationship (e.g., Bakan, 1967; Korn, 1988; Schultz, 1969), and there is a reasonably comprehensive social history of its evolution (Danziger, 1990; Walsh, 1987, 1989; Walsh-Bowers, 1995). In my view, the research relationship is rooted in both particular cultural traditions, such as the high status accorded to scientist-professionals, and internalized patriarchal power. Consequently, the standard research relationship is expressed in specific, paternalistic forms of investigative practice and report-writing codes of conduct that typically are unquestioned and constitute conventional wisdom in the discipline. Social historical inquiry indicates that the routinized depictions of the research relationship in journals are usually accurate representations of investigators' constructions of that relationship in the actual research situation (Danziger, 1990).

On the other hand, there have been some alternatives to the customary configuration of investigator domination of the research functions of designing, administering, analyzing, interpreting, and writing with the role of providing data relegated to "participants." Although rare in the past 60 years, flexibility of research roles was the norm in Wundt's studies of consciousness and in Kurt Lewin's studies at Berlin (Danziger, 1990). In the present era, there are some examples of collaboration between investigators and participants in feminist and community psychology (see reviews by Morawski & Steele, 1991; Walsh, 1987, 1989; Walsh-Bowers, 1995; Walsh-Bowers & Parlour, 1992). But in mainstream psychology, especially since 1939, active involvement by participants is rare (Walsh-Bowers, 1995). Certainly, no previous edition of the *Publication Manual* has ever identified the possibility, and the fourth edition is no exception. Indeed, in their commentary on the *Publication Manual,* Madigan et al. (1995) stated: "By mastering APA style and reading APA style reports, a student learns how a participant is to be conceptualized in contemporary psychology . . . anonymous, interchangeable, and distinct from experimenters" (p. 430). Here are the specifics of this orthodox view of research roles in the *Publication Manual*:

1. The lengthy description in item 1.09 of what the "Method" section of a research article should contain includes highly specific guidelines for each expected subsection: participants, apparatus, and procedure. For example, the authors state, "When humans are the participants, report the procedures for selecting and assigning them and the agreements and payments made" (p. 13). But the *Publication Manual* authors make clear that there is only one kind of role for participants, namely, data source. All other roles are the sole functions of psychologists or their assistants.

2. The subordinate status of citizens is reinforced by the absence of an argument anywhere for formally and explicitly acknowledging the contributions of participants to an investigator's research. For example, in item 3.89 "Author Note," only colleagues, assistants, and grants are to be acknowledged. Yet, some authors, especially in developmental journals, do include acknowledgments of participants (Walsh-Bowers, 1995). Instead, the *Publication Manual* writers only tell us, in the third guideline to reduce bias in language, that authors are to acknowledge participation by replacing the "impersonal term *subjects* with a more descriptive term when possible" (p. 49).

Ethical Standards

I take the position that ethical guidelines for investigative conduct should be integrated with revised standards for method and reporting, because in the ordinary world of research they are dynamically interconnected (Walsh-Bowers, 1995). As the literature on the social psychology of the experiment long ago showed (Rosnow, 1981), human psychological inquiry is fundamentally transactional, subject to mutual influence from investigators' and participants' biopsychosocial characteristics. For example, the gender and gender-role style of the data collector in classroom studies of gender-role stereotypes can have a marked impact on participants' responses to gender-role questionnaires (Walsh & Schallow, 1977).

Another critical dimension of the context of construction in the conduct of inquiry is the ethical "contract" that researchers engage in with their participants. Even some proponents of conventional research methodology and ethics argue that, if authors were to provide more specific and contextualized information in their research articles about such ethical considerations as informed consent, then the quality and relative accuracy of data would improve and replication would be facilitated (e.g., Adair, Dushenko, & Lindsay, 1985; Blanck, Bellack, Rosnow, Rotheram-Borus, & Schooler, 1992). In alluding to the questionable reliability of psychologists' adherence to conventional research ethics, these authors promoted a counterargument to the customary practice of excluding researchers' treatment of ethical standards from journal articles. In this regard Adair et al. (1985) stated:

> The APA *Publication Manual* only requires that authors submit a statement to the editor that the research has met APA ethical standards. This kind of certification is,

from our experience, not being followed and clearly insufficient. In short, no incentive is provided to authors to develop and improve ethical procedures or to report the practices they follow. (p. 70)

In effect, Adair et al. imply that the context of discovery, including ethical transactions, is relevant to reporting.

How then do the authors of the *Publication Manual*'s fourth edition in their compositional expectations explicitly deal with the ethical significance of methodological procedures?

1. When describing the content and organization of the method section, the authors instruct writers to "report the procedures for selecting and assigning [participants] and the agreements and payments made" (APA, 1994, p. 13). But this direction for specificity is actually quite narrow in scope, because the ethical conditions of an investigation, such as informed consent, all of which have a bearing on methodology, are excluded. Rather, under the rubric, "Economy of Expression," the *Publication Manual* authors direct writers to "weed out overly detailed descriptions of apparatus, participants, or procedure" (p. 26). "Weeding" is an unfortunate choice of metaphor when applied to the interpersonal nature of conducting psychological research. In effect, the authors' prescription contradicts the proclamation of writing about participants with sensitivity, while it simultaneously saves limited journal space for quantitative results. Thus, the "significant" business of psychologists—namely, doing quantitative research—is segregated from actual engagement with ethical principles and their applications.

2. The historical contradiction between the APA ethical guidelines for research (American Psychological Association, 1992), which in the last two editions always uses the term "participants," and the tradition established in the *Publication Manual* prevails. Despite these conflicting prescriptions, some writers have consistently avoided the impersonal term "subjects" in their journal reports, particularly in recent decades, which demonstrates the possibility for more respectful language (Walsh-Bowers, 1995). (Of course, using the more polite term "participants" can create an illusion of ethical sensitivity.) Nevertheless, the fourth edition shows the following contradictory positions:

(a) "Subjects" not "participants" appears prominently and persistently in numerous examples of preferred writing (e.g., pp. 10, 33, 38) and even once when referencing the ethical standards themselves (p. 14). Yet in "Guideline 3" for "Unbiased Language" (p. 54) the *Publication Manual* authors state: "*Participants* is preferred to *subjects*," and, as noted previously, they characterize the latter term as "impersonal."

(b) The contradictory preferences are most obvious in those passages dealing with statistical treatment of participants' data. The *Publication Manual* always uses "subjects" with reference to statistics (e.g., pp. 114, 130–131) and the enumeration of participants. In fact, participants are reduced to numerals, but raters and observers are not: "3 participants [*but* two raters, seven observers]" (p. 101).

3. In item 4.26 (p. 256), as in the third edition, the authors instruct writers to incorporate in a cover letter to a journal editor the simple statement that the writers have complied with APA's ethical standards for research. This prescription

is repeated at the very end of item 6.05 (p. 298), but here the *Publication Manual* authors identify two other acceptable means of meeting the ethical requirements: including such a statement in the manuscript text describing participants or "signing a form sent by the editor." None of these courses of action, however, provides the actual information about the investigators' implementation of ethical guidelines. Interestingly, some authors of articles in APA journals since 1939 *have* described the ethical contract they engaged in with participants (Walsh-Bowers, 1995).

4. Note that the ethical standards for research are never actually discussed in terms of reporting the research relationship. By summarizing the key principles of research ethics, the *Publication Manual* authors could have enhanced researcher awareness and encouraged psychologists to describe the nature of particular re- search relationships to which the ethical standards apply. The absence of such a discussion stands in sharp contrast to the presence of an entire unit of seven pages, item 6.05, to "Ethics of Scientific Publication," meaning plagiarism, publication credit, and the like. But even this material fails to identify exactly what the "basic ethical principles that underlie all scholarly writing" (p. 292) are. In other words, although ethical *principles and values* are absent, prescriptive *codes* of ethical conduct are fully present. The *Publication Manual*, therefore, maintains segregation of the important business of psychologists—doing quantitative research according to orthodox canons of methodology and writing in the prescribed manner—from the lived application of ethical principles.

Writing Style

Contrary to popular misconception, rhetoric is fundamental to and inescapable in all scientific report writing at least since the time of Newton: that is, the literary and rhetorical choices that authors make shape the construction of journal articles (Bazerman, 1988). Some contemporary psychologists have underscored the fact that persuasive writing plays a key role in scientific compositions (Bevan, 1991; Gergen, 1991). For example, Budge and Katz (1995) concluded their analysis of the *Publication Manual* by exhorting psychologists to become "more conscious of the literary and linguistic infrastructure of psychology and the messages communicated, intentional or not" (p. 230). What cognizance, then, do the *Publication Manual* authors give to rhetoric?

1. On page 2 the authors gravely and immediately declare that there is a tradition established in the discipline that is not to be challenged—"the scientific publishing tradition in which [writers] are about to take part." By this the authors mean that acceptable manuscripts are those that conform to "the integrity of the style" prescribed by the *Publication Manual*. The primary criterion is writing clearly and concisely. Writers are to "aim for clear and logical communication," adhering to "explicit style requirements" and using alternatives only when necessary (p. 25). The rationale given for uniformity of style is to facilitate editors' tasks and to minimize readers' distraction from "full attention to content." (See also Madigan et al., 1995, on the same points.) The rationale for brevity is to conserve journal space.

2. The prescribed writing style is impersonal, detached, objective, and rational.

Personal information and feelings must be absent, as the subjective is relegated to literature, not to science. As Madigan et al. (1995) explained, the authority of the empirical article as a text rests in the content, not in the writer or the researcher. Writers can achieve scientific authority by using "neutral" rhetoric and by "giving the persona of the writer a low profile in the text" (p. 430). Madigan et al. encouraged writers to use objective language and thereby discover "real truths" (p. 434) in their research data.

Furthermore, the *Publication Manual* authors insist that writers must not veer onto the treacherous path of mere literary devices. Creative expressions, such as "embellishment and flowery writing" (p. 27), are "inappropriate" and are clearly demarcated from scientific prose, lest readers be distracted by literary metaphors, as in item 2.12, "Linguistic Devices" (p. 46). But, as Sarason (1990) argued in his book, *The Challenge of Art to Psychology*, psychologists' overt and covert norms for composing journal articles mask writers' personal realities and discourage them from exercising their creative-writing skills by splitting "scientific" knowledge-making from literary artistry.

On the other hand, the *Publication Manual* authors promote, although mildly, "personal involvement" of writers and cultivation of their "personal style" and clearly proscribe anthropomorphisms, such as "the experiment demonstrated" in item 2.04, "Precision and Clarity." Furthermore, at several points the authors recommend writing in the active voice, but to meet *the* criterion of good writing: conciseness (e.g., p. 39).

3. Curiously, near the end of the text, the statement appears, "Style involves no inherent right and wrong" (p. 292). Then why speak with so much authority and at such great length about acceptable style? More fundamentally, how suitable are APA style and format to human psychological research in general and to other empirical methods besides the experiment and to other types of journal articles?

Gender Issues

Reflecting on the history of women in psychology, Bohan (1992) argued that using authors' full names in the reference list of an article would make the contributions of women more visible. Some women authors still might elect to use their initials to prevent prejudicial evaluation of their scholarly work, given the historical record of male bias in psychology, but the fourth edition precludes any choice. Rather, initials of the given name suffice, such as in university office directories, as is clear in all the items pertaining to references (e.g., 3.107 and Appendix 3-A). By this stance, then, the *Publication Manual* authors contribute to the status quo of women's relatively invisible place in the story of psychology.

What the *Publication Manual* does include about gender are guidelines to reduce language bias, with no further explanation: "using *man* to refer to all human beings is simply not as accurate as the phrase *men and women*" (p. 47). The best criterion for the correct language, apparently, is scientific accuracy; that is, modernist objectivity holds sway, not the ethical imperative of correcting injustice to women. Indeed, as I demonstrated previously, the *Publication Manual* recapitulates the modernist separation of ethical principles from the principal activity of the psychological scientist, namely, making objective knowledge. Furthermore, the *Publication Manual* authors do not refer the reader to revised feminist guidelines for nonsexist writing, such as those published by McHugh et al. (1986) and Stark-Adams and Kimball (1984).

THE CULTURE OF THE *PUBLICATION MANUAL*

To be sure, the *Publication Manual* contains useful information about common writing errors, guidelines to reduce bias against diverse groups, and technical information about the presentation of numerical data. For these specific purposes, the *Publication Manual* is a helpful guide. Nevertheless, replete with internal contradictions, it successfully conveys the core messages of the discipline: as scientists, we will uphold the standards of objective reason, we are in charge of the research relationship, and we will produce objective journal reports.

My principal interpretation of the *Publication Manual* as a modernist text is that psychologists remain in thrall to an institutional culture of patriarchal scientism that reverentially treats historically located conventions of investigative practice and report writing as idealized entities. As Bakan (1967) contended three decades ago, psychologists engage in methodolatry or the idolatrous worship of the experimental method. In this light, the *Publication Manual* is like sacred scripture, and its zealous advocates are like priests, ministers, and rabbis scrupulously defending the fundamentals of the Bible or the Torah. From a critical perspective on religion (Borg, 1994; Ruether, 1992, 1993), fundamentalists not only interpret scriptures literally, they absolutize good and evil, emphasize compliance with codes of purity, and regard sin as the failure to adhere to prescribed rules. Religious systems of authority, which the *Publication Manual* resembles, aim to solidify the cultural function of prescriptive codes for subjective experience and interpretations of that experience. Accepted codes then become conventional wisdom: that is, they constitute both the construction of reality and the individual's internalization of that construction. Conventional wisdom is played out in individuals' conformity with internalized prescriptions of worthy conduct.

Applied to our discipline, this critical analysis suggests that "good" psychological scientists are those who comply with the requirements of sound research and report writing as promulgated in the *Publication Manual*. In their sacred scripture, psychologists find definitive answers to their questions about putting a public face on their private methodology, because "APA style" reflects the discipline's epistemological assumptions (Madigan et al., 1995). Like the biblical stories constructed by their authors, the *Publication Manual* is an attempt by the defenders of the faith to show that, in the struggle between reason and nature, imposed rational order will prevail over the chaos of disorganized, uncontrolled, and unpredictable sensory impressions, feelings, and images. Devotion to the scientific method and its procedures will uncover Truth. Moreover, as a prominent symbol of psychologists' authority as scientists, the *Publication Manual* is closely intertwined with psychologists' very scientific identity. In fact, the *Publication Manual* ensures the distinctiveness and survival of the discipline, given that no other scientific disciplines have developed anything comparable (Bazerman, 1988; Dzinas, 1996). When literalized and proclaimed with unquestioning faith, the *Publication Manual* becomes a fundamentalist bible, providing security, comfort, and stability for its adherents. Thus, to question the legitimacy of the *Publication Manual* is to threaten the identity of the discipline and to commit heresy.

One of the central purposes of the *Publication Manual* is the indoctrination of millions of students annually in "APA style." A major theme, in fact, of Madigan et al.'s (1995) celebration of the *Publication Manual* is its key role in facilitating students' internalization of the discipline's epistemological foundations. The only sanctioned disciplinary framework, of course, is positivist psychology; no alternative forms of thinking about, conducting, and writing about psychological research are presumed to exist. Many psychology professors encourage students to purchase a copy of the *Publication Manual,* some have created psychology courses solely to teach APA style, and there are several texts on teaching it now on the market. As the centerpiece of APA's publishing industry, the *Publication Manual* has become like a catechism containing the tenets of the faith for memorization and behavioral compliance. Students are expected to master what psychologists consider to be "scientific" writing and to inhibit their inclinations to practice the rhetoric of the humanities (Madigan et al., 1995).

Some undergraduate students have informed me that in their psychology courses they are drilled in APA style and even suffer penalties of lost marks for writing in the first person, active voice; in other words, their instructors adhere to the view that the expression "it was found that" matches APA style. Moreover, the students are ordered to leave ethical information out of their research reports, because with a strict review procedure in place in the department ethics are assumed to be handled. Instead, these instructors hold up conventional journal articles for emulation, emphasizing that success in psychology graduate programs partly hinges on absorbing APA style. But some students manage to maintain a critical perspective on their indoctrination. One student described the typical research report as "written by, for, and about robots." Another student characterized the APA instructional techniques this way: "I believe that the rigid and sterile method of research reporting inadequately reflects the dynamic and interactive process of psychological research."

Community psychology graduate students whom I have taught are exposed to and practice feminist and participatory research. Many were creative writers before their immersion in undergraduate psychology. Yet even these students are strongly ambivalent about modifying enculturated injunctions to emulate "correct APA style" when they compose their thesis. The students are conflicted in part because alternative models are relatively rare in the journals, have little legitimacy, and seem ambiguous, and hence are threatening and stressful. If these students' experiences are common, what do they suggest about how psychologists educate students in constructing the research relationship in word and deed? Are the behavioral patterns that at least some psychologists evidently are demanding of students, which in other social circumstances we would typify as unreflective conformity and blind obedience to authority, harmonious with the discipline's goals of scientific discovery and the promotion of human welfare?

Dogmatic rules of report writing and investigative practice serve another institutional purpose. By inducing catechetical compliance with a uniform style these regulations enable rapid turnover and frequent publication of journal articles essential to academics' tenure and promotion. This social function in psychologists' research culture deserves critical examination (Wachtel, 1980). The production of psychological knowledge in both investigative practice and report writing cannot be unaffected by the political economy of academic psychology. In a social context of intense pressure for frequent publication of experiments, pragmatically it is far more efficient for investigators to take total control of the research enterprise, exploit participant labor, and generate depersonalized research reports. But this work ethic has a deleterious effect on the quality of the research relationship, as founding community psychologists acknowledged: They reported that research relationships with participants suffer under these conditions (Walsh, 1987).

Furthermore, journal editors, editorial policies and practices, and reviewers, as well as the authors of the *Publication Manual*, play influential roles in maintaining the political economy of psychologists' research productivity when they do not attend to authors' constructions of the research relationship. This is the spirit in which I have made recommendations for journal practices, such as in this journal (Walsh, 1989), so as to diminish the slip between the "lip and the cup," between espoused values of sensitivity to the research relationship, however construed, and actual conduct of research and report writing.

But received codes of conventional wisdom, like those embedded in the *Publication Manual*, have value only insofar as they illuminate human experience; if they do not speak authentically to actual experience, they can be changed to provide new interpretative frameworks. In fact, there is already a movement afoot in feminist and community psychology to practice a participatory research relationship and a correspondingly more relational report writing style (cf. reviews by Morawski & Steele, 1991; Walsh, 1987, 1989). Moreover, since World War II there have been such precedents in different areas of psychology (Walsh-Bowers, 1995).

I believe that we *can* produce publishable articles that demonstrate our commitment to promoting human welfare through research. A democratized research relationship and a compassionate, contextualized reporting style would truly express the *Publication Manual*'s espoused concern for sensitivity to research participants and would produce intersubjective, hence more meaningful, findings. Nevertheless, such a reorientation would necessitate political, economic, and interpersonal changes in psychologists' culture of hierarchical, professional authority.

CONSTRUCTING ALTERNATIVES

Following are suggested courses of action that echo previous calls for changing method in word and deed (Korn, 1988; McHugh et al., 1986; Morawski & Steele, 1991; Schultz, 1969; Walsh, 1987, 1989; Walsh-Bowers, 1995). But a caveat is in order. In my experience, attempting to implement these alternatives can be personally challenging. There is likely to be intense resistance to change and much defensiveness about the "bible," even among some who claim to be pushing at the margins of the discipline, given the psychological significance that traditional conceptions of science hold for psychologists. The personal is truly the political in changing the research culture of the discipline.

1. In our investigative practice, we could make the shift to a direct participation model of shared power and control to show respect to our participants, to recognize the socially constructed and intersubjective nature of research, and to learn more

about the phenomena in question. Precedents exist in the feminist literature (e.g., Fine, 1989; Lykes, 1989; Oakley, 1981).

2. In our report writing, we could create ethics sections in which we describe the research relationship. Relatedly, we could employ a personalized, contextualized approach to specify all parties in the research relationship and in the setting and to acknowledge participants' contributions. Again, there are models, especially in qualitative feminist research (cf. Olesen, 1994), in which alternative compositional forms, like a crystal displaying multiple, partial realities (Richardson, 1994), are more congruent with the content and process of feminist science.

3. In our editorial contributions to journals, we could promote changes to editorial policies and practices to encourage the flowering of alternative compositional forms and consciousness of the research relationship. Three journals have already instituted specific changes along some of these lines (*American Journal of Community Psychology, Journal of Community Psychology,* and *Canadian Journal of Community Mental Health*).

4. In our teaching and thesis supervision, we could place the inherently relational nature of psychological research and report writing at the heart of education about psychological science, thereby facilitating students' development, and our own, as sensitive scientists.

5. In our resources, we could recognize the strengths and weaknesses of the present *Publication Manual,* while continuing to create alternative forms and writing styles that suit the issues we are addressing. One hopes that the *fifth* edition of the *Publication Manual* will serve to encourage multiple methods and varied compositional forms that will do justice to the variegated and rich textures of human life, respect women's voices, and support the creativity of psychological scientists committed to innovative feminist methods.

Initial submission: December 10, 1996
Initial acceptance: March 21, 1997
Final acceptance: June 25, 1997

REFERENCES

Adair, J. G., Dushenko, T. W., & Lindsay, R. C. L. (1985). Ethical regulations and their impact on research practice. *American Psychologist, 40,* 59–72.
American Psychological Association, Council of Editors. (1952). Publication Manual of the American Psychological Association. *Psychological Bulletin, 49* (Suppl., Pt. 2), 389–449.
American Psychological Association. (1983). *Publication manual of the American Psychological Association* (3rd ed.). Washington, DC: Author.
American Psychological Association. (1992). Ethical principles of psychologists and code of conduct. *American Psychologist, 47,* 1597–1611.
American Psychological Association. (1994). *Publication manual of the American Psychological Association* (4th ed.). Washington, DC: Author.
Bakan, D. (1967). *On method.* San Francisco: Jossey-Bass.
Bazerman, C. (1988). *Shaping written knowledge: The genre and activity of the experimental article in science.* Madison, WI: University of Wisconsin Press.
Bevan, W. (1991). Contemporary psychology: A tour inside the onion. *American Psychologist, 46,* 475–483.
Blanck, P. D., Bellack, A. S., Rosnow, R. L., Rotheram-Borus, M. J., & Schooler, N. R. (1992).

Scientific rewards and conflicts of ethical choices in human subjects research. *American Psychologist, 47,* 959–965.

Bleier, R. (Ed.). (1986). *Feminist approaches to science.* New York: Pergamon Press.

Bohan, J. S. (Ed.). (1992). *Seldom seen, rarely heard.* Boulder, CO: Westview Press.

Borg, M. J. (1994). *Meeting Jesus again for the first time: The historical Jesus & the heart of contemporary faith.* New York: HarperCollins.

Budge, G. S., & Katz, B. (1995). Constructing psychological knowledge. *Theory & Psychology, 5,* 217–231.

Community Education Team. Fostering relationality when implementing and evaluating a collective drama approach to preventing violence against women. *Psychology of Women Quarterly, 23,* 97–112.

Damasio, A. R. (1994). *Descartes' error.* New York: Putnam.

Danziger, K. (1979). The social origins of modern psychology. In A. R. Buss (Ed.), *Psychology in social context* (pp. 27–45). New York: Irvington.

Danziger, K. (1990). *Constructing the subject: Historical origins of psychological research.* Cambridge, UK: Cambridge University Press.

Danziger, K. (1997a). *Naming the mind: How psychology found its language.* London: Sage.

Danziger, K. (1997b, June). *What I wish I knew in 1950.* Article presented at the annual meeting of the Canadian Psychological Association, Toronto.

Danziger, K., & Dzinas, K. (1997). How psychology got its variables. *Canadian Psychology, 38,* 43–48.

Dzinas, K. (1996, May). *The codification of "APA" style after World War II: A contextual analysis.* Paper presented at the CPA/Learned Societies meeting, St. Catharines, Canada.

Fine, M. (1989). Coping with rape: Critical perspectives on consciousness. In R. K. Unger (Ed.), *Representations: Social constructions of gender* (pp. 186–200). Amityville, NY: Baywood.

Gergen, K. J. (1991). Emerging challenges for theory and psychology. *Theory & Psychology, 1,* 13–36.

Haraway, D. (1988). Situated knowledges: The science question in feminism and the privilege of partial perspective. *Feminist Studies, 14,* 575–599.

Harding, S. (1987). *Feminism and methodology: Social science issues.* Bloomington, IN: Indiana University Press.

Keller, E. F. (1984). *Reflections on gender and science.* New Haven, CT: Yale University Press.

Kirby, S., & McKenna, K. (1989). *Experience, research, social change: Methods from the margins.* Toronto: Garamond Press.

Korn, J. H. (1988). Students' roles, rights, and responsibilities as research participants. *Teaching of Psychology, 15,* 74–78.

Kuhn, T. S. (1970). *The structure of scientific revolutions* (2nd ed.). Chicago: University of Chicago Press.

Leahey, T. H. (1992). *A history of psychology: Main currents in psychological thought* (3rd ed.). Englewood Cliffs, NJ: Prentice-Hall.

Lykes, M. B. (1989). Dialogue with Guatemalan Indian women: Critical perspectives on constructing collaborative research. In R. K. Unger (Ed.), *Representations: Social constructions of gender* (pp. 167–185). Amityville, NY: Baywood.

Madigan, R., Johnson, S., & Linton, P. (1995). The language of psychology: APA style as epistemology. *American Psychologist, 50,* 428–436.

McHugh, M. C., Koeske, R. D., & Frieze, I. H. (1986). Issues to consider in conducting nonsexist psychological research. *American Psychologist, 41,* 879–890.

Mitroff, I. I. (1974). *The subjective side of science.* Amsterdam: Elsevier.

Morawski, J. G. (Ed.). (1988). *The rise of experimentation in American psychology.* New Haven, CT: Yale University Press.

Morawski, J. G. (1992, August). *With gender in mind: The heritage of feminism in psychology.* Article presented at the annual meeting of the American Psychological Association, Washington, DC.

Morawski, J. G., & Steele, R. S. (1991). The one or the other? Textual analysis of masculine power and feminist empowerment. *Theory & Psychology, 1,* 107–131.

Oakely, A. (1981). Interviewing women: A contradiction in terms. In H. Roberts (Ed.), *Doing feminist research* (pp. 30–61). London: Routledge & Kegan Paul.

Olesen, V. (1994). Feminisms and models of qualitative research. In N. K. Denzin & Y. S. Lincoln (Eds.), *Handbook of qualitative research* (pp. 158–174). Thousand Oaks, CA: Sage Publications.

Reinharz, S. (1992). *Feminist methods for social action research*. New York: Oxford University Press.

Richardson, L. (1994). Writing: A method of inquiry. In N. K. Denzin & Y. S. Lincoln (Eds.), *Handbook of qualitative research* (pp. 516–529). Thousand Oaks, CA: Sage.

Rosnow, R. L. (1981). *Paradigms in transition*. New York: Oxford University Press.

Ruether, R. R. (1992). *Gaia and God: An ecofeminist theology of earth healing*. New York: HarperCollins.

Ruether, R. R. (1993). *Sexism and God-talk: Toward a feminist theology*. Boston: Beacon Press.

Sarason, S. B. (1990). *The challenge of art to psychology*. New Haven, CT: Yale University Press.

Schultz, D. P. (1969). The human subject in psychological research. *Psychological Bulletin, 72*, 214–228.

Smith, J. C. (1990). *Psychoanalytic roots of patriarchy: The neurotic foundations of social order*. New York: New York University Press.

Stark-Adamec, C., & Kimball, M. (1984). Science free of sexism: A psychologist's guide to the conduct of nonsexist research. *Canadian Psychology, 25*, 23–34.

Wachtel, P. L. (1980). Investigation and its discontents: Some constraints on progress in psychological research. *American Psychologist, 35*, 399–408.

Walsh, R. T. (1987). The evolution of the research relationship in community psychology. *American Journal of Community Psychology, 15*, 773–788.

Walsh, R. T. (1989). Do research reports in mainstream feminist psychology journals reflect feminist values? *Psychology of Women Quarterly, 13*, 435–446.

Walsh, R. T., & Schallow, J. R. (1977). The experimenter as a sex-role model in sex-role stereotyping. *Canadian Journal of Behavioural Science, 9*, 305–314.

Walsh-Bowers, R. (1995). The reporting and ethics of the research relationship in areas of interpersonal psychology, 1939–89. *Theory & Psychology, 5*, 233–250.

Walsh-Bowers, R. T., & Parlour, S. J. (1992). Researcher-participant relationships in journal reports on gay men and lesbian women. *Journal of Homosexuality, 23*(4), 87–104.

Wertheimer, M. (1945). *Productive thinking*. New York: Harper.

Wittig, M. A. (1985). Metatheoretical dilemmas in the psychology of gender. *American Psychologist, 40*, 800–811.

HOW OFTEN DO YOU READ THE BIBLE?

Hope Landrine
Public Health Foundation

Elizabeth A. Klonoff
California State University—San Bernardino

In his article, "Fundamentalism in Psychological Science: The *Publication Manual* As Bible," Richard Walsh-Bowers (this issue) proposes the metaphor that APA's *Publication Manual* is the bible of psychology. This is not only because psychologists tend to refer to "The" book that way or because its authors (like those of the Bible) will remain forever anonymous. Rather (he says) it is primarily because the *Manual* similarly champions a code of conduct deemed lofty and unassailable, one that the minions therefore are expected to follow religiously, with unquestioning devotion. This manual-as-bible metaphor is in fact a good and useful one in our opinion, but our reasons for thinking so differ from Walsh-Bowers'. In his view, the *Manual* is similar to the Bible in its rigid fundamentalism—in the uncompromising orthodoxy of the view of science and in the conduct that it espouses. In our view, however, that is the mere surface structure of how the two books are similar; they are similar on a deeper level as well, one that may be more important. In our view, the *Manual* is most similar to the Bible in terms of how it has been and continues to be treated and regarded by psychologists and psychology students; the *Manual* is similar to the Bible not so much in terms of the dictates it espouses but in terms of how people respond to those dictates. An analysis of this latter similarity, we believe, not only highlights the nature of the relationship between psychological publications and the dictates surrounding them, but also may elucidate the future direction of publications in our field.

First we examine how the Bible has been treated historically, and compare that to the historical treatment of the *Manual*, and highlight the similarities. Then, we briefly underscore how the Bible is treated and regarded by ordinary people and suggest that the publication *Manual* is regarded and treated similarly by the ordinary

No one we know would wish to be thanked or credited for this article.

Address correspondence and reprint requests to: Hope Landrine, Senior Research Scientist, Public Health Foundation, 13200 Crossroads Parkway North, Suite 135, City of Industry, CA 91746.

psychologist or psychology student. Finally, we note events and movements that have occurred with respect to the Bible but not yet with respect to the *Manual* and speculate on what such events may mean—by analogy—for psychology. Unlike Walsh-Bowers, who views similarities between the Bible and the *Manual* as signs of a medieval fundamentalism that is destructive to and impedes creativity and progress, we view similarities between the two books in the opposite manner.

HISTORICAL TREATMENT OF THE BIBLE AND *MANUAL*

Unlike the central text of other religions, the Bible always has been subject to criticism, critical assessment, interpretation, and reinterpretation by Christian and Jewish scholars. This is because Christians and Jews alike typically have acknowledged that the anonymous authors of the Old and New Testaments were human rather than divine. The content of the Bible has not generally been regarded—like the content of the Islamic Koran or the Hindu Veda—as transmitted directly by gods or other eternal entities, and hence it always has been considered acceptable for those with feet of clay to examine and evaluate it. For example, in the Hellenistic Age (4th century to 1st century B.C.), the Jewish scholar Philo Judaeus applied an interpretive technique called allegorism to the Old Testament to argue that its latent meaning differed from its manifest content. Likewise, the early rabbis (200 to 500 A.D.) of Palestine and Babylonia applied their own (idiosyncratic) method of textual explication and reinterpretation to the Old Testament in an effort to render it internally consistent and consistent with Judaism; these discussions are preserved as the Talmud. A variety of such (by and large noncritical but important) textual analyses of the Bible continued until the Enlightenment and the Protestant Reformation (17th and 18th centuries), at which point more critical approaches emerged. These new critical methods, developed for explicating historical and literary texts, were applied to biblical texts by the Christian philosopher Thomas Hobbes, the Jewish philosopher Baruch Spinoza, and countless others. That tradition of textual criticism and analysis of the Bible continues today and takes a variety of forms (see Brown, 1991, for a list), including hermeneutic (Bartkowski, 1996), postmodernist (Freeman, 1993), dialectical (Noble, 1993), legal-economic (Miller, 1993), feminist (Cahill, 1995; Camp, 1993; Daly, 1968, 1973; Sakenffeld, 1989), and even mathematical–computer scientific (Drosin, 1997). For example, in her now-classic texts, *Beyond God the Father* (Daly, 1973) and *The Church and the Second Sex* (Daly, 1968, 1975), feminist scholar Mary Daly provided detailed analyses of the Bible as a document written by men to reinforce and perpetuate patriarchal forms of relationships. Likewise, in his new, controversial book, *The Bible Code,* Michael Drosin (1997) presents a deconstruction of the Bible via specific algorithms to reveal another text within it: an oracle for predicting social events, such as the assassinations of John and Robert Kennedy and the Oklahoma City bombing (using this hidden code, Drosin warned others of Yitzhak Rabin's impending assassination but was dismissed as crazy).

    Thus, contrary to Walsh-Bowers' idealistic view of the Bible as a revered text adhered to with unquestioning devotion throughout history, the Bible has been questioned, criticized, analyzed, disputed, challenged, probed, interpreted, and reinterpreted by scholars. Critical, textual analyses of the Bible have not (as he implies) been tantamount to heresy but instead have been the historical (and remain the contemporary) norm. Likewise, then, contrary to Walsh-Bowers' idealistic claim that the *Manual*-as-Bible is a similarly inviolable, exalted text, the *Manual* (as he himself admits) has been criticized, analyzed, challenged, and changed. The *Manual* then is similar to the Bible in this respect and, in our view, needs to be more similar: The *Manual* needs to be subjected to the meticulous, comprehensive, critical textual analyses from multiple perspectives that are prototypical of Biblical scholarship. Psychology would benefit from treating and regarding the *Manual* more, rather than less, like the Bible.

THE ORDINARY PERSON, THE BIBLE, AND THE *MANUAL*

Everyday Christians and Jews have a Bible at home—somewhere (don't ask them to retrieve it because, to their embarrassment, their copy is old and covered with dust). It is a text that they were forced or otherwise required to study and perhaps memorize as children but have not opened since then and hence one with which as adults they remain only vaguely familiar. With the exception of the devout, few ordinary people use their Bible on a daily basis to make decisions about the conduct of their lives; few can recite passages from it accurately; and indeed, few think about it. Yet, it nonetheless remains a sacred text espousing a code of conduct for everyday life. Most Christians and Jews would say that they agree (basically, for the most part, well sort of) with that code and that they attempt (now and then, more or less, in their own way—well definitely in spirit at least) to conduct themselves in accordance with the Bible's dictates. In our everyday lives, the Bible acts not as an indispensable set of imperatives reviewed before we set out each day (as Walsh-Bowers implies) but as a global, tacit, hazy set of moral principles that are taken for granted and that are occasionally violated (when it's expedient, or when it seems justified or desirable, or when we think we can get away with it). If specific biblical passages are ever cited, it is as a last recourse for rejecting the arguments of someone we dislike for nonbiblical reasons. Psychology's relationship to the *Manual* is precisely the same.

Many psychologists and psychology students have a copy of the *Manual*—somewhere (don't ask them to retrieve it because, to their embarrassment, their copy is an old edition—but hey, how much has it changed anyway?). Undergraduate and graduate students are most aware of (and may be the few who can cite) the content of the *Manual* because they are at the stage of being forced or otherwise required to study and memorize it. Good students question, debate, and argue with their professors about the *Manual* just as young people do with their parents and religious teachers when first studying the Bible. Once we graduate, the *Manual* is shelved away somewhere and rarely opened again. With the exception of journal editors and those who must teach courses on writing in APA style, few ordinary psychologists use their *Manuals* on a daily basis to make decisions about the conduct of their research or even the writing of their articles; few can recite passages from it accurately; and indeed, few think about it. Yet, it nonetheless remains a sacred text espousing a code of conduct for professional work. Most psychologists would say that they agree (basically, for the most part, well sort of) with that code and that they attempt (now and then, more or less, in their own way—well definitely in spirit at least) to write their articles in accordance with the *Manual*'s dictates. In our everyday work, the *Manual* acts not as an indispensable set of imperatives reviewed before conducting a study or writing an article (as Walsh-Bowers argues) but as a global, tacit, hazy set of principles of scientific writing that are taken for granted and that are occasionally violated (when it's expedient, or when it seems justified or desirable, or when we think we can get away with it). If specific rules from the *Manual* are ever cited, it is as a last recourse for rejecting a manuscript or student's paper that we did not like for non-APA style-related reasons.

The contemporary, daily relationship between psychologists and the *Manual* is then a good deal like that between Christians, Jews, and the Bible—but that relationship is not the dominating, time-consuming, intimidating, energy-depleting, intrusive one that Walsh-Bowers described. Rather, we study the *Manual* and the Bible when we are young and are being indoctrinated (and criticize it at that time), and then we by and large forget about these texts, remaining only vaguely aware of them until we must use them for a specific purpose. Just as only devout fundamentalists and Biblical scholars are incessantly cognizant of the Bible and cite it frequently, so too, only editors and teachers of specific courses constantly think about or cite the *Manual*.

Thus, rather than symbolizing a repressive orthodoxy that is destructive to creativity, the similarities between the Bible and the *Manual* are encouraging: in time, psychologists may come to pay as little attention to the *Manual* as most people do to their Bible. And indeed, there is ample evidence that this is already occurring insofar as, rather than dictating and limiting our publications (as Walsh-Bowers states), the rules of the *Manual,* like those of the Bible, are being increasingly fashioned to suit our purposes—reinterpreted, violated, or simply dismissed. Empirical evidence for this is provided by the Walsh-Bowers article itself.

CONTEMPORARY AND FUTURE TRENDS: APPLYING THE *MANUAL* TO THE WALSH-BOWERS ARTICLE

Throughout the article, Walsh-Bowers repeatedly emphasizes that the *Manual* demands that published manuscripts conform to the laboratory-report format and thereby consist of the discrete sections of Introduction, Method, Results, and Discussion. Although this is indeed what the *Manual* commands, we note that the Walsh-Bowers article does not conform to that format at all (and indeed contains none of these sections) yet nonetheless is published in a journal that explicitly requires articles to conform to APA style. Obviously, the dictates regarding the appropriate format of articles can and are being violated to allow creative and divergent styles of writing. Likewise, Walsh-Bowers highlights that the *Manual* states an explicit preference for brief empirical articles, but also regards (a small number of) theoretical and review articles as tolerable. The Walsh-Bowers article, however, is neither the desired brief empirical report, nor a theoretical or review article. It is a critique—the presentation of a critical opinion without data, review, or theory—yet here it is, published in a journal that uses the *Manual* as its Bible. Clearly the codes of the ostensibly inviolable *Manual* can be ignored. Similarly,

Walsh-Bowers notes repeatedly that the *Manual* demands an impersonal, objective, neutral, detached writing style entailing the use of the authoritative voice-from-no-one and frowns on the personal voice. Yet, Walsh-Bowers uses "I" and "my" throughout his article and describes his personal experiences in some detail. Again it is clear that the rigid, stifling rules are neither so rigid nor so stifling as he claims. As a final example, Walsh-Bowers notes that the *Manual* explicitly warns against the use of creative, lively writing, dismisses this creativity as inappropriate, and demands the sterile, neutral wording of a lab report. Yet, the Walsh-Bowers article is replete with imaginative prose that entails a diversity of metaphors and allusions, including: "writers must not veer onto the treacherous path of mere literary devices"; "idolatrous worship of the experimental method"; "putting a public face on their private methodology"; "the defenders of the faith"; "the struggle between reason and nature"; and "the chaos of disorganized, uncontrolled, and unpredictable sensory impressions." Suffice it say that this does not sound like a lab report. The Walsh-Bowers article ironically violates the very dictates he purports to be inviolable.

Thus, the *Publication Manual,* like the Bible, may consist largely (as Walsh-Bowers argues) of rigid, orthodox, elitist, anachronistic, patriarchal, culturally insensitive, exclusionary, and frankly pretentious rules and examples, but these are obviously, sometimes blatantly, and increasingly ignored by authors and journal editors. Certainly, there are some journals (and all of us know which ones) that enforce rigid adherence to APA style as Walsh-Bowers argues, but just as many (and perhaps more) do not. Indeed, one APA journal *requires* authors to violate the dictates of the *Manual.* Specifically, articles published in APA's official, archival, most exalted journal, *The American Psychologist,* violate the rules in the *Manual* insofar as they are critical position papers and analyses lacking data, review, or theory and are replete with the passionate language, personal identity, and personal voice of their authors. That these characteristics are *the criteria* for articles in our most distinguished journal suggests that it is acceptable and desirable to violate the rules and that doing so is central to who we are as a discipline.

The contemporary and future trend in biblical scholarship is to focus on and publish more diverse, radical, marginal, and (frankly) downright weird (e.g., Drosin, 1997) textual analyses, critiques, and opinions. Such trends no doubt have appeared because biblical scholarship is embedded in a larger social and cultural context of diversity and conflict and of postmodernist philosophy and analytic perspectives. The Bible and our relation to it has been deeply affected by these trends, and the *Manual* (as Walsh-Bowers points out) has been similarly affected. Publications in psychology and the *Publication Manual,* like publications in religion and the Bible, are dynamic rather than static and continue to change and evolve in the larger context of change. Thus, if the *Manual* is indeed like the Bible, then one must predict not its persistent dominance, as Walsh-Bowers implies, but instead the continuing neglect of its dictates by the minions, growing dissatisfaction with its content, and increasing critiques of its purpose, relevance, importance, validity, and politics. As we continue as a discipline to change and grow within the larger social context of change, we might then hope that the *Publication Manual* really is our bible and then happily await the predictable emergence of schools of atheism and agnosticism. Hermeneutic, Marxist, feminist, and multicultural voices for change in how psychology conducts its research and in what psychology publishes can be regarded as agnostic at best. What then indeed would atheism look like?

REFERENCES

Bartkowski, J. (1996). Beyond biblical literalism and inerrancy: Conservation Protestants and the hermeneutic interpretation of scripture. *Sociology of Religion, 57,* 259–272.

Brown, R. E. (1991). A dictionary of biblical interpretation. *Heythrop Journal: A Quarterly Review of Philosophy, 32,* 77–166.

Cahill, L. (1995). Sexual ethics: A feminist biblical perspective. *Interpretation, 49,* 5–16.

Camp, C. V. (1993). Metaphor in feminist biblical interpretation: Theoretical perspective. *Semeia, 61,* 3–38.

Daly, M. (1968). *The church and the second sex.* New York: Harper Colophon.

Daly, M. (1973). *Beyond God the father: Toward a philosophy of women's liberation.* Boston: Beacon Press.

Daly, M. (1975). *The church and the second sex.* Boston: Beacon Press.

Drosin, M. (1997). *The Bible code.* New York: Simon & Schuster.

Freeman, C. (1993). The "eclipse" of spiritual exegesis: Biblical interpretation from the reformation to modernity. *Southwestern Journal of Theology, 35*(3), 21–28.

Miller, G. P. (1993). Ritual and regulation: A legal-economic interpretation of selected biblical texts. *Journal of Legal Studies, 22,* 477–502.

Noble, P. R. (1993). Synchronic and diachronic approaches to biblical interpretation. *Literature and Theology, 7,* 131–148.

Sakenffeld, K. D. (1989). Feminist biblical interpretation. *Theology Today, 46,* 154–168.

Walsh-Bowers, R. (1999). Fundamentalism in psychological science: The *Publication Manual* as bible. *Psychology of Women Quarterly, 23,* 375–393.

PUTTING THE APA *PUBLICATION MANUAL* IN CONTEXT

Nancy Felipe Russo
Arizona State University

Reading Walsh-Bowers' (this issue) article characterizing the American Psychological Association (APA) *Publication Manual* as a bible and Landrine and Klonoff's (1999) feisty commentary brought back a lot of memories. In the 1970s I was intimately involved in developing feminist critiques of the *Publication Manual* and the discussions and negotiations that led to the development of the 1977 *Guidelines for Nonsexist Language in APA Journals* (APA, 1977). I would like to share some of the insights gained from those negotiations and to put Walsh-Bowers' critique in the context of the feminist activities that were part of the process.

The *Publication Manual* is first and foremost a style manual. As Walsh-Bowers points out, language style is a powerful shaper of thought and action, which means that the *Publication Manual* can be a lever for change in the field and a means to influence how people think about research. But *Publication Manual* language is negotiated. Feminist psychologists came to the negotiation table in the 1970s and have been players in shaping the text, but other concerns affect the process as well. Efforts to change the field through the modification of *Publication Manual* language quickly run up against the hackles that arise at any suggestion that APA might try to "dictate" how to conduct research, for example.

Offering guidelines and recommendations can take one only so far. The *Publication Manual* is supposed to *reflect* the practices of the field and to represent a *consensus* on the most effective ways to present psychological theories and findings. But as Landrine and Klonoff (this issue) point out, people don't always pay attention to what the *Publication Manual* says. Further, *Publication Manual* impact is limited by the great power editors have in how they interpret and implement its recommendations. Indeed, readers are specifically told that "The *Publication Manual* presents explicit style requirements but alternatives are sometimes necessary; authors should balance the rules of the *Publication Manual* with good judgment" (APA, 1994, p. xxiii).

Thus, feminist activists targeting the publications process in the 1970s realized

Address correspondence and reprint requests to: N. F. Russo, Psychology, Box 871104, ASU, Tempe, AZ 85287-1104. E-mail: nancy.russo@asu.edu.

that changing the language of the *Publication Manual* was not enough—winning the hearts and minds of editors (and ultimately researchers) was crucial. We began to work to influence editorial appointments and editorial policy at the journal level and to widen participation in the publications process at all levels. In 1982 APA established an ad hoc Committee on Underrepresented Groups in the Publications Process, chaired by Barbara Strudler Wallston, an astute strategist, negotiator, and feminist leader (Russo, 1990).

Fortunately, unlike the Bible, trying to change the *Publication Manual* is not considered heresy. Thus, the contents of the third edition of the *Publication Manual*, published in 1978, reflects feedback received from a widely cast net that included questionnaires sent to authors, graduate departments in psychology, editors of non-APA journals, and APA production staff. In addition to reflecting current practice, the *Publication Manual* thus provides more detailed information about topics identified as problems for authors and editors. This, of course, means we have a conservative process, because the people who are "in" are the ones defining the practices and problems. The ad hoc Committee on Underrepresented Groups in the Publications Process was specifically designed to break out of that conservative mold. It also means that the practices in the field must be targeted directly if change is to occur.

Given that the *Publication Manual* is expected to reflect the field, it should not be surprising that the bulk of the *Publication Manual* deals with empirical studies. In fact, the examples that Walsh-Bowers underscores on pp. 381–382 appear after the *Publication Manual* has specifically stated that "Most journal articles published in psychology are reports of empirical studies, and therefore the next section of this chapter emphasizes their preparation" (p. 6). Reviews and theoretical articles are also discussed, however, and it is noted that "Other, less frequently published types of articles . . . include . . . discussions of qualitative methods and case studies" (p. 5). As an editor, I have found that the APA format can accommodate a wide variety of approaches (indeed, the articles in this series demonstrate this flexibility). The problems I've encountered in reporting qualitative research reflect cost and length issues and the size of the *PWQ* journal page (too small to accommodate tables of qualitative data). Using electronic means to supplement print media (or going to an all-electronic format) may resolve these issues in the future.

Walsh-Bowers rightly points out that the *Publication Manual,* like the field in general, reflects scientific perspectives and values empirical work. In identifying examples on p. 381, however, he uses one from the section dealing with documentation. In that section, the *Publication Manual* encourages people to support their statements by citing empirical work when possible, stating: "When you cite nonempirical work, make it clear in your narrative [e.g.]: Cho (1991) theorized that . . . ; Audeh (in press) argued that . . . " (p. 20). It should also be noted that many feminists have long criticized "armchair" statements about gender differences and have lambasted the failure to distinguish between statements about women's lives that are constructed from data-based findings from those unsupported by empirical data. This wording is responsive to that point of view.

Walsh-Bowers' discussion of the use of the word "participant" on p. 384 struck a particularly strong memory chord. Feminists played key roles in negotiating the use of the word "participant" in the *Publication Manual.* He points out that both "subject" and "participant" are used throughout. To understand the apparent inconsistency, it is useful to know that the term "subjects" refers to the overall category of "people and nonhuman animals" (APA, 1994, p. 14) as well as the subcategory "nonhuman animals." Thus, the wording Walsh-Bowers cites on p. 10 in the *Publication Manual* more fully reads: "the subjects, specifying pertinent characteristics, such as number, type, age, sex, and genus and species;" (APA, 1994, p. 10).

On p. 384, Walsh-Bowers leaves out some important information about feminist concerns in Guideline 3. That guideline, which is specifically titled "Acknowledge participation" states: "Write about the people in your study in a way that acknowledges their participation." It then goes on to provide some examples of how to do so, including the use of a "more descriptive term when possible—*participants, individuals, college students, children,* or *respondents,* for example (subjects and sample are appropriate when discussing statistics)" (p. 49, italics theirs). The guidelines also states that "The passive voice suggests individuals are *acted on* instead of being actors" (APA, 1994, p. 49) and that the active voice is preferable. This was an important point for feminist negotiators.

On p. 386, Walsh-Bowers raises the issue of the use of initials in references as fostering the invisibility of women in psychology. I find it ironic that in my role as editor of *PWQ* I had to decide that we could not use full names in references in this special-issue series—I advanced this argument over 25 years ago (Bernstein & Russo, 1974). In the 1980s I pushed it in meetings of the ad hoc Committee on Underrepresented Groups in the Publications Process.My position was rejected, however, when the members of the committee found out its cost and they became persuaded that as long as historical researchers had access to full names in original articles, cost issues should have priority when it came to references. Today, historical researchers have ready access to the names of authors through PsychINFO Online as well.

On p. 387, Walsh-Bowers notes the *Publication Manual* doesn't cite McHugh et al. (1986) and Stark-Adams and Kimball (1984). Rather, it refers readers to APA's 1979 *Guidelines for Nonsexist Language in APA Journals,* the basis for the current material on reducing language bias. There's a good reason for this. In 1975 APA's Education and Training Board's Task Force on Issues of Sexual Bias in Graduate Education—overwhelmed by the potential scope of its mission—focused its work on gender bias in textbook language (Task Force, 1975). This work became the basis for calls to reform psychology's language in general (see Russo & Stier, 1975). Textbook examples did not quite fit with the issues that came up in journal writing, however. So an in-house task force was formed that solicited examples of language bias in journals and developed the guidelines after consultation with feminist leaders in the field.

But feminists soon recognized that criticizing the *Publication Manual* was insufficient, as it was developed by a consensus process and would always reflect current practices. But APA sensitivities forbade anything that would look like "dictating" research approaches to the field. So Carolyn Sherif, President of Division 35, established a task force to develop guidelines for psychological research that resulted in the McHugh et al. (1986) article. Both the McHugh et al. (1986) and Stark-Adams and Kimball (1984) articles focus on the research process and not on research writing per se. Later, we pointed to these products coming from the field as justification for establishing an ad hoc Committee on Nonsexist Research. That group (which cited the earlier work) then produced abbreviated guidelines for research. These guidelines were voted on by APA's Council of Representatives and thus could be presented as a consensus document containing ways to help researchers deal with bias issues (Denmark, Russo, Frieze, & Sechzer, 1988). They are also not mentioned in the *Publication Manual.*

There is, of course, more to the story. I will post more information on the development and impact of the *Publication Manual* and feminist involvement in negotiating its language on the innovative methods Web site, at http://www.public.asu.edu/~atnfr. I invite others involved in the process to post their recollections as well.

REFERENCES

American Psychological Association. (1977). *Guidelines for nonsexist language in APA journals.* Washington, DC: Author.
American Psychological Association. (1994). *Publication manual of the American Psychological Association.* Washington, DC: Author.
Bernstein, M., & Russo, N. F. (1974). The history of psychology revisited: Or, up with our foremothers. *American Psychologist, 29,* 130–134.
Denmark, F. L., Russo, N. F., Frieze, I., & Sechzer, J. (1988). Guidelines for avoiding sexism in psychological research: A report of the Committee on Nonsexist Research. *American Psychologist, 43,* 582–585.
Landrine, H., & Klonoff, E. A. (1999). How often do you read the Bible? *Psychology of Women Quarterly, 23,* 393–398.
Russo, N., & Stier, S. (1975). A rose is a rose . . . is a four letter word. *APA Monitor, 6*(3), 15.
Russo, N. F. (1990). Barbara Strudler Wallston: Pioneer of contemporary feminist psychology, 1943–1987. *Psychology of Women Quarterly, 14,* 277–287.
Task Force on Issues of Sexual Bias in Graduate Education. (1975). Guidelines for nonsexist use of language. *American Psychologist, 30,* 682–684.
Walsh-Bowers, R. (1999). Fundamentalism in psychological science: The *Publication Manual* as bible. *Psychology of Women Quarterly, 23,* 375–392.

HEARING VOICES

The Uses of Research and the Politics of Change

Glenda M. Russell
University of Colorado

Janis S. Bohan
Metropolitan State College of Denver

This article focuses on the uses of research rather than on research methods per se. It highlights a particular feminist perspective: the importance of returning the results of research to the communities from which they derive. A theoretical rationale for psychological research on social issues argues that such work is inevitably value laden; bears implications for social change; and at its best amounts to a conversation among the researcher, the participants, and the community—one that ought to continue beyond the formal research project. This position is illustrated by two research projects and the means through which their findings were communicated back to lay communities. The unusual products of the research described here—an oratorio and a documentary video—and the process of their development are discussed.

It is by now a truism among feminist psychologists that psychological research does not proceed in a vacuum. Our growing recognition of the fact and impact of reflexivity, our emphasis on context, our awareness that the personal is political—all point to the inescapable embedment of psychological questions in sociopolitical realities. Although these awarenesses inform the framing of research questions, the choice of methodology, and the analysis and interpretation of data, we often fail to attend to the reciprocity inherent in this perspective and thereby miss the

We wish to acknowledge the assistance of the many people who enriched our understanding of the impact of Amendment 2 by completing the survey and of the allies whose comments provided such useful insights into the dynamics of taking a stand.

Address correspondence and reprint requests to: Glenda M. Russell, 2315 Broadway, Boulder, CO 80304.

logical next step: giving back to those we study the knowledge we have gained from listening to their voices. As Walsh (1989) noted, even feminist research often fails to meet the goals set out by guidelines for feminist research.

The purpose of this article is not to focus on novel research methods per se, but to encourage researchers to give thought to how their work can be of use. Accordingly, we will explore possibilities for returning the fruits of our work to lay communities, using as illustrations two products derived from psychological research. Both products emanated from research projects carried out by one of us (GR); subsequently, we have spent much time considering together their implications for psychological research and social policy and their lessons for our own work. This article brings together a description of these research projects with the substance of our joint conversations. As a framework for considering these research projects and their products, we will first explore some of the rationale underlying work of this sort. We will then briefly describe the two research projects and their major results, largely as background for understanding why and how these results were returned to the communities from which they originated. Finally, we will discuss the creative modes of "giving it back" that emerged from these projects, exploring how both the projects and their final outcome address concerns long voiced by feminist psychologists and others committed to doing work that matters in a broad social sense.

THEORETICAL BACKGROUND

Reflexivity and Psychological Research

Central to the projects described here is an awareness of the role of reflexivity in psychological research. The term "reflexivity" refers to two intertwined issues. First it points to the need for researchers to reflect on the ways in which our own and our informants' location in the world shapes our work. This includes the fact that in research we enter into relationships with our informants, and those relationships become part of the context that frames the research process. Second, reflexivity refers to the fact that when we study human beings we cannot stand apart from our own humanity; our vision is unavoidably influenced by the fact that what we see in our informants is often true of ourselves as well. Embedded in both meanings of reflexivity lies the recognition that research is not an objective rendering of reality but a form of participation in the phenomena under study (Bohan, 1996; Hertz, 1997).

Attention to reflexivity illuminates the fact that, whether or not we acknowledge it, psychological research is unavoidably influenced by factors external to the research endeavor and inevitably has consequences for social change or social stagnation as well as for individual experience. As feminists have long argued, to deny this reality does not make our work value free; it simply precludes our confronting the ethical, practical, and indeed moral underpinnings and consequences of that work. To recognize our own investment in the topics, the participants, the outcomes, and the implications of our research allows us to work more responsibly and with greater clarity of purpose.

The Psychology–Politics Dialectic

It is not only our individual positions that must be considered but broader contextual frameworks as well. An excellent analysis of the impact of sociopolitical context was offered two decades ago by Bakan (1977), who presented a thought-provoking analysis of how the very nature of this discipline has been shaped by factors external to the field itself. Bakan argued that the approach to science embraced early on by psychology—largely because it was politically expedient to do so—is grounded in the assumption that science should follow a two-step model: Knowledge ought first to be discovered through rigorous experimentation and later, should circumstances arise, be applied to the solution of problems. Bakan dubbed these bits of knowledge "fact bricks" or "fact modules."

In this view of science, fact bricks are formed, accumulated, and stored away in the warehouses of the professional literature, held against the possibility that they might be useful at some later time. Scientists and science are regarded as repositories of truth, describing the nature of realities that exist independent of themselves and their scientific endeavors and recording those descriptions largely for the benefit of other scientists.

The notion that the production and implementation of knowledge is a matter of moral and political neutrality has in fact been the target of considerable criticism, much of it from feminists (Bohan, 1992; Hare-Mustin & Marecek, 1994; Marecek, 1989; Riger, 1992; Wallston & Grady, 1992). And yet, despite such critiques, and although feminists employ new methods and richer modes of analysis, we continue to talk largely among ourselves *about* the people we study rather than *with* them. And the notion that knowledge is the province of professions and professional knowers persists, even among those of us long convinced of the social embedment of our work. In an analysis of articles published in *Psychology of Women Quarterly* and *Sex Roles,* for instance, Walsh (1989) found that less than 1% of studies reviewed indicated that results were put to use in a socially constructive manner.

In another provocative article from the 1970s, Caplan and Nelson (1973) addressed the other side of the psychology–politics dialectic, pointing to the inevitable societal consequences of psychological research. Their analysis, echoed in numerous feminist works (e.g., Kahn & Yoder, 1989; Marecek, 1989; Mednick, 1989; Unger, 1992; Wallston & Grady, 1992; Wittig, 1992, 1996), revealed the inevitable activism—whether progressive or regressive—imbedded in psychological research on social issues. This body of work suggests what a remarkable shift might occur in our work and in our understandings of social processes if we simply ask different questions. Instead of asking about race or gender differences, why not explore the problems of racism and sexism? Rather than asking if lesbian/gay/bisexual (LGB) individuals are just like heterosexual people, why not investigate the problem of heterosexism and homophobia? And, we might ask, what if we take this shift yet a step further? Instead of exploring problems, however we define them, what if we explore solutions?

Caplan and Nelson as well as others (e.g., Kahn & Yoder, 1989; Prilleltensky, 1989, 1994; Sampson, 1993) have also challenged psychologists to ask ourselves the question: *to whom* is our research, in Caplan and Nelson's terms, "useful?" In a disquieting discussion, these authors argue that it is often psychologists themselves (rather than the purported beneficiaries of our work) who benefit from particular modes of defining problems and conducting research, and from particular recommended solutions. For example, on a pragmatic level, simple, short-term research that entails straightforward statistical analysis serves well psychologists' need to have their work published, even if it does little for the population under study. In a more theoretical vein, psychologists are trained to focus on the individual; thus, when social problems are defined as individual ones, psychologists appear important to their solution. This latter issue, the tendency to define social problems as individual ones, has been widely critiqued by feminists as inimical to women for its victim-blaming potential (e.g., Bohan, 1993; Hare-Mustin & Marecek, 1994; Kahn & Yoder, 1989; Lamb, 1996; Mednick, 1989).

On the other hand, accepting rather than denying the inescapable value-laden nature of psychological research inspires us to do work that matters. Instead of storing up fact modules for possible use at some future date, we are charged to ask questions whose relevance is clear, immediate, and important. Instead of talking only to one another, we are urged to speak *with* those we want to understand and to communicate our understandings back to them. We are empowered to create work that attends to solutions that are meaningful to the real-world communities from whom we derive our understandings. What follows are descriptions of two research projects intended to address important social issues and of the products by which the insights gained through this research were returned to the community.

THE RESEARCH PROJECTS

Both of the research projects we consider here were prompted by the passage of Amendment 2 (A2), a popularly initiated amendment to Colorado's constitution that removed any legal recourse for lesbian, gay, and bisexual people who encountered discrimination based on sexual orientation. A2 was passed by voters on November 3, 1992, but never took effect because of a series of legal challenges that culminated in its being declared unconstitutional by the United States Supreme Court on May 20, 1996. In what follows, the author who conducted this research will describe the work and its outcomes.

Psychological Impact of Amendment 2 on LGBs

In the first study, I (GR) focused on the psychological impact of A2 on LGBs in Colorado and set out to document that impact by means of a survey of retrospectively self-reported measures of depression, anxiety, and trauma symptoms. (A detailed report of this and the second research project can be obtained from the first author.) The quantitative findings, drawn from 663 LGBs throughout the state, suggested that the campaign for and passage of A2 had produced decidedly negative effects on many in the LGB community (Naar & Russell, 1995; Russell, 1995). Although the quantitative results of the survey were significant, both statistically and practically, responses to the single open-ended item at the end of the eight-page survey were especially interesting. This item asked LGBs to mention anything they chose about their reaction to any aspect of A2. The 496 responses to this question suggested some of the more specific psychological and social dimensions of A2's impact on LGBs. A full-scale qualitative analysis was conducted by a team of coders (including Sylvie Naar, R. D. Perl, Sean Riley, Louis Bardach, and myself) that was notable for its diversity along major demographic measures. The analysis yielded 54 codes that served to elucidate aspects of the psychological effects of A2; these codes were in turn grouped into three major categories: elements that felt victimizing, the ways that LGBs made sense of the amendment, and risk and resilience factors associated with LGBs' reactions to it (Russell, 1997; Russell, Naar, Perl, Bardach, & Riley, 1995). The brief descriptions of the 54 codes given in Table 1 are offered as a summary of the kinds of issues suggested by the participants in the study.

Heterosexual Allies

The second study focused on heterosexual allies who had taken public stands against the passage of A2. These heterosexuals not only had to overcome the homophobic and heterosexist attitudes common in this culture, but they frequently had to challenge their own fears and to risk social opprobrium in order to take stands for LGB rights. This study was designed to explore the motivations, costs, and rewards for these heterosexuals who acted as allies of the LGB movement. Given that minimal literature on heterosexual allies existed—none of it research based (e.g., Chojnacki & Gelberg, 1995; Gelberg & Chojnacki, 1995; Larson & Wall, 1995; Powers, 1993)—it made sense to approach the topic as broadly as possible. Accordingly, I decided to conduct open-ended interviews with heterosexual allies.

In the initial phase of the project, which is the focus here, I conducted interviews with 18 heterosexual allies whose work during the A2 campaign and its aftermath had been visible to at least some segments of the broad community. These individuals represented considerable diversity in terms of age, race, ethnicity, religious affiliation, and the nature of their allied work. I anticipated broadening the study beyond these original 18 allies and conducting a thorough team-based qualitative analysis at some point (a project that is currently underway); my initial qualitative analysis of the data for this first, exploratory stage was conducted singly. I derived 18 codes from the data; these are described in Table 2.

GIVING IT BACK

With this overview of theoretical groundings and the research projects themselves as background, we move to the primary aim of this article: a discussion of giving back to the community the understandings they conferred by participating in this research. At least two issues are relevant here: to whom should the results of research be returned and by what means might this be accomplished?

The Recipients of Research

The results of research might well be offered to a wide range of constituencies. Foremost among these are the people who participated in the research project. They have the most obvious stake and should be the first to have an opportunity

Table 1

Codes for Qualitative Data on Psychological Effects of Amendment 2

ACFV	anger at Colorado for Family Values, religious right
ACHRIST	anger at Christians
AG	anger in general
AHET	anger at heterosexuals
AMEDIA	anger at media
APROC	anger at process of campaign/election
AQ	anger at gays, lesbians, and bisexuals
ASTATE	anger at state of Colorado
BA	against boycott
BARRIERS	infighting within LGB community
BF	for boycott
CCOMP	compliments for campaign against A2
CCRIT	criticisms of campaign against A2
CFV	any reference, other than anger, to Colorado for Family Values
COMM	sense of community with other LGBs, personal or abstract
DISC	actual reports of discrimination/harassment at any time
FAMR	rejection or other negative reactions from family of origin
FAMS	support from family of origin
FEAR	any reference to fear
GRASP	grasp of homophobia/heterosexism: first person perspective
HOPE	future-oriented statements of hopefulness
IHE	internalized homophobia, explicit
IHI	internalized homophobia, inferred
INSIGHT	self-analysis with insight
INVAL	discounts effects of campaign/election
ISMS	interconnections among oppressions at social/political level
ISOLATE	alienation or isolation
KIDS	any reference to children
LEAVE	desire/plan to leave Colorado
LOSS	loss or grief
MEDIA	any reference, other than anger, to media
MOVE	A2 placed in a broader political context
NOMOVE	A2 not placed in broader political context
OUT	any reference to being out of the closet
OUTL	being less out
OUTM	being more out
OVER	overwhelmed
PERSONAL	reference to personal responsibility
PRIMARY	reference to primary relationship
RECOVER	attributions to process or outcome of recovering from A2
REGRET	explicit regret for not having done enough in the campaign against A2
REPOC	attribute election results to EPOC's campaign to defeat A2

(continued)

Table 1

Continued

RINFO	attribute election results to misinformation/confusion
RLIES	attribute election results to lies told
RMIS	attribute election results to voter mistakes
SAD	depression (including specific symptoms) or sadness
SHOCK	surprise at the outcome of the election
SUPPORT	support from friends (not from family or community)
THANKS	gratitude for research study
TRAUMA	references to past traumas, images of trauma, symptoms of trauma
TRUST	references to trust of any kind
VWP	references to victims, witnesses, and/or perpetrators

to participate in the framing of its message as well as to reap any benefits from that message. In many cases, others are also candidates for receiving feedback about research projects. Individuals or agencies who are in positions to acquire greater understanding of and/or provide better services to the population under study should be considered. So, too, should people who have the potential to effect broader social and political changes affecting the population being studied. Different recipients may be best reached by varying means.

The Many Forms of "Giving It Back"

There are many ways by which research might be returned, and results of the two projects described here have been given back to the community in many ways. In the wake of Amendment 2, numerous talks based on the A2 study were given throughout the state. Both municipal response teams and response teams at Colorado colleges and universities relied on these data in organizing efforts to deal with the potential impact of the Supreme Court's final ruling. In addition, data from this study were included in American Psychological Association's (APA) *amicus curiae* brief in the Supreme Court case against A2 (APA, 1994).

Findings from the interviews with allies have proven helpful in a variety of arenas. Themes from the data have informed presentations, workshops, and trainings regarding LGB issues and, indeed, diversity in general. They have been useful in raising important issues in a course about LGB youth for heterosexual teachers, they have served as the focus of discussion in college courses on the psychology of sexual orientation, and they have been helpful in a number of clinical and supervisory situations.

Clearly, different research projects and different situations make available widely varying opportunities to convey useful information to lay communities. In the case of these two projects, the nature of the topics addressed and the communities involved, as well as the social location of the researcher, resulted in two unusual opportunities. The words and experiences of participants in the A2 study became an oratorio commissioned and performed by Harmony, Denver's LGB chorus—first

Table 2

Codes for Qualitative Data on Heterosexual Allies

CONCERNS	concerns about tactics used to promote LGB rights
COSTS	personal and social costs for taking stand for LGB rights
FAMILY	support or criticism from families of origin or chosen families
FEAR	specific fears associated with supporting LGB rights
H & H	observations about the nature of homophobia and heterosexism
INTERNAL	need to look within oneself to deal with homophobia/ heterosexism
ISMS	parallels drawn between homophobia/heterosexism and other forms of social oppression
KIDS	reports having to do with experiences of childhood or of children
MOVEMENT	perspective that sees LGB civil rights struggle as part of a larger movement
PARALLELS	comparisons between LGB experiences and those of heterosexual allies
REWARDS	rewards from working as an ally
STRENGTH	sources of strength in being an ally
Motivations for being an ally	
BUCK	buck-stops-here motivation: based on sense of basic personal responsibility
HOMOPHIL	homophilic motivation: based on contact with/concern for particular LGB individuals
JUSTICE	justice motivation: based on explicit appeal to sense of justice
PERSONAL	motivations based on personal history: specific experiences identified as critical
NIEMOELLER	motivations indicating awareness that oppression of others may ultimately pose danger to oneself
RELIGION	motivations based on religious or moral considerations

in Denver and then at an international festival of LGB choruses. The experiences of heterosexual allies heard in the second study were brought together in a documentary video produced by a local PBS affiliate and subsequently aired across the country. The experiences of research participants were reflected back to them and to the community as a whole in song and on film—individual and collective voices made available to the public through psychological research.

Throughout the development of the oratorio and the video, important concerns arose that speak both to the complexity and the rewards of doing this kind of work and to the theoretical issues and the politics of social change addressed previously. In what follows, the author who conducted these projects (GR) will explore some of these concerns, elucidating how the issues raised at the beginning of this article play out in efforts to return research to the people.

Reflexivity, Values, and Psychological Research

If indeed nothing in psychology is value free, then it is incumbent on the researcher to know as much as possible about what her or his values are and how those might influence the research project. An obvious place where values warrant attention is in the choice of the research question itself.

With respect to the study on the psychological effects of A2, my initial impulse to do this research came to me when two clients—one a lesbian and the other a heterosexual man—in consecutive sessions spoke of their distress at the amendment. I found myself thinking, "someone has got to document what this amendment has done." I had heard similar statements of distress from friends, clients, and colleagues since the election and had seen some attention to it in media reports (Booth, 1992; Johnson, 1992; Moses-Zirkes, 1993; Spring, 1992). It occurred to me that doing research on the effects of A2 might provide the LGB community with some important information that could be helpful to its process of healing. I am certain that I was motivated as well by a belief that doing this research might be helpful to me as a lesbian trying to come to terms with my own trauma from A2.

The idea for research on heterosexual allies also came to me from hearing someone else's statements. Several days after the election in the offices of the Equal Protection Campaign (EPOC), the campaign organization that worked to defeat A2 at the polls, a heterosexual woman who had been EPOC's press secretary was talking on the phone. I heard her voice take on an uncharacteristically stern tone as she said, "Listen, I know more about homophobia than most heterosexuals you'll ever meet." I knew immediately that I wanted to talk with her and other heterosexuals who had taken a stand for LGB rights. I was interested in listening to the descriptions of homophobia and heterosexism offered by heterosexuals who had been in unique positions to see how they operate. I wondered if other heterosexuals—nonallies—might be able to hear homophobia and heterosexism described by these heterosexuals more clearly than they would if LGBs were doing the describing. Ultimately, I wanted to use the enhanced understanding to improve our ability to prepare other heterosexuals to act as allies.

THE PROCESS OF GIVING RESEARCH BACK: PSYCHOLOGICAL EFFECTS OF AMENDMENT 2

The idea for an oratorio based on the data from the study on the psychological impact of A2 originated in a board meeting of "Harmony: A Colorado Chorale," a Denver-based chorus whose membership is drawn largely from the LGB community. The board had decided to commission a musical work for their performance at the July 1006 festival of the Gay and Lesbian Choral Associations of America (GALA) to be held in Tampa, Florida. Given the continuing fallout—both personal and political—from A2, the idea of a piece based on the amendment seemed fitting. I was a singing member of Harmony, and the board approached me about the possibility of basing the music on my study.

Left to my own devices, it would never have occurred to me to commission an oratorio based on this or any other research. One of the themes in the qualitative data suggested, however, that this was an important undertaking. Our coding team had named this code "Thanks"; it was one of the most frequently coded themes. This theme captured LGB respondents' appreciation for the A2 research; they expressed gratitude that someone cared enough to ask how they were affected by A2 and that LGBs' feelings on the issue would be understood. This indication that completing the survey had served as a helpful intervention for some respondents suggested that an oratorio based on the survey might also be helpful to some members of the LGB community.

As excited as I was about the prospect of a piece based on the research, I was also somewhat anxious. I felt that LGBs had entrusted me with very tender experiences regarding A2, and the prospect of allowing someone else access to the data was daunting. I asked myself what the ethics were of allowing the study to be used in this way. There was no concern about anonymity, as I did not know who had filled out the surveys in the first place. Accordingly, I sought consultation with Julie Lee-Richter of the ethics committee of my state psychological association to assure that the best interests of the LGB community would be served. Together we concluded that the composer would have access to the raw data, to my writings about it, and to discussions with me about its meaning. Direct quotations from the data would not be allowed, however, although many people might well hear lyrics reminiscent of their words because the composer would draw from the themes we had identified in the data.

I began working with Bob McDowell, the off-Broadway composer who had won the commission to write the oratorio. After reading the materials I sent him, Bob seemed to have a good understanding of the data, and his questions—mostly centering on some of the specific coded themes—suggested that he would do justice to this rich mass of data. Bob had one major question that the data did not answer fully: Where is the resolution for LGBs in the aftermath of A2? I explained several themes that had implications for resolution (see OUTM, COMM, MOVE, ISMS, FAMS, GRASP, IHE, PERSONAL, RECOVER, and SUPPORT in Table 1). I also sent Bob an article suggesting some elements of a resolution to this difficult experience (Russell, 1997).

When the time came for the chorus to begin work on "Fire," Vicki Burrichter, Harmony's director, asked me to introduce the piece to Harmony. In doing so, I emphasized how we, as a chorus, were in the position of giving back to the LGB community the pain, anger, and lessons of A2 that they had spoken of in the surveys. Performing "Fire" would be the completion of a process of receiving from the community and returning to them understandings of the pain and growth brought by Amendment 2.

"Fire" is a long and complex oratorio. It challenged the chorus both musically and intellectually. To assist the chorus in learning it, I wrote rehearsal notes describing the relationship between the qualitative themes and the oratorio's lyrics. In addition, the notes offered basic information on trauma theory and social stigma. I also worked extensively with the chorus' American Sign Language interpreter who had the formidable job of translating "Fire" for members of our deaf and hearing-impaired audience. When "Fire" was presented to a local audience in June 1996, I wrote program notes for the concert.

At last, the oratorio would be sung for its originators, the LGB community. I wanted the piece not only to reflect the community's experience, but also to add to its understanding of the A2 experience. Ultimately, I hoped that "Fire" would contribute to the community's healing. With "Fire," a traumatic event was translated into a positive statement of LGB culture.

Research Transformed: "Fire"

Bob McDowell wrote "Fire" in five parts; each part is titled with a phrase or clause from the actual data. Part I ("I was really naive . . . ") opens with a kind of dialogue between denial of homophobia and heterosexism, on the one hand, and their acknowledgment, on the other (SHOCK vs. GRASP, in Table 1). In this section, fire is a metaphor for the pervasive homophobia and heterosexism that exist and that made A2 possible.

Part Ia (" . . . they said . . . ") is a short section in which the reality of homophobia and heterosexism are revealed in a person's being fired from a job (see DISC, LOSS in Table 1). There is some debate as to the degree that A2's passage was related to the firing, reminding us that one of the impacts of anti-LGB actions, including A2, is confusion about precisely what is the cause of negative events.

In Part II ("I chose not to be active . . . "), fire becomes a new metaphor, something that needs to be tended. Without ongoing attention to political realities, fires will indeed go out (see REGRET, SAD, LOSS, TRAUMA, VWP in Table 1).

The pain of A2 is highlighted in Part III ("On November 3 . . . "), which reads like the parable of the Good Samaritan with a much different ending than in the biblical parable—no one helps. This movement captures the pain and anger that LGBs described in relation to the injustices of A2 and particularly to the failure of so many heterosexuals in the state to intervene (see especially VWP, FAMR, LOSS, SAD, TRUST from Table 1).

In Part IV (" . . . Wanted to burn down the churches."), pain gives way to anger (see ACFV, ACHRIST, AG, AHET, AMEDIA, APROC, ASTATE, TRUST, ISO-LATE, LEAVE, OVER, TRAUMA, VWP from Table 1). In some instances, the anger is a global, affective response to injustice. In other cases, the anger represents an effort to make sense of trauma. The "No! No! No!" at the end of this movement is a response, not an affirmation. We see the impulse toward self-affirmation at the very end of the fourth movement; "No!" becomes "No more No!" which becomes "No more hate!"

The transformation that began in Part IV is highlighted in Part V ("Another door was opened."). As in the first movement, this final one carries a dialogue. This dialogue seeks a resolution. How do LGBs take seriously and work to eradicate homophobia without defining ourselves in relation to those who would oppress us? Here, fire becomes a metaphor for our community, the fire that forges our commitment to work to overcome oppression (see COMM, FAMS, HOPE, MOVE, OUTM, PERSONAL, RECOVER, THANKS in Table 1).

THE PROCESS OF GIVING RESEARCH BACK: HETEROSEXUAL ALLIES

In contrast to "Fire," the process of translating research on heterosexual allies was a more straightforward venture. Unlike with the A2 data, I intended from early on for the allies data to enter the public domain in the form of a video. I worked with a producer-director, Barbara Jabaily, at a Denver PBS station and also collaborated with the grant writer for the station.

Because of the nature of this medium, I had to contend with some conflict between research and videographic interests. For instance, the expense of videotaping research interviews severely limited the questions I would be able to ask. Also, there was no way to exercise my accustomed degree of control when I was working in an area in which I was without a number of very significant skills. Moreover, it was my task to keep a consistent psychological and human focus on the project. My coproducer and I had a recurrent exchange: I would refer to the videotaped interviews as "data," and she would pointedly correct me, referring to them as "footage." This discrepancy in viewpoint reflected the tension between psychological research and videographic form that I constantly had to negotiate.

Our different perspectives notwithstanding, the working relationship between Barbara and me was rooted in a fundamental agreement about the nature of the video we wanted to make: one that focused on the internal motivations and struggles of the allies in taking their stands. That shared vision was the basis for the name we eventually chose for the video, "Inner Journeys, Public Stands" (Jabaily & Russell, 1995).

During the interviews, the presence of three participants in addition to the more familiar and comfortable dyad of interviewer and respondent took some getting used to. Framing and approaching the interviews as conversations helped. Even amid the extra people, cameras, and microphones, when I actually began to talk with each ally, we really were just two people engaged in a conversation about matters for which each of us had passion. The outside interruptions were nuisance events that usually served to shore up the working bond between us.

The qualitative analysis of the interviews provided the 18 codes (Table 2) that served as a basis for the thematic segments of the final video. In many respects, there is great overlap between the text for a documentary and a written report of qualitative research. For a video, however, in addition to selecting comments that represent a given theme well, one also has to take into account visual effects including visual continuity and extraneous factors (e.g., a fly on the wall or a bus passing), as well as the important issue of dramatic appeal.

Research Transformed: "Inner Journeys, Public Stands"

The film, "Inner Journeys, Public Stands" is 1 hour in length. The video is divided into several segments based on the codes I had identified. The segments flow from one to another without explicit demarcation so that the documentary appears seamless. Among the key messages of the video are the intimidation that allies sometimes feel (FEAR, PARALLELS in Table 2), their increasing grasp of homophobia and heterosexism (H&H), an appreciation for some of the challenges routinely faced by LGBs (FEAR, H&H, ISMS), their motives for taking stands (BUCK, HOMOPHIL, JUSTICE, PERSONAL, NIEMOELLER, RELIGION), the courtesy stigma that accrues to those who support disapprobated groups (COSTS, FEAR, INTERNAL, PARALLELS, STRENGTH), and the costs and rewards of the choice to do so (COSTS, REWARDS, STRENGTH).

One segment highlights members of the clergy who explain how their willingness to oppose A2 was rooted in religious and moral considerations (JUSTICE, RELIGION); another features individuals whose personal experiences motivated their commitment to human rights in general and to LGB rights in particular (HOMOPHIL, ISMS, PARALLELS, PERSONAL). One segment discusses homophobia and heterosexism in various racial/ethnic communities (ISMS, MOVEMENT), and another focuses on the impact of homophobia and heterosexism on children and youth (KIDS). A key section presents allies discussing how hard it often is to take unpopular stands; this part reveals the personal, internal work necessary in such circumstances (COSTS, FEAR, INTERNAL, STRENGTH). The video closes with a series of shots that focus increasingly on the strengths evoked and the rewards achieved through taking such stands (STRENGTH, REWARDS).

THE IMPACT OF RETURNING RESEARCH

Impacts on the Community

We have undertaken no formal study of the impact of the artistic products derived from these two research projects, although we can offer anecdotal support for their impact. Even as we recognize that we are more likely to hear positive than negative or indifferent reactions, it is nonetheless gratifying that numerous members of the chorus who sang "Fire" expressed pleasure at being able to sing about their experiences with A2. A number of singers and members of the audience specifically mentioned the value of having a resolution for the pain of A2 written into the piece. Further, several LGB choruses from around the country who heard "Fire" at its national debut have expressed interest in performing the piece.

Realizing, again, the selective nature of such feedback, we have also heard similarly positive responses to the video, including positive critical reviews in the local newspapers (Cornett, 1995; Ostrow, 1995). Several allies (both those featured and others) have indicated that they felt gratified to see their positions—their lives—articulated in a public forum at last. The film has been shown in classes on a variety of topics including the psychology of sexual orientation, LGB youth, multicultural psychology, and the psychology of counseling. In each case, comments from both teachers and students have been extremely positive. Finally, the video has been picked up by PBS stations across the country; in several cases, it has been aired repeatedly.

Effects on Researchers

Our experience with this research and the pleasure of giving it back have solidified our interest in seeking ways to return research results to whatever communities seem appropriate. We now strive to be more conscious of the possibilities for giving back insights and find ourselves doing so earlier in the research process. In addition, our presentations designed to provide feedback to communities often use multimedia formats. Elements from "Fire" and "Inner Journeys," for example, have complemented more traditional didactic techniques as avenues for returning the understandings gained through psychological research to the communities from which they arose.

REFLEXIVITY REVISITED

Throughout the conduct of these research projects and the process of returning their findings to the community, issues of values and reflexivity continued to arise. One important and recurrent question concerns the quandaries raised by being in a position to speak for others. This is especially a concern when one is not a member of the community in question, and caution is particularly in order when the researcher is in a privileged position vis-à-vis the group under study (for thoughtful discussions of these issues, see Alcoff, 1991–1992; Hertz, 1997; Wilkinson & Kitzinger, 1996).

Finally, the very language we use here, "returning research to the community," is problematic in that it implies a greater distance between researcher and participants than may actually exist. This language does not completely capture what the process seems to be; it is much more of a dialogue than it first appears. What is crucial is that the researcher be aware of her/his position in and the reciprocity of this process.

CONCLUSIONS

The projects described here represent the sort of research that is possible and the attention to its uses that is necessary if we heed the call reflected in feminist critiques of psychological research. These projects take seriously the importance of returning to participants and to lay communities at large the understandings we gain from them. They answer the charge to address difficult and complex social issues and are aware of the values such work inevitably bespeaks, embracing social change as a legitimate goal of psychological research. Such efforts are surely in keeping with the aims of feminist psychology.

Initial submission: December 1, 1996
Initial acceptance: March 17, 1997
Final acceptance: July 6, 1997

REFERENCES

American Psychological Association, American Psychiatric Association, National Association of Social Workers, & Colorado Psychological Association. (1994). Brief *amicus curiae Romer v. Evans*, 94–1039, U..S Supreme Court.

Alcoff, L. (1991–1992). The problem of speaking for others. *Cultural Critique, 20*, 5–32.

Bakan, D. (1977). Political factors in the development of American psychology. *Annals of the New York Academy of Sciences, 291*, 222–232.

Bohan, J. S. (1992). Prologue. In J. S. Bohan (Ed.), *Seldom seen, rarely heard: Women's place in psychology*. Boulder, CO: Westview.

Bohan, J. S. (1993). Regarding gender: Essentialism, constructionism, and feminist psychology. *Psychology of Women Quarterly, 17,* 5–22.

Bohan, J. S. (1996, August). *Strong constructionism and psychological knowledge: Who's talking about whom?* Paper presented at the annual meeting of the American Psychological Association, Toronto.

Booth, M. (1992, November 5). Therapists hear gays pour out their anguish and anger. *Denver Post,* p. 9A.

Caplan, N., & Nelson, S. (1973). On being useful: The nature and consequences of psychological research on social problems. *American Psychologist, 28,* 199–211.

Chojnacki, J. T., & Gelberg, S. (1995). The facilitation of a gay/lesbian/bisexual support-therapy group by heterosexual counselors. *Journal of Counseling and Career Development, 73,* 352–354.

Cornett, L. (1995, November 4). Video delves into allies' motivation. *Daily Camera,* p. 10A.

Gelberg, S., & Chojnacki, J. T. (1995). Developmental transitions of gay/lesbian/bisexual-affirmative, heterosexual career counselors. *Career Development Quarterly, 43,* 267–273.

Hare-Mustin, R., & Marecek, J. (1994, August). *Taking social constructionism seriously.* Symposium presented at the annual meeting of the American Psychological Association, Los Angeles, CA.

Hertz, R. (Ed.). (1997). *Reflexivity and voice.* Thousand Oaks, CA: Sage.

Jabaily, B. (Producer/Director), & Russell, G. M. (Coproducer/Interviewer). (1995). *Inner journeys, public stands* [Film]. Available from G. Russell, Coproducer.

Johnson, D. (1992, November 5). Colorado homosexuals feel betrayed. *New York Times,* p. 19.

Kahn, A. S., & Yoder, J. D. (1989). The psychology of women and conservatism: Rediscovering social change. *Psychology of Women Quarterly, 13,* 417–432.

Lamb, S. (1996). *The trouble with blame: Victims, perpetrators, and responsibility.* Cambridge, MA: Harvard University Press.

Larson, S., & Wall, L. (1995, May 21). Lesbian woman, straight man: Friends converse. *Daily Camera,* p. 3C.

Marecek, J. (Ed.). (1989). Theory and method in feminist psychology [Special Issue]. *Psychology of Women Quarterly, 13*(4).

Mednick, M. T. (1989). On the politics of psychological constructs: Stop the bandwagon, I want to get off. *American Psychologist, 44,* 1118–1123.

Moses-Zirkes, S. (1993, April). Gay issues move to center of attention. *APA Monitor,* pp. 28–29.

Naar, S., & Russell, G. M. (1995, August). Mapping the factors that mediate the effects of institutionalized trauma. In G. M. Russell (Chair), *Effects of antigay initiatives—Quantitative and qualitative analyses.* Symposium conducted at the meeting of the American Psychological Association, New York, NY.

Ostrow, J. (1995, November 7). Film looks at quiet alliance in Amendment 2 battle. *Denver Post,* p. 1E.

Powers, A. (1993, November/December). Queer in the streets, straight in the sheets. *Utne Reader,* pp. 74–80.

Prilleltensky, I. (1989). Psychology and the status quo. *American Psychologist, 44,* 795–802.

Prilleltensky, I. (1994). *The morals and politics of psychology: Psychological discourse and the status quo.* Albany, NY: State University of New York Press.

Riger, S. (1992). Epistemological debates, feminist voices: Science, social values, and the study of women. *American Psychologist, 47,* 730–740.

Russell, G. M. (1995, August). Psychological effects of Amendment 2 in Colorado: Quantitative analyses. In G. M. Russell (Chair), *Effects of antigay initiatives—Quantitative and qualitative analyses.* Symposium conducted at the meeting of the American Psychological Association, New York, NY.

Russell, G. M. (1997). *Voices of trauma, voices of hope.* Unpublished manscript.

Russell, G. M., Naar, S., Perl, R. D., Bardach, L., & Riley, S. P. (1995, August). Effects of antigay initiatives—Qualitative analyses. In G. M. Russell (Chair), *Effects of antigay initiatives—Quan-*

titative and qualitative analyses. Symposium conducted at the meeting of the American Psychological Association, New York, NY.

Sampson, E. E. (1993). *Celebrating the other: A dialogic account of human nature*. Boulder, CO: Westview.

Spring, T. (1992, December 14). Gays gird for Amendment 2 results. *Colorado Daily*, pp. 1,4,5.

Unger, R. K. (1992). Through the looking glass: No wonderland yet! (The reciprocal relationship between methods and models of reality). *Psychology of Women Quarterly, 8*, 9–32.

Wallston, B. S., & Grady, K. E. (1992). Integrating the feminist critique and the crisis in social psychology: Another look at research methods. In J. S. Bohan (Ed.), *Seldom seen, rarely heard: Women's place in psychology* (pp. 307–336). Boulder, CO: Westview.

Walsh, R. T. (1989). Do research reports in mainstream feminist psychology journals reflect feminist values? *Psychology of Women Quarterly, 13*, 433–444.

Wilkinson, S., & Kitzinger, C. (1996). *Representing the other*. London: Sage.

Wittig, M. A. (1992). Metatheoretical dilemmas in the psychology of gender. *American Psychologist, 40*, 800–811.

Wittig, M. A. (1996). Analysis, advocacy, and affirmative action. *SPSSI Newsletter, 200*, 1–2.

RATTLING CAGES—COMMENTS ON "HEARING VOICES"

Ruth L. Hall
The College of New Jersey

Bridging the gap between the personal and the political, the mantra of feminist psychology, is something feminist scholars and clinicians are committed to do. Making change in places other than within our respective institutions and associations is rare, however. Russell and Bohan challenge us to move beyond our narrow institutions and pose critical questions. As researchers, do we have any obligation to our participants? If so, how do we ensure that they benefit from their participation? Perhaps the more pertinent question to pose is what prevents us, as researchers, from giving back directly to the communities who are willing to contribute to our research?

Russell and Bohan took the additional step and gave back to their community of respondents. Their article is an excellent example of applied feminist research. The catalyst was a community's distress coupled with the researchers' willingness as helping professionals to document this distress and to aid in the healing process for the community. Their response to the question—To whom should we give back and how can this reciprocity take place?—was cogent and creative. By composing an oratorio from the gay/lesbian/bisexual community's response to Colorado's Amendment 2 (A2) and producing a documentary video of heterosexual allies' responses to A2, Russell and Bohan recognized a community's concern; heard the voices of its people; and let those voices be heard on personal, community, and societal levels. First and foremost, however, was their consideration of the audience of respondents. Many of their respondents participated as vocalists in the oratorio and as voices in the documentary. Russell and Bohan brought their research alive. Being heard is particularly important (and frequently absent) for groups whose voices are obstructed by invisibility and oppression. And the response of Russell and Bohan's participants? Someone is paying attention!

After reading their article, reflections of the work of other feminist scholars percolated in my mind. I was reminded how important it is to give back to the community of respondents and how we, as feminist scholars, must rattle the cages

Address correspondence and reprint requests to: Ruth L. Hall, Department of Psychology, The College of New Jersey, P.O. Box 7718, Ewing, NJ 08628-0718.

of "traditional" methodologies and training that potentially confine our ideas, obstruct our research, and deny us funding. I, too, was reminded how important it is to raze the wall between researcher and respondent that can prevent us from giving back to our studied communities. Feminist scholars like Russell and Bohan serve to remind us that giving back to researched communities, obtaining funding, and having our research acknowledged are not mutually exclusive.

Giving back energizes both respondent and researcher alike. While Russell and Bohan used respondents' voices as narrative to express a community's concern, Suzanna Rose employed a social action research approach to mobilize and empower lesbians and gays in Missouri (Dillon & Rose, 1996; Rose & Lisenby, 1992). In 1991, an outcry from the St. Louis lesbian/gay community erupted when the police response to the brutal attack on four gay men by 200 youths at Gay Pride Day resulted in no arrests. This event served as the catalyst for Rose and her colleague, Dennis Lisenby, to conduct training on lesbian and gay issues for police officers, the first of its kind in Missouri. A second outcome was the establishment of the St. Louis Lesbian and Gay Anti-Violence Project (AVP), cofounded by Rose, to provide counseling, referrals, and advocacy to victims of anti lesbian/gay violence. Rose currently serves as liaison for the lesbian and gay community with the St. Louis City Police Departments and as an appointed member of the Family and Domestic Violence Council of St. Louis County governments. Rose has made it her priority to give back to her community of respondents.

Russell and Bohan also remind us that we cannot stand apart from our own humanity. Michele Fine (Fine, 1996; Fine & Weis, 1996) described "working the hyphen," and asked us to "rethink how researchers have spoken of and for Others while including ourselves and our own investments, burying the contradictions that percolate at the Self–Other hyphen" (cited in Fine & Weis, 1996, p. 253). An advocate of participatory-evaluation research, Fine takes her research participants out of a passive and into an active role by engaging them in the development and interpretation of the data. Fine's particular focus on making individuals and institutions responsive to the race, gender, class, and sexual orientation concerns of her constituents and using her subjects as active participants in this process illustrates her rich and applicable style of giving back to her communities. For Fine and Russell and Bohan, the outcome of their work is a product of the researcher and the participant made possible by creating a permeable boundary between them.

I like what Russell and Bohan said about looking closely at the questions we ask and determining whether or not we should be asking different questions. Tatum's (1987) work in the school systems illustrates this point well. Tatum began teaching a Psychology of Racism course in 1980, and her book, *Why Are All the Black Kids Sitting Together in the Cafeteria?* (Tatum, 1997) shared her students' voices with each other and with educators alike. Her antiracism work, based on her experiences with Black youth in predominantly White communities, is another means she uses to give back to her research communities. She hears the stress associated with students' minority status and challenges the educators, rather than the students, to be the agents of change. Tatum invites educators to examine their own racial identity and addresses their avoidant tactics and their fears of doing so. She lays the responsibility of the work squarely on the shoulders of the appropriate group: the people with the power.

Another wonderful question posed by Russell and Bohan—to examine solutions rather than problems—is a serious challenge to researchers and to funding sources. But there are success stories. Carole Oglesby (Oglesby & Shelton, 1992) has been active in changing the world of sports for women and girls. As an administrator for the United States to the World University Games from 1975–1980, Oglesby conducted a survey of male and female student athletes in the Games and found that male athletes were more likely to receive scholarships because the female athletes were of higher socioeconomic status. Thus, many low-income women were being shut out of opportunities in sports as sports participation was most available to women who did not need financial support. Oglesby's testimony before the U. S. Senate influenced the passage of the Amateur Sport Act and did for amateur sports what Title IX did for school sports. Until women had financial support, many could not advance in sports. Oglesby found a solution and the funding to make it happen.

The application of Russell and Bohan's research served another objective. It demystified the thinly veiled perception that psychology is the study of dysfunction, illustrating that psychological research can be healthful and proactive. The authors went beyond the captive audience of undergraduate participants. And they incorporated both qualitative and quantitative research methods, demonstrating that these methods can be complementary and that both are of value.

As a teaching tool we can learn a great deal from Russell and Bohan: that our research must benefit the individuals we study; that it is not beyond any of us to give back to communities that serve as resources for our research; that we must make the commitment to do so; that we can give back in a variety of ways—at the individual, group, regional, and national levels; that we can be creative in the manner in which we give back; that it's fun to work collaboratively; that having grant money and access to media expertise is useful; and that using other areas of interest to us (e.g., the fine arts, media presentations) can provide creative avenues in which to use the research.

Fine and Weis (1996) urge us to educate ourselves and then infuse in our students the desire to give back to their research communities. Let's do that! We also need journals like *PWQ, Women & Therapy, Cultural Diversity and Mental Health, Psychological Perspectives on Lesbian and Gay Issues,* and book contracts to make the invisible groups more visible and to spread the word about the need to give back to our research communities. Although institutions may not recognize our research as meaningful if it deals with these "fringe" groups (particularly if you are a member of said group!), we cannot give up. We have many supporters including our participants. We owe it to them. Let us join adventurous colleagues like Michele Fine, Carole Oglesby, Beverly Daniel Tatum, and Suzanna Rose and rattle the cages of the academy.

REFERENCES

Dillon, J., & Rose, S. (1996, August). *Characteristics and impact of anti gay/lesbian violence.* Paper presented at the annual meeting of the American Psychological Association, Toronto, Canada.

Fine, M. (1996). *Talking across boundaries: Participatory evaluation research in an urban middle school.* New York: Bruner Foundation.

Fine, M., & Weis, L. (1996). Writing the "wrongs" of fieldwork: Confronting our own research/writing dilemmas in urban ethnographies. *Qualitative Inquiry, 2,* 251–274.

Oglesby, C. O., & Shelton, C. (1992). Exercise and sport studies: Toward a fit, informed, and joyful embodiment of feminism. In C. Kramarae & D. Spender (Eds.), *The knowledge explosion: Generations of feminist scholarship* (pp. 181–191). New York: Teachers College Press.

Rose, S., & Lisenby, D. (1992, July). *Community survey of violence against lesbian and gay men in St. Louis.* Paper presented at the Lesbian and Gay Alliance for Justice Speakout, St. Louis, MO.

Tatum, B. D. (1987). *Assimilation blues: Black families in a white community.* New York: Greenwood Press.

Tatum, B. D. (1997). *"Why are all the black kids sitting together in the cafeteria?" and other conversations about race.* New York: Harper.

THE VIEW FROM DOWN HERE

Feminist Graduate Students Consider Innovative Methodologies

Sara Jaffee, Kristen C. Kling, E. Ashby Plant, Mathew Sloan,
and Janet Shibley Hyde
University of Wisconsin—Madison

In this article, graduate students and one faculty member respond to the innovative methods presented in this issue. We identify three theoretical and methodological tensions that shape our interest in and willingness to work with these methods. The first questions whether the strengths of doing qualitative research outweigh the limitations. The second involves feminist research ideals and how attainable they are. The third explores epistemological tensions between qualitative and quantitative research. Although intrigued by the data these methods generated and by their underlying epistemology, we question the status of certain qualitative research in psychology. We contend that the criteria by which qualitative research is evaluated must be made more explicitly before quantitatively trained researchers will incorporate these methods into their own work.

Implicit in most current feminist research is the assumption that feminist methods are qualitative and go beyond the traditional research designs available in psychology. Indeed, the articles presented in these issues represent a range of innovative methods. Our task was to respond to these articles from the perspective of the up-and-coming generation of feminist researchers. We found that our discussion of the theoretical and methodological issues raised by these articles was typical of much qualitative research in that we generated nearly as many questions as conclusions.

In an attempt to make ourselves "visible" participants in the research process, we begin our discussion with a brief description of who we are and how our experiences as researchers informed our reactions to these articles. All of the

This article was written by Sara Jaffee based on discussions of the group. Aside from the first-author position, authorship was assigned alphabetically except for Janet Shibley Hyde.
  Address correspondence to: Janet Shibley Hyde, Department of Psychology, University of Wisconsin—Madison, 1202 W. Johnson St., Madison, WI 53706. E-mail jshyde@facstaff.wisc.edu.

authors, with the exception of Janet Hyde, are graduate students whose research explores various facets of gendered experience. Kristen Kling is interested in self-esteem and women's adjustment in later life. Sara Jaffee's research has focused on women's perceptions of discrimination. Ashby Plant's work examines gender stereotyping of emotion and the motivation to respond without prejudice. Janet Hyde is a faculty member in psychology and women's studies and has done research, much of it quantitative, on the psychology of women for more than 20 years. The lone sociologist among the group, Matt Sloan is interested in women's political participation and gender politics. By and large, the group has been trained almost exclusively to do quantitative research.

Some preliminary comments about our reactions are warranted. As mentioned, the articles included in these issues were chosen to represent a range of innovative methods. It is important to note that, without exception, these studies make use of qualitative methods to some degree. Although we recognize that innovative methods in the discipline span the qualitative/quantitative divide, our responses were generally guided by the qualitative nature of the research.

Our reactions to the articles presented in these issues were varied. Some of us felt hopeful that qualitative methodologies are making inroads into psychology. Some of us were unconvinced that these methods represent a significant contribution to the field. All of us were intrigued by the data these methods generated and their epistemological underpinnings. Despite our diverse responses to the articles, we identified three theoretical and methodological issues that shape our interest in and willingness to work with these methods. The first deals with the strengths and limitations of qualitative research. For us to choose these methods, the strengths must outweigh the limitations. The second involves feminist research ideals and how attainable they are. The third explores epistemological tensions between qualitative and quantitative research that inform our understanding of the place of qualitative methods in a psychological science.

STRENGTHS AND LIMITATIONS OF QUALITATIVE METHODOLOGY

The various authors who contributed to this issue have done a thorough job of describing the advantages of qualitative research. Consequently, our review of these strengths will be brief. Qualitative methods complement and extend quantitative researchers' efforts to understand what people do and think on a large scale by exploring individuals' lived experiences. By working within an inductive framework in which theory is sensitive to data, qualitative methods allow for the discovery of new information. This responsiveness to participants' understanding of their own experience is often lost in quantitative studies where the meaning of an individual's experience is typically framed by the researcher.

Qualitative methods also dovetail nicely with feminist research goals. Although many of the authors who contributed to this issue remind us that no method is inherently feminist, a number of feminist values are upheld in the qualitative methods these researchers employ. Feminist psychologists and qualitative research-ers share a belief that science can never be entirely objective or value free and that human behavior should be studied in the context of everyday interaction. Moreover, by asking questions about individuals' lived experience, qualitative methods serve feminist research goals in identifying aspects of women's and girls' psychological experience that have been ignored in traditional methods of inquiry. Finally, to the extent that qualitative methods subvert the hierarchical nature of the researcher/participant dynamic by giving participants an active role in shaping and interpreting the research question, qualitative researchers share feminist concerns with power imbalances.

All of the articles included in these issues illustrate how qualitative inquiry contributes to our understanding of psychological experience in novel ways when participants and researchers share in meaning making. For example, by allowing adolescent girls to speak about their sexual experience in their own words, Tolman and Szalacha (1999) illuminate an aspect of female sexuality that has been unexplored by the traditional focus on sexual behavior and attitudes. Reitz's (1999) analysis of interviews with male domestic-violence offenders broadens and enhances our understanding of this phenomenon by documenting the experience of domestic violence from the perspective of the batterer. Campbell and Salem (1999) offer important rape-policy guidelines in a study that asked rape-victim advocates to generate and categorize suggestions for how to improve the treatment of rape victims by legal, medical, and mental health systems. Clearly, these studies make unique contributions to psychology by correcting bias in previous research, giving voice to those not heard before, and generating new data and theory. Importantly, it is the innovative methods themselves that allow these particular contributions to be made.

As the studies included in this issue illustrate, qualitative methods provide powerful tools for elucidating how and why individuals behave as they do. As a group, we were singularly impressed with the richness of the data generated by these methods. At the same time, we found ourselves wondering how much the methods also limit what can be concluded from the data. One of our biggest concerns is the extent to which qualitative methods allow researchers to generalize their findings. Methodologies that choose to focus in depth on relatively small groups are necessarily limited in the extent to which they can generalize their findings to the population at large. For instance, although Reitz's study of batterers' experiences of being violent is a valuable contribution to the literature on domestic violence, Reitz herself acknowledges that the size of her sample and the fact that her participants were seeking treatment for abuse limits what can be learned about batterers from this group. Although her methods may elucidate the behaviors and motivations of a certain subpopulation of batterers, they cannot address the experience of batterers who do not seek treatment.

When the methods themselves necessitate the use of small sample sizes, the best researchers can do to promote generalizability is to select samples they believe are representative of a diverse population. As Weatherall (1999) points out, however, a qualitative researcher's preconceptions about the crucial dimensions of diversity may limit the representativeness of the sample s/he selects. Although it seems probable that a group of individuals who span age, race, ethnicity, gender, social class, sexuality, and religion should constitute a representative sample, there may be important elements that are not captured by such a group.

We were additionally concerned with the interpretive complexities that arise in attempting to give participants a voice in the research process. By allowing participants greater input, some forms of qualitative inquiry simply shift the problems that arise during data reduction and interpretation from the researcher to the participants. Instead of researchers' biases clouding the interpretation of data, participants' biases may do the same. For example, one researcher recently communicated to us that during a focus group, the male participants complained that the interaction was dominated by the female participants when, in fact, the female participants spent no more time talking than the males did. Male participants' preconceptions about how women do and should behave in group interactions may have biased their perceptions of the behavior of the women in the focus group. This is not to say that the task of interpretation should be left entirely to the researcher, however. Rather, we need to recognize that replacing the researcher's voice with that of the participant in no way ensures objectivity or accuracy. In other words, although a qualitative researcher may be interested in the gender dynamics of group discussions, the fact that males felt that the discussion was uneven must be tempered by the researcher's observation that it was not.

Along with our concerns about generalizability and interpretation, we were struck by the ways in which qualitative researchers who employ focus-group and interview techniques are limited by their reliance on the spoken word. Although qualitative methods allow individuals to talk about their experience in a setting that is natural and contextualized, they do not necessarily facilitate dialogue among all persons. Focus groups, for example, may silence individuals who are uncomfortable speaking in a group. In the group interactions that characterize focus-group and concept-mapping research, individuals who succumb to very real conformity pressures may begin to speak with a group voice that is not representative of their individual voices or may not speak at all. Finally, any method that relies on interviewing or group interaction to understand how and why individuals behave as they do privileges the verbally articulate. For example, in discussing her interviews with Mary, the social worker, Ceballo (this issue) observed that some individuals are less comfortable than others with talking about their feelings. Even in one-on-one interview settings these individuals may have less to say than someone who welcomes the opportunity to discuss emotional experience.

Finally, as quantitatively trained researchers, we were struck by the fact that qualitative research seems much more difficult to implement than quantitative research. For example, interviews take longer to conduct and to analyze than self-report questionnaires. Qualitative researchers who are limited to relatively small sample sizes may find it difficult to draw conclusions from their data. As Grossman, Kruger, and Moore (1999) make clear, the process of conducting qualitative studies can be emotionally draining, and it can become hard to separate one's researcher self from one's participant self. The time and effort needed to critically examine one's biases in the research process are prohibitive and not without emotional costs in some cases. Certainly, these are not reasons to stop doing qualitative research. Obviously, the extent to which researchers are affected by the process varies greatly depending on the research question; we do not suggest that all qualitative research exacts a severe emotional toll. Nevertheless, it is important to acknowledge that such concerns may prevent young researchers from incorporating qualitative methods, particularly when it is unclear how to evaluate the methods or whether their use will advance a young researcher's career.

In our consideration of the strengths and limitations of qualitative research, the group was highly impressed by researchers' efforts to integrate qualitative and quantitative methods, believing that such efforts gave researchers the best of both methodological worlds. As Tolman and Szalacha (1999) point out, qualitative and quantitative methods have traditionally been pitted against each other. To the extent that qualitative and feminist methodologies have traditionally been implicitly equated, researchers who consider themselves feminists have found themselves caught between a rock and a hard place—rejected by traditional methodologists if they employ qualitative methods and rejected by feminist methodologists if they explore feminist research questions with quantitative techniques. Two of the studies included in these issues bridge this methodological schism and illustrate the advantages of integrating qualitative and quantitative methods. Tolman and Szalacha (1999) subjected their data on girls' experiences of desire to both quantitative and qualitative methods of analysis, whereas Campbell and Salem (1999) employed concept-mapping techniques in which data generated by participants were subjected to quantitative statistical analysis and then interpreted by the participants themselves. If Tolman and Szalacha (1999), for example, had relied on qualitative analyses alone they would have been unable to estimate the magnitude of differences observed between urban and suburban girls' experiences of desire. Conversely, a singular use of quantitative analyses would have resulted in a loss of richness and complexity in the girls' responses. Such an example illustrates how integrating qualitative and quantitative methods allows us to learn far more than any one method alone can tell us. By providing exemplars of synergistic methodologies, researchers like Tolman and Szalacha (1999) and Campbell and Salem (1999) make invaluable contributions to the advancement of methodology and to the literature in their respective subfields.

FEMINIST RESEARCH IDEALS

Abolishing Hierarchies

Many of the researchers who contributed to these issues proposed that feminist research should strive to wipe out hierarchy in the research setting (Grossman et al., 1999; Weatherall, 1999). We, on the other hand, questioned whether such an ideal is attainable, much less desirable. The extraordinary difficulties of abolishing power differences within a research group of undergraduate students, graduate students, and faculty are made apparent in both the Grossman et al. (1999) and Weatherall (1999) articles. As these researchers recognize, such power differences are a fact of life within the academy. Attempts to make senior researchers and graduate students equal in the research process seemed to create as many problems as they solved. Indeed, as Grossman et al. (1999) pointed out, the existence of a feminist egalitarian ideal within a context of very real power differences actually made it more difficult to explore how power was wielded within their group.

Unlike these researchers, we contend that hierarchy can be warranted and does not necessarily leave those with less power "voiceless" in the research process. Perhaps we have simply been extremely fortunate to work within fair and well-run hierarchies. Consequently, we argue that to acknowledge that senior faculty have greater experience and expertise in the teaching and research domains does not prevent us from recognizing the different and equally valuable experiences and skills that graduate and undergraduate students may bring to the research process. Instead of striving to wipe out hierarchy, senior researchers may better serve themselves and their graduate and undergraduate students by maintaining an awareness of how they wield power and by recognizing the valuable experiences their students bring to a research question. Perhaps our own experiences working within hierarchies have been positive because the research process has been structured such that senior researchers validate our contributions and encourage the sharing of ideas.

Avoiding Invasion of Privacy

As many of the researchers included in these issues point out, hierarchies exist not only among members of a research group, but also between researchers and participants. Although one of the strengths of qualitative inquiry is that it allows researchers to delve into highly sensitive areas of human experience, researchers have to question their right to invade the privacy of their participants no matter how well intentioned the research question. Researchers' own discomfort with this dynamic is captured by a member of Grossman et al.'s (1999) research group who asked, "Who were we and what were we doing, listening to and reading the stories of women who had suffered so much?" (p. 125).

Researchers like Grossman et al. (1999) and Weatherall (1999) suggest that it is the responsibility of individuals who engage in invasive and sensitive studies to explore their own role in the development and interpretation of the research. The ideal of the self-conscious researcher is not without its own problems, however. Take, for example, the situation courageously described by Grossman et al. (1999). Their research group made important efforts to identify the ways in which group members' personal histories and issues affected the research. These efforts are to be commended for several reasons. First, as Grossman and her colleagues point out, although many feminist researchers question both the ideal and the reality of the neutral and objective researcher, there is relatively little discussion of how to make the researcher more "visible" in the process, particularly when the research question is highly sensitive. Grossman and her colleagues made several attempts to "become visible" and readily admit that mistakes were made along the way. For example, members of the research group were asked to share their experiences with physical, sexual, and emotional abuse and to write memos about their experiences in the research group. Although these efforts are to be applauded, they seemed to place less powerful members of the research group (i.e., graduate students) in the relatively uncomfortable position of having to evaluate group members who held power over them. This dynamic led us to question whether such public self-examination was truly desirable. Perhaps the research group could have accomplished its goals by asking members to reflect privately on their own experiences.

EPISTEMOLOGICAL TENSIONS

The articles included in these issues highlight the ways in which qualitative research makes new and important contributions to a field rooted in positivist epistemology. And yet, quantitative researchers still know little about how to conduct and evaluate qualitative research. Our group is a primary example. Intrigued as we were by the methods presented in this issue, we felt that we did not have the tools to evaluate them. Although the authors generally did an excellent job of framing their research and describing their methods, there was relatively little discussion about how to evaluate the methods or the results. Consequently, we were left with several questions about evaluative criteria in qualitative research. Should qualitative studies be held to the same criteria of reliability and validity as quantitative studies? If not, why? What are the alternative criteria (see Ambert, Adler, Adler, & Detzner, 1995, for further discussion)? Is all qualitative research of equally high quality and, if not, how do we distinguish the good from the bad?

Given these questions, how can we begin to facilitate dialogue between qualitative and quantitative researchers? We suggest that an important first step is for quantitative researchers to better inform themselves about qualitative methods so that they can evaluate these methods critically. That said, however, we assert that the burden of proof falls on researchers making innovative methodological advances to convince the field that such advances offer a significant contribution to what is already known. From our perspective, this involves convincing quantitative researchers that qualitative methods have as much to offer as the more traditional methods. The argument expressed by many of the authors included in these issues that qualitative methods uncover aspects of psychological experience left untouched by quantitative methods is critically important, but not sufficient. Qualitative researchers must also demonstrate the soundness of their methods before quantitative researchers can be convinced of their merit.

Such an endeavor is crucial for two reasons. First, until young researchers are convinced that qualitative methods have well-defined standards and generate novel and important data, they will not attempt to incorporate these methods into their own work. Again, our own group provides an excellent illustration of this. Regardless of how much any one of us wants to incorporate qualitative methods into our research, our immediate reaction to the articles presented in this issue was that we would have difficulty securing jobs in psychology conducting studies like the ones described. Some of us were concerned that, even if psychology departments were hiring qualitative researchers, these individuals would be treated with less respect than their quantitative peers and would have more difficulty getting tenure. If there are, in fact, "safe spaces" to conduct innovative research, we do not know where they are.

The second reason dialogue is critical is that, until qualitative researchers make explicit the criteria by which they evaluate their work, we will not be able to determine the status of these methods in the discipline. The definition of a scientific study by which quantitative researchers operate involves the systematic and replicable observation of some phenomenon. The studies included in these issues highlight the fact that there is a spectrum of qualitative research, some of which meets the traditional definition of science and some of which does not. Focusing on that which does not, we argue that research like Ceballo's (this issue) or Weatherall's (1999) that is grounded in a postmodern framework, where meaning is multiplistic, poses problems for the progress of psychology as a science. For example, Ceballo (this issue) asserts that her and Mary's differing interpretations of Mary's life narrative were "not a crisis but rather a source of richness" (p. 317). Working from this perspective, a different researcher with different biases could generate a completely new and equally valid interpretation of Mary's narrative. This lack of concern with replicability points to a very basic and irreconcilable epistemological difference between the quantitative and qualitative realms. That such qualitative studies allow researchers to generate new hypotheses and new questions is critically important, but is it sufficient for a science to progress? Until qualitative researchers explain why it is that a psychological science should concern itself with a method that does not value replicability, we will be left with the question of whether the discipline should embrace a methodology that does not adhere to orthodox scientific standards that, to some of us, seem reasonable.

CONCLUSIONS

In conclusion, our group was excited to encounter research that breaks away from traditional methods, and we were intrigued by the discussions about theory, method, and epistemology these articles generated. The fact that a major psychology journal would devote two entire issues to methodological innovation suggests to us that the discipline is becoming more open to nontraditional research. We look forward to the continued development and discussion of these methods and hope that our "view from down here" contributes to the successful incorporation of these methods in psychology.

Initial submission: August 15, 1997
Final acceptance: October 15, 1997

REFERENCES

Ambert, A. M., Adler, P. A., Adler, P., & Detzner, D. F. (1995). Understanding and evaluating qualitative research. *Journal of Marriage and the Family, 57*, 879–893.

Campbell, R., & Salem, D. A. (1999). Concept mapping as a feminist research method: Examining the community response to rape. *Psychology of Women Quarterly, 23*, 65–89.

Ceballo, R. (1999). Negotiating the life narrative: A dialogue with an African American social worker. *Psychology of Women Quarterly, 23*, 309–321.

Grossman, F. K., Kruger, L. M., & Moore, R. P. (1999). Reflections on a feminist research project: Subjectivity and the wish for intimacy and equality. *Psychology of Women Quarterly, 23*, 117–136.

Reitz, R. R. (1999). Batterers' experiences of being violent: A phenomenological study. *Psychology of Women Quarterly, 23*, 143–166.

Tolman, D., & Szalacha, L. (1999). Dimensions of desire: Bridging qualitative and quantitative methods in a study of female adolescent sexuality. *Psychology of Women Quarterly, 23*, 7–40.

Weatherall, A. (1999). Exploring a teaching/research nexus as a possible site for a feminist methodological innovation in psychology. *Psychology of Women Quarterly, 23*, 199–214.

INNOVATIVE METHODS

Resources for Research, Publishing, and Teaching

Mary Gergen
Pennsylvania State University

Joan C. Chrisler
Connecticut College

Alice LoCicero
Lesley College

A selection of innovative methods congenial to research in feminist psychology is reviewed. The methods described include collaborations, discourse analysis, ethnography, existential–phenomenological inquiry, focus groups, interviews, narrative investigations, performative methods, and the Q-sort. A brief description of undergraduate and graduate courses that emphasize these methods in their curricula follows. A bibliography of over 300 entries organized by type of innovative method is included. Journals recommended as publishing outlets for research using these innovative methods are listed with their Web sites.

For the past several decades, feminist psychologists have been critically examining the dominant empiricist tradition in psychology, one that is modeled primarily on physical-science methods (cf. M. Crawford & Gentry, 1989; M. M. Gergen, 1988;

The authors wish to thank Lisa Bowleg, Donna Crawley, Sara N. Davis, Oliva Espin, Michele Hoffnung, Louise Kidder, Lauraine Leblanc, Sue Morrow, and Stephen Small for their generosity in providing materials on pedagogy. Thanks are also extended to Julie Konik, West Chester University, who created the list of Web sites for the journals suggested as publishing outlets in this article.

Address correspondence about the research section of this article to: Mary Gergen (E-mail: GV4@psu.edu), the Department of Psychology, Penn State University, 25 Yearsley Mill Road, Media, PA 19063. Address correspondence about the teaching section to: Joan Chrisler (E-mail: jcchr@conncoll.edu), the Department of Psychology, Connecticut College, New London, CT 06320.

Gilligan, 1979; Hare-Mustin & Marecek, 1990; Marecek, 1989; McHugh, Koeske, & Frieze, 1986; Morawski, 1994; Sherif, 1987; Zalk & Gordon-Kelter, 1991). The impact of these critiques on the discipline, however, has been frustratingly minimal. As various researchers have concluded, the practices of most research psychologists remain untouched (Campbell & Schram, 1995; Fine & Gordon, 1989; Marecek, 1995). If anything, the fascination with conventional empirical methods has intensified.

In the past decade, Division 35 (The Psychology of Women) of the American Psychological Association (APA) has sponsored task forces designed to explore methodological issues and to expand the range of possibilities for research psychologists. Ten years ago, Mary Crawford chaired a Task Force on Feminist Science and Epistemology, which resulted in a bibliography of epistemology, critical analysis, and applications (M. Crawford & Marecek, 1989), published in a special issue of the *Psychology of Women Quarterly* dedicated to theory and method (Marecek, 1989). Five years later, Judith Worell and Claire Etaugh (1994) wrote about transforming theory and research in a special issue of the *Psychology of Women Quarterly*, an outgrowth of a Task Force called Feminist Visions. In 1994–1997, as a subcommittee within the Task Force on Innovative Methods, we authors addressed the issue of innovation in research and in teaching. In addition, we compiled a list of outlets for innovative work. By directly addressing the realities of "publish or perish," we hope to subvert the tendency of feminist psychologists to imitate mainstream conventions (Walsh, 1989) and to challenge the notion that only tenured professors can risk employing innovative methods. We hope to convince feminist psychologists at all stages of their careers that not only is it important for psychology to expand the range of research methods, but that there are ways in which these approaches can be rewarding in themselves, in advancing feminist values, and in gaining professional recognition.

RESOURCES FOR INNOVATIVE RESEARCH METHODS

It is perhaps foolhardy to attempt to designate what are the latest and most creative methods for doing psychological research. Innovation is a relative term, dependent on the particular historical circumstances in which one is situated. Furthermore, a familiar method in one context can be considered novel in another, especially in a field as vast and multifaceted as psychology. Thus, we must ask for some latitude in naming any method as innovative, given the multiple standards by which each might be judged. In order to maximize attention to novel methods, we have ignored the hierarchical evaluations for methodological excellence held by most mainstream psychologists, which place the laboratory experiment at the apex. According to this tradition, because experiments are designed to test hypotheses about causal relationships, no other method is as scientifically advanced and useful. Ironically, the experiment has been the target of the most trenchant criticism as well, although these attacks have been all but ignored by those committed to its merits. Joining with other critics, we take the position that the field can be greatly enriched by employing other research methods.

Because experimental methods dominate the field (e.g., required courses in

experimental methods, research standards for dissertational work, statistics requirements for all degrees—all of which are criteria for acceptance of publications within
high-status empirically oriented journals), we are omitting discussion of any new
developments in these methods within this review. Instead we hope to draw attention to methods that are often more developed in other countries, especially in
Great Britain and the Commonwealth countries. Our primary goal is to offer
exposure, not evaluation. Researchers, teachers, and students are encouraged to
explore whether a particular approach is congenial to their endeavors. We hope
that innovative research practices conducive to feminist values may result from a
synergistic integration of new and existing methods of all varieties.

As we gathered these resources, it became clear that most of them involve the
use of qualitative research methods. This should not be interpreted as an in-
principle rejection of quantitative work. Also, in the interests of space, we have
decided to omit those references in the 1989 special issue on theory and method
and its associated bibliography, published by Mary Crawford and Jeanne Marecek,
which contains resources on feminist epistemology and metatheory, reformulations
of the construction of gender, research applications, and collections of works on
gender issues from related fields. Instead we take up where they leave off, emphasizing work published since 1989. The present bibliography is not comprehensive;
we apologize for any glaring gaps in our coverage. Additional references and links
to other resources can be found on the innovative methods Web site at http://
www.public.asu.edu/~atnfr.

EPISTEMOLOGY, METATHEORY, AND CRITIQUE

Placing methods in perspective involves an understanding of how research is related
to metatheory and theory and how evaluative criteria are to be integrated into
research endeavors (Keller & Longino, 1996). As Henwood and Pidgeon (1994)
have described it, qualitative research is not merely a matter of technique, but is
related to links between epistemology and method. Therefore, a selected sample
of feminist commentaries and critiques on epistemology and metatheory is included
in the bibliography. Author positioning is also of critical concern in today's literature.
That is, how the author of the research is "situated," to borrow Donna Haraway's
(1988) well-known phrase. Sensitivity to one's position vis-à-vis one's subject matter
and one's presentations suggest reflexivity on the author's part; this recognition of
one's situatedness challenges the "God's eye view" of value neutrality, which is part
of the natural-science definition of objectivity. As Jill Morawski's (1994) *Practicing
Feminisms: Reconstructing Psychology*, a sophisticated commentary on our "liminal
science," demonstrates, reflexivity tempers the certainty of any claim one wishes
to make about one's work, as well as moves to strengthen the ethical concerns of
the author. Feminist psychologists must now ponder how to speak with others as
well as how to speak and write for others. English psychologist Erica Burman
(1990) has suggested that there are limitations to being an insider psychologist,
who speaks for one's own group, as well as to being an outsider, who may have
perspectives that are in conflict with one's respondents. The conclusion to be drawn

from this conundrum seems to be that there are no innocent productions of knowledge, and much about which to be watchful, as researcher and as reader.

An additional issue of import that indicates a shift in metatheory from the work of previous task forces is the emphasis on a postmodern, poststructuralist, or social constructionist epistemology in feminist psychology. Such a shift denotes a drastic refiguring of scientific research, such that what was formerly considered the task of gathering stable and objective facts about the social world is now regarded as the work of producing constructions within prevailing linguistic practices (K. J. Gergen, 1985, 1994). Jeanette Rhedding-Jones (1995), for example, has written about the impact of poststructuralism on qualitative research in the field of education. She emphasizes that such a stance has an effect on all aspects of research—theorizing, investigating, and presenting. There is a recognition among postmodern researchers that no interpretation of data is the "right" one, but rather one has the task of trying on different interpretations and of being willing to read and reread the data beyond any notion of a universal Truth. The writing of texts should suggest this openness, lack of certainty, and acceptance of ultimate ambiguity as well. She cautions the researcher about "staying thirsty for words, . . . writing into the text, writing against the text. In feminist poststructuralism there is all of this and a remembering for women" (p. 497).

With this invocation in mind, we have gathered together those resources that both exemplify innovation and remember women. The article is divided into three parts: a brief description and review of a selection of recent references on innovative methods, a section on outlets for the publication of innovative work, and a review of syllabi for teaching innovative methods to undergraduate and graduate students.

Innovative Methods: General Compendiums

Ideally, feminist psychologists should have at their fingertips constantly updated catalogs of innovative methods. Unfortunately, there are no resources that fit this description. Among the various handbooks, research review articles, and other edited volumes to be found in the bibliographic section, there are compendiums of research methods that are innovative within many contexts. Denzin and Lincoln's (1994) handbook is perhaps most well known and useful, although Fonow and Cook's (1991) volume is particularly oriented to feminist issues; Shulamit Reinharz's (1992) *Feminist Methods in Social Research* has been very influential. Hoshmand and Martin's (1991) work is especially important for those engaged in research in therapy. *Critical Psychology: An Introduction*, edited by Fox and Prilletensky (1997), provides interesting commentary and methodological guidance, with particular attention to issues of economic class. For a compendium of approaches dedicated primarily to feminist social-constructionist research, see *Toward a New Psychology of Gender* (M. M. Gergen & Davis, 1997).

Innovative Methods: Specific Forms

Certain methodological practices have only recently developed as innovative forms; others have been gathering momentum for a long time; still others have been familiar forms in certain enclaves of social science, but have not been transmitted to other areas. In the following, a large variety of methodological forms and related issues are described.

Collaborative Methods of Research with Participants
One of the cutting-edge issues for feminist methodologists has been a concern with the form of the relationship between participant and researcher. One approach to this issue is to create some form of collaborative bond that reduces power differences between participant and psychologist and allows some voice for the researched within the research report. The issue of whether different voices are being heard or not has been an especially keen one when cross-cultural or cross-ethnic group research is involved. One solution has been to create a form of collaborative work in which the researchers become the researched. June Crawford and her colleagues (J. Crawford, Kippax, Onyz, Gault, & Benton, 1992), using the methods of Frigga Haug (1987), describe their "memory work" with their own research group. Other approaches to confronting the dilemma of doing justice to the researched can be seen in work by Michelle Fine (1992) and M. Brinton Lykes (1994). Another fascinating example of collaboration can be seen in Patti Lather (1995) and Chris Smithies's involvement with a group of HIV-positive women, whom they have tried to help to tell their stories and to construct some forms of palliative knowledge around their deeply troubling concerns. A desktop version was published in order to hasten the completion of the book, on the urgent requests of the women involved (Lather & Smithies, 1997). (See the Community Education Team, 1999, for an example of another collaborative project).

Discourse Analysis
One of the most influential newer methods in the social sciences is focused on the analysis of the language of various texts. Instead of defining language as a clear channel for communicating information, researchers regard the text itself as a subject of scrutiny. An outgrowth of literary theory, semiotics, and postmodern rhetorics, the impulse of the research is to codify, classify, deconstruct, or interpret forms of talking and writing. Discourse analysts take a pragmatic approach to the study of language in use, that is, to what people are using language to do. Most discourse analysis accessible to English audiences has been developed in Great Britain (Burman & Parker, 1993; Parker & Burman, 1993, Potter, 1996). A great variety of research practices can be denoted as discourse analysis because the method is not fixed or rigidly codified, although conversational analysis is a highly regulated and detailed quantitative method (Psathas, 1994). Some practitioners even question whether it is a method at all (Potter & Wetherell, 1987).

Two recent collections of feminist psychology featuring discourse analysis are: *Feminism and Discourse, Psychological Perspectives* (Wilkinson & Kitzinger, 1995) and *Psychology Discourse Practice: From Regulation to Resistance* (Burman et al., 1996). Discourse analysis has been used to examine topics such as menstruation and menopause (Kissling, 1996; Komesaroff, Rothfield, & Daly, 1997), and a special issue of *Theory & Psychology* (Stam, 1996) examines the body within discourse-analysis frames (see also, Aitken & Burman, this issue; Gavey & McPhillips, this issue, for exemplars of discourse analysis.)

Ethnography

As feminist psychologists have tried to close the gap between researcher and researched, the utility of methods from other areas of the social sciences and humanities, especially anthropology and communication, has become evident. Researching people in their own settings without disturbing the fabric of their social worlds has led many psychologists to think of themselves as ethnographers, working to develop understandings of diverse social groups of which they become a part. The notion of "team ethnography," in which a group of people bring a pastiche of impressions, personal experiences, and interpretations together to create a multivocal analysis, is also in an exciting developmental stage. This form of ethnography powerfully exemplifies the situated nature of all observational reports (cf. Communications Studies 298, 1996). For a fascinating group of accounts, which demonstrates the range of ethnographic research forms and representations, see Ellis and Bochner (1996). And, just as anthropologists have been struggling with issues of representation, power, voice, and scientific validity (Clifford & Marcus, 1986; Geertz, 1983; Lutz, 1988) so too have psychologists. Michelle Fine, for one, has been especially active in exploring these issues, as well as other dilemmas that result from doing fieldwork (Fine & Weis, 1996).

Existential-Phenomenological Inquiry

This approach is found at the intersection of two philosophical strains—existentialism and phenomenology. The psychologist undertakes to discover the conscious themes accessible to individuals as they experience themselves in their everyday worlds. Although open to multiple techniques for gathering and analyzing information, the researcher is guided by several tenets that sustain the approach, for example, ways of protecting the participant's particular experiential expressions from the biases of the researcher, as well as others developed by such phenomenologists as Giorgi, Knowles, and Smith (1979) and Polkinghorne (1989). (See Reitz, 1999, for an exemplary study of men who batter.)

Interviewing and Focus Groups

Although critiques of the dominance of the scientist's perspective in experimental research are fairly common (cf. Harding, 1986; Landrine, Klonoff, & Brown-Collins, 1995), less attention has been paid to the interaction between the researchers and the researched in interview-based qualitative research designs. Some attempts to address this issue involve creating forms of interviewing that are more sensitive to the potential of power inequalities in this relationship. Margery Franklin's (1997) efforts to balance the multiple considerations involved in doing interviews with respondents who are friends is an interesting exemplar. Other issues in interviewing include concerns about question formation, the amount of control the interviewer should have over the process, and how to create interpretations of interview-derived data that both value the interviewee's words and express the perspectives of the interviewer. These inquiries seem to have no definitive answer, but must continually be explored.

Recent references to focus groups, a form of inquiry common to market research, suggest that it is becoming more prevalent in scholarly forums as well (Herndon, 1993; Krueger, 1994; Morgan & Krueger, 1997). Usually arranged as a free-form discussion about a preselected topic, the focus group is designed to raise issues, to formulate opinions, and to mold preferences. This method offers some interesting new avenues for feminist psychologists because it allows for multiple viewpoints and open, egalitarian discussions. Sue Wilkinson (this issue) provides a review and analysis of focus-group research.

Multiple, Combined, and Linked Methods

Many of the references listed in this bibliography and presented in this two-part special issue are not simple illustrations of one method. Rather they integrate diverse methods into one project. An exciting aspect of innovative methods is the potential for creating new mixes of methodologies. Thus, a new form of interviewing may be combined with a conventional method of quantitative analysis to yield a novel research form. The article by Tolman and Szalacha (1999) is an excellent example of the serial linking of the two approaches. Also in this issue, Snelling's study using Q-Methodology combines this technique with interviews. Jaffee, Kling, Plant, Sloan, and Hyde (this issue) raise potentials and problems for these combinations. Grossman, Kruger, and Moore (1999) emphasize the process aspects of evolving innovative feminist methods.

Narrative Investigations

One of the most fruitful and wide-ranging applications of a social-constructionist metatheory is narrative investigation, in which the stories people tell of their lives become the focus of research (Sarbin, 1986; Sarbin & Kitsuse, 1994). Based on the idea that cultures provide narrative resources for organizing life experiences, narrative studies focus on the ways in which this repertoire is selectively appropriated by groups of people (Rosenwald & Ochberg, 1992). Narratologists also note the ways in which scientific research as well as artistic endeavors are created as forms of stories (K. J. Gergen & M. M. Gergen, 1988). Psychologists, including feminists, in many specialties are now becoming involved with this method (Franz & Stewart, 1994; M. M. Gergen, 1992). A series on narrative as method has been introduced by Ruthellen Josselson and Amie Lieblich, who have now edited four volumes: *The Narrative Study of Lives, Vol. 1* (Josselson & Lieblich, 1993); *Exploring Identity and Gender, Vol. 2* (Lieblich & Josselson, 1994); *Interpreting Experience, Vol. 3* (Josselson & Lieblich, 1995); *Ethics and Process in the Narrative Study of Lives, Vol. 4* (Josselson, 1996). (Ceballo, this issue, also employs a narrative approach.)

Performative Psychology: Communicating in Diverse Media

Performative psychology is one of the most controversial and avant garde methods of "doing" psychology. It can either express or challenge a particular interpretation of some aspect of psychology for an audience or act as a research method to engage the audience in a coconstruction of psychological knowledge. Performative psychology uses modes of presentation taken from the arts-and-entertainment spheres of the culture. Performance techniques include improvisations, dramatic soliloquies, drawing, videos, slides, music, dance, plays, skits, poetry, mime, and any other form of presentation used in a performative event (Carlson, 1996). Performative psychology, in not privileging conceptual knowing above other forms, can be considered a bridge between experiential knowing and propositional knowing. Forms of performative psychology have been presented at the American Psychological Association meetings every year since 1995.

Forms of communicative activity bring reality to fruition. In psychology the major tool for reifying research activities and outcomes is the stylized written form that most frequently serves to summarize statistical analysis. "Good" writing is usually interpreted to mean that which conforms most closely to existing linguistic practices in the field. The *Publication Manual* (1994) of the American Psychological Association is one indicator of this regulatory aspect of the science. Writing in these particular forms tends to restrict readership to a small and select audience interested in the same topics. Within the vast majority of empirical journals in psychology and elsewhere, "gatekeepers" restrict the forms in which investigations are described (Spender, 1981). (See Walsh-Bowers' critique of the *Manual,* in this issue). Textbooks, monographs, and other forms of writing are also regulated by convention. These traditions tend to limit the extent to which authors experiment with linguistic forms. The function of writing in shaping reality is rarely discussed within graduate training or elsewhere in the field. Innovations in communication practices are beginning to crack the veneer of established practices, albeit slowly. Creative extensions of communication styles for constructing research, designed to reach wider audiences in many cases, expand the ways in which knowledge may be formed, transformed, and disseminated. Examples of transgressive writing forms also are included here as innovative methods. (See Russell & Bohan, this issue, who created an oratorio as a summative aspect of a research project.)

Q-methodology
This method is not new (Stephenson discussed Q-technique in 1953), but it has not been used extensively in feminist psychology. The Q-sort involves asking participants to evaluate a large number of statements drawn from interviews or other sources on a particular topic. The goal of the research is to look for the ways statements are distributed so as to understand which are the most significant views on a topic for the person doing the sort or to develop differentiated profiles of various kinds of people, ideas, and so on, on the basis of the distributions. Factor-analytic techniques are combined to yield generalized results. Perhaps the most well-known work in feminist psychology on Q-methodology is Celia Kitzinger's (1987) *The Social Construction of Lesbianism.* More recently, Q-sort has been promoted in an unorthodox volume on social psychology by Beryl C. Curt (1994). (See also Snelling, this issue.)

The Visual As Data
Using visual displays (iconic representations) along with texts (symbolic representations), researchers can simultaneously present diverse points of view in new and interesting ways. Psychologists have used photographs, graphic models of theoretical relations, drawings by participants and clients, films, cartoons, paintings, posters, and other artistic renderings to inscribe their research objects and findings. Blurring the boundaries of the visual and textual are the computer-based presentations that synthesize modes of presentation and use hypertext organizational principles. Moving from the print mode to the computer screen has unrealized and unimagined consequences for scientific enterprises and social relations (cf. Albright, 1996, online). Campbell and Salem's (1999) study employs concept mapping, a visual technique, in order to identify ways to improve services to rape victims.

From Research to Teaching

Selections of publications using the methods we have described are listed in the bibliography that follows under the specific topic headings. In addition, publication outlets for innovative methods are suggested. For these forms to proliferate, however, these resources must be shared, most feasibly within educational settings. For this to take place, models of teaching innovative methods are needed. In the last section of this article, some initiatives in this direction are presented. Also, Weatherall (1999) illustrates a teaching/research nexus as a model that blurs the lines between these two arenas. Updates to these items will be posted to http:// www.public.asu.edu/~atnfr.

BIBLIOGRAPHY

EPISTEMOLOGY AND METATHEORY:
COMMENTARY AND CRITIQUES

Alasuutari, P. (1996). Theorizing in qualitative research: A cultural studies perspective. *Qualitative Inquiry, 2,* 371–384.

Alcoff, L. (1994). The problem of speaking for others. In S. O. Weisser & J. Fleischner (Eds.), *Feminist nightmares—Women at odds: Feminism and the problem of sisterhood* (pp. 285–309). New York: New York University Press.

Bohan, J. S. (1993). Regarding gender: Essentialism, constructionism, and feminist psychology. *Psychology of Women Quarterly, 17,* 5–21.

Bohan, J. S. (Ed.). (1992). *Seldom seen, rarely heard: Women's place in psychology.* Boulder, CO: Westview Press.

Burman, E. (1990). The Spec(tac)ular economy of difference. *Feminism & Psychology, 5,* 543–546.

Burr, V. (1995). *An introduction to social constructionism.* London: Routledge.

Cannon, L. W., Higginbotham, E., & Leung, M. L. A. (1991). Race and class bias in qualitative research on women. In J. Lorber & S. A. Farrell (Eds.), *The social construction of gender* (pp. 237–248). Thousand Oaks, CA: Sage.

Danziger, K. (1990). *Constructing the subject: Historical origins of psychological research.* New York: Cambridge University Press.

Davis, S. N., & Gergen, M. M. (1996). Toward a new psychology of gender: Opening conversations. In M. Gergen & S. Davis (Eds.), *Toward a new psychology of gender* (pp. 1–30). New York, London: Routledge.

Ewick, P. (1994). Integrating feminist epistemologies in undergraduate research methods. *Gender and Society, 8,* 92–108.

Game, A., & Metcalfe, A. (1996). *Passionate sociology.* London: Sage.

Gergen, K. J. (1994). *Realities and relationships: Soundings in social construction.* Cambridge, MA: Harvard University Press.

Gross, B. R. (1994). What could a feminist science be? *Monist, 77,* 434–444.

Gubrium, J. F., & Holstein, J. A. (1995). Qualitative inquiry and the deprivatization of experience. *Qualitative Inquiry, 1,* 204–222.

Haraway, D. (1991). *Symians, cyborgs and women: The reinvention of nature.* London: Free Association Books.

Henwood, K., & Pidgeon, N. (1994). Beyond the qualitative paradigm: A framework for introducing diversity within qualitative psychology. *Journal of Community & Applied Social Psychology*, *4*, 225–238.

hooks, b. (1990). *Yearning: Race, gender, and cultural politics*. Boston: South End Press.

Ibanez-Gracia, T., & Iniguez Rueda, L. (1997). *Critical social psychology*. Thousand Oaks, CA: Sage.

Landau, I. (1994). Should there be separatist feminist epistemologies? *Monist, 77*, 462–471.

Macmillan, K. (1990). Giving voice: The participant takes issue. *Feminism & Psychology, 5*, 547–552.

Marecek, J. (1995). Gender, politics, and psychology's ways of knowing. *American Psychologist, 50*, 162–163.

Morawski, J. (1994). *Practicing feminisms, reconstructing psychology*. Ann Arbor, MI: University of Michigan Press.

Oyama, S. (1991). Essentialism, women and war: Protesting too much, protesting too little. In A. E. Hunter (Ed.), *Genes and gender VI. On peace, war, and gender: A challenge to genetic explanation* (pp. 64–76). New York: Feminist Press.

Parker, I., & Shotter, J. (Eds.). (1990). *Deconstructing social psychology*. London: Routledge.

Parlee, M. B. (1991). Feminism and psychology. In S. Rosenberg Zalk & J. Gordon-Kelter (Eds.), *Revolutions in knowledge: Feminism in the social sciences* (pp. 33–56). Boulder, CO: Westview Press.

PMLA: Publications of the Modern Language Association of America. (1996). The status of evidence [Special Topic]. *111*(1).

Reid, P. (1993). Poor women in psychological research: Shut up and shut out. *Psychology of Women Quarterly, 17*, 133–150.

Rhedding-Jones, J. (1995). What do you do after you've met poststructuralism? Research possibilities regarding feminism, ethnography and literacy. *Journal of Curriculum Studies, 27*, 479–500.

Rostosky, S. S., & Travis, C. B., (1996). Menopause research and the dominance of the biomedical model: 1984–1994. *Psychology of Women Quarterly, 20*, 285–312.

Sharpe, P. (1993). "Always believe the victim," "Innocent until proven guilty," "There is no truth": The competing claims of feminism, humanism, and postmodernism in interpreting charges of harassment in the academy. Part of a symposium: Constructing meaningful dialogue on difference: Feminism and postmodernism in anthropology and the academy. *Anthropological Quarterly, 66*, 87–98.

Slife, B. D., & Williams, R. N. (1995). *What's behind the research? Discovering hidden assumptions in the behavioral sciences*. Thousand Oaks, CA: Sage.

Stake, R. E. (1995). *The art of case study research*. Thousand Oaks, CA: Sage.

Stanley, L., & Wise, S. (1993). *Breaking out again: Feminist ontology and epistemology*. London: Routledge.

Steier, F. (Ed.). (1991). *Research and reflexivity*. London, Thousand Oaks, CA: Sage.

Wilkinson, S. (Ed.). (1996). Special feature: Representing the Other—Part one. *Feminism & Psychology, 6*, 43–91.

Wilkinson, S. (Ed.). (1996). Special feature: Representing the Other—Part two. *Feminism & Psychology, 6*, 167–215.

Wood, J. T. (1995). Feminist scholarship and the study of relationships. *Journal of Social and Personal Relationships, 12*, 103–120.

Worell, J., & Robinson, D. (1994). Reinventing analogue methods for research with women. *Psychology of Women Quarterly, 18*, 463–476.

INNOVATIVE METHODS: GENERAL COMPENDIA

Alasuutari, P. (1995). *Researching culture: Qualitative method and cultural studies*. Thousand Oaks, CA: Sage.

Banister, P., Burman, E., Parker, I., Taylor, M., & Tindall, C. (1994). *Qualitative methods in psychology, A research guide*. Thousand Oaks, CA: Sage.

Bartunek, J. M., & Louis, M. R. (1996). *Insider/outsider research teams.* Thousand Oaks, CA: Sage.

Berg, B. L. (1997). *Qualitative research methods for the social sciences* (3rd ed.). Needham Heights, MA: Allyn & Bacon.

Campbell, R. (1995). Weaving a new tapestry of research: A bibliography of selected readings on feminist research methods. *Women's Studies International Forum, 18,* 215–222.

Coffey, A., & Atkinson, P. (1996). *Making sense of qualitative data: Complementary research strategies.* Thousand Oaks, CA: Sage.

Creswell, J. W. (1997). *Qualitative inquiry and research design.* Thousand Oaks, CA: Sage.

Denzin, N., & Lincoln, Y. S. (Eds.). (1994). *Handbook of qualitative research.* Thousand Oaks, CA: Sage.

Ellis, C., & Flaherty, M. G. (Eds.). (1992). *Investigating subjectivity: Research on lived experience.* Thousand Oaks, CA: Sage.

Fedderman, D. F., Kaftarian, K., & Wandersman, A. (1995). *Empowerment evaluation: Knowledge and tools for self-assessment and accountability.* Thousand Oaks, CA: Sage.

Feldman, M. S. (1994). *Strategies for interpreting qualitative data.* Thousand Oaks, CA: Sage.

Fine, M. (1992). *Disruptive voices: The possibilities of feminist research.* Ann Arbor, MI: University of Michigan Press.

Fonow, M. M., & Cook, J. A. (1991). *Beyond methodology: Feminist scholarship as lived research.* Bloomington, IN: Indiana University Press.

Fox, D. R., & Prilletensky, I. (Eds.). (1997). *Critical Psychology: An Introduction.* Thousand Oaks, CA: Sage.

Franz, C. E., & Stewart, A. J. (Eds.). (1994). *Women creating lives: Identities, resilience, and resistance.* Boulder, CO: Westview Press.

Frese, P. R., & Coggeshall, J. M. (1991). *Transcending boundaries: Multi-disciplinary approaches to the study of gender.* New York: Begin & Garvey.

Gergen, M. M. (1999). *Impious improvisations: Feminist reconstructions in psychology.* Thousand Oaks, CA: Sage.

Gergen, M., & Davis, S. N. (Eds.). (1997). *Toward a new feminist psychology of gender: A reader.* New York: Routledge.

Glaser, B. G. (1993). *Examples of grounded theory.* Mill Valley, CA: Sociology Press.

Golden-Biddle, K. (1997). *Composing qualitative research.* Thousand Oaks, CA: Sage.

Hare-Mustin, R., & Marecek, J. (Eds.). (1990). *Making a difference: Psychology and the construction of gender.* New Haven, CT: Yale University Press.

Herndon, S. L., & Kreps, G. L. (Eds.). (1993). *Qualitative research: Applications in organizational communication.* Cresskill, NJ: Hampton Press.

Hoshmand, L. T., & Martin, J., (Eds.). (1995). *Research as praxis: Lessons from programmatic research in therapeutic psychology.* New York: Teachers College Press.

Jones, M. O. (1996). Studying organizational symbolism, what, how, why? *Qualitative Research Methods, 39,* 27–38.

Kenny, D. A. (1990). Design and analysis issues in dyadic research. In C. Hendrick & M. S. Clark (Eds.), *Review of personality and social psychology* (Vol. II, pp. 164–184). Thousand Oaks, CA: Sage.

Kenny, D. A., & Acitelli, L. K. (1994). Measuring similarity in couples. *Journal of Family Psychology, 8,* 417–431.

Lather, P. (1991). *Getting smart: Feminist research and pedagogy with/in the postmodern.* New York: Routledge.

Mason, J. (1996). *Qualitative researching.* London: Sage.

Maynard, M., & Purvis, J. (Eds.). (1994). *Researching women's lives from a feminist perspective.* London: Taylor & Francis.

Miles, M. B., & Huberman, A. M. (1994). *Qualitative data analysis* (2nd ed.). Thousand Oaks, CA: Sage.

Miller, G., & Dingwall, R. (Eds.). (1997). *Context and method in qualitative research.* Thousand Oaks, CA: Sage.

Mitchell, R. G., Jr. (1993). *Secrecy and fieldwork*. Thousand Oaks, CA: Sage.

Moustakas, C. (1994). *Phenomenological research methods*. Thousand Oaks, CA: Sage.

Nielsen, J. M. (Ed.). (1990). *Feminist research methods*. Boulder, CO: Westview Press.

Posavac, E. (Ed.). (1992). *Methodological issues in applied social psychology*. New York: Plenum.

Reinharz, S. (1992). *Feminist methods in social research*. New York, Oxford: Oxford University Press.

Richardson, J. T. E. (Ed.). (1996). *Handbook of qualitative research methods for psychology and the social sciences*. Leicester, UK: BPS Books.

Silverman, D. (Ed.). (1997). *Qualitative research, theory, method, and practice*. London: Sage.

Smith, J., Harré, R., & Van Langenhove, L. (Eds.). (1995). *Rethinking methods in psychology*. London: Sage.

Strauss, A., & Corbin, J. (1990). *Basics of qualitative research: Grounded theory, procedures and techniques*. Thousand Oaks, CA: Sage.

Tolan, P., Keys, C., Chertok, F., & Jason, L. (Eds.). (1990). *Researching community psychology: Issues of theory and methods*. Washington, DC: American Psychological Association.

Wilkinson, S. (Ed.). (1996). *Feminist social psychologies: International perspectives*. Buckingham, UK: Open University Press.

Wolcott, H. F. (1994). *Transforming qualitative data*. Thousand Oaks, CA: Sage.

COLLABORATIVE RESEARCH

Crawford, J., Kippax, S., Onyz, J., Gault, U., & Benton, P. (1992). *Emotion and gender*. London: Sage.

Dyck, I. (1995). Women talking: Creating knowledge through difference in cross-cultural research. *Women's Studies International Forum, 18,* 611–626.

Fine, M. (1994). Dis-stance and other stances for feminist researchers. In A. Gitlin (Ed.), *Power and method* (pp. 13–35). New York: Routledge.

Fine, M., & Weis, L. (1996). Writing the "wrongs" of fieldwork: Confronting our own research/writing dilemmas in urban ethnographies. *Qualitative Inquiry, 2,* 251–274.

Kidder, L. H., & Fine, M. (1997). Qualitative inquiry in psychology: A radical tradition. In D. R. Fox & I. Prilletensky (Eds.), *Handbook of critical psychology* (pp. 45–59). Thousand Oaks, CA: Sage.

Lather, P. (1995). The validity of angels: Interpretive and textual strategies in researching the lives of women with HIV/AIDS. *Qualitative Inquiry, 1,* 41–68.

Lykes, M. B. (1994). Terror, silencing and children: International, multidisciplinary collaboration with Guatemalan Maya communities. *Social Science and Medicine, 38,* 543–552.

Lykes, M. B. (1996). Meaning making in a context of genocide and silencing. In M. B. Lykes, A. Banuazizi, R. Liem, & M. Morris (Eds.), *Myths about the powerless: Contesting social inequalities* (pp. 159–178). Philadelphia: Temple University Press.

Parker, S., Nichter, M., & Ritenbaugh, C. (1995). Body image and weight concerns among African American and White adolescent females: Differences that make a difference. *Human Organization, 54,* 103–114.

Pennebaker, J. W., Paez, D., & Rime, B. (Eds.). (1997). *Collective memory of political events*. Hillsdale, NJ: Lawrence Erlbaum.

Small, S. A. (1995). Action-oriented research: Models and methods. *Journal of Marriage and the Family, 57,* 941–955.

Thom, K. (1992). Therapeutic distinctions in on-going therapy. In S. McNamee & K. J. Gergen (Eds.), *Therapy as social construction* (pp. 116–135). London: Sage.

Wang, C., Burris, M., & Xiang, Y. P. (1996). Chinese village women as visual anthropologists: A participatory approach to reaching policymakers. *Social Science and Medicine, 42,* 1291–1400.

DISCOURSE ANALYSIS

Albright, J. M. (1996). Of mind, body and machine: Cyborg cultural politics in the age of hypertext. http://www-scf/usc/edu/~Albright/index.html

Belgrave, L. L., & Smith, K. J. (1995). Negotiated validity in collaborative ethnography. *Qualitative Inquiry, 1,* 469–486.

Billig, M. (1991). *Ideology and opinions: Studies in rhetorical psychology.* Thousand Oaks, CA: Sage.

Burman, E., Aitken, G., Alldred, P., Billington, T., Goldberg, B., Gordo Lopez, A., Heenan, C., Marks, D., & Warner, S. (1996). *Psychology discourse practice: From regulation to resistance.* London: Taylor & Francis.

Burman, E., & Parker, I. (Eds.). (1993). *Discourse analytic research.* New York: Routledge.

Capps, L., & Ochs, E. (1995). *Constructing panic: The discourse of agoraphobia.* Cambridge, MA: Harvard University Press.

Chrisler, J. C., & Levy, K. B. (1990). The media construct a menstrual monster: PMS in the popular press. *Women & Health, 16,* 89–104.

Coupland, N., & Nussbaum, J. (Eds.). (1993). *Discourse and lifespan identity.* London: Sage.

Curt, B. C. (1994). *Textuality and tectonics: Troubling social and psychological science.* Milton Keynes, UK: Open University Press.

Davies, B., & Banks, C. (1992). The gender trap: A feminist poststructuralist analysis of primary school children's talk about gender. *Journal of Curriculum Studies, 24,* 1–25.

Garcia, A. M. (1991). The development of Chicana feminist discourse, 1970–1980. In J. Lorber & S. A. Farrell (Eds.), *The social construction of gender* (pp. 269–287). Thousand Oaks, CA: Sage.

Gilfoyle, J., Wilson, J., & Brown [no initial] (1992). Sex, organs and audiotape: A discourse analytic approach to talking about heterosexual sex and relationships. *Feminism and Psychology, 2,* 209–230.

Gubrium, J. F., & Holstein, J. A. (1990). *What is family?* Mountain View, CA: Mayfield.

Harré, R., & Gilett, G. (1994). *The discursive mind.* London: Sage.

Harré, R., & Stearns, P. (Eds.). (1995). *Discursive psychology in practice.* London: Sage.

Henwood, K. L. (1993). Women and later life: The discursive construction of identities within family relationships. *Journal of Aging Studies, 7,* 303–319.

Henwood, K. L., & Phoenix, A. (1996). "Race" in psychology: Teaching the subject. *Ethnic and Racial Studies, 1,* 1–12.

Hertz, R. (Ed.). (1997). *Reflexivity and voice.* Thousand Oaks, CA: Sage.

Jensen, R. (1996). Knowing pornography. *Violence Against Women 2,* 82–102.

Josselson, R., Lieblich, A., Sharabany, R., & Wiseman, H. (1997). *Conversation as method: Analyzing the effects of growing up communally on later relationships.* Thousand Oaks, CA: Sage.

Kissling, E. A. (1996). Bleeding out loud: Communication about menstruation. *Feminism & Psychology, 6,* 481–504.

Komesaroff, P., Rothfield, P., & Daly, J. (Eds.). (1997). *Reinterpreting menopause. Cultural and philosophical issues.* New York: Routledge.

Malson, H., & Ussher, J. M. (1996). Bloody women: A discourse analysis of amenorrhea as a symptom of anorexia nervosa. *Feminism & Psychology, 6,* 505–521.

Marecek, J. (1993). Disappearances, silences, and anxious rhetoric: Gender in abnormal psychology textbooks. *Journal of Theoretical and Philosophical Psychology, 13,* 114–124.

Maynard, M., & Purvis, J. (Eds.). (1994). *(Hetero)sexual politics.* London: Taylor & Francis.

Messner, M., & Sabo, D. (Eds.). (1994). *Sex, violence and power in sports.* Freedom, CA: Crossing.

Miles, L. (1993). Women, AIDS, and power in heterosexual sex: A discourse analysis. *Women's International Forum, 16,* 497–511.

Odeh, L. A. (1993). Post-colonial feminism and the veil: Thinking the difference. *Feminist Review, 43,* 26–37.

Parker, I., & Burman, E. (1993). *Discourse analytic research: Repertoires and readings of texts in action*. London: Routledge.

Potter, J. (1996). *Representing reality: Discourse, rhetoric and social construction*. London: Sage.

Psathas, G. (1994). *Conversation analysis: The study of talk-in-interaction*. Thousand Oaks, CA: Sage.

Stam, H. J. (Ed.). (1996). The body and psychology [Special Issue]. *Theory & Psychology, 6*(4).

Widdicombe, S., & Wooffitt, R. (1995). *The language of youth subcultures: Social identity in action*. London: Harvester Wheatsheaf.

Wilkinson, S., & Kitzinger, C. (Eds.). (1995). *Feminism and discourse: Psychological perspectives*. London: Sage.

ETHNOGRAPHY

Agar, M., & MacDonald, J. (1995). Focus groups and ethnography. *Human Organization, 54*, 78–86.

Atkinson, P. (1990). *The ethnographic imagination: Textual constructions of reality*. New York: Routledge.

Behar, R. (1996). *Vulnerable observer: Anthropology that breaks your heart*. Boston: Beacon Press.

Bell, D., Caplan, P., & Karim, W. J. (Eds.). (1993). *Gendered fields: Women, men and ethnography*. London: Routledge.

Bochner, A. P., & Ellis, C. (1996). Taking ethnography into the twenty-first century. *Journal of Contemporary Ethnography, 25*, 3–5.

Communication Studies 298. (1996). Fragments of self at the postmodern bar. *Journal of Contemporary Ethnography, 25*, 6–20.

Davis, K. (1995). *Reshaping the female body; The dilemma of cosmetic surgery*. New York: Routledge.

Denzin, N. K. (1997). *Interpretive ethnography: Ethnographic practices for the 21st Century*. Thousand Oaks, CA: Sage.

Ellis, C., & Bochner, A. P. (Eds.). (1996). *Composing ethnography: Alternative forms of qualitative writing*. Thousand Oaks, CA: Alta Mira Press.

Ekins, R., & King, D. (Eds.). (1996). *Blending genders: Social aspects of cross-dressing and sex-changing*. New York: Routledge.

Erickson, K., & Stull, D. (1997). *Doing team ethnography*. Thousand Oaks, CA: Sage.

Gerald, R. A. (Ed.). (1997). *Explorations in ethnoarchaeology*. Albuquerque, NM: University of New Mexico Press.

Hey, V. (1996). *The company she keeps: An ethnography of girls' friendship*. Bristol, PA: Open University Press

Kleinman, S., Copp, M. A., & Henderson, K. A. (1997). Qualitatively different: Teaching fieldwork to graduate students. *Journal of Contemporary Ethnography, 25*, 469–499.

Letherby, G. (1995). "Dear researcher": The use of correspondence as a method within feminist qualitative research. *Gender & Society, 9*, 576–593.

Odzer, C. (1994). *Patpong Sisters: An American woman's view of the Bangkok sex world*. New York: Blue Moon Books.

Prus, R. (1996). *Symbolic interaction and ethnographic research: Intersubjectivity and the study of human lived experience*. Albany, NY: State University of New York Press.

Root, D. (1996). *Cannibal culture: Art, appropriation, and the commodification of difference*. Boulder, CO: Westview.

Sanday, P. (1990). *Fraternity gang rape: Sex, brotherhood and privilege on campus*. New York: New York University Press.

Stanley, L. (1995). *Sex surveyed 1949–1994: From Mass-Observation's "Little Kinsey," to the National Survey and the Hite Reports*. London: Taylor & Francis.

Stack, C. (1996). *Call to home: African Americans reclaim the rural south*. New York: Basic Books.

Van Maanen, J. (Ed.). (1995). *Representation in ethnography*. Thousand Oaks, CA: Sage.

Visweswaran, K. (1994). *Fictions of feminist ethnography.* Minneapolis, MN: University of Minnesota Press.

EXISTENTIAL PHENOMENOLOGICAL INQUIRY

Daniluk, J. C. (1993). The meaning and experience of female sexuality: A phenomenological analysis. *Psychology of Women Quarterly, 17,* 53–69.
Giorgi, A., Knowles, R., & Smith, D. L. (Eds.). (1979). *Duquesne studies in phenomenological psychology: Vol. 3.* Pittsburgh, PA: Duquesne University Press.
Osborne, J. W. (1990). Some basic existential-phenomenological research methodology for counsellors. *Canadian Journal of Counselling, 24,* 79–91.
Polkinghorne, D. (1989). Phenomenological research methods. In R. S. Valle & S. Halling (Eds.), *Existential phenomenological perspectives in psychology: Exploring the breadth of human experience* (pp. 41–60). New York: Plenum.

INTERVIEWING AND FOCUS GROUPS

Cannon, L. W., Higginbotham, E., & Leung, M. L. A. (1991). Race and class bias in qualitative research on women. In J. Lorber & S. A. Farrell (Eds.), *The social construction of gender* (pp. 237–248). Thousand Oaks, CA: Sage.
Chirban, J. T. (1996). *Interviewing in depth.* Thousand Oaks, CA: Sage.
Devault, M. (1990). Talking and listening from women's standpoint: Feminist strategies for interviewing and analysis. *Social Problems, 37,* 96–116.
Franklin, M. (1997). Making sense: Interviewing and the narrative representation of women artists' work. In M. Gergen & S. N. Davis (Eds.), *Toward a new psychology of gender* (pp. 99–116). New York: Routledge.
Henwood, K. L. (1993). Women and later life: The discursive construction of identities within family relationships. *Journal of Aging Studies, 7,* 303–319
Herndon, S. L. (1993). Using focus group interviews for preliminary investigation. In S. L. Herndon & G. L. Kreps (Eds.), *Qualitative research: Applications in organizational communication* (pp. 39–45). Cresskill, NJ: Hampton Press.
Hochschild, A. R. (1997). *The time bind: When work becomes home and home becomes work.* New York: Metropolitan Books/Henry Holt & Co.
Hollway, W., & Jefferson, T. (1997). Eliciting narrative through the in-depth interview. *Qualitative Inquiry, 3,* 53–70.
Holstein, J. A., & Gubrium, J. F. (1995). *The active interview.* Thousand Oaks, CA: Sage.
Kessler, S., & McKenna, W. (1985). *Gender: An ethnomethodological approach.* Chicago: University of Chicago Press. (Original work published in 1978)
Kessler, S. J. (1990). The medical construction of gender: Case management of intersexed infants. *Signs: Journal of Women in Culture and Society, 16,* 3–26.
Krueger, R. A. (1994). *Focus groups: A practical guide for applied research.* Thousand Oaks, CA: Sage.
Kvale, S. (1996). *InterViews: An introduction to qualitative research interviewing.* Thousand Oaks, CA: Sage.
Kvale, S. (1996). The 1,000-page question. *Qualitative Inquiry, 2,* 275–284.
Mishler, E. (1991). Representing discourse: The rhetoric of transcription. *Journal of Narrative and Life History, 1,* 255–280.
Morgan, D. L., & Krueger, R. A. (Eds.). (1997). *Focus group kit* (Vols. 1–6). Thousand Oaks, CA: Sage.
Opie, A. (1992). Qualitative research, appropriation of the "other," and empowerment. *Feminist Review, 40,* 52–69.

Plumbo, M. A. (1995). Living in two different worlds or living in the world differently: A qualitative study with American Indian nurses. *Journal of Holistic Nursing, 13,* 155–173.

Riessman, C. K. (1991). When gender is not enough: Women interviewing women. In J. Lorber & S. A. Farrell (Eds.), *The social construction of gender* (pp. 217–236). Thousand Oaks, CA: Sage.

Way, N. (1995). "Can't you see the courage, the strength that I have?" *Psychology of Women Quarterly, 19,* 107–128.

Weiss, R. (1994). *Learning from strangers: The art and method of qualitative interview studies.* New York: Free Press.

Zeeland, S. (1996). *The masculine marine: Homoeroticism in the U.S. Marine Corps.* Binghamton, NY: Haworth Press.

MULTIPLE, COMBINED, AND LINKED METHODS

Crawford, M. (1995). *Talking difference: On gender and language.* London: Sage.

Fielding, N. G., & Fielding, J. L. (1986). *Linking data.* Thousand Oaks, CA: Sage.

Gergen, M. (1988). Towards a feminist methodology. In M. Gergen (Ed.), *Feminist thought and the structure of knowledge* (pp. 87–104). New York: New York University Press.

Hickson III, M., & Jennings, R. (1993). Compatible theory and applied research: Systems theory and triangulation. In S. L. Herndon & G. L. Kreps (Eds.), *Qualitative research: Applications in organizational communication.* Cresskill, NJ: Hampton Press.

Steckler, A., McLeroy, K. R., Goodman, R. M., Bird, S. T., & McCormick, I. (Eds.). (1992). Integrating qualitative and quantitative methods [Special Issue]. *Health Education Quarterly, 19*(1).

NARRATIVE INVESTIGATIONS

Chase, S. E. (1995). Taking narrative seriously: Consequences for method and theory in interview studies. In R. Josselson & A. Lieblich (Eds.), *Interpreting experience: The narrative study of lives* (Vol. 3, pp. 1–26). Thousand Oaks, CA: Sage.

Diversi, M. (1998). Glimpses of street life: Representing lived experience through short stories. *Qualitative Inquiry, 4,* 131–147.

Franz, C., & Stewart, A. (1994). *Women creating lives: Identities, resilience and resistance.* Boulder, CO: Westview Press.

Gergen, M. M. (1992). Life stories: Pieces of a dream. In G. Rosenwald & R. Ochberg (Eds.), *Storied lives* (pp. 127–144). New Haven, CT: Yale University Press.

Goldner, V., Penn, P., Sheinberg, M., & Walker, G. (1990). Love and violence: Gender paradoxes in volatile attachments. *Family Process, 29,* 343–364.

Gorman, J. (1993). Postmodernism and the conduct of inquiry in social work. *Affilia, 8,* 247–264.

Hinchman, L. P., & Hinchman, S. K. (Eds.). (1997). *Memory, identity, community; The idea of narrative in the human sciences.* Albany, NY: SUNY Press.

Josselson, R. (Ed.). (1996). *Ethics and process in the narrative study of lives* (Vol. 4). Thousand Oaks, CA: Sage.

Josselson, R. (1996). *Revising herself; The story of women's identity from college to midlife.* New York: Oxford University Press.

Mishler, E. (1995). Models of narrative analysis: A typology. *Journal of Narrative and Life History, 5,* 87–123.

Personal Narratives Group (Eds.). (1989). *Interpreting women's lives: Feminist theory and personal narratives.* Bloomington, IN: Indiana University Press.

Plummer, K. (1995). *Telling sexual stories.* New York: Routledge.

Sarbin, T. R. (Ed.). (1986). *Narrative psychology: The storied nature of human conduct.* New York: Praeger.

Sparkes, A. C. (1996). The fatal flaw: A narrative of the fragile body-self. *Qualitative Inquiry, 2,* 463–494.

Squire, C. (1994). Safety, danger, and the movies: Women's and men's narratives of aggression. *Feminism & Psychology, 4,* 547–570.

Vaz, K. M. (1997). *Oral narrative research with black women.* Thousand Oaks, CA: Sage.

Weingarten, K. (1994). *The mother's voice: Strengthening intimacy in families.* New York: Harcourt Brace.

PERFORMATIVE PSYCHOLOGY: COMMUNICATING IN DIVERSE MEDIA

Barry, D. (1996). Artful inquiry: A symbolic constructivist approach to social science research. *Qualitative Inquiry, 2,* 411–438.

Billig, M. (1994). Repopulating the depopulated pages of social psychology. *Theory & Psychology, 4,* 307–335.

Blumenfeld-Jones, D. S. (1995). Dance as a mode of research representation. *Qualitative Inquiry, 1,* 391–401.

Carlson, M. (1996). *Performance, a critical introduction.* New York: Routledge.

Case, S. E. (1997). *The domain-matrix; Performing lesbian at the end of print culture.* Bloomington: Indiana University Press.

Case, S. E, Brett, P., & Foster, S. L. (Eds.). (1995). *Cruising the performative: Interventions into the representation of ethnicity, nationality, and sexuality.* Bloomington, IN: Indiana University Press.

Cochran, L. (1986). *Portrait and story: Dramaturgical approaches to the study of persons.* Westport, CT: Green.

Donmoyer, R., & Yennie-Donmoyer, J. (1995). Data as drama: Reflections on the use of readers theater as a mode of qualitative data display. *Qualitative Inquiry, 1,* 402–428.

Dudek, S. (Ed.). (1996, Fall/Winter). Performative psychology [Special Issue]. *Psychology and the Arts.*

Finley, S., & Knowles, J. G. (1995). Researcher as artist/artist as researcher. *Qualitative Inquiry, 1,* 110–142.

Gergen, M. (1990). From mod masculinity to post-mod macho: A feminist re-play. *Humanist Psychologist, 18,* 95–104.

Krug, K., & Piller, P. (1996). Sex, lies and hypertext—Two feminists' review of Landow's hyper/text/theory. *Organizations, 3,* 576–585.

Lather, P., & Chris, S. (1997). *Troubling with angels: Women living with HIV and AIDS.* Boulder, CO: Westview Press.

Mienczakowski, J. (1996). An ethnographic act. The construction of consensual theater. In C. Ellis & A. P. Bochner (Eds.), *Composing ethnography: Alternative forms of qualitative writing* (pp. 244–266). Thousand Oaks, CA: Alta Mira Press.

Mienczakowski, J., Smith, R., & Sinclair, M. (1996). On the road to catharsis: A theoretical framework for change. *Qualitative Inquiry, 2,* 439–462.

Morris, R. C. (1995). All made up: Performance theory and the new anthropology of sex and gender. *Annual Review of Anthropology, 24,* 567–592.

Smyth, A. (1991). The floozie in the jacuzzi/The problematics of culture and identity for an Irish woman. *Feminist Studies, 17,* 7–28.

Tierney, W. G. (1995). (Re)Presentation and voice. *Qualitative Inquiry, 1,* 379–390.

Ussher, J. M. (1994). Sexing the phallocentric pages of psychology: Repopulation is not enough. *Theory & Psychology, 4,* 345–352.

Q-METHODOLOGY

Kitzinger, C. (1987). *The social construction of lesbianism.* London: Sage.

Kitzinger, C., & Stainton Rogers, R. (1985). A Q-methodological study of lesbian identities. *European Journal of Social Psychology, 15,* 167–181.

Senn, C. Y. (1996). Q-methodology as feminist methodology: Women's views and experiences of pornography. In S. Wilkinson (Ed.), *Feminist social psychologies: International perspectives* (pp. 77–89). Buckingham, UK: Open University Press.

Stainton Rogers, R. (1991). *Explaining health and illness*. Hemel Hempstead, UK: Harvester Wheatsheaf.

Stainton Rogers, R., Stenner, P., Gleeson, K., & Stainton Rogers, W. (1995). *Social psychology: A critical agenda*. Cambridge, MA: Blackwell.

THE VISUAL AS DATA

Ball, M. S., & Smith Gregory, W. H. (1992). *Analyzing visual data*. Thousand Oaks, CA: Sage.

Curtis, B. (1994). Men and masculinities in American art and illustration. *Masculinities, 2,* 10–37.

Gergen, K. J., & Gergen, M. M. (1991). From theory to reflexivity in research practice. In F. Steier (Ed.), *Method and reflexivity: Knowing as systemic social construction* (pp. 76–95). London: Sage.

Harper, D. (1994). On the authority of image: Visual methods at the crossroads. In N. Denzin & Y. Lincoln (Eds.), *Handbook of qualitative research* (pp. 403–412). Thousand Oaks, CA: Sage.

Radnofsky, M. L. (1996). Qualitative models: Visually representing complex data in an image/text balance. *Qualitative Inquiry, 2,* 385–410.

Tufte, E. R. (1990). *Envisioning information*. Cheshire, CT: Graphics Press.

Wang, C. (1994). Photo as voice. *Health Education Quarterly, 21,* 171–186.

SAGE SERIES ON QUALITATIVE RESEARCH METHODS

Sage Publications (Thousand Oaks, CA) has developed a series, "Qualitative Research Methods," of 35 short publications, ordered by number:

1. *Reliability and Validity in Qualitative Research* by Kirk/Miller
2. *Speaking of Ethnography* by Agar
3. *The Politics and Ethics of Field Work* by Punch
4. *Linking Data* by Fielding & Fielding
5. *The Clinical Perspective in Fieldwork* by Schein
6. *Membership Roles in Field Research* by Adler & Adler
7. *Semiotics and Fieldwork* by Manning
8. *Analyzing Field Reality* by Gubrium
9. *Gender Issues in Field Research* by Warren
10. *Systematic Data Collection* by Weller/Romney
11. *Meta-ethnography: Synthesizing Qualitative Studies* by Noblit/Hare
12. *Ethnostatistics: Qualitative Foundations for Quantitative Research* by Gephart
13. *The Long Interview* by McCracken
14. *Microcomputer Applications in Qualitative Research* by Pfaffenberger
15. *Knowing Children: Participant Observation with Minors* by Fine & Sandstrom
16. *Focus Groups as Qualitative Research* by Morgan
17. *Interpretive Biography* by Denzin
18. *Psychoanalytic Aspects of Fieldwork* by Hunt
19. *Ethnographic Decision Tree Modeling* by Gladwin
20. *Writing up qualitative research* by Wolcott
21. *Writing Strategies: Reaching Diverse Audiences* by Richardson
22. *Selecting Ethnographic Informants* by Johnson
23. *Living the Ethnographic Life* by Rose

PUBLISHING INNOVATIVE METHODS

In recent years the development of new journals aimed at specialized niches in the social sciences has greatly expanded. On the innovative-methods Web site, http://www.public.asu.edu/~atnfr, we have posted a long (though not exhaustive) list of journals that publish reports of research using methods that are innovative in psychology. For those seeking outlets for their reports, it may be a helpful (and encouraging) place to start.

The following list is made up of journals that are illustrative of several types found on the longer list, and one set we excluded from the longer list. The set listed that follows, excluded from the Web list, includes journals focusing on theory and methodology. We included on the Web site a long list including journals exclusively reporting studies using methods psychologists might find innovative, journals consistently including some reports using methods psychologists might find innovative, and journals that have had some reports of research using innovative methods in recent issues. Examples of each kind are found in the following list. There have been many articles *about* innovative methodologies in a great variety of journals included in the PsychInfo database. (A search for the word "qualitative," for example, in the years 1995 through present yielded over 2,000 hits!) There now appears to be little doubt that the discipline of psychology will extend some degree of acceptance, at least, to reports using innovative methods.

JOURNALS FOCUSING ON THEORY AND METHODOLOGY ITSELF

Human Studies http://kapis.www.wkap.nl/kapis/CGI-BIN/WORLD/journalhome.htm?0163-8548

Theory & Psychology http://www.sagepub.com

EXAMPLES OF JOURNALS DEDICATED TO EXCLUSIVELY REPORTING STUDIES USING METHODS INNOVATIVE TO PSYCHOLOGY

Discourse and Society http://www.sagepub.com/

Journal of Constructivist Psychology Taylor & Francis http://ksi.cpsc.ucalgary.ca/PCP/PCP.html#RTFT0C8

Journal of Pragmatics Elsevier http://www.elsevier.nl/inca
Narrative Inquiry http://www.benjamins.nl
Qualitative Health Research http://sagepub.com/

EXAMPLES OF JOURNALS THAT HAVE CONSISTENTLY INCLUDED SOME REPORTS USING INNOVATIVE METHODOLOGIES

American Journal of Orthopsychiatry http://www.amerortho.org/Birth http://www.blacksci.co.uk/
Journal of Counseling Psychology http://www.apa.org
OMEGA Journal of Death and Dying http://www.baywood.com/site/new2/viewbook.cfm?id=100140&c=
Social Science and Medicine http://www.elseview.nl/locate/socscimed

JOURNALS THAT HAVE HAD SOME REPORTS OF RESEARCH USING INNOVATIVE METHODS IN RECENT YEARS

Child Development http://srcd.org
Family Process http://familyprocess.org/volume36.html
Psychology and Health http://www.gbhap-us.com/journals/340.340-top.htm
Sport Psychologist http://ted.educ.sfu.ca/Society/Journal/

Electronic Journal

The Qualitative Report An electronic journal dedicated to qualitative research and critical inquiry. Online address: www.nova.edu/ssss/QR/index.html

Editor, Ron Chenail, School of Social and Systemic Studies, Nova Southeastern University, 3301 College Ave., Fort Lauderdale, FL 33314. Email: ron@nsu.acast.nova.edu

Web sites

*Cybergrrl Webstation http://www.cybergrrl.com/cg.html Includes articles, movie and book reviews, and more. Houses many other feminism-related sites.
*Feminist Majority Foundation http://www.feminist.org Includes a "Feminist Research Dialogue" in the Feminist Research Center. Also features a wealth of original research by the Feminist Majority Foundation, as well as links to other feminist sites. Feminist University Network contains listings of hundreds of feminist students and faculty with their contact information and research and organizing interests.
*Library Resources for Women's Studies http://sunsite.unc.edu/cheryb/women/librcws.html Provides links to university and research center libraries across the United States that contain references to women's studies.
*Nordic Institute for Women's Studies and Gender Research http://www.uio.no/www-other/nikk/ Includes research and networking among Nordic women and others who are interested in their projects and in cooperative work

*The Women's Studies Reference Roadmap http://women-www.uia.ac.be/women/roadmap/women/w0000000.html From University of Antwerp, Belgium, contains links to women's studies Internet sites around Europe. Also contains a relatively complete directory of mailing lists and Usenet newsgroups talking about women's studies and feminism.

TEACHING ABOUT INNOVATIVE METHODS

When our subcommittee began its work, one of the first steps we took was to issue a call for syllabi and other class materials from courses that included innovative research methods. We sent the call twice (about 6 months apart) to various psychology and women's studies email discussion lists; the call included a request that it be forwarded to other appropriate lists. We also personally contacted colleagues whom we knew were doing innovative research on the assumption that they would also teach their students about it. We did this, of course, because we thought that having access to model syllabi would encourage more feminists to design and teach courses that include innovative methodologies.

Our call was greeted with great enthusiasm, yet it did not produce the results we expected. Dozens of faculty from a wide variety of social science fields responded to say that they would love to teach a course on innovative methods or include information about them in their standard courses. These eager professors begged us to send them whatever we found as soon as possible and to provide them with advice and assistance in designing or redesigning their courses. Despite repeated public Internet postings and private telephone calls, we were only able to get syllabi from nine courses. Clearly, more of us would like to teach innovative methods than are actually doing it!

The syllabi for undergraduate courses (Research Methods in Psychology, Method of Psychology II: Non-Experimental Methods, Qualitative Methods, Feminist Research Methods, Feminist Styles of Inquiry) came from faculty in psychology and women's studies. The courses were conceptualized as broad introductions to research methodologies, and the instructors tried to expose students to as wide an array of methods as possible. They discussed the pros and cons of each method and included readings or lectures on epistemology. The women's studies courses included readings on feminist critiques of the experimental method. Standard courses on research methods for psychology majors generally focus on the experimental method, and there is usually not much time to cover alternatives. Therefore, we were interested in the strategy used at one college, where research methods is a year-long course. The fall semester focuses on the experiment; the spring semester is then free to focus on alternative methods. Although the students probably get the message that the experiment is more important than other methods, this is an effective way for feminist faculty to ensure that students learn about and have a chance to try alternative, and even innovative, methods without having to argue with traditional colleagues about the value of teaching new methods. Everyone can be satisfied as she or he can claim that "our students get twice as much methodological training as the average psychology major."

The graduate courses (Qualitative Methods & Theory, Qualitative Research

Methods, Advanced Qualitative Research, Bridging the Gap Between Research and Action) came from faculty in psychology, counseling, and family studies. These courses were more narrowly construed. They focused on teaching one or a few methods in some depth, and all of the instructors required the students to plan and carry out a small research project using one of the techniques they learned. Class time was spent in large part discussing readings and reporting on progress with their projects. We were especially intrigued with the course on action research because the instructor included readings on communicating research results to the media and to legislative bodies. We all hope that our research will make a difference, but students who are explicitly trained in how to testify before boards and committees, how to write for the popular press, how to write press releases, and how to call for and speak at a press conference may be more likely than most to realize their goals.

The methods taught in the nine courses include action research, archival research, case study, content analysis, correlational study, ethnography, focus group, interviewing, narrative analysis, observation, oral history, survey research, and visual data analysis. Some of these methods are obviously more innovative than others. Some are qualitative, others quantitative, and some (e.g., content analysis, surveys) can be done either way. What all of these methods have in common is that (with the exception of correlations) they are all used less commonly in psychology than are experiments. The instructors of the undergraduate research methods courses teach from the stance that all methods have value. The educated researcher is expected to choose the one that is most likely to answer the question of interest.

The instructors share the philosophy that learning by doing works best. Even in courses that do not require students to conduct a study of their own design, students gain experience using the methods in structured assignments. Here are some examples of assignments: conduct and transcribe a structured interview; write an ethnographic description of a social event; carry out a content analysis designed by the instructor (e.g., personal ads, Saturday morning TV commercials); during a class break go to a randomly assigned campus location, conduct an observation without taking notes, and return to class prepared to describe what was happening and how it felt to be an observer.

The courses were similar in paying significant attention to ethical issues and most were also explicit in their attention to issues of gender, race, and class, variables that experimenters often ignore or attempt to "control." Women's studies courses devoted time to considering whether or not "feminist methods"; courses on qualitative research seemed to favor grounded theory. Several courses addressed the possibility of viewing the participants as research collaborators. The instructors also attended to technological advances. The graduate courses included information about and practice with computer packages for qualitative analysis, and several undergraduate courses required students to search the World Wide Web for information or to participate in email discussion lists.

Although we did not collect enough syllabi to provide a comprehensive packet of models, we did find many interesting ideas in the ones we examined, and we hope that these ideas and the readings we suggest throughout this article will be sufficient to inspire faculty to construct their own courses. Articles that will be of interest to instructors in designing or redesigning courses are supplied in the Suggested Readings list. We also recommend the following journals, which regularly publish about feminist pedagogy: *Feminist Teacher, Transformations,* and *Women's Studies Quarterly.*

SUGGESTED READINGS

Ewick, P. (1994) Integrating feminist epistemologies in undergraduate research methods. *Gender & Society, 8,* 92–108.
Maher, F. A., & Tetreault, M. K. T. (1994). *The feminist classroom.* New York: Basic Books.
Stanton, D. C., & Stewart, A. J. (Eds.). (1995). *Feminisms in the academy.* Ann Arbor, MI: University of Michigan Press.
Vaz, K. M. (1992). A course on research issues on women of color. *Women's Studies Quarterly, 20,* (1/2) 70–85.

Initial submission: June 1, 1997
Final acceptance: October 1, 1997

REFERENCES

Aitken, G., & Burman, E. (1999). Keeping and crossing professional and racialized boundaries: Implications for feminist practice. *Psychology of Women Quarterly, 23,* 277–297.
Albright, J. M. (1996). *Of mind, body and machine: Cyborg cultural politics in the age of hypertext.* Unpublished manuscript, Dept. of Sociology, University of Southern California, Los Angeles, CA 90089. Also available at Web site: http://www-scf/usc.edu/~albright/index.html
American Psychological Association. (1994). *Publication manual of the American Psychological Association.* Washington, DC: Author.
Burman, E. (1990). The Spec(tac)ular economy of difference. *Feminism & Psychology, 5,* 543–546.
Burman, E., Aitken, G., Alldred, P., Billington, T., Goldberg, B., Gordo Lopez, A., Heenan, C., Marks, D., & Warner, S. (1996). *Psychology discourse practice: From regulation to resistance.* London: Taylor & Francis.
Burman, E., & Parker, I. (Eds.). (1993). *Discourse analytic research.* New York: Routledge.
Campbell, R., & Salem, D. A. (1999). Concept mapping as a feminist research method: Examining the community response to rape. *Psychology of Women Quarterly, 23,* 67–92.
Campbell, R., & Schram, P. J. (1995). Feminist research methods. A content analysis of psychology and social science textbooks. *Psychology of Women Quarterly, 19,* 85–106.
Carlson, M. (1996). *Performance, A critical introduction.* New York: Routledge.
Clifford, J., & Marcus, G. E. (Eds.). (1986). *Writing culture: The poetics and politics of ethnography.* Berkeley, CA: University of California Press.
Communication Studies 298. (1996). Fragments of self at the postmodern bar. *Journal of Contemporary Ethnography, 25,* 6–20
Community Education Team. (1999). Fostering relationality when implementing and evaluating a collective-drama approach to preventing violence against women. *Psychology of Women Quarterly, 23,* 95–110.
Crawford, J., Kippax, S., Onyz, J., Gault, U., & Benton, P. (1992). *Emotion and gender.* London: Sage.
Crawford, M., & Gentry, M. (Eds.). (1989). *Gender and thought: Psychological perspectives.* New York: Springer-Verlag.
Crawford, M., & Marecek, J. (1989). Feminist theory, feminist psychology: A bibliography of epistemology, critical analysis, and applications. *Psychology of Women Quarterly, 13,* 477–492.
Curt, B. C. (1994). *Textuality and tectonics: Troubling social and psychological science.* Buckingham, UK: Open University Press.
Denzin, N., & Lincoln, Y. S. (Eds.). (1994). *Handbook of qualitative research.* Thousand Oaks, CA: Sage.

Ellis, C., & Bochner, A. P. (Eds.). (1996). *Composing ethnography: Alternative forms of qualitative writing.* Thousand Oaks, CA: Alta Mira Press.

Fine, M. (1992). *Disruptive voices: The possibilities of feminist research.* Ann Arbor, MI: University of Michigan Press.

Fine, M., & Gordon, S. M. (1989). Feminist transformations of/despite psychology. In M. Crawford & M. Gentry (Eds.), *Gender and thought: Psychological perspectives* (pp. 146–174). New York: Springer-Verlag.

Fine, M., & Weis, L. (1996). Writing the 'wrongs' of fieldwork: Confronting our own research/ writing dilemmas in urban ethnographies. *Qualitative Inquiry, 2,* 251–274.

Fonow, M. M., & Cook, J. A. (1991). *Beyond methodology, Feminist scholarship as lived research.* Bloomington, IN: Indiana University Press.

Fox, D. R., & Prilletensky, I. (Eds.). (1997). *Handbook of critical psychology.* Thousand Oaks, CA: Sage.

Franklin, M. (1997). Making sense: Interviewing and the narrative representation of women artists' work. In M. Gergen & S. N. Davis (Eds.), *Toward a new psychology of gender* (pp. 99–116). New York, London: Routledge.

Franz, C. E., & Stewart, A. J. (Eds.). (1994). *Women creating lives: Identities, resilience, and resistance.* Boulder, CO: Westview Press.

Gavey, W., & McPhillips, K. (1999). Subject to romance: Heterosexual passivity as an obstacle to women initiating condom use. *Psychology of Women Quarterly, 23,* 349–367.

Geertz, C. (1983). *Local knowledge: Further essays in interpretive anthropology.* New York: Basic Books.

Gergen, K. J. (1985). The social constructionist movement in modern psychology. *American Psychologist, 40,* 266–275.

Gergen, K. J. (1994). *Realities and relationships: Soundings in social construction.* Cambridge, MA: Harvard University Press.

Gergen, K. J., & Gergen, M. M. (1988). Narrative and the self as relationship. In L. Berkowitz (Ed.), *Advances in experimental social psychology* (Vol. 21, pp. 17–56). New York: Academic Press.

Gergen, M. M. (1988). Toward a feminist metatheory and methodology in the social sciences. In M. Gergen (Ed.), *Feminist thought and the structure of knowledge* (pp. 87–104). New York: New York University Press.

Gergen, M. M. (1992). Life stories: Pieces of a dream. In G. Rosenwald & R. Ochberg (Eds.), *Storied lives* (pp. 127–144). New Haven, CT: Yale University Press.

Gergen, M. M., & Davis, S. N. (Eds.). (1997). *Toward a new psychology of gender.* New York: Routledge.

Gilligan, C. (1979). Women's place in man's life cycle. *Harvard Educational Review, 49,* 431–446.

Giorgi, A., Knowles, R., & Smith, D. L. (Eds.). (1979). *Duquesne studies in phenomenological psychology: Vol. 3.* Pittsburgh, PA: Duquesne University Press.

Grossman, F. K., Kruger, L. M., & Moore, R. P. (1999). Reflections on a feminist research project: Subjectivity and the wish for intimacy and equality. *Psychology of Women Quarterly, 23,* 117–135.

Haraway, D. (1988). Situated knowledges: The science question in feminism and the privilege of partial perspective. *Feminist Studies, 14,* 575–599.

Harding, S. (1986). *The science question in feminism.* Ithaca NY: Cornell University Press.

Harding, S. (Ed.). (1987). *Feminism and methodology.* Bloomington, IN: Indiana University Press.

Hare-Mustin, R., & Marecek, J. (Eds.). (1990). *Making a difference: Psychology and the construction of gender.* New Haven, CT: Yale University Press.

Haug, F. (1987). *Female sexualisation: A collective work of memory* (E. Carter, Trans.). London: Verso.

Henwood, K., & Pidgeon, N. (1994). Beyond the qualitative paradigm: A framework for introducing diversity within qualitative psychology. *Journal of Community & Applied Social Psychology, 4,* 225–238.

Herndon, S. L. (1993). Using focus group interviews for preliminary investigation. In S. L. Herndon & G. L. Kreps, (Eds.), *Qualitative research: Applications in organizational communication* (pp. 39–45). Cresskill, NJ: Hampton Press.

Hoshmand, L. T., & Martin, J. (Eds.). (1995). *Research as praxis: Lessons from programmatic research in therapeutic psychology*. New York: Teachers College Press.

Jaffee, S., Kling, K. C., Plant, E. A., Sloan, M., & Hyde, J. S. (1999). The view from down here: Feminist graduate students consider innovative methodologies. *Psychology of Women Quarterly, 23*, 423–430.

Josselson, R. (Ed.). (1996). *Ethics and process in the narrative study of lives. Vol. 4*. Thousand Oaks, CA: Sage.

Josselson, R., & Lieblich, A. (Eds.). (1993). *The narrative study of lives. Vol. 1*. Thousand Oaks, CA: Sage.

Josselson, R., & Lieblich, A. (Eds.). (1995). *Interpreting experience: The narrative study of lives. Vol. 3*. Thousand Oaks, CA: Sage.

Keller, E. F., & Longino, H. E. (Eds.). (1996). *Feminism and science*. New York: Oxford University Press.

Kessler, S. J., & McKenna, W. (1985). *Gender: An ethnomethodological approach*. Chicago: University of Chicago Press

Kissling, E. A. (1996). Bleeding out loud: Communication about menstruation. *Feminism & Psychology, 6*, 481–504.

Kitzinger, C. (1987). *The social constructionism of lesbianism*. London: Sage.

Komesaroff, P., Rothfield, P., & Daly, J. (Eds.). (1997). *Reinterpreting menopause: Cultural and philosophical issues*. New York: Routledge.

Krueger, R. A. (1994). *Focus groups: A practical guide for applied research*. Thousand Oaks, CA: Sage.

Landrine, H., Klonoff, E. A., & Brown-Collins, A. (1995). Cultural diversity and methodology in feminist psychology: Critique, proposal, empirical example. In H. Landrine (Ed.), *Bringing cultural diversity to feminist psychology: Theory, research, and practice* (pp. 55–75). Washington, DC: American Psychological Association.

Lather, P. (1995). The validity of angels: Interpretive and textual strategies in researching the lives of women with HIV/AIDS. *Qualitative Inquiry, 1*, 41–68.

Lather, P., & Smithies, C. (1997). *Troubling the angels: Women living with HIV and AIDS*. Boulder, CO: Westview.

Lieblich, A., & Josselson, R. (Eds.). (1994). *Exploring identity and gender, Vol. 2*. Thousand Oaks, CA: Sage.

Lutz, C. (1988). *Unnatural emotions*. Chicago: University of Chicago Press.

Lykes, M. B. (1994). Terror, silencing and children: International, multidisciplinary collaboration with Guatemalan Maya communities. *Social Science and Medicine, 38*, 543–552.

Malson, H., & Ussher, J. M. (1996). Bloody women: A discourse analysis of amenorrhea as a symptom of anorexia nervosa. *Feminism & Psychology, 6*, 505–521.

Marecek, J. (Ed.). (1989). Theory and method in feminist psychology [Special Issue]. *Psychology of Women Quarterly, 13*(4).

Marecek, J. (1995). Psychology and feminism: Can this relationship be saved? In D. Stanton & A. Stewart (Eds.), *Feminisms in the academy* (pp. 101–132). Ann Arbor: University of Michigan Press.

McHugh, M. C., Koeske, R. D., & Frieze, I. H. (1986). Issues to consider in conducting nonsexist psychological research. *American Psychologist, 41*, 879–890.

Morawski, J. (1994). *Practicing feminisms: Reconstructing psychology*. Ann Arbor, MI: University of Michigan Press.

Morgan, D. L., & Krueger, R. A. (Eds.). (1997). *Focus group kit* (Vols. 1–6). Thousand Oaks, CA: Sage.

Parker, I., & Burman, E. (1993). *Discourse analytic research: Repertoires and readings of texts in action*. London: Routledge.

Polkinghorne, D. (1989). Phenomenological research methods. In R. S. Valle & S. Halling (Eds.), *Existential phenomenological perspectives in psychology: Exploring the breadth of human experience* (pp. 41–60). New York: Plenum.

Potter, J. (1996). *Representing reality: Discourse, rhetoric, and social construction.* London: Sage.

Potter, J., & Wetherell, M. (1987). *Discourse and social psychology.* London: Sage.

Psathas, G. (1994). *Conversation analysis: The study of talk-in-interaction.* Thousand Oaks, CA: Sage.

Reinharz, S. (1992). *Feminist methods in social research.* New York: Oxford University Press.

Reitz, R. R. (1999). Batterers' experiences of being violent: A phenomenological study. *Psychology of Women Quarterly, 23,* 143–146.

Rhedding-Jones, J. (1995). What do you do after you've met poststructuralism? Research possibilities regarding feminism, ethnography and literacy. *Journal of Curriculum Studies, 27,* 479–500.

Rosenwald, G., & Ochberg, R. (Eds.). (1992). *Storied lives.* New Haven, CT: Yale University Press.

Russell, G. M., & Bohan, J. S. (1999). Hearing voices: The uses of research and the politics of change. *Psychology of Women Quarterly, 23,* 403–418.

Sarbin, T. R. (Ed.). (1986). *Narrative psychology: The storied nature of human conduct.* New York: Praeger.

Sarbin, T. R., & Kitsuse, J. I. (Eds.). (1994). *Constructing the social.* London: Sage.

Schutz, A. (1964). *Collected papers.* The Hague: Martinus Nijhoff.

Sherif, C. (1987). Bias in psychology. In S. Harding (Ed.), *Feminism and methodology* (pp. 37–56). Bloomington, IN: Indiana University Press.

Snelling, S. J. (1999). Women's perspectives on feminism: A Q-methodological study. *Psychology of Women Quarterly, 23,* 247–266.

Spender, D. (1981). The gatekeepers: A feminist critique of academic publishing. In H. Roberts (Ed.), *Doing feminist research* (pp. 186–202). New York: Routledge.

Stam, H. J. (Ed.). (1996). The body and psychology [Special Issue]. *Theory & Psychology, 6*(4).

Stephenson, W. (1953). *The study of behaviour: Q-technique and its methodology.* Chicago: University of Chicago Press.

Tolman, D. T., & Szalacha, L. A. (1999). Dimensions of desire: Bridging qualitative and quantitative methods in a study of female adolescent sexuality. *Psychology of Women Quarterly, 23,* 9–42.

Walsh, R. T. (1989). Do research reports in mainstream feminist psychology journals reflect feminist values? *Psychology of Women Quarterly, 13,* 433–444.

Walsh-Bowers, R. (1999). Fundamentalism in psychological science: The *Publication Manual* as bible. *Psychology of Women Quarterly, 23,* 375–392.

Weatherall, A. (1999). Exploring a teaching/research nexus as a possible site for feminist methodological innovation in psychology. *Psychology of Women Quarterly, 23,* 201–218.

Wilkinson, S. (Ed.). (1996). *Feminist social psychologies: International perspectives.* Buckingham, UK: Open University Press.

Wilkinson, S. (1999). Focus groups: A feminist method. *Psychology of Women Quarterly, 23,* 221–244.

Wilkinson, S., & Kitzinger, C. (Eds.). (1995). *Feminism and discourse: Psychological perspectives.* London: Sage.

Worell, J., & Etaugh, C. (Eds.). (1994). Transformations: Reconceptualizing theory and research with women [Special Issue]. *Psychology of Women Quarterly, 18*(4).

Zalk, S. R., & Gordon-Kelter, J. (Eds.). (1991). *Revolutions in knowledge: Feminism in the social sciences* (pp. 33–56). Boulder, CO: Westview Press.

INDEX

NOTES

NOTES

NOTES

NOTES

NOTES

NOTES

NOTES

NOTES

NOTES